GROC's CAND

THE CYCLAD

Includ

SYROS, MYKONOS, P

SIKINOS, FOLEGANDROS, SANTORINI,

ANAFI, AMORGOS,

The Small islands of DONOUSSA,

KOUFONISSI, SHINOUSSA & IRAKLIA,

ASTIPALAIA, TINOS, ANDROS, SIPHNOS,

MILOS, SERIFOS, KITHNOS & KEA

with excursion details to

DELOS, ANTIPAROS, THIRASIA & KIMOLOS

As well as

The Mainland Ports of

PIRAEUS, RAFINA & LAVRIO

For the package & villa holidaymaker,
backpacker & independent traveller
whether journeying by air, car, coach, ferry-boat or train.

by

Geoffrey O'Connell

Published by

Ashford

1 Church Road
Shedfield
Hampshire
SO3 2HW

Geoffrey O'Connell's highly personalised style of writing encompasses books on yacht building and maintenance, humour, travel as well as a magnum opus concerning the history of Southwick village, where he and fellow traveller and wife, Rosemary, live in a Georgian house on a centuries-old Hampshire estate.

They regard themselves as geriatric, if very knowledgeable backpackers whilst ferry-boating about the Greek islands gathering information for the next guidebook.

One of the CANDID GUIDE Series

CONTENTS

Please do not forget that prices are given as a guide only and relate to the year in which the book is written. In recent years not only lodging and 'troughing' costs, but also transport charges, particularly ferry-boat fees, have escalated dramatically. The increased value of most other currencies to the Greek drachmae has compensated, to some extent, for apparently inexorably rising prices.

In an effort to keep readers as up-to-date as possible regarding these and other matters, I have introduced **GROC's GREEK ISLAND HOTLINE**. *See* elsewhere for details.

The series is entering its seventh year of publication and I would appreciate continuing to hear from readers who have any additions or corrections to bring to my attention. As in the past, all correspondence (except that addressed to 'Dear fifth' or similar endearments) will be answered.

I hope readers can excuse errors that creep (well gallop actually) into the welter of detailed information included in the body text. In order to keep the volumes as up-to-date as possible, the period from inception to publication is kept down to some six months which does result in the occasional slip up......

ILLUSTRATIONS

The Candid Guides unique

'GROC's Greek Island Hotline'

Available to readers of the guides, this service enables a respondent to receive a bang up-to-the-minute update, to supplement the extensive information contained in a particular Candid Guide.

To obtain this paraphrased computer print-out, covering the Introductory Chapters, Athens, Piraeus & the Mainland Ports as well as any named islands, up to twenty five in number, all that is necessary is to:-

Complete the form below, enclosing a payment of £1.50 (to include postage), and send to:-

Willowbridge Publishing, Bridge House, Southwick Village,
Nr.Fareham, Hants. PO17 6DZ

Note: The information will be of no use to anyone who does not possess the relevant, most up to date GROC's Candid Greek Island Guide. We are unable to dispatch the Hotline without details of the guide AND which edition. This information is on the Inside Front Cover.

Planned departure dates ....
....

Mr/Mrs/Miss ....

of..

....

I possess: **GROC's Greek Island Guides**	Edition	I require: **GROC's Greek Island Hotline**
to:	....	to: ....
....	....	....
....	....	....
....	....	....
....	....	....
....	....	....

and enclose a fee of £1.50. Signature..Date ....

I appreciate that the 'Hotline' may not be dispatched for up to 7-10 days from receipt of this application.

INTRODUCTION

This volume is the second edition of the Cyclades, one of seven in the very popular and proven series of GROC's Candid Guides to the Greek Islands. The rationale, the *raison d'etre* behind their production is to treat each island grouping on an individual and comprehensive basis, rather than attempt overall coverage of the 100 or so islands usually described in one volume. This obviates attempting to do justice to, say, Ios in amongst an aggregation of many other, often disparate islands.

Due to the vast distances involved very few, if any, vacationers can possibly visit more than a number of islands in a particular group, even if spending as much as four weeks in Greece.

It is important for package and villa holiday-makers to have an unbiased and relevant description of their planned holiday surroundings rather than the usual extravagant hyperbole of the glossy sales brochure. It is vital for backpackers and ferry-boat travellers to have, on arrival, detailed and accurate information at their finger tips. With these differing requirements in mind factual, 'straight-from-the-shoulder' location reports have been combined with detailed plans of the major port, town and or city of each island in the group, as well as topographical island maps.

Amongst the guides generally available are earnest tomes dealing with Ancient and Modern Greece, a number of thumbnail travel booklets and some worthy, if often out-of-date books. Unfortunately they rarely assuage the various travellers' differing requirements. These might include speedy and accurate identification of one's position on arrival; the situation of accommodation as well as the whereabouts of a bank, the postal services and tourist offices. Additional requisites probably embrace a swift and easy to read resumé of the settlement's main locations, cafe-bars, tavernas and restaurants; detailed local bus and ferry-boat timetables, as well as a full island narrative. Once the traveller has settled in, then and only then, can he or she feel at ease, making their own finds and discoveries.

I have chosen to omit lengthy accounts of the relevant, fabulous Greek mythology and history. These aspects of Greece are, for the serious student, very ably related by authors far more erudite than myself. Moreover, most islands have a semi-official tourist guide translated into English, and for that matter, French, German and Scandinavian. They are usually well worth the 300 to 500 drachmae (drs) they cost, are extremely informative in 'matters archaeological' and are quite well produced, if rather out of date, with excellent colour photographs. Admittedly the English translation might seem a little quaint (try to read Greek, let alone translate it) and the maps are often unreliable, but cartography is not a strong Hellenic suit!

Each **Candid Guide** is finally researched as close to the publication date as is possible. On the other hand, in an effort to facilitate production of this volume, as early as possible in the forthcoming year, it has been found necessary to omit any information that requires waiting until the springtime of the year of publication. These details, often available as late as March, April or even May, and which include up to date air, ferry-boat and train fares, are 'punched' into the **Hotline**, for details of which read on. Naturally, any new ideas are incorporated but, in the main, the guides follow a now well proven formula.

Part One introduces the particular island group and details the relevant mainland ports from which ferry-boat connections can be made. Part Two includes a detailed description of each island, the layout being designed to facilitate quick and easy reference.

With this edition, the long planned decision has been implemented to split out the Introductory chapters and Athens City into a separate guide. With the continued improvement and expansion of the island chapters, not only was the sheer volume of information becoming unwieldy but innumerable readers, who wished to take along two or three guides, were humping about hundreds of pages of duplicated chapters. In years gone by it was almost mandatory to include Athens in any Greek island guide book as the capital city was pivotal for most forms of travel. Now that all the island groups have one or more, international airports, it is possible to travel direct, without recourse to Athens. Even if there isn't a convenient international facility, many travellers' only sight of Athens is the two airports where they transfer to a domestic flight for the onward leg. *There is nothing permanent except change (by courtesy of Heraditus 540-475 BC).*

The exchange rate has fluctuated quite violently in recent years and at the time of writing the final draft of this guide, the rate to the English pound (£) was hovering about 260drs. Unfortunately prices are subject to fluctuation, usually upward with annual increases varying between 10-20%. Happily the drachma tends to devalue by approximately the same amount.

Recommendations and personalities are almost always based on personal observation and experience, occasionally emphasised by the discerning comments of readers or colleagues. They may well change from year to year and be subject to different interpretation by others.

The series incorporates a number of innovative ideas and unique services which have evolved over the years and include:

The Decal: Since 1985 some of the accommodation and eating places recommended in the guides display a specially produced decal to help readers identify the particular establishment. The decals are dated so a reader can identify the relevancy of the recommendation. The current issue is the third (1989-91). Previous ones have been 1984-85 & 1986-88.

GROC's Greek Island Hotline: An absolutely unique service available to readers of the Candid Guides. Application enables purchasers of the guides to obtain a summary detailing all pertinent, relevant comments and information that have become available since the publication of the particular guide – in effect, an up-to-date update. The Hotline is constantly being revised and incorporates bang up-to-the-moment intelligence. A payment of £1.50 (incl. postage) enables a respondent to receive the paraphrased computer printout in respect of the various guides, with an upper limit of twenty five islands, in addition to Athens and the various mainland ports. An interested reader only has to complete the form, or write a letter, requesting the Hotline, enclose the fee and post to Willowbridge Enterprises, Bridge House, Southwick Village, Nr Fareham, Hants PO17 6DZ.

Travel Insurance: A comprehensive holiday insurance plan that 'gives cover that many other policies do not reach....' See elsewhere for details.

The author (and publisher) are very interested in considering ways and means of improving the guides and adding to the backup facilities, so are delighted to hear from readers with their suggestions.

Enjoy yourselves and 'Ya Sou' (welcome).

Geoffrey O'Connell 1989

ACKNOWLEDGMENTS

Every year the list of those to be formally thanked grows and this edition shows no diminution in their number which has forced the original brief entry from the inside front cover to an inside page.

Contributors who assisted with my Cyclades research, for this second edition, include Anne Merewood, Liz & David Drummond-Tyler and Han Warr.

Apart from those numerous friends and confidants we meet on passage, there are the many correspondents who are kind enough to contact me with useful information, all of who, in the main, remain unnamed.

Rosemary who accompanies me, adding her often unwanted, uninformed comments and asides (and who I occasionally threaten not to take next time), requires especial thanks for unrelieved, unstinting (well almost unstinting) support, despite being dragged from this or that sun kissed beach.

Although receiving reward, other than in heaven, some of those who assisted me in the production of this edition require specific acknowledgement for effort far beyond the siren call of vulgar remuneration! These worthies include Graham Bishop, who drew the maps and plans, and Viv Hitié, who controls the word processor.

Lastly, and as always, I must admonish Richard Joseph for ever encouraging and cajoling me to take up the pen – surely the sword is more fun?

The cover picture of a windmill (The Chora, Sikinos) is produced by kind permission of GREEK ISLAND PHOTOS, Willowbridge Enterprises, Bletchley, Milton Keynes, Bucks.

Hozoviotizza Monastery, Amorgos. Acknowledgement to Anne Merewood.

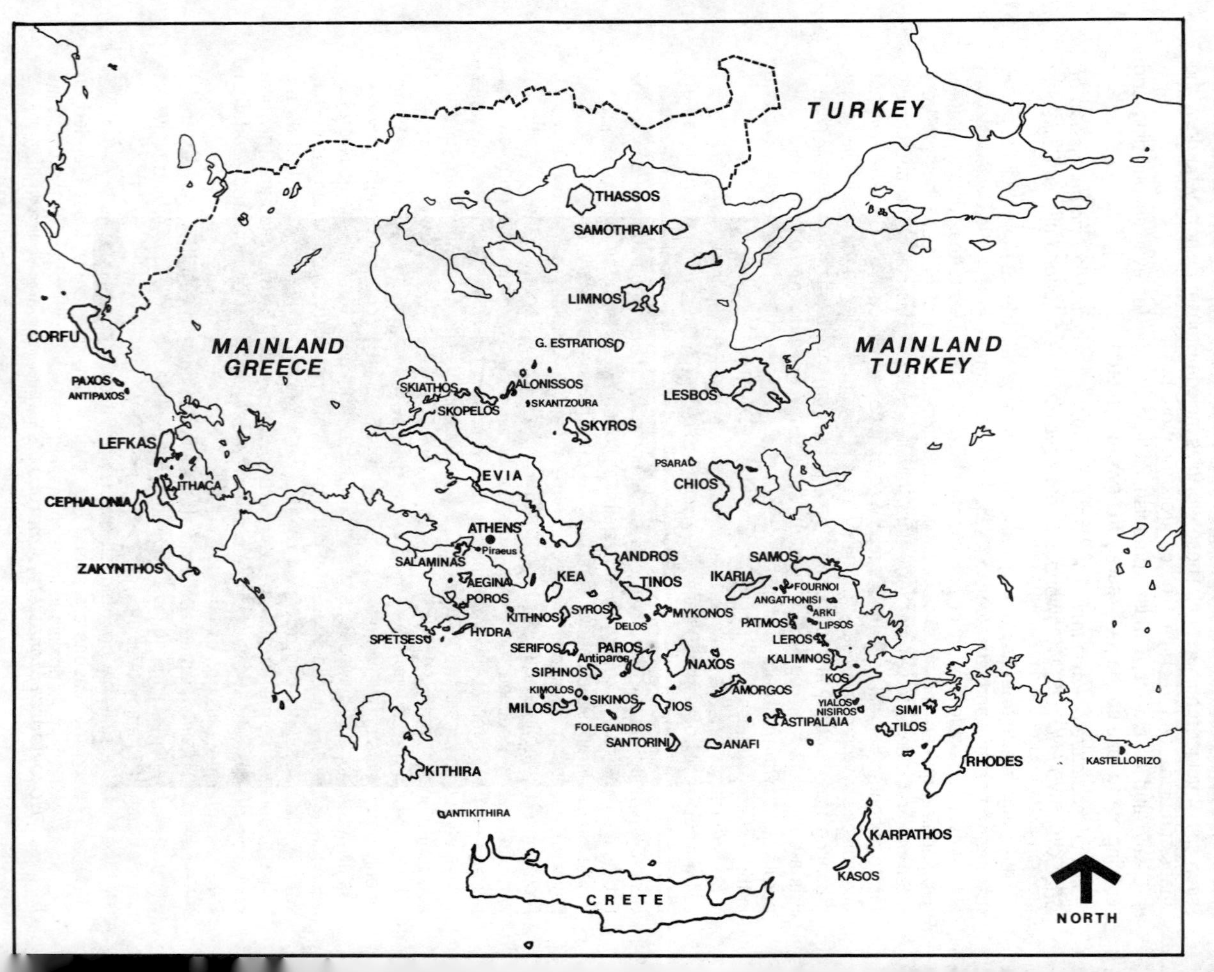

THE GREEK ISLANDS

1 PART ONE
Introduction to the Cyclades Islands (Kiklades, Kikladhes, Kykladen, Κυκλαδες)

Fair Greece! Sad relic of departed worth! Immortal, though no more; though fallen, great! Byron.

A loosely knit scattering of some twenty four inhabited islands set in the Aegean stretching south towards Crete, west beneath the island of Evia and east towards the island groupings that edge the Turkish mainland.

They range in size from tiny to large; arid to verdant; gentle hills to mountainous; plain-featured to beautiful and *au naturel* to Western sophistication. In fact, the Cyclades offer almost every possible hue, shade and variety of Greek island. Due to their diverse nature, geographical spread and accessibility from the mainland port of Piraeus, they are very often the first islands to which a ferry-boat traveller aspires. This can be no bad choice, for, to misquote Samuel Johnson, "a man who cannot find solace in the Cyclades will not find solace anywhere in Greece". Certainly there is a magic quality to the islands, whether steaming past the rocky fastness of their perimeter or urgently bustling into port. Whether it is a cool, clear morning; a hot, motionless, steamy afternoon or, perchance, a deep purple night with the lights of other steamers and scattered island settlements winking in the distant darkness.

No two islands are the same, but rarely are they so entirely different that each port of call will not recall both similarity and dissimilarity to others in the chain. Two impressions, amongst all the others, will surely prevail – the wind and the granite mountainsides. Generally, during the summer, the gusts come and go, but from the middle of July to the middle of September the *Meltemi* blows almost continuously from the north.

The almost impossible choice of islands on offer ranges from, say, Mykonos (once a haunt of the 'beautiful people', still chic but now more a holiday centre for voyeurs); Naxos (a wild, mountainous north and gentle, beach fringed south) to the simple, still comparatively untouched, charm of Kimolos or Sikinos. The final selection can only depend on the travellers own sensibilities but, whatever his or her fancy, the Cyclades will surely fulfil them all and the siren call will undoubtedly echo down the years to return and return and...

It would be a travesty not to sound a warning note. The simple, naive, primitive Greece of only thirty years ago (so appealing to voyagers in the past, but born of grinding poverty) has all but disappeared. Mass tourism is not entirely to blame, for once the decision had been made that the Greeks should be pitchforked into the 20th century then the curtain was slowly but surely rung down on the past, and rightly so. But all is not lost as the Greek people, in the main, retain their exuberance and simple charm, in addition to which centuries old customs, ways and manners have not changed or disappeared altogether – 'Plus ca change, plus non ca change'.

I trust the following chapters will assist travellers, planning to visit the Cyclades, in the formulation of their arrangements. I hope they experience the same love affair that I have been privileged to enjoy over the years.

I have made a possibly controversial decision, which is to include Astipalaia in the Cyclades. I hope my reasons are sound but, even if not, they are at least founded on practicality. Certainly Astipalaia is infinitely easier to reach from certain of the Cyclades islands, than from the Dodecanese, with which it is usually bracketed. Additionally its geography and Chora are distinctly Cycladean, bearing little, if any, similarity to any of the Dodecanese islands. I accept that Patmos (alone of the Dodecanese) has a Chora, but a 'fortified monastery Chora', nothing like the typical, Cycladean, hilltop capital town.

The history of the islands grouped together under the loose geographical ties of the Cyclades is, as elsewhere in Greece, confusing, to say the least. Even the nomenclature and number of islands in the group has been the subject of much change and alteration over the years. Certainly, by about 1000 BC, the Ionians from the west coast of Greece had imposed their worship of Letos on Delos, as well as imbued the island with various myths honouring Apollo. Thus, for a time, tiny Delos became the most important island in the whole Aegean. At about this time the Cyclades (or *Kyklos*), referred to the twelve or fifteen islands circled around Delos, but now refers to an administrative area including some thirty or so islands.

Settlement of the Cyclades can be traced as far back as 7000 BC but the earliest, easily identifiable period of occupation was between 3000-2600 BC. An early attraction, to outsiders, was the volcanic mineral obsidian, centred on Milos island. By about 2000 BC the Minoans of Crete were in command and had established large settlements on the islands of Milos and Santorini. They were followed by the Mycenaeans, a Dark Age and then the Ionians. In their turn these invaders were routed by the Persians in 490 BC, who were on their way to a naval 'punch-up' with the City-State of Athens. This event took place at Salamis. The Persians lost, after which, naturally enough, the Athenians created an Empire, although they had the cunning to call it a League or Confederation. The Cycladian islands baulked against this regime, but were brought back into line by Athens under the guise of a Second Confederation. From then on times were turbulent, with the Egyptian Ptolemies and others variously emerging winners, until the Romans cropped up in 197 BC. The latter allowed the patriarchs of Rhodes island to run the show, taking the reins of power back again, until their own empire fragmented in AD 395. The Cycladians were then left to the ravages of various invading hordes. The Byzantine Empire, which remotely involved itself in the Cyclades, received a bloody nose in the early 1200s from Crusaders who, instead of sorting out the Arabs and Jerusalem, found an easier target in Constantinople, which they laid waste. The Venetians, who had been keeping a close eye on events, took over the Cyclades, as well as other bits of Greece including Crete, Rhodes, some of the Dodecanese and the Ionian islands. The Venetians parcelled up the various islands and handed them out to their ruling families. One of these patriarchs, having taken the title of Duke of Naxos, sided with the Franks and managed to hang on to that particular island until the 1560s, by which time most of the other islands had been lost to the Turks. Not a nation to give in easily, the Venetians pursued a running battle with the Turks, taking back this or that island until they irrevocably lost Crete in 1669. However, one outpost, Tinos, remained in Venetian hands until the early 1700s. If all this were not enough, during the middle 1600s, English ships captain adventurers, with letters of patent from Charles I, raided various Cycladean islands for antiquities. With the Turks firmly at the helm in the Aegean, a hundred years of peace ensued until the Russians and Turks pitched into each other in 1770. The Russians annexed numerous of the islands, for the next five years, after which the Turks took over again, until 1821. In this year the Greeks kicked over the traces once and for all and painfully and slowly drove out their erstwhile overlords, with the resultant formation of the independent Greek State.

The principle religion is Greek Orthodox, but with Catholic enclaves left over from the Venetian occupation.

A number of the Cycladean islands produce their own wines, the most renowned of which are those of Santorini.

Before tackling the individual islands, it is helpful to break them down into smaller geographical sections, taking into account the ferry-boat lines of communications. The upshot is that the Cyclades can be split into East and West chains, with their own East and West wings. The eastern chain includes Syros, Mykonos, Paros, Naxos, Amorgos,

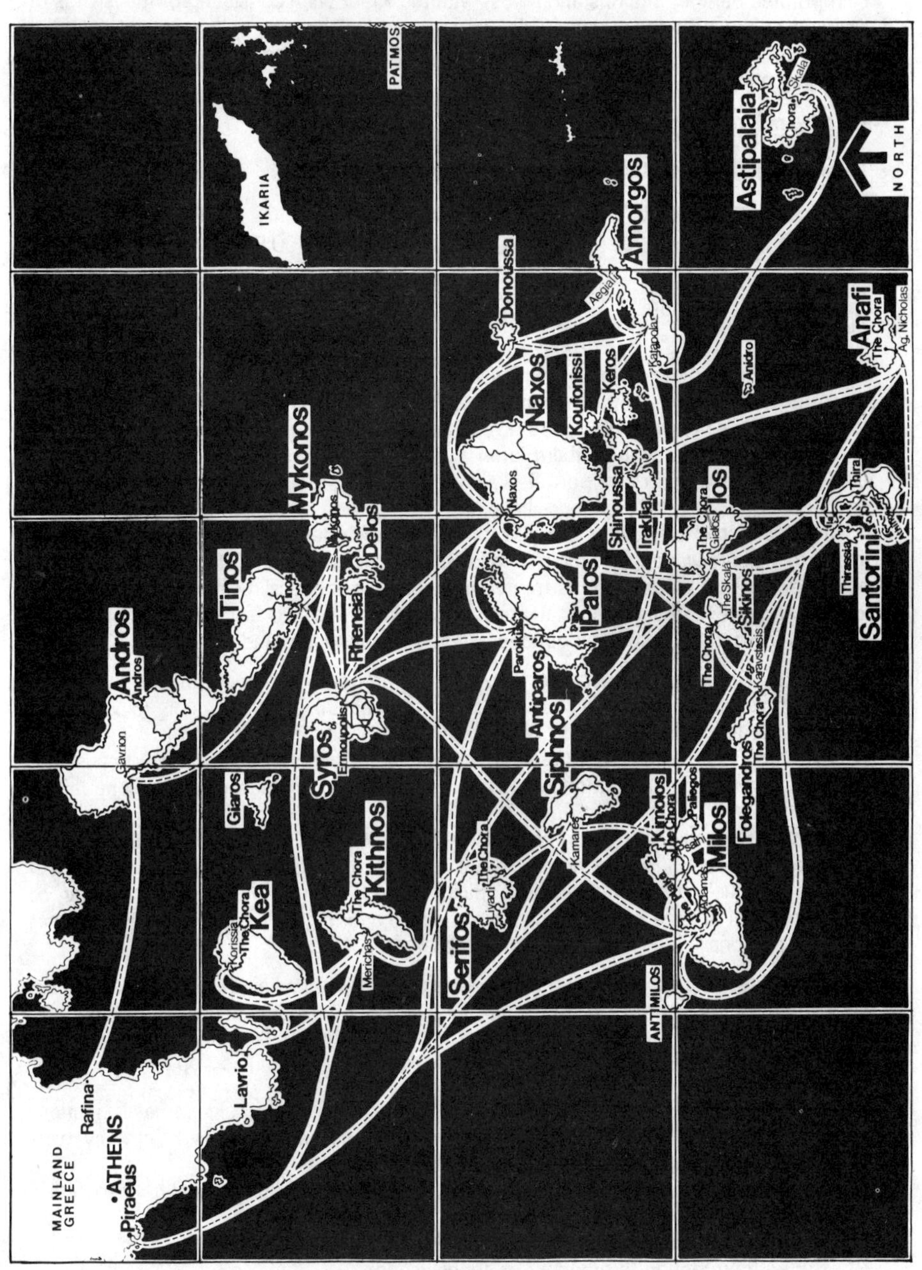

Illustration 1 The Cyclades Islands

Ios and Santorini, with the East wing taking in Andros and Tinos. The western chain incorporates Serifos, Siphnos and Milos, with the West wing consisting of the islands of Kea and Kithnos. To these generalities must be added the other islands, as well as the various connections and excursions, but at least this arrangement enables me to establish a starting point.

For the statistically minded:

The monthly average temperatures of Naxos island are:

		Jan	Feb	Mar	Apr	May	June	July	Aug	Sept	Oct	Nov	Dec
Average air temperatures	C°	12.4	12.5	13.4	16.3	19.6	23.2	24.8	25	22.7	20	17	14
	F°	54	54	56	61	67	74	77	77	73	68	63	57
Sea surface temperatures (at 1400hrs)	C°	15	15	15	16.8	19	22.2	24	23.5	22.7	20	17.4	15.5
	F°	59	59	59	62	66	72	75	74	73	68	63	60

A rather incomplete map of the Cyclades is produced by *Clyde Surveys Ltd*, now marketed by *Bartholomews*. The best, inexpensive, general map of the area is printed in Greece by *Delta Publications*.

At the end of this chapter there is an alphabetical list of the islands included in the book, their major town and port(s), as well as a quick reference resumé of ferry-boat connections.

The island chapters follow a format, which has been devised and developed over the years, to make the layout as simple to follow as is possible, without losing the informative nature of the text. Each island is treated in a similar manner, allowing the traveller easy identification of his (or her) immediate requirements. The text is faced by the relevant port and town maps, with descriptions tied into the various island routes.

Symbols, Keys & Definitions Below are some notes in respect of the few initials and symbols used in the text, as well as an explanation of the possibly idiosyncratic nouns, adjectives and phrases, to be found scattered throughout the book.

Where and when inserted, a star system of rating indicates my judgement of an island, and possibly its accommodation and restaurant standards, by the inclusion of one to five stars. One star signifies bad, two basic, three good, four very good and five excellent. I must admit the ratings are carried out on whimsical grounds and are based purely on personal observation. For instance, where a place, establishment or island receives a detailed 'critique' I may consider that sufficient unto the day... The absence of a star, or any mention at all, has no detrimental significance and might, for instance, indicate that I did not personally inspect this or that establishment.

Keys The key *Tmr*, in conjunction with grid references, is used as a map reference to aid easy identification of this or that location on port and town plans. Other keys used in the text include *Sbo* – 'Sea behind one'; *Fsw* – 'Facing seawards'; *Fbqbo* – 'Ferry-boat quay behind one'; *BPTs* – 'British Package Tourists' and *OTT* – 'Over The Top'.

GROC's definitions, 'proper' adjectives & nouns: These may require some elucidation, as most do not appear in 'official' works of reference and are used with my own interpretation, as set out below:
Backshore: the furthest strip of beach from the sea's edge. The marginal rim separating the shore from the surrounds. *See* **Scrubbly**.
Benzina: a small fishing boat.
Chatty: with pretention to grandeur or sophistication.
Dead: an establishment that appears to be 'terminally' closed, and not about to open for business, but...

Donkey-droppings: as in 'two donkey-droppings', indicating a very small, hamlet. *See* **One-eyed**.
Doo-hickey: an Irish based colloquialism suggesting an extreme lack of sophistication and or rather 'daffy' (despite contrary indications in the authoritative and excellent *Partridges Dictionary of Slang!*).
Downtown: a rundown/derelict area of a settlement – the wrong side of the 'railway tracks'.
Ethnic: very unsophisticated, Greek indigenous and, as a rule, applied to hotels and pensions. *See* **Provincial**.
Gongoozle: borrowed from canal boat terminology, and is the state of very idly and leisurely, but inquisitively staring at others who are involved in some busy activity.
Greasy spoon: a dirty, unwholesome cafe-bar, restaurant or taverna.
Great unwashed: the less attractive, modern day mutation of the 1960s hippy. They are usually Western European, inactive loafers and layabouts 'by choice', or unemployed drop-outs. Once having located a desirable location, often a splendid beach, they camp under plastic and in shabby tents, thus ensuring the spot is despoiled for others. The 'men of the tribe' tend to trail a mangy dog on a piece of string. The women, more often than not, with a grubby child or two in train, pester cafe-bar clients to purchase items of jewellery.
Note the above genre appears to be incurably penniless (but then who isn't?).
Grecocilious: necessary to describe those Greeks, usually bank clerks or tour office owners, who are making their money from tourists but are disdainful of the 'hand that feeds them'. They appear to consider holiday-makers as being some form of small intellect, low-browed, tree clambering, inferior relation to the Greek homo-sapiens. They usually can converse passably in two or three foreign languages (when it suits them) and habitually display an air of weary sophistication.
Hillbilly: another adjective or noun, similar to 'ethnic', but applied to describe countryside or a settlement, as in 'backwoods'.
Hippy: those who live outside the predictable, boring (!) mainstream of life and are frequently genuine, if sometimes impecunious travellers. The category may include students or young professionals taking a sabbatical and who are often 'negligent' of their sartorial appearance.
Independents: vacationers who make their own travel and accommodation arrangements, spurning the 'siren calls' of structured tourism, preferring to step off the package holiday carousel and make their own way.
Kosta'd: used to describe the 'ultimate' in development necessary for a settlement to reach the apogee required to satisfy the popular common denominator of package tourism. That this state of paradise on earth has been accomplished, will be evidenced by the 'High St' presence of cocktail or music bars, discos, (garden) pubs, bistros and fast food. 'First division' locations are pinpointed by the aforementioned establishments offering inducements, which may include wet 'T' shirt, nightdress or pyjama bottom parties; air conditioning, space invader games and table top videos, as well as sundowner, happy or doubles hours.
Local prices: *See* **Special prices**.
Mr Big: a local trader or pension owner, an aspiring tycoon, a small fish trying to be a big one in a 'small pool'. Despite being sometimes flashy with shady overtones, his lack of sophistication is apparent by his not being Grecocilious!
Noddies or nodders: the palpable, floating evidence of untreated sewage which has been discharged into the sea.
One-eyed: small. *See* **Donkey-droppings**.
Poom: a descriptive noun 'borrowed' after sighting on Crete, some years ago, a crudely written sign advertising accommodation that simply stated POOMS! This particular place

was basic with low-raftered ceilings, earth-floors and windowless rooms, simply equipped with a pair of truckle beds and rickety oilcloth covered washstand – very reminiscent of typical Cycladean cubicles of the 1950/60s period.

Provincial: usually applied to accommodation and is an improvement on **Ethnic**. Not meant to indicate, say, dirty but should conjure up images of faded, rather gloomy establishments with a mausoleum atmosphere; high ceilinged Victorian rooms with worn, brown linoleum; dusty, tired aspidistras as well as bathrooms and plumbing of unbelievable antiquity.

Richter scale: borrowed from earthquake seismology and employed to indicate the (appalling) state of toilets, on an 'eye-watering' scale.

Rustic: unsophisticated, unrefined.

Schlepper: vigorous touting for customers by restaurant staff. It is said of a skilled market schlepper that he can 'retrieve' a passer-by from up to thirty or forty metres beyond the stall.

Scrubbly: usually applied to a beach or countryside and indicating a rather messy, shabby area.

Special prices: A phrase employed to conceal the fact that the price charged is no more, no less than that of all the other bandits, no, no competitors. **Local prices** is a homespun variation designed to give the impression that the goods are charged at a much lower figure than that obtainable elsewhere. Both are totally inaccurate, misleading misnomers.

Squatty: A Turkish or French style ablution arrangement. None of the old, familiar lavatory bowl and seat. Oh no, just two moulded footprints edging a dirty looking hole, set in a porcelain surround. Apart from the unaccustomed nature of the exercise, the Lord simply did not give us enough limbs to keep a shirt up and control wayward trousers, that constantly attempt to flop down on to the floor, awash with goodness knows what! All this has to be enacted whilst gripping the toilet roll in one hand and wiping one's 'botty' with the other hand. Impossible! Incidentally, ladies should (perhaps) substitute blouse for shirt and skirt for trousers, but then it is easier (I am told) to tuck a skirt into one's waistband!

Way-station: mainly used to refer to an office or terminus, stuck out in the sticks and cloaked with an abandoned, unwanted air.

Cyladean islands described include:

Island name(s)	**Capital**	**Ports** (at which inter-island ferry-boats & Flying Dolphins dock)	**Ferry-boat/Flying Dolphin connections** (**EB**=excursion boat; **FB**=ferry-boat; **FD**=Flying Dolphin; **M**=mainland).
Amorgos	The Chora	Katapola	**FB:**Aegiali(Amorgos),Donoussa,Koufonissi, Shinoussa,Iraklia,Naxos,Paros,Mykonos Syros,Piraeus(M)/Rafina(M). **FB:**Astipalaia,Kalimnos,Kos,Nisiros, Tilos,Simi,Rhodes.
		Aegiali	**FB:** *See* Katapola.
Anafi (Anaphi, Anaphe)	The Chora	Ag Nikolaos	**FB:** Santorini,Sikinos,Folegandros,Milos, Naxos,Paros,Piraeus(M). **FB:** Ag Nikolaos(Crete),Sitia(Crete),Kasos, Karpathos,Rhodes.
Andros	Andros	Gavrion	**FB:** Tinos,Syros,Mykonos,Rafina(M).
Antiparos (Andiparos)	Antiparos (Kastro)		**EB:** Paros.
Astipalaia (Astypalaia, Astypalea, Astipalea)	The Chora	Skala	**FB:** Amorgos,Naxos,Syros,Piraeus(M). **FB:** Kalimnos,Kos,Nisiros, Simi,Rhodes.

Delos (Dhilos, Dilos)			**EB:** Mykonos & Tinos.
Donoussa (Dhenoussa, Dhonoussa, Donousa)	Donoussa	As capital	*See* Amorgos.
Folegandros (Pholegandros, Polycandros)	The Chora	Karavostassis	**FB:** Sikinos,Ios,Santorini,Naxos, Paros,Syros,Piraeus(M). **FB:** Milos,Kimolos,Siphnos,Serifos,Kithnos **FB:** Anafi,Ag Nikolaos(Crete),Sitia(Crete), Kasos,Karpathos,Chalki,Rhodes.
Ios (Nios)	The Chora	Gialos	**FB:** Folegandros,Sikinos,Naxos,Paros, Santorini,Mykonos,Siphnos,Serifos, Tinos,Piraeus(M). **FD:** Paros,Naxos,Mykonos. **FD:** Santorini,Iraklion(Crete).
Iraklia	The Chora	Ag Georgios	*See* Amorgos
Kea (Tzia)	The Chora (Ioulis)	Korissia	Lavrio(M)/Rafina(M)* *Height of season only.
Kimolos (Kimilos)	The Chora	Psathi	*See* Milos.
Kithnos (Kythnos Thermia)	The Chora (Kithnos)	Merichas	**FB:** Serifos,Siphnos,Milos,Kimolos, Syros,Piraeus(M). **FB:** Lavrio(M). **FB:** Kea,Tinos,Andros,Rafina(M).
Koufonissi (Koufonisia, Koufonisi)	Koufonissi	As capital	*See* Amorgos.
Milos (Melos,Milo)	The Plaka	Adamas	**FB:** Kimolos,Siphnos,Serifos,Kithnos, Syros,Rafina(M)/Piraeus(M). **FB:** Kimolos,Folegandros,Sikinos,Ios, Santorini,Anafi,Ag Nikolaos(Crete), Sitia(Crete),Kasos,Karpathos,Rhodes.
		Pollonia	**EB:** Kimolos.
Mykonos (Myconos, Mikonos, Miconos)	Mykonos	As capital	**FB:** Tinos,Andros,Paros,Syros Santorini,Anafi,Crete. **FB:** Rafina(M)/Piraeus(M). **FD:** Paros,Ios,Santorini,Iraklion(Crete).
Naxos	Naxos	As capital	**FB:** Ios,Sikinos,Folegandros,Paros, Santorini,Iraklia,Shinoussa,Koufonissi, Donoussa,Amorgos,Astipalaia, Kalimnos,Kos,Rhodes. **FB:** Syros,Piraeus(M)/Rafina(M). **FD:** Paros,Ios,Santorini,Iraklion(Crete). **FD:** Mykonos.
Paros (Paros)	Paroikias	As capital	**FB:** Naxos,Ios,Sikinos,Folegandros, Santorini,Anafi,Iraklion(Crete). **FB:** Ikaria,Samos. **FB:** Donoussa,Amorgos,Koufonissi, Shinoussa,Iraklia. **FB:** Amorgos,Astipalaia,Nisiros,Kalymnos, Kos,Tilos,Simi,Rhodes,Chalki, Karpathos,Kasos,Crete. **FB:** Mykonos,Tinos. **FB:** Piraeus(M). **FD:** Naxos,Mykonos. **FD:** Ios,Santorini,Iraklion(Crete).

			EB: Piraeus(M). **EB:** Antiparos & Siphnos.
Rheneia	Rheneia		**EB:** Mykonos.
Santorini (Santorine, Thira, Thera)	Thira (Phira Fira)	Thira, Ia, Athinos	**FB:** Ios,Naxos,Paros,Sikinos,Folegandros, Siphnos,Serifos,Mykonos,Syros,Milos, Kimolos,Piraeus(M). **FB:** Anafi,Ag Nikolaos(Crete),Sitia(Crete), Kasos,Karpathos,Chalki,Rhodes. **FD:** Ios,Paros,Mykonos,Naxos. **FD:** Iraklion(Crete).
Serifos (Seriphos)	The Chora	Livadi	**FB:** Siphnos,Milos,Kimolos,Sikinos, Folegandros,Ios,Santorini,Syros,Piraeus(M). **FB:** Kithnos,Rafina(M).
Shinoussa (Schinoussa, Skhinoussa, Skinoussa)	Shinoussa	Mersini Bay	*See* Amorgos.
Sikinos	The Chora	The Skala (Alopronia)	*See* Folegandros.
Siphnos (Sifnos)	Apollonia	Kamares	**FB:** Serifos,Kithnos,Milos, Rafina(M)/Piraeus(M). **FB:** Milos,Kimolos,Ios,Santorini. **EB:** Paros.
Syros (Siros)	Ermoupolis	As capital	**FB:** Paros,Naxos,Ios,Santorini,Tinos, Mykonos,Sikinos,Folegandros,Milos, Siphnos,Serifos,Kythnos. **FB:** Ikaria,Samos. **FB:** Iraklia,Shinoussa,Koufonissi,Donoussa, Amorgos,Astipalaia,Kalimnos,Kos, Nisiros,Tilos,Simi,Rhodes. **FB:** Rafina(M)/Piraeus(M).
Tinos	Tinos	As capital	**FB:** Andros,Mykonos,Syros,Rafina(M). **FB:** Piraeus(M). **EB:** Delos.

2 PIREAUS (Pireas, Pireefs) & Other Ports including Rafina & Lavrio

Fortune and hope farewell! I've found the port, you've done with me; go now with others sport. From a Greek epigram.

Tel prefix 01. Piraeus is the port of Athens (Illustrations 2, 3 & 4) and the usual ferry-boat departure point for most of the Aegean islands. The town's layout is confusing on first acquaintance, but now very unlike the old Piraeus as portrayed in the film *Never on a Sunday*. The bawdy seaport cafes, tavernas and seedy waterfront have been replaced by smart shipping offices, banks, tree planted thoroughfares, squares and parks.

Arrival at Piraeus will usually be by bus or Metro, unless arriving by sea when the choice of transport may well be a ferry-boat or hydrofoil (Well, it would be a long, tiring swim, wouldn't it?).

ARRIVAL BY BUS From Syntagma Sq (Athens), Bus No. 40 arrives at Plateia Korai (*Tmr* C3), but in truth that is rather an over simplification. For a start the bus is absolutely crammed, especially early morning, and it is very difficult to know one's exact whereabouts, which is germane as the bus hurtles on down to the end of the Piraeus peninsula. The first indicator that the end of the ¾ hour journey is imminent is when the bus runs parallel to the Metro lines. The second is crossing a wide avenue at right-angles (Leoforos Vassileos Georgiou), after which signs for the *Archaeological Museum* indicate that it is time to bale out.

From Plateia Korai, north-west along Leoforos Vassileos Georgiou (Yeoryiou) leads to the Main (Grand or Central) Harbour (*Tmr* D2); south-east progresses towards Limin Zeas (Pasalimani) (*Tmr* C/D4) and east towards Limin Mounikhias (Tourkolimano) (*Tmr* B5), the latter two being marina harbours. Limin Zeas is where the Flying Dolphins dock.

From Omonia Sq (Athens) Bus No. 49 arrives at Ethniki Antistaseos (*Tmr* C2); from the East airport, (a yellow) Bus No. 19 (but often numberless) arrives at Plateia Karaiskaki (*Tmr* C/D2). This latter Square (Akti Tzelepi) is a main bus terminal. The note in brackets regarding the No. 19 bus should point out that all the other buses are blue.

Another service (Bus No. 101) arrives at Theotoki St (*Tmr* E/F3/4), from whence head north-east towards Sakhtouri St, on which turn left in a northerly direction to reach the southern end of the Main Harbour waterfront.

ARRIVAL BY METRO Piraeus Metro station (*Tmr* 1C1/2), the end of the line, is hidden away in a large but rather inconspicuous building, flanked by Plateia Loudovikou. It could well be a warehouse, an empty shell of an office block, in fact almost anything but a Metro terminus. Passengers emerge opposite the quayside, towards the north end of the Grand Harbour.

If catching a ferry almost immediately, it is probably best to make a temporary headquarters by turning right out of the Metro building, following the quay round to the left and 'falling' into one of the three or so cafe-bars set in the harbour-facing side of a sizeable quayside block of buildings. The importance of establishing a shore base, or bridgehead, becomes increasingly apparent whilst attempts are made to locate the particular ferry-boat departure point.

To obtain tickets also turn left (*Fsw*) out of the Metro station and follow the quayside round. One of the first major landmarks is Karaiskaki (or Akti Tzelepi) Sq (*Tmr* C/D2), fronted by large, shipping office buildings surmounted by a number of neon lit signs. These advertising slogans change from year to year but the point is that they are eye-catching. Proceed along the quay road (Akti Posidonos), between the Streets of Gounari and Ethniki Antistaseos, (*Tmr* C2), keeping the waterfront to the right. Reference to **Ferry-Boat Ticket Offices, A To Z** gives details of various ticket offices.

The Port police are located in a quayside shed and must be regarded as favourites to dispense fairly accurate information in respect of ferry-boats. Any information received is best tucked away for future comparison with the rest of the advice acquired.

ARRIVAL BY FERRY Reorientate using the above information, but bearing in mind that ferries dock all the way round the Grand Harbour, from the area of the Metro Station (*Tmr* 1C1/2) as far down as the Olympic office (*Tmr* 8D3).

ARRIVAL BY FLYING DOLPHIN The hydrofoils dock at Limin Zeas Harbour. *See* **Flying Dolphins, A To Z**.

ARRIVAL BY TRAIN Peloponnese trains pull up at the same terminus building as the Metro (*Tmr* 1C1/2), whilst trains from Northern Greece 'steam' into the far (north-west) side of the Grand Harbour (*Tmr* 19D/E1/2).

THE ACCOMMODATION & EATING OUT

The Accommodation Although I have never had to doss (or camp) out in Piraeus, I am advised that it is not to be recommended. There are just too many disparate (desperate?) characters wandering about.

Close by the Metro Station are the:-

Hotel Ionion (*Tmr* 4C2) (Class C) 10 Kapodistrion. Tel 417 0992

Directions: Turn left from the Metro station (*Fsw*) along the quay road, Kalimasioti St, and left again at the first turning.

The hotel, halfway up on the right, is noticeable by the prominent sign promising *Family Hotel and from now on Economical Prices*. But is it, with a single room sharing a bathroom charged at 2080drs & a double room, also sharing, 3160drs?

The Delfini (*Tmr* 5C2) (Class C) 7 Leoharous St. Tel 412 3512

Directions: As above, but the second turning left.

Singles cost 2500drs & doubles 3500drs, both with bathroom en suite.

Hotel Elektra (*Tmr* 6C2) (Class E) 12 Navarinou. Tel 417 7057

Directions: At the top of Leoharous St, turn right on to Navarinou St and the hotel is at the end of the block.

Recommended as being very comfortable and convenient. During the season a single room costs 1190drs & a double 1540drs (1st April-30th Sept), both sharing the bathroom.

Whilst in this neighbourhood, a seedy, rather slovenly but cheap option is the:

Hotel Aenos (Enos) (*Tmr* C2) 14 Ethniki Antistaseos. Tel 417 4879

Directions: As above and from Odhos Navarinou cross over Gounari St, past the street market area to Ethniki Antistaseos.

Rooms share the bathrooms, with a single costing 950drs & a double 1250drs.

Follow the quay road of Akti Posidonos round to the right, along the waterfront of Akti Miaouli as far as Odhos Bouboulinas, the side street prior to Odhos Merarkhias. Turn up Bouboulinas St.

Youth Hostel No. 1 (*Tmr* 24D3) 8 Filonos St.

Directions: As above and on the right, between the 3rd and 4th lateral street, including the Esplanade.

An unofficial, large, very seedy looking establishment with, surprise, surprise, Youth Hostel dormitory style accommodation at Youth Hostel prices.

Further on along the waterfront Esplanade, towards the Custom's office (*Tmr* 14D/E3), and close by the Church of Ag Nikolaos, advances to the bottom of Leoforos Charilaou Trikoupi (*Tmr* D3). This street runs south-east and is amply furnished with cheaper hotels including the:-

Capitol Hotel (*Tmr* 7D3) Class C) Ch. Trikoupi/147 Filonos Sts. Tel 452 4911

Directions: As above.

A single room costs 1800drs & a double room 2400drs, both en suite.

Glaros Hotel (Class C) 4 Ch. Trikoupi. Tel 452 7887

Directions: as above.

Single rooms are en suite and start at 1500drs, while a double room, sharing a bathroom, costs

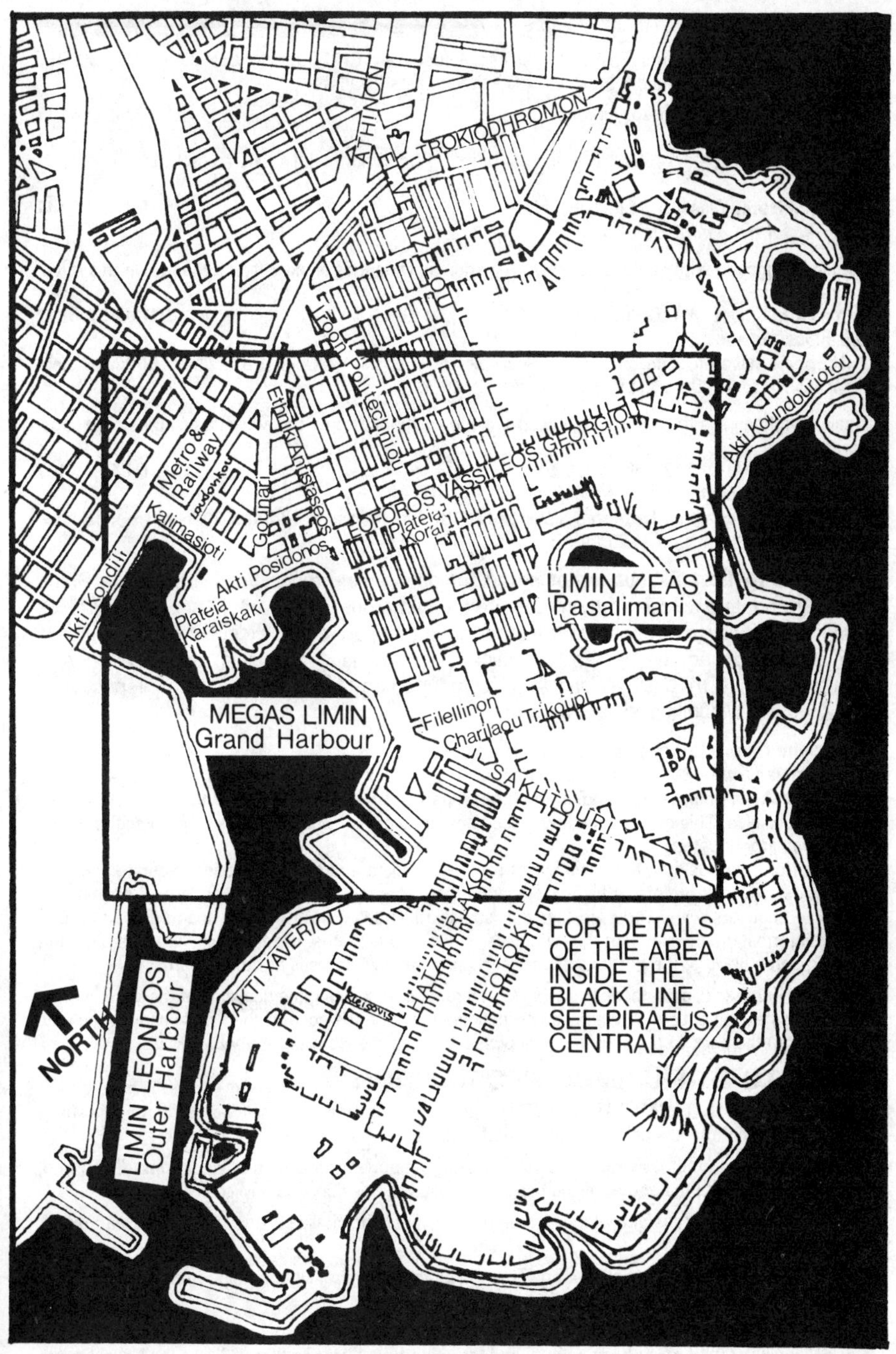

Illustration 2 Piraeus Port & Town

1725drs & en suite 2025drs. These charges rise, respectively, to 1650drs for a single & 1900/2225drs for a double room (1st June-31st Dec). A breakfast costs 250drs.

Serifos Hotel (Class C) 5 Ch. Trikoupi. Tel 452 4967
Directions: as above.

A single room costs 1450drs & a double room 2150drs, both with en suite bathrooms and the:

Santorini Hotel (Class C) 6 Ch. Trikoupi. Tel 452 2147
Prices as for the *Serifos Hotel*.

Forming a junction with Leoforos Charilaou Trikoupi is Notara St along which turn left. On this street is sited the:

Faros Hotel (Class D) 140 Notara St. Tel 452 6317
Directions: As above.

All rooms have en suite bathrooms. A single room costs 1200drs & a double 1600drs, rising, respectively, to 1300drs & 1700drs (1st July-31st Dec).

Again at right angles to Leoforos Charilaou Trikoupi, is Kolokotroni St on which are situated, amongst others:

Aris Hotel (Class D) 117 Kolokotroni St. Tel 452 0487
Directions: As above.

A single room sharing a bathroom is charged at 1000drs & en suite 1260drs. A double room sharing costs 1400drs & en suite 1630drs.

The Eating Out Piraeus is not noted for outstanding rendezvous around the Grand Harbour and its encircling terrain, despite the numerous restaurants, tavernas and cafes that line the quayside roads. On the other hand there are some excellent eating places in the area bordering the eastern coastline of the Piraeus peninsula, bounded by Akti Moutsopoulou (*Tmr* C/D3/4) and Akti Koumoundourou (*Tmr* B5) encircling (respectively) the Zeas and Mounikhias Harbours.

Especially recommended is the classy:

Delligiannis (*Tmr* 20B5) 1 Akti Koundouriotou. Tel 413 2013
Directions: A very pleasant setting, in the 'pretty' part of Piraeus, up on the hill to the south-west of Limin Mounikhias. This overlooks a few million pounds worth of private yachts lying to anchor in the attractive harbour setting.

Apart from the position, the selection of food is excellent and there is outside seating as well as that inside, which resembles a high-class saloon bar. The service is quick, friendly and honest. For instance, enquirers will be advised that the 'souvlaki flambe' is nothing more than souvlaki on fire! 'Inside information' advises that the 'birds liver in wine' is delicious, despite being listed as a starter. Costing some 500drs, the portions are larger than most main courses at other tavernas.

On Plateia Karaiskaki, a number of cafe-bar/restaurants stretch along the quayside of the large building that dominates the square. A white van sometimes parks on the edge of the Plateia early in the day, selling, from the back of the vehicle, small pizzas and feta cheese pies for about 100drs.

THE A TO Z OF USEFUL INFORMATION

AIRLINE OFFICE & TERMINUS (*Tmr* 8D3) The Olympic office is sited halfway along the Esplanade of Akti Miaouli, at the junction with Odhos II Merarkhias.

BANKS The most impressive is the vast, imposing emporium housing the **Macedonia & Thrace**, which rests opposite the corner of the Esplanade roads of Posidonos and Miaouli (*Tmr* 9C2).

BEACHES Between Zeas and Mounikhias Harbours, opposite Stalida island. Also *See* **Beaches, A To Z, Athens**.

BREAD SHOPS One on Loudovikou Sq (*Tmr* 10C2) and others on Odhos Kolokotroni (*Tmr* 21C2/3) and Charilaou Trikoupi (*Tmr* 21D3).

BUSES Two buses circulate around the peninsula of Piraeus. One proceeds from Roosevelt Sq to Limin Mounikhias, and on to Neon Faliron, and the other from Korai Sq (*Tmr* C3), via the Naval Cadets College, to Limin Zeas. Bus No. 905 connects the Metro station to the Flying Dolphin quay, Limin Zeas. *See* **Arrival by Bus, Introduction** for other details.

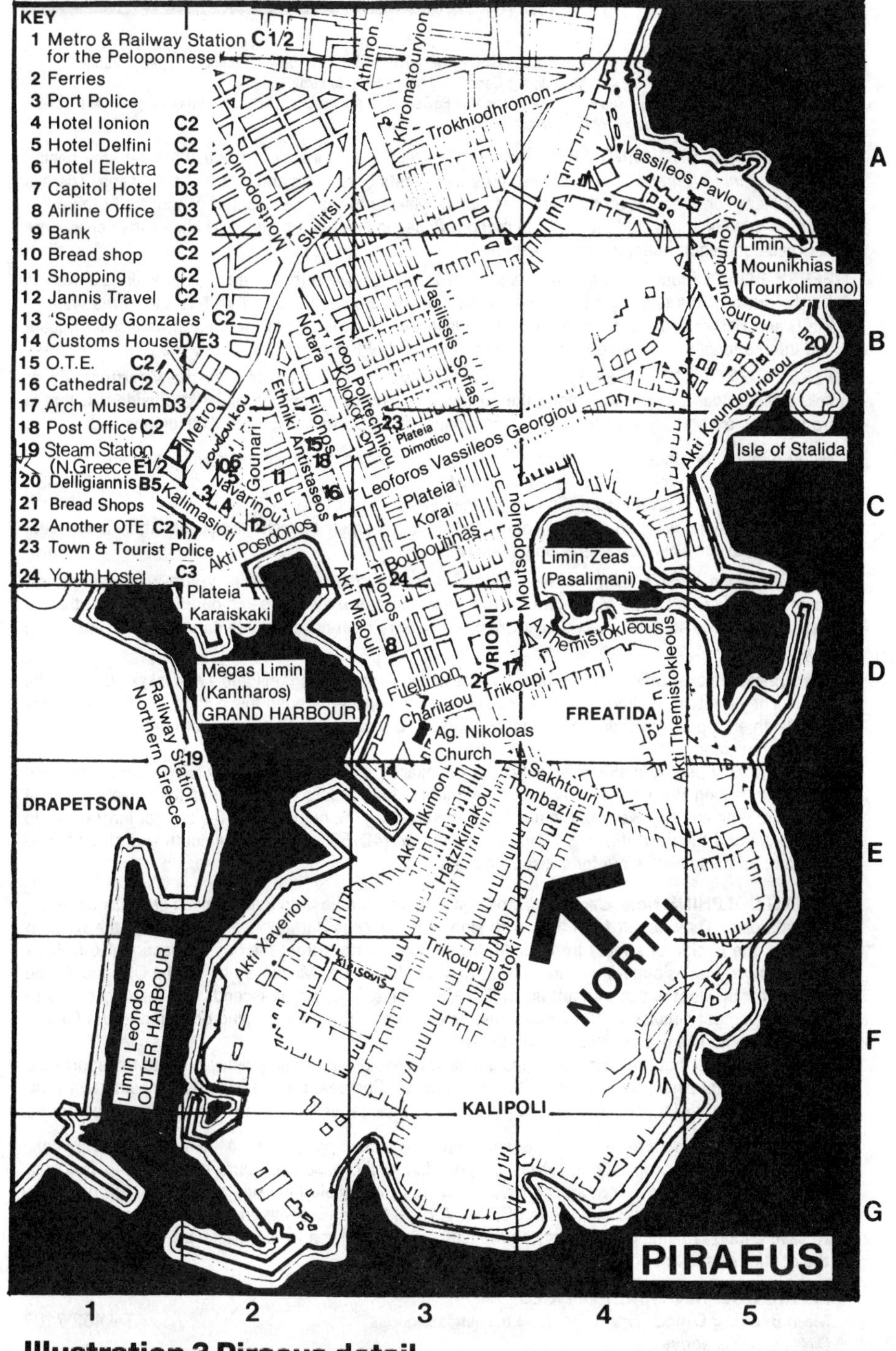

Illustration 3 Piraeus detail

Trolley Buses

No. 16 **I. Drosopoulou(Ag Troiada Cathedral** – *Tmr* 16C2), Ag Ioannis Rentis (NE Piraeus Suburb).

No. 17 Skouze St, Akti Miaouli, Ag Georgios (NW Piraeus suburb).

No. 20 P Skylitsi (Neo Faliro), Leoforos Vas Pavlou, Akti Kountourioti, Leoforos Vas Georgiou, Akti Kondili, Drapetsona (W Piraeus suburb).

COMMERCIAL SHOPPING AREA (*Tmr* 11C2) There is a flourishing and busy Market area behind the *Macedonia & Thrace Bank*, hemmed in by the streets of Gounari and Ethniki Antistaseos. There is an excellent supermarket on the corner of Odhos Makras Stoas, if a shopper cannot be bothered to visit the various shops and stalls of the market. Prices in Piraeus are generally higher than elsewhere in Greece and shop hours are as for Athens.

FERRY-BOATS Most island ferry-boats leave from the quayside that stretches between Akti Kondili (to the north of the Grand Harbour), Karaiskaki Sq, Akti Posidonos and Akti Miaouli (to the west of the Grand Harbour). As a general rule the Aegean ferries depart from the area of Karaiskaki Square and International ferries leave from the south or far end of the Akti Miaouli quay road.

FERRY-BOAT TICKET OFFICES Yes, well, at least they lie 'extremely thick' on the waterfront. Ticket sellers 'lie in wait', all the way along the quayside streets of Kalimasioti and Akti Posidonos, that is from the Metro station, past the Gounari St turning to the bottom of Ethniki Antistaseos.

My two favourite offices are situated at opposite ends of the spectrum, as it were, and are:

Jannis Stoulis Travel (*Tmr* 12C2) 2 Gounari St Tel 417 9491

Directions: Located on the right (*Sbo*) of Gounari St.

The owner, who wears a rather disinterested air, is extremely efficient and speaks three languages, including English. This business is only open 'office' hours.

His fast talking, ever smiling, 'speedy Gonzales' counterpart occupies a wall-to-wall stairway on Kalimasioti St (*Tmr* 13C2). My regard for the latter operator may well be coloured by the fact that he was the man who sold me my first ever Greek island ferry-boat ticket, more years ago than I am willing to concede

There are two ticket offices on the harbour side of the large building on Plateia Karaiskaki, beyond the cafes. They are two of almost 'dozens' of ticket offices spaced around this edifice. Other alternatives include an enterprising vendor of tickets who lurks, from early morning, amongst the ferry-boat stalls on Akti Posidonos.

It is probably best to make enquiries about the exact location of a particular ferry's departure point when purchasing the tickets. It has to be admitted the vendors tend to refer to a ship's point of departure with any airy wave of the hand. When searching the quayside for the correct ferry-boat, do not go beyond the Port offices & Custom house (*Tmr* 14D/E3), towards the south end of the Grand Harbour, as these berths are for cruise ships only.

FLYING DOLPHINS Note, *Ceres* hydrofoils only service the Eastern Peloponnese and islands of the Argo-Saronic. They depart from the south side of Limin Zeas Harbour, so allow $\frac{3}{4}$hr for the walk up and over the hillside of streets from the Metro station. Do not forget the bus connection (No 905), if time is short. Foot-sloggers will find it best to walk down Akti Miaouli as far as the Olympic Airline office (*Tmr* 8D3), at which turn left up Odhos Merarkhias. This street ascends and then descends to the large, almost circular port of Limin Zeas, where turn to the right keeping on round to the far end of the harbour. The hydrofoil quay is on the left.

One problem is that the Flying Dolphins are used by various package holiday firms to transport their clients to, for instance, the islands of Poros, Hydra and Spetses, but the early bird should get a seat. These craft are well equipped with lavatories, a snackbar as well as central and aft viewing platforms.

The terminus is conveniently overlooked by the patio of a large, modern cafe-bar/restaurant/zacharoplasteion which is open during the essential hours of the Flying Dolphins' operation. Mind you it is not inexpensive. Two Nes meh ghala (and not a lot of ghala) cost some 250drs and two toasted sandwiches 500drs. A breakfast is also served but I have never been able to save enough to indulge this fancy... One plus point is that the ladies toilets are very clean, even if the gentlemens is not so spotless.

FLYING DOLPHIN TICKET OFFICES

Main Booking Office (*Tmr* C/D4) 8 Akti Themistokleous Tel 452 7107

Directions: As above.

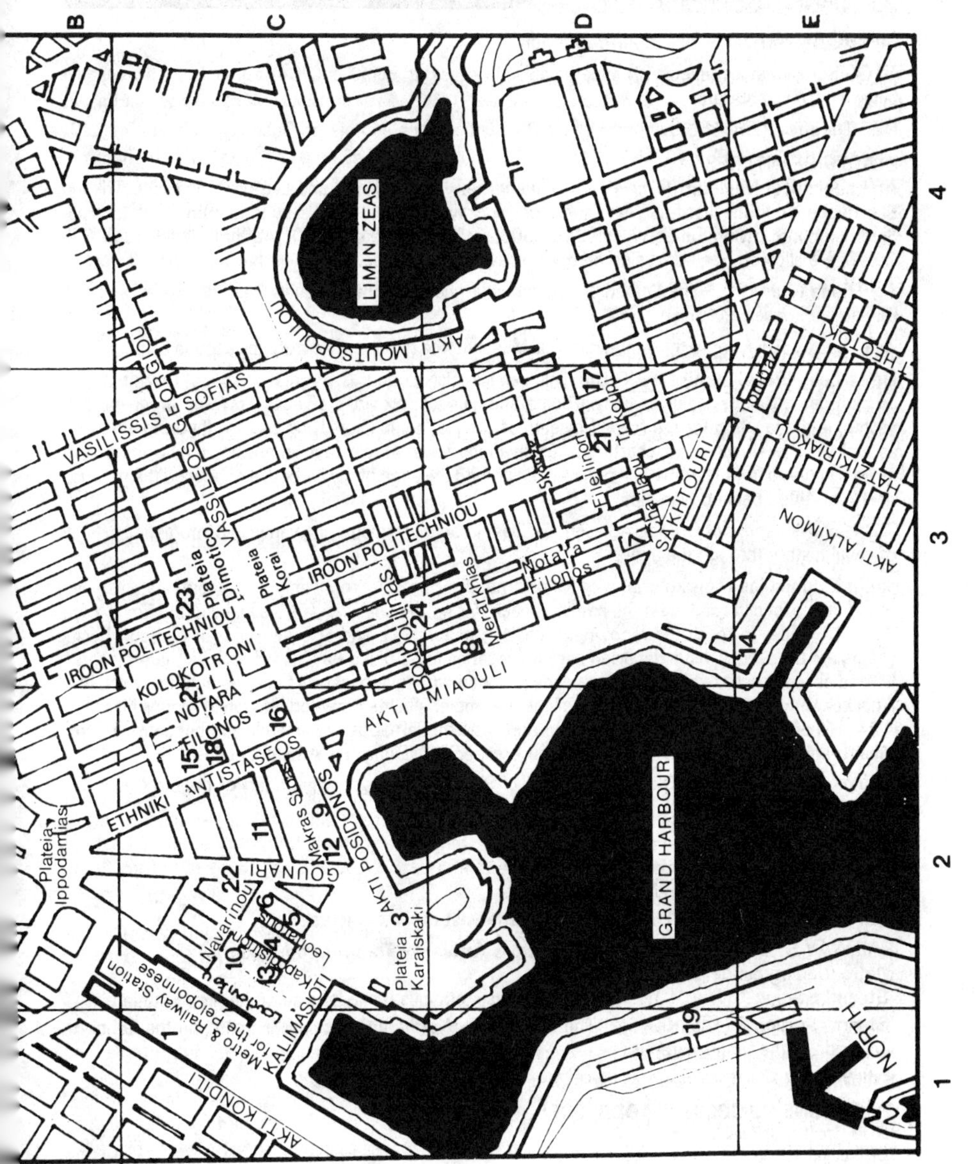

Illustration 4 Piraeus inset

METRO *See* **Arrival by Metro, Introduction.**

NTOG Somewhat inconveniently situated at Limin Zeas Harbour (*Tmr* C/D4), and only open weekdays between 0700-1500hrs.

OTE The office (*Tmr* 15C2) is north of the Post Office, with another on Odhos Navarinou (*Tmr* 22C2).

PLACES OF INTEREST

Archaeological Museum (*Tmr* 17D3) Situated between Filellinon and Leoforos Charilaou Trikoupi Sts. Reopened in the last few years and reportedly well laid out, with easy to identify exhibits. Open Summer months: Mon-Sat between 0845-1500hrs; Sun & holidays 0930-1430hrs; closed Tues. Only Greeks are allowed free admission here, as elsewhere in Greece, foreigners having to pay 200drs.

Ag Triada (*Tmr* 16C2) The Cathedral was rebuilt in the early l960s, having been destroyed in 1944. Distinctive, mosaic tile finish.

Zea Theatre Adjacent to the Archaeological Museum, the remains date from the second century BC.

Limin Zeas (Pasalimani) (*Tmr* C/D4) This semicircular harbour is of great antiquity. Now it is lined by high-rise buildings, shelters fishing boats and caiques, provides a yacht basin for larger, modern yachts, is the location for the Naval Museum of Greece, contains a Flying Dolphin (hydrofoil) terminal as well as a base for yacht charterers. Excavations have shown that, in ancient times, there were several hundred boat sheds which radiated out around the edge of the harbour and housed the *triremes*, the great, three-banked warships.

The Naval Museum of Greece Adjacent to Zeas Harbour and displaying varied and interesting exhibits of naval history through the ages.

Limin Mounikhias (Tourkolimano or Mikrolimano) (*Tmr* B5). From Limin Zeas, continue north-east round the coast cliff road, past the bathing beach (*facing the tiny island of Stalida*) and the Royal Yacht Club of Greece, to reach the renowned, 'chatty', picturesque and also semicircular harbour. Racing yachts are believed to have departed here for regattas in Saroniko Bay, as far back as the 4th century BC and as they do to this day. The quayside is ringed with tavernas, cafes and restaurants which form a backcloth to the multi-coloured sails of the assembled yachts crowded into Limin Mounikhias.

The Hill of Kastela overlooks the harbour and has a modern, open-air, marble amphitheatre, wherein theatre and dance displays are staged, more especially during the Athens Festival

Filonos Street (*Tmr* B/C/D2/3) The 'Soho' of Piraeus, espousing what's left of the old *Never on a Sunday* atmosphere for which the port was once famed.

POLICE

Port On the quay bounded by Akti Possidonos.
Tourist & Town (*Tmr* 23C3) Dimotico Square.

POST OFFICE (*Tmr* 18C2) On Filonos St, north-west of the Cathedral.

RAILWAY STATIONS *See* **Arrival by Metro** & **Arrival by Train, Introduction.**
Metro (Underground) (*Tmr* 1C1/2).
'Steam' Station 1 (*Tmr* 1C1/2) The Peloponnese terminus is the far side of the Metro station.
'Steam' Station 2 (*Tmr* 19D/E/2) The terminus for Northern Greece and situated on the far, north-west side of the Grand Harbour.

SWIMMING POOL Adjacent to Limin Zeas Harbour.

TELEPHONE NUMBERS & ADDRESSES

NTOG (*Tmr* C/D4) Zeas Marina	Tel 413 5716
Port Authorities	Tel 451 1311
Taxi rank	Tel 417 8138

OTHER MAINLAND PORTS For the Cyclades.

RAFINA (Illustration 5) Tel prefix 0294. A noisy, clamorous, smelly, busy seaport, with an excellent bus service to Athens.

ARRIVAL BY BUS The buses park on the dual carriageway (*Tmr* 1C4) that curves up from the large Ferry-boat Quay (*Tmr* 2D1/2). The office is a small hut, towards the top and on the right (*Sbo*) of this thoroughfare. Timetables are stuck in the window.

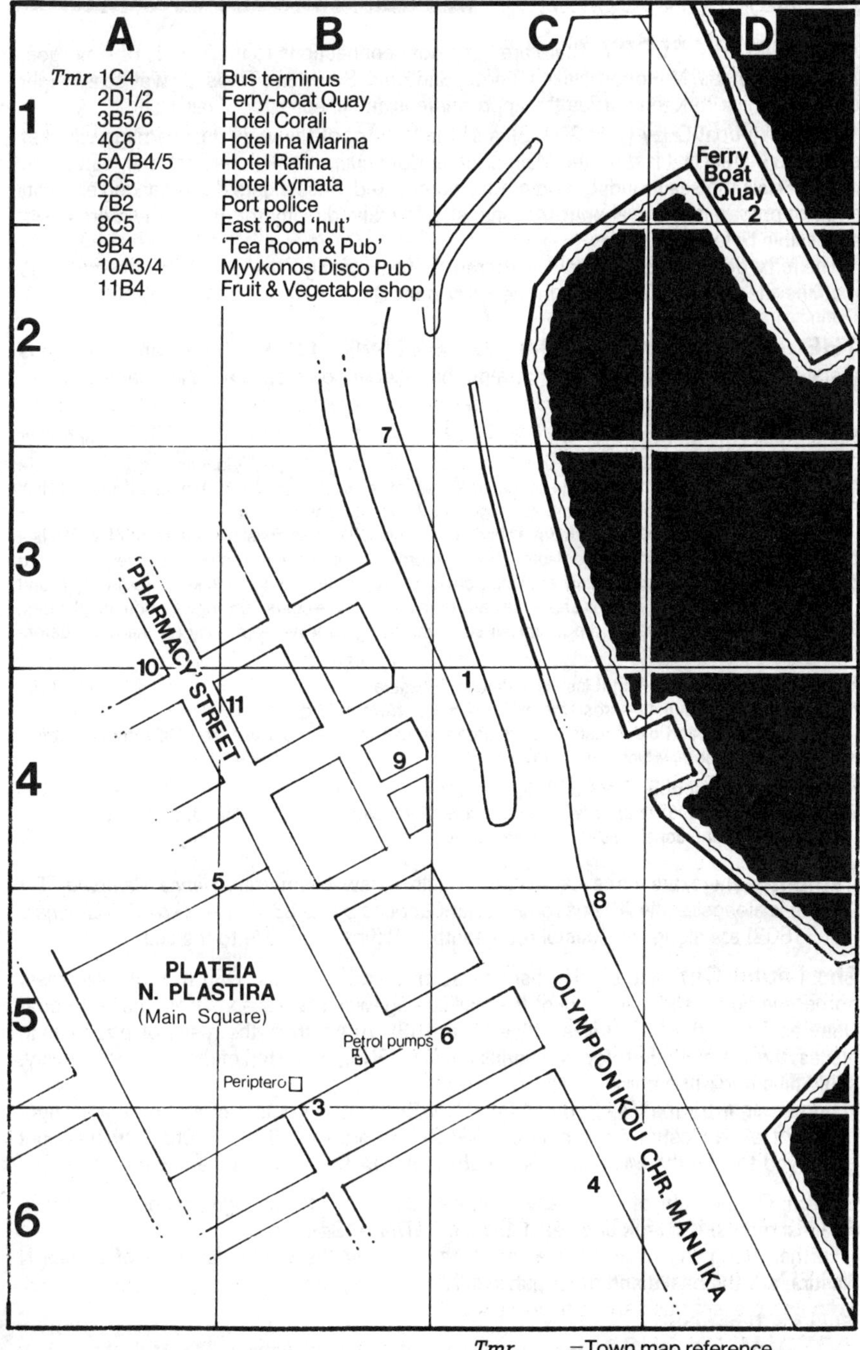

Illustration 5 Rafina

Tmr =Town map reference
Fsw =Facing seawards
Sbo =Sea behind one
Fbqbo =Ferry-boat Quay behind one

ARRIVAL BY FERRY There are ferry-boat connections to the islands of Amorgos, Andros, Evia, Ios, Mykonos, Naxos, Paros, Santorini, Syros and Tinos, as well as a 'height of season' link to Kithnos (*See* the appropriate island chapter for details).

The Ferry-boat Quay (*Tmr* 2D1/2) is at the bottom of the wide dual carriageway that climbs to Plateia N. Plastira, the Main Square. Continuing to the left (*Sbo*), the waterfront road follows the sea round, but do not be sidetracked. Passengers disembarking at night, and not prepared to travel on to Athens, should make directly for one of the more easily accessible hotels.

The ferry-boat ticket offices are scattered about in amongst the restaurants and tavernas that line the thoroughfare up from the Ferry-boat Quay.

THE ACCOMMODATION & EATING OUT There are numerous restaurant/tavernas doing a roaring trade, but accommodation is another matter.

The Accommodation

Hotel Corali (*Tmr* 3B5/6) (Class D) 11 Plateia N Plastira. Tel 22477

Directions: From the top end of the Ferry-boat Quay dual carriageway, half-right across a small square and the hotel is on the left-hand side of the large pedestrian square (that now blocks off the old High Street). A couple of petrol pumps are set down on the far left corner of this square.

A grey, urban, soulless, rather down-at-heel, but clean, 1920s establishment in front of which is a periptero. The high ceilinged, linoleum floored rooms share the cavernous, massively equipped bathrooms. You know, cast iron cisterns supported on very large cast iron brackets, 25mm pipes and mahogany lavatory seats. Rooms share the bathroom and a single costs 1560drs & a double 2400drs. The Madam does not live on the premises so, if intending to leave early, pay up the night before departure.

Hotel Rafina (*Tmr* 5A/B4/5) (Class E) 2 Plateia N Plastira. Tel 23460

Directions: Almost directly across the pedestrian way from the *Hotel Corali*.

Greyer, scruffier and older than its counterpart across the way, but cheaper. Only double rooms, sharing the bathroom, which cost 1600drs.

Hotel Kymata (*Tmr* 6C5) (Class D) Plateia N Plastira. Tel 23406

Directions: Prior to the *Hotel Corali*, over a row of pizza-joints and rather difficult to spot.

Similar prices and conditions to the *Hotel Corali*.

Camping There are three campsites, within a few kilometres. *Rafina Camping* (Tel 23118) is alongside the Athens road, whilst *Cococamp* (Tel 23413) and *Kokkino Limanaki* (Tel 31602) are along the coastal road south of Rafina and close to the sea.

The Eating Out Side-by-side fish restaurants and tavernas, with rooftop balconies, border the right-hand side (*Sbo*) of the dual carriageway that ascends from the Ferry-boat Quay as far as the Port police office (*Tmr* 7B2). Apart from the mass of pizza eating places, the late night, hot-dog, soft-drink hut (*Tmr* 8C5), at the top of the dual carriageway, could fill a nook or cranny.

Some might try the *Tea Room & Pub* (*Tmr* 9B4), at the outset of and on the far right of the Plateia N Plastira. Open between 0800-1200hrs and 1900-2400hrs. Others might be moved to visit the *Mykonos Disco Pub* (*Tmr* 10A3/4) – and some might not!

General On the right of 'Pharmacy' St (thus named due to the high proportion of these establishments) is a Fruit and vegetable shop (*Tmr* 11B4).

Further along the main avenue, or more correctly the pedestrian way of Plateia N Plastira, are the banks and other public services.

Buses & Timetables

Athens buses depart from 29 Mavrommateon St (Tel 821 0872) at:-

0545, 0610, 0630, 0645, and then every half-hour to 1445, 1500, 1515, and then every half-hour to 1945, 2030, 2100, 2145, 2230hrs.

Rafina buses depart at:
0540, 0615, 0645, 0715, 0745, 0820, 0850, 0930, 0950 and then every half-hour to 1350, 1430, 1450, 1520, 1550, 1630, 1650, and then every half-hour to 2050, 2140, 2230, 2300hrs.
One-way fare 140drs, duration 1hr.

Ferry-Boats & Timetables (Tel 29300)

Day	Departure Time	Ferry-boat	Ports/Islands of Call
Daily	0830hrs	Marmari	Marmari(Evia).
	1000hrs	Karistos	Karistos(Evia).
Mon	0030hrs	Bari Express	Syros, Mykonos.
	0745hrs	Eptanissos	Gavrion(Andros),Tinos,Syros.
	1430hrs	Marmari	Marmari(Evia).
	1600hrs	Kithnos	Gavrion(Andros).
	1700hrs	Bari Express	Gavrion(Andros),Tinos,Mykonos.
	1715hrs	Karistos	Karistos(Evia).
	1800hrs	Marmari	Marmari(Evia).
	1900hrs	Alecos	Syros,Paros,Naxos.
Tues	0745hrs	Eptanissos	Gavrion(Andros),Tinos,Mykonos.
	1430hrs	Marmari	Marmari(Evia).
	1600hrs	Kithnos	Gavrion(Andros).
	1700hrs	Delos	Syros,Paros,Naxos,Ios,Santorini,Anafi.
	1700hrs	Bari Express	Gavrion(Andros),Tinos,Mykonos.
	1715hrs	Karistos	Karistos(Evia).
	1800hrs	Marmari	Marmari(Evia).
Wed	0745hrs	Eptanissos	Gavrion(Andros),Tinos,Mykonos.
	1430hrs	Marmari	Marmari(Evia).
	1600hrs	Kithnos	Gavrion(Andros).
	1700hrs	Bari Express	Gavrion(Andros),Tinos,Mykonos.
	1715hrs	Karistos	Karistos(Evia).
	1800hrs	Marmari	Marmari(Evia).
	1900hrs	Alecos	Syros,Paros,Naxos.
Thurs	0745hrs	Eptanissos	Gavrion(Andros),Tinos,Mykonos.
	1430hrs	Marmari	Marmari(Evia).
	1600hrs	Kithnos	Gavrion(Andros),Tinos,Syros.
	1700hrs	Delos	Syros,Paros,Naxos,Aegiali(Amorgos), Katapola(Amorgos).
	1700hrs	Bari Express	Gavrion(Andros),Tinos,Mykonos.
	1715hrs	Karistos	Karistos(Evia).
	1800hrs	Marmari	Marmari(Evia).
Fri	0745hrs	Eptanissos	Gavrion(Andros),Tinos.
	1515hrs	Marmari	Marmari(Evia).
	1600hrs	Kithnos	Gavrion(Andros).
	1700hrs	Delos	Syros,Paros,Naxos.
	1715hrs	Bari Express	Gavrion(Andros),Tinos,Mykonos.
	1730hrs	Karistos	Karistos(Evia).
	1800hrs	Eptanissos	Gavrion(Andros),Tinos,Mykonos.
	1900hrs	Marmari	Marmari(Evia).
	1900hrs	Alecos	Syros,Paros,Naxos.
Sat	0030hrs	Kithnos	Kymi(Evia),Ag Estratios,Limnos,Kavala(M).
	0745hrs	Eptanissos	Gavrion(Andros),Tinos,Mykonos.
	0815hrs	Bari Express	Gavrion(Andros),Tinos.
	0900hrs	Delos	Syros,Paros,Naxos,Aegiali(Amorgos), Katapola(Amorgos).
	1515hrs	Marmari	Marmari(Evia).
	1715hrs	Bari Express	Gavrion(Andros),Tinos,Mykonos.
	1730hrs	Karistos	Karistos(Evia).
	1830hrs	Marmari	Marmari(Evia).
Sun	0745hrs	Eptanissos	Gavrion(Andros),Tinos,Mykonos.
	1130hrs	Kithnos	Kithnos.
	1700hrs	Delos	Syros,Paros,Naxos.
	1700hrs	Marmari	Marmari(Evia).

1700hrs	Karistos	Karistos(Evia).
1830hrs	Bari Express	Gavrion(Andros).
1900hrs	Eptanissos	Gavrion(Andros).
2100hrs	Marmari	Marmari(Evia).
2130hrs	Karistos	Karistos(Evia).

Third class, one-way fares: Rafina				
	to Marmari	405drs;	duration	1hr.
	to Karistos	600drs;		
	to Andros	675drs;	"	1½hrs.
	to Tinos	1500drs;	"	4hrs
	to Syros	980drs;	"	3½hrs.
	to Mykonos	1200drs;	"	5hrs.
	to Paxos	1050drs;	"	5hrs.
	to Naxos	1225drs;	"	6½hrs.

LAVRIO (Lavrion) (Illustration 6) Tel prefix 0292. A messy town and 'savaged' port that probably once possessed a graceful Italianesque waterfront. The mute remains of the latter are represented by several crumbling 'neo municipal' buildings and a few tired, dusty palm trees.

The little harbour is host to a mix of speedboats and small commercial craft. Off the messy, quarried headland to the right (*Fsw*) is a stranded cargo ship, that must have cut the corner rather too tightly. Offshore is the private island of **Makranisos**, mysteriously not included in any Cycladian details.

ARRIVAL BY BUS The Athens buses pull up on the edge of a large, grandiose park and inter-related maze of squares, interlaced by sweeping streets. There is a Bus office (*Tmr* 1A3).

ARRIVAL BY FERRY The shabby Ferry-boat Quay (*Tmr* 2E2/3) is shared with other commercial interests and the way along the finger pier is blocked by piles of 'this-and-that'.

The small, dilapidated and crowded ticket office is converted from the remains of a concrete stucco restaurant and is surrounded by broken-down wire fences and crushed concrete posts. It services the **FB Ioulis Keas II** and **Kithnos**, sells a map/guide book of Kea island and opens about an hour prior to scheduled sailing times.

Note, despite any advice, even from the main NTOG office in Athens, it is usually necessary to return to Lavrio to connect between the islands of Kea and Kithnos. The **Ioulis Keas II** does not go on from one to the other, but makes a separate trip, via Lavrio. The **Kithnos** does call at Kea whilst *en route* to Kithnos, once a week.

THE ACCOMMODATION & EATING OUT

The Accommodation Almost unbelievably, even the official manual lists accommodation. This may well not matter too much as Lavrio is not a place to stay.

The Eating Out There are a number of cafe-bars and taverna/restaurants. A very convenient establishment is the:-

A La Marinara (*Tmr* 3D3)
Directions: On the edge of the Harbour and a convenient spot to fritter away a few hours, being in sight of the Ferry-boat Quay. Unfortunately most of the food is pre-packaged but the spaghetti bolognese is reasonably priced, as is a bottle of Amstel.

On the way round from the Restaurant to the Ferry-boat Quay is a pavement mounted shrine, close by which is a Meccano-like, metal and wood trip boat jetty.

An inexpensive, but horribly named alternative is the:-
Lido Fast Food (*Tmr* 4A5)
Directions: At the Ferry-boat end of the High St, close to the Sounio roundabout.

Cafe-bar To Moypagio (*Tmr* 5D1)
Directions: To the left-hand side of the Harbour (*Facing the Ferry-boat quay, with the park behind one*).
A small cafe-bar on the roadside and complete with convenient toilets.

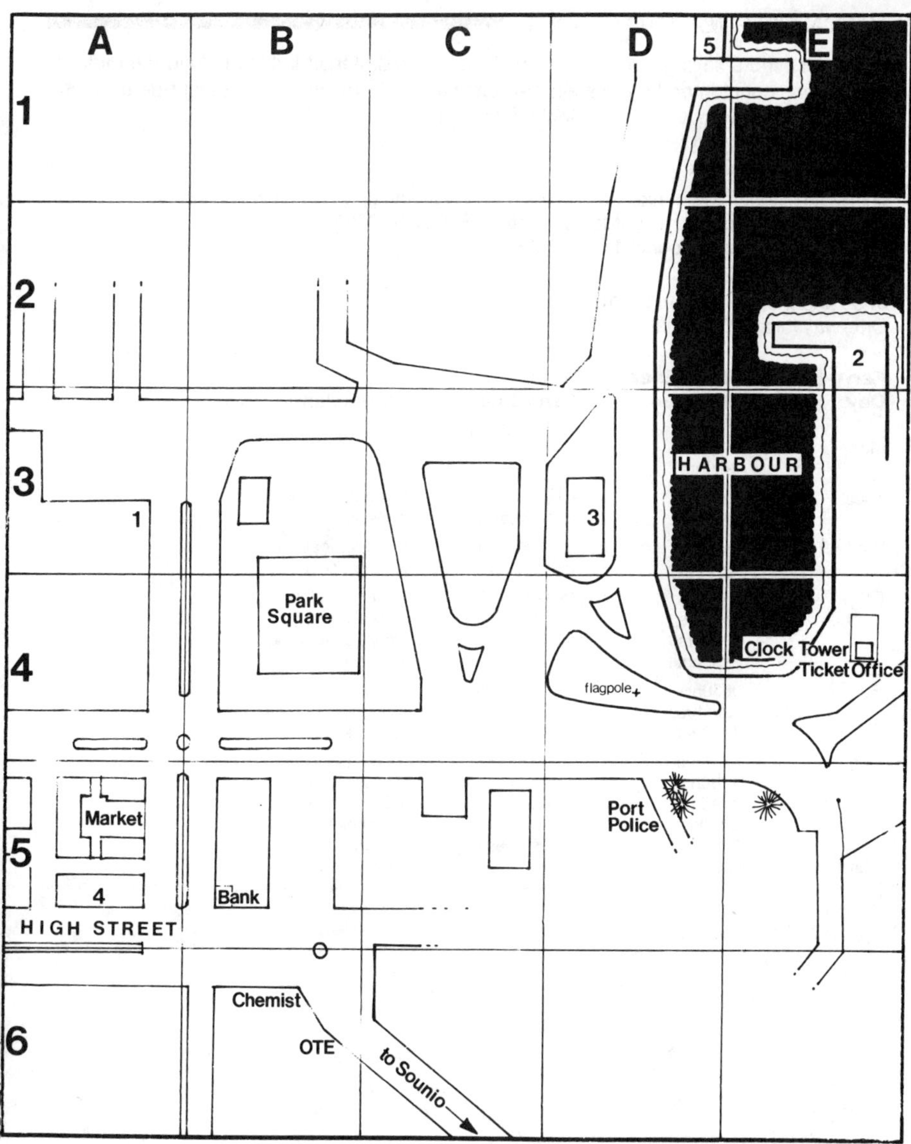

Illustration 6 Lavrio

Tmr 1A3	Bus office
2E2/3	Ferry-boat Quay
3D3	A La Marinara Restaurant
4A5	'Lido Fast Food'
5D1	Cafe-bar To Moypagio

Tmr =Town map reference
Fsw =Facing seawards
Sbo =Sea behind one
Fbqbo =Ferry-boat Quay behind one

Perhaps Lavrio's saving grace is the small, lovely, old Market lurking behind the High St. A charming conglomeration of stalls set out in a cruciform with ancient night-time lighting and a rather impressive donkey drinking trough.

Buses & Timetables

This is the Athens to Sounion bus, which travels via Markopoulo & Lavrio(Lavrion).
Athens buses depart from 14 Mavrommateon St (Tel 8213203) at:-
0630, and then every hour to 1730, 1900hrs.

Lavrio buses depart at:-
0730 and then every hour to 2130hrs.
One-way fare: 290drs; duration 1¾hrs.

Ferry-boats & Timetables (Tel 25249)

Day	Departure time	Ferry-boat	Ports/Islands of Call
Mon	0830hrs	Ioulis Keas II	Korissia(Kea).
	1900hrs	Ioulis Keas II	Korissia(Kea).
Tues	0830hrs	Ioulis Keas II	Merichas(Kithnos).
	1900hrs	Ioulis Keas II	Korissia(Kea).
Wed & Thurs	0830hrs	Ioulis Keas II	Korissia(Kea).
	1900hrs	Ioulis Keas II	Korissia(Kea).
Fri	0830hrs	Ioulis Keas II	Merichas(Kithnos).
	1500hrs	Ioulis Keas II	Korissia(Kea).
	1900hrs	Ioulis Keas II	Korissia(Kea).
	2100hrs	Kithnos	Korissia(Kea).
Sat	0830hrs	Ioulis Keas II	Korissia(Kea).
	1230hrs	Ioulis Keas II	Merichas(Kithnos).
	1900hrs	Ioulis Keas II	Korissia(Kea).
Sun	0830hrs	Ioulis Keas II	Korissia(Kea).
	1700hrs	Kithnos	Korissia(Kea).
	1745hrs	Ioulis Keas II	Korissia(Kea).
	2030hrs	Kithnos	Gavrion(Andros).
	2145hrs	Ioulis Keas II	Korissia(Kea).

Third class, one-way fares: Lavrio to Kea 555drs; duration 2½hrs
to Kithnos 830drs; " 4hrs.

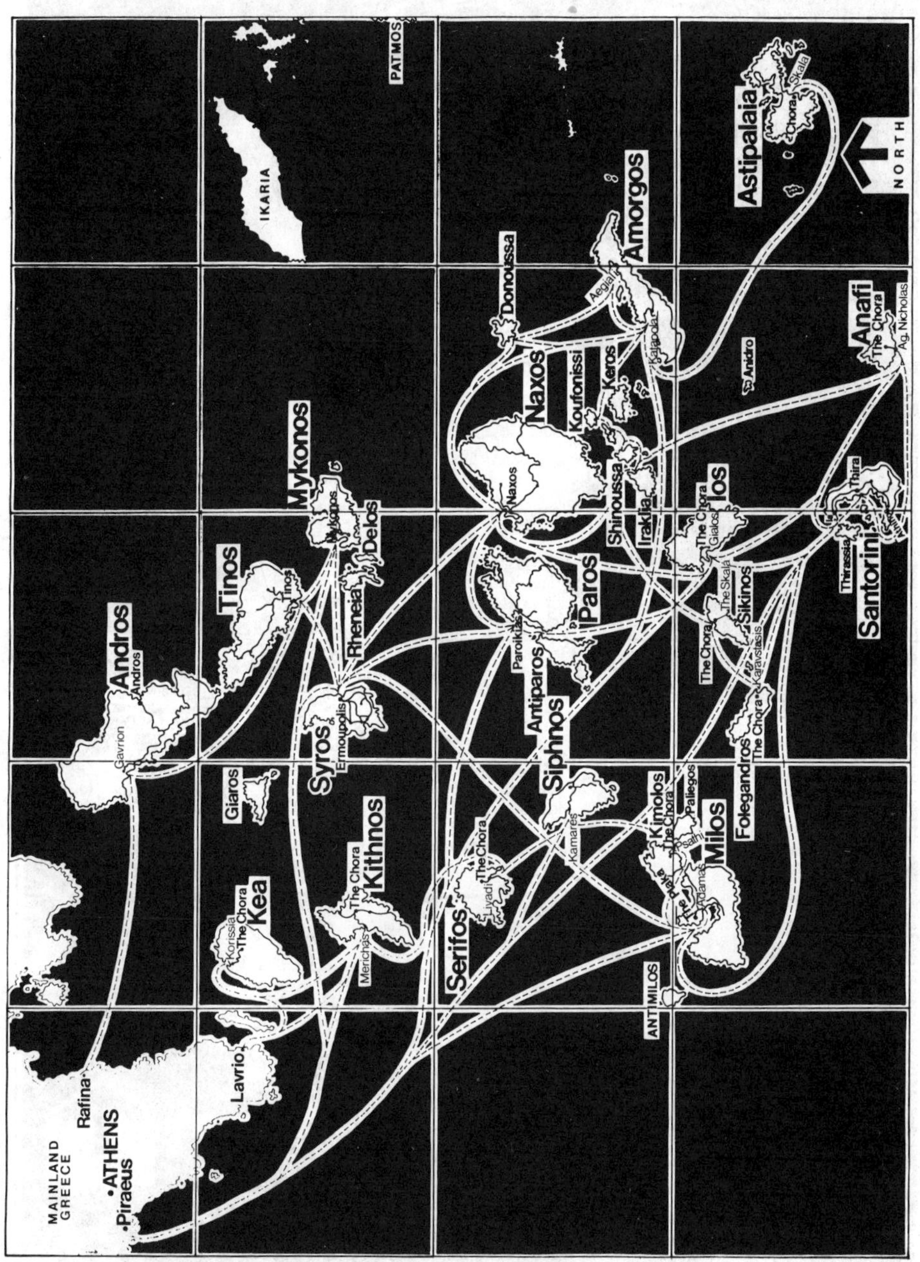

Illustration 7 The Cyclades islands

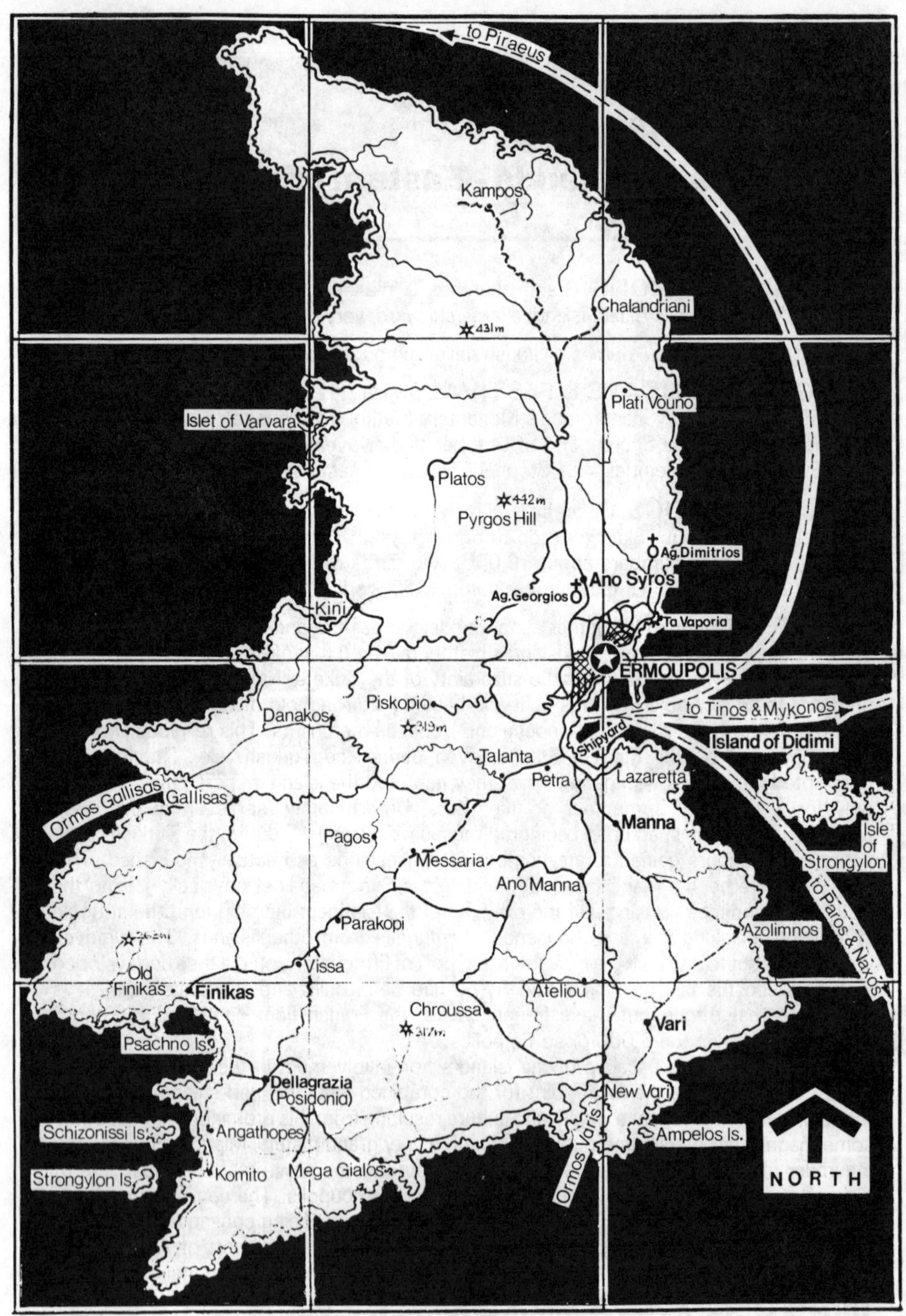

Illustration 8 Syros island

PART TWO

3 SYROS (Siros, ΣΥΡΟΣ) ★★★
Cyclades Islands - Eastern chain

FIRST IMPRESSIONS Grand churches & mansions; shuttered houses; paved roads; balconies; a rocky, bare island; a large shipyard; very drinking water-short & saline.

SPECIALITIES 'Loukoumes' (Turkish delight); nougat; octopus; Roman Catholicism.

RELIGIOUS HOLIDAYS & FESTIVALS include: 25th September – The appearance of the Virgin Mary, Faneromenis Monastery (Catholic & Orthodox procession); 26th October – St Dimitrios Church; end of October/early November – 'Apanosyria' Festival, Ano Syros; 27th December – St Stephen, Gallisas. Feasts also at Kini and Finikas.

VITAL STATISTICS Tel prefix 0281. Syros, the legal and administrative centre of the Cyclades, is about 18km from top to bottom and 10½km wide with an area of 87sq km. The population numbers about 19,000, two-thirds of whom live in the main town and port of Ermoupolis. Of that number some 1350 work in the shipyards.

HISTORY Mentioned by Homer as 'abounding in pasture and wine, rich in sheep and corn'. Yes, well, not so now. The island's history mirrored that of the rest of the Cyclades until, in 1207, Syros came under the suzerainty of the Duke of Naxos. In this period the medieval town of Ano Syros was built and became a stronghold of Roman Catholicism, a faith brought to the island by Genoese and Venetian merchants. This religious anomaly was supported by the King of France, even during the Turkish rule. The Russians interrupted the latter's occupation when they captured the island in 1770, even if it was only for a period of some four or five years. Unfortunately, some antiquities were plundered, which finished up in Leningrad museums. Strangely, during the Turkish occupation the islanders gained a rare number of concessions and actually flourished. This may well have been a major factor in deciding the Syriots against physically joining the 1821 Independence uprising. On the other hand the islanders did help fund the struggle in addition to taking in many thousands of refugees from other islands. The fugitives immediately set to and built the new town and port of Ermoupolis, on the then undeveloped area between the hill, on which Ano Syros had been built, and the sea's edge. It is interesting that throughout these fraught years, the French fleet continued to keep a watching brief over the 5,000 or so Catholics.

Despite, or perhaps because of the island's non-involvement in the War of Independence, Syros became the focal point for the combined industrial and shipping thrust of the new State. The immense wealth and culture resulting from this prominence bequeathed some magnificent private and public buildings, a very grand plateia, Miaoulis Square, and a number of splendid churches. These all contribute to the now present atmosphere of graceful, faded and long-lost elegance in 'up-town' Ermoupolis. The decline of coal vis-a-vis oil fired power for ships, in the early 1800s, had far reaching consequences for the island. Initially, merchant shipping relocated to Piraeus, the home port of Athens. The inevitable upshot of this was the slow but remorseless run-down in industrial activity and subsequent closure of many of the cotton mills, tanneries, iron foundries, factories and warehouses. With a lot of Government encouragement the shipyard has remained active and prosperous.

GENERAL Over the past ten or twelve years, little has changed and Syros remains quintessentially a Greek island, with few publicised attractions for the tourist. Admittedly there are now more much needed hostelries, but not a lot else has altered. It appears to be central government policy to keep the Neorion Shipyard fully manned. To this end leisure activities and job opportunities, including work in hotels, restaurants and all the associated services that could woo the workers away from the maritime industry, are positively discouraged. Probably because of these strictures, Syros has retained much of the charm and essence of Greek island life which mass tourism has, elsewhere, ravaged and restructured.

So, why does Syros not receive more 'rave notices' from travel writers, why does the average guide afford this pleasant refuge (from the more characteristic Cycladean hurly-burly) only a page? Surely it should rate as an appealing island at which to stop off? Can it be that the lack of 'standard' tourist pre-requisites – namely discos, international jewellery and souvenir shops and 'Safari' evenings – has detracted from the island's native charm?

Of course there are shortcomings, including the lack of an adequate beach at Ermoupolis; water has always been in short supply; mosquitoes can be a nuisance, if the proper precautions are not observed; the bus service is adequate, but no more, and the night life in Ermoupolis is non-existent (goody). As against these possible deficiencies, accommodation is generally inexpensive; there are splendid beaches at Old Vari, Dellagrazia, Finikas, Gallisas and Kini, all with accommodation to hand; the *Volta* on Ermoupolis's main square is a nightly and colourful event; there is a swinging disco at Gallisas and the taxi service is excellent.

The islanders are a colourful people and each year or two, a different hue dominates.

ERMOUPOLIS: capital & main port (Illustration 9) From a distance the twin hills overshadowing Ermoupolis have an attractive look, even if the surrounding mountains are bare and unappealing. The one to the left is topped off by a Catholic cathedral and the one to the right by a blue domed Orthodox church.

The islet of Didimi stands off from the bay, often with a ship at anchor in the roads. The southern headland is named Lazaretta and was once a quarantine stop (and is the origin of our word Lazaretto). A closer inspection of the port does not present a pretty sight. To the left (*Sbo*), the curve of the bay is occupied by the shipyard, a floating dock as well as other industrial workings whilst further round, to the far left, are a row of large oil storage tanks. If this were not enough, the untidy buildings bordering the Esplanade and parallel side streets conceal the glory of the magnificent Main Square. Moreover the three or four storey Venetian homes of the Upper Town are also hidden from view.

Referring back to my general definition of a Greek Town, the port's rubbish is still brought down from the precipitous, stepped, upper levels (apparently battened to the hillsides) by donkeys with large, circular panniers strapped to their flanks. Naturally enough, I suppose, the garbage is then tipped on to the quayside, where the donkeys spread it about in their efforts to get a good meal. Later, much later, when the resultant mess is nicely churned up, the rubbish truck arrives!

The upper reaches of the town are well worth exploring. Old, paved roads and endless, wide, arduous steps 'march' up and down the steep hillsides. Unfortunately, many of the houses are shuttered and in partial ruins. This seems a great pity but the ever present bogey of inheritance and bequests to religious orders tends to 'encourage' this neglect.

ARRIVAL BY FERRY A reliquiae of the once pivotal role of Syros as well as its continuing dominant administrative status, is highlighted in the island still remaining on many ferry-boat schedules. Despite this, the lead position as the epicentre of the Cyclades 'network' has been taken over by Paros.

Ferries berth on the right-hand (*Sbo*) side of the port, from close by the Customs office (*Tmr* 1D5) down as far as the Bus terminal (*Tmr* 2C3/4). The boats are met by owners

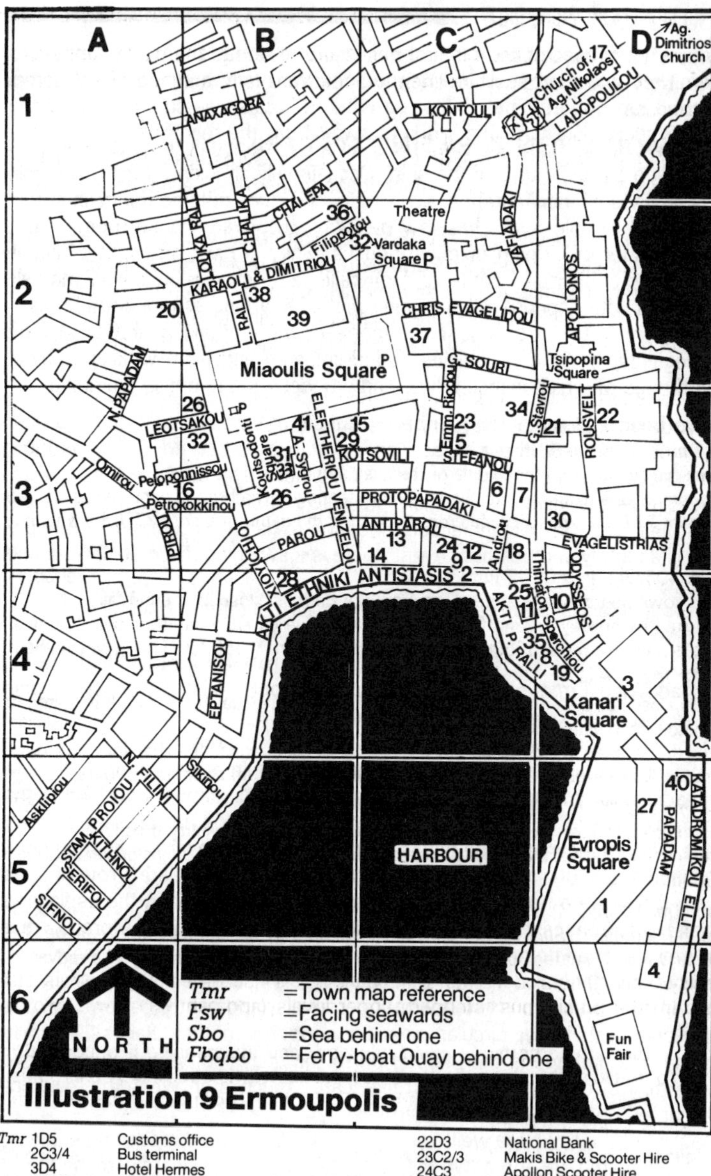

Illustration 9 Ermoupolis

Tmr 1D5 Customs office
2C3/4 Bus terminal
3D4 Hotel Hermes
4D5/6 Hotel Nisaki
5C3 Yanni's Guest House
6C3 Nick's Rooms
7C/D3 Tony's Pension
8D4 Hotel Syrii
9C3/4 Mama Anna's Pizza Place
10D4 Pension Apollon
11C/D3/4 Hotel Aktaeon/Syros Travel
12C3/4 Hotel Ellas
13C3 Hotel Mykonos
14B/C3 Hotel Athina/Banque Agricole de Greece
15B/C3 Central Rooms
16A/B3 Pension Antik
17D1 Ag Nikolaos Church
18C3 Kafeneion Nisiotissa
19D4 Taverna Ta Fiarrera
20A/B2 Souvlaki O Manos
21C/D3 Commercial Bank
22D3 National Bank
23C2/3 Makis Bike & Scooter Hire
24C3 Apollon Scooter Hire
25C/D3/4 Bookseller
26 Bakers
27D5 Municipal Tourist office
28B3/4 Kaba's Drink Shop
29B/C3 Cake & Drink Shop
30C/D3 Tranzit Stores
31B3 Small shop
32 Cinemas
33B3 Town police
34C2/3 Disco Margarita
35C/D4 Teamwork
36B/C1/2 Ladies Hairdresser
37C2 OTE
38B2 Museum
39B2 Town Hall
40D4/5 Port police
41B3 Post Office
P Periptero

of accommodation but to disembark it is first necessary to dodge the wild stampede of nougat-vendors. They wield large, white linen wrapped baskets, and charge the ramps as they drop into place.

THE ACCOMMODATION & EATING OUT Fortunately there is now much more accommodation available than in the past. Occasionally an island, for no particular reason, spawns an unusual manifestation, evolving peculiarities outside the main stream of development. For example Syros has few pensions or private house rooms, but a disproportionate number of lodging or guest-houses. They are not an entirely suitable substitute, often being converted from large, high ceilinged Victorian houses elementally divided up and with an atmosphere rather reminiscent of boarding school dormitories.

The lower category hotels are almost a bygone genre – creaking and dilapidated buildings with neglected reception cubicles, faded linoleum and paintwork and shared bathrooms, the fittings of which evince Edwardian grandeur and primitive plumbing.

The Accommodation Close by the Ferry-boat Quay are the:-

Hotel Hermes (*Tmr* 3D4) (Class B), Plateia Kanari Tel 28011
Directions: Across the square from the middle of the quay and on the right (*Sbo*).

Pricey and discourage 'one-night' stands. Single rooms, sharing the bathroom, cost 1900drs & with an en suite bathroom 2770drs, whilst double rooms, sharing the bathroom, cost 2770drs & with an en suite bathroom 3630drs.

Hotel Nisaki (*Tmr* 4D5/6) (Class C) 2 E Papadam Tel 28200
Directions: Further towards the southern headland from the *Hermes*, close by the fun-fair.

Often block-booked by holiday-making Greeks. All rooms have en suite bathrooms with a single priced at 2650drs & a double room 3250drs, increasing to 2925drs & 3600drs (1st July-15th Sept).

Hotel Syrii (*Tmr* 8C/D4) (Class B)
Directions: Actually classified as a pension which overlooks the Esplanade Akti P Ralli, but is entered from Odhos Thimaton Sperchiou, the street behind.

The crumbling exterior does not do justice to the pleasant accommodation. The airy front rooms overlook the harbour. Double rooms, with an en suite bathroom, start off at about 2500drs.

Hotel Aktaeon (*Tmr* 11C/D3/4) (Class E) Akti P Ralli Tel 22675
Directions: In the middle block, immediately across the Esplanade from the Ferry-boat Quay.

Some of the rooms are massive and all have to share the bathrooms, with a single priced at 800drs and a double 1300drs.

Pension Apollon (*Tmr* 10C/D3/4) 8 Odysseos St Tel 22158
Directions: From the right-hand (*Sbo*) side of the Esplanade, an alley beside the *Hotel Aktaeon* (*Tmr* 11C/D3/4) leads to Odhos Thimaton Sperchiou. The other side of this is another alley which advances to the scooter-noisy Odhos Odysseos. The pension, on the left, is embellished by the painting of a sleeping giant and is operated by a piratical looking, but honest, young partnership, who also run Apollon Scooter Hire.

The large, old, rather ethnic house is clean, pleasant and inexpensive if decorated in 'standard Greek Youth Hostel' fashion. For instance the hallway is adorned by a large fish net full of starfish, shells and other 'ocean artifacts'. A double room with washbasin and sharing a hot shower costs 1400drs.

Hotel Ελλασ (Hellas) (*Tmr* 12C3/4) (Class E) Antiparou Tel 22519
Directions: Edging the Esplanade road, across from the Bus terminal, with the entrance at the rear.

Provincial, if not grotty, and rather smelly. The double rooms, sharing the bathroom, cost 1400drs.

Hotel Mykonos (*Tmr* 13C3/4) (Class E) 18 Antiparou Tel 28346
Directions: Further along narrow Odhos Antiparou to the left (*Sbo*), in the next block.

'Provincial' in the extreme and all rooms share the facilities. A single room is charged at 1000drs & a double 1400drs, but add 100drs per shower use.

Pension Athina (*Tmr* 14B/C3/4) (Class D) Tel 23600
Directions: Above the Banque Agricole de Greece which borders the Esplanade. Entry is at the rear, from the alleyway Odhos Antiparou.

A much more pleasant choice than either the *Hellas* or *Mykonos*. Double rooms only, sharing the bathroom facilities. A front room costs 1600drs, a room at the back 1200drs, which rates increase to 2400drs & 2000drs (1st June-31st Oct).

A few streets back from the waterfront are yet more options. These include:-

Nick's Place (*Tmr* 6C3) No 14 Androu Tel 24451

Directions: Androu Lane branches off from the crook in the Esplanade, opposite the Bus terminal. The accommodation is three blocks back and on the left (*Sbo*).

A rather blasé character, Nick owns another establishment. Comments and prices as for other Ermoupolis guest-houses.

Tony's Pension (*Tmr* 7C/D3)

Directions: As for *Nick's Place*, but the opposite side of the street.

A worldly-wise young man, in his middle 30s, runs this well established pension, but finds it difficult to get up in the mornings. Clean and airy, with a splendid, winding staircase. Facilities include an informal book exchange, tourist information, map of the island, bus and ferry timetables, as well as a breakfast room at which only coffee is available, despite 'the blurb'. A double room costs about 1500drs, including the use of the shower.

Yanni's Guest House (*Tmr* 5C3) (Class B) 2 Emm Riodou Tel 28665

Directions: The entrance is in a side lane off a 'back-street', three back and parallel to the waterfront, towards the right or ferry-boat side of the port. From *Nick's* continue south along Odhos Androu and turn left along Odhos Stefanou. The first right is a lane and *Yanni's* is the first door, on the right.

The aged but clean, rambling old house with definite Simiot features has changed little over the last nine or ten years, experiencing only a 'minor' adjustment in ownership. Originally a flower-power inspired dwelling, it still possesses innumerable notices stuck up all over the place, including some advising of young Yannis's whereabouts. The main door is let into the side street wall of the building. The entrance gives way to stone steps covered in by a glass sided conservatory. A notice board has details of bus timetables, a sketch of the town and shopping information. Through the door at the top and the office is to the left and the dark main hall to the right. Yanni has added the house next door. The (smelly) communal toilet/shower block, walled patio and gardens are down the steps beyond the office. Best not to be 'caught short' in the night as it is quite a 'stumble' from the bedrooms, including the short but steep flight of steps. A simple double room costs from 1600drs, rising to 1900drs with, if desired, continental breakfast charged at 250drs and everything extra. A shower costs 100drs, a machine full of clothing cycled by the pension staff works out at 650drs. The 'Che-Guevarra' moustachioed proprietor can 'forget' the original rate quoted and sometimes, half-heartedly, attempts to overcharge. This is perhaps understandable, as the rates harden the later in the day that guests arrive. Room No 6 is one of two rooms with a double bed, but kitchen smells tend to seep through the locked, interconnecting door.

Central Rooms (*Tmr* 15B/C3) (Class C) Plateia Miaoulis Tel 28509/22275

Directions: At the top of Odhos Eleftheriou Venizelou (*Facing the square*) and to the right, amongst the colonnades edging the road.

Reasonable but rather 'dormitory like' with double rooms, sharing the bathrooms, costing 1500drs. Hot showers are free between 1600-2100hrs.

Pension Antik (*Tmr* 16A/B3) Odhos Petrokokkinou

Directions: At right-angles to the Esplanade is Odhos Xioy, the 'Market Street'. From this the third turning left angles away and the accommodation is on the right.

'Syros quaint', chattily decorated with spidery red paint. The owner is usually, nay always absent.

Rather more up-market, expensive hotels are represented by the:-

Hotel Europe (Class C) 74 Stam Proiou Tel 28771

Directions: In the road above, one back and parallel to the down-town commercial quay, away to the left (*Sbo*) of the Harbour . Some 200m from the top of the 'Market St' (Odhos Xioy), alongside the Church of the Assumption. Pleasantly situated overlooking the bay, although it does edge the main road out of town. The view includes the lighthouse Islet of Didimi and often a tanker at anchor, seemingly forever steaming around the headland.

The building has a 1950s, faded elegance and is constructed around a lovely courtyard. The rooms are carpeted and well appointed, even if the floor coverings are rather faded and the walls show evidence of salt damp. The hotel is run by Teamwork Travel (*Tmr* 35C/D4). Single rooms, sharing the bathroom, start off at 2500drs & en suite 2800drs, whilst double rooms en suite are charged at

3500drs, which rates increase, respectively, to 2850drs, 3250drs & 4300drs (16th June-15th Sept). Teamwork are not above 'negotiating' when a client evinces disinterest.

Hotel Vourlis (Class A) 5 Mavrogordatou Tel 28440

Directions: Another excellent, if very expensive establishment is situated beyond the Church of Ag Nikolaos (*Tmr* 17D1), on the east cliff of the town. The hotel is on the left, unfortunately situated on a dangerous left bend, about and around which there tends to be a lot of 'car hooter'.

This luxury hotel (well pension actually) has been created from a splendidly proportioned, 19th century mansion. Both the public rooms and bedrooms are beautifully appointed and furnished. All rooms have en suite bathrooms. Single rooms cost 2800drs & doubles 3600/4000drs, which charges increase, respectively, to 3200drs & 4000/5000drs (1st April-31st May) and 4000drs & 4800/6000drs (1st June-30th Sept). A continental breakfast costs 300drs and an English one 600drs.

The Eating Out Syros is remarkably short of above average tavernas or restaurants and prices are in the run-of-the-mill range. Mind you, the main feature of an Ermoupolis evening is to sit at one of the numerous cafe-bars on the periphery of the Main Square and watch the colourful and extensive *Ramblas*, which goes on for hours. After nightfall Plateia Miaoulis almost resembles St Marks Square in Venice and the most sought-after (and expensive) cafe-bars are on the Town Hall side. There are also a row of establishments bordering the road edging the south side of the square. The most reasonably priced (and unhygienic?) is probably the one beneath *Central Rooms* (*Tmr* 15B/C3) where two Nes meh ghala cost 140drs... but ware cockroaches! The next door cafe-bar, with an awning covered terrace across the street, alongside the Rotunda, serves mainly pizza and spaghetti dishes. At the far, right-hand (*Sbo*) corner, a taverna owner possesses a Heath Robinson charcoal grill from which, in the evenings, he serves octopus portions accompanied by a glass of ouzo.

On the far left-hand (*Sbo*) side of Plateia Miaouli, beside a flight of steps is:-

Souvlaki O Manos (*Tmr* 20A/B2)

Directions: As above.

These souvlaki are the 'slab of meat' version, not giro. Sandwiches are also sold.

Another snackbar recommendation is the:-

Kafeneion H Nisiotissa (*Tmr* 18C/D3/4) Odhos Androu

Directions: In the narrow lane that branches off the Esplanade, opposite the Bus terminal, the entrance to which is barred to vehicles by bollards. The cafe-bar is beneath the sign *Breakfast, Fruit Juice, Toast*.

A narrow fronted kafeneion/bar. The pleasant owner serves a good breakfast with fruit juice and toast just as the sign proclaims. Two Nes meh ghala, two yoghurts and honey cost 400drs.

Towards the pier head, close by the *Hotel Hermes* (*Tmr* 3D4) is the:-

Taverna Ta Γiarrera (Giannena) (*Tmr* 19C/D4)

Directions: As above.

Well patronised by Greeks, serving a varied menu and extremely convenient for the ferries. A meal for two of tzatziki, bean salad, feta, a collation of cooked meats (including liver, heart, kidney & etc. – offal really), 2 plates of chips, a beer, a lemonade, bread & service cost 750drs. A noteworthy feature is the 'trap' side window from which are served souvlakis, costing 80drs.

Also on the Esplanade, to the left (*Sbo*) of the *Hotel Hellas* is:-

Mama Anna's Pizza Place (*Tmr* 9C3/4)

Directions: As above.

The title gives away the 'culinary bent'. An unexceptional meal for two of tzatziki, spaghetti & mince, veal & chips, a plate of feta and two beers cost about 1000drs.

Nothing can replace Γ*olia* and I cannot really forgive George for departing the shores of Syros. How can a man put his personal life and love before my readers' gourmet requirements? I obviously misjudged him, but if anyone out there knows just where he is, running a restaurant in Canada, then please let me know. It might be worth the cost of a flight to sample his food again. In the meantime the only 'heights' taverna is:-

Cafe Tembelis

Directions:From the left-hand side of Plateia Miaoulis (*Facing the Town Hall*) is a quarter of an hour,

100 steps climb up, ever up to the second metalled road at right-angles (or 12th turning to the left from the square). Follow the paved street to the left as far as a sharp right turn, where select the steps to the right, along Anastasseos St. The taverna, for some obscure reason named cafe, is 200m further on, to the left.

Run by a husband and wife team and packed with locals. An indulgent meal for a couple of 2 plates of liver, 2 helpings of giant beans, a Greek salad, tzatziki, 2 bottles of retsina, bread and service cost 1460drs.

THE A TO Z OF USEFUL INFORMATION

BANKS

The Commercial Bank (*Tmr* 21C/D3) Odhos G Stavrou.
Directions: To the right (*Sbo*) of the Harbour quay, the narrow lane (Odhos Androu), opposite the Bus terminus, crosses Protopapadaki St. It then bends to the right, where it joins two other streets, forming an upside down 'Y'. Changes personal, Eurocard backed cheques.

Other banks include the **National Bank** (*Tmr* 22D3), in the lateral road edging the Commercial Bank, on Odhos Rousvelt/Kalomenopoulou, and the **Banque Agricole de Greece** (*Tmr* 14B/C3/4) bordering the Esplanade.

BEACHES The only 'nearly' beach is to the right of the town, up and beyond the twin spired and domed Church of Ag Nikolaos and keeping to the right. Turn right down the sloping, angled and stepped concrete pathway that zig-zags down to sea-level. Here is a rock edged concrete pathway from which small piers jut into the sea. This edges the foot of the cliff-face into which are set a few cave-like store/dwellings. The path leads to a fairly large, concrete jetty. Up against the cliff-side is the *Asteria Beach Bar*. This delightful spot is used by the locals and *cognoscenti* visitors from which to swim and sub-aqua.

There are narrow, stony, pebbly beach coves behind the *Hotels Hermes* (*Tmr* 3D4) and *Nisaki* (*Tmr* 4D5/6), which, despite their generally unsatisfactory nature, are often crowded. The sea is clean, in stark contrast to the Harbour which is very murky. *See* **Excursion to Ag Dimitros Church**.

Perhaps it is worth mentioning that there is a 'local' swimming pool by the Harbour breakwater. It was complete with a set of water polo nets.

BICYCLE, SCOOTER & CAR HIRE There are a number of firms renting scooters but none hiring out cars. This is not surprising as the road system is not very extensive and the bus system is reasonably widespread.

Apollon Scooter Hire (*Tmr* 24C3/4) Odhos Antiparou Tel 26366
Directions: Along Odhos Androu (what isn't?) from the Esplanade, opposite the Bus terminal, and first turning on the left into the narrow lane that runs parallel to the waterfront. On the left and one beyond the back entrance to the *Hotel* Ελλασ.

The proprietors are very helpful. Haggle and they may drop the Vespa scooter rate to a daily rate of 1500drs, with further savings for 2-3 days hire... and the tank may well be full of petrol!

Makis Bike & Scooter Hire (*Tmr* 23C2/3) Emm Riodou St.
Directions: In the narrow street next door to *Yanni's Guest House*.

Two small scooters or one (big) Vespa cost 1500drs a day. Two for the price of one...

There are mopeds for hire from a Esplanade Tour office, close to the Bus terminal (*Tmr* 2C3/4), and two more on the Esplanade, beyond Kaba's Drink (*Tmr* 28B3/4).

BOOKSELLERS (*Tmr* 25C/D3/4) Edges the Esplanade, in the area of the Bus terminal. An international newspaper shop with various language paperbacks stacked in wire racks.

BREAD SHOPS One (*Tmr* 26B3) on the main shopping street, Odhos Protopapadaki, to the left (*Sbo*) of the High St (Odhos Eleftheriou Venizelou or Ermou). The bread is good quality. Another Baker (*Tmr* 26A/B2/3) is opposite the periptero at the left-hand (*Sbo*) corner of Plateia Miaoulis. They both serve fresh cheese pies.

BUSES A widespread network covers the island and the summer season schedule is excellent. The Terminus (*Tmr* 2C3/4), or more accurately the 'park-up', is to the right (*Sbo*) of the Esplanade. One of the buses is 'middlingly' antique with a radiator grill resembling a Wurlitzer organ.

Bus timetable Note this is the basic, spring schedule.

Ermoupolis Town to Dellagrazia (Posidonia),Finikas, Gallisas & Talanta

Daily	0645hrs	Dellagrazia,Finikas,Gallisas & Talanta.
	0800hrs	Talanta,Gallisas,Finikas,Gallisas,Talanta.
	1000,1115hrs	Manna,Parakopi,Dellagrazia,Finikas,Gallisas,Talanta.
	1245hrs	Talanta,Gallisas,Finikas,Dellagrazia,Parakopi,Manna.
	1345hrs	Manna,Parakopi,Dellagrazia,Finikas,Galissas,Talanta.
	1505hrs	Talanta,Gallisas,Finikas,Dellagrazia,Parakopi,Manna.
	1615hrs	Manna,Parakopi,Finikas,Dellagrazia,Mega Gialos,Vari.
	1745hrs	Talanta,Gallisas,Finikas,Dellagrazia,Parakopi,Manna.
	2000hrs	Manna,Parakopi,Finikas,Dellagrazia,Mega Gialos,Vari.

Ermoupolis Town to Manna, Vari & Mega Gialos

Daily	0645hrs	Manna,Vari,Mega Gialos,Dellagrazia, Finikas,Gallisas,Talanta.
	0730hrs	Manna,Vari.
	1000hrs	Manna,Vari,Mega Gialos.
	1245hrs	Manna,Vari.
	1400hrs	Manna,Vari,Mega Gialos.

Ermoupolis Town to Kini

Daily 0645, 1415hrs

Ermoupolis Town to Ano Syros

Daily 0745, 1030, 1130, 1230, 1345, 1600, 1830hrs.

Ermoupolis Town to Ano Manna, Vissa & Chroussa

Daily 0645, 1400hrs.

Note the bus timetable is not only stuck up in the window of the cafe across the Esplanade from the Bus terminal, but all over town.

COMMERCIAL SHOPPING AREA Not only is there a thriving Street Market, that occupies the length of Odhos Xioy, but a shop-filled High St (Odhos Eleftheriou Venizelou or Ermou) as well as a main shopping street Odhos Protopadaki. The Market is a splendidly colourful affair and noteworthy must be the fish shop with a dinghy full of fish at the front of the stall. Particularly useful shops include Nikas, a well equipped, small supermarket with a range of meats on display located at the waterfront end of the 'Market St'; Kaba (*Tmr* 28B3/4), an excellent wine, beer and spirits shop, some from the barrel, around the corner to the left (*Fsw*) from the Esplanade end of the 'Market St'; a Cake & Drinks shop (*Tmr* 29B/C3), on the right, Main Square end of the High Street, which sells cold bottled water and wedding dresses (if a client should so desire); Tranzit Stores (*Tmr* 30C/D3), a good, general store also stocking dairy products, at the right-hand (*Sbo*) end of the main shopping street; a small shop (*Tmr* 31B3) selling loose olives and cheeses, situated in a tiny square off the bottom left of the Main Square, one turning prior to Odhos Xioy, and a small Mini-Market & Grocers, close by Ag Nikolaos Church (*Tmr* 17D1), on a corner of the tree filled, raised square.

CINEMAS A summer months, open-air Cinema (*Tmr*) 32A/B3) is located across the road from the bottom of the left-hand (*Sbo*) corner of the Main Square. Another, enclosed Cinema, (*Tmr* 32B/C2) is to the right and behind the Town Hall, across a square dominated by the now neglected Apollon Theatre, supposedly a La Scala look-alike.

DISCOS The Disco Margarita (*Tmr* 34C/D2/3) is on the left of Odhos G Stavrou.

EMBASSIES, CONSULATES & VICE-CONSULS I can only recall the Dutch Consulate, next door to *Tony's Pension* (*Tmr* 7C/D3).

FERRY-BOATS Syros is still, nominally, the hub of the Aegean ferry-boat system, although for all practical purposes Paros has now taken over this role. Notwithstanding there are still a great number of cross connections made here. Incidentally, another pivotal island is Mykonos. Additionally there are 'Express' and small passenger boats, outside the scope of government controls, that make various scheduled island journeys. Ferries to and from Piraeus are boringly numerous.

Ferry-boat timetable (Mid-season)

Day	Departure time	Ferry-boat	Ports/Islands of Call
Daily	1230hrs	Panagia Tinou	Tinos,Mykonos.
Mon	0400hrs	Bari Express	Mykonos.
	2230hrs	Alecos	Paros,Naxos.

Tues	2030hrs	Delos	Paros,Naxos,Ios,Thira*(Santorini),Anafi.
Wed	1215hrs	Hellas Express	Paros,Naxos,Ios,Sikinos,Folegandros, Ia(Santorini),Thira*(Santorini),Crete.
	1215hrs	Ikaros	Evdilos(Ikaria),Karlovasion(Samos),Vathy(Samos).
	1315hrs	Olympia	Naxos,Katapola(Amorgos),Ios,Thira*(Santorini).
	1815hrs	Schinoussa	Paros,Naxos,Donoussa,Aegiali(Amorgos).
	1900hrs	Alecos	Paros,Naxos.
Thur	2030hrs	Delos	Paros,Naxos,Aegiali(Amorgos),Katapola(Amorgos).
	2115hrs	Olympia	Paros,Naxos,Katapola(Amorgos),Aegiali (Amorgos),Astipalaia,Kalimnos,Kos,Nisiros, Tilos,Simi,Rhodes,Kastellorizo.
Fri	1815hrs	Schinoussa	Paros,Naxos,Koufonissi,Katapola(Amorgos), Aegiali(Amorgos),Donoussa.
	2030hrs	Delos	Paros,Naxos.
Sat	1230hrs	Delos	Paros,Naxos,Aegiali(Amorgos), Katapola(Amorgos).
	2230hrs	Alecos	Paros,Naxos.
	2115hrs	Nireus	Paros,Naxos,Iraklia,Shinoussa,Koufonissi, Katapola(Amorgos),Aegiali(Amorgos), Donoussa,Astipalaia.
Sun	2030hrs	Delos	Paros,Naxos.
	2400hrs	Apollo Express	Paros,Naxos,Ios,Ia(Santorini), Thira*(Santorini),Crete.

*Santorini ports should include Athinos or maybe Thira or maybe both..!

Please note these tables are detailed as a GUIDE ONLY. Due to the time taken to research the Cyclades, it is IMPOSSIBLE TO 'match' the timetables or even boats. So don't try cross pollinating...

FERRY-BOAT TICKET OFFICES The Esplanade buildings from Plateia Kanari, on the right (*Sbo*) of the Harbour, all the way round to the High Street (Odhos Eleftheriou Venizelou) are sprinkled with ticket offices representing the various ferry-boat companies. To pick one or two might appear invidious but, naturally, I will comment (as usual).

Syros Travel 18 Akti P Ralli Tel 23338
Directions: In the ground floor of the *Hotel Aktaeon* (*Tmr* 11C/D3/4).

Mr Kouzoupis widely publicises the benefits of his office but negates all this self-acclaim with a cock-sure, 'wait until I'm good and ready' attitude.

With the choice of offices, customers do not have to endure this cavalier approach. Other firms include one between the *Hotel Mykonos* (*Tmr* 13C3/4) and the Banque Agricole de Greece (*Tmr* 14B/C34). This is run by a courteous and dignified old boy. He can well fulfil most enquiries and represents the *Pension Athina*.

A helpful office is that on the right (*Sbo*) of the Esplanade, beneath the sign 'Tourist Information Officer':-

Teamwork (*Tmr* 35C/D4) Akti P Ralli Tel 23400
Directions: As above.

Run by the energetic, if commercially obsequious and wily Panayiotis Boudouris who will answer all or any enquiries, from which he might turn a drachmae. Apart from being an agent for the **CF Naias**, they have flats and villas to let and represent the *Hotel Europe*, which Mr Boudouris manages. Any show of reluctance to take up residence at the hotel can result in a significant lowering of the initially quoted rate. A nod is as good as a... The office is open Monday to Saturday between 0900-1400hrs & 1700-2000hrs and Sunday between 0900-1330hrs.

HAIRDRESSERS Barbers are plentiful and there is a Ladies Hairdresser (*Tmr* 36B/C1/2) on the right of the road between the old Theatre and the Church of Ag Nikolaos.

LAUNDERETTE None, but three dry cleaner/laundries, two on Odhos Protopapadaki and the other close by, on Odhos Androu.

MEDICAL CARE

Chemists & Pharmacies Numerous. Open shop hours but closed Saturday and Sundays. There is a night and weekend rota service for emergencies.

Dentists There is a dentist at No 19, Sperchiou (*Tmr* C/D3/4), on the 2nd floor and another in

Odysseos St (*Tmr* D3/4), one block past the *Apollon Pension* on the left (*Heading towards Evagelistrias St*). The latter's weekday clinic is open between 0930-1300hrs & 1600-2000hrs.

Doctors Odhos Stefanou (*Tmr* C3) hosts a doctor whose surgery is 'at the ready' between 1030-1230hrs (Mon-Thurs), 1030-1230hrs & 1730-1930hrs (Fri) and 0930-1200hrs (Sat). The building also houses the services of a Psychiatrist. There is a second practitioner in Odhos Antiparou, between the Hotels *Mykonos* & *Athina*, and open Mon, Wed & Fri between 0900-1100hrs & Mon, Tues & Thurs between 1700-1900hrs.

Hospital The Hospital is close by the roundabout, on the south side of the port, beside the Manna main road.

NTOG (*Tmr* 27D5) Actually a Municipal Tourist office located in the 'arched' building edging Plateia Evropis. For some obscure reason the powers that be have limited the opening hours to weekdays between 1200-1300hrs!

OTE (*Tmr* 37C2) On the right-hand, top edge of Plateia Miaoulis. In the summer the office is open daily between 0600-2400hrs.

PETROL There are a number of filling stations south of the town.

PLACES OF INTEREST

Cathedrals & Churches

Church of Ag Nikolaos (*Tmr* 17D1) A beautiful, twin spired Orthodox Church with a gold striped, blue domed roof in front of which is a raised, rectangular, tree planted garden. The church, named after the patron saint of sailors, possesses a monument to the Unknown Warrior carved by a well known Greek sculptor. The road divides around the church which marks the start of the 'Old Quarter', known as 'Ta Vaporia' or 'The Ships'. In this area are an above average number of graceful, balustraded, balconied mansions. Some of the architecture in this area is fascinating as evidenced by No 28 Odhos Apollonos.

Two churches (or more correctly one church and a cathedral) dominate Ermoupolis, one each being mounted on top of the twin hills that tower over the port. On the left-hand (*Sbo*) hilltop is the old city of Ano Syros, founded in the 1300s, and the:-

Cathedral of St George A Roman Catholic place of worship dating back to medieval times. Most of the inhabitants of this fascinating settlement, which is only accessible to pedestrians, are the descendants of former merchant Catholic settlers. The religious tone was maintained by Capuchin and then Jesuit monks. The Capuchins founded a convent in 1535.

The right-hand hill of Vrontado is topped off by the:-

Church of Anastasis This embraces the Greek Orthodox faith and possesses some fine, very old icons. There are wonderful views out over the sea and distant islands of Tinos, Delos and Mykonos.

To the left of the far side of the Plateia Miaoulis leads to lovely staircases of steps, some with self-rooting saplings scattered about, and an Orthodox church, beautifully draped with bougainvillea. The house and shop lined streets in this area pleasantly wind down and around to the waterfront.

Cemetery, British Beside the road to Ano Syros and on the left, beyond the Church of St Georgios, which is noticeable for its tall bell and clock tower. The cemetery is well maintained but kept locked. Of the one hundred or so buried here, some fifty were victims of torpedo attacks on a British transport ship during the First World War.

Museum (*Tmr* 38B2) Let into the rear of the Town Hall and entered from Odhos L Ralli. Exhibits include items from surrounding islands but many Syriot island artefacts found their way into overseas museums. Open daily (except Tues) between 0900-1500hrs, Sundays & holidays 0930 - 1430hrs.

Plateia Miaoulis (*Tmr* B2) Veritably a magnificent, marble paved square. The far side is edged by resplendent public buildings including the Museum, Town Hall and Library. In the basements are a row of smart cafe-bars facing out over the plateia, the tables and chairs of which are spread out beneath scattered trees and palms. Anyone of these is ideal to view the evening entertainment – observing the endless and energetic *Ramblas*.

In stark contrast, bordering the road edging the south side of the square are a row of seedy, colonnaded buildings, the ground floors of which are also occupied by a number of cafe and restaurant bars. They have awning covered areas on the edge of the square, to the right of the statue of Admiral Miaoulis (a revolutionary hero) and the Rotunda bandstand.

Theatre (*Tmr* C1/2) I mention the Apollon Theatre as it is supposed to be modelled on the world famous La Scala in Milan. The theatre may well be a miniature La Scala but the forelorn, shuttered, decrepit looking building, edged on one side with palm trees, now appears to be a repository for an assortment of junk. The unpainted, undecorated interior is a total contrast of bare concrete and wooden chairs with no other furnishings. A local amateur dramatic society puts on one or two productions each year.

Town Hall (*Tmr* 39B2) This well proportioned, massive, neo-classical building dominates the Plateia Miaoulis. The central columned entrance is pleasantly balanced by corner towers.

POLICE
Port (*Tmr* 40D4/5) Behind the buildings which edge Evropis Square, on the right (*Sbo*) of the Harbour.
Town (*Tmr* 33B3) In the narrow square, Plateia Koutsodonti, off the lower left-hand (*Sbo*) side of the Plateia Miaoulis. Their squad car and or Landrover often completely obstructs the street. Unfriendly, unhelpful and regard tourists with total disdain.

POST OFFICE (*Tmr* 41B3) On the left-hand corner (*Sbo*) of the High St and Plateia Miaoulis.

TAXIS A very busy and well subscribed rank on the edge of Plateia Miaoulis – where else? The fare structure is detailed at the head of the line of taxis which include numerous Mercedes vehicles.

TELEPHONE NUMBERS & ADDRESSES

Bus terminus (*Tmr* 2C3/4)	Tel 22575
Hospital	Tel 22555
OTE (*Tmr* 37C2)	Tel 24099
Police, town (*Tmr* 33B3)	Tel 22610/22620
Post Office (*Tmr* 41B3)	Tel 22590

TOILETS There is a vast, old-fashioned, very clean facility to the right of the Harbour, a few buildings down from the Customs office (*Tmr* 1D5). To the left, men, to the right, ladies. An attendant oversees proceedings and sells the toilet paper. Another mens public lavatory is tucked away in a narrow alley behind the *Hotel Mykonos* (*Tmr* 13C3/4). It certainly is public... and very smelly.

TRAVEL AGENTS *See* **Ferry-boat Ticket Offices**.

WATER DRINKING The island is water-short but there is a desalination plant (that works) with a distribution office alongside *Yanni's Guest House* (*Tmr* 5C3). Conservation is necessary and includes switching off the water during the day and a generally rather miserly attitude in respect of its use. In most accommodation showers are charged as an extra, hot or cold, as is the utilisation of clothes washing machines. A relic of days of yore is the old boy whose large horse, bedecked with bells, pulls a big, four wheeled cart supporting a water tank decorated with 'murals'. The tap water can be very chalky or brown, salty and froths(!). Bottled water is a good buy.

EXCURSIONS TO ERMOUPOLIS TOWN SURROUNDS

Excursion to Ag Dimitrios (circa 2km) From the upper port keep to the right of Ag Nikolaos Church out along the cliff road. Beyond the *Hotel Vourlis* is the Disco Sunrise and a turning off to Ano Syros.

Prior to reaching the church, a track leads down to a small, shingle beach with two squatters' cabins on the foreshore.

Ag Dimitrios is a colourful, Byzantine style church, erected in the 1930s close by the cliff-edge. The 'wedding cake' building is balustraded and arched with squared stonework, fiddly stone framed doors and windows. The whole is capped by the familiar, red tiled cupola with upturned edges. The courtyard makes a pleasant picnic spot.

Excursion to Ano Syros It is possible to mount the hundreds of steps, setting out from the left (*Sbo*) of the far, top side of Plateia Miaoulis. This leaves a large school on the right, just behind and to one side of the Town Hall. But why not go by taxi or bus and save the exhausting, hour long climb. Certainly the medieval town and its Roman Catholic Cathedral should be visited. (*See* **Places of Interest, A To Z, Ermoupolis Town.**)

ROUTE ONE

To Kini & back to Ermoupolis Town via Dellagrazia (Posidonia) (35km) Both high and low (quay) roads south from Ermoupolis Town join at a roundabout. The low or harbour road is remarkable for the fact that ships awaiting their turn at the repair yard are moored in such a way as to tower over the 'back street' route.

The first section of the main road, which circles the bottom of the bay, is dominated by the shipyard and various warehouses. It is not a particularly pretty sight, unless one is an industrial archaeologist with particular interest in the 19th century.

Keeping to the left leads to:-

MANNA (3km from Ermoupolis Town) Not even a hamlet, or for that matter a particularly attractive site but there is a large petrol station. At each end is a stony cove, if a visitor must swim. There is a surfaced road that reconnects, farther on along, with the main Manna to Vari road, but beware at the junction as the irregular surface can cause a nasty moment.

VARI (NEW) (9km from Ermoupolis Town) Pleasantly spread out with some small shops, a phone box and a Saturday night disco (The Disco Caravel).

The road wanders on to:-

OLD VARI (10km from Ermoupolis Town) Most maps do not make a distinction but there are two developments with the seaside hamlet of Old Vari nestling at the end of Ormos Varis.

A pretty, interesting and squalidly attractive place to stay. The sandy beach of the small, enclosed cove has some rubbish on the foreshore. The sandy sea-bed is weedy and there may well be a slight, but pervading smell of spilt diesel fuel. This is related to the fishing fleet anchored at the far right of the bay (*Fsw*). The left-hand (*Sbo*) headland is topped by an impressive, castellated mansion.

Four tavernas edge the backshore which is planted with shady arethemusa trees. One back from the shore road is the *Hotel Romantica* (Class C, tel 61211), where all rooms have en suite bathrooms, with a single costing 1500drs & a double 2800drs, increasing to 2000drs & 3600drs (1st July-31st Aug), and the *Hotel Domenica* (Class C, tel 61216), which edges the road down to the cove, where a single room en suite is priced at 2960drs & a double room en suite 3460drs. The clean *Hotel Emily* (Class D, tel 61400) edges the narrow beach. Here a single room, sharing the bathroom, is priced at 1300drs & a double room 1600drs and en suite 1900drs, which rates increase, respectively, to 1500drs, 1900drs & 2200drs. A bar/restaurant has a patio set into the sea.

The main road, now mostly at or about sea-level, skirts the indented, rocky coves hereabouts and is lined with many new bungalows and chalets. The countryside is surprisingly well vegetated, similar to west island Karpathos, in the Dodecanese, but with the difference that the road is in good condition.

The *Hotel Akrotiri*, (Class C, tel 42141), seemingly set down in the wilderness, is only five minutes walk from a very pleasant, sandy cove close by the Church of Ag Thekla (14km from Ermoupolis Town). There is some kelp and,at the far end,caiques and benzinas are overlooked by the *Hotel Alexandra* (Class C, tel 42540), where all rooms have en suite bathrooms, with a single room costing 2050drs & a double 2600drs, increasing to 2800 & 3650drs (1st July-31st Aug).

The other side of the peninsula headland is the '2 donkey droppings' hamlet of:-

MEGA GIALOS (14km from Ermoupolis Town) Here a lot of villas are being built.

DELLAGRAZIA (Posidonia) (12km from Ermoupolis Town) Confusingly known by both names. The colonial style town is very interesting with some almost whimsical mansions enclosed by large railings and once owned by wealthy shipowners. The streets are gracefully tree-lined, all in amongst which new construction is underway. There is a definite aroma of money.

The bright blue church, close by the junction with the Vissa road, is most unusual with the campanile separated from the main building, so much so that it forms a separate gateway.

The road cuts down to the coast at the left side of a large bay. A paved road passes by a small, clean, sandy beach with thin horizontal, biscuit-like rocks in the shallows, overlooked by the *Hotel Possidonion* (Class B, tel 42100). The hotel rooms all have en suite bathrooms, with a single room charged at 2500drs & a double 3200drs, which prices increase to 3000drs & 3800drs (1st May-30th June & 1st-30th Sept) and 4100drs & 5000drs (1st July-31st Aug).

In the lee of the headland of Diakoftis is a caique harbour/cove, beyond which is a small army barracks. The other side of the bluff is the very small, lovely, underrated seaside hamlet of:-

ANGATHOPES (14km from Ermoupolis Town) The inhabitants obviously make an effort to keep the locale clean and tidy. Pleasant swimming with an islet close to the shore and, tucked into the crook of the headland, the low, rather ugly, concrete box-like *Hotel Delagrazia* (Tel 42225), which is actually a Class B pension. Apart from the *Delagrazia*, there is a new hotel, now possibly complete, a local wind surfing club and pedaloes.

From Angathopes an unpaved track makes for a deserted spot, place-named **Komito** on the maps. In reality this is simply where the path runs out on a relatively clean, shingly, sand and pebble beach on which are a few lumps of tar. The backshore is bordered by a thick grove of arethemusa and olive trees but no taverna or houses. On the headland to the left is a 'Dr No' house and to seawards, a 'Dr No' island. 'Informed rumour' confirms my impression as to the 'Dr No' nature of the left-hand headland. The property is said to belong to an English wheeler-dealer, international commodity oil broker. Further chatter infers that the luxury yachts seen sneaking into the bay, the other side of the headland, belong to other oil men and rich Arabs. Well rumour would, wouldn't it?

Back at the junction, west of Dellagrazia, the right turning leads to:-

FINIKAS (12km to Ermoupolis Town) The lovely, family holiday location of Finikas and Dellagrazia almost run into each other. A curving, narrow, tree lined beach edges the bay-hugging road. 'Fixtures and fittings' include hotels, bars, a mini-market, some ***Rooms***, a benzina quay, wind surfers and *Finikas Furnishing Apartments* (*sic*).

Following the road round the bay leads, almost immediately, to:-

OLD FINIKAS A spacious fishing boat and caique quay complete with two shower-heads, all set in a rocky cove with a sliver of sand. The rustic taverna, upon which paeans of praise have been heaped, doubles up as a barbers. A beer and a mezes of fish, cheese, tomato, olives and bread cost 150drs. The menu includes huge omelettes.

On the outskirts of Finikas is a petrol station and the main road leads inland towards Vissa. After about two-thirds of a kilometre, a left-hand turning proceeds northwards in the direction of:-

GALLISAS (9km to Ermoupolis Town) A one-time hippy hide-out, the resort has gradually been cleaned up by the inhabitants. A small hard core of overseas tradesmen and professional craftsmen have abandoned their cave dwellings and 'gone legitimate'. Alan Grove, a jewellery maker now with a shop in the village, is a committed, and vociferous spokesman for this colony of expatriates. He will help, where possible, in English, German, French or Greek.

Sited on the junction of the Finikas to Ermoupolis road and the turning to Ormos Gallisas, are ***Rooms*** and innumerable mini-markets (well at least three).

The profusely bamboo groved, paved approach road to the bay passes the extremely smart looking *Hotel Francoise* (Class C, tel 42000) where all rooms have en suite bathrooms, with a single charged at 1890drs & doubles 2670drs, increasing to 2480drs & 3895drs (1st July-10th Sept). There is mini-golf, a number of shops, the Disco Aphroditi, ***Rooms*** and Villas to Let. I am advised, and have confirmed, that English based Lisanne Bates (telephone contact 01 995 2356) rents a villa in the village.

At the entrance to the beach is the notice 'Dear Visitors, Well come to our village of Gallisas. You must know camping on the beach is forbitten (*sic*). You can camp only in the two campings work here.' The 'campings' are *Camping Yianna* (Tel 42418), with a reception, small shop and a disco, and *Two Hearts*. One correspondent waxed enthusiastically in respect of the latter which is positioned behind the small hills adjacent to the beach and 300m from the bus stop. The toilet and shower blocks are kept clean and the water is hot. There is a small kitchen, as well as a bamboo shaded terrace on which to sit, eat, read, play cards or converse. A self-service restaurant caters for the inner person and a mini-market the consumer urge. The owner is very friendly. The per person, per day charges are 350drs, per tent 150drs and tent hire costs 300drs.

The broad, large, curving, gently shelving, sandy beach is edged by tufted scrub. On the left, where the road runs out, is the *Green Dollars Bar* (yes Green Dollars), a popular rendevous for the overseas expatriates who languish hereabouts. Pedaloes lurk.

To the left is a benzina quay and beyond that, behind the church, is a nudist beach, a freshwater spring and caves that still provide a dwelling for the influx of the 'great unwashed' that continue to set up home in Gallisas, for the summer months. Alan refers to them as dedicated migrants but I suppose it depends upon your standpoint – I'm a boring middle class 'wrinkly'.

Continuing on the road back to Ermoupolis, after about 2km a junction with the Kini road forks off to the left, through the village of **Danakos**, and on to another fork. The left option leads down to the pleasant settlement of:-

KINI (9km from Ermoupolis Town) The approach to the curving beach of sand, laced with pebbles, is spanned by two 'laid back' tavernas. To the left (*Fsw*), over a small headland, is a sandy cove and to the right, the main body of the village. Several tavernas jut into the sea and to the far right is a fishing boat mole and moorings.

Prior to the beach is the new, clean looking *Hotel Ελπιδα* (Class D, tel 71229), where all the rooms have en suite bathrooms, a single room cost 1600drs & a double 2500drs, increasing to 2500drs & 3200drs (1st July-15th Sept). Opposite, set back behind railings, is a very smart snackbar with ***Rooms*** but... The lady in charge appears not to wish to let her one double room, urging all enquirers to go to the hotel! Those fortunate enough to prise this jewel from 'her apartment' crown will only have to pay 1200drs a night for a room with en suite bathroom which, despite her protestations "no hot water", has a solar heated shower! Stranger and stranger.

In addition, a big addition, there is:-

Marcos Rooms 49 Kini Beach Tel (an Ermoupolis No) 25632

Run by Marcos Kalogeras and his family, this lovely accommodation is very clean, pleasant and well presented with the rooms encircling a courtyard. The owner or a family member is usually present. Double rooms en suite cost 1600drs.

The road from Kini back to Ermoupolis winds pleasantly up on to the spine of the hills that dominate the skyline above the port. The fork to the left 'blunders' into a large OTE installation.

Best to fork right and wander steeply down through beautifully rural countryside, past the turning to **Piskopio** and, to the right, a deep meandering gorge spattered with farmsteads set in the steep sided defile.

ROUTE TWO North of Ermoupolis Town and Ano Syros, the surfaced road climbs on to the dry, unwelcoming backbone of the mountain range that fills out this end of the island. In reality this leads nowhere. When the road surface breaks down, becoming difficult and stony, a number of rocky tracks and paths tempt the voyager. They appear to head in the direction of this or that tantalisingly glimpsed, distant sea bays. These 'siren-calls' whimper to an end in some farmyard, and not hidden, undiscovered beaches.

Unloading at Paros for the new season. Acknowledgement to David & Liz Drummond-Tyler.

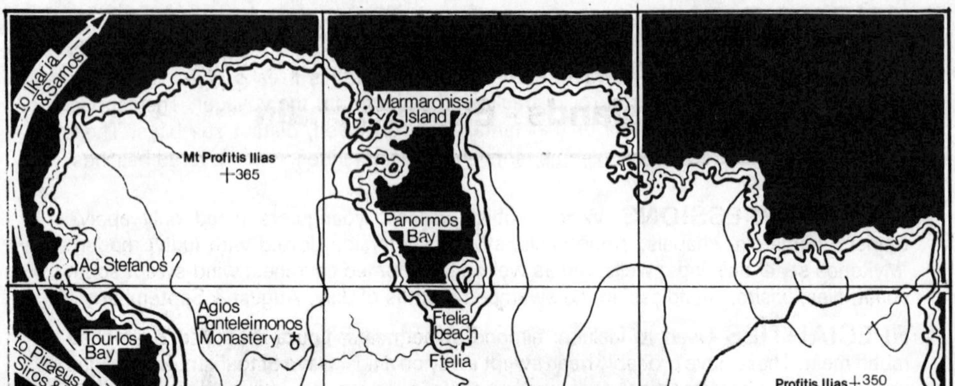

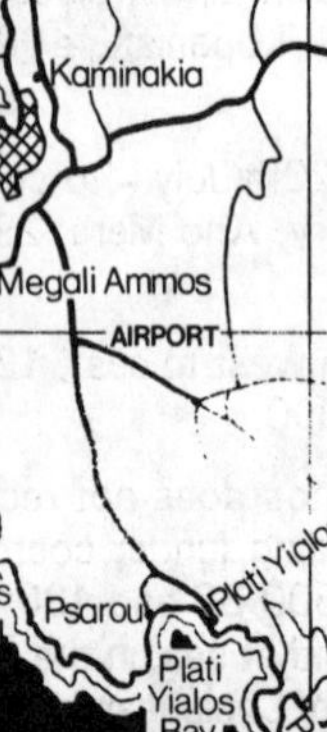

Illustration 10 Mykonos island & Delos island

4 MYKONOS (Myconos, Mikonos, Miconos) Delos (Dhilos, Dilos) & Rheneia Cyclades Islands - Eastern chain

Straights ★★
Gays ★★★★

FIRST IMPRESSIONS Wind; rubbish; discos; youngsters (need only apply); tourists; numerous chapels; stone walls; stony countryside dotted with (ugly) modern 'Mykonos style' buildings; wells; red as well as blue domed churches; wind-swept south coast; flies; 'visitor friendless' in the swamped months of July, August & September.

SPECIALITIES Used to include: almond sweetmeats; Louza-seasoned & smoked rabbit meat. These have probably been swept away on a tidal wave of tourism. Specialities encouraged by the same tidal wave, now include: hand-woven items; discos; souvenir shops; tourists; Gays & boutiques as well as manganese ore & 'Kopanisti', a very creamy, pungent cheese.

RELIGIOUS HOLIDAYS & FESTIVALS include: 20th July – to celebrate the Prophet Elias; 15th August – Virgin Mary, Tourliani Monastery, Ano Mera; 29th August – St John the Baptist.

VITAL STATISTICS Tel prefix 0289. Some 18km from west to east, 12½km north to south, with an area of about 75sqkm & a population of 4000.

HISTORY Possibly due to the proximity of Delos, Mykonos does not receive many early historical mentions. The islanders gained infamy by siding (under coercion?) with the Persians, during the wars with the Athenians, between 500 BC and 480 BC. These culminated in famous Greek victories on land, at Marathon, and at sea, in the naval battle of Salamis. Mykonos followed the historical path of a number of Cycladean islands joining, or being 'co-opted', into the Delian League. This was organised by Athens, with the central funds originally 'banked' on Delos island. This arrangement hampered the Athenians ability to get their hands on the cash, quickly enough. Thus the Treasury was transferred to Athens, in 450 BC. Oh ho, ho!

After the eclipse of the Athenian empire and absorption into the Macedonian Kingdom, Mykonos followed the general drift of the regions. The Romans slowly gained the ascendency from about the last century BC, until the fourth century AD. As a result of the void created by the collapse of the Roman dominion, there was a fair amount of piratical rape and pillage, although the Byzantine Empire was nominally in control.

The Venetians took over in the early 12th century but power was wrested from them, in 1537, when the Turk Barbarossa invaded. During the Turkish occupation, the islanders expanded their fleets and piracy became an island occupation, even an enterprise. Not only did the shipping activities increase the wealth but the merchants were also active in purchasing Aegean pirates booty. Nothing more than fences really! Perversely it is said that no extensive fortifications were built, despite its pivotal position in the sea-lanes, due to the islands overall poverty. But this is not entirely consistent with the facts that, in the 17th and 18th centuries, Mykonos provisioned various foreign naval fleets active in this area of the Aegean.

The skills and wealth were put to good use when the Mykoniots threw their energy into the Greek War of Independence (1821-1828). They contributed some 22 ships armed with a total of 132 cannon. A heroine of the time was the indefatigable and remarkable woman, Manto Mavrogenous, who helped organise the defence of the island against Turkish reprisal raids.

The overall change in emphasis and direction of the shipping world resulted, here as elsewhere in the Aegean, in a general and steady decline of the island's wealth and population. This downward trend reached its nadir by 1950. From being nothing more than a 'stepping stone' to the archaeological riches of adjacent Delos, the naive, simple, white cubist simplicity of Mykonos Port and Chora, combined with some relatively far-flung but gloriously sandy beaches, came to the attention of European sophisticates. They were followed by the rich, 'beautiful people' who were, in their turn, succeeded by a train of vassals. Some of these were hedonists of a particular bent, as the holiday-making, sun-seekers that now pack the island, appear to divide into two camps (sorry) – the sexually deviant and those who come to observe the phenomena. This of course, like many of my sweeping statements, is an over-simplification and I would not wish to encompass, damn or mislead those heterosexuals who are still attracted by the (now surely tarnished) magic still associated with the island.

GENERAL Mykonos is a conundrum. Either tourists will love it, and their personality profile might well indicate they were unmarried, in their middle 20s, enjoyed dressing up and were not island *aficionados*, or they will despise the place. Scott Fitzgerald's hero in *The Great Gatsby* ghosted in and out of the 1920s 'beautiful people', who drove everywhere in large Cadillacs or Buicks. In strict contrast callers to Mykonos do so on crowded ferry-boats or aircraft. But it is a more prosaic and egalitarian society than the privileged who originally discovered and patronised the island, in the early 1960s.

Visitors should not forget to pack their glad-rags. Evenings in Mykonos Town are spent parading the Esplanade and guessing who might be straight – that is easier, there are less of them!

As the Greeks so nicely put it, 'In the springtime we inflate the island and tow it to its mooring place. At the onset of winter we deflate it and bring it back...'.

MYKONOS: capital & port (Illustration 11) This is one of the few Cycladean island Chora's set in comparatively flat surrounds, not winding up the contours of a steep hillside with the town perched atop. In this respect Mykonos is similar to Paros, but almost the whole town is a startlingly colourful, dazzlingly white and cubist Chora with a plethora of whitewashed lanes, steps and houses. The problem is that the street layout is inordinately complicated and it is extremely easy to get lost. Furthermore any resemblance between Mykonos and other Greek islands is purely coincidental.

The port area/harbour Esplanade is, in stark contrast to the Chora, disappointingly grubby and unattractive. Additionally the 'suburbs' (and countryside for that matter) are, on the whole, messy and indiscriminately peppered with what would appear to be a standard Mykoniot 'prefab' villa. These appear to have been cast in a blancmange mould.

ARRIVAL BY AIR There are numerous domestic connections as well as some daily international flights. To reach Mykonos Town, about 3km distant, the usual Olympic bus drops clients off at the airline office (*Tmr* 19C/D1/2) for 50drs. Taxis cost 220drs.

ARRIVAL BY FERRY The Ferry-boat Quay is set down on the far left (*Sbo*) of the Harbour, a rather inconveniently distant walk to the centre of the town.

Mind you, this is not the first hurdle to be crossed. The hordes of disembarking travellers have to run the gauntlet of throngs of islanders frantically thrusting details of accommodation in their faces. Potential clients are plucked at, pushed and jostled by the frenzied Room owners, who unusually have pictures of their houses, pensions or hotels displayed on placards. Even early and late in the summer season this can prove quite a daunting prospect but I am assured, by a tour guide girlfriend, that the scenes in July and August are almost frightening.

To facilitate movement of clients and their baggage, three wheeled trucks are utilised, more especially where the accommodation is 'out of town', because the Chora is barred to traffic.

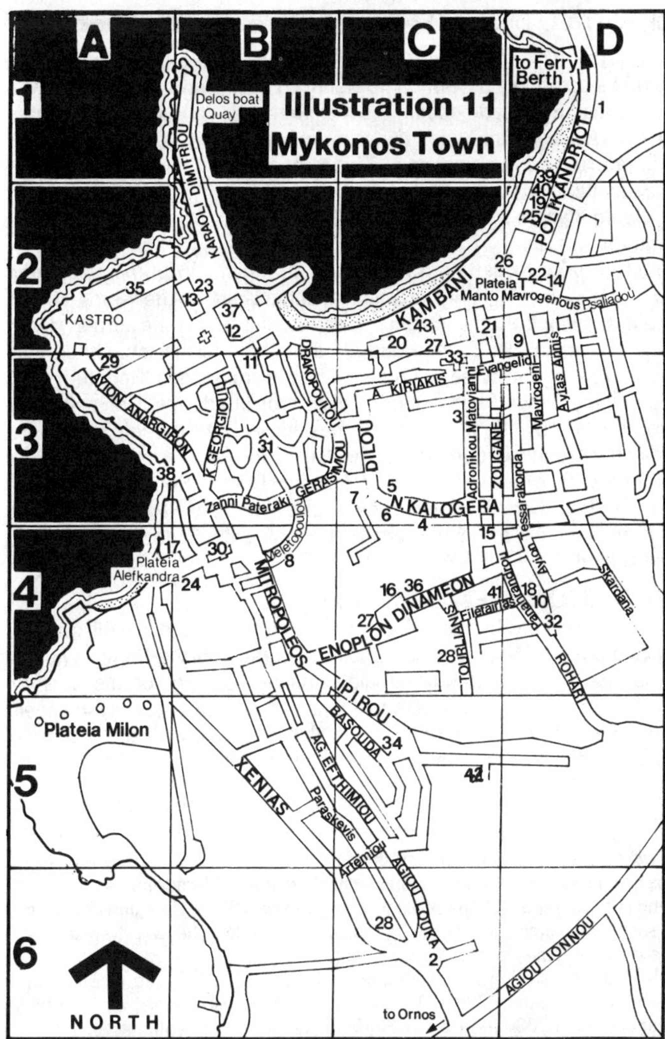

Tmr 1D1	Bus station A	26C/D2	Babis Pandazopoulos Ticket office
2C6	Bus station B	27	Aegeon Centre Ticket offices
3C3	Hotel Karbonis	28	Launderettes
4C3/4	Hotel Philippi	29A2/3	Paraportian Church
5C3	Hotel Zorzis	30B4	Metropolis Cathedral
6C3/4	Hotel Marios	31B3	Four Gossiping Churches
7B/C3/4	Hotel Maria	32D4	Koutsomboles Church
8B4	Rooms	33C2/3	Ag Kyriaki Church
9C/D2/3	Hotel Delfines	34C5	'Church of the Cat'
10D4	Hotel Karbonaki	35A2	Folklore Museum
11B2/3	Snackbar Pita	36C4	Popular Museum
12B2	Taverna Nikos	37B2	Town Hall
13A/B2	OTE	38A/B3	Skarpa Ouzerie
14D2	Taverna Antonini	39C/D1/2	Port police
15C/D3/4	Lotus Restaurant	40D1/2	Post Office
16C4	El Greco's Restaurant	41C/D4	Spilia Taverna
17A/B3/4	Restaurant Pelican	42C5	Police station
18C/D4	Rooms Despina Dantou	43C2/3	Sea & Sky Ticket office
19C/D1/2	Olympic Airline office	T	Taxi rank
20C2/3	Banks		
21C/D2/3	Baker		
22D2	Souvlaki Snackbar/Mad Club	*Tmr*	=Town map reference
23B2	Municipal Tourist office	*Fsw*	=Facing seawards
24A/B4	Catholic Church	*Sbo*	=Sea behind one
25C/D1/2	Aris Yiannakakis Ticket office	*Fbqbo*	=Ferry-boat Quay behind one

The Bus station (A) (*Tmr* 1D1) for Ftelia Beach, Ano Mera, Kalafatis Beach and Ag Stefanos is conveniently located beside Odhos Polikandrioti, the road that connects the Ferry-boat Quay to the broad Esplanade edging the main body of the Harbour. The other buses to, for instance, Ornos and Plati Yialos depart from an irregular square (*Tmr* 2C6), at the far end of the Chora, just off the 'ring road'. This terminus is signposted throughout the Chora, which is fortunate as the maze-like convolutions of the town's lane layout can prove quite puzzling. Room owners from far afield push their guests on to the appropriate bus whilst the luggage follows on.

For those not 'captured' prior to getting off the quay, turn right (*With the sea to the right*) past The Pigeon Club, an Archaeological Museum and a church. After some 200m, the road curves sharp left, away from the Harbour. It is possible to 'cut the corner' down some steps to the right to rejoin the 'Beach Road' (Polikandrioti) further on. Others will walk round the corner, following the sweep of the road to the crossroads. Here turn right down the steep slope along Odhos Polikandrioti. These crossroads are a messy affair being surrounded on all sides by 'Rent A Vehicle' businesses. On the left is a white building (with the standard rounded corners to the flat roof), terrace and stone wall enclosed yard festooned with signs variously proclaiming 'Drinks, Rooms With Bath, Autorent Motorbikes, We Rent Cars & Bikes at Low Prices, We Rent Bikes, Motorbikes For Rent Here' and Auto Rent A Car'. If you should be in any doubt there are rooms, drinks, food and vehicle hire!

THE ACCOMMODATION & EATING OUT

The Accommodation Unless pre-booked, this really is an island to avoid in the months of July, August and September. Whatever, the choice is to stay in the Chora, with all that entails, while the less rich and trendy should consider heading for the country locations, where it is quieter, easier to get personal washing done and usually cheaper. This is a comparative statement as accommodation in Mykonos Town is very expensive and in the country, just costly. Visitors may well be asked for up to double the official room rates.

In the Chora are the:-

Hotel Karbonis (*Tmr* 3C3) (Class D) Adronikou Matoyianni St Tel 22217
Directions: From the Esplanade, about midway round is Odhos Adronikou Matoyianni, a turning off Plateia Manto Mavrogenous between the shops of Best Gold Store and Greek Light Jewellery. This street is sprinkled with shops, restaurants, chemists and doctors. The hotel is beyond the church (on the right), as is *Jimmy's All Night Restaurant*, and on the right.

Single rooms are only available, sharing the bathrooms and start off at 1355drs whilst double rooms sharing cost 1805drs & en suite 2080drs. These rates increase, respectively, to 1805drs & 2260/2440drs (1st-30th June) and 2080drs & 2530/3340drs (1st July-15th Sept).

O Megas (Grocery Store), Adronikou Matoyianni St
Directions:One block back towards the Harbour, on the same side of the street as the hotel above.

This store has details of accommodation both in the Chora and outside town.

Where Odhos Adronikou Matoyianni makes a junction with Odhos N Kalogera, turn right and on the left is:-

Hotel Philippi (*Tmr* 4C3/4) (Class D) 32 N Kalogera St Tel 22294
Directions: As above with lovely gardens.

All rooms share the bathrooms with a single priced at 1510drs & a double 2025drs, increasing to 1915drs & 2700drs (1st July-30th Sept).

Further along, on the right, is the:-

Hotel Zorzis (*Tmr* 5C3) (Class C) N Kalogera St Tel 22167
Directions: As above.

Rumoured to be 'male friendly', the manager promises 'Private bath, hot water and lots of fun'! Only double rooms are available, all with en suite bathrooms. They kick off at 2710drs, increasing to

4070drs (16th May-30th June & 21st Sept-31st Oct) and 6320drs (1st July-20th Sept). At this price there would have to be masses and masses of fun!

Diagonally opposite is the:-
Hotel Marios (*Tmr* 6C3/4) (Class C) 5 N Kalogera St Tel 22704
Directions: As above, but across the road.

Rather less expensive than its other 'C' class rivals. Single rooms are only available with en suite bathrooms. They start off at 1990drs, double rooms sharing cost 1955drs & en suite 2710drs. These prices increase, respectively, to 2485drs, 2225drs & 3160drs (16th May-15th June) and 2890drs, 2680drs & 3795drs (16th June-10th Oct).

Odhos N Kalogera curves right into Odhos Dilou. A lane leads off to the left and on the left-hand corner is the:-
Hotel Maria (*Tmr* 7B/C3/4) (Class D) 18 N Kalogera St Tel 22317
Directions: As above.

The double room prices are almost 'Mykonos reasonable'. A double room, sharing a bathroom, is charged at 1460drs, increasing to 2590drs (1st July-10th Sept).

Back at the junction with Odhos Dilou, a sharp turning left wanders into Ag Gerasimou. By keeping left on to Odhos Meletopoulou and on the left, next door to a chapel, is:-
Rooms (*Tmr* 8B4) Odhos Meletopoulou Tel 22731
Directions: As above.

Nice looking two storey house with courtyard, gardens and verandah. Usual rates.

Two other hotels worthy of a mention include the:-
Hotel Delfines (*Tmr* 9C/D2/3) (Class D) Odhos Mavrogeni Tel 22292
Directions: To the right (*Sbo*) from Plateia Manto Mavrogenous (*Tmr* C/D2) and on the right.

A double room en suite starts off at 3000drs.
and the:-
Hotel Karbonaki (*Tmr* 10D4) (Class D) 21 Panahrandou Tel 23127
Directions: Sounds like a fizzy drink really and opposite the junction of Panahrandou and Filetairias Sts. Located by proceeding along Odhos Adronikou Matoyianni, crossing over Odhos Kalogera, jinking left after the *Restaurant Lotus* and right by *Vengera's Bar* which leads on to Panahrandou St. The hotel is on the left, prior to Koutsomboles Church (the four churches in one).

Single rooms, sharing a bathroom, start at 1400drs & en suite 1700drs whilst double rooms sharing cost 1800drs & en suite 2100/2500drs. These prices increase, respectively, to 1700drs, 1900drs, 2150drs & 3000/3200drs (16th May-25th June) and 1850drs, 2150drs, 2250drs & 4600/5400drs (26th June-26th Sept).

Rooms Despina Dantou (*Tmr* 18C/D4) 17 Panahrandou St Tel 23117
Directions: Next door to the *Karbonaki* and opposite the outset of Filetairies St. This latter is a 'classic' of external coloured staircases.

No 17 is a pretty, two storeyed house in a quiet location. The outside staircase has a turquoise handrail and gives access to the accommodation. The rooms are not out of the ordinary but they are airy, clean and fitted with a washbasin (soap and towel provided). A narrow balcony at the rear of the house allows washing to be hung out to dry. The bathrooms are clean but the shower is a tiny room with no hooks, thus a bather's clothes and towel can also get wet. Mama Despina is old, carbuncled and very pleasant. A single room is charged at 1500drs & a double room 1800drs.

See **Paradise Beach** for details of the only official campsite.

The staff of the Municipal Tourist office (*Tmr* 23B2) are helpful and speak fair English, when open. They have a list of most of the accommodation available and will place callers.

Nancy, an American girlfriend, assures us that at the hotel in which she stayed for almost a month, only she and the manager were 'straight', so bear in mind your preferences when selecting accommodation. A nod's as good as a wink...

The Eating Out Expensive, there is no other word for it, and generally small portions. Furthermore restaurants and tavernas fill comparatively early due to the press of tourists being topped up with cruise-liner passengers. On the other hand snackbar prices are reasonable, with a good souvlaki pita costing 65drs. A very good, convenient *Souvlaki Snackbar* (*Tmr* 22D2) borders Plateia Manto Mavrogenous in the ground floor of the building which also houses the Mad Club. Two tasty stick souvlakis and a lemonade cost 200drs. Another particularly 'filling' example is served by a small *Snackbar* (*Tmr* 11B2/3) 20m down the alley alongside the shop of Y Voulgaris, almost at the other end of the Esplanade. Incidentally, this is signposted 'For Exchange National Bank of Greece' (but this bank has long closed). The snackbar is at the end of a cul-de-sac, on the left.

Further on down the alley and on the right is:-

Taverna Nikos (*Tmr* 12B2)

Directions: As above or left at the tatty administration block housing the OTE (*Tmr* 13A/B2), down the street and almost opposite a small chapel.

Recommended and for Mykonos must rate very well, but note the caveat 'for Mykonos'. There certainly is a fair selection on offer – including spinach and cheese pie, fried zucchini, as well as an assortment of salads. Main courses include the usual moussaka (350drs), pastitso, stuffed tomatoes, meatballs, stuffed eggplant, all priced at 300drs. Also on offer are roast beef (320drs), 'succulent' roast lamb (335drs) and various chops and steaks. A meal for two will set diners back about 1300drs including a bottle of retsina, but note that only the large Cambas retsina is available, costing 260drs a bottle. The other wines are damned expensive.

Reputably the best and most popular taverna in town is:-

Taverna Antonini (*Tmr* 14D2)

Directions: On the left (*Sbo*) of Plateia Manto Mavrogenous. This square, with a railed off bust to the forefront (celebrating the island's heroine), has the Mad Club on the left-hand corner, and the Piano Club blocking off the bottom side.

The tables are crammed on to the pavement and climb the steps into the building. A meal for two of moussaka, 1 haricot beans, a Greek salad, half bottle of retsina and bread costs about 1400drs.

Whilst in Plateia Manto Mavrogenous, there is, next door to the Baker (*Tmr* 21C/D2/3), a highly recommended eatery, the:-

Restaurant H Klimataria

Directions: As above.

I am advised that this restaurant, literally translated 'The Grape Vine', is the only remaining truly Greek taverna left in town. An interesting menu at reasonable prices, reasonable for Mykonos that is.

Lotus Restaurant (*Tmr* 15C/D3/4)

Directions: On the main street of Adronikou Matoyianni across Odhos Kalogera and on the left.

Narrow, bistro-ish, 'hole-in-the-wall' and serving good soups.

Continuing into Odhos Enoplon Dinameon, which bends round to the right, gives access to an area which is really bewitchingly lovely at night with electric lighting skilfully used to highlight the buildings, paved streets and surroundings. Beyond the Popular Museum (*Tmr* 36C4) and on the right, opposite the Three Wells, is:-

El Greco's (*Tmr* 16C4)

Directions: As above.

A mouth-watering but extremely pricey menu.

One of the most picturesque and photographed locations must be that of the:-

Restaurant Pelican or **Alefkandra** (*Tmr* 17A/B3/4)

Directions: From the OTE building (*Tmr* 13A/B2), Odhos K Georgouli winds towards the Plateia Milon (Windmill Sq). Half-way is an area on the right containing a number of churches, past which leads to a scrubbly beach. *The Pelican* is on the right, at the start of a row of buildings that border and jut out over the sea.

Splendidly situated and not overly expensive.

Spilia Taverna (*Tmr* 41C/D4)

Directions: From the outset of Odhos Filetairias (opposite *Rooms Despina Dantou* (*Tmr* 18C/D4), the taverna is up a couple of steps in a narrow, 'hole in the wall' on the right, across the street from the second, dark red painted staircase.

A pleasant and quiet establishment. Tzatziki and a tasty moussaka, with vegetable garnish, bread and 2 beers for a couple cost about 1100drs.

THE A TO Z OF USEFUL INFORMATION

AIRLINE OFFICE & TERMINUS (*Tmr* 19C/D1/2) In a block to the far right (*Fsw*) of the Harbour. This building also contains the ticket office of Aris Yiannakakis (*See* **Ferry-boat Ticket Offices**), the Post Office as well as the Port Authorities.

In common with other Olympic offices, the staff often display signs of hardly controlled strain. In addition to the usual stresses, there is a daily crop of tourists attempting to change their tickets, flying times, destinations *ad nauseam*. As this is a desperately busy office, even in May and October, the quiet chaos (often not so quiet) can be imagined! Open daily between 0740-1700hrs.

Aircraft timetable (Mid-season)

Mykonos to Athens (& vice-versa)
At least seven flights a day.
One-way fare: 5020drs; duration 50mins.

Mykonos to Rhodes

Mon, Wed, Fri & Sun	1310hrs
Return	
Mon, Wed, Fri & Sun	1440hrs

One-way fare: 7270drs; duration 1hr 10min.

Mykonos to Samos

Wed, Thurs, Sat & Sun	1520hrs
Return	
Wed & Sat	1850hrs
Thurs & Sun	1810hrs

One-way fare: 5460drs; duration 40mins.

Mykonos to Santorini

Daily	0840hrs
Return	
Mon, Tues, Thurs & Sat	1220hrs
Wed, Fri & Sun	1140hrs

One-way fare: 3980drs; duration 40mins.

Mykonos to Chios

Mon & Fri	1520hrs
Return	
Mon & Fri	1835hrs

One-Way fare: 6050drs; duration 55mins.

Mykonos to Crete (Iraklion)

Mon	1555hrs
Tues, Thurs & Sat	1310hrs
Return	
Mon	1725hrs
Tues, Thurs & Sat	1440hrs

One-way fare: 6710drs; duration 1hr 10min.

BANKS Two major Banks (*Tmr* 20C2/3), almost side-by-side and in the same building which is centrally located on the Esplanade, next door to the Church of Ag Nikolaos. They only keep the usual banking hours, Monday to Friday which is quite surprising, considering the frantic internationalism of the Port. Apart from the to-be-expected crush of the 'resident' holiday-makers, there are seven or eight cruise liners a day, plus Delos island visitors. One or two Ferry-boat Ticket offices offer simple exchange facilities, but do not forget the Post Office (*Tmr* 40D1/2).

BEACHES To the right of the Harbour (*Fsw*), beyond the Post Office building (*Tmr* 40D1/2) and backed by Odhos Polikandrioti, is a delightful, narrow, small but very sandy beach. At the height of the season it must be very, very crowded but early and late in the year has surprisingly few visitors.

Beneath Windmill Sq (Plateia Milon) (*Tmr* A5) is a small, narrow but stony bit of scrubbly foreshore with some sand.

Towards the far end of the Harbour wall, beyond the Banks (*Tmr* 20C2/3), is a strip of sandy foreshore. This is used by local fishermen to beach their caiques and small benzinas, but those keen enough could have a quick dip.

Many town residents take the various excursion boat trips to Paradise and Super Paradise Beaches. At least one correspondent declared that the trip wasn't worth the 'sand'.

BICYCLE, SCOOTER & CAR HIRE There are two concentrations of activity. One is at the crossroads on the way round from the Ferry-boat Quay and the other is 'Scooter Alley' (*Tmr* C6), either side of the Ornos/Psarou road, at the south edge of the town. Both are rather messy areas. Recommendations include:-

Ioannis Zouganelis (*Tmr* C6) Tel 23427
Directions: The last outfit on the right of the street, in the direction of Ornos.

Don't be put off by his 'more than usually' disinterested attitude. He is a straightforward, honest chap and the rates are reasonable. The 24 hour hire of a scooter costs 1200drs and a moped 800drs. Naturally two or three days rental brings the price down.

See **Arrival By Ferry** for the other area of enquiry, at the Ag Ioannou and Stefanou crossroads. Diagonally opposite this site, on the right of the slope down to the Harbour beach road, is a Rent A Car firm.

BOOKSELLERS International newspapers and paperbacks are sold in Odhos Kambani, behind the Bank (*Tmr* 20C2/3) building. (I am aware that this is another Odhos Kambani!). A Kiosk (*Tmr* B2) is sited on the Esplanade, opposite the Delos boat Quay and they have an excellent selection of English paperbacks.

BREAD SHOPS Mykonos Bakery (*Tmr* 21C/D2/3) is situated on the far corner of the large building on the right (*Sbo*) of Plateia Manto Mavrogenous.

BUSES A comprehensive service, the timetable details of which are difficult to unearth. In theory these are supposed to be chalked on blackboards at each and every bus stop but... The Police (*Tmr* 42C5) will advise. As discussed under **Arrival By Ferry** there are two terminals:-
A. Polikandrioti Beach road (*Tmr* 1D1)
and
B. 'Plateia Plati Yialos' (*Tmr* 2C6).

Bus timetable (Mid-season)
A. Terminal
Mykonos to Ano Mera & (some on to) Kalafatis Beach(K)
Daily 0710(K), 1000, 1025(K), 1230(K), 1400, 1700(K), 2030hrs(K).

Mykonos Town to Ag Stefanos
Daily 0815, 1000, 1100, 1200, 1315, 1400, 1600, 1700, 1800, 1900, 2000, 2100hrs.

B. Terminal
Mykonos Town to Plati Yialos & Psarou
Daily 0800, 0930, then 'about every half-hour, depending on when the bus fills up', until 1900, 2000, 2100, 2200, 2300hrs.

Mykonos Town to Ornos & (some on to) Ag Yiannis Beach(Y)
Daily 0745, 1100(Y), 1200, 1300, 1400(Y), 1600(Y), 1700(Y), 1800(Y), 1900, 2000(Y), 2200hrs(Y).

CINEMAS None. The locals explain, with many a chuckle, "we watch videos now"!

COMMERCIAL SHOPPING AREA There is very little that cannot be purchased. Naturally the internationalism of visitors, rather than Greek island requirements, is reflected in the number of shops selling jewellery, fur coats, knitwear, shoes and clothes as well as art, hair and beauty salons, picture galleries and fashion shops.

Most of the essential pre-requisites can be found on the major streets of Adronikou Matoyianni, Enoplon Dinameon, Mitropoleos, Ag Efthimiou and Ag Louka, as well as the ancillary lanes of Kambani, A. Kiriakis, Evangelidi and Zouganeli.

DISCOS A profusion, probably more than on any other island, which speaks volumes (speaks volumes...!). It is best to establish the particular bent, quirk and or character of this or that disco, it may well help to save everyone unnecessary embarrassment. Those readers not 'in the picture' should curl up with an Enid Blyton book – not with Enid Blyton, she's dead...

Establishments include:-

Apollo's Disco. 2001 Odhos Pasaliadou, beside the Piano Bar, Plateia Manto Mavrogenous.
La Mer Disco. The Alefkandra Sq end of Odhos K Georgouli.

Caprice Disco Bar. In the same area as the *Restaurant Pelican*, prior to the Catholic Church (*Tmr* 24A/B4) and off Odhos K Georgouli.
City. Off K Georgouli St.
Kastros Bar. Classical music and comparative serenity. Close by the area known as Kastro, on the bluff beyond the Delos boat quay, overlooking the seafront at the top end of the Venice Quarter. They serve their own version of Irish Coffee, imaginatively named – Kastro.
Mad Club. Centrally situated, on the corner of Plateia Manto Mavrogenous. A popular spot.
Pierros Disco Bar. Opposite Ag Nikolaos Church. The gayest bar in town... I am reliably advised.
Pigeon House Club. Ag Stefanou St, almost on the Ferry-boat Quay.
Rainbow Disco. Along Odhos K Georgouli and at the outset of Odhos Matropoleos.
Remezzo. Alongside the junction formed by Ag Stefanou, Ag Ioannou and Polikandrioti Sts, on the way to the Ferry-boat Quay.
TKs. At the commencement of Odhos K. Georgouli, behind the OTE/Municipal Tourist office building.
Yacht Club. Well, not really. The peaked cap, pressed slacks, 'yellow-wellie' brigade would 'become Wodehouse purple-faced' at the very suggestion. Its only connection with a yacht must be the situation, close by the Ferry-boat Quay. Dancing, drinking (and debauchery) until the early hours.

And many, many more... including Windmill Disco, Scandinavian Bar and Irish Bar.

FERRY-BOATS Not a major ferry-boat port but a very useful island from which to reach the Eastern wing of the Cyclades (the islands of Andros and Tinos). Mykonos is also on the East chain schedules, with easy links to Paros, from whence there are convenient, local craft connections with the Western chain island of Siphnos.

Ferry-boat timetable (Mid-season)

Day	Departure time	Ferry-boat	Ports/Islands Call
Daily	0115hrs	Schinousa	Piraeus(M).
	1415hrs	Panagia Tinou/ Naias II	Tinos,Syros,Piraeus(M).
Mon	0630hrs	Bari Express	Syros,Rafina(M).
	1430hrs	Olympia	Naxos,Santorini,Anafi,Ag Nikolaos(Crete).
Tues	0500hrs	Bari Express	Tinos,Andros,Rafina(M).
	1400hrs	Eptanissos	Tinos,Andros,Rafina(M).
Wed	0500hrs	Bari Express	Tinos,Andros,Rafina(M).
	1400hrs	Eptanissos	Tinos,Andros,Rafina(M).
Thurs	0500hrs	Bari Express	Tinos,Andros,Rafina(M).
	1400hrs	Eptanissos	Tinos,Andros,Rafina(M).
Fri	0500hrs	Bari Express	Tinos,Andros,Rafina(M).
Sat	0515hrs	Bari Express	Tinos,Andros,Rafina(M).
	0600hrs	Eptanissos	Tinos,Andros,Rafina(M).
Sun	0515hrs	Bari Express	Tinos,Andros,Rafina(M).

One-way fares: Mykonos to Piraeus 1365drs; duration 5½hrs
to Rafina 1200drs 5hrs.

Hydrofoil timetable (Mid-season)

Day	Departure time	Hydrofoil	Ports/Islands Call
Wed	1415hrs	Nearchos	Paros,Ios,Santorini,Iraklion(Crete).

Please note these tables are detailed as a GUIDE ONLY. Due to the time taken to research the Cyclades, it is IMPOSSIBLE TO 'match' the timetables or even boats . So don't try cross pollinating...

FERRY-BOAT TICKET OFFICES A number of Esplanade offices, but my own favourite is:-
Aris Yiannakakis (*Tmr* 25C/D1/2) In the same block as the Post Office, and on the far right (*Fsw*). The staff are very helpful and lack that dismissive attitude cultivated 'here and there' on the Greek islands.

Other offices include:-
Babis Pandazopoulos (*Tmr* 26C/D2) Bordering Plateia Manto Mavrogenous, next door to the Mad Club.
Aegeon Centre This firm has two offices, one (*Tmr* 27C2/3) on Odhos Adronikou Matoyianni and the other (*Tmr* 27C4), just before Three Wells, across from the Popular Museum.

Sea & Sky Travel (*Tmr* 43C2/3). Supposedly even more helpful and friendly than Yiannakis, you take's your pick.

HAIRDRESSERS A veritable plethora. In such a cosmopolitan spot it would be unendurable for the ladies to have to go without their weekly visit to the hairdressers, wouldn't it! In any case 'the sea plays havoc...!'

LAUNDERETTE There are now two (at least). One (*Tmr* 28C4) is on Odhos Tourlianis and the other (*Tmr* 28C6) on Odhos Xenias, just north of the Plateia Plati Yialos Bus terminal. At this latter charges are 400drs for a machine load, 600drs for a full machine and the lady will iron and fold. Open daily between 0930-1300hrs & 1800-2000hrs, but closed Sundays.

LUGGAGE STORE None, so almost everybody piles their cases and backpacks around the statue on Plateia Manto Mavrogenous.

MEDICAL CARE

Chemists & Pharmacies Plentiful and often named 'Drug Stores'. Ugh! They include Kousathanos, Markantonakis and Stainatopoulos. Usual weekday hours and closed weekends but a rota is in operation, the information about which is displayed in the various shop windows.

Dentists Two are officially listed – A Drakopoulou (Tel 22503) in town and G Economou (Tel 22994) at Ornos.

Doctors A veritable rash of medical men including: Nikolos Michael in Odhos Adronikou Matoyianni (Tel 23026) and S Prodromidi also in Odhos Adronikou Matoyianni (Tel 22005).

Hospital More a very large clinic, to the left (*Sbo*) of Adronikou Matoyanni, beyond the crossroads with Odhos Kalogera.

MUNICIPAL TOURIST OFFICE (*Tmr* 23B2) Now the Tourist police have disappeared into the maws of the Town police (*Tmr* 42C5), the authorities have erected a small 'box' on the front of the OTE building. Climb the wooden steps and turn right but not left as that will harass a veterinary surgeon who occupies the other half of the 'box'. The usual informative details and open during the height of season months between 0830-2030hrs.

OTE (*Tmr* 13A/B2) Open weekdays between 0730-2100hrs and possibly also open some summer month weekends.

PETROL There is a Petrol Filling station on the road to Ano Mera, close to the town.

PLACES OF INTEREST

Cathedrals & Churches One informed source maintains that the building of the innumerable churches and chapels was funded from wealth accrued by fishing and piracy! Well, there you go.

Paraportian Church (*Tmr* 29A2/3) A most unusual, whitewashed structure cobbled together from four separate chapels,over the centuries,and situated on the Kastro bluff, beyond the OTE.

Metropolis Cathedral (*Tmr* 30B4) Orthodox faith.

Catholic Church (*Tmr* 24A/B4) Blue domed and white walled.

'The Four Gossiping Churches' (*Tmr* 31B3) Quaintly named, if nothing else, and south down the lane from the OTE.

Koutsomboles Church (*Tmr* 32D4) Known as the Four Churches. Why do they not also gossip?

Ag Kyriaki (*Tmr* 33C2/3) Just off the Esplanade, to the left (*Sbo*) of the Bank building and possessed of some very old icons.

Eklissoula Ton Ghatlou (*Tmr* 34C5) More colloquially known as the Church of the Cat.

Delos island Undeniably top of the excursion hit parade. *See* **Excursion To Delos island.**

Museums

Archaeological Towards the eastern or Ferry-boat Quay end of the Port. Five small rooms display, amongst other items, an unusual collection of ancient vases and pithoi between 2500 and 4500 years old; a 7th century BC pithoi, with reliefs depicting the Trojan War; a selection of 1st and 2nd century BC funeral jewellery and headstones, from adjacent Rheneia island, once the graveyard or Necropolis for Delos island, and a marble statue of Hercules. Open daily between 0900-1500hrs; Sun & holidays 0930-1630hrs & closed Tuesdays. The entry fee is 200drs.

Folklore (*Tmr* 35A2) Towards the sea side of the OTE building. A square, whitewashed, 18th century mansion with contrasting wooden shutters and doors, an external staircase and a low, curved roof building butted on the side. Once owned by the Kyriazopoulos family and displaying memorabilia,

artefacts, commemorative items, furniture, furnishings, utensils, books and documents of the past. Open daily between 1730-2030hrs; Sun & holidays 1830-2030hrs. Entrance is free.
Mykonos Library (*Tmr* C2) To the rear of the Bank building (*Tmr* 20C2/3), on the corner adjacent to Ag Kyriaki Church. A collection of Hellenistic coins and 18th/19th century seals.
Naval Adjacent to the Popular Museum (*Tmr* 36C4) and open the same hours.
Popular (*Tmr* 36C4) On Odhos Enoplon Dinameon, prior to the Three Wells fountain. Local exhibits and open daily between 1030-1230hrs & 1900-2100hrs.
Popular Art Museum In the Galatis or Venetian Mansion.

Tria Pigadia or Three Wells (*Tmr* C4) Three carved fountain heads sited on the right of the picturesque Odhos Enoplon Dinameon (*From the direction of Odhos Adronikou Matoyianni*).

Harbour Esplanade & Chora The wide, curved, paved, traffic-less waterfront of the harbour, comprising the streets of Akti Kambani and Al Mavrogenous, circles round from Plateia Manto Mavrogenous (*Tmr* C/D2) to the Town Hall (*Tmr* 37B2). The Esplanade is where the majority of the action takes place. Those that ceaselessly parade up and down are observed by the cafe-bar clients who endlessly look on from the various establishments that sprawl across the wide thoroughfare. Participants in this twenty four hour merry-go-round vary from the outrageous to the 'Oh my goodness'... and beyond! The not particularly attractive waterfront, is edged by a harbour wall and narrow beach (off which moor a wide selection of boats).

On the other hand, the Chora that stretches away from the Esplanade is startlingly, almost painfully beautiful. The 'doll-like' houses, which are festooned with flowers and plants, external steps, stairs and colourful balconies, edge and spill out on to the streets and lanes. These thoroughfares vary from wide to the extremely narrow. The flagstones are prettily picked out with whitewash, as they wander and wind their way through the town. The setting is most attractive at night when the darkness is brilliantly lit by dazzlingly illuminating, concealed electric lighting. The jostling crowds that throng the streets, bazaars, boutiques, bars, shops, tavernas and restaurants do so in surroundings of colourful and vivid brightness, alluring shadows and purple darkness. Particularly attractive spots include:-
Alefkandra (*Tmr* A/B4) Popularly known as the Venice Quarter, the houses of which unevenly edge the sea with their dissimilar, railed and roofed balconies projecting over the water. At night the cafe-bars and tavernas, at the *Skarpa Ouzerie* (*Tmr* 38A/B3) end of the buildings, throw out daubs, pools and splashes of luminescence into the shades of enveloping blackness. Further south and overlooking this beautiful spot is the:-
Plateia Milon (*Tmr* A5) A 'Windmill Square' on which four 'dead', round,mill buildings (with their now forever still, projecting, circular sail frameworks) resemble silent Martian monsters, temporarily halted in a terrestrial invasion. I write 'dead' but they are occasionally 'switched' on for the benefit of summer tourists. Only the sails rotate, there being no internal workings.

Another Mykonos sight is:-
Petros The island pelican, but not the original bird. Nonetheless, the present incumbent (accompanied by a posy fisherman who stands around to be included with the bird in the endless photographs) has earned his share of popularity and interest. This has, naturally, waned somewhat. Naturally? Well, some of the specie of homo-sapiens that now visit the island would probably out do and up stage a pink elephant, even if one did appear on the waterfront. Whilst on the subject, it reminds me of the rumour, only a rumour, that the original Petros took it upon himself to give up the delights of Mykonos and fly the nest, as it were, landing on Tinos. The Tiniots, unable to believe their luck, pampered the truant, in an effort to keep him on the island 'ground-staff', claiming him as their own. The Mykoniots, when they discovered this underhand behaviour, took out a law suit to retrieve the miscreant. The elected judge, with the wisdom of Solomon, is said to have instructed the Mykonos fisherman, who was supposed to be the birds ex-keeper, to endure a mock savaging. On seeing his master being beaten, the pelican went to the beleaguered man's aid thus establishing, without doubt, his true home.

Cruise Liners Bearing the mind the overwhelming popularity of the island, it is not surprising that Mykonos is on the cruise liner circuit. This naturally widens the holiday sporting activities to include passenger spotting and watching. An unfortunate side effect of their daily visitations is a further increase in the overcrowding, still higher prices and even less room at the tables of the inns.

POLICE

Port (*Tmr* 39C/D1/2) Their office is towards the Ferry-boat end of the Harbour, at the far end of the building which contains the Post Office.

Town (*Tmr* 42C5). Their office now incorporates the Tourist police who 'shack up' with the immigration authorities.

POST OFFICE (*Tmr* 40D1/2) In a building that also houses the Port police and Olympic Airways offices. Open for stamps and exchange weekdays between 0730-2000hrs; Sat 0800-1500hrs and Sundays 0900-1530hrs.

TAXIS (*Tmr* T) They rank on Plateia Manto Mavrogenous (*Tmr* C/D2). A board advises the base line figures of the official tariffs including:-
Mykonos Town to Ag (San) Stefanos from 200drs; Tourlos 160drs; Ano Mera 400drs; Metaliou 700drs; Kalafatis 650drs; Plati Yialos 280drs; Ornos 240drs; the Airport 220drs & St John 300drs. Note that all sorts of extras are charged (luggage, hours, etc).

TELEPHONE NUMBERS & ADDRESSES

Bus station	Tel 23360
First Aid	Tel 22274
Municipal Tourist office (*Tmr* 23B2)	Tel 23990
Olympic office (*Tmr* 19C/D1/2)	Tel 23404
OTE (*Tmr* 13A/B2)	Tel 22155
Police station (*Tmr* 42C5)	Tel 22482, 22235
Taxis, rank (*Tmr* T)	Tel 22400
Taxis, radio	Tel 23700

TOILETS Few facilities, but there is one to the side of the OTE building (*Tmr* 13A/B2).

TRAVEL AGENTS & TOUR OFFICES *See* **Ferry-Boat Ticket Offices, A To Z**.

ROUTE ONE

To Ag Stefanos (4km) This route progresses north from the Ferry-boat Quay, edging the west coastline, initially skirting an ugly quarry at **Kaminakia**.

TOURLOS (2km from Mykonos Town) A broad bay with four coarse sand coves and some kelp. At the near end is the *Hotel Sunset* (Class D, tel 23013), also known as *Iliovassilema*. All rooms have en suite bathrooms with a single room costing 1915drs & a double room 2395drs, increasing to 2530drs & 3160drs (1st-20th July & 21st Aug-30th Sept) and 3205drs & 4010drs (21st July-20th Aug). The *Sunset* is followed by *Pension Tourlos Beach* (Class B, tel 22306), with similar rates. At the far end is the *Pension & Restaurant Matheus*. Rent-A-Bike is present.

AG STEFANOS (4km from Mykonos Town) A 'chatty', busy, coarse sand beach, with the plush bungalows of the *Hotel Alkistis* marching up the hillside and three restaurants edging the backshore, at the far end. The foreshore is kelpy and Ag Stefanos is on the flight path to the Airport! Other 'attractions' include pedaloes, Rent-A-Bike, ***Rooms*** and on the right entering the village, the *Hotel Artemis* (Class C, tel 22345). A single room cost 2020drs & a double 2685drs, increasing to 2925drs & 3585drs (1st July-30th Sept). A 'bus blackboard' detailing the timetables is present.

ROUTE TWO

To Anno Mera (& beyond to Tarsana, Kalafatis & Ag Anna Beaches) (8km) At the outset it must be pointed out that, bearing in mind the popularity of the island, both the signposting and roads are appalling. This road climbs out of Mykonos Town through the messy outer ring of development, past the petrol station and a car-breakers (yes a car-breaker). Frankly I don't find the Mykonos countryside at all attractive. The authorities can exercise little, if any, control over house building as the landscape is indiscriminately scattered with the standard Mykonos 'housepack' – a white cube with blancmange mould rounded roof edges and a decorative chimney.

If a matchless example of my 'prejudice' is required, beyond the turning off to the Monastery of Ag Panteleimonos, the town rubbish dump is possibly the most unattractive of its type that I have seen. The road edge containment is made up of a fence of beaten out, flattened, rusty oil drums, discarded cookers and refrigerators. The only plus point is that the tip is not bordering sea-cliffs. Incidentally my obsession with 'dead buses' is satiated by an example way down in the fields to the left.

Ftelia Beach (5km from Mykonos Town) A turning to the left and a bare kilometre down the steeply inclined road. The thoroughfare is initially surfaced but becomes a rough, if sandy, track. This winds over a messy, scrubbly plain about which are scattered 'in sequence' car tyres, possibly a local lads, dirt-track motorbike circuit. The large, indented Bay of Panormos, skirted by many chapels, is as attractive as the landward is unattractive. The right-hand (*Fsw*) side is mucky but to the left there is a very pleasant, clean, coarse sand beach, with some tar. This sweeps round to the *Restaurant Ftelia* whose unattractive building is set into the hillside. Alongside the restaurant is a horrid, rubbishy area signed 'Parking Reserved For Surfers'. This seems an unnecessary stricture considering the surrounding acres and acres of waste ground.

It is thought provoking to realise that this was the site of an ancient town and port.

Back on the main road, the next settlement is:-

ANO MERA (8km from Mykonos Town) The rather confusing layout of this large, sleepy village, which is dominated by a monastery campanile, would appear to have simply happened. Ano Mera is one of the saving graces of the island.

On the approach, a sharp left takes off past Paleokastrou Monastery into a northern hinterland on the slopes of Mt Kourvousia. In actual fact Paleokastrou was a convent, or as the maps rather prettily put it a Women's Monastery.

Keeping to the left of the settlement, along a wide, dusty track, or 'bypass', leads towards the beaches of Ag Anna, Kalaftis and Tarsana, of which more later.

Keeping to the right at the major fork gives way to two short roads, the low and the high, into the centre of the village. The high road leads on to a large circular square, almost a roundabout, around which the village is scattered. At the far or east side of the square is a Clinic, with a post-box inside the entrance and opposite which is a periptero with a telephone. There are three or four tavernas, a good bakery, a supermarket and a squatty Public WC (or toilets for our American friends). The latter is certainly one of the most revolting facilities in all of Greece. A number of the taverna signs are in English.

To the right (*Mykonos Town behind one*) is the:-

Tourliani Monastery A 16th century house of worship behind a very high, fortified wall, above which peeps a campanile and rises a 'wedding-cake-stand' tower. The solid, arched doorway let into the outer wall leads on to a spacious courtyard and, to one side of the cloistered perimeter, a simple two room museum.

Prior to leaving matters religious, as detailed previously, the turning to the left immediately prior to Ano Mera proceeds to the picturesque:-

Monastery of Paleokastrou (8½km from Mykonos Town) More correctly a Nunnery or Convent. It certainly is a place of quiet tranquillity. The flag-stoned courtyard is dominated by a large tree, from a branch of which is suspended a bell to summon the worthy.

Elia Beach (8km from Mykonos Town) From the centre of Ano Mera proceed across the village, leaving the roundabout to the right. It is possible to take the road signposted Ackari Beach (Agari), but only if a traveller wishes to switch back up and over uncharted, unmade, wall-lined tracks for miles and that double back towards the west. Otherwise turn left at the very expensive *Hotel Ano Mera* (Class A, tel 71215), a 'sore-thumb' construction that juts out of the bleak, stone walled surrounds, prior to the now long, wide, downward track to the beach. Note that any signposting runs out alongside the hotel, becoming nothing more than red paint blobs and crude arrows. Steeply descending, the road passes, on the left, an interesting, unfinished, uninhabited building, styled on a windmill but with a large, stone, first storey patio. Possibly it was to be a nightspot.

The lovely, broad, coarse sand beach is surrounded by hillsides. The foreshore is clean, even though some scattered kelp is piled about here and there. There are two tavernas to the left of the track that runs out on the backshore of the beach. Many who stay in Mykonos town taxi out daily to enjoy the delights of this spot.

Kalo Livadi Beach (10km from Mykonos Town) Continue along the Ano Mera 'bypass' and select the next surfaced road to the right, signed 'Kalo Livada Beach Hotel'. Then turn first left on to a track which descends steeply, switching from unpaved to paved surfaces at the particularly steep sections or tight bends.

The beach is very long, pleasant, sandy and (out of the height of season months) secluded. Towards the left-hand (*Fsw*) end is the referred to accommodation, *Kalo Livadi* (Class D, tel 71298). This is actually a set of beach bungalows with alternate blue and red painted doors. This alternate colour scheme is to be seen elsewhere on Mykonos. A double room costs 2260drs, increasing to 2710drs (1st July-10th Sept). There is also a taverna, but nothing else.

Returning once again to the Ano Mera 'by-pass', eastwards advances after another 2km to a right-hand turning which bears off along an unsurfaced road to:-

TARSANA (12km from Mykonos Town) The long, clean, coarse sand beach, with some kelp, slowly curves around the very clear sea's edge of the bay.

To the far left (*Fsw*) is the extremely expensive *Hotel Aphroditi* (Class B, tel 21367) constructed in a series of cubes up the foothill of the backing hillside. The hotel runs a cocktail bar, no hush my mouth a beach taverna distanced about 100m from the small cliff edging the bay. The hotel serves lunch-time meals from hay-boxes and pampered guests pick over this or that delicacy. Casual visitors are discouraged from bestowing their custom by being charged outrageous prices.

There are a few pedaloes scattered about as are some bamboo beach sun shelters.

On the way in, at the far right (*Fsw*) of the bay are the twin peaks of Cape Kalafatis. The other side of the Cape is:-

AG ANNA (12km from Mykonos Town) Not the Paradise beach Ag Anna, but a small bay and fine shingle beach, with a line of tar and some kelp bordering the sparkling sea. The location is rather ramshackle with, for instance, a lorry water tanker body abandoned on the backshore.

Both Ag Anna and Tarsana beaches are backed by gentle but unexciting, scrubbly slopes. Most importantly, out of the height of season, they are almost deserted.

Returning to the main road, it is really not worth going any further eastwards, although the oft mentioned Profitis Ilias, the highest island point at a lowly 351m, is in this direction. The one or two beaches that can be spied way down on the right (or south coast) cannot be reached by road. Additionally the never-out-of-the-ordinary countryside becomes a positively lunar panorama riddled with old quarry workings. The very eastern end of the island is uninhabited mountain moorland with the armed forces in occupation. Offshore is Dragonissi islet, famed for its sea worked caves in which seals have their lodgings.

ROUTE THREE

To Psarou, Plati Yialos, Paradise & Super-Paradise Beaches (4km) On a steep, downward section of the road to Plati Yialos beach, a backwards facing turning to the right curves round to:-

Psarou Beach (4km from Mykonos Town) The final, unsurfaced approach is through screens of bamboo petering out in the car park of *Hotel & Restaurant Psarou*. A sign declares 'Parking in the Garden', actually a field. A single-file footpath leads down the side of the Restaurant to emerge on the extreme right-hand (*Fsw*) side of the beach. The coarse sand beach is scattered with straw sun umbrellas and deck chairs. Swing-top litter bins line the shore. At the far end of the cove is a beach taverna. Water sports include hang gliding, wind surfing and pedaloes. There is a smart milieu to this location which is fairly crowded, even early and late in the year.

Plati Yialos Beach (4km from Mykonos Town) The surfaced road swoops steeply down besides the expensive *Hotels Petinos* (Class C, tel 23680) and *Platis Gialos Beach* (Class D, tel 22913). The *Petinos* has a diving club.

The thoroughfare peters out on a rough, small vehicle park at the extreme right of the lovely, narrow, curved, coarse sand beach set in a cove which terminates in a 'butterfly wing' of rocky outcrops at the far left-hand side. The near end of the beach is 'planted' with beach umbrellas and deck chairs, the whole edged with bar/taverna/restaurants. The second beach taverna, the pleasant *Agrogiali*, where cheerful service is the 'order of the day', serves an agreeable lunchtime meal for two of Greek salad, chips, bread and 2 bottles of beer at a cost of 800drs.

An expensive feel, no water sports and crowded, even early and late in the summer. To the right, around a low cliff-edge, is a jetty from which there are 'continuous' daily boat trips to Paragka, Paradise Beach (and Camping), Super Paradise Beach, Agrari and Elia beaches, with a one-way fare to Paradise Beach costing 75drs. There are also excursions to Delos Island and Mykonos Caves (Dragonissi islet).

The first hotel on the way into the village has Greek dancing every Saturday night and despite the costly ambience, a couple of coffees are reasonably priced.

Buses to Mykonos Town depart from 0810 & 0945hrs and then 'when they're full', the last bus leaving at 2310hrs. The signposted bus stop is 200/300m up the hill from the beach.

There is a footpath from Plati Yialos to:-

Paradise Beach Here nude bathing is allowed and there is the very popular *Paradise Beach Taverna*. This acclaim is well founded on freshness, price, quality and selection. Paradise Beach can also be reached along a track from a right-hand spur off the Airport road. The official campsite, *Paradise Camping* (Tel 22129), is open from April to October. Charges are 230drs per person plus 120drs for a tent.

A difficult trek can be made to:-

Super Paradise Beach Here gather the majority of the more unnatural, if 'beautiful' young men who sunbathe and disport themselves 'in the starkers'.

ROUTE FOUR

Ornos & Ag Yiannis (4km) The road, almost for the whole of its length, borders the sea's edge. The initial part of the route passes through the 'suburbs' of Mykonos Town with package tour hotels dotted about and a pleasant beach.

About half-way to Ornos, there is a development at:-

MEGALI AMMOS (1½km from Mykonos Town) A splendid beach edged by horizontal biscuit rock. To landward there are cubic, condominium chalet hotels set into the hillside, one painted cardinal red and overlooked by blue coloured units. There is a taverna at the Mykonos Town end of the beach.

The main road curves to the right, skirting the nearside of Korfos Bay, the beach of which is indescribably filthy being covered in all manner of rubbish and the backshore of which is used as a municipal civil engineering dump. Additionally the general noise would indicate the presence of an electricity generating station.

Not much further on is a major fork in the road. If driving a scooter beware, as the surface hereabouts is loose gravel. The left-hand turning snakes along to:-

Ornos Beach (3½km from Mykonos Town) The road passes, on the right, the *Hotel Asteri* (Class D, tel 22715), where all rooms have en suite bathrooms with a single room costing 2260drs & a double 2710drs, increasing to 2710drs & 3615drs (1st-31st July) and 3160drs & 4515drs (1st Aug-5th Sept); Rent-A-Car & Motor Byke, on the left, and *Bistrot Boheme* (*sic*), on the right.

The coarse sand beach, with some kelp, is edged by four taverna/beach restaurants as well as, to the left (*Fsw*), the *Port Ornos Restaurant* and *Ornos Beach Hotel* (Class B, tel 22243). This latter is extremely expensive with a single room kicking off at 3870drs & a double room 4400drs, increasing to 4090drs & 4570drs (1st-30th June) and 5040drs & 6280drs (1st July-30th Sept). Some benzinas and powered motorboats are moored.

To the right is the extensively refurbished *Club Mikonos* (formerly the Paralos Beach Hotel) which heralds itself as 'The leading holiday resort of the Greek Islands' – a statement which will intrigue some other hoteliers. At the far end is a taverna with a painted fish fascia where they, somewhat languidly, serve a reasonable range of middlingly expensive fare. A coke costs 90drs and a 'tost' 100drs. Also on this section of the beach are a few beach umbrellas.

Buses depart for Mykonos Town at 0810, 1010, 1120, 1210, 1320, 1420, 1620, 1710, 1910, 2010 and 2210hrs.

Returning to the fork in the main road (incidentally around a cemetery), the right-hand route snakes up a hillside. It borders, on the right, what was obviously once planned as a village development. Despite the winding nature of the road, it follows the curve of the bay. On the last, sharp right-hand bend a track sallies forth towards Cape Alogomandra, at the extreme tip of the Bay of Ornos, but peters out in another hill-bound, discontinued development.

After the apex of the bend, on the left is the:-

Pension Elefteria (Class E) Tel 23090

Directions: As above. The good lady's card describes it as the *Hotel Kostas*. Actually it is a pleasantly situated pension, overlooking Ornos beach to which a convoluted track descends. There is a bus stop right outside the door.

Mrs Theochari and her husband's English is limited but their daughter, a good looking, well-built lass, has an excellent command of the language and will somewhat disinterestedly converse with foreign guests, when necessary. Breakfast, if required, is taken in the family kitchen off which open out the family bedrooms. A large double room with spacious en suite bathroom starts off at 1800drs increasing, with the onset of summer, to 2500drs. A double room sharing a bathroom costs 1500drs in the high season.

Continuing, the road leads over the hillside, only to drop down on the reverse side to:-

Ag Yiannis (4km from Mykonos Town) A dramatic location with some development, including the excellently situated *Manoula's Beach Hotel*.

The rocky bay has a tiny beach of coarse sand, rocks and kelp. There are a few bamboo sun umbrellas, old pedaloes and one taverna, to the left, beyond which are another two coves. But it is to the right of the bay that the eye is drawn. Here a small chapel and stone jetty jut out into the sea, edged by a rocky headland. A few caiques are moored to the quay. Unfortunately, close to, the scene is not as attractive as it appears from a distance. Some rock blasting has cleared a track round the headland, to the right of the chapel, but with little effect as it leads nowhere.

EXCURSION TO DELOS ISLAND (Dhilos, Dilos)

The sacred island 'super-spot' of the Aegean and the envy of the rest of the Cyclades who would dearly love to have Delos as their own adjunct. Steal it, they would tow it away... if they could. Tinos ensures it gets in on the act and runs pleasure cruises, but Mykonos has the stranglehold on this most valuable tourist property.

Lizards are everywhere and Delos is arid.

ARRIVAL BY CAIQUE In the summer months craft depart daily from a Mykonos Town quay, close by the OTE office (*Tmr* 13A/B2). The boat trips set out at between 0830-0900hrs and the voyage takes some ½ hour. The round trip costs about 400drs each and to go ashore costs another 200drs. Guided tours cost 2000drs. Some 3-4 hours is allowed on the island and the caiques and trip boats begin the return journey from midday on. Tourists are not allowed (legally) to stay overnight or camp out and the *Hotel Xenia* is only for the use of bona-fide archaeologists.

Due to the complexities of the excavations it is probably preferable to join a guided party. The average visitor can only hope, in the short time available, to absorb part of the rarified atmosphere and wonder at the vast extent of the wild flower and weed bestrewn ruins in which nestle marvellous mosaics, terraces, cisterns and from which sprout rich outcrops of statues, stoas, columns, crepidoma, shrines and altars.

The amazing site includes a sacred harbour and lake; temples to Apollo and the Athenian; houses of the Naxians, Poseidoniasts, Cleopatra, Dionysos, Tritons, Masks and Dolphins; sanctuaries; sacred ways; porticos; the Terrace of Lions; the Theatre and Mt Kynthos.

A historical review shows that the island was occupied as long ago as 3000 BC. Even prior to the arrival of the Ionians, in 1000 BC, Delos was obviously a religious centre with a thriving port. The Ionians really gave an impetus to the island's sacred importance. They imported the mythological Cult of Leto. She was the mother of both Artemis (or Diana), Goddess of hunting, woodlands and associated with fertility as well as being a Moon-Goddess, and Apollo, God of music, poetry, archery, prophecy and healing.

But as now, 'a good little earner' was usually too much temptation for others not to poke their 'sticky fingers' into the action. It only took a few centuries for the Athenians to muscle in on the act. They joined the local Masons (well not really), more a United Nations of the Aegean and known as the Delian League. The central funds of this association were deposited on Delos. In the meantime an Aegean bully-boy, Polykrates, tyrant of Samos and conqueror of the Cyclades, in an effort to impress the Gods, attached the larger, adjacent island of Rheneia to Delos by chains. These were stretched across the 1000m channel separating the two, thus binding and dedicating Rheneia to Apollo. Show-off!

After this unpleasant fellow's departure (522 BC), the Athenians got back to work with a will in the 'corridors of power'. Probably one of their chaps became Hon Treasurer because lo and behold, in 454 BC, the funds were transferred to Athens, for safe keeping. Oh yes! And when they got their hands on the money to what purpose do you think it was put? Beefing up the navy, building castles and fortifications? On no. One Perikles frittered the loot – sorry, bank balance – on repairing damage incurred during Persian invasions, and tarting up Athens. Well, well.

It only took a further few years of manoeuvring and disruptive activity (28 actually) for the Athenians to convince the islanders that Delos should be purified. This was actually the second ritual cleansing, one other having taken place in 543 BC. This time the proposed event was lent urgency as the Athenians adjudged that an epidemic plaguing their city was due to the Gods' anger. It also had the effect of distancing the existing Delos residents from their ancestors, thus breaking possible hereditary ties, and any claim on the now missing money.

To propitiate the Gods, and loosen the Delians grip, not only was it decreed that all the tombs had to be removed, to Rheneia island, but that no further deaths or births could take place on Delos. Inhabitants would, in future, have to carry out these necessary bodily functions on Rheneia!

In an effort to rid themselves of the troublesome and despotic Athenians, the islanders appealed to the Spartans for support. When the Athenians heard of this they deported all the inhabitants, in 422 BC, and caused the leaders to be murdered. Despite this, the Athenians, suffering severe reversals in the Peloponnesian wars, agreed with the soothsayers and allowed the islanders to return to Delos. To show who was top dog though, Athens landed a delegation on Rheneia island from whence they threw across an olden-day, wooden equivalent of the modern-day Bailey bridge, over which they marched in triumph. Known as putting a 'frightener' on.

Between about 404 and 394 BC, after the Athenians had been defeated by the Spartans, Delos revelled in a period of independence. This was followed by further interference from Athens. In about 315 BC, with the Egyptians now in charge of the Aegean, the island commenced probably its most prosperous era with the Romans appearing on the scene, about 250 BC. In 166 BC the Roman authorities let the Athenians loose, granting free-port status to Delos in order to curb the power of Rhodes, and turned a blind eye to the wholesale deportation of the islanders, once again. They must have felt like yo-yo's. Additionally the tenor of the great religious festivals was subtly altered and they became truly secular events, reminiscent of those epic 1960's Cecil B De Mille extravaganzas. It is said that up to 10,000 slaves were sold every day of a festival. The decline, when it set in, was very rapid and began in 88 BC. Delos, caught up in the 'spin-off' of King Mithridates' war against Rome, was sacked and razed to the ground, the treasury robbed and the inhabitants murdered or taken into slavery.

Despite attempts to rebuild, repopulate, erect a fortification (in 66 BC) and resuscitate the flagging religious importance of the island, it was a downhill slide. So much so that when the Athenians, in the 3rd century AD, attempted to sell the place off there were no takers. Since this low point, over the centuries the island's visitors have been a mixture of shepherds, pirates and builders from Mykonos, Tinos and Syros. The latter appropriated much basic construction material. This fact is borne out when the plaster work is chipped off older buildings on the aforementioned islands, revealing a block of ancient marble.

Naturally, the Venetians, Turks and British 'borrowed' a number of the more attractive statues, carvings and marbles. Finally, in 1872, French archaeologists started the work that still goes on today.

The Layout The following brief discourse will not replace the services of a good guide or an extensive archaeological description, but here goes. The various sites are, in the main, identified.

From the modern-day landing mole, with the Sacred Harbour to the left and Commercial Harbour to the right, straight ahead is:-

The Agora (or Square) of the Competialists Competialists were Roman merchants, freed men and slaves, who worshipped the God of crossroads (Lares or Compita). The other merchants that traded here were formed into associations depending upon their religious affiliations, including Apollo and Hermes, to name but two. The Square also acted as a boundary between the Sacred area to the left, or north, and the Commercial area to the right, or south.

To the left, from the Square, leads along the Sacred Way, with, on the left-hand, the:-
Stoa* of Philip Built by Philip V of Macedon in 210 BC. 71m by 11m with 16 fluted Doric columns.
** A portico, or as in this case, a section of roofed colonnade.*

and on the right-hand the:-
South Stoa Erected in the 3rd century BC. 66m by 13m with 28 Doric columns, the rear of which was divided into some 14 shops and through which was the:-

Agora of the Delians

The path of the Sacred Way is impeded by the:-
Propylaea of the Sanctuary of Apollo** Built by the Athenians during the 2nd century BC and once packed with altars, temples and statues.
***A gateway and or entrance to a temple.*

These included the:-
Okos* of the Naxians** A 6th century BC construction with central columns.
****A house.*

Temple 'C' To the right of the Naxian House and possibly dating back to the Mycenaean era.

Statue of Apollo Or the Collossus of the Naxians. Well, really only the base of what was once a very large Kouros**** of the God and supposedly knocked off its perch by a giant bronze palm tree. The Venetians and others vandalised the marble statue and bits are exhibited here and there.
*****A male statue.*

Further along the now wide Sacred Way are, on the right, three temples, the:-
Great Temple The Temple of the Delians on which construction started between 480 and 470 BC, at the outset of the Delian League, stopped when the 'naughty' Athenians transferred the funds back to Athens and only restarted in the 3rd century BC. The interior was divided into Pronaos (vestibules), Cella (the main body of the temple) and the Opoisthodomos ('the room at the rear' – often a strong-room).

Temple of the Athenians Built about 425 BC, the Cella originally had seven statues mounted on a semi-circular pedestal
and
Poros Temple Dating back to the 6th century BC. This temple was the treasury of the Delian League until the funds were 'relocated' to Athens. In front of the temple are two bases.

Beyond the last temple is an arc of five treasuries or small temples. In the same circular sweep, arching back behind the **South Stoa**, are the remains of three buildings and to the east of which is the:-
Monument of the Bulls This 67m long by 9m wide building could well require renaming as it probably housed a trireme as a votive offering, celebrating victory in some ancient sea battle.

Across the Sacred Way from the three temples are a scatter of more temples edged by the:-
Stoa of the Naxians Built in the 6th century BC and forming the south-west boundary of the Sanctuary and which, at its far (north) end closes with the:-

Okios of Hieropoieon & Andros Houses dating back to the 6th century BC, to the right and north of which are the remains of an unremarkable Stoa alongside and around which was the:-

Sanctuary of Artemis In which is the Temple of Artemis, rebuilt three times on the same site, and north of which is the:-

Thesmophorion A 5th century BC temple built in three sections. The centre one is a courtyard and converted by early Christians into a place of worship.

Close by, to the east, is the:-
Ekklesiasterion So named because it was in this building that the Delos Council or Assembly met.

From here it is only a short skip and a jump to a building, originally an office and house, but into which, at a later date, the Romans built a bath in the ruins.

Continuing in an easterly direction is the:-
Stoa of Antigonus Marks the northerly edge of the Sanctuary. Built in the 3rd century BC and 120m in length.

To either side are extant the remains of a number of statue bases, buildings, sanctuaries, shops, fountains and tombs, the most thought provoking of which must be through the gateway in the north-east corner of the Sanctuary. The guide books coyly refer to the mutilated statues as 'bases embellished...', 'marble phalli...' and 'marble bases designed to support statues...' They mark the site of the:-
Sanctuary of Dionysos The plain fact is that the remains are 'ginormous' genitalia of which only the testicles and a stump remain. When complete they must have made a most interesting sight!

The gateway give access to the:-
Museum Naturally, the repository of the archaeological finds on both Delos and Rheneia. That is the finds that have not been appropriated by Athens (ever plunderers!).

North of the Sanctuary is the area surrounding the:-
Sacred Lake Now devoid of water but as it was built sometime ago, I suppose that is acceptable – perhaps somebody removed the plug! The sacred nature is attributable to mythology and is the place where Leto gave birth to Apollo whilst clinging to a palm tree. Swans once graced the holy water. Alongside is the:-

Terrace of the Lions From the original nine or so, some five magnificent specimens remain crouching. Originally a gift from the islanders of Naxos in the 7th century BC, one of the missing statues resides in Venice.

To the south of the Lake (in between the Stoa of Antigonos and the Lake) was the:-
Agora of the Italians A largish, open courtyard, 110½m by 69m, once edged by marble columns and a colonnaded gallery, constructed by Italian merchants in about 110 BC. The exterior was circled by shops.

To the west are variously, and in order, the Temple of Leto, Temple of the 12 Gods and the Stoa of Poseidon (probably a 2nd century market hall).

To the north-west of the Lake is the:-
Institution of the Poseidoniasts of Berytos That's a mouthful. Originally constructed by shippers and traders from Syria who were followers of a pagan god that they linked with Poseidon.

Other remains in this area include the House of Diadumenos, the House of Comedians, Granite Palaestra and the Lake House. Further to the north-east are the Gymnasium, Stadium, Xystos track, Stadium Quarter and the Synagogue.

Back, as they say, at the landing mole, and straight ahead (east) is the Theatre Quarter. This comparatively cramped residential area rises towards the Area of Sanctuaries through which the Theatre Road threads its way past, amongst others, the House of Cleopatra and Discourides, the House of Dionysos, and the House of the Trident. Other buildings of note (beyond the Theatre) include the Houses of the Dolphins and the Masks.

A number of these Houses possess outstanding mosaics whilst the street not unnaturally leads to the:-

Theatre Rather a disappointment compared to other examples throughout Greece, but with splendid views. Built in the 3rd/2nd century BC with a capacity for about 5500 people. Perhaps the most interesting fact is that the theatre surrounds was used to collect and distribute rain-water to the adjacent and intriguing Theatre Cisterns which serviced some of the settlements water requirements.

Alongside the Theatre is a building possibly once used as a hotel. A path, or Sacred Way, climbs Mt Kynthos (110m) from the area of the Museum past, on the left, the:-

Sanctuaries of the Foreign Gods These included Syrian and Egyptian sanctuaries.

Beyond, alongside and clustered about the Heraion are a Samothrakeion and three Serapeion shrines. Further on up the Mountain are various shrines and sanctuaries including the Grotto of Herakles (Hercules), formed by huge slabs of stone.

To sum up, Delos must be one of the most enchanting, dramatic and awe-inspiring of all the Greek archaeological sites.

EXCURSION TO RHENEIA ISLAND Some Mykonos travel agencies (Sea & Sky Travel office) run trips to Rheneia, which is a completely uninhabited island and otherwise can only be reached by private yacht – or trips from Tinos. The tours stop at the island beach for picnics/barbecues. Sea & Sky offers 'a long half-day' excursion including food for 2½ thousand drachmae.

Mykonos Town. Acknowledgement to Anne Merewood.

A Santorini based pack animal 'carrying the can'.

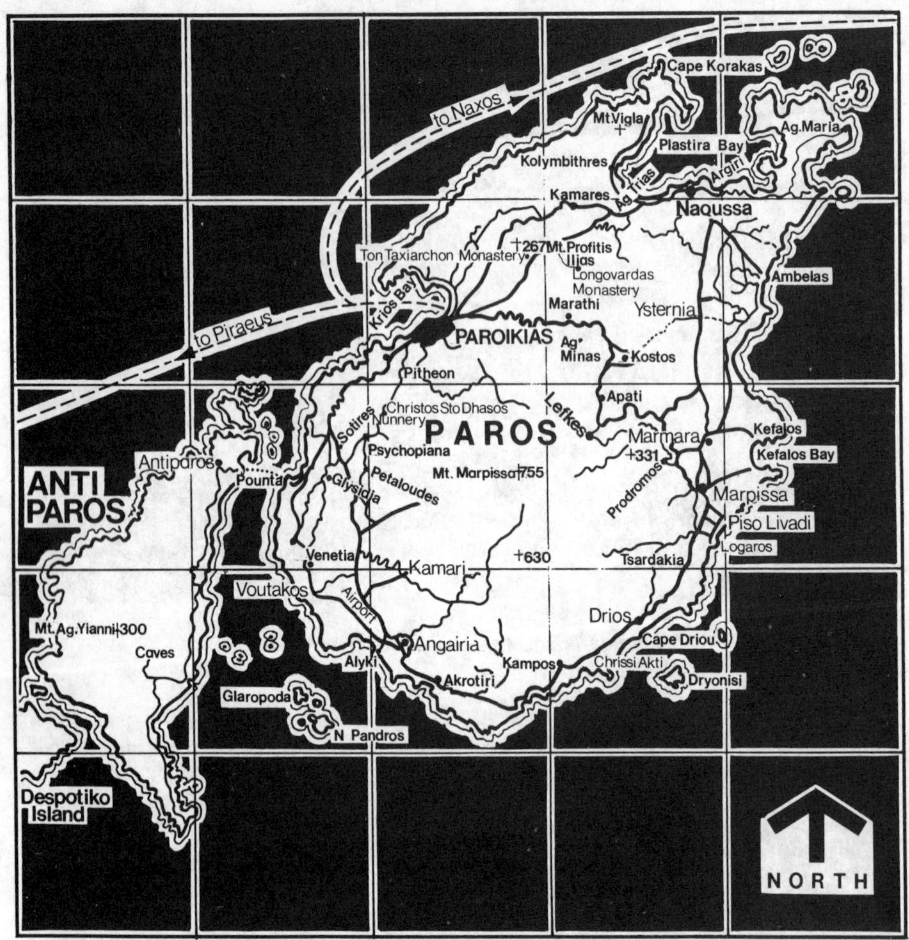

Illustration 12 Paros & Antiparos islands

5 PAROS & ANTIPAROS (Andiparos) Cyclades Islands - Eastern chain

Paroikias (main) Port ★★
Rest of the Island ★★★

FIRST IMPRESSIONS Travel agents/tourist offices; port bustle/ferry-boats; car hire; English; discos; self-service; Old Quarter; lack of mountains; cultivated countryside; indented coastline.

SPECIALITIES Marble quarrying; a red wine; agriculture.

RELIGIOUS HOLIDAYS & FESTIVALS include: July – Festival of fish and wine; 15th August – Fair and Festival of Panaghia Ekatontapyliani, Paroikias; 23rd August – Festival, Naoussa; 24th September – Festival of Panaghia Myrtidiotissa Thapsanon, Mt Ag Pantes.

VITAL STATISTICS Tel prefix 0284. The island is 21km from north-east to south-west and up to 16½km across, totalling some 190sq km in area. The population numbers about 7,000, of which some 3,000 live in and around the main port, town and Chora of Paroikias (Paros).

HISTORY Apart from the usual Neolithic remains, the most interesting site is Saliangos islet. Saliangos is located north of Antiparos island, in the narrowest point of the channel between the two islands. Here has been revealed a complete Neolithic settlement, dating from 4000 BC.

During the years between 2000-1500 BC, the island traded extensively with Crete. Conquest by the Ionians resulted in the arts flourishing and a great age of prosperity with colonies being established on Thassos and the Dalmatian coast. Architochos, the poet who created *iambic* verse, achieved fame in both poetry and war, dying during a battle with the citizens of Naxos (654 BC). He was deified by Parians for some years.

The island supported the Persians during the conflict with Athens – and after the Greek victory at Marathon (490 BC) were inevitably at the receiving end of a punitive raid instigated by Athens. The Athenians recruited one Miltiades to undertake the mission but he failed, incurring a mortal wound while attempting to seize a holy relic, one of the objects necessary to ensure success. His son was left to pay the fine levied by the Athenians resulting from his father's failure. Oh dear, the cost of the sins did visit the son. Island marble was exported far and wide for both sculptures and building work and the general affluence continued through to the period of domination by the Romans.

The island re-emerged into the spotlight of history with the establishment of the Church of Panaghia Ekatontapyliani. This church was reputedly founded, in the third century AD, by St Helena (the mother of Constantine the Great, the Byzantine Emperor) whilst she was voyaging to the Holy Land.

A savage raid by Arabs, in the early 9th century, left the island depopulated until the arrival of the Venetians, in the early 1200s. During their rule castles were built at Paroikias, Naoussa and Kefalos. In fact a couple of particularly devastating pirate raids resulted in the capital being relocated, for a time, at Kefalos. In 1537, the Turkish Admiral Barbarossa precipitated the beginning of the end for the Venetians with a savage attack. This resulted in the Turks capturing the island, which finally came under their direct administration, in 1560. The Turks did not have it all their own way, a state of affairs which led to the citizens of Paros 'getting the thick end of the stick' in a number of Venetian reprisal raids. Despite the Turks reputation for savagery, they were extremely liberal with regard to religious freedom. During their suzerainty some thirty monasteries were established.

The Russo-Turkish War (1770-74) resulted in the arrival of the Russian fleet who anchored at Naoussa for a winter. After the War of Independence, the Mykonos heroine, Manto Mavrogenous, settled on Paros.

GENERAL The island has been a popular holiday-makers destination for many years and obviously has had to adapt to cope with the increasing summer hordes. Most islands can contend with reasonable numbers of disparate groups of people but Paros has taken on board package tourists in very large numbers. They, by the very composition and style of their vacationing, create inordinate demands on the inhabitants and amenities, more especially at Paroikias. Easily visible manifestations include the high incidence of seaside hotels, car hire firms, as well as restaurants offering *Meal A, Meal B* and so on. Surprisingly the Old Quarter or Chora of the town remains relatively untouched by the shallow impression a two week visitor can inflict. It has been pointed out that many of the buildings have been appropriated by Athenians whose shops now retail nothing more than tourist goods, in one guise or another. The still unspoilt character may be due to package tourists being bussed to (and from) their hotel, at the other end of the bay, from which bars and beach they venture not.

The countryside, in which are set some attractive, small villages, is absolutely delightful.

PAROIKIAS (Parikia, Paros): capital town & main port (Illustration 13) Low-lying and possibly the busiest Greek island port in the Aegean. The Esplanade has lost any charm it once possessed. Even the picturesque windmill opposite the Ferry-boat Quay, once occupied by the Tourist police, now looks abject and forlorn in the surge of steamship passengers that ebbs and flows across the waterfront. Not all is dross – the Old Quarter that lies behind the Esplanade is still a lovely maze of lanes, alleys and steps. Naturally intensive tourism has proved very penetrative but the infiltration is not as extensive as on Mykonos, but should that be the yardstick?

ARRIVAL BY AIR The airfield at Alyki is almost the other side of the island, some 12km from Paroikias. The facility still only caters for the more rudimentary, Olympic Airways 'Ford Transits with wings on'. The 'baggage claim', albeit beneath quite a smart sign, is still a plank resting on two concrete blocks but there are rumours of direct flight charter craft.

ARRIVAL BY FERRY Rarely can a Ferry-boat Quay (*Tmr* 1D1) be so conveniently located. But it needs to be to cope with the enormous flow of passengers resulting from the island's pivotal role in the ferry-boat system. Apart from being on the 'main line' route linking Syros, Ios and Santorini, connections can be made with the Western chain (by small passenger ferries to Siphnos); to Naxos for the scattering of Eastern islands, comprising Iraklia, Shinoussa, Koufonissi, Donoussa, Amorgos and Astipalaia, as well as Mykonos for the Eastern wing of islands (Andros and Tinos).

The number of passengers has necessitated the erection of large 'cages' in which those about to embark are kept penned. Those disembarking make the short walk to the Esplanade roundabout, at the end of the quay. Representatives of hotels, pensions and private house accommodation, both in and out of town, clamour for clients, swarming over the alighting passengers. Many of the touts carry smart colour photo 'brochures'. Note that owners of the more desirable Chora accommodation do not have to bother to join in this scrum, except at the very beginning and end of the summer season.

To the left (*Sbo*), along the waterfront hugging Esplanade leads to the newly developed, northern suburbs of Paroikias, growth necessitated by the sharp increase in the number

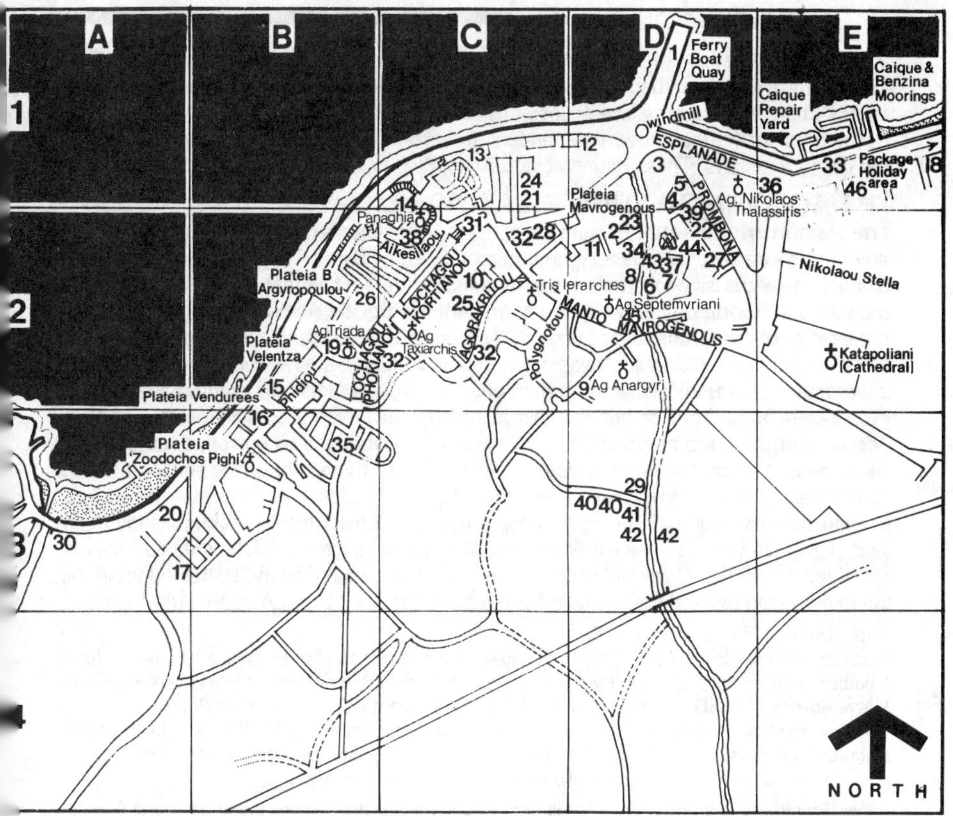

Illustration 13 Paroikias

Tmr	
1D1	Ferry-boat Quay
2D1/2	Tourist police
3D1	Paros Travel Agency
4D1/2	Hotel Kontes
5D1	ITS Travel Agency
6D2	Pension Constantine
7D2	Rooms
8D2	Rooms
9C/D2/3	Rooms
10C2	Rooms Mimikos
11D2	Hotel Gregory
12C/D1	OTE
13C1	Scopas Travel Agency
14B/C1/2	Rooms
15B2/3	Rooms
16B2/3	Rooms
17A/B3	Rooms
18E1	Rooms
19B2	Taverna Thanassis
20A/B3	Restaurant Limanaki
21C1/2	Commercial Bank
22D2	Hotel Parko
23D1/2	Cyclades Tourist Agency
24C1/2	Self Service Marios
25C2	To Tamarisk Restaurant
26B/C2	May Tey Restaurant
27D/E2	Olympic Airline office
28C/D1/2	National Bank
29D3	Acropolis Motorbikes
30A3	Rent a Car/Motorbike
31C1/2	Bookshop
32	Bakers
33E1	Bus terminal
34D2	Supermarket
35B/C2/3	Drop Art Gallery
36D/E1/2	Public toilets
37D2	Laundry
38B/C1/2	The Kastro
39D1/2	Post Office
40D3	Rooms
41D3	Hotel Margarita
421D3	Hotel Galinos/Louiza
43D2	Restaurant Aligaria
44D2	Restaurant Dimitris
45D2	Taverna Kyriakis Moshoulis
46E1/2	Budget Rent A Car

Tmr =Town map reference
Fsw =Facing seawards
Sbo =Sea behind one
Fbqbo =Ferry-boat Quay behind one

of package holiday-makers. To the right, the waterfront road bends around to the left and then curves slowly back, all the while edging the Old Quarter, on the left, to which various steps and squares give access.

A number of 'in-the-know' independent travellers make straight for outlying seaside and inland locations. These might include Alyki, Piso Livadi or the small port of Naoussa.

THE ACCOMMODATION & EATING OUT

The Accommodation If by some mischance a traveller is not offered accommodation almost immediately, there is a signboard to the left of Paros Travel Agency (*Tmr* 3D1), listing many of the island's hotels and telephone numbers. The other side of the roundabout and half-right (*Sbo*), opens out into a large park-like Square (Plateia Mavrogenous). Here is the office of the Tourist police (*Tmr* 2D1/2). Note a dried up, concreted river-bed splits the area into two dissimilar sized portions. Wandering across Plateia Mavrogenous, towards the Chora, will more often than not 'flush out' the offer of accommodation.

There are a plethora of hotels, a large number of which are tour-operator booked. Despite this, there are plenty of D and E class establishments to go round, as there are pensions and ***Rooms*** – with the possible exception of the height of the season months. That latter caveat applies anywhere in the Aegean, let alone the Cyclades. It has been pointed out that much of the Paros accommodation opens late and closes early in the year. This may well be because Athenians own many of the establishments and they do not wish to travel until the winter gales are out of the way. One indisputable fact is that the mid-season rates almost double for the peak season period. A nasty little habit.

Hotel Kontes (*Tmr* 4D1/2) (Class D) Tel 21246

Directions: In the block of buildings, at the apex of the corner formed by Odhos (almost Leoforos) Prombona and the square, half-left (*Sbo*) from the end of the Ferry-boat Quay. Rather masked by Paros Travel Agency (*Tmr* 3D1) and to the right of ITS Travel Agency (*Tmr* 5D1). A noisy area.

A fairly modern building. A single room, sharing the bathroom, costs 1020drs & with an en suite bathroom 1270drs, a double room, sharing 1700drs & en suite 1800drs. These rates increase, respectively, to 1300/1700drs & 2050/2270drs (16th June-30th Sept).

Odhos Prombona is a rich vein of hotels which range along the right of the street (*Sbo*) from the Esplanade all the way to the Olympic Airways office. They include the:-

Hotel Oasis (Class C) Tel 21227

Directions: As above.

All rooms have en suite bathrooms with a single room charged at 1600drs & a double 2250drs, increasing to 3200drs & 4000drs (1st June-30th Sept).

Hotel Parko (*Tmr* 22D2) (Class E) Tel 21782

Directions: As above.

All rooms have to share the bathrooms. A single room costs 1500drs & a double room 1800drs. These prices rise to 2800drs & 3400drs (1st July-15th Sept).

and the:-

Hotel Kypreou (Class D) Tel 21383

Directions: As above.

Only double rooms. which have to share the bathrooms, starting at 1800drs and escalate to 3500drs (11th June-20th Sept).

Pension Constantine Passos (*Tmr* 6D2)

Directions: Proceeding initially half-right, as if towards Plateia Mavrogenous diagonally across the Esplanade roundabout, it is necessary to turn left before the concrete river-bed (either side of Paros Travel, (*Tmr* 3D1). This opens out into an irregular shaped plateia with a colourful, low walled, triangular garden in the centre, and bounded, on the right, by the river-bed. The far side is edged with two restaurants and a Dry Cleaners. From the bottom, left-hand corner a narrow street bends round to the right opening out into another irregular, oldish, small and slightly sunken square. The cracked paving appears to mask broken drains and when the summer is at its hottest the mosquitoes and smells prove interesting! Mrs Passos's pension is at the far right-hand side.

The establishment is impersonal but the rooms are spacious, the shared bathrooms clean and well equipped, the water hot and there is a communal fridge on each landing. A single room is charged from 1000drs and a double room 1500drs. The bedroom doors tend to close with a hollow bang, day and night.

Rooms (*Tmr* 7D2)
Directions:Next door and prior to the aforementioned *Pension Passos*.
Same rates and comments regarding the surrounds.

Rooms (*Tmr* 8D2)
Directions: Back at the 'River-bed' Plateia, the summer-dry, concrete lined water-course is used as a pedestrian way. This accommodation is beyond the far right corner of the square.
Double rooms from 1500drs.

Continuing along the river-bed progresses to the main 'arterial' lane of Manto Mavrogenous which bridges the stream bed. Climb the 'doo-hickey' steps, turn right on Odhos Manto Mavrogenous and then quarter left along the narrow lane that branches off across crossroads and past the Church of Ag Anargyri, on the left. Just beyond the side turning, on the right, is ***Rooms*** (*Tmr* 9C/D2/3). Continuing in a south-west direction, the lane jinks,after which there is a turning off to the left. This latter connects with 'River-bed alley'. It is of course, possible to continue south along the river-bed from Odhos Manto Mavrogenous. Close to the junction, on the right, are a pair of ***Rooms*** (*Tmr* 40D3) and the:-

Hotel Margarita (*Tmr* 41D3) (Class D) Tel 21563
Directions: As above and on the right.
All rooms have en suite bathrooms with a single costing 1125drs & a double 1810drs, increasing to 2260drs & 3615drs (1st July-31st Aug).

Just around the corner, south or right on the 'river-bed' is the:-
Hotel Galinos/Louiza (*Tmr* 42D3) (Class C) Tel 21480
Directions: As above.
This is actually two hotels, one either side of the river-bed, the *Galinos* and the *Louiza*, run as one and owned by the same proprietor. The *Galinos* has an 'in house' restaurant. The hotel mini-bus or a red estate car may well meet the ferries. All rooms have en suite bathrooms. All single rooms cost 2270drs & a double 2710drs, increasing to 2710drs & 3200drs (1st-30th June & 1st-30th Sept) and 3600drs & 4050drs (1st July-31st Aug).

Returning to the 'confluence' of the river-bed and Odhos Manto Mavrogenous, advancing west on Manto Mavrogenous passes the fountain of Mavrogenous 'A' and the Church of Ag Septemvriani (on the right), two lanes and the Church of Tris Ierarches (on the left). The next left turning, Odhos Agorakritou, is beneath a covered way. Keeping round to the right leads into a dead-end, small square, on the left of which is:-

Rooms Mimikos (*Tmr* 10C2) Tel 21437
Directions: As above.
Clean, some of the rooms have balconies and all share the bathrooms. A single room starts at 1500drs & a double 2000drs which includes the cost of showers.

Back at the main, park-like Plateia Mavrogenous,on the far left is the:-
Hotel Georgy (*Tmr* 11D2) (Class C) Plateia Mavrogenous Tel 21667
Directions: As above. The hotel is over a cafeteria.
All rooms have en suite bathrooms with a single room priced at 2270drs, a double 3200drs, increasing to 3500drs & 4500drs (1st July-30th Sept).

From the far side of Plateia Mavrogenous, past the Banks on the left, along the street, over a crossroads, which jinks around an excellent grocery on the left, advances to Odhos Lochagou Kortianou. This 'main' lane parallels the Esplanade for a distance, prior to curving round on to Plateia Velentza on the edge of the Esplanade.

Hotel Dina (*Tmr* B2) (Class E) Tel 21325
Directions: As above but on the slow right-hand curve in the street as it bends round to Velentza Square, prior to (another) Mavrogenous Fountain and (on the other side of the street) the Church of Ag Triada.
This excellent accommodation doesn't have any single rooms. Double rooms have en suite bathrooms and cost 2160drs, increasing to 2920drs (1st July-30th Sept).

Back at the Ferry-boat Quay roundabout, proceeding southwards to the right (*Sbo*) along the Esplanade, beyond the OTE office (*Tmr* 12C/D1) and a chapel is the:-

Scopas Travel Agency (*Tmr* 13C1)

Directions: As above and on the left (well it would have to be wouldn't it...).

Apart from the usual travel agency functions this cavernous office advertises ***Rooms***.

In the Old Quarter or Chora, amongst the castle walls and tower, are a couple of beautifully positioned, 'town provincial' houses, offering accommodation in a very lovely part of Paroikias. To find them, where the Esplanade curves to the left, beyond Scopas Travel Agency (*Tmr* 13C1), the second flight of steps climbs into the Chora and leads, on the right, to a rectangular terrace (once a temple). Along the narrow lane left (or eastwards) from the terrace and one of the ***Rooms*** (*Tmr* 14B/C1/2) is on the left. Further on down the alley and sharp right at the square (close by the Churches of Ag Aikaterini and Panaghia) along the lateral lane and the other ***Rooms*** is on the right. Double rooms, sharing the bathroom, are priced from 1500drs.

Further south along the Esplanade is ***Rooms***,at the end of the terraces, above the Rendez-Vous Bar. Beyond Plateia Velentza are:-

Rooms (*Tmr* 15B2/3)

Directions: As above, on the near corner of the next square, Plateia Vendurees, over a 'local' kafeneion.

and:-

Rooms (*Tmr* 16B2/3)

Directions: As above, but on the far side of Plateia Vendurees, in the first block, above the *Pizzaria Europa*, next door to the *Souvlaki Asteras*.

The Esplanade runs into the long, rectangular Plateia 'Zoodochos Pighi'*, from which a street, that was or is a river-bed, winds obliquely off from the far, left-hand corner. Beyond the Rex Open Air Cinema, up the third lane to the left (opposite *Hotel Kato Yialos*) and on the right-hand side is ***Rooms*** (*Tmr* 17A/B3)

Returning to the Ferry-boat Quay roundabout (*Tmr* D1), the new, broad, waterside Esplanade loops off on a gentle semi-circular route round the bay, in a north-easterly direction. Alongside Panos Rent-A-Car, on the right beyond some waste ground and opposite a caique repair yard and moorings, is ***Rooms*** (*Tmr* 18E1). Further on, prior to the *Asterias Hotel* and over the top of a Rent-A-Car & Motorbyke outfit is ***Rooms***. Beyond the *Asterias Hotel*, a rough track ascends the slope, there being a sign indicating that 60m up the path are *Rooms Icarus*. From hereon along the Esplanade and beyond the *Hotel Stella*, is a veritable warren of package holiday hotels in almost every nook and cranny.

A correspondent has recommended: the *Hotel Stella* (Class C, tel 21502), with expensive en suite double rooms costing 3160drs, increasing to 4065drs, owned by Costas Antoniades,and where he was awoken by a mower cutting the front lawn; and the adjacent *Hotel Paros* (Class C, tel 21319) managed by Alex, a young and efficient lady with a perfect command of English, where all rooms have en suite bathrooms, with a single room priced at 1355drs & a double 2000drs, rising to 1805drs & 2350drs (1st-30th June & 1st-30th Sept) and 3200drs & 4065drs (1st July-31st Aug). Both can offer rooms with sea-facing balconies.

The side-street rising gently from the Esplanade, between the *Hotel Zannet* and the *Taverna Katerina*, leads past three separate houses with accommodation, on the left. These include ***Rooms***, the:-

Hotel Cyclades (Class C) 22048

Directions: As above, on the right.

All rooms have en suite bathrooms with a single charged at 2100drs & a double 2500drs, increasing dramatically to 3250drs & 3900drs (1st July-31st Aug)

and the:-

Hotel Hellinikon (Class E) Tel 21429

Directions: As above, on the left.

Only double rooms en suite, which start at 2260drs, rising to 3800drs (1st June-15th Sept).

Still on the Esplanade road, now edging a beach with a grove of trees, and on the right is the *Pension Piertzovani*, followed by the:-

Hotel Livadia (Class D) Tel 21597

Directions: As above.

Not quite as shown in some old photographs, but was that ever thus. Single rooms sharing a bathroom cost 1090drs, double rooms sharing 1810drs & double rooms en suite 3435drs. These charges increase to 1900drs & 20890/4335drs (1st July-31st Aug).

**Not the official name I know, but any designation is better than none.*

Beyond *Rooms Violetta* and more ***Rooms*** is:-

Camping Koula

Directions: As above.

Open from April to October and facilities include a restaurant, mini-market, bar, cooking facilities, hot water and a shower/toilet block. Shaded by trees but low-lying. The per person charge is 300drs.

Hotel Alkion (Class C) Tel 21506

Directions: Beyond the campsite, sporting a warning of the dire consequences should a visitor be found in a bedroom!

The classification is surprisingly high, probably because the sign for the the hotel is ancient! A single room with en suite bathroom costs 1360drs, a double room, sharing the bathroom, costs 1540drs & en suite 2265drs, rising, respectively, to 2265drs & 3620/4260drs (11th July-31st Aug).

Beyond the *Alkion* is a signpost pointing down a track to the 'tucked-up' *Rooms To Let Shower*. From hereon the waterfront peters out, only to stutter briefly into life again, alongside yet another hotel. Opposite a sliver of sandy beach (*See* **Beaches (No 3), A To Z**), is the 'dead' – *Paros Camping*

Camping *See* **The Accommodation**.

The Eating Out Naturally I should preface my remarks by advising readers that the following comments are purely personal, sweeping, all-embracing observations but I am sure I do not need to reiterate these caveats. Perhaps it should be restated that I make judgements from a particularly opinionated point of view, that I might be considered mean and greedy, and that one of the criteria is comparison with that which is available within, in this instance, the other Cyclades islands. Having got that off my chest, I must draw attention to the Chapter's introductory remarks in which I commented on the manifestation of restaurants offering 'Chinese style' Greek Meal A, Meal B and so on. Paros proliferates an abnormally high incidence of 'low-life' eating places – self-service and fixed-menu tat. Astonishingly there are still a few middle-of-the-road, honest-to-goodness tavernas whilst at the other end of the scale are some very expensive restaurants, complete with linen table-cloths, flowers and menus that do not list prices.

One splendid old-world example is:-

Taverna Thanassis (*Tmr* 19B2) Tel 21091

Directions: Signposted from Plateia B Argyropoulou, or from Plateia Velentza take the 'Main Street' from the bottom left corner (*Sbo*) then the first left and on the first right-hand corner.

A small square building which is unfortunately bereft of a patio, terrace or garden, but in a desert of gourmet emporiums... Perhaps on the pokey side with huge barrels in the rafters against the far wall. Thanassis, the portly proprietor (now possibly tourist-weary after years in the heat of the kitchen), Roula, his wife, and their son administer proceedings. The small number of chairs and tables fill up very quickly, so arrive early. The usual pressures on the available space are exacerbated by one or two package holiday reps who bring along selected clients for an evening – 'Keep it under your hat – I'll show you a really local taverna'. A wide ranging menu, the food is prepared daily, so is fresh, if a little on the oily side. Kalamari stew for one (440drs), a Greek salad (150drs), chicken & potatoes (300drs), bread (20drs each) and a retsina from the barrel (100drs) all for 1030drs. Keftedes for 2, a large Greek salad, bread and 2 jugs of retsina cost 700drs.

Recommended (that is recommended to me) as true tavernas have been the *Restaurant Aligaria* (*Tmr* 43D2), run by a rotund host who creates a super atmosphere to accompany the good food (main meals 300drs a dish), the:-

Restaurant Dimitris (*Tmr* 44D2)

Directions: Both the *Dimitris* and the *Aligaria* are on the route round to *Pension Constantine Passos* (*Tmr* 6D2), on opposite sides of the street.

The Dimitris is patronised by Greeks and tourists alike. However, it is rumoured that the young, quiet proprietor is guilty of reheating food cooked earlier in the day, if not the day before! A meal for two of tzatziki (140drs), stifado and macaroni (450drs), papoutsaki (290drs), a half litre of very interesting, deep red, sweetish wine from the barrel (140drs) and bread (20drs each) cost 1060drs.

The last of this trio of honourable mentions is the *Taverna Kyriakos Moshoulis* (*Tmr* 45D2). Offers an appetising looking menu, is reasonably lively and borders Odhos Mano Mavrogenous, on which its tables and chairs are spread about, close by the 'river-bed' alley. Also on Odhos Manto Mavrogenous, about 60m before the crossroads with Lochagou Kortianou St, is *Taverna H Steki*. This establishment's tables spill out into the street, beneath a tree or two. Inexpensive and good value.

Symptomatic of the Paros 'fast-tourist-taverna' is the:-
Restaurant Limanaki (*Tmr* 20A/B3)
Directions: Towards the far, south-west end of the Esplanade, beyond Plateia 'Zoodochos Pighi' and on the left, opposite a tree lined, sand and shingle beach.

A sample of the offerings might include a set meal – 'Todays Spesial (*sic*) of red mullet, Greece salat (*sic*), yoghurt garlic-tzatziki'. Service can be surly, the food poor and overcharging is not unknown.

This particular stretch of waterfront, all the way back to Plateia B Argyropoulou, is 'knee-deep' in the above style of taverna/restaurant.

A number of the fast food establishments include fish and chips in their offerings, yes fish and chips. There are any number of souvlaki snackbars spread about the main squares with prices of 90/100drs for a souvlaki pita. Various establishments, from year to year, claim they are the 'Best in Paros'.

Self Service Marios (*Tmr* 24C1/2)
Directions: On the west side of Plateia Mavrogenous. The Commercial Bank, on the corner, is followed by the *Argonauta Restaurant* – linen table-cloths, no prices on the menu (a particular hate of mine this) and a smoothie proprietor who expresses the utmost surprise when a prospective client has the temerity to ask for a price list. Next door is *Self Service Marios Special Souvlaki*.

Although self-service (another of the banes of my life), the system here is comprehensive, polite, quite reasonably priced and operates from morning through to late in the evening. Patronised by Greeks and usually very busy with a nice patio across the street, on the edge of the park, a few seats on the pavement and ample room inside for chilly evenings. The range on offer encompasses breakfast, cakes, snacks and light suppers.

In the north-east, 'package holiday' end of the harbour are a number of taverna/restaurants of which I would select the:-
Taverna Katerina
Directions: As above.

A wide variety of food on offer at lower than average prices.

There are, as advised, one or two very smart restaurants which are usually outside the scope of my research (and pocket) but this does not mean one or two should not be highlighted. They include:-
To Tamarisk Restaurant (*Tmr* 25C2) Odhos Agorakritou.
Directions: In giving directions I may well commence from an easy starting point but naturally readers will, once their sense of direction and orientation has taken over, find simpler, shorter routes than I describe. From the Church of Panaghia Katapoliani (*Tmr* E2) or from the 'river-bed' pedestrian way, walk along Odhos Manto Mavrogenous in a north-westerly direction. Proceed past Mavrogenous Fountain 'A' and the Church of Ag Septemvriani (on the right), two alleyways and the Church of Tris Ierarches (on the left). The turning beneath an archway leads on to Odhos Agorakritou. The *Tamerisk*, with very neat, tree planted gardens, is on the right.

The menu includes 'Filet Mignon' which I'm sure is very nice, but need I say more? I won't cop out. An evening meal here is a delight with courteous, polite service and excellent food. A repas for two of a tomato & zucchini dish (delicious), 1 pork & beef kebab (very good), 1 pork chop with saute potatoes (tasty), bread, a large bottle of retsina, 2 big filter coffees and 2 cognacs cost 2300drs, which is not that expensive for an all-meat meal. Recommended.

Also in this area, back a few metres and left into a 'Cul-de-sac Plateia' leads to the rear entrance of an extremely smart restaurant. Staying on Odhos Manto Mavrogenous, in the direction of the crossroads with Odhos Lochagou Kortianou, passes the discreet front entrance. Credit cards accepted, candles in delicate lamp-holders, folded linen napkins – splendid, but....

Another very pleasant, but very expensive restaurant that should be mentioned is *Creperie/Bistro Balcony* edging Odhos Lochagou Kortianou. On the far, left-hand corner of Plateia Mavrogenous (*Fbqbo*) is an excellent zacharoplasteion that serves up 'mentionable' pies and highly recommended bougatses.

Prior to *Bistro Balcony*, an alley branches right from the junction of Odhos Lochagou Kortianou and Phokianou, opposite the Church of Taxiarchis. On the corner is the *Levantis*, a Lebanese/Greek/French restaurant and tea room (A what?). On the left of the alley, opposite an Antique Carpet shop and the Church of Panaghia Eleoussa, is the *May Tey Restaurant* (*Tmr* 26B/C2), serving Oriental food in Western decor, brightly lit and stylish – and not very Greek!

THE A TO Z OF USEFUL INFORMATION

AIRLINE OFFICES & TERMINUS (*Tmr* 27D/E2) The Olympic office is at the far end of Odhos Prombona. Turn half-left (*Sbo*) from the Ferry-boat roundabout, and beyond the *Hotel Oasis*, the Post Office, several Rent-A-Car outfits, as well as the *Hotels Parko* and *Kypreou*. The office is open between 0800-1530hrs.

Aircraft timetables (Mid-season)
Paros to Athens

Mon, Wed, Fri & Sat	0750, 0815, 1245, 1550, 1810, 1835hrs
Tues, Thurs & Sat	1040, 1240, 1615hrs
Tues, Sat & Sun	1905hrs
Return	
Mon, Wed, Fri & Sun	0645, 0710, 1140, 1445, 1705, 1730hrs
Tues, Thurs & Sun	0645hrs
Tues, Thurs & Sat	0935, 1300hrs
Tues, Sat & Sun	1800hrs

One way fare: 5610drs; duration 45mins.

Paros to Iraklion (Crete)

Tues, Thur & Sat	1405hrs
Return	
Tues, Thur & Sat	1510hrs

One-way fare: 7710drs; duration 45mins

Paros to Rhodes

Tues, Thur & Sun	0750hrs
Return	
Tues, Thur & Sun	1120hrs

One-way fare: 8770drs; duration 1hr.

BANKS The **National Bank** (*Tmr* 28C/D1/2) is on the far left-hand (*Fbqbo*) corner of Plateia Mavrogenous. It is more than a pleasure to report that the service is swift and smiling. Travellers cheques and Eurocheque card backed personal cheques are cashed. Normal banking hours. The **Commercial Bank** (*Tmr* 21C1/2) is on the opposite corner.

BEACHES Two or perhaps three small beaches – depending on how one regards the treatment of the north-east end of town.

Beach 1. To the south-west, furthermost point of the Esplanade, opposite Plateia 'Zoodochos Pighi'. Not very large, being fairly narrow and of no great length, exposed to the sea but pleasantly tree-lined on the roadside edge. Sand mixed with shingle. A plus point is that this end of the harbour is almost exclusively in the hands of the independent travellers who stay in the Port and Chora quarters. Thus it is less crowded than the other two beaches, at the north-east, package holiday sector of the large, curving bay. They include:-

Beach 2. Rather narrow and small, but plentiful coarse sand mixed with shingle. Copiously tree lined and edged by the road, across which are a stretch of taverna/restaurants and hotels. This proximity ensures crowding,with the sun worshippers intermingled by lots of jolly beach footballers. Picnickers will be mobbed by cats. Beach beds cost 100drs.

Beach 3. The aforementioned beach runs out alongside a low retaining wall which meanders into a long, but very narrow strip of scrappy sand and shingle sprinkled with bits of tar. There is some tree cover. Beach beds lurk at the broader, near section and wind surfers at the far, narrow end.

BICYCLE, SCOOTER & CAR HIRE
Budget Rent A Car (*Tmr* 46 E1/2)
Directions: Across the Esplanade from the Bus terminal.
Accepts payment by *Barclaycard*.

East of the Bus terminal (*Tmr* 33E1), are two Rent-A-Car firms, one of whom offers scooters (of which more later, as the saying goes). The usual range of vehicles include the increasingly popular beach buggies, that is increasingly popular with the hirer, nobody else. Another 'Rent-A-Car' street is Odhos Prombona (*Tmr* D1/2), the thoroughfare that forms the right-hand (*Sbo*) side of a fairly large park.

The scooter hire situation is possibly the worst I have ever experienced. For instance the two previously detailed car hire firms on the north-east Esplanade each advertise along the lines, 'We have 90 scooters' with a few smart versions propped up across the road. In actuality they are simply, fronting for a set-up at the back of the town. I very nearly wrote 'set-down', as the 'disorganisation' is a wire-fenced, back street shambles. The compound contains possibly as many as a 100 scooters, but out of this number about half are being repaired, a quarter are totally useless and some are on hire. This usually leaves about 6 'clapped out' units considered fit for use. The 'office' is a greasy lean-to, and the oily overall clad owner attempts to obtain payment in advance, as well as a hirer's passport. Tell them to forget it – one or the other. Rates tumble from about 2000drs to 1500drs a day, with some bargaining, but carefully check the intended conveyance and insist upon the supply of a spare tyre and plug.

Not all is lost though as there are at least two 'independents'.

Acropolis Motorbikes (*Tmr* 29D3)

Directions: Across the junction of the ways north of the *Hotel Galinos/Louiza*.

A reputable office, manned, well 'girled' really, by a pleasant and helpful lass.

The other is:-

Rent A Car/Motorbyke (*Tmr* 30A3)

Directions: At the south-west end of the Esplanade, alongside Disco 7 and a dry river-bed.

The pleasant, committed young proprietor speaks good English and although, or perhaps because, he is a small operator, hires out well maintained units.

BOOKSELLERS A well stocked shop (*Tmr* 31C1/2) on the right of Odhos Lochagou Kortianou, not far from the crossroads with Odhos Manto Mavrogenous.

BREAD SHOPS The Baker (*Tmr* 32C1/2), on the left of the street off the far end of Plateia Mavrogenous, opposite the Commercial Bank, featured in the BBC television series 'Mediterranean Cookery'. The fee must have been satisfactory as the establishment has been modernised. Health fiends might note that brown bread is baked late in the mornings. The back lane of Odhos Agorakritou embraces a Baker (*Tmr* 32C2), the other side of the road and beyond the *To Tamarisk Restaurant*. There is a Baker (*Tmr* 32B/C2) on the 'Commercial St' of Lochagou Phokianou, between a supermarket and the *Hotel Dina* as well as yet another baker in the package holiday area.

BUSES The Bus terminal (*Tmr* 33E1) is located on the Esplanade, about 200m to the east of the Ferry-boat Quay. The ticket office is simply a shack, immediately prior to the bus lay-by. Note that the owner of the periptero, close by, speaks English and is very helpful.

Opposite is a 'Left Luggage' office – open daily between 0800-2000hrs, with a charge of 100drs for 24hr storage.

Bus timetable

Pariokias (Paros Port) to Angairia via Ag Irine, Petaloudes, Airport, Alyki.

Daily 0700, 0800, 1100, 1300, 1400, 1600, 1800hrs

Return journey

Daily 0715, 0815, 1115, 1315, 1415, 1615, 1815hrs

Paroikias to Drios via Marathi, Kostos, Lefkes, Prodromos, Marpissa, Piso Livadi, Logaros, Chrissi Atki (Golden Beach).

Daily 0800, 0900, 1000, 1100, 1200, 1300, 1400, 1500, 1600, 1800hrs

Return journey

Daily 0700, 0900, 1000, 1100, 1200, 1300, 1500, 1600, 1700, 1900hrs

Paroikias to Naoussa

Daily 0800, 0900, 1000, 1030, 1100, 1130, 1200, 1300, 1400, 1500, 1600, 1700, 1800, 1900hrs

Return journey

Daily 0730, 0830, 0930, 1000, 1030, 1100, 1130, 1200, 1230, 1330, 1430, 1530, 1630, 1830, 1930hrs

One-way fare 90drs.

Paroikias to Pounta via Ag Irine

Daily 0730, 1000, 1200, 1400, 1600hrs

Return journey

Daily 0815, 1015, 1215, 1415, 1615hrs

One-way fare 70drs.

There are also separate buses to Petaloudes (Valley of the Butterflies) for which *See* **Route Two**.

CINEMAS At the north-eastern end of the Esplanade and prior to the beach is a turning to the right, alongside the *Hotel Stella*. This leads to the Cine Paros. At the other end of the Esplanade, from Plateia 'Zoodochos Pighi' along the 'old river-bed street', at the far, top, left-hand corner and first left leads to Cine Rex.

COMMERCIAL SHOPPING AREA The 'High St', Odhos Lochagou Kortianou, runs into Odhos Lochagou Phokianou. This latter street curves around on to Plateia Velentza and constitutes the Commercial Shopping Area. From the outset to the finish, in a south-westerly direction, passes Diplos Supermarket, a large, varied stock and inexpensive; 'Excellent Grocery', ... if they say so; 'The Tea Pot', a chic spice shop in a side lane to the left, and a Supermarket. These are interspaced with two bakers and a number of fruit and vegetable shops.

There is a large Supermarket (*Tmr* 34D2) on the edge of the square to the left (*Fbqbo*) of the river-bed .

I rarely detail shops ranging from Art Galleries, through Fur and Fashion to Jewellery Emporiums for a number of reasons. Not least of these is that they bear little relationship to the Greece I am trying to prise open for the reader... Apart from which they are not slow in coming forward in the normal course of events, being more than a little publicity conscious. But I must mention:-

Drop Art Gallery (*Tmr* 35B/C2/3)

Directions: Located on Odhos Lochagou Phokianou, but proceed straight on in a southerly direction, not following the curve of the street round to the Plateia Velentza. The lane jinks past the Church of Ag Vithleem and the shop is in a slight recess, on the right. My notes simply say 'everything for everybody's pocket'. Certainly some inexpensive but tasteful prints help fill the presents list without having to resort to the usual mass produced junk.

Close to the Drop Art Gallery is a Herbarium. Yes, well...

DISCOS Quite a number including a clutch at the far, south-west end of the Esplanade, beyond Plateia 'Zoodochos Pighi'. These include Hesperedes, the Irish Bar, Disco 7 and Easy Going, with Disco Psarades on Plateia B Argyropoulou.

There are a number of extremely trendy and smart cocktail bars including Pebbles & Statue, close by the Old Quarter Castle, and looking out to sea. The terrace of this latter establishment sports 'Habitat-like' slatted furniture and 1930s style cocktail glasses and prices reflect these 'attributes'.

FERRY-BOATS A very, very busy port with possibly the largest number and widest choice of island connections of any Aegean island.

Ferry-boat timetable (Mid-season)

Day	**Departure time**	**Ferry-boat**	**Ports/Islands of Call**
Daily	Throughout the day		Piraeus(M).
Mon	0130hrs	Apollo Express	Naxos,Ios,Sikinos,Folegandros,Thira(Santorini).
	1330hrs	Naxos	Naxos,Ios,Thira(Santorini).
	2230hrs	Nireas	Katapola(Amorgos),Aegiali(Amorgos), Astipalaia,Kalimnos,Kos,Nisiros,Tilos,Simi, Rhodes,Chalki,Diafani(Karpathos),Karpathos, Kasos,Sitia(Crete),Ag Nikolaos(Crete).
	2230hrs	Alecos	Naxos.
Tues	0100hrs	Hellas Express	Ios,Thira(Santorini).
	1330hrs	Naxos	Naxos,Koufonissi,Katapola(Amorgos).
	1345hrs	Aegeon	Ikaria,Karlovasion(Samos),Vathy(Samos).
	1345hrs	Apollo Express	Naxos,Ios,Thira(Santorini).
	2030hrs	Delos	Naxos,Ios,Thira(Santorini),Anafi.
Wed	1330hrs	Hellas Express	Naxos,Ios,Sikinos,Folegandros,Ia(Santorini), Thira(Santorini),Iraklion(Crete).
	1330hrs	Aegeon	Piraeus(M).
	1345hrs	Apollo Express	Naxos,Ios,Thira(Santorini).
	1930hrs	Schinoussa	Naxos,Donoussa,Aegiali(Amorgos),Katapola (Amorgos),Koufonissi,Shinoussa,Iraklion(Crete).
	2230hrs	Alecos	Naxos.

Thur	1330hrs	Naxos	Naxos,Ios,Thira(Santorini).
	1345hrs	Aegeon	Ikaria,Karlovasion(Samos),Vathy(Samos).
	1345hrs	Apollo Express	Naxos,Ios,Thira(Santorini).
	2030hrs	Delos	Naxos,Aegiali(Amorgos),Katapola(Amorgos).
	2230hrs	Olympia	Naxos,Katapola(Amorgos),Aegiali(Amorgos), Astipalaia,Kalimnos,Kos,Nisiros,Tilos,Simi, Rhodes,Kastellorizo.
Fri	1330hrs	Hellas Express	Naxos,Ios,Ia(Santorini), Thira(Santorini),Iraklion(Crete).
	1330hrs	Aegeon	Piraeus(M).
	1930hrs	Schinoussa	Naxos,Koufonissi,Katapola(Amorgos), Aegiali(Amorgos),Donoussa.
	2030hrs	Delos	Naxos.
	2230hrs	Apollo Express	Naxos,Ios,Thira(Santorini).
	2230hrs	Alecos	Naxos.
Sat	1230hrs	Delos	Naxos,Aegiali(Amorgos),Katapola(Amorgos).
	1330hrs	Naxos	Naxos,Ios,Thira(Santorini).
	1345hrs	Aegeon	Ag Kirikos(Ikaria),Vathy(Samos).
	2230hrs	Nireas	Naxos,Iraklia,Shinoussa,Koufonissi,Katapola (Amorgos),Aegiali(Amorgos),Donoussa,Astipalaia.
Sun	0130hrs	Apollo Express	Naxos,Ios,Ia(Santorini).
	1330hrs	Hellas Express	Naxos,Ilos,Ia(Santorini),Thira(Santorini), Iraklion(Crete).
	1330hrs	Aegeon	Piraeus(M).
	2030hrs	Delos	Naxos.

In addition there are:-

Daily		Megalochari	Ios,Santorini.
		Megalochari	Mykonos,Tinos.

Between May-Sept inclusive, the following service operates:-

Mon, Wed,& Fri*	1600hrs	Yiannis Latsos/ Magarita	Siphnos.

* Note in the height of season months of July & August this service operates daily with a commensurate alteration to the departure time.

Hydrofoil timetable (Mid-season)

Mon	1430hrs	Nearchos	Naxos.
	1600hrs	"	Ios,Santorini,Iraklion(Crete).
Wed	1215hrs	"	Mykonos.
	1545hrs	"	Ios,Santorini,Iraklion(Crete).
Fri	1030hrs	"	Ios,Paros,Naxos.
	1700hrs	"	Iraklion(Crete).

Please note these tables are detailed as a GUIDE ONLY. Due to the time taken to research the Cyclades, it is IMPOSSIBLE TO 'match' the timetables or even boats . So don't try cross pollinating...

FERRY-BOAT TICKET OFFICES It has been pointed out that the Port police (off the plan in square F1 – if there was an F1) helpfully chalk up a full list of all the ferry-boats, their destinations and times, each day. Their office borders the north-east Esplanade, beyond the Bus terminus.

The amazing activity generated at the few Paroikias Port ticket offices would turn many another, more leisurely, less active operator, on other islands, green, very green with envy.

The prime location is occupied by:-

Paros Travel Agency (*Tmr* 3D1) Tel 21582

Directions: Immediately across from the Ferry-boat Quay, occupying an island site.

Possibly the rudest most disinterested office it has been my wont to encounter, but they almost monopolise the very busy trade. A blackboard under the verandah advertises the daily sailings of the craft for which they act, whilst large boards, on the outside of the office wall, indicate the weeks activity. The very speed of service can lead to mistakes so, however poor the attention and however annoying it must be for the staff, prospective passengers should ensure their instructions are clearly understood, prior to paying for tickets. Money will not be refunded for any incorrect or mistaken purchase. This caveat is not unique to this office, but applies everywhere. The agency advertises a tourist bus trip 'Round of Paros by Bus Every Day', and a daily coach tour to Petaloudes (Butterfly Valley) (*See* **Route Two**).

ITS Travel Agency (*Tmr* 5D1) Tel 21869

Directions: To the left (*Sbo*) of Paros Travel.

More polite but very tied in with the package holiday trade, acting as agents for *Sun-Med*.

Cyclades Tourist Agency (*Tmr* 23D1/2)

Directions: Past the periptero on the far edge (*Fbqbo*) of the dry river-bed and sharp left along the low retaining wall.

The problem is that Paros Travel has matters almost entirely wrapped up. Two other offices worthy of note are detailed under **Travel Agents & Tour Offices, A To Z**.

LAUNDRY A Dry Cleaners (*Tmr* 37D2) is sited on the square to the left of the river-bed, fairly close to the Ferry-boat Quay and a launderette is located in the package tourist area.

LUGGAGE STORE *See* **Buses, A To Z**. Paros Travel (*Tmr* 3D1) operates a left-luggage service.

MEDICAL CARE

Chemists & Pharmacies Not a surplus but there are a few located in and around Plateia Mavrogenous and along the High St, Odhos Lochagou Kortianou and Phokianou. There is a good Pharmacy on the far edge of Plateia Mavrogenous, close by the *Self Service Marios* (*Tmr* 24C1/2).

Clinic Opposite and across the road from the town's public lavatory block (*Tmr* 36D/E1/2), which is on the left edge of the park to the left (*Sbo*) of the Ferry-boat Quay.

Dentists Two, one a Mr N Kiriafanos and another, Mr E Triantafilou, whose surgery is next door to *Self Service Marios* (*Tmr* 24C1/2). The weekday hours are between 0900-1300hrs & 1800-2000hrs, by appointment.

Doctors At least two doctors, one a Dr Kebabis and the other, a Frenchman, Dr Roger Hamusse whose surgery is next door to *Self Service Marios* (*Tmr* 24C1/2). Weekday hours are between 0900-1230hrs & 1800-2000hrs.

NTOG None. *See* **Tourist Police, A To Z**.

OTE (*Tmr* 12C/D1) Keep right (*Fbqbo*) along the Esplanade in a south-west direction and almost immediately on the left. The rear of the office backs on to the edge of Plateia Mavrogenous. Surprisingly small for such a busy, international island and not open at weekends or holidays – yet! Open weekdays between 0730-2200hrs.

PETROL There are a number of filling stations on the Naoussa road.

PLACES OF INTEREST

Cathedrals & Churches

The Cathedral Church of Panaghia Ekatontapyliani (Katapoliani) (*Tmr* E2) Despite or perhaps because of the pre-publicity, I find the stories attached to the church far more interesting than the building itself. The text books display an alarming uniformity respecting the origins, reasons for the name and legends associated with the church. The most recent research suggests that it is positioned on the site of a very early place of Christian worship. This was added to over the centuries, with another two or three religious buildings tacked on to the original structure. Certainly in the 6th century AD a major tidy-up and rebuilding took place, incorporating the earlier works and topping off with the then fashionable domed basilica. Badly damaged in 1733 by earthquake, the structure was the subject of a considerable restoration in the early 1960s. The alternative name 'Katapoliani' is thought to be a derivation of the common-place Cycladean *Katapola* – or low ground.

Now to legend which postulates that the church was founded in AD 326 by St Helena, the mother of Constantine the Great. 'Ekatontapyliani' is popularly supposed to refer to a 100 doors, but a moments reflection causes the windows to be counted, as well. Even so I doubt the addition. Perhaps the best story revolves around the architect/builder. This 'legends' that the master builder employed an apprentice, one Ignatius, to oversee the work. The beauty of the finished job so enraged his employer that, in a fit of jealous rage, he attempted to throw Ignatius off the roof. In a last, desperate grasp the apprentice seized the architect and they both plunged to their death on the patio below. Well there you go! Dress modestly – no shorts. Opening hours are between 0800-1200hrs & 1600-2000hrs.

There are a clutch of 16th and 18th century churches in the area of the Kastro (*Tmr* B/C1/2). The latter sits atop the lowly hill now named after the fascinating colonnaded Church of Ag Konstantinos. Additionally there are a number of enchanting, old churches scattered about the town including the:-

Church of Ag Nikolaos Thalassitis (*Tmr* D/E1/2) A small, 17th century structure, but now rather forlorn and isolated being situated on the broad pavement to the side of the Esplanade road, left (*Sbo*) of the Ferry-boat Quay .

From the Cathedral Church of Panaghia Ekatontapyliani (*Tmr* E2), the time-worn street of Manto Mavrogenous starts off by the school, opposite which are the *Church of Ag Nikolaos* (1823) and the *Frangonastiro Monastery*, once a Capuchin order and built in the 18th century. Further along on the right is the *Church of Ag Septemvriani*, built in 1592 and possessing a pleasingly carved, stone door lintel. On the left is the *Church of Tris Ierarches*, dated 1695. Beyond the turning left into Odhos Lochagou Kortianou, in a parallel lane, is the *Church of Ag Athanassios* (1695). On the right are the *Churches of Ag Onouphrios* and *Ag Markos*. Where the two lanes join up again are the *Churches of Taxiarchis* (1633) and *Ag Nikolaos* (1823). Beside the bend round to Plateia Velentza is the *Church of Ag Triada*. But this is only a sampling as there are more, many more for the aficionado.

Kastro (*Tmr* 38B/C1/2) Very little is left of this 13th century fort except a tower and a piece of wall which incorporates some rather strange, circular stones and blocks of varying thickness. The whole seems oddly incompatible, which may be explained by the fact that much of the material came from the ruins of the ancient Temple of Demeter. In the shadow of the wall is the tiny Church of Ag Anna.

Fountains 'Sprinkled' (sorry) along the length of Manto Mavrogenous, Lochagou Kortianou and Phokianou are three lovely water fountains dedicated to the War of Independence heroine, Manto Mavrogenous.

Museum Adjacent to the school playground, across the way from the Church of Ekatontapyliani (*Tmr* E2). A display of island finds, with one or two notable pieces including a 5th century BC statue of the Winged Nike and a segment of the Parian Codex. Open weekdays (except Tues) between 0845-1500hrs & weekends between 0900-1400hrs.

POLICE

Tourist (*Tmr* 2D1/2) Their office used to be romantically located in the solitary windmill, a central feature of the Esplanade road roundabout. Now they are more prosaically situated on the left-hand (*Sbo*) edge of Plateia Mavrogenous, up a flight of steps to the upper storey of the block, a few down from the office of the Cyclades Tourist Agency. One feels that the service has been emasculated in the move. Certainly the romantic swagger associated with the officers, years ago, has now been replaced by a more sober, grey countenance. Still very helpful but of course normal office hours with a lunch time siesta. In the meantime the thatch of the now empty windmill is deteriorating.

POST OFFICE (*Tmr* 39D1/2) On Odhos Prombona, diagonally to the left (*Fbqbo*), towards the Church of Panaghia Ekatontapyliani and on the corner of the side-turning to the right, down the side of the *Hotel Oasis*. Transacts full currency exchange transactions, including Eurocheques and travellers cheques and one of the only places at which to buy stamps. This may sound an obvious statement but on the islands it is generally easy to purchase them at a number of other locations, including peripteros, but not on Paros.

TAXIS The rank is close by the periptero, on the left side of the road that cuts diagonally across the Plateia Mavrogenous.

TELEPHONE NUMBERS & ADDRESSES

Clinic	Tel 21235
Dentist	Tel 21552

Doctor	Tel 21256
Olympic office (*Tmr* 27D/E2)	Tel 91256
Police, port	Tel 21240
Police, tourist	Tel 21673
Police, town	Tel 22221
Taxi rank	Tel 21500

TOILETS (*Tmr* 36D/E1/2) A very smart, clean facility to the left (*Sbo*) of the Ferry-boat Quay, beyond the small church on the right-hand side of the Esplanade and to the right down the broad avenue flanking the park. An attendant in attendance (what else?) and clients have to pay for toilet paper.

TRAVEL AGENTS & TOUR OFFICES *See* **Ferry-boat Ticket Offices, A To Z**, in addition to which there are:-

Polos Tours Tel 22093
Directions: Bordering the Esplanade to the right (*Sbo*) of the Ferry-boat Quay, alongside the OTE (*Tmr* 12D1).

Handles international boat and plane travel. Considering their comparatively helpful attitude, in comparison to one or two of the other offices, mores the pity that they are not involved in domestic business. Having written that, there is a suggestion this office is, or will be, selling ferry-boat tickets. They do act as agents for apartments, hotels and ***Rooms***. Additionally they 'Fotocopy'.

Scopas Travel Agency (*Tmr* 13C1) Tel 22300
Directions: Further on along the south-west Esplanade and on the left – well to be on the right would involve getting very wet feet.

An enterprising firm in a dark, deep-set office. Apart from travel excursions, they operate a baby-sitting agency.

EXCURSION TO PAROIKIAS PORT SURROUNDS

Excursion to Krios Bay & Beach (3½km) The *cognoscenti* tend to head out of the port as fast as is possible and this is one convenient option.

The Krios beach water-taxi moors to the left (*Sbo*) of the Ferry-boat Quay. This boat service, between Paroikias and the Disco Krios Restaurant, is advertised as running every 15mins, between 0930-0300hrs (next day). For landlubbers the Esplanade road to the north-east hugs the sea's edge all the way to the far end of the bay. Continue along the beach, past Primatsa Beach Bar and the incongruous sight of a red, English telephone box, devoid of telephone, set in the grounds of the Coffee Shop Aktaia. At this point the beach becomes a sandy, tree lined walk. Further on, the beach disappears and a footpath continues round the shoreline, passing several new buildings being constructed on the headland behind. There are signs to Sun Appartments and Villa Gorgy. The path eventually climbs over the headland, allowing good views across the bay to Paroikias, and shortly drops down to the *Disco Krios Restaurant*. This establishment serves light meals and grills with spaghetti bolognese (350drs), yoghurt, honey and fruit (300drs) and fruit salad (200drs) on the menu, as well as cocktails (300drs) and ice-creams (250drs).

Next door is the Krios Beach Club and SOS Shop, as well as decent looking toilets. Continuing on over another slight headland, the path passes *Camping Krios* and Scandinavian Restaurant Cocktail Bar, which mark the start of the long, sandy bay. The beach is fairly narrow and is backed by sand dunes with sea holly and low hills behind. A short way along are two new apartment blocks, *Niriides Studios*, owned by Olympic Holidays, and, behind these, *Anna Apartments*. A little further along the beach is the *Restaurant Snack Bar* ΝΑΛΑΤΕΣΤΑ and one or two other buildings, one of which has an ice-cream kiosk at the garden gate.

ROUTE ONE

To Naoussa (& beyond) (11km) The route passes through pleasant, rolling countryside, dotted with small dovecotes, farms, hamlets and the occasional taverna. The main road from the port leads off from the park, to the left (*Sbo*) of the Ferry-boat Quay, and divides around the slopes of Profitis Ilias about a kilometre out of town. The left-hand route proceeds via the village of **Kamares**. The right-hand fork passes, on the left, the **Monastery of Ton Taxiarchon**, which was constructed in the 16/17th centuries and has one or two icons in the church. Further on, to the right, is a track to the **Monastery of Longovardas** where whitewashed buildings, built in 1638, surround the church with cells encircling the cypress tree planted rectangle. There is a library and a sign advising 'Open 9.30-1230 No Womens'. Attempts to gain admittance are often met by a taciturn papa who indicates a white house some 2km distant, across the valley, where Father Josephus speak English good'.

The two roads link up again at the village of **Agia Trias (about 8km from Paroikias Port)**. After another 1½km, the road joins the coast at Plastira Bay. There is a junction with an unmade track that angles off to the left, encircling the bay around to the north (for details *See* **Excursions to Naoussa Port Surrounds**). A few metres further along the route, to the right, are the nicely laid out, if somewhat isolated *Bungalows Naoussa*, followed by the smart *Hotel Ippokampous* (Class B, tel 51223).

From about this point there is a splendid panorama across the bay, with a tiny chapel capped islet set in the bay and the horn of the encircling peninsula of Mt Vigla forming the backcloth.

NAOUSSA (Naousa):- fishing village (Illustration 14) On the outskirts of the settlement a junction is made with the Ambelas/Piso Livadi road. There is a fuel station and quite a lot of development, which includes low-rise flats, several restaurants and a few hotels.

The downhill section of the road passes a small cove and shingle beach with some ***Rooms*** splendidly sited, on a small headland, overlooking the foreshore. Proceeding to the centre of this very pleasant fishing village, a Greek St Ives, there are, on the right, some six houses with ***Rooms***.

The heart of Naoussa is over the bridge that spans the wide, summer-dry river-bed, although it is possible to use the concreted ford to the left. Locals park their cars beneath the bridge, for, apart from the shade, the surfaced river-bed is used as a thoroughfare. In fact, the area beneath the bridge is actually marked out with white lines to facilitate compact parking.

The harbour is formed by large, rocky boulders which stretch around the small headland, incorporating a ruined Venetian Castle, to form a 'U' shaped port. The agreeably messy main quay and inner harbour have an intimate, friendly atmosphere, with the far end of the main quay dominated by a small chapel and edged by tavernas. The nearside, on which are plonked down two churches, is lined with parked cars. The main harbour hosts modern tourist craft and yachts. Where vehicles allow, the concrete and paved surface is littered with nets spread out to dry as well as bulky bundles of stowed nets dotted about here and there. The small caique harbour is crowded by caiques which press up to the seawall and hemmed in by an assorted collection of varying sized cubic buildings

Once an excellent spot to make for directly on landing at Paroikias. But the knowledge has spread, and lovely Naoussa has a considerable band of followers, so much so that the connecting bus is usually very crowded, so be quick.

The tiny 'Old Quarter' is a charming maze of lanes and alleys, down which the swallows swoop in a never ending display of aerial acrobatics.

THE ACCOMMODATION & EATING OUT

The Accommodation There is an abundance of private houses with accommodation as well as an adequate number of hotels. The (expensive) prices are on a par with those of Paroikias.

Either side of the road into Naoussa there is a widespread scattering of ***Rooms*** and on the left, prior to the main bridge and close by the seafront, is ***Rooms*** (*Tmr* 1A2).

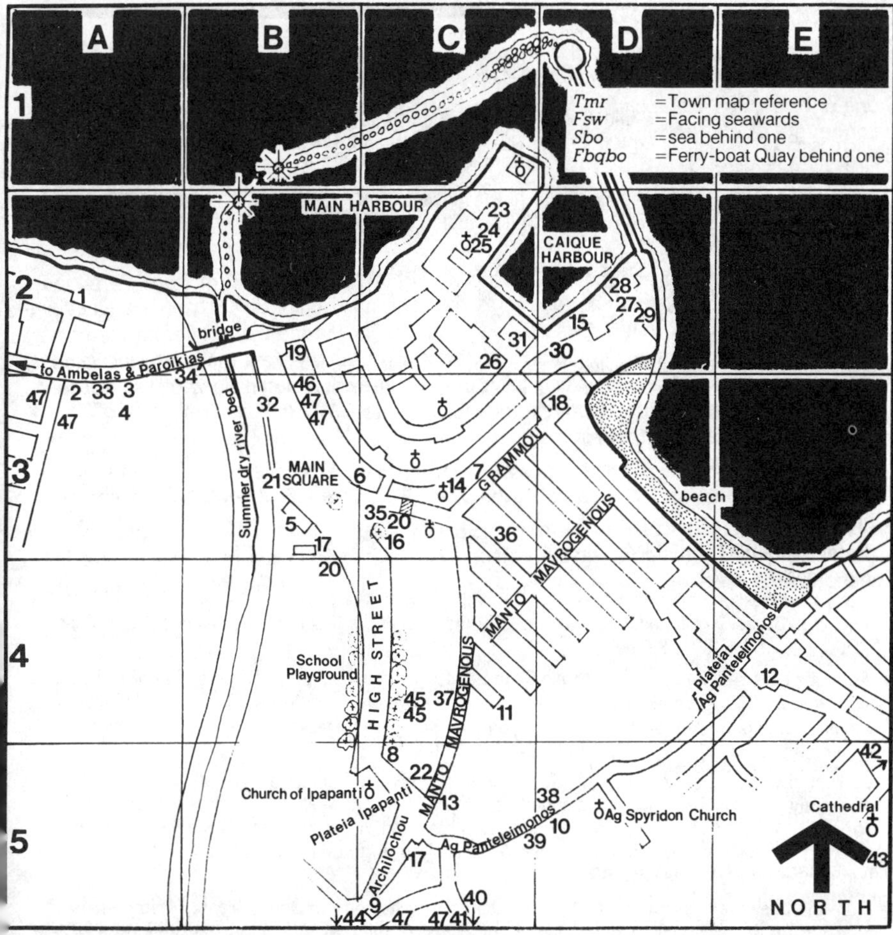

Illustration 14 Naoussa

Tmr 1A2	Rooms/Restaurant Meltemi
2A2/3	Hotel Atlantis
3A2/3	Hotel Drossia/Pub Phillipe
4A3	Hotel Madaki
5B3/4	Hotel Aliprantis
6B/C3	Gavalos Tours
7C3	Rooms Sofia
8C4/5	A N Spirou Scooter Rental
9B/C5	Rooms
10C/D5	Hotel Minoa
11C4	Rooms
12E4	Rooms
13C5	Christos Taverna
14C3	Quick Snacks
15D2	National Bank
16C3/4	Car & Motorbike hire
17	Bakers
18C/D2/3	Grocer/Fruit shop/Dentist
19B2/3	Chemist
20B/C3/4	Clinic/Doctor
21B3	OTE
22C5	Post Office
23C2	Ouzerie Kargas
24C2	Taverna Mouragio
25C2	Barbarossa Cocktail Bar
26C2/3	Supermarket
27D2	Happy Octopus Taverna
28D2	Remezzo Cocktail Bar
29D2	Disco Chez Linardo
30C/D2/3	Kosmos Cafe-bar
31C/D2/3	To Limani Snackbar
32B3	Telephone Kiosk
33A2/3	Car Hire
34A/B2/3	Launderette
35B/C3/4	Zacharoplasteion
36C3/4	Kaba/Drinks shop
37C4	Hairdresser
38C/D5	Pension Stella
39C/D5	English School
40C5	Kafeneion
41C5	Pension Christina
42E4/5	Rooms
43E5	Bungalows
44B/C5	Town police
45C4	(Two) Tavernas
46B2/3	Quick Snacks
47	Rooms

By the roadside, on the right, is the:-

Hotel Atlantis (*Tmr* 2A2/3) (Class C) Tel 51209

Directions: As above.

All rooms have en suite bathrooms. A single room is priced at 2170drs & a double 2350drs, increasing to 3250drs & 3480drs (21st May-20th June) and 4785drs & 4875drs (21st June-30th Sept).

In the side-street behind the *Atlantis* are several houses (*Tmr* 47A2/3) with accommodation:-

Hotel Drossia/Pub Phillipe (*Tmr* 3A2/3) (Class D) Tel 51213

Directions: As above.

Single rooms kick off at about 1600drs & doubles 2400drs.

and the:-

Hotel Madaki (*Tmr* 4A3) (Class E) Tel 51475

Directions: As above.

Comparatively reasonably priced. A single room with en suite bathroom costs 1900drs, a double room sharing a bathroom 1500drs & a double room with en suite bathroom 2000drs, increasing, respectively, to 2180drs & 1700/2270drs (1st-30th June & 16th-30th Sept) and 2620drs & 1820/2720drs (1st July-15th Sept).

Once over the bridge, the broad 'High Street', which doubles up as the Square, opens out to the right. On the left (*Sbo*), beyond a *Quick Snacks* outfit (*Tmr* 46B2/3), are several ***Rooms*** (*Tmr* 47B3) and on the right the:-

Hotel Aliprantis (*Tmr* 5B3/4) (Class C) Tel 51571

Directions: As above.

A prime location. All rooms have en suite bathrooms with a single room charged at 1875drs & a double 2250drs, which prices increase to 2250drs & 2700drs (21st May-30th June) and 3375drs & 4050drs (1st July-30th Sept).

From the left-hand, far edge of the Main Square (*Sbo*), just beyond Gavalos Tours (*Tmr* 6B/C3), a lane curves away half-left beneath an archway. Beyond the church of Ag Nikolaos Mostratou (on the right), Odhos Grammou makes off to the left. Beyond another *Quick Snacks – Spaper* (yes, Spaper) and O Dimitris, the barbers shop, is *Rooms Sofia* (*Tmr* 7C3)

Back at the Main Square, the High St ascends to the right (*Sbo*), curving gently up-hill between pleasantly tree lined pavements and edged, for the first part, by tavernas. Towards the top end of the street is a school playground, on the right. From the head of the street, the road bends to the left, around the Church of Ipapanti on to Odhos Archilochou, to the right. Beyond and behind a cocktail bar, on the left is ***Rooms*** (*Tmr* 9B/C5).

From the three-way junction of the High St, Odhos Archilochou and Odhos Manto Mavrogenous, the street of Ag Panteleimonos curves round the top side of the port. Almost immediately, a small lane heads south from Ag Panteleimonos St, past a kafeneion (*Tmr* 40C5) advertising billiards, to:-

Pension Christina (*Tmr* 41C5) (Class B) Tel 51017

Directions: As above.

A few pleasant looking, modern, cuboid apartments spaced out around a large, open courtyard, entered through double gates. All rooms have en suite bathrooms with a single costing 2110drs & a double 2530drs, increasing to 2410drs & 2890drs (1st-30th June & 1st Sept-10th Oct) and 3390drs & 4065drs (1st July-31st Aug).

Returning to Ag Panteleimonos and proceeding eastwards advances to:-

Hotel Minoa (*Tmr* 10C/D5) (Class C) Tel 51309

Directions: As above and on the right, prior to Ag Spyridon Church.

Recommended to us as clean, serving good meals and having en suite bedrooms with pleasant balconies. My notes also say wood/tiles/marble – sometimes, I wonder what I am on about? Furthermore, the establishment is relatively inexpensive with a single room priced at 1750drs & a double 2900drs, rising to 2150drs & 3350drs (1st July-30th Sept).

Almost opposite the *Minoa* is the:-

Pension Stella (*Tmr* 38C/D5) (Class D) Tel 51317

Directions: As above and behind the buildings edging the street, approached down an alley.

Of pleasant appearance and moderately priced. All rooms have en suite bathrooms with a single charged at 1600drs & a double 2300drs, increasing to 1800drs & 2700drs (1st June-30th Sept).

In these 'upper reaches' is other accommodation including the beautifully sited but expensive ***Rooms*** (*Tmr* 11C4), off Odhos Manto Mavrogenous; ***Rooms*** (*Tmr* 12E4) on up a pace or two in the climb towards the Cathedral and the windmills, from Plateia Ag Panteleimonos – a small square with a statue and garden; *Bungalows* (*Tmr* 43E5), south of the Cathedral and handy for the Disco Cave(!), also tucked behind the Cathedral, and ***Rooms*** (*Tmr* 42E4/5) down a side-street to the north-east of the Cathedral. A double room in this latter, a small cottage costs 1300drs.

The Eating Out There are numerous establishments but, as for the accommodation, eating out is generally very expensive, especially in those eateries spaced out around the waterfronts. The broad High St narrows down as it curves uphill, towards the Church of Ipapanti. At the widest it is lined, on both sides, with tree shaded tavernas, with a couple of more traditional tavernas (*Tmr* 45C4) towards the upper end.

Plateia Ipapanti is at the top of the High St, to the left of Ipapanti Church. Across the road, and also on the left, is:-

Christos Taverna (*Tmr* 13C5)
Directions: As above, next door to a water fountain.
Comes well recommended, but is costly, very costly.

The main quay is edged by tavernas at the top or northern end and the adjacent caique harbour is lined with cafe-bars and tavernas. Of these, the very popular *Kosmos Cafe-bar* (*Tmr* 30C/D2/3) is at the right (*Fsw*), or south, side of the caique harbour, the seats and tables of which 'nestle' up to the National Bank. To the east of the *Kosmos* is the *Restaurant* Το Υσλαστοσ Χταποδι (Happy Octopus) (*Tmr* 27D2), a simple looking bistro (which accepts Barclaycard!). Opposite is the *Remezzo Cocktail Bar* (*Tmr* 28D2). Around to the left (*Fsw*) of the *Kosmos* is the *Limani Snackbar* (*Tmr* 31C/D2/3), reputed to be cheaper but having the appearance of an English country pub, rather than a Greek taverna.

On the main harbour quay are the *Soumes Kargas* (*Tmr* 23C2), which proclaims it is a traditional ouzerie and serves grilled octopus with an ouzo; the *Taverna Mouragio* (*Tmr* 24C2), specialising in fish dishes, and the *Barbarossa Cocktail Bar* (*Tmr* 25C2)...adept at cocktails.

The Main Square is edged by a *Quick Snacks* bar (*Tmr* 46B2/3), a direct competitor to a self-same named establishment in Odhos Grammou, *Quick Snacks – Spaper* (*sic*) (*Tmr* 14C3). As could be expected, a snackbar serving toasties and other hand-held munchies. Also bordering the Main Square is a Zacharoplasteion (*Tmr* 35B/C3/4). This sells delicious looking cakes and serves ice-cream sundaes on their patio.

THE A TO Z OF USEFUL INFORMATION

BANKS The **National Bank** (*Tmr* 15D2) is on the right (*Fsw*) of the caique harbour. A very small branch, only open the usual weekday hours.

BEACHES The one to the west or left of Naoussa is pleasant, if rather stony and 'inflicted' with some biscuit rock. The backshore has the occasional boat keel to the sky and trailers scattered about.

The other beach, to the south or right of the town and officially designated the Town beach, is frankly disappointing. No, it is a disaster. The narrow shore is flanked by the peeling and unpainted backs of buildings. Unfortunately, the locals tend to dump their building materials here and, although sandy, it is also stone and rubbish littered with a resident clutch of domestic chickens that shelter in amongst the various bits of driftwood.

See **Excursions to Naoussa Port Surrounds**.

BICYCLE, SCOOTER & CAR HIRE There is a **Car Hire** business (*Tmr* 33A2/3), on the right, prior to the bridge; a **Car & Motorbike** company (*Tmr* 16C3/4) at the top end of the Main Square as well as **AN Spirou Scooter Rental** (*Tmr* 8C4/5).

BOOKSELLERS Gavalos Tours (*Tmr* 6B/C3) transacts book swop.

BREAD SHOP There are two Bakers, one (*Tmr* 17B3/4) bordering the Main Square and the other (*Tmr* 17C5) tucked away on the left of Odhos Archilochou, on the far side of the Church of Ipapanti.

BUSES The terminal, more a turn round, is on the Main Square. *See* **Buses, A To Z, Paroikias**.

COMMERCIAL SHOPPING AREA None but the back lanes have a sprinkling of fruit and vegetable shops, with a concentration in the area of the caique harbour. One particular Grocer/Fruit shop owner (*Tmr* 18C/D2/3) takes his produce inside during the afternoon siesta – a sorry commentary on the light fingered tendencies of the tourists. A Supermarket (*Tmr* 26C2/3) 'lurks' in the area of the port and a Kaba (*Tmr* 36C3/4), or drinks shop, hides away in a side-street between Grammou and Manto Mavrogenous Sts. There are two peripteros on the Main Square.

DISCOS Two, Disco Cave, beyond and behind the Cathedral and Disco Chez Linardo (*Tmr* 29D2) beyond the caique harbour.

FERRY-BOATS None, but there are trip-boats to other locations on Paros and Mykonos islands. Tickets and details from the usual firms (*See* **Travel Agents & Tour Offices**).

HAIRDRESSER (*Tmr* 37C4) Bordering Odhos Manto Mavrogenous.

LAUNDRY A launderette (*Tmr* 34A/B2/3) 'twins' with a tourist gift/card shop named La Palma, close to the bridge. Is it my imagination or is this part of the same chain as the tourist shop of the same name, opposite the Paroikias Bus terminal?

MEDICAL CARE
Chemists & Pharmacies (*Tmr* 19B2/3) Immediately on the left of the Main Square and provides exchange facilities!.
Clinic (*Tmr* 20B/C3/4) At the top, left-hand (*Sbo*) end of the Main Square, in the fork of the roads. Weekday opening hours are between 0900-1230hrs & 1800-2000hrs.
Dentist (*Tmr* 18C/D2/3) Above a Grocer/Fruit shop.
Doctor (*Tmr* 20B/C3/4) On the right (*Sbo*) of the 'confluence' of the Main Square and High St.

OTE The Main Square has a concrete, 'periptero' style OTE (*Tmr* 21B3). Close by is a telephone kiosk (*Tmr* 32B3) from which international calls can be made. A shop, the bridge side of the *Hotel Drossia/Pub Phillipe*, has a metered phone.

PETROL There is a filling station on the junction of the road to Ambelas and Paroikias.

POLICE (*Tmr* 44B/C5) On the left (*Sbo*) of Odhos Archilochou, on the way out of Naoussa.

POST OFFICE (*Tmr* 22C5) Across the road from the Church of Ipapanti.

TAXIS Rank on the Main Square.

TELEPHONE NUMBERS & ADDRESSES

Clinic (*Tmr* 20B/C3/4)	Tel 51216
Police (*Tmr* 44B/C5)	Tel 51202

TOILETS Yes, beyond the National Bank (*Tmr* 15D2), on the mole leading out to the ruined fort.

TRAVEL AGENTS & TOUR OFFICES
Gavalos Tours & or **Nissiotissa Tourist Office** (*Tmr* 6B/C3) Tel 51480
Directions: The office is on the left (*Sbo*) of the Main Square.
Cathy and or Kostas 'dish up' attentive assistance. Services include booking hotel and room accommodation, apartments or bungalows, tours, trips and excursions, car-rental, ferry-boat tickets (domestic and international), left-luggage *ad infinitum*, as well as book swop.

Katerina Simitzi Tel 51444
Directions: Located on the Main Square.
All as for Nissiotissa, but for Cathy/Kostas read Katerina.

In the last few years the original, aforementioned couple of Main Square offices have been supplemented by **Ballos Tours**, **Simitian Tours** and **Fimi Travel**, the other side of the Main Square in the ground floor of the *Hotel Aliprantis*.

A closing note for those travellers who might want to earn a drachma or three. Perhaps the English School (*Tmr* 39C/D5) in Odhos Ag Panteleimonos, close by the *Hotel Minoa*, might have a vacancy for the literate – I won't apply.

EXCURSIONS TO NAOUSSA PORT SURROUNDS

Excursion to the North Peninsula/Ormos Langeri (about 6km) The road curves around the back of the port from the Ambelas junction to:-

AG ARGIRI (1km from Naoussa Port) A sandy beach overlooked by the *Hotels Kalypso* (Class C, tel 51488) and *Cavos* (Class C, tel 51367), as well as the *Batistas* and *Ioli Holiday Apartments*.

The surfaced road degenerates into a track. Keep to the left or west side of the peninsula in the low-lying, softly undulating countryside amongst which are set the occasional apartment buildings for rent. Mind you they are rather out of the way.

After about 3½km, a lump of land projecting into the bay is tenuously connected by a sandy causeway.

At the northern end there is a lovely, sweeping, sandy beach backed by dunes and low, windswept trees.

Almost at the far east-north-east of the peninsula is **Ag Maria** (circa 3km from Naoussa Port) a nice, quiet, unspoilt, sandy beach with a small taverna.

Excursion to Kolymbithres Beach, Ag Giannis Detis & beyond (7½km) Proceed along the Paroikias road as far as the junction beyond *Naoussa Bungalows*. Here a wide, rough surfaced track forks off to the right. This curves round the rocky sea-shore of the bay, past *Restaurant Avra/Shop & Bar* as well as *Apartments & Rooms Anna*. Up a side track, to the left, is the *Hotel Kouros* (Class C, tel 51000), which has a restaurant and bar.

Further on along the main route is:-

Camping Naoussa

Directions: As above on the left.

Well laid out, with a shower block, reception, mini-market and bar. One has to consider the low-lying nature of both the river and the swampy surrounds, and then ponder about the possible mosquito problem.

The track now turns towards the sea and beach area known as:-

Kolymbithres (3km from Naoussa Port) Famed for the unusual wind and sea scoured rocks on the water's edge. The marshy land hereabouts has a sandy foreshore almost continuously washed over by the sea. The beaches are haphazardly wired off and signposted private, apart from one public access also signed, as is 'Nudist Beach 3km'. There is a windsurfing school operating from the nearest strip of shore.

After the final right-hand curve of the Kolymbithres beach, the route climbs into a rocky hillside, past *Bungalows Asteria* to the left, one of several expensive looking developments on the hillside above, and some patchy development centred around an old farmstead and the *Taverna Vigla*. At this point a track to the right descends to a tiny, idyllic, sandy beach with a taverna.

A kilometre or so further on, past a massive new development, is a 'bit of beach' from which viewpoint, across the bay, Naoussa glitters white in the distance. This is followed by a surprisingly large caique repair yard on the foreshore, more a levelled area than a formal boatyard, in the lee of the very large Chapel of Ag Giannis Detis. The chapel surmounts a headland beyond which is a small, shady cove with a simple hut taverna. However idyllically quiet and deserted the spot may appear out of the height of season, there are sail boards stacked up. Additionally the chapel has a signboard requesting people not to sunbathe, and certainly not 'starkers', in their grounds.

To the left, across the narrow neck of the land hereabouts, the seascape is reminiscent of a rocky Guernsey inlet.

A small hut taverna is plonked down a little above a bare circular area, almost in the form of a roundabout, from which a track climbs away across craggy scenery towards the lighthouse on Cape Korakas.

Excursion to Ambelas (4km) The road from the outskirts of Naoussa forks, after 1¼km. The right-hand road progresses to Piso Livadi and the left to:-

AMBELAS (4km from Naoussa Port) On first entering this once charming fishing hamlet, with a small taverna and pleasant beach, there are ***Rooms*** and a mini-market on the left.

Ambelas is now the proud possessor of several hotels and apartments, including the *Hotel Ambelas* (Class C, tel 51324), where double rooms with en suite bathrooms are charged at 1950drs, increasing to 2200drs (1st July-31st Aug).

Just past the *Ambelas* is a large refectory like taverna with an old chapel incorporated into the building.

To the right (*Fsw*) of the quay is a sandy beach edged by the *Taverna Damionos*. To the left of the quay is a tiny, sand and shingle cove and at the end of the track are *Apartments Helen* and *Hotel Christiana* (Class C, tel 51573) with a taverna. Other holiday accommodation is being built. Behind the quay are telephone facilities, available between 0800-1200hrs & 1700-2100hrs. Buses to Naoussa depart at 0915 & 1315hrs.

The whole village is open and scattered, there is even a vineyard between the *Hotel Ambelas* and the sea and an olive grove on the opposite side of road. Unfortunately in the late evening it totally lacks atmosphere.

The road from Naoussa to Piso Livadi (*See* **Route Two**) passes through rolling agricultural countryside with large enough fields for farming machinery to be utilised, rather than donkeys. Olive groves and pine trees are occasionally dotted about, in clumps.

ROUTE TWO

From & back to Paroikias (a southern circular route) via Pounta, Alyki, Drios & Lefkes (47km) From Paroikias the south Esplanade road climbs up and around the *Hotel Xenia* (Class B, tel 21394), interestingly incorporating an old windmill, and then heads off towards some popular beaches. Of these, the first signposted beach is a pleasant, sandy cove, which unfortunately breaks into shingly sand, with some kelp and general rubbish scattered about.

From hereabouts some of the more energetic sand-searchers walk up and along the hillside to the left (*Fsw*), climb over a stone wall by the red painted metal gates and down to a nice, sandy cove.

Above this small bay and down below the main road is:-

Parasporos Camping (2½km from Paroikias Town) bar, restaurant and mini-market.

In this area, to the left of the main road, are the remains of the Asklepieion (shades of Kos?), an ancient Medical School. Pitheon, indicated on some maps, is across country, south of the Asklepieion and marks the site of an ancient temple.

At about 3km a beefy sign points along a rough track to the right and offers much including camping but...! This side route descends across country past the Chapel of Ag Irini (4½km from Paroikias Town) to a lovely location with the island of Antiparos in the middle distance. The tree edged beach with some kelp, degenerates into pebbles and then rocks. Facilities include various water sports which take in wind surfers (600drs per hour), fun boards (1000drs per hour), pedaloes (500drs per hour), canoes (300drs per hour) and water skiing (1500drs per hour). The track comes to an end in a farmyard by an almost entirely sea-swept, small, sandy cove edged by a stone wall and trees. There are a few benzinas to the right. The farm, which has chickens, geese, pigs and turkeys as well as growing bananas, pineapples, olives, oranges and lemons, forms a backcloth to the cleared campsite right next to the beach. It is sheltered by palm trees and an olive grove, and there is access to the almost private, sandy beach. The farm has its own restaurant and bar for the campers' benefit.

Annoyingly there is no way through for wheeled transport and it is necessary to retrace ones footsteps, or wheels as the case may be.

On the main road again, after about 4km, a fork in the road allows the left turn to lead through the village of **Sotires** and on to:-

PETALOUDES (8km from Paroikias Town) Note that it is quicker and more direct to get to Petaloudes on the secondary road,via the large Nunnery of Monastiri Christos Sto Dhasos and the village of **Psychopiana**.

This luxuriantly vegetated valley was once part of the estate of a rich, landed Paros family. It is thickly wooded and has a constantly running stream, which is vital to attract the butterflies and moths. The situation brings to mind the more famous valley on Rhodes island. The best time of year to visit is early summer. Despite the island bus company running a service, Paros Travel of Paroikias also operates tour buses.

Returning to the main road, after some 5km, with Antiparos looming large, there is another fork in the road. The right-hand turning leads down a fast and wide road to:-

POUNTA (Punda, Punta) (6km from Paroikias Town) Yes, well! A rather Mexican hamlet... One extremely smart hotel is to the right, there are a couple of tavernas, a cafe, *Bar Pounta* and a damned big quay.

The *raison d'etre* for the spot is the trip boat shuttle connections to and from the island of Antiparos (*See* **Excursion to Antiparos**).

Returning to the main road, the route parallels the coastline around to:-

ALYKI (12km from Paroikias Town) Once an area of salt pans, some evidence of which remains, and a small fishing boat port, which happily is still sparsely developed.

There are two hotels, a few cafe-bars, tavernas, several restaurants, a disco and a lovely, tree lined sandy beach. The *Cafe-bar Apollon*, has ***Rooms*** and opposite is a periptero, at the angle in the beach. There are ***Rooms*** across from the other corner of the beach elbow and accommodation at the *Hotel Angelaki* (Class C, tel 21985), sited on the furthest headland to the left (*Fsw*). The *Angelaki* only has double rooms with those sharing a bathroom costing 1700drs & those with an en suite bathroom 2000drs, which prices increase to 2300drs & 3000drs (1st July-31st Aug). Not only does a reader recommend the hotel, but also the *Taverna Angelaki* which is in front of the hotel. The food was acclaimed and the prices were low. An ouzo is accompanied by a large plate of mezes, which may or may not be charged.

The *Hotel Afroditi* (actually a Class B Pension, tel 21986) charges 1850drs for a single room, sharing the bathroom, and 2100drs for an en suite double room. These rates increase to 2260drs & 3100drs (1st July-15th Sept).

There appear to be many apartments available in the area.

There are continuing rumours that the unsurfaced road from Alyki is to be dealt with, but no evidence yet. The unpaved surface bumps and grinds to:-

DRIOS (22km from Paroikias Town) On the western approaches to this lovely, small, village holiday resort are a couple of hotels as well as ***Rooms***. Opposite the latter is a track down to the sea beyond the *Taverna Angiri* and some ***Rooms***.

It is easy to drive past the main body of the hamlet which lies hidden to the right side of the road. The turning to the beach, several hundred metres along the road, is close by *Cafe Lake* and a large, modern, drinking water fountain, on the opposite corner. The faded sign, which may or may not be visible, points past an English look-alike, tree shaded village pond, alongside which the locals while away the day (and night) in a kafeneion shaded by a thick awning of tree branches. The gently inclined lane down to the seafront, runs straight and true, hemmed in by high stone walls attractively tree and flower planted. At the small, shingle sand beach the lane turns sharply left.

The high, steep retaining wall on the beach side of the road is planted with mature trees. Across the road, in the angle of the bend in the road, is the surprisingly large, barn-like and 'laid-back' *Restaurant Kyma*. Meals and accommodation are available.

To the right (*Fsw*) back along the coastline are two low-key hotels, one of which is the

Avra (C Class, tel 41016), where a double room sharing a bathroom costs 1810drs & with en suite bathroom 2260drs, increasing to 2260drs & 2900drs (1st July-15th Sept).

On the left of the quay road, towards the small fishing boat mole used by a few benzinas and caiques, is the rather incongruous Art Club.

Close by, at Cape Driou, there is evidence of long established habitation, for carved in the rocks are some ancient, ships slipways.

A little further along the main route, the package holidaymakers needs have been thoughtfully catered for at:-

CHRISSI AKTI (23km from Paroikias Port) Signposted imaginatively 'Golden' this and 'Golden' that. The track off the main road bends past, on the left, the bamboo shaded *Restaurant Zina* (smelling strongly of burnt cooking oil) to run out on the backshore, in between two hotel/restaurants. By the way, the beach really is 'Golden'.

A crudely painted signpost pointing to the left, along the beautiful, sandy beach, proclaims *Apartments/Rooms*. In this direction is a backshore taverna.

Once again on the main road, beyond the hamlet of **Tsardakia**, a couple of turnings off, lead down to:-

LOGAROS (22km* from Paroikias Town) A comparatively underdeveloped and sparse settlement, spread along a narrow bay and lovely, sandy beach. There are a few ***Rooms*** and tavernas with a 'huddle' at the tree edged, right-hand end (*Fsw*). These include the *Logaras Beach*.

Around the headland is the increasingly popular:-

PISO LIVADI (21 km from Paroikias Town) A pleasant, lively, fishing port, which is, just, holding off the usual ravages inflicted by organised holiday firms. One street in, one street out with a right-angled waterfront.

The short, narrow peninsula down-leg on the left-hand side (*Fsw*) (of the right-angle) is lined with a few, three storey tavernas and hotels, backed by a steep hillside. It terminates on a concrete quay, beyond which a rocky breakwater curves into the sea. The right-hand side encompasses the beach which is edged by a few, two storey taverna buildings with ***Rooms***,followed by the southward, tree lined road.

Many ***Rooms*** (the most inexpensive are up the hillside, above the quay on the left-hand side), tavernas and restaurants as well as two travel agents, a yacht charterer, Kafkis Captain Travel & Navigation,and a mini-market.

Reasonably priced ***Rooms*** are available over the *Restaurant Bolas*. Food and drink in the port is that 100drs or so more expensive, which is due as much to the presence of affluent yacht charterers as it is to package holiday-makers. The *Georges Roof-Top Restaurant* comes highly recommended but is open evenings only. The menu includes such unusual dishes (unusual for island Greece) as T-bone steak, 'George's Steak Special' (with a cream, mustard and pepper sauce) and vegetarian dishes, such as zucchini and spinach pies. Furthermore, the prices are, or were, reasonable.

There is a helpful Information office, Perantinos Travel & Tourism Agency, on the left at the road junction, entering from the Marpissa direction. If the owner is not in his office he can usually be found lounging in one or other of the nearby tavernas.

There is an open-air cinema, the Kine Makis, where locals make up most of the audience and entrance costs some 250drs.

The beach is sandy with some shingle but towards the far,right-hand end there is more shingle and pebbles in the shallows and some kelp.

Hotels include: the *Andromachi* (Class B Pension, tel 41387), where all rooms have en suite bathrooms, a single costing 1900drs & a double 2260drs, increasing to 3025drs & 3250drs (21st June-20th Sept); *Marpissa* (Class B Pension, tel 41288), with shared bathrooms, single rooms charged at 1650drs & a double 2000drs, rising to 2000drs & 2600drs (1st July-15th Sept); *Amaryllis Beach*

**Note distances are now in a clockwise direction not counter-clockwise as heretofore.*

(Class C, tel 41410), with en suite bathrooms, a single priced at 2000drs & a double 3000drs, increasing to 2500drs & 3500drs (1st June-30th Sept); *Leto* (Class C, tel 41283), only double rooms with en suite bathrooms costing 2000drs, which increases to 2900drs (1st-19th July & 21st-31st Aug) and 4000drs (20th July-20th Aug); *Lodos* (Class C, tel 41218), with double rooms en suite charged at 2260drs, rising to 3160drs (16th July-15th Sept); *Logaras* (Class C, tel 41389), where double rooms en suite are charged at 2080drs, which increases to 2650drs (1st July-31st Aug); *Pisso Livadi* (Class C, tel 41309), only doubles en suite which cost 1945drs & 2710drs (1st July-31st Aug); *Vicky* (Class C, tel 41333), where single rooms share the bathrooms at a price of 1400drs & doubles sharing cost 2050drs & doubles en suite 2650drs, rising to 1800drs & 2600/3350drs (1st July-15th Sept); *Dimaras* (Class E, tel 41324), with only double rooms en suite at a price of 1715drs, which increase to 2060drs (1st-9th July & 26th-31st Aug) and 2685drs (10th July-25th Aug); *Koralli* (Class E, tel 41289), with double rooms en suite costing 3000drs; *Lena* (Class E, tel 41296), with an en suite double room charged at 1500drs and 3000drs (1st June-30th Sept) and the *Maya* (Class E, tel 41390), only double rooms en suite costing 1800drs & 3000drs (1st July-31st Aug).

Three hundred and fifty metres along the Marpissa road is *Captain Kafkis Camping* (Tel 41479) where the charge is 300drs per person.

From Piso Livadi the road system in the region of the spread out villages of both **Marpissa** and **Marmara** is complicated and the signposting poor. Both settlements date from early times and are endowed with a multiplicity of churches. There is petrol at pretty, quiet Marpissa, as well as a Post Office, tavernas, ***Rooms***, a disco and an excellent baker. Both have a road down to the Bay of Kefalos, where there is now only a tiny scattered settlement on the left-hand side and a large headland to the right. The bay is truly dramatic but unfortunately the foreshore is pebbly.

The onset of the lovely cross-country mountain road, passing through fertile agricultural countryside, is marked by a large, untidy quarry at the roadside, near the village of:-

PRODROMOS (14km from Paroikias Town) Also known as Draghoulas. It is a very good example of a Cycladian fortified village with the outer walls of the perimeter houses forming a defensive rampart. The settlement is on a side road and entry is from the east, via an arched gateway flanked by two churches.

To the left of the main road's steep climb, way up on the left, on the mountain crest, are a number of windmills, one or two of which are still working.

LEFKES (10km from Paroikias Town) A lovely mountainside village to one side of the main road with a massive *Xenia Hotel* (Class B, tel 71248).

From Lefkes the road, beyond *Apati*, bypasses **Kostos** and winds around to:-

MARATHI (5km from Paroikias Town) Famed for the marble quarries which date back to antiquity. They are located on the Lefkes side of the hamlet, to the left, in the direction of the small 17th century Monastery of Ag Minas. There are extensive underground workings with evidence of the old quarrying tools engraved in the rock.

EXCURSION TO ANTIPAROS ISLAND (Andiparos) Tel Prefix 0284. This small, unforgiving island is 12km from top to bottom and up to 6km wide, with an area of about 40sq km and a population numbering some 650.

It is common practice to treat Antiparos as a 'bolt on goody' to Paros, but it is bigger than, for instance, Folegandros and is a holiday area in its own right. A day-trip excursion hardly does it justice.

Trip-boats run from Paroikias and have their schedules fixed to the side of the boat. The trip takes between ¾ and 1 hour at a cost of 340drs for the return trip.

The other departure point is Pounta on the west coast of the island from whence the short sea journey takes about ten minutes. The craft involved are fast, sturdy passenger boats and a small, 'perfectly formed' car ferry. During the summer months the scheduled services shuttle backwards and forwards, rolling and pitching uncomfortably in the narrow channel. The bus from Paroikias always connects with a sailing which departs at 0820hrs, and every hour thereafter until 2020hrs, at a return trip cost of 120drs. In days of yore, passengers wishing to cross were supposed to open the small chapel door to signal the Antiparos ferry-man (who must have had bloody good eyesight!). I suspect, nowadays, readers will find the chapel door locked. 'Chapel door openers' will probably be charged with 'intent to thieve'.

There is only one settlement of any size, the fortified town of **Antiparos**, or Kastro, separated from the lagoon-like Ferry-boat Quay, by a few minutes walk. The island's hotels, pensions, rooms, restaurants, tavernas and kafeneions are gathered about the quay, the town and the connecting road.

On the sea-front is a small branch of the National Bank, open between 0930-1130hrs, but only for the height of summer months. The quayside road leads, through a building site, towards the island's campsite, *Camping Antiparos* (Tel 61221). There is another route described later on in the text. At the north end of the harbour is *H Avra Restaurant* and *Rooms to Let*, beyond the streets of 'Peace' and 'Life'. There is also accommodation at *Mike's Place*, overlooking the sea. At the north end of the shallow lagoon is a narrow, hard sand beach, backed by trees. 'Camping and nudding' (*sic*) is not permitted.

The 'High Street' of the town is at right-angles to the quayside road and is a surprisingly long, gently rising street. As one advances so it becomes less given over to tourists' needs (such as a travel agent providing a scheduled minibus service to the Cave of Antiparos) and more concentrated on the requirements of the local population. This road 'houses' a bread shop, which also sells hot cheese pies for 70drs, a zacharoplasteion and two or three general stores. In particular, there is a Clinic, opening between 0915-1215hrs & 1730-1900hrs. Higher up, beyond the village school, is a Post Office which provides exchange facilities. Dotted throughout the length of the road are tavernas and sundry eateries.

At the top of the street is a T-junction. To the left the road bends past an open square bordered by various cafes, cocktail bars, restaurants and shops. This is not as bad as it sounds as most of the establishments are small and unobtrusive. The narrow village street continues, beyond an OTE, ***Rooms***, the Red Lion, which offers 'darts, cocktails, music, quality'! The latter, almost unresistable attractions, are closely followed by the Oasis kiosk (ice-creams) and lastly the Paradise Night Club, beyond which the road is well and truly in the countryside, on the way towards the Cave of Antiparos.

Returning to the T-junction, a right turn leads past the Fabrike Pub, which proclaims 'musik, coktils, koffees' (*sic*), and then on out of the settlement. One kilometre or so of dirt track, across fields and through herds of goats, advances past a pretty, double-barrelled chapel to the Luna Disco, set incongruously next to, if not part of, an untidy working farm. The track continues through the farmyard down to a rocky coastline, indented with shallow, sandy coves. A small, bushy headland divides this bay from the next, which has a benzina jetty and is backed by the camping site and a Fun Pub – 'Breakfast all morning, disco all night'. An aforementioned track leads back to the quay.

Hotels include:- the *Korali* (Class E, tel 61236), close to the Ferry-boat Quay, behind the chapel, where all rooms have en suite bathrooms with a single costing 1500drs & a double 2100drs, increasing to 1900drs & 2900drs (11th June-31st Aug); *Mantalena* (Class D, tel 61206), with a single room, sharing a bathroom, costing 1355drs, a double room sharing 1810drs & a double room with en suite bathroom 2260drs, prices which increase to 2080drs & 2260/3160drs (10th July-31st Aug); *Anargyros* (Class D, tel 61206) and the *Chryssi Akti* (Class C, tel 61206), where all rooms have en suite bathrooms, a single room costs 1810drs & a double 2260drs, increasing to 2710drs & 3160drs (10th July-31st Aug).

Incidentally, everything on the island is a walk or a boat trip including the:-

Cave of Antiparos The track from the Kastro is in good condition but it is a 1½-2hr tramp and on a hot day... The other method of getting there is by trip boat which depart from the port at a return cost of some 600drs.

The cave is sited close to the top of Mt Ag Yianni and the arduous climb from the docking area takes up to ½ hour. During the summer months donkeys can ease the slog, at a cost, and a makeshift cafe looks after the 'inner' man or woman.

The cave's attractions are the stalactites and stalagmites, the fame of which has been well known for centuries. Bits of the calcified 'mites' are to be found displayed not only on the island but, it is suggested, as far away as a Russian museum. This 'piracy' must date from the Russian occupation, in the 1770s. Entrance is alongside a small chapel and modern-day descent into the cave is made rather easier by the deployment of some four hundred concrete steps, in place of the ropes that used to be the *modus operandi*.

For hundreds of years visitors have been 'carving' their names, one such dating back to the 14th century. Another inscription on a stalagmite, engraved in 1673, records the use of the dank and dark antechamber as a place of worship and the particular stalagmite as an altar. This ceremony was staged by a French ambassador to Turkey who transported not only his retinue but, it is documented, some islanders. The congregation totalled about 500 celebrants who all had to be 'roped down'! It must have been quite a feat to organize this spectacular.

The despoilation caused by centuries long graffiti and collectors' depredations was, it is said, made worse during the Second World War. Then the Occupation Axis troops caused further damage with hand grenades used to flush out partisan guerillas who used the cave as a place of refuge.

Antiparos Town from the Ferry-boat Quay. *Acknowledgement to David & Liz Drummond-Tyler.*

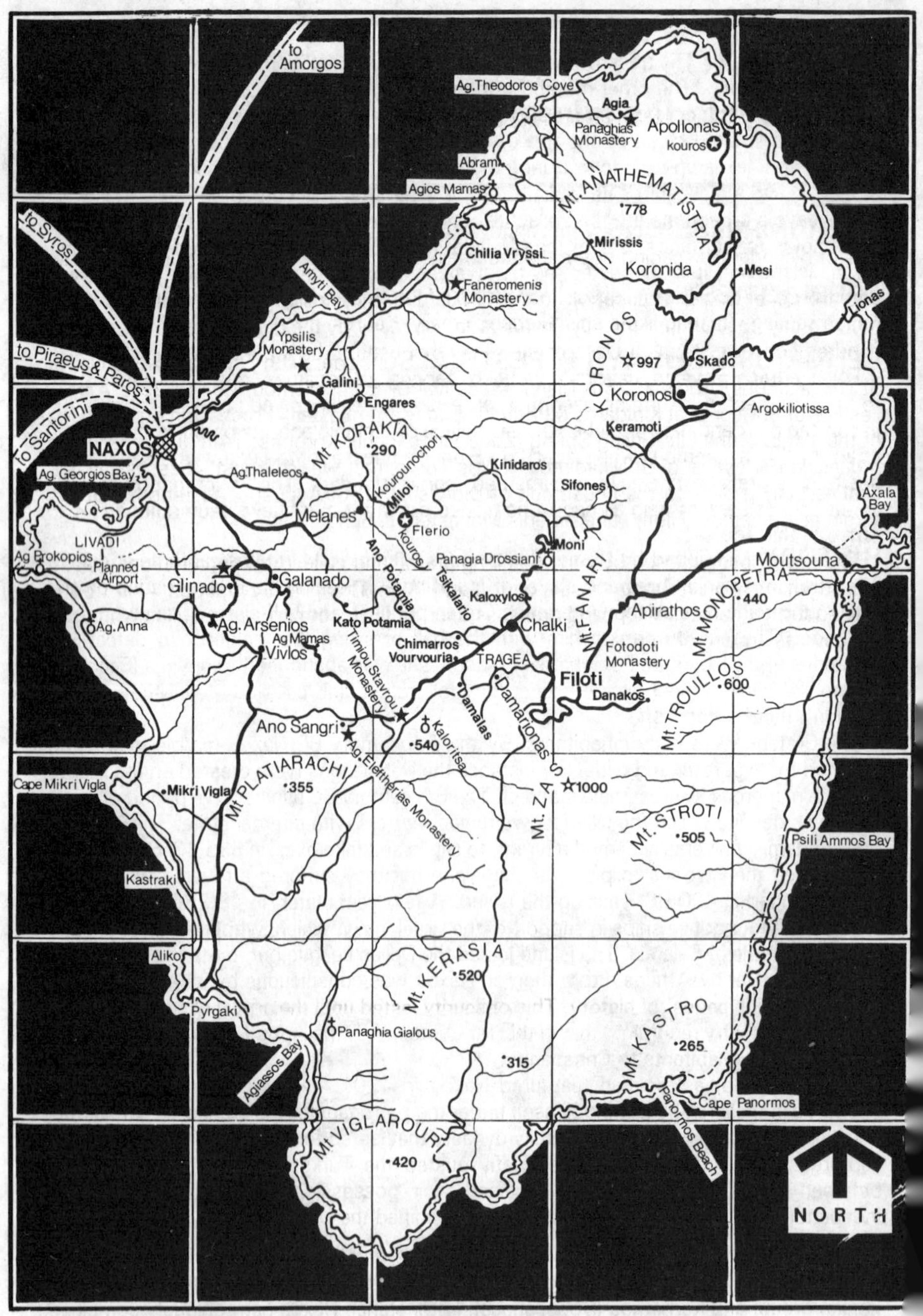

Illustration 15 Naxos island

6 NAXOS ★★★★
Cyclades Islands - Eastern chain

FIRST IMPRESSIONS Venetian towers; tourist development; river-beds & waterfalls of oleanders cascading down the mountainsides; lizards; donkeys & mules; eagles.

SPECIALITIES Kitron liqueur (made from lemon tree leaves); white Promponas wine; Naxos sausage (tasting like a shish-kebab); emery; Kouros.

RELIGIOUS HOLIDAYS & FESTIVALS include: 10th February – Festival of St Charalampos, Angidia; 25th March – Festival of Evangelismou, Chalki; 23rd April – Festival of St George at Kinidaros & Potamia; Friday after Easter – Procession & pilgrimage of the Virgin of the Life-Giving Spring (Zoodochos Pighi), Koronos; 14th July – Religious procession & festival of St Nikadimos, Naxos Town; first week August – Festivals & folk dances (dating back to the pagan cult of Dionysus); 15th August – Assumption of the Virgin at Apipathos, Filoti, Faneromenis Monastery & Sangri.

HISTORY Mentioned by Homer (Zia or Zeus Island). Its mythological fame is due to Theseus, an Athenian hero and slayer of the Minotaur, leaving his lover Ariadne on the island whilst she was asleep. Ariadne, a Cretan princess and half-sister to the Minotaur, had aided Theseus by arming him with the ball of string that helped him defeat the mysteries of the labyrinth. For whatever reason, she was abandoned. Dionysus (Bacchus, the god of wine) arrived on the scene, they fell in love and coupled – well they would, wouldn't they?

The Cretans were early inhabitants. By the 7th century BC Naxos marble was being sculpted for export far and wide. For instance the Delos Lions were created on the island, as were numerous Kouros (male statues). The 6th century BC ushered in a period of great affluence, despite which the silly fellows ruined matters with internal strife. This allowed one Lygdamis, universally named a tyrant, to slip in and take over, in 535 BC. Some exiles encouraged the Persians to pitch for the island but they suffered a reverse which their fleet revenged in 490 BC, sacking the island. A few years later, in 480 BC, the Naxiots sneaked off four or five ships in support of the Greek navy, which 'whopped' the Persians at the sea battle of Salamis. The island joined the Delian League but, on trying to opt out, were taken over by Athens. From then on Naxos was conspicuous by its absence from even the 'inside pages' of history. This obscurity lasted until the arrival of the Venetians, apart from an entry recording, that in the 1st Century AD, the Apostle, St John of Patmos converted the inhabitants to Christianity.

Marco Sanudo, a Venetian, captured Naxos in 1207. Perversely he left his Italian overlords in the lurch by putting himself under the patronage of the Franks. Whatever his loyalties, he established a strong family dynasty that lasted for 359 years, until the Turks captured the island. The Russians briefly ousted the Turks, but only for four years, between 1770-1774. The Turks regained their possession until the Greek War of Independence (1821-1827), after which Naxos joined the United Greece.

GENERAL Overall Naxos is probably one of the most attractive and beautiful of the Greek islands. I would rank it along with other favourites that include Lefkas and Ithaca (Ionian group) and Karpathos (Dodecanese). For instance Naxos harmoniously combines the majestic mountain beauty of Crete with the intensively cultivated, agricultural plains and miles of sweeping golden sands of Rhodes. The northern part of the island is green, verdant and very beautiful, with the summer-dry river-beds a riot of tumbling, flowering oleander bushes. The high central plain, centred around Chalki, is mainly planted with large, prolific, old olive groves. In the drier, but still green south-west, almost the whole length of the coast is golden beaches intermittently broken up by rocky headlands. The near totally deserted south-east coast, rimmed by mountains, is a moorland vista edged by a rocky waters edge regularly, if widely, interspersed by delightful, sandy coves.

Because of the island's mineral and agricultural resources, Naxos did not have to woo 'The Tourist'. However, partly due to the cessation of the emery industry, it has now jumped on the holiday bandwagon and tourist complexes are springing up all along the south-west coast as well as at Apollonas. Gone are the bamboo tents of wild camping hippies from the beaches beyond Ag Anna – it is no longer secluded and quiet enough for them. *Thomson Holidays*, with all that their ilk entails, arrived, with a vengeance, in 1988, describing the island as 'The new 'in' place... relax by day, party by night'. Coincidentally the interior of the island is opening up, with many of the dirt roads being widened and surfaced.

Long may Naxos and its amiable inhabitants prosper, but hurry, an airport is under construction. The army have been building it since 1986, blowing up Stelida, the mountain south of Naxos Town overlooking Ag Georgios Bay, to provide the hard core. Progress, happily, has been slow, since the runway keeps sinking into the salt flats, south of Livadi, on which it is being built (surprise, surprise). It is rumoured, though, that the donor of the land will be claiming it back, if the construction is not completed soon. The same source also indicated that it may be large enough to be an international airport, but that is unlikely.

NAXOS: capital town & port (Illustration 16) Naxos Town is a busy, commercial seaport with, tacked on the sides, as it were, holiday resorts around the corner. The one towards the north end is still fairly small and more of a residential suburb than a rowdy, package tour complex. However, the small town springing up behind Ag Georgios Beach is a veritable warren of holiday accommodation, both completed and under construction. It is now truly a tourist 'new town' with all facilities. A conference centre, catering for up to 450 people, is available on the ring road at the Mathiassos Village Bungalow complex!

Behind the waterfront an extensive, almost Medieval Old Quarter stretches up the hillside. This is of much greater complexity and interest than, say, Paros. Apart from size, one of the greatest differences between the two is that the Paros Chora is 'light and sun' whilst the Naxos Chora is darker and more secretive. No whitewash here, that is strictly for the tourists. Sadly, the shops and facilities within the Old Town are changing their character to satisfy 20th century demands.

ARRIVAL BY FERRY More than adequate connections with the other islands. Although Naxos is not quite such an important terminus as, say, Paros, it is the springboard for the scattered Eastern Cycladic islands of Iraklia, Shinoussa, Koufonissi, Donoussa, Amorgos and Astipalaia. The massive quay (*Tmr* A2/3), on which passengers are coralled in roofed pens, merges with the Esplanade at the northern end. This is not inconvenient as the ferries are met by a respectable number of accommodation owners and the bus terminal is at this end of the waterfront, on the expansive 'Bus Terminal Square'.

THE ACCOMMODATION & EATING OUT

The Accommodation Possibly no other island town is able to offer as much accommodation as Naxos but due to the maze-like nature of the Old Quarter, locating many of the ***Rooms*** requires diligence. Additionally, hotels in the holiday areas of town are block booked by package tour operators, Dutch and German as well as English. Thus they are unavailable in the height of the season months. Off-season, however, the owners of these hotels are as likely as any others to meet the ferries and offer their rooms to all-comers.

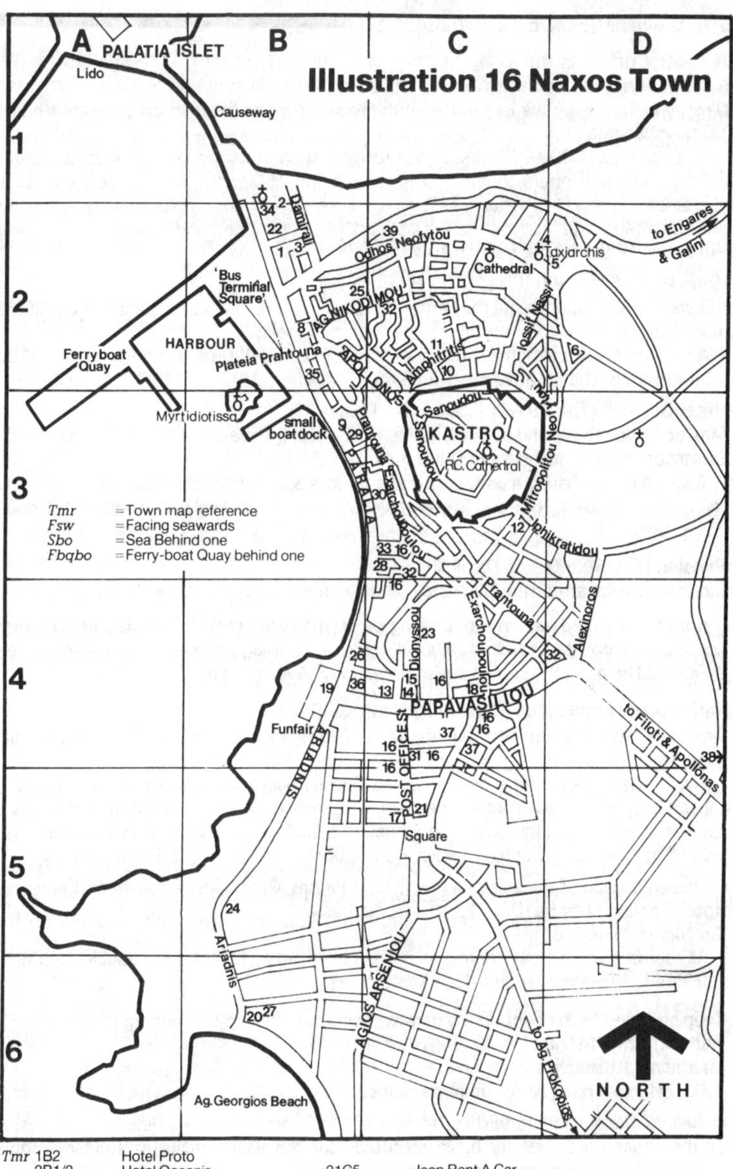

Illustration 16 Naxos Town

Tmr 1B2	Hotel Proto		
2B1/2	Hotel Oceanis	21C5	Jeep Rent A Car
3B2	Pension	22B1/2	Naxos Tourist Centre
4C/D2	Hotel Anna	23C4	Rooms
5C/D2	Hotel Apollon	24B5	Pension Ariadne
6C/D2/3	Pension Anna Maria	25B/C2	Restaurant Stamata
7B/C2/3	Rooms	26B/C4	Zacharoplasteion Aktaio
8B2	Cafeteria Pharos Elpidas	27B6	Pension Glaros
9B/C2/3	Kali Kardia Restaurant	28C3	International shop
10C2/3	Hotel Dionyssos	29B/C3	Commercial Bank
11C2	Hotel Panorama	30B/C3	Mike's Bikes
12C/D3	Hotel Renetta	31C4/5	Post Office
13C4	Credit Bank	32	Bakers
14C4	Katerina's Burger Shop	33B/C3/4	St Anna Travel
15C4	Doctor	34B1/2	Bus office
16	Rooms	35B2/3	ZAS Travel
17C5	Restaurant Fotis	36B/C4	OTE
18	Laundries	37C4/5	Hairdressers
19B4	National Bank	38D4/5	Clinic
20B6	Kavouri Restaurant	39B/C1/2	Police

A central office is the:-

Naxos Tourist Information Centre (*Tmr* 22B1/2) Tel 24358

Directions: Bordering the Esplanade, at the end of the parade of shops and eateries flanking the 'Bus Terminal' Square.

Open between 0800-2100hrs. A well-run operation catering more for 'independents' than package holiday-makers. It offers to find rooms (from about 1500drs), provides detailed and accurate information concerning ferries, bus times and tours, sells postcards and used books at relatively expensive prices. Left-luggage facilities are available at 100drs per item, and local and international phone calls can be made, the former costing 10drs.

Hotel Proto (*Tmr* 1B2) (Class D) 13 Protopapaki Tel 22394

Directions: Almost opposite the Ferry-boat Quay, across the wide expanse of Esplanade and above a motorbike hire firm.

All rooms share the bathrooms. A single room costs 920drs & a double room 1390drs, rising to 1110drs & 1670drs (16th June-15th Sept).

Hotel Oceanis (*Tmr* 2B1/2) (Class D) 11 Damirali St Tel 22436

Directions: As above and at the top or left-hand end (*Fbqbo*), of a street, one back and parallel to the Esplanade and on the left-hand side.

A single room sharing a bathroom costs 950drs & a double room sharing 1500drs, whilst a double room en suite costs 1850drs. These rates increase, respectively, to 1500drs & 2200/2800drs (1st June-30th Sept).

Pension (*Tmr* 3B2) Odhos Damirali

Directions: Almost behind the *Proto*, on the same side as the *Oceanis*, about centre of the street.

A crudely painted sign in red lettering proclaims 'We serve coffee, Rooms, hot showers, clothes washed here, douche chaud'. Additionally there is a left-luggage service available daily between 0600-2400drs. The hotel is run by a smiley-faced lady. Average rates.

Hotel Anna (*Tmr* 4C/D2) (Class E) 58 Neofytou St Tel 22475

Directions: As above and on the left, about 200m along the gently curving, badly surfaced road of down-town Naxos.

It is rather more a two storey, low-rise Guest House, with sea views. The old lady, of Romany appearance, oversees a spotless pension, personalised with nice touches. The lovely double rooms have small en suite bathrooms. Shared use of a kitchen is allowed. This establishment is constantly praised by readers. A double room costs 2000drs, increasing to 2500drs (1st July-30th Sept).

On the same side of the street, a few metres further along, behind Taxiarchis Church, is the:-

Hotel Apollon (*Tmr* 5C/D2) (Class C) 61 Neofytou St Tel 22468

Directions: As above.

All rooms share the bathrooms, with a single priced at 1170drs & a double 1550drs, increasing to 1170drs & 1750drs (1st July-15th Sept).

Keeping round to the right up the narrow, rising lane forking,left and on the right is:-

Pension Anna Maria (*Tmr* 6C/D2/3)

Directions: As above.

Double room rates as for other pensions.

In general, independents wishing to stay in Old Quarter accommodation, as opposed to the better hotels, must accept pretty basic standards for the same prices as modern rooms in the fairly characterless holiday areas. You pays yer money...

Rooms to Let (*Tmr* 7B/C2/3)

Directions Located in Odhos Persephones, not far from and below *Hotels Dionyssos* & *Panorama*. The large, blue painted 'Rooms to Let' is clearly visible from the Ferry-boat Quay. There are directions painted on the walls of the lanes leading to it from Plateia Prantouna (*Tmr* B2).

This is a purpose built (early 70s?) block of eight rooms, sharing two bathrooms and 'a bit' of kitchen area. The flat roof is also available in the height of the season. By today's standards, the rooms are rather basic with concrete floors but are large and well maintained. They are run by Despina, a very friendly Mama, who lives on the lower floor with her husband and sons. Her husband captains the little ferry-boat, **Daphne II**, which fetches the *Thomson* holiday-makers from Mykonos airport, as well as running excursions to Delos and Santorini. Double rooms cost, from 1200drs.

A relation of Despina's also has ***Rooms*** available, across the lane from *Hotel Dionyssos* and opposite the entrance to *Anixis*. A door in the wall leads into a tiny courtyard, with two open flights of stairs leading off. The one to the right serves a pleasant sun terrace overlooking Apollo's Gateway and the sea, whilst the one to the left leads to an enclosed landing and three small double rooms, which are clearly used by the family in the winter. The room to the left has twin beds and a balcony with fine views of the entrances to the two aforementioned hotels and the distant monastery and mountains beyond. The shared 'bathroom' is situated under the other flight of steps, with the toilet at the lowest point. Gentlemen not endowed to stallion proportions would find limbo-dancing lessons an advantage! Double rooms cost from 1200drs.

An interesting example of the Old Quarter genus '*Hellene Domicilius*' is the:-
Hotel Dionyssos (*Tmr* 10C2/3) (Class D) 110 Persefonis St Tel 22331
Directions: From Plateia Prantouna select Odhos Apollonos, off the far right-hand corner, and the third alley to the left. It is possible to follow the stencilled 'hand', but this is not an infallible method as the winter whitewashing tends to obscure some of the pointers.

In piratical days of yore, or possibly, and more accurately, Dickensian England, the less-than-winsome proprietor would have put one in mind of the overseer of a boy chimney sweep. The area is pleasant enough and the premises have a splendid rooftop terrace. Accommodation on offer starts with tiered bunks in an arched, darkened cellar, around which are dotted oilcloth covered, rickety card tables, but for 500drs a night what can a traveller expect? A double room sharing the bathroom kicks off from 1200drs, whilst an en suite room starts at 1500drs. More a hostel than a hotel.

Fairly close by are the:-
Hotel Anixis (Class D) 330 Amfitritis St Tel 22112
Directions: As above and on the corner of the square.

Distinctly smarter than the 'Dinosaur', no hush my mouth, the *Dionyssos*, but then one pays more. A single room, sharing a bathroom, costs 1300drs, a single with en suite bathroom 1500drs, a double sharing 1500drs & a double en suite 2200drs. These rates increase, respectively, to 1600/1800drs & 1800/2800drs (21st June-30th Sept).
and the:-
Hotel Panorama (*Tmr* 11C2) (Class C) Amfitritis Kastro Tel 22330
Directions: As above but one block to the north.

A single room, sharing the bathroom, is priced at 1250drs, a double sharing 1750drs & en suite 2050drs, increasing, respectively, to 1560drs & 2300/2700drs (1st July-15th Sept).

From the *Hotel Dionyssos*, in a clockwise direction, Odhos Mitropolitou Neofytou circles the Kastro area of the Old Quarter. Beyond the junction with Odhos Iphikratidou is the:-
Hotel Renetta (*Tmr* 12C/D3) (Class C) Tel 22952
Directions: As above.

The friendly, smiling proprietress Maria is active in procuring guests for her hotel, which is situated in a very attractive area of winding alleyways and lanes. She will always stop likely looking travellers. En suite double room rates rise from 2000drs to 2700drs (1st July-15th Sept).

Branching off the south of the Esplanade is Odhos Papavasiliou, which ascends from the waterfront. Odhos Dionyssou is a side-street to the left (*Sbo*), on the right of which is:-
Rooms (*Tmr* 23C4)
Directions: As above.

The first floor of this building is given over to three airy rooms and a nicely tiled bathroom, with the family living above. A double room costs 1300drs, off season.

There are more ***Rooms*** next door.

From the south end of the Esplanade, alongside the National Bank (*Tmr* 19B4), a narrow street climbs to level out in an area used as a lorry park. From here the road proceeds on towards the package holiday end of the town.

Pension Ariadne (*Tmr* 24B5) (Class B) 1 Ariadnis Tel 22452
Directions: As above and on the east, inland side of the street, close to the curve in the road.

A long, single storey, barrack like building with rather old, ill fitting doors and windows. A vociferous Alsatian guard dog allows entry to the Reception, which is just beyond the extent of his restraining chain! The manager, Despina Kitini, appears to have links with other establishments in town. A double room with en suite bathroom costs from 2000drs.

Continuing on along Ariadnis St and off to the left, behind the *Taverna Kavouri*, is the:-

Pension Glaros (*Tmr* 27B6) Tel 23131
Directions: As above.

Very comfortable and quiet, with a splendid view across Ag Georgios Beach. The owner, J. Frantzeskos, is working hard to prepare another accommodation close by. All rooms have en suite bathrooms, a single costing 1750drs & a double 1990drs. These prices increase to 2000drs & 2350drs (1st May-30th June & 1st-30th Sept) and 2750drs & 3250drs (1st July-31st Aug).

To the left of Ariadnis St a grid layout of urban style streets give access to a 'litter' of hotels, most of which are block-booked by the tour companies.

Camping At the far end of the gently curving, sandy Ag Georgios Beach is the *Cafe-Bar/Disco Flisvos*, from which a 1000m track leads to:-

Camping Naxos Tel 23501
Directions: As above but due to the distance involved, it is best to use the camp bus which, as they do on many islands, meets the ferry-boat arrivals.

All the usual facilities including hire of tents. A word of warning involves the general surrounds, which is towards the old salt flats or Alikes. This is an area of ever intensifying development which was once low-lying land, criss-crossed by stagnant drainage ditches with all the attendant problems of insects and unsatisfactory aromas.

Camping Apollon
Directions: A new 200 pitch campsite has been built 2.8km from Naxos Town, along the road to Ag Prokopios, on the opposite edge of the salt flats from the airport.
For details *See* **Ag Anna, Route Three**.

Camping Maragas is an even further distance, beyond Ag Anna.

The Eating Out A number of the Esplanade cafe-bars, tavernas and restaurants offer 'numbered' breakfasts, listed 1, 2 & 3 and featured as 'English, Scandinavian, Continental and Normal' fare. One even 'chronicles' baked beans – how Greek! Blessings must be offered that, strangely, this habit has not spread to midday or evening meals, only applying to breakfasts. Before leaving the subject, I hope visitors will not patronise restaurants that eschew the legal requirement of displaying a controlled price list... surely it is an oversight!

Before settling down at the trough, for those who require an aperitif, why not try the:-

Cafe-bar Andonis Dionysos
Directions: From the Ferry-boat Quay, turn right (Fbqbo) and beyond Plateia Prantouna, a few doors up from ZAS Travel (*Tmr* 35B2/3) on the Esplanade.

A hefty ouzo and pieces of octopus BBQ'd on a charcoal grill cost 100drs. A number of the brutes are caught just across the way, in the harbour, tenderised by the continuous slap, slap of their being banged against the quay wall and then hung out to dry.

Cafeteria Faros Elpidas (*Tmr* 8B2)
Directions: Almost on the edge of the small main square, Plateia Prantouna.

Friendly, good service with a range of breakfasts, cakes, pastries, ice-creams and drinks.

Kali Kardia Restaurant (*Tmr* 9B/C2/3)
Directions: Bordering the Esplanade, to the left (*Sbo*) of the Commercial Bank.

Excellent, reasonably priced food and very drinkable retsina. Fish, kebabs, kalamares (300drs) and steaks are available. A meal for two of stuffed tomato & pepper (200drs), papoutsaki (300drs), chicken & potatoes (250drs), bread (20drs per head) and ½litre of barrel retsina (100drs) cost 790drs. Another of kid & macaroni (400drs), moussaka (300drs), horta (100drs), bread and wine cost 940drs.

To the right (*Sbo*) of the Commercial Bank, beneath the 'Upstairs We Sell & Buy Used Books' is the *Taverna Psestaria*, which prepares 'Meat produced in our Farma (*sic*)'. A small, inexpensive, family-run taverna in traditional style.

Off to the right (*Sbo*) of Plateia Prantouna and on the left is a popular pizza eating place with the chairs and tables on a raised patio.

Praised by a particularly valued correspondent is:-

Taverna 'Pantelias'
Directions: Valued he may be, but his descriptive powers were restricted to: 'in the alley road running

parallel to the waterfront but 'one-block back' as it were'. I call it Pantelias because a gentleman of that name appears to own it... and I could discover no other name.

Consists of two rooms knocked into one and very busy with locals. No pretensions and a happy place. A sample meal of 1 helping of stuffed tomatoes (2 and very good), 1 succulent pork chop, a helping of deep fried kalamares, 1 plate of potatoes, a green salad, bread and one litre of retsina (2 500gm bottles of kortaki) cost 1380drs.

From the far left (*Sbo*) side of Plateia Prantouna, Odhos Ag Nikodimou, the Old Market Street, curves sharply and gently climbs, passing beneath covered arches. This advances past, on the left, some steps down to a pleasant square bounded by churches on two sides and the commended *Restaurant Stamata* (*Tmr* 25B/C2). Further along Odhos Agios Nikodimou jinking to the right, then left (and right and left...?) progresses to the:-

Manolis Taverna

Directions: As above... or simply follow the wall stencilled directions.

This is a reasonable priced taverna with a garden on the left, a chapel alongside, and the kitchen on the right of the narrow lane. Run by friendly, cheery Manolis, his South African wife Vivi and abetted, if that's the word, by Litzia (7) and Aleko (5). Another daughter Letarina aged about twelve is rather slow but delightful. They are assisted by the waiter Iannis who gets hotter and hotter and redder and redder, dashing from garden to kitchen and vice-versa. Delightful people but the standard of food varies. A taramosalata, 2 chicken & chips, 1 large salad and 2 kortaki retsina cost 1000drs. On another occasion 1 tzatziki, 2 fried kalamaries (disappointing), 2 chips, 2 500gm retsina (barrel retsina, but not 'ready') and bread was priced at 980drs.

The same reporter also 'carried on' about:-

Restaurant Vassilis

Directions: In the 'alley complex', but quite close to *Manolis* and the waterfront.

Recently 'done up' and redecorated. The longish narrow room has doors to alleys at both ends. Perhaps rather pretentious with its new decor but most friendly and serving a delicious evening meal. A 'trough' for two of 1 taramosalata, 1 tzatziki, 2 enormous helpings of mouth wateringly fresh marides (fried 'just right'), salad (crisp, fresh), tomatoes, chips, 2 jugs of retsina (well carafes actually and more than a litre total I'm sure), and bread cost 1080drs. The veal is 'favourably mentioned'.

Almost opposite the *Vassilis*, beneath an archway, is the highly recommended *Taverna Lucullus*. This is reputed to be the oldest traditional establishment, serving the largest souvlaki in town, on a wooden chopping board.

A typical example of a tourist coffee-bar is 'Panteboy', a name that probably confuses many a foreigner. The word is pronounced rendez-vous! This one serves enormous, delicious-looking bowls of yoghurt and fruit salad.

Zacharoplasteion Aktaio (*Tmr* 26B/C4)

Directions: The far, south end of the Esplanade, beneath the *Hotel Koronis*.

Comfortable seats and well frequented by locals.

Beyond the Rent-A-Car firm alongside the above establishment, is a *Souvlaki Pita Bar*.

Further on and left up Odhos Papavasiliou and, on the left is *Katerina's Burger Shop* (*Tmr* 14C4) where a mikro beer costs the same as a larger bottle elsewhere.

Across the road is the side turning of 'Post Office' St which, not surprisingly, leads past the Post Office to open out on a large, unequal sided square formed by the various roads that branch off. On the right-hand, nearside is:-

Restaurant Fotis (*Tmr* 17C5)

Directions: As above.

A small, 'greasy-spoon' with ***Rooms*** above.

Across the square and on the same side are two rather tourist orientated eateries, the *Cafe-bar Rose Restaurant* and the *Marabou Restaurant*. Sample prices at the latter include moussaka (300drs), briam (260drs), octopus with pasta (350drs) and chicken moussaka in lemon sauce (280drs), all garnished with french fries or rice and carrots! Beers cost 90drs or 100drs.

At the town end of Ag Georgios Beach is the:-

Kavouri Restaurant (*Tmr* 20B6)

Directions: As above.

One of the best beach tavernas encountered anywhere. At both lunchtime and evenings there is always a wide variety of ready-made dishes plus excellent grills. Not the most inexpensive place but very good, splendid value, delicious food.

For bathers the provision of showers is a noteworthy point.

THE A TO Z OF USEFUL INFORMATION

BANKS The **Commercial Bank** (*Tmr* 29B/C3) edges the Esplanade, a few yards down from the Harbour. Eurocheques cashed.

BEACHES Not only does Naxos town possess one of the finest beaches of any Cycladic island but the south-west coast of the island is almost one long, sandy beach.

At the north end of the town, either side of the causeway to Palatia islet, on which stands the reworked marble Gate of Apollo, are:-

Beach 1: On the left of the causeway. More a place for a quick dip but obviously favoured as a lido for there are the remains (not Roman) of a faded, bamboo faced beach bar as well as changing rooms. Like a moth, these flicker briefly but frantically to life at the height of the season.

Beach 2: To the right of the start of the causeway. A scrubbly bit of old beach.

But do not be down-hearted for the jewel in Naxos's crown is:-

Beach 3: Ag Georgios Beach, to the south-west of the town, is now bordered, at the near end, by package holiday hotels. A long, curving, sandy bay with a gently shelving sea bottom and very clear water, the first section of which is edged by a wall and a few spindly trees. Beyond the *Kavouri Restaurant* is a new hotel and the old Disco Asteria has disappeared beneath an extension to the *Hotel Asteria*. The first bit of foreshore is kelpy and the sea very shallow. Half-way round there are pedaloes and sun-beds for hire and the Disco Infinity, beyond which is the Paradise Bar & Disco. The far end of the really attractive sweep of sand is marked by the Day Club, with its distinctive mock windmill and from where surfboards can be hired. The bay magnificently curves on towards Cape Moungri.

BICYCLE, SCOOTER & CAR HIRE The hirers of two wheeled, powered conveyances are wary men and bearing in mind the mountainous and large nature of the island, this is not surprising. Unless a moped or scooter is in good condition it simply will not carry two on the more adventurous journeys. The balance of choice must be weighted towards a Jeep or beach buggy. The 'going' day rate for a 50cc moped is 1800drs.

From the bottom of the Ferry-boat quay (*Tmr* B2), almost across the Esplanade and beneath the *Hotel Proto* (*Tmr* 1B2) is the smart office of **Theoharis**. Behind *Hotel Proto* is **Rent the Mobike**, which particularly mentions the big off-road machines, as well as the more modest varieties. This establishment also specialises in yacht service and 'diving' works!

The Esplanade spawns a number of outfits including **Mike's Bikes** (*Tmr* 30B/C3). This was once a garage and is located beneath an Art Gallery. Perhaps the most 'fertile ground' for scooters is in 'Post Office' St – in fact almost next door to the Post Office (*Tmr* 31C4/5) where there are two firms side-by-side. Where 'Post Office' St breaks into a large square, there is the very smart:-

Jeep Rent A Car (*Tmr* 21C5)
Directions: As above.

This firm is run by a very helpful and informative young chap, called Chris, who speaks perfect English. A buggy costs 6000drs a day all in (except petrol), rising to 8000drs in the height of summer months and 1500drs buys enough petrol for the day. The vehicles appeared to be well maintained, which is more than could be said of one hired at greater cost from the smart firm (Buggy for Fun) in the side-street near Zacharoplasteion Aktaio (*Tmr* 26B/C4).

BOOKSELLERS To the right-hand (*Sbo*) of the far side of Plateia Prantouna, and on the left, is a good foreign language book and paper shop. Along the Esplanade towards the Ferry-boat Quay, past *Pharos Elpidas Cafeteria* (*Tmr* 8B2), the *'Chora Cafe-Bar'* and an alleyway and on the right is:-

Mr Melissino's A card, gift and dress shop of which naught, but he is the brother of George, the author of the only available island guide. Naturally enough, this publication is on sale here. The guide is old fashioned in style, but the photographs are well worth the purchase price. Mr Mellissino also sells stamps.

A most interesting venue on Odhos Paralia, the Esplanade, two narrow lanes beyond the Commercial Bank (*Tmr* 29B/C3) is:-

Upstairs We Sell & Buy Used Books Upstairs it is, because, as with quite a lot of the Esplanade, the ground floor of the back of any building is the first floor of the front. The business sells jewellery and dresses but as the charming owner declares the books are his 'trap'. And what a trap with three full shelves of English, French and German books.

There is another 'We Sell Used Books' in the Old Quarter, off to the right of Odhos Ag Nikodimou.

BREAD SHOPS One Baker (*Tmr* 32B/C2) is in the Old Quarter, to the right of Odhos Ag Nikodimou and on the left , just before *Manolis Taverna*. Along the Esplanade, Odhos Paralia, and close by Santa Anna Travel (*Tmr* 33B/C3/4), stencilled signs on the walls lead the way up steep steps to a Bakery (*Tmr* 32C3/4) on the right of an irregular square. There are a couple of ***Rooms*** behind the aforementioned Travel Agency.

Odhos Papavasiliou ascends from the south end of the Esplanade. Along the next street to the right (*Sbo*) of Papavasiliou, beyond the 'Post Office' St, is a baker on the left approaching the square. Yet another Baker (*Tmr* 32C/D4) is located on the dog-leg in Odhos Papavasiliou, at the top of the steep rise from the waterfront, at the junction with Odhos Prantouna.

BUSES The Bus office (*Tmr* 34B1/2) is not quite where indicated on some island maps, but a little to the north, beyond a small public garden. The buses turn and park around the very large square at the bottom of the Ferry-boat Quay.

Bus timetable

This is the height of the season. During the spring and autumn timetables fall off and exclude many 'tourist only' locations. Unless stated otherwise, all times are daily:

Naxos to Ag Anna (SW coast)
0730, 0800, 1000, 1100, 1200, 1300, 1400, 1600, 1700, 1800, 1900hrs
Return journey
0800, 0930, 1030, 1130, 1230, 1330, 1430, 1630, 1730, 1830, 1930hrs
One-way fare: 90drs.

Naxos to Agiassos Bay (SW coast)
1200hrs
Return journey
1800hrs

Naxos to Apirathos (Centre island)
0830, 1100, 1300, 1900hrs
Return journey
0730, 0845, 1200, 1530, 1900hrs

Naxos to Apollon (N coast)
0830, 1000, 1100, 1300hrs
Return journey
0630, 1100, 1430, 1700, 1800hrs
One-way fare: 360 drs.

Naxos to Chalki (Centre island)
0830, 1100, 1200, 1300, 1900hrs
Return journey
0705, 0750, 0905, 1220, 1550, 1920hrs
One-way fare: 130drs

Naxos to Damarionas (Centre island)
1200hrs
Return journey
0710hrs

Naxos to Filoti (Centre island)
0830, 1100, 1200, 1300, 1900hrs
Return journey
0700, 0745, 0900, 1215, 1545, 1915hrs

Naxos to Komiaki
0830, 1100, 1300hrs
Return journey
0700, 1130, 1500, 1830hrs

Naxos to Koronos (N centre island)
0830, 1100, 1300hrs
Return journey
0715, 1145, 1515, 1845hrs

Naxos to Lionas (NE coast)
1200hrs
Return journey
1800hrs
One-way fare: 180drs.

Naxos to Melanes (Kouros) (E of Naxos Town)
1200, 1530hrs
Return journey
0700, 1230, 1600hrs
One-way fare: 70drs.

Naxos to Moutsouna (E coast)
1300hrs
Return journey
1800hrs
One-way fare: 180drs.

Naxos to Pyrgaki via Kastraki (SW coast)
0900, 1100, 1300, 1600hrs
Return journey
0930, 1140, 1340, 1600hrs

Naxos to Ano Sangri (SE of Naxos Town)
1200hrs
Return journey
0715, 0900hrs

Naxos to Tripodes (Vivlos) (SE Naxos Town)
0900, 1100, 1300, 1600hrs
Return journey
0730, 0940, 1150, 1350, 1600hrs

Naxos to Danakos, Keramoti (Centre island)
Mon, Wed & Fri 1200hrs
Return journey
Mon, Wed & Fri 0700hrs

Naxos to Kinidaros (Centre island)
Mon, Wed & Fri 1200hrs
Return journey
Mon, Wed & Fri 0700hrs
One-way fare: 130drs.

Naxos to Potamia (Centre island)
Mon, Wed & Fri 1430hrs
Return journey
Mon, Wed & Fri 0700hrs
One-way fare: 90drs.

Naxos to Engares (NE of Naxos Town)
Mon, Wed & Fri 0730, 1200hrs
Return journey
Mon, Wed & Fri 0800, 1230hrs

COMMERCIAL SHOPPING AREA It should be borne in mind that Naxos Town was a busy, commercial port serving a large, self-sufficient island, long before tourists arrived in any numbers. It is therefore possible to buy virtually anything in the town, and even the shops on the seafront can provide goods ranging from an olive oil press to a chic little cocktail dress. The Chora or Old Quarter provides a 'fertile ground' of shops. These are, in the main, interspersed along the narrow, climbing, tumbling alleys of Odhos Ag Nikodimou and Odhos Apollonos, both of which radiate off Plateia Prantouna. One particular shop that draws attention is the old man who sells sponges and decorative shells towards the far end of Odhos Ag Nikodimou. On the left of Odhos Apollonos, as it climbs towards the Museum, is an imposing cavernous shop advertising 'We have Naxos Cheese, Honey, Wine'. Somewhere in the alleys towards The Kastro is an isolated, small shop signed 'Smal Supermarket' (*sic*). The interior must be all of 8ft square but appears to have virtually everything a shopper could possibly want. This is often run by Jan, who is all of 9 years old. She is extremely efficient, knowing where everything is kept. Jan laboriously writes down every item and price, and meticulously adds up the bill, checking and rechecking. This may well work out differently each time, but always wrong in her favour. She will go far that young lady!

The Esplanade has a number of mini-markets and supermarkets. The most comprehensive and reasonably priced is south of Santa Anna Travel Agency (*Tmr* 33B/C3/4) and is recognizable by the turnstiles, which are to aid the owners keep an eye on the customers. This store closes on Wednesday afternoon and all day Sunday, a detail which reminds me to stress that Naxos has not allowed tourism to affect the old siesta habits, after which many businesses do not reopen. Incidentally, most of the supermarkets display a most unwelcome sight, a silent comment on the habits of the more light-fingered holiday-makers, namely signs requesting tourists to leave all their bags outside.

DISCOS There is now at least one in the Old Quarter, behind ZAS Travel and a few doors up from the Municipal Lavatories, and several in the 'Tourist Quarter'. *See* **Beaches, A To Z.**

FERRY-BOATS A busy port and important stepping stone to the far Eastern Cycladian islands of Iraklia, Shinoussa, Koufonissi, Donoussa, Amorgos and Astipalaia.

Ferry-boat timetable (Mid-season)

Day	Departure time	Ferry-boat	Ports/Islands of Call
Mon	1100hrs	Hellas Express	Paros,Piraeus(M).
	1230hrs	Ios(Express)	Ios,Santorini.
	1700hrs	Apollo Express	Ios,Sikinos,Folegandros,Santorini.
	2200hrs	Schinoussa	Iraklia,Shinoussa,Koufonissi,Donoussa, Aegiali(Amorgos),Katapola(Amorgos).
Tues	1000hrs	Schinoussa	Paros,Syros,Piraeus(M).
	1230hrs	Apollo Express	Paros,Syros,Piraeus(M).
	1330hrs	Ios(Express)	Mykonos.
	1600hrs	Naxos	Iraklia,Shinoussa,Koufonissi,Amorgos.
	1800hrs	Alekos	Paros,Syros,Rafina(M).
	2400hrs	Delos	Ios,Santorini,Anafi.
Wed	1000hrs	Naxos	Paros,Syros,Piraeus(M).
	1030hrs	Delos	Paros,Syros,Rafina(M).
	1230hrs	Ios(Express)	Ios,Santorini.
	1430hrs	Apollo Express	Ios,Santorini.
	1530hrs	Hellas Express	Ios,Sikinos,Folegandros,Santorini.
	2200hrs	Schinoussa	Iraklia,Shinoussa,Koufonissi,Donoussa, Aegiali(Amorgos),Katapola(Amorgos).
	2200hrs	Apollo Express	Paros,Piraeus(M).
Thurs	1000hrs	Schinoussa	Paros,Syros,Piraeus(M).
	1230hrs	Hellas Express	Paros,Syros,Piraeus(M).
	1330hrs	Ios(Express)	Mykonos.
	1500hrs	Naxos	Ios,Santorini.
	1800hrs	Alekos	Paros,Syros,Rafina(M).
	2400hrs	Delos	Amorgos.
Fri	0745hrs	Delos	Paros,Syros,Rafina(M).
	1030hrs	Naxos	Paros,Piraeus(M).
	1330hrs	Ios(Express)	Mykonos.
	1430hrs	Hellas Express	Ios,Santorini.
	2200hrs	Schinoussa	Iraklia,Shinoussa,Koufonissi,Donoussa, Aegiali(Amorgos),Katapola(Amorgos).
	2400hrs	Delos	Paros,Rafina(M).
	2400hrs	Olympia	Amorgos,Astypalaia,Kalimnos,Kos,Rhodes.
	2400hrs	Apollo Express	Ios,Santorini.
Sat	1000hrs	Schinoussa	Paros,Syros,Piraeus(M).
	1100hrs	Hellas Express	Paros,Piraeus(M).
	1230hrs	Ios(Express)	Ios,Santorini.
	1500hrs	Naxos	Donoussa,Amorgos,Koufonissi,Shinoussa,Iraklia.
	1515hrs	Delos	Amorgos.
Sun	0745hrs	Delos	Paros,Syros,Rafina(M).
	0930hrs	Olympia	Syros,Piraeus(M).
	1000hrs	Naxos	Paros,Piraeus(M).
	1130hrs	Apollo Express	Paros,Piraeus(M).
	1330hrs	Ios(Express)	Mykonos
	1430hrs	Hellas Express	Ios,Santorini.
	1800hrs	Alekos	Paros,Syros,Rafina(M).

The diabolical **Marianna** has been replaced by the **Skopeletis**, which returns to its Katapola(Amorgos) base at 1500hrs, Mon & Wed. For more accurate, detailed ferry-boat connections to Iraklia, Shinoussa, Koufonissi,

Donoussa, Aegiali & Katapola(Amorgos) See the relevant island descriptions. It is almost impossible to tie in the separate details - it would need a year or two on a large IBM main frame computer!

In addition there is a hydrofoil service:-

Hydrofoil timetable (Mid-season)

Mon	1500hrs	Nearchos	Paros,Ios,Santorini,Iraklion(Crete).
Wed	1320hrs	Nearchos	Mykonos.
	1530hrs	Nearchos	Paros,Ios,Santorini,Iraklion(Crete).
Fri	1330hrs	Nearchos	Paros,Ios,Santorini,Iraklion(Crete).

Duration: to Mykonos 50mins
Ios 1hr
Iraklion 4hrs.

Please note these tables are detailed as a GUIDE ONLY. Due to the time taken to research the Cyclades it is IMPOSSIBLE TO 'match' the timetables or even boats . So don't try cross pollinating...

FERRY BOAT TICKET OFFICES A number of ticket agencies spread along the Esplanade but, as on most islands, one agency occupies the 'limelight'. Here that is:-

ZAS Travel (*Tmr* 35B2/3) Tel 23330

Directions: Located beneath the Town Hall (ΔΗΜΑΡΕΙΟΝ), almost opposite the caique quay that forms the south-side of the Harbour.

A 'switched on', efficient staff run the office which handles most ferries, including the **Skopelitis**, and changes currency. This company organises a day-long, round the island excursion bus with a few hours stop at Apollonas and a multi-lingual commentary.

Two other ticket offices, more involved in trip boat and excursion traffic, are the:-

Santa Anna Travel Agency (*Tmr* 33B/C3/4)

Directions: Two-thirds of the way along the Esplanade from the Ferry-boat Quay. Often does not open in the evening.

and the:-

Travel Centre of Naxos

Directions: Close to the OTE (*Tmr* 36B/C4).

A good office for a general spread of information, including accommodation.

In the square at the south of 'Post Office' St, (*Tmr* C5), there are two more travel agents. The first, **Mika Tours**, shares premises with 'The Jeep Rent A Car' (*Tmr* 21C5), and appears to sell tickets for all main ferry services as well as local tours. The second is almost next door, on the corner, and is the *Thomson* agent. It advertises such delights as 'Beach BBQ', 'A night feast in a Greek village', 'sunset cruise' and 'sight-seeing tours of the island'. Super!

HAIRDRESSERS At least two Ladies Hairdressers (*Tmr* 37C4/5), both accessible along the first left-hand turning (*From the Port*) from the 'Post Office' St. A nice barber operates from a small, 'back street' shop (*Tmr* B/C2/3) in Odhos Prantouna. A hair and beard trim costs about 200drs.

LAUNDRY There is a Laundry in a basement next door to the Post Office (*Tmr* 31C4/5). This one will do a plain wash and dry, as well as ironing, if required. Another two are also in or accessible from Odhos Papavasiliou. One is on the left (*Sbo*) (*Tmr* 18C4) of the street and the other is next door to the first Ladies Hairdresser (*Tmr* 37C4/5) previously mentioned.

LUGGAGE STORE A number, including two on Odhos Damirali, one at the *Pension* (*Tmr* 3B2), another opposite the *Hotel Oceanis* (*Tmr* 2B1/2), and yet one more at the Naxos Tourist Information Centre (*Tmr* 22B1/2) (*See* **The Accommodation**).

MEDICAL CARE

Chemists & Pharmacies One, Nik Dellaroca, is on the town side of the 'Bus Terminal' Square (*Tmr* B2) and another is close by the OTE (*Tmr* 36B/C4).

Clinic (*Tmr* 38D4/5) Located in a bland, new medical centre to the left of the main Filoti road out of Naxos Town, close to where the bypass branches off.

Dentists There are three listed, Bardanis (Tel 22317), Mamouzelos (Tel 22315) and Sofia Kritikou (Tel 23771). One Dental surgery is in the little cul-de-sac parallel to and west of Odhos Dionyssou (*Tmr* C4) (which may or may not be one of those whose telephone numbers I list).

Doctors Kastritsios (Tel 22308), Sofigitis (Tel 22302) and Venieris (Tel 22557). One Doctor's surgery (*Tmr* 15C4) is in the street that branches off Odhos Papavasilou, opposite 'Post Office' St, a turning flanked by a Credit Bank (*Tmr* 13C4) and *Katerina's Burger Shop* (*Tmr* 14C4). It is on the right and also may or may not be one of those whose telephone numbers I list!

OTE (*Tmr* 36B/C4) At the far end of Odhos Paralia, the Esplanade road, just before the *Hotel Ermis*. Despite being the largest island in the Cyclades, this office only opens weekdays between 0730-2200hrs and is closed weekends, 'high-days' and holidays.

PETROL One filling station is Esplanade sited, another at the outset of the Engares road and one on the ring road which stays open late evening, even on Sundays.

PLACES OF INTEREST

Cathedrals & Churches

The Church of Myrtidiotissa Possibly the first island church seen by a visitor, as the little chapel picturesquely sits on a tiny islet to one side of the Harbour.

There is a veritable clutch of churches as well as the Orthodox Cathedral to the north of the Old Quarter (*Tmr* C2).

The Catholic Cathedral (*Tmr* C3) A lovely building with a boldly domed roof in the rather small, claustrophobic Kastro Square. It is located at the centre of the old Kastro walls, breached at the old gateways, but is not very well signposted. It was originally built in the 13th century and 'restored' in the 16th/17th centuries. Recently it has been re-restored – back to the original!

The Kastro (*Tmr* C3) There is not a lot left and the only real evidence is the Venetian houses, many which possess heraldic devices, built into the old walls and forming a picturesque ring of medieval buildings. Within these is a beautiful area, a jumble of paved streets, an ancient cistern, the Catholic Cathedral, the Museum, the Palace of Sanudo and other attractive buildings.

Chora The Old Quarter is quite extensive, radiating out from the epicentre of the steep hilltop, Kastro, around which the lanes, alleys and arched walkways wind tortuously. Unlike Mykonos and Paros, the Old Quarter has not been 'tarted up' for the delectation of tourists. In fact, the Administration appears to actively discourage sightseeing by continuously digging up various lanes!

Museum It is rather tucked away but is reached by initially facing (*Sbo*) and then keeping round to the right of the Catholic Cathedral on the main Kastro walkway. Now open after some years of restoration, the exhibits include a collection of Cycladic idols and bead jewellery, Mycenean pottery and a Roman mosaic, as well as jewellery, pottery and sculptures.

Close by is the one-time French Ursuline Convent.

Temple Rather inescapable to ferry travellers as it prominently caps Palatia islet which the boats round. Not so much a temple, more a single gateway, reputably of the Temple of Apollo, which was probably started in the 5th Century BC. Frankly the site is a rather messy scatter of discarded, fallen lumps of masonry, set amongst heather clumps and once enclosed by a now trampled wire fence at the foot of which were the occasional, defunct floodlight.

POLICE (*Tmr* 39B/C1/2) The office is a minute or so walk from the 'Bus Terminal' Sq, close to the junction of Odhos Neofytou and the Engares road. They certainly are conspicuous by their absence, even on an election night, some years ago, with all the emotional build-up involved and the odd chap hurling the occasional stick of dynamite about – in the direction of a politically dissenting fellow citizen. On that exciting, tumultuous evening they were only to be observed simply putting in place the night-time signs barring Esplanade traffic.

POST OFFICE (*Tmr* 31C4/5) On the left-hand side of the major street, to the right (*Sbo*) of Odhos Papavasiliou and named, for convenience sake, 'Post Office' St.

TAXIS No particular rank as they are located at a number of strategic points throughout the town including the 'Bus Terminal Sq' (at the Ferry-boat Quay end of the Esplanade), in the area of the junction of the Esplanade road and Odhos Papavasiliou and in and around the package holiday end of town.

TELEPHONE NUMBERS & ADDRESSES

Clinic (*Tmr* 38D4/5)	Tel 22346
Police (*Tmr* 39B/C1/2)	Tel 22100
Taxis	Tel 22444

Note Doctors & Dentists phone numbers are detailed under **Medical Care, A To Z**.

TOILETS From Prantouna Sq (*Tmr* B2), ascend Odhos Prantouna for a few metres and on the left is a municipal facility including showers (hot water) and toilets. My notes simply read 'Richter scale 7'. Ugh! I'd better point out that for a 'pourboire' (or tip) the lavatory person ensures a better class of toilet compartment.

TRAVEL AGENTS & TOUR OFFICES *See* **Ferry-boat Ticket Offices & The Accommodation.**

Excursion (on foot) to Ag Prokopios & Ag Anna *See* **Ag Anna, Route Three**.

ROUTE ONE

To Apollonas via Galini & Abram (circa 30km) Possibly, one of the prettiest routes I have travelled, on any Greek island, with magnificent, majestic and stunning scenery, even if the outset is rather inauspicious.

The Galini/Engares road heads off from the north end of the Esplanade keeping left at the first fork, alongside the *Cafe-Bar Restaurant Elli*. The rough surfaced road rises quite steeply past high-rise apartments leaving the town ring road to the right. It it unfortunate that the 'Town Hall' does not forego the right to site the town's rubbish dump in such a way as to make a most unsightly mess and ensure the pollution of at least one bay. Well, there you go! From **Galini** (5km from Naxos Town) a dirt road leads off to the defunct **Monastery of Ypsilis**, once converted into a castle/church.

Beyond the villages of Galini and **Engares** (8km), the road is unsurfaced. On the left, a lovely valley runs down to a large, shingly beach foreshore with a bamboo bestrewn, shrub growing backshore. On the left (*Fsw*) is a narrow band of discontinuous small rocks in the extremely clear sea. The other side of the small headland bifurcating the (river) valley, is a pretty, small, very sandy beach. The backshore is cluttered with storm-tossed rubbish in amongst the sand dunes, all overlooked by a few unobtrusive houses built on the gentle hillsides.

The bay is followed by a tiny 'U' shaped cove with a large church alongside the road junction. The shore of this lovely location is shingle and the sea bottom consists of weed covered, small rocks. Beyond the bluff a larger bay marks the start of a rocky, low cliff edge stretching away in the distance.

The road cuts slightly inland passing over a bridge which spans a boulderous river-bed. The latter is attractively beflowered with oleanders and for much of the summer, runs with water. Upstream of the bridge is a small waterfall.

Just before the road cuts inland towards the Monastery of Faneromenis, there are two bays at **Pahia Ammos**. These have shingly foreshores, and a stony sea-bed with sand in places. There are a few dwellings around them and two tavernas, down separate tracks to the left. One of these is run by an elderly couple who have opened up the front room of their small holding, as a dining room, in order to earn a few extra drachmas from the tourists. Callers may be offered meat, pasta, kefalotiri, feta and wine by the farmer's wife, in a delightful situation on their tree and oleander lined verandah overlooking a pleasant fertile valley. The second one, which has opened up in competition, offers 'GRHHK Breakfast, Saλads, Wine, Home Made Cees-Soft, Drinks, Beer Cold 40M' (*sic*).

The route advances past the **Monastery of Faneromenis** (approx 14km from Naxos Town) on the left, but now no longer a working community, and beyond which is the 'donkey dropping' hamlet of:-

CHILIA VRYSSI (16km from Naxos Town) Here is a steep valley with a bay at the bottom and offshore an islet. A few small terraced vineyards adorn the slopes. A little further on a steep, rough track leads down to a lovely, small cove, unfortunately marred by a rather ugly building, at the bottom of a valley cleft. There is another, smaller offshore islet. Possibly undomesticated vines grow on the valley slopes, some of them in terraces. This is followed by a large cove, the land behind which is cultivated all the way down to the rocky foreshore. Beyond the large cove, on the right of the road, is the flower-decked *Country Taverna*.

Another kilometre or so along this marvellous, coast-hugging road, skirting the indented shoreline at a height, and a track leads down to:-

Abram Beach (20km from Naxos Town) In the summer-time the river of this agricultural valley is almost stagnant. On the left (*Fsw*) is a small chapel overlooking the pebble beach, with a sandy backshore. From this ascends (in the style of a large concrete steps) the:-

Pension Efthinios Tel 22997

Directions: As above.

Mama Athena, who presides over the business, has a small amount of English – enough to take a booking over the phone, as long as a caller is explicit. She is friendly and may well invite casual (but interested) callers in for a cup of Greek coffee, accompanied by a cold glass of water. The verandah is now bamboo covered, with modern sculptures gracing the edge and a built-in BBQ in one corner. A simple, old-fashioned room, costs between 1500drs and 2000drs, depending upon the time of year, but at the height of the season regulars are likely to occupy most of the available accommodation. An idyllic spot for the 'get away from it all – I know this little spot..'

On this section of the road to Apollonas the air is rich with the mellifluous sounds of goat-bells and the almost deafening, sawing of the grasshoppers. Three kilometres or so further along the stony, rough track and way down below is the small, shingle/kelpy cove of **Ag Theodoros** in a beautifully poetic setting. The track down is identified by a rusty, unreadable sign by a building.

Beyond Ag Theodoros, the road climbs into the mountains, with views on the left of wooded ravines, terraced vineyards on the higher slopes and the occasional house. In wintertime, some of these ravines must sport tremendous waterfalls.

AGIA (25km from Naxos Town) Another 'single donkey dropping' scattering of farmsteads, more a slight thickening out than a collection of buildings, adjacent to the **Monastery of Panaghias**. The location is again perfectly lovely, high on the mountainside overlooking a small indented bay in which are moored 2 or 3 fishing boats.

APOLLANAS (30km from Naxos Town) A once lovely, sleepy, archetypal island fishing boat port situated on a bay sheltered by high mountainsides. Unfortunately the place is fast becoming a resort in its own right, with vast amounts of building work taking place. Postcards from yesteryear show large areas of greenery between the buildings, especially the church, but these have now all but disappeared beneath whitewashed concrete. Apart from Excursion buses, that roll in and out during the daylight hours, an increasing number of holiday-makers and independent travellers overnight in the village.

The bay is split into two by a rocky projection, on which are built four changing rooms. To the right (*Fsw*), is the main, wide, shingly beach, with some kelp, stretching away to the far edge of the bay. The port and a small, sandy beach are to the left. Both beaches display 'Nudism Forbidden' signs and the sea is sparkingly clear.

The short, paved quayside of the port (most other streets being rough surfaced) is edged with shops, tavernas and restaurants, intermixed with and behind which are ***Rooms***. For instance, the last four taverna/restaurants prior to the fishing boat quay, have accommodation. Particularly recommended is *The Falcon*, for which ascend the steps from the harbour wall that finish up on a small plateia overlooking the sea. On this headland a French girl lets out a room with en suite bathroom, a fridge and balcony with views over the garden and the sea. In fact there is plenty of overnight accommodation with rooms to be found in most of the back streets. Double rooms cost 1600drs, on average. Hotels include the Class C *Aeolos* and the Class E *Aegeon, Atlantis* and *Kouros*, two of which border the main beach.

The *Kouros*, is one of the main beach hotels and advertises alongside the bus stop 'Good room every time hot showering', an attractive thought. It was being rebuilt in 1988 and when complete will be a multi-storey hotel. Despite this there is still only a track, down a muddy stream bed and across a marsh, to the *Kouros*. Rumour, just a rumour suggests this is because the couple who run the accommodation, though both from the island, weren't born and bred in Apollonas. Thus the locals refuse to vote a road... To the nearside of the *Kouros* is the large, canteen-like *Restaurant Marina's*. This was being enlarged in 1988.

Above the rock that divides the bay, is the path to the famous stone carved 'Kouros'. To the side of this track is the *The Old House* with double rooms to rent, sharing the bathroom. In addition to accommodation, the Old House offers metered telephone facilities between 0800-1200hrs and 1600-2100hrs. Opposite is a doo-hickey, hole-in-the-wall 'Local Supermarket'.

Further up the road, next to the pleasant, old school building, which is still in use, is the newly constructed *Hotel Aeolos*. The extent of the village is increasing, with several more buildings being built along this road.

Of the waterfront tavernas, the *Restaurant Paradise*, close to the bus stop, is run by Costas and his wife Kalopi, helped by their two metrios. It has been recommended, almost deified, by one reader. He (Richard), or more correctly his wife (Susan), was of the opinion that their pistachio here equalled one prepared at Psili Amos Beach, Patmos, in 1983. (Richard assured me that the management committee had not ceased to carry on about this particular Patmos pistachio since consumed. I wonder if Rosemary is related to Susan..?). A super pistachio for two, an excellent salad, bread and 2 kortaki retśina, all preceded by 2 ouzos, cost 1020drs.

The second waterfront taverna has 'gone trendy' and is now more a rock beat cocktail bar. The third along, *Nikos*, is reasonably priced. The fourth taverna, *Restaurant Fantasia*, is run by a nice, ordinary, elderly couple who also have ***Rooms*** available. A meal of two tasty omelettes, a Greek salad, bread and a half litre of retsina cost 452drs.

The mini-market is run by Costas who lived in Camden Town, London for a time and he not only helps with information but runs a second-hand book trade. Additional shopping facilities include a kiosk devoted solely to toiletries, on the waterfront, just beyond the 'mini-market'.

It is worth bearing in mind that until comparatively recent times Apollonas was rather remote and inaccessible and the inhabitants relaxed, 'laid-back' attitude reflects this one-time isolation. For instance, the eating places quite often run out of this or that without being unduly concerned and it is necessary to accept what is on offer.

At the end of the quay, around to the left, an area has been surfaced on which the Excursion buses park. At the far side, is a toilet block, an eye-watering, 'Richter scale 10' little facility.

When the day tourists have all departed the locals occasionally stage a football match on the beach.

Hotels, which all have en suite bathrooms, include the:- *Aeolos* (Class C, tel 81388) with a single room priced at 1600drs & a double 2000drs; *Atlantis* (Class E, tel 81203), where a single room is priced at 950drs & a double 1430drs, increasing to 1200drs & 1800drs (1st July-31st Aug) and *Kouros* (Class E, tel 81340) which only has double rooms costing 1700drs, rising to 2000/2500drs (1st July-31st Aug).

A short way off the main road route to Naxos Town (via Filoti) is signposted the **Kouros of Apollonas**. This remarkable but abandoned, incomplete marble figure was sculptured in about 650 BC and was probably destined for Delos island. It is approximately 10½m in height and lies in a long deserted quarry. Close by, opposite the quarry entrance, are the remains of the Venetian Fort of Kalogeros which either gave its name to the north-eastern region or (surprise, surprise) vice-versa.

ROUTE TWO

To Apollonas via Galanado, Chalki, Filoti & Apirathos (54km) The first section of the main road route to Apollonas is unremarkable, passing through agricultural countryside all the way to the lower slopes of the central mountain range. The foothills commence after about 8km, close by the 8th century Ag Mamas Church. This is down a path to the left and was once the Cathedral of Naxos, possessing some remarkable 7th century icons. The road gently ascends to the hamlets of:-

SANGRI (10km from Naxos Town) Kato Sangri possesses the remains of a Venetian castle whilst **Ano Sangri** boasts the **Monastery of Ag Eleftherios**. This latter became a *Krifo Scholio*, a secret school for Greek children, during the Turkish occupation, and now houses a Folk Museum. There is also an ancient archaeological site and beyond, still on the main Chalki road, the 16th century **Monastery of Timiou Stavrou** as well as the 14th/15th century Church of Kaloritsa, which possesses a number of original frescoes.

Detour to Ormos Agiassos(Circa 10km) Prior to **Timiou Stavrou Monastery**, a dirt road heads due south to end up on the shores of Agiassos Bay, with Panaghia Gialous Church almost in the centre of the beach. Here, as elsewhere at other out-of-the-way Naxos locations, there is a (overseas) Holiday Bungalows development – to the right of the bay (*Fsw*). There is no doubt it is off the beaten track. Any further south would necessitate an amphibious outfit. Pyrgaki is around a bluff to the right, but only accessible on foot, to the very brave and the arid slopes of Mt Viglarouri blocks off travel to the left.

Returning to the main route, from the 'Sangri's' the road passes through **Vourvouria** to:-
CHALKI (Chalkio) (16m from Naxos Town) This pretty village is at a high altitude, set down on a great plain of very old olive trees. On the Filoti side of the village both bread and petrol are available. There are a number of fortified tower-houses, including the outstanding Pirgos Frangopoulou.

Encircling Chalki are a number of hamlets and interesting locations including, from the north-west in an anticlockwise direction, Apano Kastro – a Venetian Castle; Tsikalario (Tsingalario) – ancient monuments; towards Damarionas – the 12th century Church of Panaghia Protothroni, which possesses some restored frescoes; Kaloxylos – the highly rated Church of Ag Trias, and towards Moni, the 8th century Church of Drossiani, from whence some of the frescoes have been removed to Athens for 'safe keeping'.

From the enchanted olive tree forests of the Plain of Tragea, this route becomes truly dramatic with the craggy, towering mountains dwarfing the surrounding countryside and providing tremendous vistas. Still climbing, the road passes through the largest village of the island:-

FILOTI (19km from Naxos Town) This unremarkable settlement is situated well up on the flank of Mt Zas.

At about 22km from Naxos Town, a right-hand fork advances to:-
DANAKOS (24km from Naxos Town) Known for the fast flowing streams, which in years gone by powered a number of waterwheels, but famous for the Byzantine sculptures at the **Monastery of Fotodoti**, which is above the village, to the north.

APIRATHOS (Apeiranthos) (27km from Naxos Town) This settlement is quite pretty and was supposed to have originally been settled by Cretans.

Detour to Moutsouna(12km) To the right, a badly potholed, winding road dramatically snakes and plunges down through the dry, broom and sage growing mountainside. In the middle distance are the islands of **Makares** and, behind them, Donoussa set in the sparkling cobalt sea. To the right, a dry river-bed gorge, overflowing with oleanders, plunges all the way to:-

MOUTSOUNA (39km from Naxos Town) As with the other eastern coastal village of Lionas, the *raison d'etre* is, or more correctly was, the quarrying of emery. The stone was bucketed down aerial cable-ways from the workings riddling the surrounding mountainsides to the surprisingly massive works and docking quays, for outbound shipment.

The village is 'one-eyed' with a scruffy taverna to the left of the approach road. Beyond, on the waterside, are some deserted warehouses and workings as well as two small tramp steamer quays (between which is a 'tablecloth' sized beach). Further on, to the right is a small, sandy, shingle beach set in rocks.

Prior to Moutsouna, while still on the downward slope, and through a gateway to the left, a track makes across the neck of the headland to a large beach with groves of trees at either end.

From Moutsouna 'a detour on a detour' is to take the track due south, which edges the coastline for some 14km. This jaunt is not for the faint-hearted, nor for those who like there to be a definite goal to any trip.

In the first kilometre, there are three small coves varying from pebble to fine shingle then, *en route*, a gate, yes a five bar gate, similar to those that shut off English fields, followed by various small coves. The wide track jolts on, with rocky coast to the left and mountain foothills to the right.

The surrounds become sandy dunes with much moorland gorse on the approach to:-

PSILI AMMOS (47km from Naxos Town) A spread-out agricultural backyard through which the road bends and in which a surprising amount of private house development is taking place. This is despite there not being an apparent focal point or, for that matter, any visible trade being carried out. Beyond the hamlet is a big, sand dune backed beach.

From hereon the surface of the track becomes rougher and the width narrower, passing the occasionally lovely cove here and there, until the coastline proceeds to curve around Cape Panormos. Here the track becomes decidedly rough in patches, struggling on to decant and run out in the lovely fastness of the small cove and beach of **Panormos**. A church, a dwelling house, a fishing caique often moored and nothing else. Additionally, whatever is written, maps may detail or a reader is told, this is the end of the road. Any further progress must be made on foot.

Returning to the main route at Apirathos, another 5km to the north is the:-

Detour to Kourounchori (19km) Turning to the left heads westwards on an unsurfaced, road which proceeds through **Sifones**, past a 'T' junction connection to **Moni** and on to:-

KINIDAROS (16km from Naxos Town) A very 'backyard' village to the north of which the Church of Ag Artemios is built on or over the remains of a Temple to Diana.

Beyond Kinidaros, prior to the hamlet of Miloi, and to the left, is the area known as:-

FLERIO (9km from Naxos Town) Here are ancient marble quarries and another Kouros. This is a later sculpting than the Apollonas Kouros and a mere 6.40m in height. Close by this Kouros is a most delectable garden with a minute restaurant – if that is not too grand a word for it. A little old lady and her son tend a very small shed and some 3 tables under a vine trailing trellis, surrounded by roses, hollyhocks, margarites, snapdragons et al, as well as a cistern with goldfish – a veritable garden of delights. The old lady is sweet (but businesslike) and can produce beer, ouzo, retsina and simple mezes.

Miloi is followed by the village of **Kourounochori** (8km from Naxos Town) where are the remains of a Venetian castle. From Kourounochori there is a choice of routes via Engares or the village of **Ag Thaleleos**, which has a 13th century church of the same name.

Back on the main route, once again, and the next village on the road to Apollonas is:-

KORONOS (36km from Naxos Town) A 'stepped' town scrabbling up the mountain sides and renowned for its emery mines. A turning off to the right ½km prior to Koronos, proceeds east to the village and Church of Argokiliotissa which, on Easter Friday, plays host to hordes of worshippers.

Detour to Lionas (8km) From Koronos a branch road to the right initially describes large loops, which increasingly tighten up, descending steeply down the mountainside past evidence of extensive quarrying, to the erstwhile port of:-

LIONAS (44km from Naxos Town) An oleander planted river-bed passes two now 'dead' tavernas at the outset of the village, which is set in a steep sided gorge. The immediate, central area is simply waste ground with the remnants of very large, old houses dotted about. A number of new, more humble dwellings are built into both sides of the gorge. The beach at the bottom of the bay is made up of large pebbles washed over by the startlingly clear sea-water. This rather strange place does not go out of its way to encourage the casual visitor.

Returning to Koronos, the main route proceeds through the 'one donkey-dropping' village of **Skado** from whence an unmade track also connects with the coastal village of Lionos BUT it does not join up with the surfaced road from Koronos, so beware!

KORONIDA (Komiaka) (43km from Naxos Town) Part of the road through Koronida becomes a rough track and the village is noted, if for nothing else, for being the island village built at the highest altitude, some 700m. Not unnaturally there are splendid view more especially as the mountains fall rapidly away to the coastal plain and Apollonas. It may be of interest that Koronida, and the surrounding hamlets, are renowned for their wine and, it is said, Klephtic folk songs dating back to the Turkish occupation.

The surrounding countryside is particularly lush and lovely, the road being shaded by bowers of trees and cleft by mountain streams. Apart from the distractions of the view, it is necessary for travellers to keep their wits about them as, about halfway down the steep descent, the road unexpectedly reverts to rough track, for a stretch. Nasty.

ROUTE THREE

To Pyrgaki via Glinado, Vivlos (Tripodes) (21½km) or a walk to Ag Anna via Ag Prokopios (1½hrs) The first part of the vehicle route, in the direction of Galanado, is as described under **Route Two**. Incidentally, whilst describing that route I did not draw attention to the large area of land bounded by the sea and the prominent rock headland known as Stelida and Livadi. Once an area of salt flats or 'Alikes', the flat land is intensively farmed, with bamboo fences dividing up the small individual plots of land. After 5½km, the right-hand turning should be followed for the:-

Detour to Ag Anna (6½km) On the approaches to **Glinado** (6km from Naxos Town) is the 17th century **Monastery Ag Saranta** possessing some fine post-Byzantine icons. A few kilometres on is **Ag Arsenios** (8km from Naxos Town). The friendly inhabitants of this small village make up for any difficulties experienced in negotiating the approach. This is through extensively cultivated land, over a rough, narrow track, tightly hemmed in by bamboo 'hedgerows' through which it seems unlikely that a bus could negotiate – but it does.

AG ANNA (12km from Naxos Town) Both sides of the lane are being built on prior to widening out and spilling on to the sandy, rather bedraggled, narrow waterfront. There is a large quay alongside which a converted but decrepit, listing and possibly abandoned landing craft is berthed. Flanking the access road,where the bus pulls up, are two 'lived-in' tavernas. The bearded proprietor of the left-hand (*Fsw*) establishment, also owns the:-

Hotel Anna (Class C)

Directions: To the rear of the cafe restaurant.

This accommodation is surprisingly smart. Double rooms with en suite bathroom are priced at 1925drs, rising to 2540drs (1st July-15th Sept). The garden, which the owner proudly encompasses with an expansive wave of the hand, is now formally laid out with paths and flower beds.

During the summer there is a caique service from Naxos Town to Ag Anna, departing Naxos on the hour, between 1000hrs and 1900hrs, returning from Ag Anna on the half-hour. The fare is 150drs. The **Skopelitis** 'claims' to run occasionally between Ag Anna and Piso Livadi(Paros), but this has not been confirmed.

The curving, narrow, sandy foreshore, which doubles up as an 'Esplanade', stretches away to the right of the quay, all the way to Ag Prokopios.

To the left (*Fsw*) of the quay the bay curves quite sharply around to a low headland hill, topped by a small chapel. This almost creates a lagoon, the beach of which is sandy, if messy. Continuing to the left along the sandy track, over the base of the small dune headland, spills on to the north end of a great, sweeping sandy beach backed by tufted sand dunes in which are set clumps of low trees and gorse. In the lee of the chapel headland, amongst the dunes thickly planted with marine pines, and scattered along the beach backshore is a certain amount of 'wild' camping. The conveniently located, if provincial *Taverna Paradiso*, with a tree shaded patio, is well patronised by all and sundry. At the rear of the establishment are some old fashioned showers and toilets, which are put to extensive use, especially by the campers. The occasional summer months bar 'sets up shop' along the beach track and there is at least one licensed, reasonably well appointed campsite with satisfactory showers/toilet block.

Effectively the beach stretches all the way from Ag Prokopios, in the north, as far as Pyrgaki, in the south-west, with the occasional headland protruding into the Aegean, forming great bays sprinkled with a few coves.

To Ag Prokopios & Ag Anna from Naxos Town on foot (1½hrs) This is an easy walk – it can almost be done barefoot throughout – which an increasing number of sun and sea worshippers seem to be undertaking. The route follows the beach round Ag Georgios Bay, past *Flisvos Bar* (Day Club), where the signposted track for *Camping Naxos* heads away from the beach. Further round the bay is a 'bit of track', a few metres from the sea, which heads over the little spit of land to the next bay. The track is now simply the narrow, sandy 'beach' of this (next) bay, which is more of a lagoon, protected by a submerged reef or sand bar across its wide mouth. In calm weather this becomes almost stagnant water, not recommended for bathing. However the sand dunes above the strip of soft sand provide superb sun-traps, particularly if the meltemi is in evidence.

Beyond the lagoon, the path joins the 'proper' road to Ag Prokopios. This is on a causeway above the salt flats, which bypasses Camping Naxos and the airport site, half a mile or so to the left. A little way to the right, the dirt road (which is a bus route in summer) turns to the left, away from the sea, round the corner of the salt flat. If this is not under water (and frequented by interesting wading birds rather than tourists) there's a hundred metre short-cut across the corner, starting at about where the lagoon path joins the road. Note that straight on leads to where they are quarrying rock for the airport runway. Although there appears to be some holiday development in that direction, and there is a stony beach over the next headland, it is currently a militarily forbidden area.

Within a couple of hundred yards the road passes the large:-

Camping Apollon Situated on a small hill, 3km from Naxos Town and 800m away from the beach. The campsite, which opened in July 1988, is very large and has many facilities. These include four clean sanitary blocks; a mini-market; cooking places; a travel office; spacious lots to pitch a tent beneath wooden roofs providing plenty of shade; a self-service restaurant, with cheap but good food; a free camp bus service to Naxos and back, several times a day and coinciding with ferry-boat arrivals, and a lack of mosquitoes! Prices per person are 300drs and 150drs for a tent.

Beyond the campsite, the road climbs, for about ½ kilometre beside farm fields to a crest, below which lies:-

AG PROKOPIOS The descent passes several ***Rooms*** and there are a couple of single storey blocks on the right, end on to the road. The second of these has stone tables built into the sea-facing verandah. Their double rooms cost 1500drs, with a private bathroom, whilst those at the back, with no verandah or sea view, cost 1000drs, again with a private bathroom. Some of the bathrooms are of an 'interesting nature', registering a good 8 on the Richter scale.

Further down, round the bend, and on the left is the older *Hotel Sophia* (Class E, tel 23982) with nice gardens and a sea-facing verandah. Rooms here cost from 1500drs with shared bathroom and shared use of the kitchen. The first taverna on the left, has a periptero outside from which international calls can be made. The second taverna on the left is called *Hideaway*, and one on the right advertises 'Greek cooking' (what do the others serve, one wonders?). Where the road finally reaches the beach there is a taverna on either side. The one on the left (*Fsw*) looks decidedly dead. The beach is a lovely sweep of coarse whitish sand set in a circular bay round to the right. As it is noticeably shelving and faces southwards, it is quite sheltered from the meltemi, and good swimming is to be had in the clear water, untroubled by fine sand.

To the left, the narrow track continues along a low cliff towards Ag Anna, past newly constructed blocks of rooms, a couple of small tavernas and the makings of a disco. The sweep of Ag Prokopios sand ends in an untidy, stone and sand beach. An outcrop of rock marks the start of the finer sand of Ag Anna beach stretching all the way to that settlement's quay. The track bends away from the beach for a few metres, behind some of the many new buildings being thrown up, before returning to form a 'Beach Esplanade' in front of the shack-like buildings, which include a supermarket, a few tavernas and the Santa Anna Travel Agency, although this latter appeared closed for some of 1988.

Returning to the main road route to Pyrgaki, from Ag Arsenios the road rolls over the gently sloping countryside to:-

VIVLOS (or Tripodes) (9km from Naxos Town) The question of the totally disparate names is all to do with the change in the agricultural emphasis of the village. The modern name, for the now thriving agricultural community is Tripodes, but the old name stubbornly refuses to 'lie down and die', despite dating back to the days when the village was famed for its wine.

Prior to the village, signposts invitingly lure the unwary voyager to turn right towards the **Plaka Beach**. The thought is indeed beguiling but resist the temptation. If the siren calls cannot be resisted... take a right fork from the heights of Vivlos. This joins the detour to the broad, intensively worked agricultural plain which opens out below, bounded by a rocky outcrop to the right. Also to the right are the remains of a medieval tower and the Church of Ag Mattheos, built on earlier Christian ruins. In the distance is the shimmering outline of Paros island. A ridged, concrete path descends to the plain where an adventurer's problems really start. The landscape is criss-crossed with boulderous and rutted tracks, most of which are hemmed in by high bamboos and thick vegetation, blocking out any possible sight of and clue how to reach the sea. Every so often a donkey, its load and owner pops out from this or that 'tunnel' with a friendly 'Yassas', only to disappear as suddenly. Best to approach this beach from the Ag Anna end, don't you know!

From Vivlos, after some 15km, is a signpost to:-

CAPE MIKRI VIGLA (18km from Naxos Town) The track wanders along to the coast through a farmstead, the backs of various dwellings and fenced fields.

The way forks with the right-hand turning advancing towards the north of the cape. A once deserted, small, coarse sand beach, is cradled in the curve of the land bounded by upwards sweeping dunes and the turquoise sea. The beach is now backed by an 'imaginative' development. Admittedly the concept appears highly professional, tasteful and up-market, but none-the-less...

The gently ascending, gorse growing and spring-turf moorland that rises to the lighthouse topped cape, sprouts a monstrously large taverna plonked down to the left of the beach, but that's progress, isn't it? Interestingly enough, the area is obviously on an established goat and sheep herd walk. Besides the taverna is a water well with a sign, in English, 'This water is drinking. Please keep clean'. Some hope. These Cycladean wells are interesting in that, instead of the more usual raised stonework of the neck, the top is almost flush with the ground and surrounded by a low walled catchment area. Part of this is compartmented off to keep an open drinking trough topped up, with the rest of any overflow channelled back into the well.

South of the large headland of Mikri Vigla leads to the top end of a magnificent, huge, coarse sand sea-shore that sweeps all the way past Kastraki as far as Alyko. Some tar is in evidence and part of the shallow sea-bed is made up of horizontal slabs of biscuit rock. There is a small taverna conveniently tucked into the lee of the rocky headland.

KASTRAKI (17km from Naxos Town) This hamlet edges the large beach described above and on the shore of which is plonked down, almost in the middle of nowhere, the rather 'doo-hickey' *Zorbas Taverna*. This provides a focal point of fun, lust – no hush my mouth, drinking, eating and basic accommodation at inexpensive prices.

ALYKO (19km from Naxos Town) En route, the road passes by large inland lagoons beyond which is some chalet development. Perhaps the most surprising site (and sight) is at a fork in the road, at about 20km. More correctly after a short drive along a right-hand turn, the surfaced road of which sweeps through a forlorn gate and collapsed gatepost on to a large, sand-duned headland. Over this is spread an enormous, unfinished, deserted development which basks in the sun overlooking a lovely cove and the sea to the south of the cape. Possibly this massive dream was embarked on during the Colonels regime, for locals reckon it demised some 19 years ago. Worth a visit if only to view a magnificent folly, now only accommodating lizards and other lowly life forms.

The main road edges the rocky coastline which is broken up by three coves, the first two pebbly, the last smaller but sandy.

PYRGAKI (21½km from Naxos Town) This is more a map place name than a settlement. Despite this, there is a very smart, multi-cellular, elaborate holiday complex set into the sloping, arid hillside. Occasionally swashbuckling inmates of this European 'fat-cats' development brave the elements and wander the ½km back up the road to a 'saving-grace', small, simple, roadside taverna. This 'Alice-Springs' watering hole serves basic drinks and meals, set in a tree-shaded yard across from the sea. Super!

Pension Koufoupoulos (Tel 23365/22249) is along a track, about 500m beyond the taverna. The owner (of the same name) is a personable young man, fascinated by all aspects of foreign espionage! Some double rooms are equipped with a kitchenette, dining table, chairs, fridge, all manner of cutlery and crockery and en suite bathroom facilities, as well as a balcony. A superbly decorated and equipped establishment with an out of season room rate of 2000drs per night.

To expand on the three coves, the first, at the Alyko end, has large pebbles and is somewhat rocky. Across the road is a swamp. The second cove is pebbly with rocks some 50m out to sea. The third, in the shadow of the referred to complex, is beautiful but shadeless sand. The whole bay of this sun drenched corner has clear and clean sea and, despite the close proximity of 'development on the hill', there are more often than not few, if any, people on the beach.

As one reader suggested, why not bus here and walk back to town? Well it cuts down on drinking time, that's why not.

Pyrgaki is a nice note on which to end the description of this still lovely island.

The pass-boat connection, Sikinos. *Ackowledgement to David & Liz Drummond-Tyler.*

Naxos Town. *Acknowledgement to David & Liz Drummond-Tyler.*

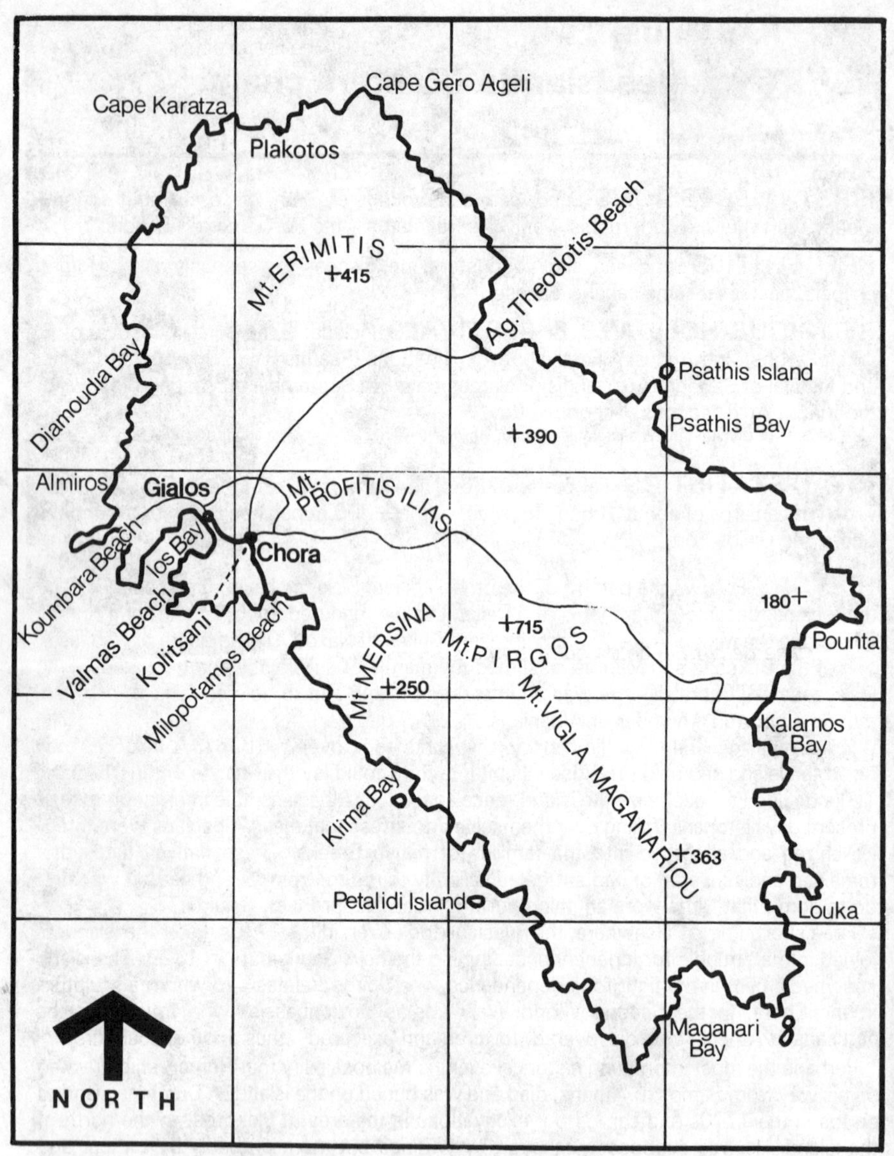

Illustration 17 Ios island

7 IOS (Nios)

The young in heart ★★★★★
The rest of us ★★★

Cyclades Islands - Eastern chain

FIRST IMPRESSIONS Sand, sea, sun, youngsters, fun, discos (almost synonymous aren't they?); wind; rubbish; only 3 settlements – the Port, Chora & Beach.

SPECIALITIES Sand, sea, sun, youngsters, fun, discos – (no seriously folks); Homer; chapels; pasteli (sesame cake) & cheese.

RELIGIOUS HOLIDAYS & FESTIVALS include: 22nd June – Festival of St John, Pyrgos; 2nd August – Festival of Ag Theodotis, Psathis Bay; 29th August – Feast and festival of St John (Ag Yiannis), Kalamos Bay; 8th September – Feast and festival of the Virgin, Ag Theodotis, Theodotis Bay.

NB it has to be admitted that the information about which panayieri is where, when and to whom is very confusing.

VITAL STATISTICS Tel prefix 0286. The island is 18km in length, up to 10km wide with an area of about 105sq km. Most of the 1,300 population live in or around the Chora and Gialos Port.

HISTORY Follows the pattern of the other, adjacent islands having been colonised by the Ionians; became a member of the Delian League; endured Egyptian and then Roman rule and,in the Middle Ages, the omnipresent Dukes of Naxos. On the death of Nicolas II, one of the Dukes, a son Marcos, assumed the mantle of suzeraintiy and built a now long lost castle on 'Chora Hill'. He was an interesting fellow and to bolster the lack of native muscle, imported a number of Albanians.

In line with general Cycladic history, the Turks took over in 1536/37. In 1558 they razed the island and sold off those inhabitants they could lay their hands on. In 1579 the Turks decided to recolonize the island, once again with Albanians. It is interesting to read present day historians 'falling over themselves' to stress that these Albanians were totally Hellenized and absorbed into the families of native Greeks. These natives had either remained undiscovered or had struggled valiantly to return, from far and near. It wouldn't do to admit that Niots were anything but the 'true-blue' product, would it?

For a short time, as elsewhere, the Russians took over, in the 1770s. Later the islanders joined in the struggle for Independence, joining the new Greek state in 1829. The island spawned a hero in the fight for independence, one Spiros Valetas – to whom a sculpture in the Chora. In the Second World War, Kostas Bouloubassis, who fought for the partisans in Athens, was discovered, tortured and executed – thus another sculpture.

Perhaps the most interesting historical event is the possibility that Homer, shipwrecked on his way from Samos to Athens, died and was buried on the island. A Dutchman landed on Ios in the 1770s and carried out excavations in the area of Plakotos, to the north of the island. He was supposedly inspired by writings but more probably by rumour and legend. Perhaps in mind of the tourist trade to come, he supposedly found Homers grave, even down to a detailed inscription. Strangely the original headstone disappeared but perhaps our Dutchman dug up another tomb? Additionally the exact location, as described by various authorities, is the subject of some doubt. I must own up to not having made the pilgrimage so have to rely on others for the details. Some relate that it is in and around Mt Pirgos but I am fairly certain the site is on the northern slope of Mt Erimitis, where a commemorative engraved stone has been erected. Interestingly it is postulated that the coast at Plakotos marks the spot of an ancient city, long ago engulfed by the sea.

To the present-day visitor it may well seem unbelievable that an earthquake, in 1951, caused Gialos Port to be totally devastated. In fact there was every chance that the island would become deserted. Fortunately the lure of prosperity held the natives rooted to the spot as the trickle of overseas visitors, that started in the 1960s, became a deluge. It is interesting to contemplate that, in the 1970s, most passengers had to be taken on and off the ferry-boats by caique (as they still have to be, to this day, on neighbouring Sikinos). Even up until 1979/80 only one or two passenger boats docked each week.

GENERAL The Ios of the 1960s 'flower-power' generation graduated through the 'great unwashed' of the 1970s to emerge, in the 1980s, still as a young peoples island, but that of the clean-cut, solid-limbed, college students. On the other hand... Residents have recently expressed much disquiet about drugs, drunkenness, litter and thieving, more especially in and around the young and penniless.

The original dirt track from Gialos Port to Milopotamos Beach, via the Chora, may have made way for a dusty but surfaced road; the bus may now turn round at Milopotamos Beach on a concrete pad, rather than duck-boards; the majority of beach sleepers may have been herded into official campsites, but the bedrock of a young peoples paradise remains. Admittedly Gialos is better organised (and has expanded a little); the Chora has spread across the road from the Old Town and the buildings at Milopotamos Beach have increased, a little. But what could ruin the magnificent sweep of this great sandy bay? Mosquitoes and rubbish may be an irritant but for the young hedonist the day-time lazing on this sun drenched shore, the early evening animation of cafe-bar conversation and the frenzy of dusk to dawn disco dancing in the Chora still proves an undiminished magnet. It is intriguing that, despite the worldly-wise nature of much of the holiday-makers' delights, there remains a charmingly naive quality to the atmosphere.

The older generations (those over 30 years of age!), perhaps seeking less active diversions, can rest assured that there are other, almost deserted, locations than those referred to above. Added to which, even Milopotamos and its environs become almost deserted once the first ear-splitting crescendo of the discos' strangled beat echoes through the narrow alleys and lanes of the Chora.

Ios is not only for the fledgling adult, with sex, sun, and souvlaki, in any order. The young in heart may well find the place irresistibly, excitingly attractive and the more mature traveller need not stay away and miss the undoubted charms of this sparse but lovely island. An added advantage is that years of holiday-making by the impecunious British has held prices down – to such an extent that Ios is noticeably one of the least costly of the popular Cyclades islands. Note I write 'popular', for the less visited islands of, say, Amorgos and Sikinos are even more reasonably priced.

GIALOS (Ormos Iou): the port (Illustration 18) There are a number of Greek island ports at which arrival by ferry is even more exciting than usual, forever remaining a magical moment. These include, at random, Vathi (Ithaca), Simi, Astipalaia, Siphnos and Ios.

Incoming boats thrust through the horns of land that almost pinch off the harbour bay. The neck of the entrance bends round to the right, and on the elbow, there is the small, pretty Byzantine Church of Ag Irinis perched on a rocky outcrop. This church is proclaimed as a classic example of its genre. The sturdy bell tower is pierced by the characteristic, elongated, curved arches; the quintessential domed roof is topped off with a small cross and the cupola is pierced by thin plates of horizontal rock forming steps. Incidentally the latter imbue it with the appearance of a Second World War sea mine.

High above the Port, the white cubes of the Chora peep out from around the sides of its hilltop fastness.

As in other Ios matters even the name of the port is in some doubt. Certainly Gialos appears rather disembodied and disjointed, which is not so surprising considering, that

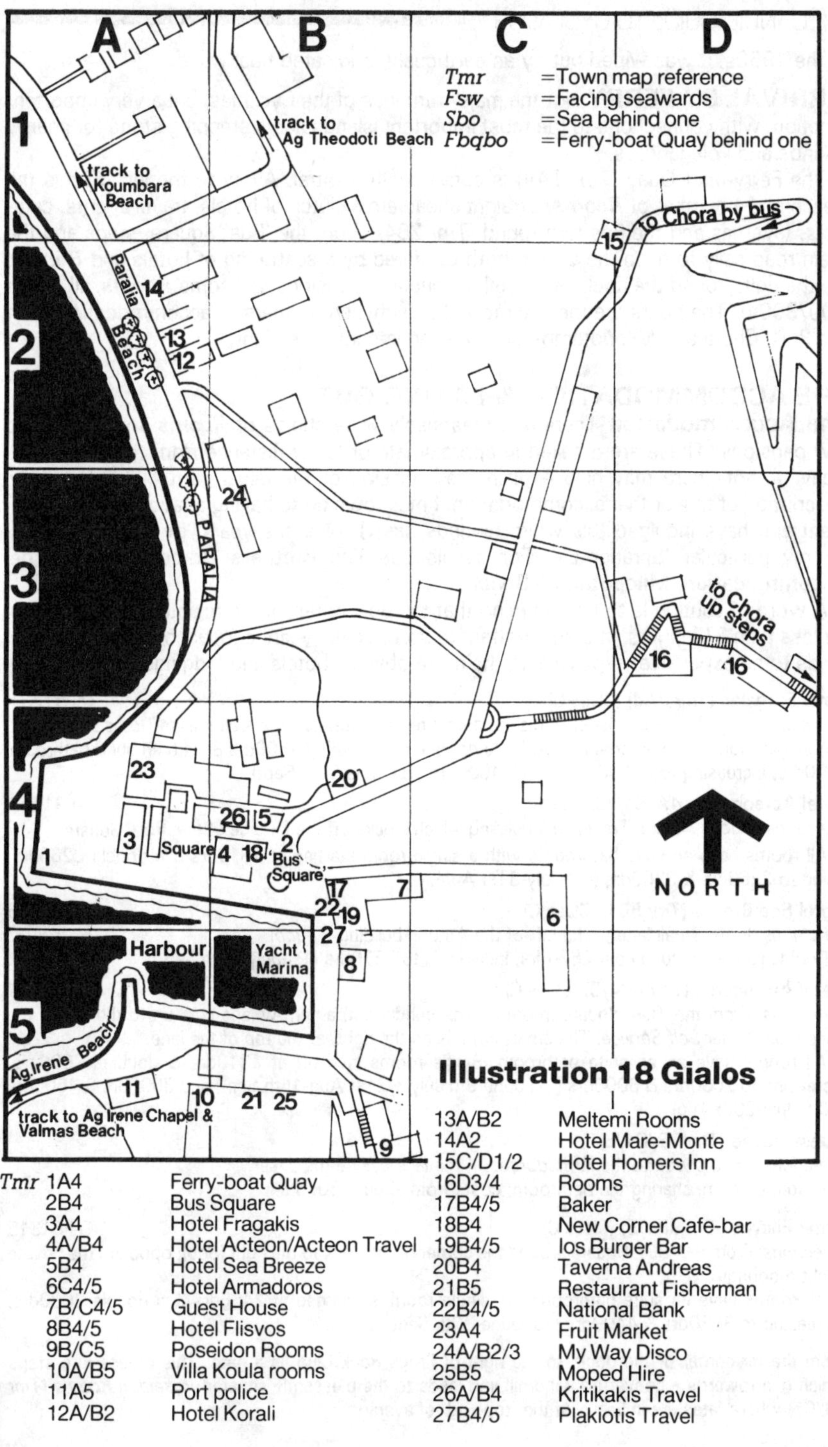

Illustration 18 Gialos

Tmr			
1A4	Ferry-boat Quay	13A/B2	Meltemi Rooms
2B4	Bus Square	14A2	Hotel Mare-Monte
3A4	Hotel Fragakis	15C/D1/2	Hotel Homers Inn
4A/B4	Hotel Acteon/Acteon Travel	16D3/4	Rooms
5B4	Hotel Sea Breeze	17B4/5	Baker
6C4/5	Hotel Armadoros	18B4	New Corner Cafe-bar
7B/C4/5	Guest House	19B4/5	Ios Burger Bar
8B4/5	Hotel Flisvos	20B4	Taverna Andreas
9B/C5	Poseidon Rooms	21B5	Restaurant Fisherman
10A/B5	Villa Koula rooms	22B4/5	National Bank
11A5	Port police	23A4	Fruit Market
12A/B2	Hotel Korali	24A/B2/3	My Way Disco
		25B5	Moped Hire
		26A/B4	Kritikakis Travel
		27B4/5	Plakiotis Travel

in the 1950s, it was wiped out by an earthquake originated tidal wave.

ARRIVAL BY FERRY Not the major terminus of the Cyclades, but a very important junction, with connections to the most important islands and a stepping stone for nearby Sikinos and Folegandros.

The Ferry-boat Quay (*Tmr* 1A4) is conveniently central. Away to the left (*Sbo* is the beach and a number of ***Rooms***. Straight ahead are a clutch of hotels, travel agents, cafe-bars, tavernas and the Bus turn-round (*Tmr* 2B4). From the 'Bus' Square, steps and the main road sally forth to the Chora, both bordered by a scattering of hotels and ***Rooms***. To the right, round the dock, is a hotel, a couple of pensions and some ***Rooms***, all within 200/300m. The boats are met by more than sufficient owners of accommodation from the Port, Chora and Milopotamos Beach, even late into the night.

THE ACCOMMODATION & EATING OUT

The Accommodation There is a reasonably wide choice of ***Rooms*** and hotels but few pensions. These are detailed in approximate order of distance from the Ferry-boat Quay. A note here may help explain the omission of the usual garrulous and wordy description of this or that accommodation. I must own up to having a favourite establishment and have indulged this whim (sounds nasty), over the years, by simply heading for my particular 'Shrangri-La'. For details *See* **The Brothers Draco Pension, The Accommodation, Milopotamos Beach**.

A word of caution is to bear in mind that the port hoteliers are reluctant to let a room for less than 2/3 nights. In stark contrast to six or seven years ago, accommodation here tends to be expensive, especially at the more obvious hotels and lodgings.

Hotel Fragakis (*Tmr* 3A4) (Class C) Tel 91231
Directions: In the building closest to disembarking ferry-boat passengers,alongside *Doras Bar*.

A single room en suite, costs 1600drs, a double room sharing 1500drs & with en suite bathroom 2000drs, increasing to 3200drs & 2500/4000drs (1st June-30th Sept).

Hotel Acteon (*Tmr* 4A/B4) (Class D) Tel 91207
Directions: Above Acteon Travel, in a building which blocks off the far side of the 'Port' Square.

All rooms have en suite bathrooms with a single room starting at 1810drs & a double 2260drs, rising to 2260drs & 3250drs (1st July-31st Aug).

Hotel Sea Breeze (*Tmr* 5B4) (Class C) Tel 91285
Directions: In the small lane to the left of the Acteon building (*Fbqbo*).

Double rooms en suite cost 2620drs, increasing to 3570drs (1st July-30th Sept).

Hotel Armadoros (*Tmr* 6C4/5) (Class C) Tel 91201
Directions: From the 'Bus' Square (more a mini-roundabout) a narrow lane cuts up to the left of the garish *Ios Burger Self Service*. The smart hotel is on the right, at the top of the lane.

All rooms have an en suite bathroom. Single rooms kick off at 1310drs & doubles 2000drs, increasing to 2000drs & 3000drs (1st June-9th July & 21st Aug-15th Sept) and 3000drs & 4500drs (10th July-20th Aug).

Guest House (*Tmr* 7B/C4/5)
Directions: On the way to the *Armadoros*, on the lane beside the baker.

A double room, sharing the bathroom, costs from about 1500drs.

Hotel Flisvos (*Tmr* 8B4/5) (Class C) Tel 91315
Directions: From the 'Bus' Square around the corner of the dock to the right (*Sbo*), opposite the private yacht moorings.

All rooms have en suite bathrooms. A single room is charged at 2465drs & a double 2080drs, increasing to 3520drs & 4400drs (1st June-30th Sept).

From the far corner of the dock, to the right of Frogs Rock Club, is a path. This breaks into steps which rise towards a converted windmill and leads to the pleasantly situated *Poseidon Rooms* (*Tmr* 9B/C5) where rates are in line with the 'top end' of average.

Further on round the dock, on the other side from the Ferry-boat Quay and behind *Skipper's Bar*, is:-
Villa Koula Rooms (*Tmr* 10A/B5)
Directions: As above.

Despite being a high season *Sun Med* slot, Koula, the extremely pleasant, accommodating (sorry) landlady still has room at the inn. And she will consider 'one night stands' (whoops – its not that sort of place!). The most acceptable double rooms, complete with wardrobes, have somewhat smelly en suite bathrooms, wherein the toilet header tank takes hours (yes, hours) to fill. Rates vary from about 1500drs, out of season, to 3000drs at the height of summer. In addition to Koula's niceness, this is a quiet location.

Back at the Ferry-boat Quay and away to the left (*Sbo*) is the Port beach – where some hardier souls stretch out for the night, and:-
Hotel Korali (*Tmr* 12A/B2) (Class C) Tel 91272
Directions: Beyond the 'ranch-like' My Way Disco and on the right, almost opposite the middle of the beach, which is tree edged hereabouts.

Double room rates are the Class C average.

Meltemi Rooms (*Tmr* 13A/B2)
Directions: Positioned between the *Korali* and the *Restaurant/Taverna Aphroditi* and fronted by a pleasant rose garden edging the road. The young girl of the house speaks English.

Nicely situated accommodation at average prices.

Hotel Mare-Monte (*Tmr* 14A2) (Class C) Tel 91564
Directions: Third building along from the *Meltemi Rooms*, that is beyond the *Aphroditi Taverna* and the *Marina Bistro*.

All rooms have en suite bathrooms, with a single priced at 2500drs & a double 3100drs, which charges increase to 3600drs & 4700drs (16th June-15th Sept).

Incidentally, at the far end of the beach are a number of very smarty accommodation cubes strung out at right-angles to the shore.

Back at the Ferry-boat Quay... from the 'Bus' Square the one and only road makes off for the zig-zag climb to the Chora. A hundred metres or so along the initially gentle incline, at the left-hand bend is a choice of route. The road continues on to the left whilst, almost straight ahead, a broad, stepped, paved and well shaded path takes a more direct route to the Chora.

The main road can 'offer' the *Pension Olga* and the:-
Homers Inn Hotel (*Tmr* 15C/D1/2) (Class C) Tel 91365
Directions: As above and on the left.

The cost of a double room, en suite, rises from about 2400drs to 3500drs.

The *Inn* is followed by *Stelios Pension*.

The steps are a more fruitful source of accommodation with at least two ***Rooms*** (*Tmr* 16D3/4) on the right. The first is:-
Ouravia's Rooms
Directions: As above.

Run by a friendly woman (called Ouravia) with one or more gold teeth. She lives in a very pleasant house on the right (and lets some rooms there) whilst there are other rooms in a block on the other side of the steps, along a dirt track which hairpins down to the road (and continues across the latter to the port beach). The main building incorporates a bar edging the steps, with the accommodation behind. Breakfast is served in the bar, mainly to package punters booked in by one of the big operators. A double room costs the average.

Further on up the flight is:-
Hotel Moschonas No 662 Tel 91218
Directions: As above, on the left at a crook in the path. Provincial and more a pension than a hotel with a 'single-minded' landlady.

Some rooms have an en suite bathroom, some share the bathroom, with double room rates starting at 1500drs. Emphatically uninterested in one night stands!

Camping

Ios Camping Tel 91329
Directions: Beyond the Port police office (*Tmr* 11A5) and some 50m along Ag Irene Beach. This latter is a narrow sliver of picturesque squalor on which a number of small boats are beached, in various

states of disrepair, and flotsam laps the waters edge.

A reasonable, average site, which is very convenient for the ferry-boats.

The Eating Out There are numerous mediocre cafe-bars, a number of bars, quite a few forgettable restaurants/tavernas and, regrettably, a rather garish hamburger joint. Far be it for me to crib, but on a general note it is a fact that the Ios Greek salad is a particularly poor thing, there rarely being any olives nor for that matter onion nor... The Baker (*Tmr* 17B4/5) sells excellent doughnuts for 80drs. The coffee served in the snackbar alongside the front of Acteon Travel is perfectly foul.

Probably the best value, neatest cafe-bar is the:-

New Corner (*Tmr* 18B4)

Directions: Behind and to one side of Acteon Travel.

Outside tables and chairs and, despite the remarkable neatness and rather chic feel to the place, quite reasonably priced, and thus popular. The service is extremely slow, even by Greek standards, the proprietor is rather precious and any complaints in respect of quality or content are contemptuously ignored. A coffee pot, allowing 1½ cups, costs 80drs, a yoghurt 55drs, a Continental breakfast 150drs and an English breakfast of bacon & eggs 200drs. Open between 0800-1430hrs & 1930-2400hrs. During the closed hours a self-service window opens, around the corner in the narrow alley. Apart from the caveats above, the place is 'blinded' from a view of the Ferry-boat Quay.

Ios Burger Self-Service (*Tmr* 19B4/5)

Directions: From the 'Bus' Square, around to the right of the dock.

Disturbingly modern looking, with yellow signs. My prejudices might well be 'showing' as it has to be admitted, that I favour neither hamburgers nor self-service! A large burger costs 250drs.

Taverna Andreas (*Tmr* 20B4)

Directions: On the left, at the outset of the main road, opposite the water fountain.

More a snackbar really, with a reasonable priced if rather limited number of offerings.

Restaurant Fisherman (*Tmr* 21B5)

Directions: On the far side of the Harbour from the Ferry-boat Quay, almost behind the pretentious *Skippers Inn*.

Almost always well patronised by fishermen (well, well). Basic, reasonably priced food and recommended by a number of people.

Convenient to ferry-boat watchers is the *Restaurant Fragakis*, they of hotel fame (*Tmr* 3A4), where is served average priced, run of the mill food.

To the left (*Sbo*) of Kritikakis Travel (*Tmr* 26A/B4) is the:-

Restaurant Pizzeria

Directions: As above.

A meal for two of 2 beers, 1 bacon omelette, 1 lamb chops with chips, 1 portion of local cheese (bland) & a bottle (720ml) of retsina cost 1390drs.

THE A TO Z OF USEFUL INFORMATION

BANKS The National Bank (*Tmr* 22B4/5) is boxed in between the Baker and *Ios Burger*. It only throws open the doors for the summer months of June to September when it opens the normal weekday hours. *See* **Acteon Travel, Ferry-boat Ticket offices, A To Z** and the **Post Office, A To Z, The Chora**.

BEACHES

Beach 1. Ag Irenes On the right of the Harbour (*Sbo*). Really more a narrow foreshore, cluttered with small boats and benzinas, in various states of decaying repair, and littered with rubbish. Not recommended.

Beach 2. Valmas To reach this beach skirt Ag Irene's and take the steps up to and then the track around the Chapel of Ag Irene's. The twenty minute walk along the stony path, which clings to the top of the cliff edge, passes one or two pocket handkerchief sized plots of sand hemmed in by the sea washed rocks. The trek ends some way above the nearside of the small, sandy beach, which is set in the cleft of a cove. On the opposite side is a cluster of buildings amongst which is a small, simple taverna. It is necessary to clamber down to the backshore of the quite steeply sloping and sharply narrowing beach, on which are set two large wells. The chosen few, *cognoscenti* regulars sunbathe in the nude, lying just beyond the startlingly and appealingly clear sea-water.

The slow moving taverna owner can be difficult or, to put it more plainly, pretty awkward. The limited choice of drinks and Greek salad available are not inexpensive, but almost everything has to be transported by sea. Very regular 'regulars', with some Greek, may possibly be able to rent a room to one side of the taverna, but only if the proprietor really takes to you – no promises.
Beach 3. The Port Beach is round to the left (*Sbo*) from the Ferry-boat Quay. The narrow beach is fine shingle backed by scrubbly grass with two separate clumps of trees. The far end is tatty.
Beach 4. From the far end of the Port Beach, a rough, stony track winds to the left, round the coastline of the bay. It then climbs up and over the neck of the rocky, scrub grass and low gorse covered land which separates Ios Bay from Koumbara Beach. Here, to seaward, is a small chapel on the edge of a rocky bay. Beyond a rocky caique mole is a curving cove with a lovely, coarse sand beach. The stony backshore ends in a short isthmus with, at its extremity, a low islet seemingly sunbathing in the sparkling sea-water. To the right of the neck of land are a couple of very small, stony and sand coves. Both the beach areas appear deserted but closer examination reveals that the boulderous cairns dotted about are the 'beach huts and rooms' of itinerant campers. 'Wild' campers also occupy the few low caves formed by overhanging rocks. The water is clean and crystal clear although there is some tar scattered about. The beach is very quiet and the needs of the scattered population are catered for by two tavernas, the one with the large patio, across the track from the sea, being recommended. On the sea side of the track is a small, doorless shack-like building, with a filthy interior, that was probably once a 'squatty'.

BICYCLE, SCOOTER & CAR HIRE A small moped hire outfit operates from beyond the yacht marina (*Tmr* 25B5). But who pays the asking rate of 1500drs a day, even if it does include a tankful of petrol, on an island with dozens of buses and almost nowhere to go?

BOOKSELLERS A shop on the quay side of the 'Port' Square doubles up as an international newspaper vendor, foreign language bookshop, small store and ferry-boat ticket office. The restless owner keeps a vigilant watch for light-fingered shoppers and browsers.

BREAD SHOPS One Baker (*Tmr* 17B4/5) edges the far side of the 'Bus' Square. This shop also sells bottled water, honey and milk.

BUSES The buses park on the 'Bus' Sq (*Tmr* 2B4), close to the Harbour, furthest from the Ferry-boat Quay.

There are some three buses for the one and only bus route from the Port to the Chora and on to Milopotamos Beach. They operate daily between 0730-2330hrs, every 20mins. The Port to Milopotamos Beach journey costs 60drs and the drivers herald their arrival and departure with a blast of the horn.

COMMERCIAL SHOPPING AREA None, not unnaturally, bearing in mind the small size of the settlement. Facing the Ferry-boat Quay is a Fruit Market (*Tmr* 23A4), more a stall, positioned alongside a supermarket. Various gift shops hide away in the alley to the side of Acteon Travel.

DISCOS Oh yes. Ios must have nearly as many sophisticated discos as it has chapels, but from these few lines please do not misconstrue the comment. They are concentrated in the Chora and need not impinge on those who do not wish them to encroach. The Port's only contribution to this concentrated cacophony is My Way (*Tmr* 24A/B2/3), on the near edge of the Port beach. It only opens for the height of season months.

FERRY BOATS Located almost at the epicentre of the Cyclades, Ios is not the busiest, nor the most important port of call but it is definitely near the top of the pile. Furthermore it is a very convenient staging post for the islands of Sikinos and Folegandros as well as connecting with the Western chain of Milos, Serifos and Siphnos, the Eastern wing of Tinos and, of course, the pivotal islands of Paros, Naxos, Mykonos, Syros and Santorini. There is also a hydrofoil style catamaran link with Crete.

Ferry-boat timetable (Mid-season)

Day	**Departure time**	**Ferry-boat**	**Ports/Islands of Call**
Mon	0900hrs	Thira II	Naxos,Paros,Piraeus(M).
	1500hrs	Ios(Express)	Santorini.
	1600hrs	Kimilos	Santorini.
	1700hrs	Georgios Express	Sikinos,Folegandros,Santorini.
	2030hrs	Kimolos	Siphnos,Serifos.

Tues	1000hrs	Ios(Express)	Paros,Naxos,Mykonos.
	1030hrs	Georgios Express	Naxos,Paros,Syros,Piraeus(M).
	1330hrs	Megalohari	Santorini.
	1800hrs	Santorini	Sikinos,Folegandros,Santorini.
Wed	1000hrs	Megalohari	Paros,Mykonos,Tinos.
	1030hrs	Santorini	Naxos,Paros,Syros,Piraeus(M).
	1500hrs	Ios(Express)	Santorini.
	1600hrs	Thira II	Santorini.
	1615hrs	Georgios Express	Santorini.
Thur	0900hrs	Thira II	Naxos,Paros,Piraeus(M).
	0930hrs	Georgios Express	Naxos,Paros,Piraeus(M).
	1730hrs	Santorini	Santorini.
Fri	0900hrs	Santorini	Naxos,Paros,Piraeus(M).
	1000hrs	Ios(Express)	Paros,Naxos,Mykonos.
	1330hrs	Megalohari	Santorini.
	1630hrs	Thira II	Sikinos,Folegandros,Santorini.
Sat	0230hrs	Georgios Express	Santorini.
	0930hrs	Georgios Express	Naxos,Paros,Piraeus(M).
	1000hrs	Megalohari	Paros,Mykonos,Tinos.
	1045hrs	Thira II	Naxos,Paros,Syros,Piraeus(M).
	1500hrs	Ios(Express)	Santorini.
	1730hrs	Santorini	Santorini.
Sun	0400hrs	Georgios Express	Santorini.
	0830hrs	Kimolos	Sikinos,Folegandrso,Milos,Kimolos, Siphnos,Serifos,Piraeus(M).
	0930hrs	Georgios Express	Naxos,Paros,Piraeus(M).
	1000hrs	Ios(Express)	Paros,Naxos,Mykonos.
	1200hrs	Daphne II	Santorini.
	1600hrs	Daphne II	Paros,Naxos.
	1615hrs	Thira II	Santorini.
	1930hrs	Santorini	Naxos,Paros,Piraeus(M).

In addition to the above there is the:-

Hydrofoil timetable (Mid-season)

Mon	1330hrs	Nearchos	Paros,Naxos.
	1700hrs	Nearchos	Santorini,Iraklion(Crete).
Wed	1115hrs	Nearchos	Paros,Mykonos.
	1645hrs	Nearchos	Santorini,Iraklion(Crete).
Fri	1130hrs	Nearchos	Paros,Naxos.
	1600hrs	Nearchos	Santorini,Iraklion(Crete).

The Nearchos is a hydrofoil catamaran. The journey to Iraklion is reputed to be uncomfortable, if fast, even in fairly calm sea conditions. The craft has one huge cabin, similar to a Jumbo jet, into which all the passengers are locked. The expensive 4 hour trip costs 2440drs.

Please note these tables are detailed as a GUIDE ONLY. Due to the time taken to research the Cyclades, it is IMPOSSIBLE TO 'match' the timetables or even boats'. So don't try cross pollinating...

FERRY-BOAT TICKET OFFICES

Acteon Travel & Tours (*Tmr* 4A/B4) Port Square Tel 91207

Directions: Dominates the north end of the 'Port' Square, as should the 'Mr Big' of the business.

The large, smart office extends through the building from front to the back. That fronting the 'Port' Square deals with tours, change facilities, including foreign exchange and travellers cheques, bus tickets to various European capitals, In addition to which there is a metered phone and no end of information. They quote bus tickets to London (presumably from Athens), via Italy. Other capitals on offer include Milan, Munich, Paris, Amsterdam, Brussels, Zurich and Frankfurt. In addition, there are cheap flights to London. Another useful front office service is a notice board for personal messages. It is a pity that the staff have, over the years, proved to be both abrupt and rude, sometimes extremely unpleasant.

The jewel in this company's particular crown operates the 'hatch' at the rear, facing the 'Bus' Sq, alongside the *New Corner Cafe-bar*. I first met Andreas Vasiliades many years ago, when he was supremo of the local ferry-boat department, in the main office. In those days he used to operate two visitors books, one for all and sundry and the other for the Irish! Pressures on space has resulted in his department being moved to the rear where he dispenses tickets and information in a confident, quick-fire manner. Andreas, now 50 plus years young, is a 'smiley' Greek Cypriot with a highly developed sense of humour. He could well be English, his mastery of the language is so complete. Probably a 'born again' character long before it became fashionable, Andreas will recall his waiter days in London when he was a fast moving, fast talking, fast living gambler. That is until his own 'Road to Damascus' when a steward on the fated Cruise Liner Laconia. On its maiden voyage, after an overhaul and change of name, the ship foundered, in December 1963, off the island of Madeira. Andreas survived his Atlantic dunking – after a number of acts of bravery saving passengers' lives.* From then on he became a reformed personality, or so he will tell a listener, but I'm not so sure that there isn't a twinkle in his eyes. He has developed a theory of longevity, based on the necessity to ingest copious amounts of water. To this he attributes his fitness, of which he is so assured, that he will throw out a running challenge to any doubters. If he has a 'tiny fault', or two, Andreas is not as attentive a listener as perhaps he could be. Another little quirk is his tendency to dissuade the more adventurous from visiting the smaller islands of Sikinos and Folegandros, with dismissive, derogatory asides – Sikinos – 'full of hippies, dirty, no money' (once true I suspect but now totally incorrect). Perhaps his throw away line in respect of the Chora was particularly apt when, in answer to some question about the night life there, he snapped.. 'If you must go to that jungle'. Certainly a man whom it has been a pleasure to meet.

Incidentally, before completing this panegyric, the rear office offers a baggage store facility at 30drs per piece for a 12hour period and sells the only usable island map available for about 150drs. Tours on offer include the Ag Theodotis excursion (*See* **Excursions to Gialos Port Surrounds**). The front office opens seven days a week between 0800-2230hrs and the back hatch between 0800-2100hrs.

Kritikakis Travel Agency (*Tmr* 26A/B4) Tel 91254

Directions: This business is in the alley to the side of Acteon Travel.

The office sells tickets for another inter-island 'African Queen', the **MV Ios**, now laughably with the suffix 'Express'(!) and the pleasure boat **Magaro**, which plies back and forth to Maganari Beach (*See* **Excursions To Gialos Port Surrounds**). They are Olympic agents, change money and have a metered telephone.

Plakiotis Travel Agency (*Tmr* 27B4/5) Tel 91277

Directions: Around the Harbour and beyond the *Ios Burger Cafe-bar*.

Perhaps the most interesting consideration in respect of this agency is the little brochure they produce, more especially the photograph on the inside front cover, above the thumbnail map of the Cyclades. The picture shows an old view of the Harbour prior to the dock or Ferry-boat Quay being built. This explains the present-day, truncated, rather pathetic state of Ag Irene's Beach. It was obviously once the far end of a much larger, sandy cove. Another plus is that the Ios Club musical programme is displayed on the notice board. An evening there is a must, for further details of which *See* **Discos, A to Z, The Chora,**.

LUGGAGE STORE *See* **Acteon Travel, Ferry-boat Ticket offices, A To Z.**

MEDICAL CARE Don't be ill in the Port – the only medical care available is in the Chora, about 1km up the hill.

POLICE *See* **The Chora.**

POST OFFICE *See* **The Chora.**

TAXIS Rumoured to lurk on the quay, but I cannot 'press a taramosalata to my heart' and own up to ever observing the rank. A reader reports the fleeting glimpse of a vehicle. In any case, the bus service is so excellent, and the roads so minimal, that there is really no necessity to contemplate their use.

TELEPHONE NUMBERS & ADDRESSES *See* **The Chora.**

TOILETS A number of the older travel books refer to there being only one unusable, unflushable toilet. Despite this being blown up many years ago, it is still impossible to find any toilet facility. The desperate must use those of obliging cafe-bar and taverna owners. Whilst on this note, in the area of the dock there is quite a pong.

******The story has been related by David Marchbanks in his book 'The Painted Ship' published in 1964.*

TRAVEL AGENTS & TOUR OFFICES *See* **Ferry-boat Ticket offices.**

EXCURSIONS TO GIALOS PORT SURROUNDS

Not so much the exact surrounds (for which *See* **Beaches, A To Z**) but two locations that most logically fit the text here.

Excursion to Ag Theodoti Beach The rough, stone path was once only used by the devoted for a particular panayieri. It has now been engineered sufficiently to accommodate a mid-summer, daily 'Red-Bus' service. Incidentally, the state of the road is used as an excuse not to run the excursion until numbers make the trip financial feasible! Our old friends Acteon have cornered this particular commodity, selling tickets from the 'rear hatch'... 'for Pease and Nature Lovers... Huge sandy beach... Rooms and Restaurant... Rooms. Indian Huts'. The one-way fare costs 500drs for the 45 minute journey and a return ticket can be used whenever required. Departures for the height of summer months are scheduled at 1000hrs & 1200hrs, returning at 1700hrs & 1900hrs. Huts and double rooms cost about 1500drs a night. Naturally the promotion of this large bay and valley has ensured that it can now hardly be an exclusive jewel of a find but that's life... despite the fact that its perfect for peace and nature lovers!

Excursion to Maganari Beach Only accessibly by trip boat. The Kritikakis Travel office handles the pleasure boat **MV Margaro**, which departs at 1000hrs and returns at 1700hrs. The 50 minute journey costs 800drs for a return ticket but it is possible to arrange for an overnight stop, returning the next day. The story behind the original development there, the subsequent degeneration and the slow reversal of fortunes would make a story in itself. Enough to say that the hotel, restaurant and disco are now operating correctly, if expensively.

For lovers of Natural History it is, or was, here (and Milopotamos Beach) that, in the month of August, the local cuttlefish made a lemming-like beach assault, throwing themselves out of the sea in order to lay their eggs. It is doubtful nowadays if they would be able to find any clear space...!

THE CHORA: capital (Illustration 19) Also known as the 'Village' or the 'Jungle'. The main road bypasses the pretty, hill clambering settlement and buses decant travellers on a dusty, bedraggled square to one side of the Chora. On the right-hand (*Port behind one*) edge of the 'Bus' Square is the rather unimposing, tired looking Town Hall (*Tmr* 1B4) behind which, on a gently rising slope, the untidy overflow development of the Chora has had to take place.

From the 'Bus' Square (*Tmr* 2B3/4), the Chora is reached along a short, walled causeway skirting the dusty recreation ground and terminating at the imposing Cathedral Church of Evagelismos (or Annunciation) with its pretty, light blue domes. Behind the Cathedral is Ag Evagelismos Square (*Tmr* 3B2/3).

Even during daylight hours there is a thinly veiled suggestion of youthful, vibrant energy, a scarcely concealed warning of the frenetic activity that bursts asunder once darkness descends. An analogy might be a heavyweight champion weight-lifter who attempts to disguise his bulging muscles in a size too small, tight fitting 'T'shirt.

In the morning hours the majority of the Chora visitors sit around at the various cafe-bars, irresistibly reminding one of a party of revellers who have been to a really excellent, late night party – which is in fact almost to a man and woman what they are. Midday and afternoon, the sun worshippers tumble down to Milopotamos Beach to bathe away the excesses of the night before. Once resuscitated they bundle back into the Chora to gather strength for another evening's assault on the auditory and pleasure senses. This movement of bodies resembles a mass migration. Even in broad daylight almost every other doorway emits sound and light in varying degrees of mind-numbing intensity.

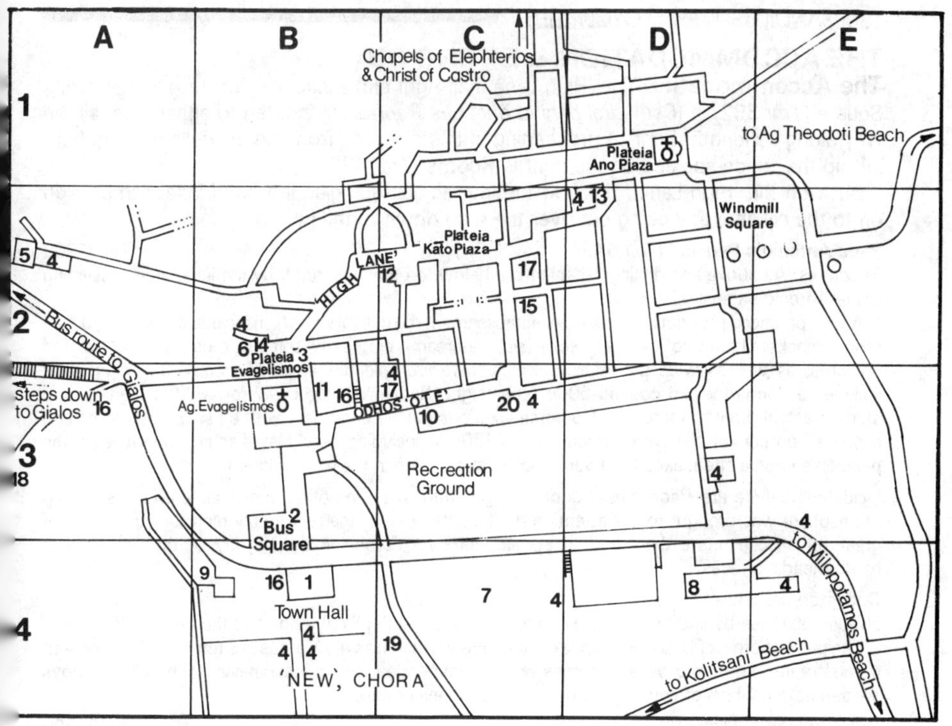

Illustration 19 The Chora

Tmr	=Town map reference
Fsw	=Facing seawards
Sbo	=Sea behind one
Fbqbo	=Ferry-boat Quay behind one

Tmr	
1B4	Town Hall/Doctor/Police/Post Office
2B3/4	Bus Square
3B2/3	Plateia Evagelismos
4	Rooms
5A2	Papa Antonios Pension
6B2/3	Hotel Philippou
7C4	Hotel Aphroditi
8D4	Hotel Parthenon
9A/B3/4	Olympic Flame Restaurant
10C3	Restaurant Romantica Zachar
11B2/3	Shoe shop
12B/C2	Restaurant Antonis
13C/D1/2	Taverna
14B2/3	National Bank
15C2	Commercial Bank
16	Laundries
17	Bakers
18A3	Ios Club
19B/C4	ΨΗΣΤΑΡΙΑ ΚΩΣΤΟΠΟΥΛΟΣ
20C2/3	OTE

Oddly enough, despite many of the ingredients that go to make up the Chora being the very ones which should bring Greek island lovers out in a rash – and cause the very old to write letters to *The Times* – it is almost impossible not to be infected with the atmosphere generated. I realise that this is a contradiction in definitions but there it is. And this is despite the inordinate number of fashion and jewellery shops, bars, discos and pubs that dominate the pretty, rising and falling, swaying alleys and lanes. Oddly enough, even in this 'jungle,' it is only necessary to climb to the upper reaches of the village to slip gradually out of the 20th century into the Greece of old, with donkeys unexpectedly emerging from picturesque passageways.

The climb up the ever ascending alleys to the little chapel that tops the wedding cake of a town is particularly pleasant. (*See* **Places of Interest, A To Z**).

THE ACCOMMODATION & EATING OUT

The Accommodation The 'High Lane' half-right and ascending from Ag Evagelismos Square (*Tmr* 3B2/3) (*Cathedral behind one*) has ***Rooms*** signposted to either side, all the way along its length. Prior to proceeding in this direction from Ag Evagelismos Sq, half-left up the cul-de-sac and on the right is **Rooms** (*Tmr* 4B2).

Back on the 'High Lane', the first turning, an acute angled left-hand lane, climbs high on to the hill above, looking out over the road down to the Port.

Papa Antonio's Pension (*Tmr* 5A2) Tel 91309
Directions: As above and distinguishable from below, on the main road, by the large sign acclaiming 'Papa Antonio's Pension'.

A well-practiced proprietor runs a busy establishment the delights of which include a common/dining room, snacks, filtered coffee, 'very sexy (*sic*) ice-cream', clothes washing at a cost of 150drs, and upwards, as well as wide patios from which there are splendid views. Accommodation on offer includes a dormitory bed costing 600drs per night. Rather incongruously for what is manifestly a student establishment, there are also some luxurious double bedrooms with en suite bathrooms and a private portion of the patio which cost 3,150drs, including breakfast. Lastly but not least the pension's hillside site makes for a very cool location, even in the hot summer months.

Incidentally, there are ***Rooms*** next door to *Papa Antonio's*. One other establishment in this rarified atmosphere was brought to our attention by 'Pamela', one of the regrettably diminishing number of great British characters that used to spread out over Europe in the heyday of the Empire. Her recommendation was:-

Dormitory Pension
Directions: Close by and below the hill-topping Chapels of Ag Elephterios and the Christ of Castro.

The patron Lefteris Platais, who speaks fluent French, and his wife Maroussais run the establishment. If you are into dormitory beds, it comes well recommended, and is inexpensive. The girls and boys are separated, which of course may or may not suit everyone.

Hotel Philippou (*Tmr* 6B2/3) (Class C) Tel 91290
Directions: On the corner of Ag Evagelismos Square. The only hotel in the Old Chora, the rest being on the opposite side of the main road.

A double room en suite costs 2700drs, rising to 3750drs (1st July-31st Aug).

At the far, top of the 'High Lane' and around to the left, on Odhos Ano Piaza, is:-

Rooms (*Tmr* 4C/D1/2)
Directions: As above, opposite the Orange Club.

A double room sharing a bathroom costs from 1200drs in mid-season.

Back at Ag Evagelismos Sq and edging round the Cathedral, as if proceeding back to the 'Bus' Sq, a lane (nicknamed 'Odhos OTE') parallels the main road (*In the direction of Milopotamos*).

Rooms (*Tmr* 4C/D2/3)
Directions:As above, and on the far side of the OTE.

Average room rates.

By carrying on along this lane, almost to the far end of the village, there is a turning to the right, which is more a track, back to the main road.

'Pension No Problem' (*Tmr* 4D3)
Directions: As above, half-way along the track, and on the left, is the once magnificent, odd looking, old house. The grounds are encircled by the track and next door is the School.

The owner of this ramshackle and 'provincial' establishment is an extremely nice man. Rudimentary rooms, mid-season, cost 630drs for a single or 1200drs for a double, sharing the distinctly antediluvian bathroom.

In the 'New Town', that is the modern-day development behind the Town Hall (*Tmr* 1B4), there are a clutch of hotels and ***Rooms*** including three separate houses to the rear of the Town Hall (*Tmr* 4B4).

Hotel Aphroditi (*Tmr* 7C4) (Class D) Tel 91546
Directions: Right of the main road, further along from the Town Hall, in the Milopotamos Beach direction.

All rooms have en suite bathrooms, with a single room costing 1650drs & a double 2000drs, rising to 3000drs & 3700drs (1st July-31st Aug).

Rooms (*Tmr* 4C/D4)
Directions: To the right (*Chora behind one*) or nearside of the block containing 'Coco's Place Bar', and up a flight of steps.

Hotel Parthenon (*Tmr* 8D4) (Class E) Tel 91275
Directions: Still further along in the Milopotamos direction from the Town Hall, behind Up Down Disco and alongside the Disco PN

. All rooms have en suite bathrooms. A single room is priced at 1650drs & a double 2000drs, increasing to 2900drs & 3500drs (1st July-31st Aug).

Rooms (*Tmr* 4E3/4 & 4E3)
Directions: One house is the other side of the Disco PN and the other is back on the Chora side of the main road, opposite to the street down from the *Hotel Parthenon*.

The Eating Out Innumerable places to fill the inner man or woman but many are mainly memorable, simply for the awfulness of their nomenclature and or offerings. These must include *Olympic Flame Pizza Spaghetti* (*Tmr* 9A/B3/4) next door to which is the *Captains Table* offering 'Original English Fish And Chips'. Oh goody! Others in the 'table of dread' might embody the Why Not? Pub. The management extol the virtues of its Hellenic kitchen which, incidentally, serves chicken curry, chilli con carne, Alfredos spaghetti (what?), goulash... and 'low prises'(*sic*) How Greek! It also proclaims in the publicity blurb that... 'In fact (it) has no equivalent anywhere else in the world'. Yes... Not to be forgotten is the Sweet Irish Dream Snackbar

Now for the recommendations:-

Romantica Zachar (*Tmr* 10C3)
Directions: On Odhos 'OTE', and the same side as the OTE office, below street level.

Popular, if expensive, with good breakfasts and pizzas.

Antonis Restaurant (*Tmr* 12B/C2)
Directions: From Plateia Ag Evagelismos, half-right along the 'High Lane' and on the right, on the corner of the first small square.

Although rather a 'barn of a place' there are pleasantly sited tables and chairs on a small square to the right of the street. Not only are souvlakis sold from a side window, but they put on a good value 'Special of the Day'. The menu is rather limited. A meal for two of spaghetti & meatballs, feta, bread, a bottled water and retsina cost 900drs.

In the 'High Lane', prior to *Antonis*, a cluster of establishments, comprising the Why Not? Pub, Kalimera Cocktail Bar and The Jazz Club, operate under an umbrella of self-publicity, if not the same management. Not loathe to hide their light, under anything, they print a 'Time Out' publicity broad sheet. In glowing terms, this describes the wild, heart pumping, breathtaking delights available at their various establishments. These embrace a Video Cinema Bar, serving cocktails including one named 'Orgasm' and another 'Foreplay' (I can only guess that the videos must be blue movies), and late night drinking at the Kalimera Bar, where the gratifications include 'happenings'. The Jazz Club, not to be outdone, lists its own version of orgasmic cocktails. That's enough of that!

There are two reasonably priced tavernas opposite each other at the top of the 'High Lane', where it joins Ano Piaza alley. The left-hand establishment is a:-

Taverna (*Tmr* 13C/D1/2)
Directions: As above and across the way from the Orange Bar.

Serves a reasonably priced meal from a limited menu. A meal for two of 2 meatballs with potatoes, 2 plates of beans, bread and 2 beers cost 880drs. A young, serious countenanced son waits on the tables and the establishment becomes deservedly busy in the evenings.

THE A TO Z OF USEFUL INFORMATION

BANKS The National Bank of Greece (*Tmr* 14B2/3) is on Plateia Evagelismos, next door to the *Hotel Philippou*. The **Commercial Bank** (*Tmr* 15C2) is right (*Port behind one*) of the 'High Lane', just beyond the Baker & confectioners. This latter bank accepts personal cheques backed by a Eurocard.

BEACHES The magnificent Milopotamos Beach is no further away than many a port beach.

Kolitsani Beach: A road starts out from opposite the Fanari Disco, which runs out on to the track from behind the Town Hall (*Tmr* 1B4). The walk takes about 15minutes and the beach is pebbly and well sheltered. A half-hearted local keeps a Cantina open most afternoons.

BOOKSELLERS On the right of the 'High Lane', about half-way along.

BREAD SHOPS There is a Baker/cake shop (*Tmr* 17C2) beyond Plateia Kato Piaza, and on the right, and another (*Tmr* 17B/C2/3) on the left of Odhos 'OTE',

BUSES Pull up on the square close to the Town Hall (*Tmr* 1B4). The drivers use the occasion for a long-winded natter. (*See* **Buses, A To Z, Gialos**).

COMMERCIAL SHOPPING CENTRE Based on the 'High Lane' and Odhos 'OTE', with almost the whole of the lower Chora a market place. A couple of shops deserve a mention. One in the narrow lane that encircles the Cathedral is a Shoe shop (*Tmr* 11B2/3) called 'Step On Ios – Shoes for Everyone'! The other, bordering the 'High Lane', between Plateia Kato Plaza and Plateia Ano Piaza, is the small, almost poky 'Nicholas Store Handicrafts, at No 26. The very pleasant proprietor is most helpful and sells, at reasonable prices, some unusual and extremely nice tiles and cups with Ios scenes and characters. My favourite is one which depicts an old man wearing traditional clothes and footwear (the owner's now deceased father).

DISCOS Almost a growth industry, that is if there aren't already enough in the Chora. But there is one establishment which everyone should visit. And should readers (rightly) doubt my recommendation, then they should see my postbag endorsing:-

The Ios Club (*Tmr* 18A3) Very often loudly heralded events and or places are disappointing in actuality, but not so the Ios Club. Approached by a track to the left of the steps down to the Port, the spectacular setting is high above and looks out over Ormos Iou towards distant Sikinos island. Within the high, roofless wall the layout is a small, informal, rocky amphitheatre and entrance costs 100drs per person. Clients are given a shell or bead which acts as a credit towards the cost of the first drink. For example, two people pay 200drs to get in but the baubles reduce the price of an Export Henninger and orange juice to just 20drs. To reinforce the impression that the club is not a rip-off, should a spectator purchase another drink, the management only charge 120drs for a can of beer. I realise that if I was in a taverna and was even offered a can of beer, let alone charged 120drs, then I would probably break out in spots, but this is an institution of exceptional merit. In my enthusiasm I have not explained that for the hour or so spanning the setting of the sun, the club plays a programme of appropriate classical music. And there can be no finer Cyclades location from which to watch the beauty of the setting sun. After the magic, dying moments of the sunset, the music reverts to more popular beats.

Incidentally, the town plans referring to the Up Down disco have incorrectly listed the title, which posterity will be pleased to note is the Upside Down.

FERRY-BOAT TICKET OFFICES *See* **Travel Agents & Tour Offices, A To Z.**

HAIRDRESSERS At least a couple, with one on Kato Piaza Square.

LAUNDRY There are two, but neither are Coin-op. One, 'Laundry-Taylor' (*Tmr* 16B3), is up the first stepped alleyway to the left of Odhos 'OTE', heading towards the OTE. Closed between 1300-1600hrs. The other laundry (*Tmr* 16A3), is at the beginning of the track to the Ios Club, at the far end of the building housing the Sweet Irish Dream Snack Bar... Like everything else in the Chora, this laundry plays loud music and is open at night!

LUGGAGE STORE *See* **Acteon Tours, Ferry-boat Ticket offices, A To Z, Gialos**.

MEDICAL CARE

Chemists & Pharmacies Only one specialist chappie on the island let along the Chora, on Odhos Ano Piaza (*Tmr* D1) almost opposite the Orange Bar.

Clinic *See* **Doctor**

Dentist One beside the ΤΗΣΤΑΡΑΙΑ ΚΩΣΤΟΠΟΥΛΟΣ (*Tmr* 19B/C4) in the 'New Chora'.

Doctor Conveniently situated in the Town Hall (*Tmr* 1B4). Did you know... doctors are drafted to the islands for a fixed period – a sort of punishment for all the money they will make in the years to come in the more lucrative suburbs of large Greek mainland towns. It is said of the present incumbent that he was posted to Ios years ago and, against the run of play, opted to stay on. But he is now, much to all and sundries consternation, rumoured to be considering departing for halycon fields – greener drachmae pastures.

OTE (*Tmr* 20C2/3) Half-way along and on the right of Odhos 'OTE' and flanked by Kritikakis Tours on the near side and ***Rooms*** on the far side. Only open weekdays between 0730-1500hrs.

PETROL None. Moped hirers include a tankful in the rental.

PLACES OF INTEREST Yes, well. In the welter of silence that accompanies this subject, I found very comforting the remains of the old, donkey driven water pump on the Milopotamos side of the Town Hall. Donkeys used to have to walk round and round a track circumscribing the well with a wooden shaft strapped to their back and the other end hafted into a socket on top of the mechanical arrangement capping the water bore. This particular example is now unusable because a road has been constructed tight to one side of the well top. It is reassuring to see how 'chaps' used to have to survive. It gives one a warm glow to think of the tap at home, if you get my drift.

The climb up and the Chora hilltop are notable, not only for the dramatic views, more especially of the Port area, but for the three churches. The approach is via Ag Gremmiotissa Church.

Churches & Cathedrals

Ag Gremmiotissa A pleasant, flagstone yard surround the church with an attractive campanile and a solitary, rather lean, palm tree planted one side of the whitewash outlined courtyard. Ag Gremmiotissa is famed for its icon of the Virgin about which, not unnaturally, there is woven a fable. It appears that a devout, Christian Cretan 'freedom fighter' set afloat an icon and a lamp, in order to save the holy relics from Turkish oppressors. The caique finished up at Ios. The islanders put the seaborne icon in a local chapel but every morning it was mysteriously found at a different location. Finally somebody twigged that it was best to let it stay where it finished up and built Ag Gremmiotissa Church, from whence it is supposed to be possible to see Crete...

Above Ag Gremmiotissa, on the way to the topmost chapel, is the *Church of Christ of Castro* and on the very highest rocky point, picked out in whitewash, is the:-

Chapel of Ag Elephterios Once pleasantly decorated by frescoes but both Elephterios and Castro have been allowed to fall into disrepair and the interiors are supposed to be ruined. The exteriors are almost 'panstick' thick with whitewash One intriguing rumour suggests the existence of a tunnel from Elephterios to a safe haven some hours away. The builders would have required nuclear blasting to get through the rock or an act of God. Maybe...

Windmill Square Once known as Plateia Plano or Upper Square and originally laid out with circular, paved winnowing groundworks. The three windmills presently stand mutely silent on an unattractive, raised area now flanked by two disco bars. Well that's progress, isn't it?

There are also rumours of a ruined 15th century fort about 2½ hours walk from the Chora.

POLICE The office is located in the Town Hall (*Tmr* 1B4). Definitely a 9 to 5 'set of chaps' but that is a Greek 9 to 5 which roughly translated, gives weekday hours between 0800-1200hrs & 1400-1800hrs. At the height-of-the-summer-season there is a weekend presence.

POST OFFICE In the Town Hall (*Tmr* 1B4). As elsewhere they carry out exchange transactions.

TAXIS *See* **Taxis, A To Z, Gialos**.

TELEPHONE NUMBERS & ADDRESSES

Doctor (*Tmr* 1B4)	Tel 91246/91227
Police, town (*Tmr* 1B4)	Tel 91222
port	Tel 91264

TOILETS An average facility to the left from Kato Piaza Sq (*Tmr* C2) (approaching along the 'High Lane' from Plateia Ag Evagegelismos). There is another Public toilet to the Port side of the Town Hall.

TRAVEL AGENTS & TOUR OFFICES From Plateia Evagelismos along the 'High Lane', immediately beyond Plateia Kato Piaza (*Tmr* C2) and in the next building to the left is:-

Plakiotis Travel Change but not personal cheques.

Further on, beyond the next turning right, with one office on the right and one down the alley to the right, are the offices of:-

Acteon Travel Only pale shadows of the Gialos office.

Kritikakis Tours Alongside the OTE office (*Tmr* 20C2/3).

From the Chora the road winds along the heights prior to a zig-zagging descent from a rocky promontory above the nearside of:-

MILOPOTAMOS BAY: the beach (Illustration 20) The view out over the bay reveals one of the greatest sweeps of beach in the Cyclades. It has to be admitted that the magnificence of the 'spread' is accentuated by the approach being from on high, as it were. The extraordinarily wide, long, slow curve of glorious sand is framed in a broad fertile plain bordered by a large range of mountains and, on the far side, by rocky hillsides encircling the bay. High above the beach, alongside the main road, is a small chapel from the side of which almost every professional photographer takes a panoramic view of Milopotamos Beach. Close to sea level is an imaginative, if somewhat 'OTT', mini-walled estate set down below on a bluff. This house is complete with castellated walls as well as large statues of horses and figures, and is rumoured to be owned by a wealthy Frenchman.

The near, or Chora side of the bay, has experienced some development in the last seven or eight years but the central plain and far end of the beach remain almost unchanged. Allowing for my obvious partiality I consider Milopotamos Beach has actually improved during this period. Certainly on the credit side is that the most undesirable elements have been discouraged from camping out on the backshore.

It is pleasing to observe how much the donkey is still in evidence, here being utilised in their traditional role as pack-animals for the transport of goods to the far end of the beach. Unfortunately the other creature much in evidence is the mosquito.

I have indicated a partiality in respect of accommodation on Ios island and have to own up to landing and heading straight for the *Brothers Dracos Taverna*. Their establishment is admirably sited on the very nearest edge of this almost obscenely lovely, broad swathe of sandy beach that stretches on for in excess of a kilometre, and edges a beautifully clear sea with solid sand bottom. Although during the height of summer months the foreshore does get almost jam-packed with sun worshippers, even at its most crowded the far end is almost always practically empty. But whatever the midday situation, by late afternoon the beach empties as if all the day's visitors have been hoovered up. In general terms the far end of the beach is the preserve of the topless (and bottomless), as are the nearside slab-like rocks around to the right of the bay (*Fsw*). The middle ground is occupied by a Windsurf School, sand-seated, circled groups of folk-singing youngsters as well as the more active playing almost every variety of game known to 'beach groupies'. The near end of the beach is more often than not used by locals. Unbelievably a man cleans the beach daily but, as with the rest of the island, rubbish is a problem. Here it is assiduously swept up, collected, packed in bins and plastic bags but then left where stacked, only to be spread all over the place... to be collected up all over again...

Some things change. The rocky goat path from the area of the 'heights' mounted *Acropolis Hotel* has, at its lower end, become a wide, very steep, dusty swathe; the beach duck-boards, that the buses used to turn round and park on, have been replaced by a concrete pad and the arid hillside to the right of *Dracos Taverna* (*Fsw*) is covered by an extremely expensive, tasteful hotel complex ascending the steep slopes, complete with a swimming pool (yes a swimming pool, beside this of all beaches). The unofficial campsite, that used to lay out along the low concrete wall, now part collapsed, has been done away with. The original, now rather run-down facility half-way along the beach, has been supplemented by another site.

THE ACCOMMODATION & EATING OUT

The Accommodation Whilst on the bus from the Chora it is quite on the cards that 'likely looking' passengers will be offered accommodation by the fulsome lady conductress, or one of her colleagues. Her pension is located high on the hillside, on the right-hand side of the road and prior to the *Hotel Acropolis*. There is often a bus parked on the large forecourt. The building is kept spotless.

The Pension Acropolis (Class E) Tel 91303

Directions: Close to the cliff edge, on the hilltop overlooking Milopotamos Beach and to the right of

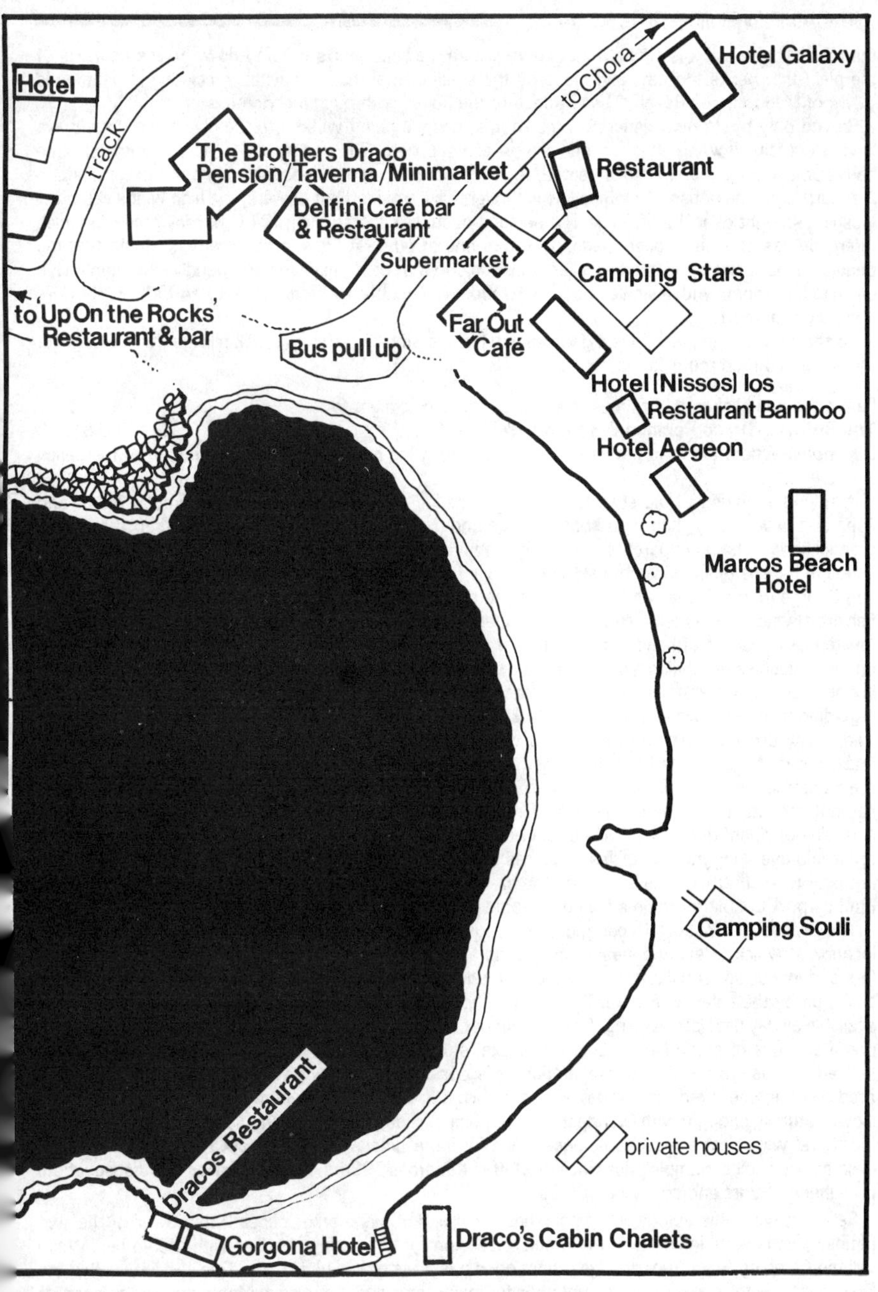

Illustration 20 Milopotamos Beach

the road. The pension is situated just about where the road starts to wind down to the nearside of the plain that backs the bay, and close by the small chapel that is inevitably included in panoramic views of Milopotamos Beach. The entrance to the house is through a concrete arch.

Served only by its own generator, the rooms, despite being wired into the circuit, do not always have electricity flowing thus paraffin lamps are supplied. The rooms are spacious with en suite bathrooms and the water is solar heated. Ground floor bedrooms almost all open on to the large patio that surrounds the house. A clothes line is thoughtfully provided but beware, the high winds can blow washing straight over the cliff-side The pension overlooks the startling 'OTT' holiday home to which reference has previously been made. This was one of our first 'digs' and there is no doubt that the pension is both clean and in an excellent position, and that the family are very friendly. All rooms have en suite bathrooms with a single priced at 1000drs & a double 1800drs, rising to 1400drs & 2500drs (1st July-5th Sept).

To the front of the pension is a goat track which scrambles down the rock hillside thus cutting out the circuitous road route to the beach.

I am of course blinkered but I must own up to heading straight for:-

The Brothers Draco Pension & Taverna (& Mini-Market) Tel 91243

Directions: Where the road peters out on the beach in the near right-hand (*Fsw*) corner of the beach and bay.

A splendid mixture of old style taverna and pension, developed over the years first by Mama and Papa and now run by their twin sons, George and Yianni (and their wives) with hindrance from the grandchildren. The grandparents still help in the taverna (and run the mini-market of which more later), although Papa is really only interested in his daily fishing expeditions. On these he is accompanied by son George who helps lay and haul the nets. A side benefit of this activity is that family-caught fresh fish are always on the menu, and a little cheaper than elsewhere. It has to be admitted that Yianni, the taverna twin, can be offhand at first, but as a reader agreed, he improves, if only after a long lecture on the difficulties of running a restaurant, the unwillingness of staff to work, the punitive taxes on staff imposed by the Government and the unreasonableness of tourists. This latter may include a homily regarding a girl, who when presented with 20 dishes to choose from, didn't like any – to which Yianni said, "Why do you come to Greece?". So, says Yianni, he stays small and in the winter works as a mechanic in Athens. The best positioned accommodation is the original line of first floor balcony rooms, complete with small en suite bathrooms that face out over the bay. This is not to say that time has not accentuated some of the usual 'Greek Room Idiosyncrasies' – no toilet roll; doors that shut and will not open; doors that will not shut and suspect drainage with the occasional concrete block or tile laid over long missing grilles of access traps. Incidentally, I assume this contemporaneous lid is not only to seal off the smells, but to stop clients tripping, or even disappearing down the plug hole. But I carp. A double room en suite costs about 1600drs.

The Dracos two patio terraces must be almost unrivalled for position and make an incomparable location at which to enjoy a meal or simply sip a drink or two (or three or four). The straightforward fare and insouciant service (okay, easy-going, still a euphemism for casual) has been given a bit of a shake-up by the splendid *Far Out* (for details of which read on). Enough to say that food and drink is available all day until late evening, from the almost self-service servery abutting the top patio. The pre-prepared trays of stuffed tomatoes, moussaka, stuffed aubergines or spaghetti bolognese are best tackled as close to the time of preparation as is possible. In common with most Greek tavernas, the food can become 'tired' as the day wears on. That is certainly so, where and when the turnover is slow. Naturally enough, with Grandpapa's overriding piscatorial enthusiasm, fish is a speciality and the 'Brothers' will select a reasonably priced dish for impecunious clients. As always, kalamares are an inexpensive choice. Sample prices include stuffed tomatoes 199drs, a plate of fishes 300drs, spaghetti bolognese 199drs and souvlakia 400drs.

Before leaving this eulogy, the family has a cellar-like mini-market beneath the lower of the two patios. This is quite in line with the Greek obsession for competing head-on with each other. When will the *Camping Stars Supermarket* owner open a taverna or has he already? One certainty is that the Dracos shop is the cheapest in Milopotamos for many items and they also sell international newspapers at the height of the season. It is another sad marginalia to add that the family have found it necessary to erect a sign reading 'Shoplifters will be Prosecuted', the necessity for which is underlined by the spelling being correct! Yianni speaks excellent English, George sufficient, but as I am totally incapable of sorting out which 'twin has the Toni...' it is no earthly use my identifying them. Enough to say that from the ever smiling grandmama, dour papa, the friendly, if sometimes preoccupied twin brothers to their wives and children, it is difficult to find a more genuine family.

After that fulsome testimonial... it is necessary to point out that there are other, more than adequate establishments including the *Hotel Galaxy* which I am fairly certain is package booked. But all is not lost.

Hotel (Nissos) Ios (Class D) Tel 91306

Directions: To the waterfront side of *Camping Stars*.

The daily rate for a double room, with en suite bathroom, ranges from 1450drs to 2350drs (1st July-31st Sept).

The Hotel Aegeon (Class E) Tel 91392

Directions: To the left-hand of the road, a 100 metres or so along the backshore, and distinguished by an arched entrance to the grounds.

Double rooms, with a bathroom en suite, cost 1630drs, increasing to 2300drs (1st July-31st Aug).

Marcos Beach Hotel (Class E) Tel 91571

Directions: Behind and slightly to the right (*Sbo*) of the *Hotel Aegeon*.

Rooms have en suite bathrooms. Single rooms cost 2000drs & double rooms 2500drs, increasing to 2300drs & 2900drs (16th June-25th Aug) and 2150drs & 2700drs (26th Aug-31st Oct).

Attractively situated at the far end of the bay are the:-

Gorgona Hotel Tel 91307

Directions: As above.

Offers very basic, sparse, over-priced rooms from about 2250drs en suite. One room for four is available at a cost of about 5500drs.

and the

Dracos Restaurant

Directions: As above.

Distant cousins of our favourite Milopotamos family, but there all resemblance ceases. The standard accommodation is at the rather sleazy end of the scale, as is the establishment, with a double room en suite from 1500drs, but the water is cold. They also own, round to the right (*Fsw*) and on the edge of the backshore, a very pleasant development of Cabin/Chalets with a two bed unit costing 3500drs per night (including breakfast).

Camping There is a choice of two campsites:-

Camping Stars Tel 91302

Directions: On the left of the main road, about 50m prior to the shore. The entrance stands back from the road's edge.

This is an excellent, well managed, smart site, as one would expect of the small, gold toothed, smiling proprietor who has owned the supermarket alongside for as long as I can remember. I have to add here that a recent, to be trusted correspondent was less than flattering '...a very disappointing experience... dirty, crowded and noisy'. It is a proud management boast that there is 'perpetual hot water' to service the toilet block. The per person charge is 300drs per head plus 80drs charge for the tent. Tents are available for hire at 160drs per day. The reception block has a bank of security lockers and a post box on the office wall.

The other flank of the small square is taken up by a Restaurant/Cafe with steps to the fore.

The other (original site) is:-

Camping Souli 91554

Directions: About halfway along the backshore, to the left (*Fsw*) of the road from the Chora.

This rather tatty site is located in a low-lying area which must be prone to mosquitoes. The proprietress is charming but, despite being less expensive, *Camping Stars* must have knocked her trade more than a little. A night costs 200drs and she hires tents for 150drs, when necessary. There are excellent individual shelters to protect tents from the wind. Facilities include a toilet block and reception, open daily between 0800-1300hrs & 1700-200hrs. Entertainment facilities include 2 ancient pinball tables. A dining area serves beer at a cost of 80drs, a 'big beer' 100drs and some snacks.

The Eating Out A number of establishments have been covered in the descriptions of accommodation, but these did not include the:-

Delfini Cafe-Bar & Restaurant

Directions: Between the road and *Brothers Draco*, and behind which is the *Hotel Delfini*.

Advertises 'Specialities', which include fish & chips (200drs) and hamburgers & chips (180drs).

Mmh! Neat enough and, at the height of season, fills up, as does everywhere in Milopotamos.

At any other time the *Delfini* has to compete with the:-

Far Out Cafe

Directions: Flanks the left (*Fsw*) of the main road where it runs out on the beach.

The place almost defies description, and is probably one of the slickest operations I have encountered in Greece. The main body of the building, edging the very large terrace, houses an incredibly efficient self-service operation. Not only is the choice imaginative but the standard of food is excellent, even if portions might be considered on the small side. The self-service even extends to the bread and the bottles of drinks stocked in a cold cabinet. There is a separate 'Tost Snack Bar'. Service starts early morning with a full breakfast, including bacon and eggs, costing 300drs and terminates late at night, but the food often runs out early evening. Food on offer can include soup, egg meat-loaf, moussaka, stuffed tomatoes, pasta, macaroni pie, meat balls & rice, spaghetti bolognese, chicken, green beans, potatoes & tomatoes, potatoes & peas and Greek salad. Prices for a plate or helping include moussaka 250drs, spaghetti sauce 230drs, spaghetti with meat sauce 190drs, stuffed tomatoes 190drs and Greek salad 150drs. Bottled drinks tend to be expensive.

The terrace is crammed with youngsters of every shape, size, colour and creed. Loudspeakers belt out non-stop pop until the evening video show. Yes, not one but two video shows a night, with one of the films being a full length feature. The massed audience simply sit goggle-eyed and glued to their seats with the velvet darkness of the night closed down round the patio, almost like a curtain. I have to admit that the Far Out is not exactly my scene but is obviously rather popular. Rumour, only rumour, suggest that the light-fingered brigade operate on the terraces. One very useful service is the provision of a notice board for personal messages.

Another establishment is:-

Up On The Rocks

Directions: Along the wide track edging the right-hand side of the bay (*Fsw*). This starts out alongside the *Draco Brothers Taverna*.

Once very popular and certainly spotlessly clean but the menu is limited and the prices average.

THE A TO Z OF USEFUL INFORMATION

BANKS None. *See* **Acteon Travel, Travel Agents & Tour-Offices, A To Z**.

BOOKSELLERS Camping Stars Supermarket stocks a good range of paperbacks and the Draco Brothers mini-market a number of international newspapers and books.

BREAD SHOPS No baker but the two shops sell rolls and bread.

BUSES They pull up on the beach, heralding both arrival and imminent departure by enthusiastic horn blowing. *See* **Buses, A To Z, Gialos** for details of timetables.

CHEMISTS The shops sell the more mundane items, otherwise it is necessary to go to the Chora.

COMMERCIAL SHOPPING AREA Of course none but the merits of the Draco Brothers Mini-Market have already been discussed. Camping Stars Supermarket is well stocked with a wide range of goods. Another mute commentary on the light fingered nature of the tourists is that the proprietor of the latter establishment deploys his elderly parents to watch over the stock displayed in front of the shop. There is now a third Mini-Market in the bowels of the *Hotel Delfini*, behind the *Delfini Restaurant*. How on earth the 'Beach' can support three shops I really don't know, but the old Greek habit of just not being able to resist rushing in whenever anyone else seems to be making an honest drachmae still thrives.

DISCOS Apart from **Far Out's** non-stop clamour, nearly all the discos are concentrated in or around the Chora.

MEDICAL CARE *See* **The Chora**.

TOILETS There is no public block and it is necessary to use the relevant 'offices' of the various restaurants/tavernas and cafe-bars. *Far Out* has a very accessible facility.

TRAVEL AGENTS & TOUR OFFICES Surprisingly, there are two offices (but they only open for the months of June through to early October).

Acteon Tours: This is positioned on the corner of the *Far Out*. Open daily only between 1330-1730hrs. Does exchange and moped hire.

and:-

Kritikakis Travel The office is alongside the third mini-market, in the basement of the *Hotel Delfini*.

Christos sto Dhasos, Paros. *Acknowledgement to David & Liz Drummond-Tyler.*

Ag Irini Bay campsite, Paros. *Acknowledgement to David & Liz Drummond-Tyler.*

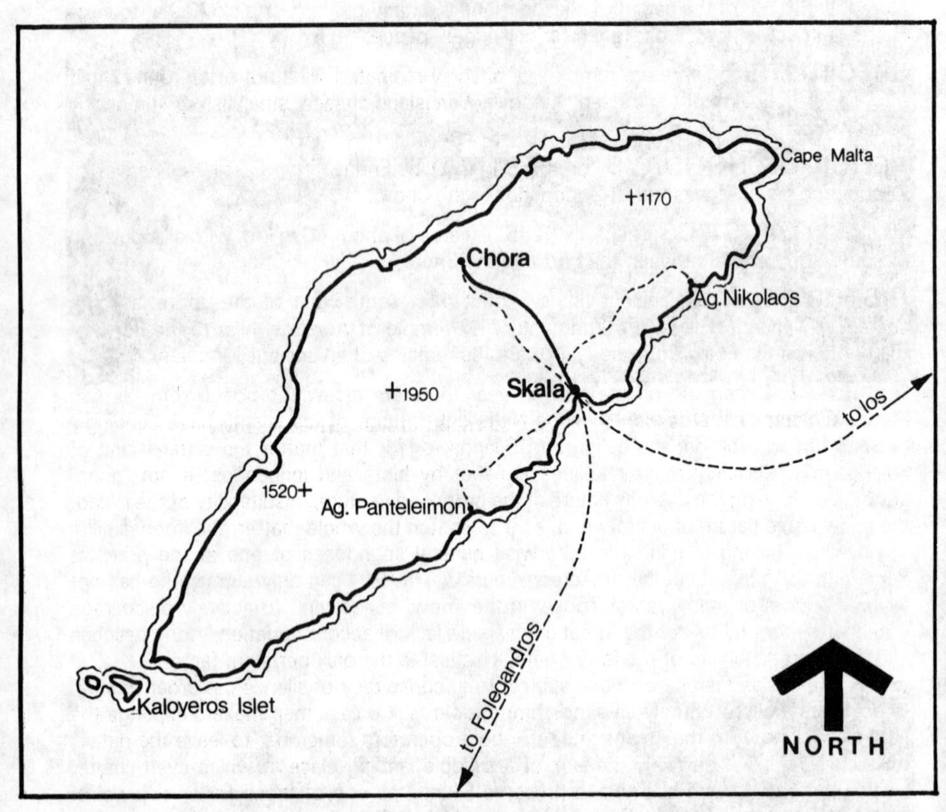

Illustration 21 Sikinos island

8 SIKINOS ★★★★★
Cyclades Islands - Eastern chain

FIRST IMPRESSIONS Few cats; dry, but comparatively verdant countryside; plentiful water wells but slimy water; donkey & mule trains; a handful of tourists – no more than 20 out of the height of season months, at any one time; no clothes or tourists shops, just some postcards; few flies; partridges; peace.

SPECIALITIES There are rumours of a highly resinated wine not often found other than on Sikinos – I'm not surprised; Xinogalo – an island cheese; small fish drying on the Skala roofs.

RELIGIOUS HOLIDAYS & FESTIVALS: Friday after Easter – Festival of Zoodochos Pighi, Monastery of Zoodochos Pighi, Chora.

VITAL STATISTICS Tel prefix 0286. An area of about 40sq km, with a population of some 300 spread between the Port and the Chora.

HISTORY Settled in ancient times. About 4km south-west of the Chora is a 5th century AD church built over a 2nd century BC temple of Apollo, whilst to the north of the Chora, on the coast at Palaiokastro, are the remains of an ancient sanctuary.

GENERAL Depending on the time of year, there are a few trip-boats from Ios and Santorini. I am of the opinion that the Niots (inhabitants of Ios island) have cunningly decided not to promote the delights of Sikinos, or for that matter the sister island of Folegandros. Certainly most enquiries are met by hints and innuendos, if not 'open' advice, cataloguing the dubious nature of the proposed venture, unsuitability of the island, the undesirable nature of visitors and, as if to scotch the whole matter, the impossibility of docking. Bearing in mind the otherwise general soundness of one of the principle deprecators Andreas (yes he of Acteon Tours & Travel), I can only surmise he has not visited Sikinos for many years! Those 'in the know' at Ios tend to actively discourage potential visitors by talk of the 'great unwashed', lack of accommodation, stony beaches and the unpredictability of the ferry-boats. This last is the only pertinent factor.

Maybe the island is one of those subject to a 'conspiracy of silence', in order to keep the delights a secret. Surely an almost impossible task unless map makers expunge the particular island from their maps and ferry-boat operators remember to leave the details off their schedules. Certainly the lack of a suitable landing place at which even charter yachts can easily berth has helped preserve Sikinos as one of those finds, a 'jewel of island uniqueness' set in the Cycladean sea beset by tourist hordes.

The symmetry of the port and its beach bordering the lovely cove is fully complemented by the bewitching, 'old world' Chora of outstanding, simple, agricultural beauty.

It is a pity that the link between the two places, on a narrow, paved mule-track, has been blasted and bulldozed asunder to form a wide dirt road. Despite this, the traveller often remains faced with an ever upward climb to the Chora (taking about an hour) as the brand new bus runs somewhat spasmodically. The service revolves around ferry-boat arrivals, and there are few, if any, other vehicles and no taxis. Regretfully, the coming of mechanised transport has reduced the number of mule trains. Donkeys and mules are still widely used, off the main route, to transport all normal loads, which include drinking water to those houses without a well, all and every day.

The dramatic landscape is colourful, almost verdant, with a surprising amount of agriculture. There are water wells everywhere which are constantly replenished by spring water trickling from the surrounding hillsides. Once a 'resort' for exiled Communists, the isolation and interbreeding of the island has resulted in a hereditary physical deformity, the Sikinos jaw, akin to the deafness of Astipalians.

THE SKALA: harbour (Illustration 22) Also known as Alopronia and really only a semi-circular cove with a caique quay and small settlement to the left (*Sbo*), a broad, sandy beach to the centre and a thin ribbon of development to the right. Prior to the preoccupation of the Colonels Junta with tourism, and the inception of widespread development of the islands, Sikinos was regarded as a rather uninteresting, forced port of call. Mind you this was when Ios was described as 'lesser-known', quiet and off the beaten-track!

ARRIVAL BY FERRY To date, the quayside is too small for the smallest ferry (even if the cove was deep enough) so the inter-island boats 'pull up' in the mouth of the harbour. Passengers and freight are transferred to one of two 'pass-boats' to complete the journey. This is a haphazard operation, without allowing for the natural Greek ability to make any act or sequence of events infinitely more difficult than need be. There is no doubt that it is a great help if the sea state is calm and those of a nervous disposition should try to ascertain the ferries particular method of exit. Some urge passengers out of side doors in the car hold, which requires a short climb down a rope ladder into one of the waiting but bucking boats. Those wearing a backpack should unshoulder it prior to disembarking. Other ferries lower the stern car ramp against which the shore craft bump and scrunch. The excitement reaches fever point whilst packages of almost every conceivable commodity, bundles of black dressed old ladies, small children with young mothers, string-tied suitcases and cardboard boxes, as well as the occasional domestic animal are bundled over. The short journey to the quay costs 100drs a head, but I'm not sure who should pay whom? Accommodation is usually proffered by Room owners, even whilst 'gathering strength' on the inter-island ferry and a traveller will almost certainly be approached on the 'pass-boat' trip.

The isolation of Sikinos will be completely eroded if the oft threatened construction of a new Ferry-boat Quay comes to fruition.

THE ACCOMMODATION & EATING OUT Naturally, there is not a very wide choice of either.

The Accommodation

Pension Koundouris (*Tmr* 5D2) Tel 51232

Directions: From the quay (*Tmr* 1B2/3), proceed along the sea wall past the *Kafeneion/Cafe-bar Meltemi Tmr* 2C2), on the left, a large post-box concealing the now 'dead' water fountain (*Tmr* 8C/D2/3) and mount the steps between the small *Cafe-bar/Loukas Rooms* (*Tmr* 3D2) on the left and *Rooms Flora/Cafe* (*Tmr* 4D2/3) on the right. The rising, stepped alley turns sharp left around the back of the buildings and the pension is on the left.

In the unlikely event of not having been previously accosted, it is best to make enquiries in the taverna. This is on the ground floor and to the nearside of the steps up to the accommodation. The owner, genial, if possibly lecherous Panayotis Kountouris, is no fool and he and his son-in-law 'accost' the incoming ferries, gathering prospective clients under their wing, like mother hens. He invites his 'chicks' to a coffee in the taverna whilst the rooms are made ready and to introduce himself and the family. His wife is rather stern faced, if not unfriendly. A double room, sharing the simple bathroom facility, which does not enjoy the luxury of hot water, costs between 1000-1700drs.

The taverna unfortunately does not possess a patio or terrace but the food is reasonable as are the prices. Incidentally this is the case for all of Sikinos, that is lack of terraces and inexpensive meals. The house retsina (an island brewed, 'little killer') is served in milk bottles (a dead ringer for the British version), with a pine cone for a stopper. Certainly less cloudy than the Karterados (Santorini) brew, it has a similar consistency to the Gavrion (Andros) and Siphnos variations. At times retsina is not available and the 'house' wine is a palatable, 'rough and ready' rose, dry but fruity. The limited menu includes fried small fish (250drs), spaghetti bolognese (225drs), Greek salad (200drs), bread (30 or

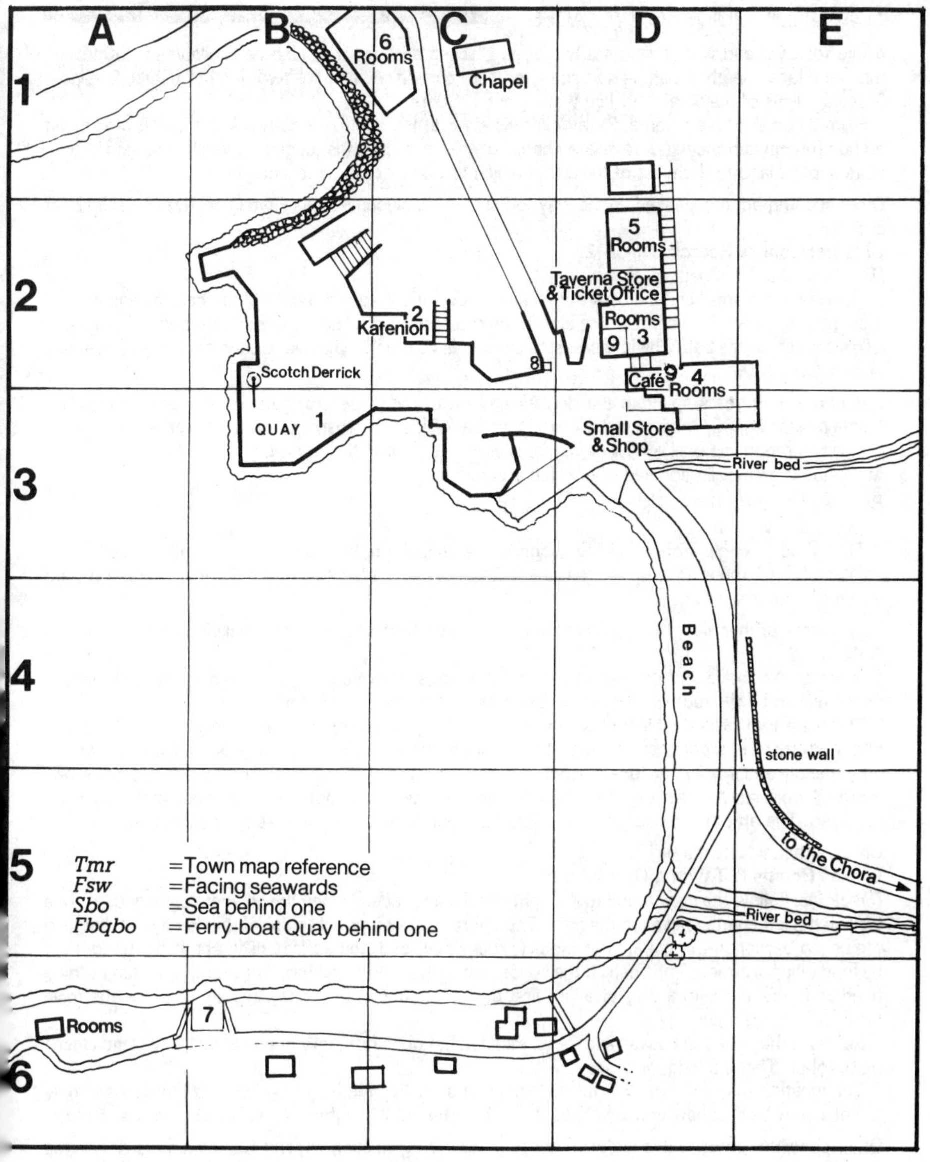

Tmr =Town map reference
Fsw =Facing seawards
Sbo =Sea behind one
Fbqbo =Ferry-boat Quay behind one

Illustration 22 Skala

Tmr 1B2/3	Quay		
2C2	Kafenion/Cafebar Meltemi	6B/C1	Rooms
3D2	Cafe-bar Loukas & Rooms	7A/B6	Loukas Rooms & Taverna
4D2/3	Rooms Flora/Cafe	8C/D2/3	Postbox/Water fountain
5D2	Pension/Taverna Koundouris	9D2	Cafe (with telephone)

40drs for two) and wine (100drs a half litre). Chicken and rice may also be available at 250drs. as may be a local meatball dish, lemon soup and curd cheese. A meal for two of small fishes, 2 salads, 2 beers, slices of melon and bottled water cost 1200drs.

From a corner of his taverna, Panayotis runs a store, the sole ferry-boat ticket office as well as an *ad hoc* foreign currency and travellers cheque exchange facility (he juggles as well!). The family own quite a lot of land to the west of the island which can only easily be reached by boat.

Other accommodation passed on the way to Panayotis includes *Rooms Flora* (*Tmr* 4D2/3, tel 51214) and:-

Cafe-bar/Loukas Rooms (*Tmr* 3D2)

Directions: As described.

The rooms are small and the bathroom tiny, however it is pleasant, with a broad balcony and several thoughtful touches. These embody a sink in the room, towels, a mirror, lots of worthwhile hooks and a light switch by the bed. The low pressure shower is cold only. The mid-season price is an extremely reasonable 1400drs.

It is only a few years ago that the donkey and mule trains used to 'park up' alongside the water fountain (*Tmr* 8C/D2/3). Here water containers were filled for transportation to the various dwellings. It is sad to report the well is now dry and it is almost obscured by a post-box.

Alongside is an initially cobbled lane which ascends the hillside.

Rooms (*Tmr* 6B/C1)

Directions: As above.

The modern, single storey building is opposite a chapel, on the sea side of the path. It overlooks a small harbour, around the corner from the main quay. A lovely situation on the low hill with distant views of Santorini island.

Fifty metres further along this lane and up a rough path to the right are two buildings set back.

Rooms

Directions: As above and the first of the two dwellings. There are no signs to help, but the place is distinguished by the red-painted surrounds to its blue doors and windows.

There are two large double/treble rooms to let. The young proprietor also crews one of the pass-boats, so there is a good chance that these will be offered before the shore is reached. His wife is very friendly and speaks reasonable English. The rooms have a wash-basin, or rather a shallow stone sink and work surface, but other facilities are shared. There is no hot water, but soap and towels are provided. The official mid-season rate is 2000drs, but negotiation can result in a reduction.

On the other side of the bay is:-

Loukas Rooms & Taverna (*Tmr* 7A/B6)

Directions: Follow the quay round to the right (*Sbo*) then proceed along the concrete path, with a stone wall on the left and the beach to the right. The Chora road swings off to the left but keep right, hugging the beach backshore. In the area of the dry, rocky river-bed, the surface of the path has broken up, beyond which a street climbs behind the houses along this side of the bay. The prettily situated building overhangs the sea with a very pleasant first storey terrace and is approximately opposite the main quay, across the cove.

Run by father and son Loukas and recommended but does not really open up until July – and closes by October. That's a long, hard season!

The location may be attractive but the menu is slim. Even late August/early September the only 'entries' may be spaghetti and meatballs. A lunch for two of 2 spaghetti, a beer and bread cost 400drs.

Other possible rooms in this direction are to be found by walking beyond *Loukas Rooms & Taverna* right through the settlement to one or two footpaths which lead over the low headland. In the next rocky cove (no bathing here without a crash helmet, and it would take a brave sailor to bring a boat into the little jetty) is a small development of three buildings, right on the foreshore.

Rooms, Restaurant Stella & Lenia

Directions: As above and the largest, two storey building.

Offers breakfast, but only open for the height of season months. It certainly is an 'away from it all' holiday spot, but it's not somewhere to head on spec!

About ½km up the Chora road, on the left, is a surprisingly large collection of buildings 'labelled':-

Cafe Restaurant H Chora

Directions: As above.

There is an accommodation block behind the restaurant.

For other accommodation *See* **The Chora**, but it is a long trudge if the bus doesn't meet the ferry, which is often the case...

The Eating Out Many of the establishments have been referred to in *The Accommodation*. It is noteworthy that there are no price tariffs here or in the Chora. Order, smile and pay up, you will not be 'turned over'.

Kafeneion/Cafe-bar Meltemi (*Tmr* 2C2)
Directions: On the quay.

A locals haunt. The handsome, dark skinned Mr Chalkea (of Cretan appearance) and his family eye up newcomers with a hard, disinterested stare. The family might, no will, unbend in time. A Greek breakfast for two costs 380drs and a dinner for two of 1 small plate of fish, meatballs & chips, a Greek salad, bread and a bottle of wine cost 1550drs. The patron is a busy man as he 'trebles up' as an island muleteer and a shore to ferry boatman.

The fishermen sort out their nets on the quay in front of the Kafeneion.

The small cafe (*Tmr* 9D2) beyond the postbox possesses the port's metered telephone.

THE A TO Z OF USEFUL INFORMATION

BANKS None but Panayotis, he of *Pension Koundouris* (*See* **The Accommodation**), changes travellers cheques. Naturally his rate reflects the less rigid constraints experienced outside the conventional banking system... The Chora Post Office changes Postcheques, Eurocheques and Travellers cheques.

BEACHES The splendid Skala beach fills the bottom of the bay. It is a comparatively generous sweep of sand and a backshore of pebbly sand on which are scattered some small boats, boat trailers and beer crates. The shore is backed by a narrow, stone laid path that sweeps up to the Chora (after a long, steep climb). Further along is a dry river-bed, close by which is an incongruously sited, abandoned, squatty toilet block. The other side of the river-bed is a flat grass field which has a marshy appearance. At the far end of the bay the sea bottom is rocky and the narrow foreshore is big pebbles with a pleasant grove of trees on the backshore.

A good number of years previously, a group of hippies discovered Sikinos and the convenient camping area, behind and to the far side of the beach. The residents erected the 'squatty' but must have decided, in the end, that it was best to exclude the 'Great Unwashed'.

In August, a caique runs day-trips to the sandy Ag Georgios beach, ½hr north of Skala, at a cost of 300drs each way. Occasionally a caique will run to the pebble beach of Ag Panteleimonas, some 20 minutes away.

BREAD SHOPS The bread is baked in the Chora and brought down by bus, daily – if it is running.

BUSES With the completion of the Chora road, a new bus now provides a daily service between the port and the Chora. The vehicle was brought to Sikinos, in 1988, by the son of Nikos Margetis, who is owner of the *Kastro Cafe* in the Chora. Appropriately there is a picture of this hard won, 20th century possession in the cafe. The son, of course, is the island's bus driver.

Bus timetable
The bus is based in the Chora and the schedule depends on the time of year. The minimum service is a twice-daily round trip departing from the Chora at approximately 0700hrs & 1500hrs, returning half an hour later. In the busy months this is stepped up to forays at 0700, 0830, 1100, 1400, 1600, 1900 & 2100hrs. The bus also ties in with ferry-boat arrivals.

DISCO Believe it or not, yes. *See* **Route One**.

FERRY BOATS As described, they anchor in the bay.

Ferry-boat timetable (Mid to high season)

Day	Departure time	Ferry-boat	Ports/Islands of Call
Mon	1700hrs	Apollo Express	Folegandros,Santorini,Ios,Naxos, Paros,Piraeus(M).
Tues	0300hrs	Milos Express	Ios,Santorini.
	1000hrs	Apollo Express	Ios,Naxos,Paros,Piraeus(M).
	1800hrs	Georgios Express	Folegandros,Santorini.
	2000hrs	Milos Express	Folegandros,Milos,Siphnos,Serifos,Piraeus(M).

Wed	0930hrs	Milos Express	Folegandros,Kimolos,Milos,Siphnos, Serifos,Kithnos,Piraeus(M).
	1000hrs	Georgios Express	Ios,Naxos,Paros,Syros,Piraeus(M).
	1730hrs	Hellas Express	Folegandros,Santorini,Iraklion(Crete).
Thurs	1000hrs	Hellas Express	Ios,Naxos,Paros,Syros,Piraeus(M).
Fri	2100hrs	Golden Vergina	Santorini,Anafi,Ag Nikolaos(Crete),Sitia(Crete), Kasos,Karpathos,Diafani(Karpathos), Chalki,Rhodes
Sat	0730hrs	Milos Express	Ios,Santorini.
	2000hrs	Kimolos	Ios,Santorini.
Sun	0900hrs	Kimolos	Folegandros,Kimolos,Milos,Siphnos, Kithnos,Piraeus(M).
	0930hrs	Milos Express	Folegandros,Kimolos,Milos,Siphnos, Serifos,Kithnos,Piraeus(M).
	2000hrs	Golden Vergina	Folegandros,Kimolos,Milos,Piraeus(M).

Please note these tables are detailed as a GUIDE ONLY. Due to the time taken to research the Cyclades, it is IMPOSSIBLE TO 'match' the timetables or even boats . So don't try cross pollinating...

FERRY-BOAT TICKET OFFICES As detailed, Papa Panayotis operates the only ticket office from the General store section of his pension/taverna (*Tmr* 5D2). The relevant timetables are stuck up on the walls of the taverna.

MEDICAL CARE Best not to be ill, at all.

POLICE & POST OFFICE *See* **The Chora**.

ROUTE ONE

The Port to the Chora It used to be a one hour uphill trudge but now there is the bus. The route has been bludgeoned into a broad dirt road with, here and there, remnants of the rock-slab track showing through, as the new road follows the course of the old. The original stepped path, still used by locals, ascends to the left-hand part of the Chora.

The Chora road passes the 'squatty toilet block', to the right; an extensive private house on the left; a little further on, the Generating Station almost immediately beyond which is Disco Sikinos. I think I am correct to say that the founders of this facility were refugees from the Ios disco scene. Certainly the delights of this unexpected entertainment centre were once advertised at the *Far Out Cafe* (Milopotamos Beach, Ios). Despite appearing totally unattended, closer inspection, through the broken glass of its closed door, reveals the place to be surprisingly pleasantly fitted out. A tiny square room has a small bar, the front of which, as well as the walls, is faced with varnished bamboo. A fishing net is slung from the ceiling, holding a few, large sea shells and starfish, to give an effective and tasteful 'fishing boat' atmosphere.

Beyond the disco, at about that part of the route where the upward climb becomes serious, is the surprisingly large *Restaurant H Chora*, above which are ***Rooms***.

At about the half-way stage there still remains part of a small, shady spinney, all that is left of a once welcoming spring and a water well.

THE CHORA/KASTRO The upper, mountain community almost divides into two, sprawling and dipping down across a central, sunken, saddle ridge. Strictly speaking the right-hand (*Skala behind one*) village is the Kastro, the left-hand one is the Chora. Dominating the saddle, where the old path, as distinct from the old road, scrambles up to the Chora, is the school (ΔΗΜ ΣΧΟΛΕΙΟΝ).

Truly, this must be one of the loveliest examples of an island 'working' town still extant. I stress working because agricultural pursuits take place almost to the core of the settlement. This is particularly so in the 'left-hand' Chora where prolificate henhouses, pigsties, donkey pens and mule sheds in and amongst the dwellings. Behind stone walls, hidden by rises in the ground, clouds of chaff indicate when the crops are being winnowed. There are a number of now defunct windmills stretched along the escarpment, facing out over and high above the sea, beyond the tumbling, brown, parched mountainside.

The new road sweeps round to the left of the right-hand village and up to the saddle. Keeping straight on is the older, concrete road past the Post Office. This has a metered telephone and is open weekdays between 0800-1430hrs .

The old road ends at a T-junction. Taking the right lane and turning almost immediately left and right again leads to the baker's, an inconspicuous cottage affair with a plastic-strip curtain across the doorway. Ignoring the immediate left and right sallies forth to *To Kaminia Taverna*. This signposted taverna is run by a smiley, friendly mama. She has to summon her grown-up daughter to calculate the mathematics of any bill and to translate. There is no patio or terrace and entrance is through a curtain. Behind *To Kaminia* is *Loukas Rooms*, a clean looking pension. To the left, prior to *To Kaminia*, is Odhos Zoodochos Pighi, the name being neatly carved on a marble plaque attached to the side of a house. This path ascends the remainder of the mountain to the once fortified:-

Monastery Zoodochos Pighi The last part of the track across the rocky surface is indicated by whorls of whitewash and passes a rough hewn grave, presumably that of a long departed monk.

The high walls of the building enclose a very pretty, flower planted courtyard in front of the attractive campaniled chapel. There is extensive restoration underway. For those without the time to obtain the key, the locked gates necessitate climbing through the yet unrestored ruins of the monks' living quarters, to the right of the building. There are marvellous all-round views over the sea to the north, the Chora and, to the south, down the tumbling valley to the distant port. The key is available from the patron of the 'School Plateia' Kafeneion, Nikos Margetis – he who is father of the bus driver.

Back at the T-junction, selecting the left-hand lane leads past a couple of grocery stores, on the left, and two cafe-bars on the right. In the second of the latter 80drs will buy half a litre of excellent retsina from the barrel. Further down this lane, and off to the right is a narrow street overhung by a grapevine trellis in which is the *Cafe-bar Taverna To Κλιματαρια* or, logically enough, the Vine. The taverna's comfortable, orange coloured plastic chairs are scattered about. This is the 'island hot spot' despite which the menu is limited and the service slow. Menu offerings include 'Olish variety' and 'Cakes Spoon'! The owner is a rather flat faced, bluff man with a deeply buried sense of humour. His eleven year old daughter waits on the tables. A lunch of 'olish' variety (which turns out to be a large mezes), a Greek salad, bread and a soda water cost 550drs.

Just before this taverna, on the right, is a veritable Aladdin's Cave of a general store, where it is possible to buy anything from cheese to knitting wool. Close to is the *Kafeneion* of Nikos Margetis who is extremely helpful to tourists, especially those who join him in admiration of the bus, pictures of which adorn his cafe-bar. He has double rooms, with en suite bathroom and hot water available, at a cost of between 1500-1900drs.

Beyond the narrow street of the *Cafe-bar To Κλιματαρια* is a large, pleasant square around the main church, after which the lane drops to the saddle and the 'School Plateia'. Here is the settlements public well and drinking trough, the scene of much early morning 'donkey' work (oh dear). Whilst the villagers draw water to transport it on pack animals to the upper dwellings, the donkeys and mules are also watered for the day.

The bus stops twice, once close by the Post Office and the second time on the 'School Plateia' which is used as the turn-round point.

The 'left-hand', smaller 'village', or Chora, is connected to the central 'School Plateia' by a long flight of steps. These rise from close by a chapel, on the one side, and a flour miller's on the left. The old steps to Skala make off down the hillside from the side of the faded, disproportionately large school. The overriding impressions in the Chora is still one of donkeys, more often than not coralled in various crumbling buildings or, for that matter, any nook and cranny, as well as of jasmine and cacti. There are many dilapidated dwellings and tiny alleys wander off here and there in a higgledy-piggledy network of lanes. Quite frankly it would not be a surprise if the 'Magnificent Seven' came riding in. Apart from donkeys this 'village' houses the Police station.

On an island where the paths remain in constant use by the natives and their animals, there is the possibility of a number of excellent walks. These are not for the aged, infirm, faint-hearted or anyone with the sense to collapse in the nearest taverna, but it does offer an alternative to the new road.

WALK ONE

The Port to the Chora/Kastro (1hr 40mins) This route starts out on the road along the back of the beach. At the end of the stone wall take to the hills up a bulldozed track to the left (*Sbo*). This was a footpath winding up through the scrubland to the Chapel of Panaghia, high above the port. It is as if someone approached the road builders and said, 'While you've got the bulldozer here, mate, how about improving our path to the chapel?' So instead of a narrow, well-worn path there is a broad swathe of splintered rock and mangled bushes and roots – more difficult to negotiate than the original path, especially as thorn bushes are haphazardly springing up. It is a very stiff climb. Just before the crest of the hill, the track charges to the left through a wall and dips down and up to the chapel.

Passing to the right (*Sbo*) of the chapel, the old mule path mercifully takes over, and the going from hereon is relatively easy – easier on the feet, in fact, than the rough surface of the main road. A few metres beyond the chapel is a well, which in common with others away from the new road, is in frequent daily use. Beyond the well, the path takes to a stone staircase on the left (ignore the bit of path into an enclosure ahead) for a short, sharp ascent, at the top of which it opens out and continues in the same direction as before, keeping close to a wall on the right. On this section the path is not so well defined. Fairly soon the track contours round a fold in the mountain and comes to another well, below sheer cliffs. At this point in particular, one could be forgiven for doubting if the Chora will ever be reached, as the path turns away from it and several mountain spurs are in the way. Fear not, as the track easily skirts each fold of the mountain, descending to cross even the most impassable-looking of ravines by a dramatic and well-engineered stone staircase. All the while the views are spectacular, whether of the sea and neighbouring islands (Ios and Santorini) or of the terraced slopes below.

The last part of the route is through terraced olive groves, past a Tinos-like dovecote and an interesting double well, before climbing steps to the 'School Plateia'.

To follow this route from the Chora, take the broad steps down from and alongside the school and turn right just before they end at a left-hand turn with a rounded wall. To continue down these steps puts one on a path which drops to the valley floor by a chapel and then climbs to rejoin the main road, about a third of the way down (*See* **Route One**).

A few minutes after taking the right turn, beyond the wells, a path descends to the left, on a right-hand bend (and therefore goes straight on!), and takes a lower route to the port. Continue along the contour to the right for the high road, as described. I know, I know... why not catch the bus?

WALK TWO

The Chora to Episkopi (1¼ hours) Episkopi is the 5th century AD church built over a 2nd century BC temple of Apollo, although other authorities speak of it as having originally been a Roman temple or a 3rd century AD Heroon (temple-tomb).

From the 'School Plateia' a dirt track skirts round to the right of the left-hand part of the village. After passing under a water pipe, supplying a farm far down below to the right, this turns left, back into the village. A mule track continues straight on and this leads straight to Episkopi, following the folds of the coastline high above the sea. A couple of well-worn tracks fork off right downhill, but these are to be ignored. Just about when hope of locating Episkopi is fading, it appears on the skyline, on a plateau before the southern heights of the island. Its dome, somehow reminiscent of a lemon-squeezer, sits incongruously on the solid block of the temple.

The Byzantine church, which was remodelled after earthquake damage shortly before 1673, is badly decayed, having been stripped of its treasures by 'foreigners', and is now in an advanced state of collapse. A complex timber framework has been constructed inside to support the structure, but with gaping cracks in the masonry, and one of the supporting pillars way off vertical, for how much longer?

Although the church is situated on the northerly coast of the island, there is a fine view down a steep valley all the way to the sea to the south. In fact, it is quite easy to see Episkopi, gleaming a creamy white in the sunshine, from as far away as the ferry between Sikinos and Folegandros.

To return to the Chora, instead of simply retracing one's steps, walkers can consider giving free rein to their internal 'mountain goat'. At the end of the flattish area, on which the church is built, where the approach path bends leftwards to follow the coastline, a narrow footpath on the right strikes up the hill. With Episkopi behind one, and the sea to the left, after a short, steep climb the path opens out onto a reasonable donkey path heading straight for the Chora. It runs roughly parallel to the lower path but offers even more splendid sea views. These take in Folegandros to the rear, Siphnos in the distance to the left, followed by Antiparos and Paros, Naxos far ahead and Ios, seemingly just beyond the Chora. About half-way back to the Chora is a chapel with a pretty, double-barrelled roof.

WALK THREE (North-east)

The Port to Ag Nikolaos Chapel & Cove (50 minutes) The destination is a delightful little cove, the other side of a couple of headlands, to the north-east of the port. However, it is necessary to start in almost the opposite direction by following the main road to the Chora, as far as the Generating Station. Opposite this, to the left-hand side of an abandoned bulldozer and Volvo truck, is a footpath. This was probably a mule track before the road and house construction, at this point, virtually obliterated it. The path strikes off uphill, at an acute angle to the road, immediately crossing a car track from opposite the Sikinos Disco to some houses on the right. The mule track climbs, passing to the right of a house, with a triple-arched verandah and upstairs terrace, and two further, newly built buildings in a line up the hill. The track disappears round the back of the last of these (ignore the inviting-looking footpath to the right) and continues to ascend, parallel to the road and flanked by a low stone wall.

Shortly beyond a point level with the aforementioned *Restaurant/Rooms H Chora* complex, the track joins another track skirting the hill from left to right and flanked by a stone wall above. Turn right on to this latter track, which is more of a path at this point. At last facing the sea, follow it to climb and cross the hill saddle behind the large headlands above Skala. From this viewpoint are magnificent panoramas of the Chora to the rear, of the Harbour bay below and to the right, and of Ios island and town straight ahead.

From here the track gently descends over scrubland towards some broad, cultivated terraces and is then funnelled into a walled mule track. This advances between some more scrubland, unworked terraces, disused farm buildings and a well, on the right. The last section of this easy descent is alongside a well-tended olive grove and a small, newish house. After which, the path tumbles down the hillside for the last hundred metres to the tiny Chapel of St Nikolaos and the sheltered cove below.

Inside, the chapel is almost bare, except for an altar screen with three or four paintings of St Nikolaos and a lectern-cum-table in the centre. cluttered with candle ends, incense and a few coins. Unusually, there are no matches, so anybody wishing to light the customary candle to the patron saint of sailors, before entrusting themselves to the pass-boat for the ferry, will have to take their own.

The cove is at the mouth of a dry river-bed, which, a little further up the valley, appears to be lined with polished marble and is overhung by oleanders. The sheltered beach is of flat stones and coarse sand, and is flanked by layered rocks affording good sunbathing, with fine views of Santorini in the distance.

The path beyond this cove is not obvious, but it is possible to continue up over the next headland to **Dialiskari Beach**. This is sandier and provides good swimming.

WALK FOUR (South-east)

The Port to Ag Panteleimon Chapel & Beach (1 hour) The start of the route is the lane from Skala bay past *Rooms To Let* (*Tmr* 6B/C1). Initially cobbled, the lane becomes a dirt track on the edge of the village and then reverts to the original mule track, beyond a cluster of smart new buildings. This snakes through walled fields and terraces to a point level with a rectangular spit of land jutting into the sea. Here a broad track joins from the left and begins to climb around to the right of the low hill ahead. It is necessary, however, to veer slightly to the left, following the course of the wall. The path hereabouts is broad slabs of rock between widely spaced walls.

Part way up, by a farm building on the left, the left-hand wall ends and the ground widens out. Ignore the path to the left, skirting the coast, and continue straight up the slabs of rock, keeping close to the right-hand wall. There is an obvious, wide gap on the skyline at which to aim. After a while the path funnels down in between two walls and is stepped in places. When the path opens out, yet again, keep straight on or slightly to the left (the two possible routes rejoin each other after a few metres). Where the terrain changes, commence to contour round to the left of the mountain spur, across open scrubland. The path is not always obvious where it crosses rocky ground.

Having rounded the spur, the path closes in again. It descends for a metre or ten and then turns sharply right to cross over a saddle, allowing the first view of the chapel, on the other side of a steep valley. After a short descent, the path bears right to contour inland up the valley for a little way and then descends steeply down stone steps. At the foot of these, a hairpin turn to the left, by an evergreen thicket, advances on the rough path down the side of the gully to the small, stony beach.

A few metres beyond the turn for the beach is a small, roofless stone hut on the right, and not far beyond this, on the apex of a left-handed hairpin bend, a track joins from the right, supposedly from the Chora. After the hairpin bend there is a short, sharp, rocky staircase climb, with the Chapel of Ag Panteleimon, is just around the corner.

The path continues beyond the chapel, following the coastline. It may even go right round the island – you never know your luck! The route just described, though, is probably as much of a country hike as most walkers would require. The description might sound a bit messy but its actually an easy route to find and never too strenuous. Other than a circular route of several hours via the Chora, there's only the same path back again.

A taverna guest, Astipalaia. Acknowledgement to Anne Merewood.

A Chora cafe-bar, Amorgos. Acknowledgement to Anne Merewood.

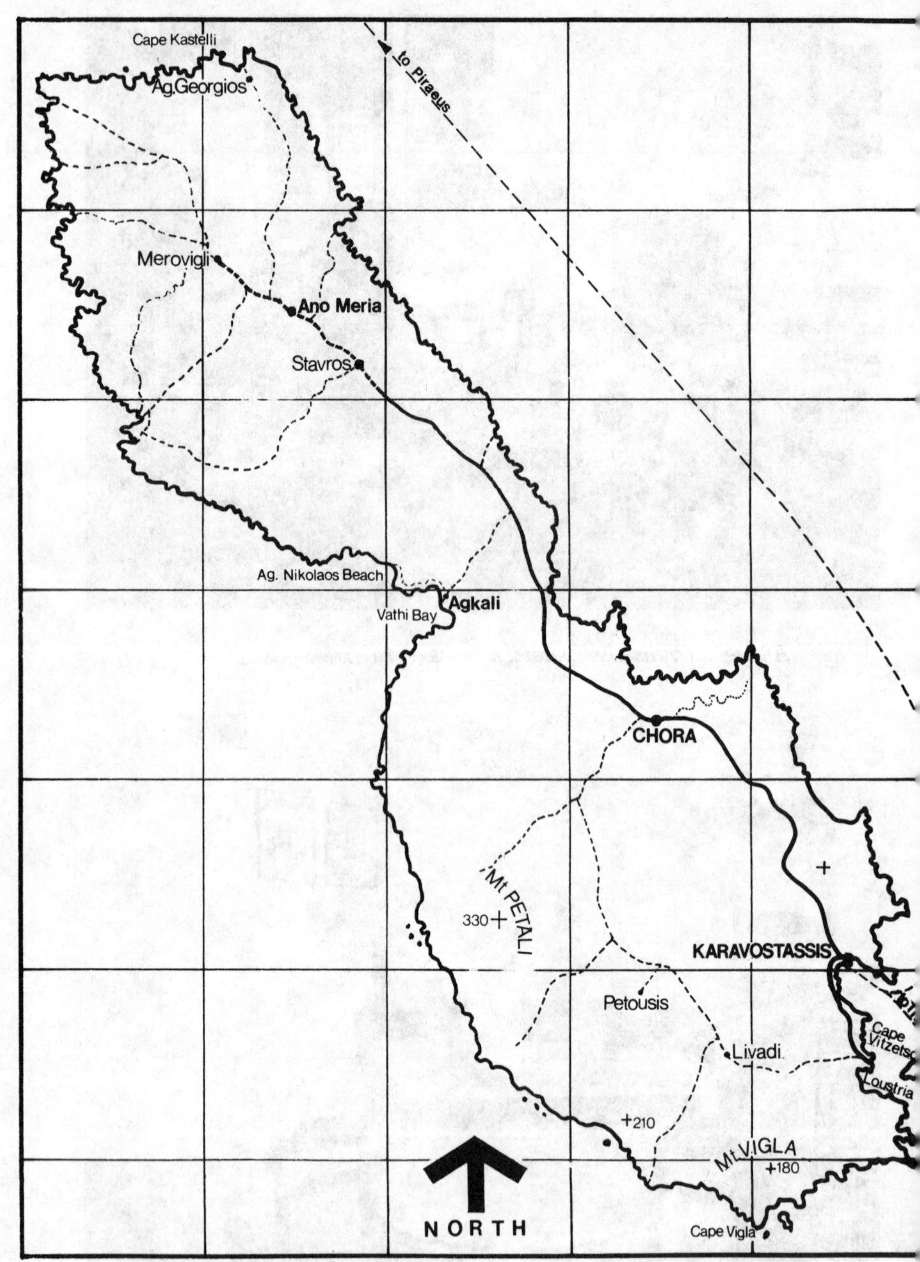

Illustration 23 Folegandros island

9 FOLEGANDROS (Pholegandros, Polycandros) Cyclades Islands - Eastern chain

★★★★

FIRST IMPRESSIONS Arid, terraced mountain slopes; water short; Danish holiday-makers; lack of flies; shops open late; few cats; no taxis; a 'Santorini' Chora.

SPECIALITIES Koukoulas, distinctive women's hats.

RELIGIOUS HOLIDAYS & FE TIVALS include: None that are only relevant to the island.

VITAL STATISTICS Tel prefix 0286. Some 12km long, orientated NW/SE, up to 4km at the widest and under 1km at the narrowest, with an area of about 35 sq km. The population numbers some 700, spread between Karavostassis' port, the Chora and the northern settlement of Ano Meria.

HISTORY The usual mixture of Dorians, Cretans, Romans (who used the island as a place of exile), Venetians and Turks.

GENERAL Folegandros is usually lumped together with Sikinos at the tail-end of an Ios chapter. This is a travesty. Both islands deserve a separate chapter and are almost totally dissimilar. For example, the 'proper' ferry-boat quay at Karavostassis Port has allowed Folegandros to become a much more sophisticated location than Sikinos with the to be expected increase in the number of tourists. These are 'topped-up' by a series of Danish inspired, teaching holiday-courses during the months of June, July and August, an influx which has resulted in a comparatively hefty increase in prices.

There are several hotels in the Chora, even if the owners are apparently disinterested in procuring guests. There are a number of tavernas in the port, even if the patrons appear lukewarm to tourists. Perhaps the arid nature of the land imparts some of its stern, unyielding characteristics to the islanders? They are, in general, reserved and appear at first to lack the traditional Greek warmth. But have no fears, for only a slight scratch to the 'skin' reveals a very rural, rustic, old-world island charm. The 'mains' drinking water is only turned on for a few hours in the morning, but it is necessary as most of the wells 'dish up' slimy water. Despite these irritating and minor shortcomings Folegandros must still rate as one of the more idyllic Cyclades islands.

Once away from the simply beautiful and verdant Chora, the remaining countryside and few villages are delightful, agricultural backwoods. The lack of other than generally inferior beaches is, I would like to think, more than adequately offset by the island's other attractions. These include the stunning, 'Santorini-like' scenery to the north of the Chora, the latter being perched precipitously close to the edge of the east coast mountainsides that plunge steeply into the surrounding sea; the simple, fishing hamlet of Agkali, nestling at the foot of an almost dry river gorge; as well as the quiet, unsophisticated, northern cluster of inland agrarian hamlets, strung along the spine of the mountain range, that make up Ano Meria.

A last, general warning is not to visit out of the very short summer season (July-September) – many of the accommodation and eating places are closed and the bus timetables are severely curtailed.

KARAVOSTASSIS: port (Illustration 24) The approach to the port from Sikinos island is marked by a number of rocky outcrops. The quay is set in a craggy inlet of the large bay, imparting an impression of claustrophobia and clutter. The bay is generally untidy with most of the development crammed into a stretch on the right (*Sbo*). There is a certain amount of 'creeping infill' round the nearside of the beach. There are no shops, a hotel, one taverna, a cafe-bar taverna, a kafeneion, a 'canteen' periptero and everything closes for the siesta.

ARRIVAL BY FERRY The surprisingly large Ferry-boat Quay (*Tmr* 1E1) is situated on the extreme right of the Harbour (*Sbo*). The waterfront leads quickly into the heart of the tiny port development, with all the impression of a messy, hot 'Yukon' frontier town, especially the area rising up the hillside to the right of the quay.

Due to the lack of choice and general disinterest evinced by the port owners of accommodation, who do not even bother to meet the ferry-boats, it is one of the few islands where I can wholeheartedly endorse heading straight for the Chora. It is not entirely true to say that visitors disembarking are not met, as some Room owners sidle up to stragglers in the street.

Both the 'private' and 'state' buses meet ferry-boat arrivals.

THE ACCOMMODATION & EATING OUT Karavostassis does not have a surfeit of either accommodation or eating places and the height of summer presence of a disproportionate number of Danes has hardened up prices, especially in the Chora. It may be of interest to know their classes include 'body consciousness' and 'dream interpretation'!

The Accommodation Probably the best private house options are around the bay, on the road towards *Camping Livadia* (of which more later).

Rooms (*Tmr* 3C6)
Directions: Walk along the quay past the fishermens' 'bus shelter' (*Tmr* 4D1), where lines and hooks are daily baited, up the 'Esplanade' chicane, beyond the chapel to the left, the Bus stop/turn round point to the right (*Tmr* 5C1), left along the tree shaded, concreted backshore track, past the *Restaurant Kati Allo* (*Tmr* 6A3) and the *Hotel Aeolus* (*Tmr* 2A3/4) on the right. The curve of the bay passes a little shrine (*Tmr* 7B5), on the right, behind which are a few buildings – one probably uncompleted ***Rooms***, and on to a laid stone road surface. The chalet is on the right (Phew!).

The Papa, an unsmiling, middle-aged 'Sancho Panza', is recognisable by the small motorcycle he rides and without which he is rarely seen. It has a box fixed behind the pillion seat. He also wears an Italian style, Colonial pith helmet, seen extensively on the Dodecanese islands. The other half is a a smiley Mama. Rates range from 1300-2000drs for a double bedroom, sharing the bathroom.

At the junction of the Chora road and the concrete track 'Esplanade', that skirts the bay, is a sign to 'Alissideri traditional villas for rent. Greek rooms in a traditional house'. This establishment is on the hillside between *'Rooms' Sancho Panza'* (*Tmr* 3C6) and *Taverna on the Rocks* (*Tmr* 12D6).

Hotel Aeoulus (*Tmr* 2A3/4) (Class C) Tel 41205
Directions: As above, but about centre of the 'U' of the bay.

Of posh appearance with formal gardens and terraces but not outrageously expensive and in a pleasant situation. All rooms have en suite bathrooms with a single priced at 2000drs & a double 2500drs, increasing to 2500drs & 3000drs (1st July-31st Aug).

In this neck of the woods the *Restaurant Kati Allo* (*Tmr* 6A3) also offers accommodation and there are some ***Rooms*** between the restaurant and the Chora road.

Back on the quay road are a couple more, rather 'doo-hickey' alternatives, namely:-
Rooms (*Tmr* 8B1)
Directions: Fronting the 'High Street'. The bungalow is the last building on the right, the far side of which is a rock wall and then fields.

The old lady demands the going rate (1200-1800drs) for a double room but will not entertain less than three days stay. The bathroom and washbasin is an open air affair.
and:–
Rooms (*Tmr* 10B1)
Directions: A street behind the aforementioned accommodation. Wander up the fairly steep, unmade

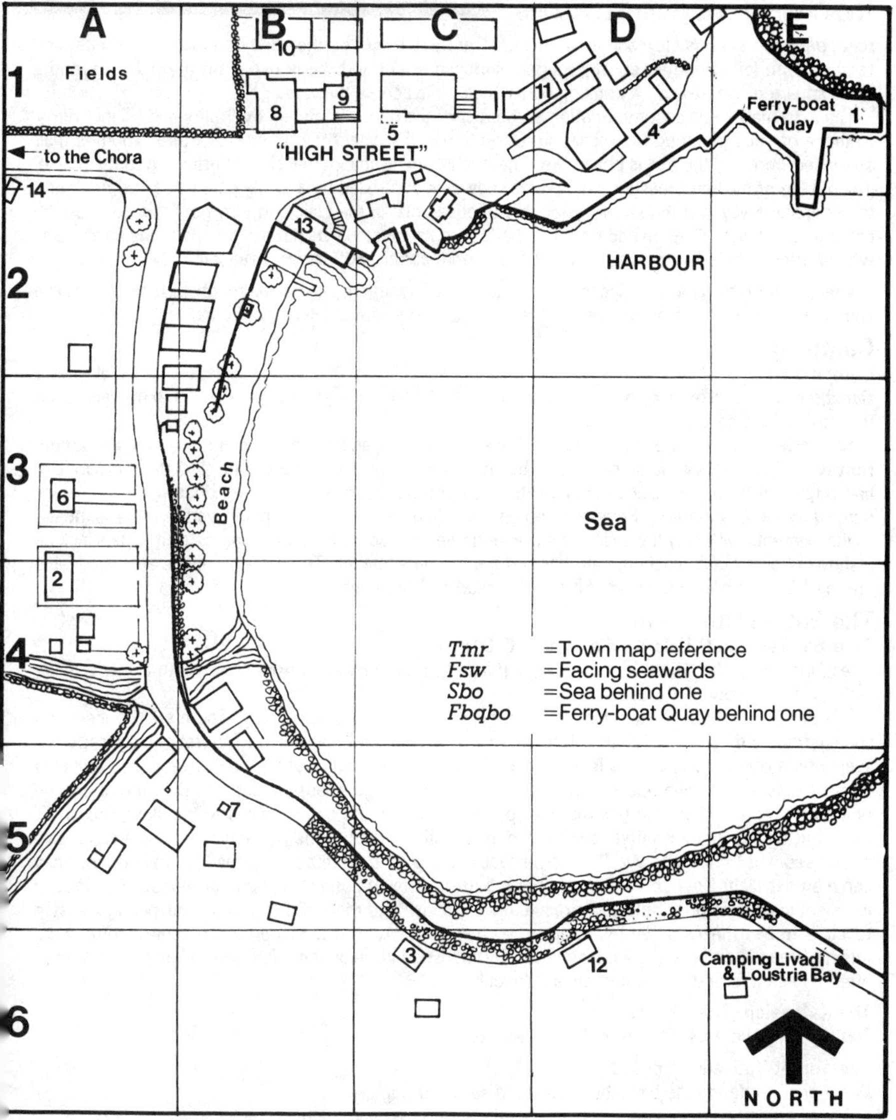

Illustration 24 Karavostassis

Tmr 1E1	Ferry-boat Quay	8B1	Rooms
2A3/4	Hotel Aeolus	9B/C1	Kafeneion
3C6	Rooms 'Sancho Panza'	10B1	Rooms
4D1	Fishermans shelter	11C/D1	Cafe-bar Taverna H Kalo Kardia
5C1	Bus stop	12D6	Taverna on the Rocks
6A3	Restaurant/Rooms Kati Allo	13B2	Evangelos Bar
7B5	Shrine	14A1/2	Canteen/periptero

road, between the Bus stop and a Kafeneion (*Tmr* 9B/C1), set on the edge of a municipal shelter and terrace. Turn left, along an equally roughly surfaced street and the house is on the right, beyond a small square of wasteland. A drinking water hydrant is across the way.

The extremely basic accommodation at the rear of the house is owned by 'Henry and Minni Crun' – to those of you old enough to recall the 'Goon Show'. I suspect the primitive, raftered room is their spare bedroom and the bed is board-like. The 'bathroom' is an external shed abutting on to the house. The dribble of the low pressure, cold water shower is controlled by a single gate valve and the 'bath' water drains away into the street, through a 'mouse-hole' in the wall, and why not? It is quite on the cards that, whilst walking to and from the 'bathroom', a guest will be nuzzled by one of the local mules who is often hobbled in the street. The double room costs 1500drs, mid-season.

In keeping with the general reticence regarding accommodation, across the rough surfaced street is a substantial house with ***Rooms*** but the owner makes no effort to advertise the fact.

Camping

Camping Livadia Tel 41203

Directions: *See* **Route One**, but for those not prepared to turn a page or two, it is a 2km walk round the curve of the bay.

Where an island is as short of accommodation as Folegandros, a campsite is a distinct option. However, this particular location means being rather cut off from 'Town life' and the surrounding, unlovely countryside does not compensate. On the other hand the site's van does meet the ferries parking by the Bus terminal. Being located on the side of an arid hill, Camping Livadi is rather exposed to the elements with only the shade of still young trees and some covered areas. Site amenities include a shower/toilet block, kitchen, cafe-bar and a small mini-market. The cafe-bar prices are reasonable but the facility is only open from June to the middle of September.

The Eating Out

Cafe-Bar Taverna H Kalo Kardia (*Tmr* 11C/D1)

Directions: From the 'High St' to the right (*Fbqbo*) up an angled, narrow street with a few outside tables which almost fill the alley.

The patron is rather taciturn and dour but his smiley wife is very friendly. There are 'house-rules' and customers must not insult the status of the establishment by asking for ice-creams, cigarettes or even a pure orange juice – "This is a kafeneion". Oh and don't queue at the 'bar', even if in a pressing hurry, it does upset mine host who dismisses 'counter-loungers' out of hand. As the time of a ferry-boat arrival approaches, the taverna fills up, despite which the patron sticks to his slow, measured pace, but with an underlying sense of panic. It is, without doubt, one of the cleanest tavernas I have patronised and I once observed him order out a group who were accompanied by their dogs. They serve an excellent Greek breakfast of bread, butter, jam and coffee, yoghurt and honey. The food is excellent and some prior notice can result in various fish and meat dishes being available. A pleasant touch is to see mezes served with an ouzo. A meal for two of fish soup (scorpaena scrofa), 2½kg retsina, bread, 2 coffees and 2 ouzos cost 1850drs Good value but bills vary due to 'suspect' addition, often, I hasten to add, in the customers' favour.

The Kafeneion (*Tmr* 9B/C1)

Further along the 'High St', but diffident service.

Restaurant Kati Allo (*Tmr* 6A3)

Directions: Bordering the backshore concrete surfaced track.

A well organised restaurant, with large patio terrace, serving the usual fare at reasonable prices.

Taverna Xakia On The Rocks (*Tmr* 12D6)

Directions: The far side of the bay. A simple, hut-like building, in a pleasant situation, affording a wonderful view when the sun sets, the last of the rays brightly illuminating Sikinos island. Even the Port looks pretty from the terrace.

I am a great one for dishing out travel rules and principles but often am to be found wanting in their execution. No better example than here at '*...on the Rocks*', which you certainly will be if you do not establish their menu prices before ordering!

Evangelos Bar (*Tmr* 13B2)

Directions: Bordering the 'High St' down narrow steps to the left (*Fbqbo*).

The nicely situated bar is set in a converted boat shed with the wide, shallow slipway now doubling up as a terrace. 'Chatty' setting and a 'chatty' proprietor, who speaks good English, the whole overlaid by taped music all of which results in 'chatty' prices. There are sea urchins in the shallows.

THE A TO Z OF USEFUL INFORMATION

BANK *See* **The Chora**.

BEACHES The main beach fills the bottom of the small bay, is tree-edged and rather scrubbly with a shore made up of big pebbles. The first metre or so of the sea-bed is made up of rather slimy stones beyond which the bottom is sandy and the water very clear. The elements are so propitious that a strong swimmer can make for Dio Adelfia, the nearest of the two islets set down in the bay.

Over the headland to the left (*Fsw*) of the quay are two beaches set in the adjoining, large bay. The far one is a coarse sand cove crowded in by quite high cliffs, but almost impossible to reach. The closer of the two is another coarse sand beach with a sea bottom of big stones, just over the neck of the headland. The latter is a very difficult scramble, added to which the port's rubbish is tipped over the low cliff-edge to the left of the cove. On the port side of the headland, half-left of the quay, is a very small cove with a broad, shingly sand beach.

For other beaches *See* **Route One**.

BUSESApart from the official service, there is a 'pirate' 12 seater, a bright green Mercedes Benz bus (similar to a 'Transit Van' with windows). This parks close by the *Cafe-bar Taverna H Kalo Kardia* (*Tmr* 11C/D1), whilst the 'proper' bus stops close to the bus stop (*Tmr* 5C1) (well it would...). Both buses meet the ferries and, if they cannot cope with the number of passengers, return for stragglers. The owner/driver of the 'pirate' bus is a member of one of the two families who own most of the Chora.

The timetables are complicated by the differing methods of operation. The official buses run between the port and the nearside of the Chora and operate a separate service from the far side of the Chora to Ano Meria, with a stop-off at the top of the track down to Agkali. The 'pirate bus' also runs from the port but turns off along a narrow lane that circumnavigates the pedestrian Chora. This route emerges at the far, north side of the Chora and then proceeds on to Ano Meria. Being an owner-driver he really crams them in, so much so that the 'Guiness Book of Records' would probably like to monitor his activities.

Bus timetable (Mid-season)
'State' Bus

Karavostassis Port to the Chora
Daily 0740, 0940 & hourly to 1440, 1710, & hourly to 2310hrs.
Return journey
Daily 0730, 0930 & hourly to 1430, 11710 & hourly to 2300hrs.

Chora to Ano Meria via a roadside stop for the Agkali track
Daily 0800, 0900, 1045 (to Agkali stop off), 1215, 1500, 1840, 2100hrs.
Return journey
Daily 0645, 0945, 1100 (from Agkali stop off), 1300, 1800(Agkali), 1915hrs.

'Pirate' Bus
Karavostassis Port to Ano Meria via the Chora (far side) and Agkali track.
Daily 0845, 1030, 1200, 1445, 2045hrs.
Return journey
Daily 0945, 1130, 1300, 1545, 2145hrs.

One-way fares: Karavostassis to the Chora 70drs; duration Karavostassis to Ano Meria ¾hr.
In addition to the above, buses meet the ferries. Timetables are posted by Karavostassis Ferry-boat Quay (*Tmr* 1E1) and the Chora 'Water Wells' Sq (*Tmr* 2D3/4).

COMMERCIAL SHOPPING AREA Yes, well. There is an important contribution to the ports trading in the shape of a 'Canteen' (*Tmr* 14A1/2). This is a concrete box periptero edging some waste ground to the left of the outset of the Chora road. Sells cigarettes, beer, ice-cream, cheese-puffs, chocolate, orange drinks and bottled water.

FERRY-BOATS There is a remarkably good service considering the remoteness of the island until comparatively recent years.

Ferry-boat timetable (Mid-season)

Day	Departure time	Ferry-boat	Ports/Islands of Call
Mon	1800hrs	Apollo Express	Santorini.
Tues	0200hrs	Milos Express	Sikinos,Ios,Santorini.
	0900hrs	Apollos Express	Sikinos,Ios,Naxos,Paros,Piraeus(M).

	1900hrs	Georgios Express	Santorini.
	2100hrs	Milos Express	Milos,Siphnos,Serifos,Piraeus(M).
Wed	0900hrs	Georgios Express	Sikinos,Ios,Naxos,Paros,Syros,Piraeus(M).
	1830hrs	Hellas Express	Santorini.
Thur	0900hrs	Hellas Express	Sikinos,Ios,Naxos,Paros,Syros,Piraeus(M).
Fri	2000hrs	Golden Vergina	Sikinos,Santorini,Anafi,Ag Nikolaos(Crete), Sitia(crete),Kasos,Karpathos, Diafani(Karparthos),Chalki,Rhodes.

Please note these tables are detailed as a GUIDE ONLY. Due to the time taken to research the Cyclades it is IMPOSSIBLE TO 'match' the timetables or even boats . So don't try cross pollinating...

FERRY-BOAT TICKET OFFICES *See* **The Chora**. A lady 'sets up' a stool at the outset of the quay, prior to a ferry-boat's arrival.

OTE, POST OFFICE, POLICE & TRAVEL AGENTS *See* **The Chora**.

PLACES OF INTEREST On the gate of the *Restaurant/Rooms Kati Allo* (*Tmr* 6A3) is a notice advertising boat trips to Agkali and St Nikolaos Beach. Departure 1115hrs, returning at 1800hrs.

TAXIS None.

WATER The island's drinking water is available from water hydrants and taps,here and there, but these are only turned on between 0930-1100hrs. It is therefore not a bad idea to obtain one or two bottles of mineral water.

Excursion To Loustria Bay (2km) The track curves round the far side of the bay, past Cape Vitzetzos. To the south of the latter are, down below, two rather inaccessible and tiny coves with grey, coarse sand beaches. The route peters out on the nearside of a scrubbly, unlovely, grey sand and shingle beach alongside a grove of arethemusa bush trees. These groves spread along and shelter the backshore of the beach. The hardier souls who camp in amongst the trees and bushes cause the environs to be very messy and latrine-like. The sea bottom is weedy with a tendency to being slimy and the far end consists of slate stones, pebbles and biscuit rock. Nude bathing.

From Loustria Bay is a pleasant walk up a fertile valley to the hamlet of **Livadia**.

Camping Livadi (*See* **The Accommodation**) is set back from the far end of the beach on the lower, shadeless slopes of the hillside, but at least the last part of the track is concrete surfaced.

ROUTE ONE

To the Chora (2½km) A winding ascent through granite mountains to a fairly flat, gently undulating, rock surfaced plain, the fields of which are divided up by stone walls. The private bus turns off before the Chora, alongside a building that was once a 'Souvenir' shop. Surely a strange place for such a business, out in the barren countryside?

THE CHORA: capital (Illustration 25) A Chora of water wells and churches.

The main road ends at the south-east side of the Chora on the sloping 'Bus' Square (*Tmr* 1E4), where the 'State' bus 'terminuses. The far side is edged by pleasant, two storey houses. To the left, across an undulation in the lie of the land, on a low hillside, is a maze of stone walls, enclosures and old stone dwellings – reminiscent of a Minoan settlement. Maybe it was. On the right is an acute angled path that scrambles up the hillside to a Monastery and, on the coast,the Chrissospilia Cave (for which a guide is recommended). A wall edges cliffs which fall sharply away to the sea and from this high point there are marvellous views. In the angle formed by the plateia wall and the Monastery path is a monument.

This Chora may well be one of the most beautiful in the Cyclades and certainly the Old Quarter/Kastro is much photographed. There are the usual features of whitewashed buildings and churches but unusually the village is spread out, not being confined by the restrictions of a crowded hillside. There are two, not one, large squares, both fully shaded

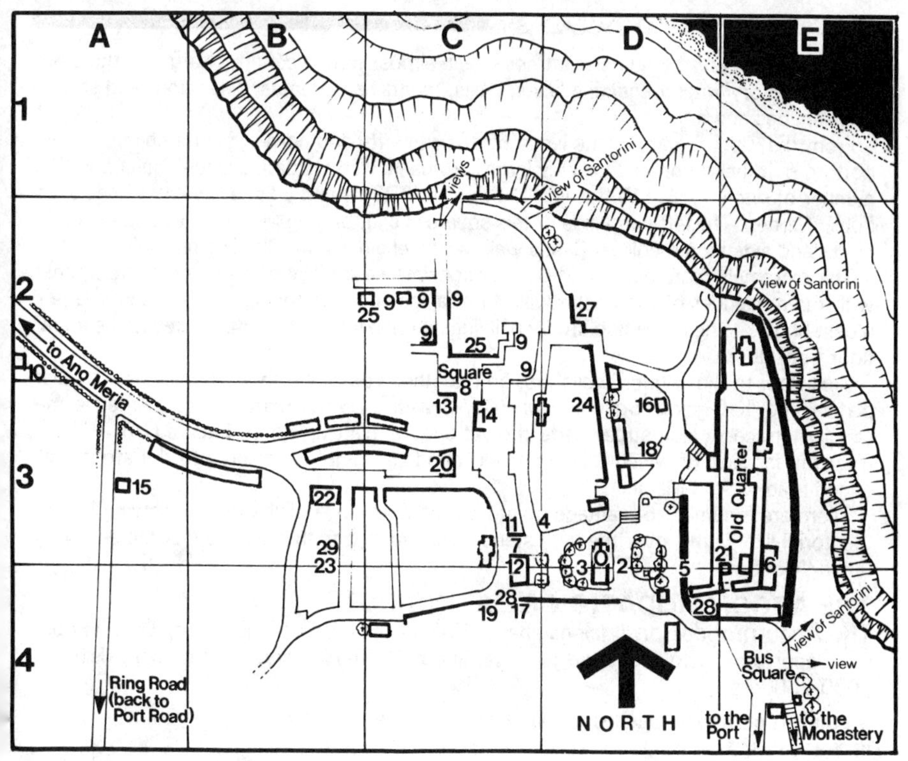

Illustration 25 The Chora

Tmr	1E4	'Bus' Square
	2D3/4	'Water Wells'Square
	3D3/4	'Kafeneion' Square
	4C/D3	Restaurant H Piatsa
	5D3/4	Rooms
	6E3/4	Hotel Danassis
	7C3/4	'Small' Sq
	8C2/3	'Post Office' Square
	9	Rooms
	10A2/3	Hotel Fani-Vevis
	11C3	Restaurant O Kritikos
	12C3/4	Butcher
	13C2/3	Cafe-bar/Taverna
	14C3	Cafe-bar/Rooms
	15A3	Cafe-bar
	16D2/3	Baker
	17C/D4	Grocer
	18D3	Supermarket
	19C4	Gift shop
	20C3	Tourist shop
	21D/E3/4	Tourist office
	22B/C3	'Dead' Ticket office
	23B3/4	Clinic
	24D2/3	OTE
	25C2/3	Post Office
	26B/C2	Hotel Odysseas
	27D2	Pizza Coffee
	28	Greengrocers
	29B3/4	General store

Tmr =Town map reference
Fsw =Facing seawards
Sbo =Sea behind one
Fbqbo =Ferry-boat Quay behind one

by the branches of the numerous trees which almost form a canopy. Naturally, there are the 'mandatory' interconnecting lanes, wells, fountains, tavernas, kafeneions and shops, of all shapes and sizes.

From the 'Bus' Square a lane leads off the top left-hand corner, past a church, to the bottom right-hand corner of a very large, profusely tree shaded, irregular square with a number of water wells ('Water-Wells' Sq) (*Tmr* 2D3/4) and a large, oval, wall-enclosed Public Garden. The left-hand side of this square is shut off by two churches and the dark, right-hand side by a medieval Castle wall, which encloses the Old Quarter.

The extremely picturesque Old Quarter consists essentially of two paved streets that, with the remainder of the Castle wall, form a rectangle enclosing some of the village's oldest houses. These are two storey buildings with external stone staircases to the upper floor front doors.

Next door to the 'Water-Wells' Sq, on the other side of the two churches, is a smaller plateia, the 'Kafeneion' Square (*Tmr* 3D3/4) with a pretty, mature, tree planted semi-circular terrace. A side-street leads into yet another plateia, 'Small' Square (*Tmr* 7C3/4), from the far side of which a lane curves round to the left, running into the stone wall edged road to Ano Meria.

There are a number of vantage points on the north side of the Chora allowing lovely, 'Santorini-like' views over the very steep, terraced slopes that tumble into the sea, way down below.

THE ACCOMMODATION & EATING OUT

The Accommodation A fair number of ***Rooms*** and even a hotel or two. 'Oveh'! Room rates approximate to the island average, about 1200-1500drs, early season, rising to 2000-2500drs.

On the left of the approaches to the Chora, from the port, is:-

Rooms O Pavlos
Directions: As above, immediately prior to both the boundary sign for the Chora and the windmills.

A largish 'complex' of house and garden, at the end of which are two inward facing, single storey blocks of rooms opening on to the terrace.

There are also ***Rooms*** advertised shortly before the 'Bus' Sq, on the right (*Port behind one*). Opposite them, to the left of the road, is a large hotel under construction.

Rooms (*Tmr* 5D3/4)
Directions: On the right-hand side of the 'Water-Wells' Sq, close to the 'tunnel' into the Old Quarter.

The long, low raftered bedrooms reflect the property's age for these houses originally formed part of the Venetian Castle walls.

Hotel Danassis (*Tmr* 6E3/4) (Class E) Tel 41230
Directions: Through the 'tunnel' from the 'Water-Wells' Sq (*Tmr* 2D3/4), along the alley, through another covered archway and the building is in the far corner.

A splendid example of a walled Cycladean hotel or pension (what do you mean 'a splendid example of a walled Cycladean...!'?). The owner keeps the showers locked against payment of extra drachmae. Only double rooms, sharing a bathroom, are available which cost 2100drs. The landlady is smiley and there is an extensive, pleasant roof terrace for sunbathing. Room No. 5 is narrow and whitewashed but some of the others are rather dark.

From the 'Small Square' (*Tmr* 7C3/4) proceeding up the lane to the right (*Port behind one*) of *Restaurant O Kritikos* (*Tmr* 11C3) advances to ***Rooms*** (*Tmr* 9C/D2/3) just beyond the church and on the left.

Approaching 'Post Office' Square (*Tmr* 8C2/3), the Cafe-bar (*Tmr* 14C3) on the right has ***Rooms*** and to the right of the Post Office (*Tmr* 25C2/3) is a 'blind' alley on the right of which are ***Rooms*** (*Tmr* 9C/D2).

To the left (*Port behind one*) of 'Post Office' Sq, a gently downhill street heads north to a spaced out, flat area. Here are comparatively modern buildings with ***Rooms*** (*Tmr* 9C2) to either side. A little further on the street runs out. From this viewpoint are splendid panoramas over the terraced, sloping mountainside that plunges precipitously into the sea. A lateral street to the left has buildings with ***Rooms*** (*Tmr* 9B/C2) and beyond some waste ground the:-

Hotel Odysseas (*Tmr* 26B/C2) (Class E) Tel 41239
Directions: As above and on the left.

There are no balconies or terraces and the accommodation outside of the main building is probably not worth the price. Single rooms, sharing a bathroom, cost 1400drs & with an en suite bathroom 1850drs, whilst a double room sharing costs 1850drs & with an en suite bathroom 2300drs, which rates increase, respectively, to 1850/2300drs & 2300/2750drs (1st July-15th Sept).

Hotel Fani-Vevis (*Tmr* 10A2/3) (Class B) Tel 41237
Directions: Bordering the Ano Meria road, just beyond the stop for the 'pirate' bus, close by the junction with the 'ring road'.

Actually classified as a pension. Whatever, it is a substantial, smartly refurbished old building in an excellent situation. No single rooms available. Double rooms, sharing a bathroom, cost 2050drs & en suite 2500drs, increasing to 2500 & 2800drs (15th June-15th Sept).

The Eating Out The Chora possesses a number of excellent kafeneions, cafe-bar restaurants and tavernas. More often than not the waiters are rather disdainful, sometimes surly. Establishments include:-

Cafe/Restaurant O Kritikos (*Tmr* 11C3)
Directions: Spanning the third, 'Small' Square. I write spanning because the restaurant proper is one side of the plateia but operates in conjunction with a Butcher (*Tmr* 12C3/4) opposite. This is a strange butcher's shop selling ice-cream, and has a kitchen in the back, but as to the working arrangement...?

The tables and chairs are pleasantly spread about against the church wall side of the square but the service is rather 'laid back', if not offhand and some of the food below par. The old boy, with a huge moustache, and a girl work very hard. A meal for two of 2 pork chops & chips, a Greek salad, 2 x ½kg retsina and 2 ouzos cost 1200drs.

On the north-east corner of the same square is another establishment, the:-
Restaurant H Piatsa (*Tmr* 4 C/D3)
Directions: As above, with a pleasant, raised terrace and a roomy interior, overlooking the two squares.

A few casserole dishes are available in the early evening, but the main concentration is on grills, barbecued to order in the street. The waiters appear cheerful and helpful enough but one suspects they are rather disdainful of tourists – somehow there is an aura of artificial *bonhomie* rather than true Greek hospitality. A meal for two of barbecued pork chops (400drs each), salad (170drs), tzatziki (120drs), bread (20drs each) and a half-litre of retsina (120drs) cost 1250drs.

Cafe-Bar/Taverna Nikos 'with Garden' Restaurant (*Tmr* 13C2/3)
Directions: Diagonally across the square from the Post Office.

No tables and chairs in front of the taverna, but an agreeable, if rather heavily shaded, low slung trellis and walled garden patio at the back. This very pleasant establishment is run by a friendly family and opens daily between 0900-1500hrs & 1800-2300hrs. Inside the cafe-bar is a very interesting picture of Karavostassis dated 1977, as well as some other excellent black and white photos of old Folegandros. The menu is only in Greek but the smiley Mama is very helpful. Menu prices include bean soup 180drs, cheese pie 180drs, tzatziki 120drs, salad 120drs, chicken & chips 250drs, lamb chop 400drs & a pork chop 450drs. A meal for two of 2 lentil soups (very nice), 1 macaroni with meat sauce (tasty, herby but cold), a meat rissoto (bland but hot), 2 x ½kg retsina, 2 coffees and 2 ouzos cost 1780drs.

Opposite is a neat:-
Cafe-Bar (*Tmr* 14C3)
Directions: As above.

'Equipped' with external bench seats and serves a reasonably priced breakfast as well as boiled eggs. Oh, by the way the butter is actually butter, if you see what I mean.

Recommended as the most up-market establishment in Folegandros, and located on 'Water Wells' Sq (*Tmr* 2D3/4) is the *Restaurant Kathforia*. It is reported to serve well presented, good, but expensive food ...and no cheap wine is available. The *Pizza Coffee* (*Tmr* 27D2) is situated beyond the OTE and on the other side of the alley.

At the far, west-end of the Chora, at the outset of the Chora 'ring road', is a:-
Cafe-Bar (*Tmr* 15A3)
Directions: As above.

Interesting because the young, pleasant Greek, married to a Danish girl, is very knowledgeable and erudite in respect of Greek classical music.

THE A TO Z OF USEFUL INFORMATION

BANKS None *See* **Post Office** or **Ferry-boat Ticket Offices, A To Z.**

BREAD SHOPS (*Tmr* 16D2/3) Actually a baker, across the lane from the Castle Wall, on the street north-east of 'Water-Wells' Sq, and distinguishable by the piles of gorse brush stacked outside.

BUSES *See* **Buses, A To Z, Karavostassis Port.**

COMMERCIAL SHOPPING AREA No central conglomeration but a rather pleasant sprinkling of shops to satisfy most needs. These include a Grocer (*Tmr* 17C/D4), who sells a fairly wide range of 'goodies'; a brand new Supermarket (*Tmr* 18D3); a modern General store (*Tmr* 29B3/4); several Greengrocers (*Tmr* 28C4 & 28D/E4) and an excess of butchers, but this is often the way in the older Greek towns. Maybe that is why the Butcher in the 'Small' Square (*Tmr* 7C3/4) has entered the restaurant trade? There are, a number of souvenir shops which include a small Gift shop (*Tmr* 19C4) and tasteful Tourist shop (*Tmr* 20C3).

DISCOS I only list the matter because there are innumerable signs directing prospective clients towards the 'Music Bar Deaf Seagull' (*sic*) but I never found it. And why deaf? Maybe the intensity of sound resulted in the loss of hearing!

FERRY-BOAT TICKET OFFICES There is an office (*Tmr* 21D/E3/4, tel 41273) situated in the Old Quarter. The owners have pretensions to becoming an NTOG. I found the lady, Maraki Lizardoy, very helpful, whilst others prefer to deal with her husband. Mrs Lizardoy has passable English. They change travellers cheques and foreign currency (notes only) in addition to dispensing a wide range of information. The office is definitely open between 1800-2100hrs (with a hint that, during the summer rush, there could be 'morning surgery').

On the left heading towards the Ano Meria road is a 'dead ticket office' (*Tmr* 22B/C3)

MEDICAL CARE

Chemists & Pharmacies The shops and stores stock the basic necessities.

Clinic (*Tmr* 23B3/4) At the west side of the Chora. The doors open Mon, Tues, Thurs & Fri between 0900-1200hrs, and Mon, Wed & Fri also between 1830-1930hrs.

OTE (*Tmr* 24D2/3) A small, cell block of a single storey building on the left of the narrow alley branching off the top left-hand corner of the 'Water-Wells' Plateia (*Tmr* 2D3/4). To help distinguish the otherwise totally inconspicuous office there is a large black sign painted with an arrow mounted almost opposite the building. A friendly lady gives a personal service but it is hardly an OTE, more a 'front-room'. Sometimes open weekday mornings (but the doors are closed if there is no business) and in the evenings after 1800hrs.

POST OFFICE (*Tmr* 25C2/3) A 'doo-hickey' office in a row of houses on the edge of an irregular shaped square. There are some phones and full exchange facilities.

ROUTE TWO

To Ano Meria (5km) It is quite feasible to walk from the Chora to Ano Meria, the tramp along the spine allowing full appreciation of the stunning scenery. However, it is totally exposed to the full force of the Meltemi, when it blows. The walk can also take longer than expected, as villagers are quite likely to invite hikers in for a cup of coffee. The equally likely offer of a mule for hire enables lost time to be regained...

On the other hand, there is a bus... The narrow concrete road rises and falls along the high ridge of the mountain range which falls away either side towards the coast. After 2½ km there is a pedestrian track to the seaside settlement of:-

AGKALI The buses pull up at the top of the path, the start of which is distinguishable by an ugly, concrete box of a bus shelter, on the edge of a large water-well catchment.

The steep 1km, 20 minute walk down the valley cleft is on a laid stone path which alternates with an unmade track. The lower reaches course along a river-bed, dry except for a seeping spring and one or two crude wells. The final descent is through massed oleanders, before breaking out on to the scrubbly, coarse sand, pebble littered backshore of the cove, hemmed in by steep hillsides set in Vathi Bay. At the bottom of the path there is drinking water cistern with two taps but the water is 'soapy'.

Houses, tavernas and ***Rooms*** are let into both hillsides. On the right-hand side (*Fsw*), at beach level, is a concrete block built shed, humorously labelled OTE, which does in truth contain a telephone (of sorts). The simple beach taverna on the right is run by a nice couple. They serve good mezes with a drink and will knock up reasonably priced meals to demand. A meal for two of 2 omelettes, a plate of chips, 3 small melanouri (oblada melanura), 2½kg retsina, bread, 2 bottles of soda, 2 coffees and 2 ouzos cost a very inexpensive 920drs.

Above this beach taverna is a restaurant with ***Rooms***, where the owner allows sleeping on the roof terrace. Apart from the inevitable meatballs, omelettes, tzatziki and Greek salad, the Mama or Papa will dash down to the fishing boat quay with a washing up bowl and a few thousand drachmae. A delicious meal for two of three grilled, sardine-like fish (300drs), an exquisite, light and fluffy omelette (80drs), 1 tzatziki (120drs), bread (30drs), a bottle of beer (85drs) and retsina (110drs) cost 725drs.

Also to the right is the concrete fishing boat quay. To the left of the cove is the hamlet's concrete toilet block set on a plinth of rock. Around the projecting cliff rock, behind the toilet facility, is a very small cove and at this end the beach and sea-bottom consists of small pebbles. It is often rather windy here and the water rough, but the main beach and sea are clean, with a coarse sand foreshore and a sea bottom made up of biscuit rock and pebbles.

Visitors may well be pestered by a toothless old man, Manolis. He tries to persuade tourists to hire donkeys at 200drs a person for the ride back to the bus stop. He does not take no for an answer and becomes visibly miffed when his string of 'thoroughbreds', waiting patiently by the wells at the foot of the path, are ignored.

A half-hour cliff walk to the west or right (*Fsw*) leads to:-

Ag Nikolaos A nice sandy beach with a taverna that opens up at the height-of-the-season. Despite the 'wild' camping, the location is kept clean with the rubbish collected into one single dump.

There is a scenic route back to the Chora. Adjacent to the backshore wells, a path strikes off to the right (*Sbo*), climbing steeply for a short stretch. It then gently works its way up and along the side of a narrow valley cleft, on the other side of the hill from the main path to the bus stop. The track rejoins the road about half-way back to the Chora.

Returning to the main road and continuing northwards, after another 2½ km the route spills into the village of:-

ANO MERIA More a string of connected, neat, agricultural hamlets formed by huddles of dwellings, spread out and straggling along the rounded and extensively terraced, but arid mountain tops. The road becomes track almost as soon as the first outpost is reached. Cattle, donkeys and goats are very much in evidence, herds of which appear to ebb and flow through the village tended by women and children. The bus conveniently parks for ¼ hour alongside a prominent taverna. From the little supermarket at Stavros, the baker is perched on the brow of a hill, up a little track to the left of the road, above and beyond the enormous Church of Profitis Ilias. It is as if the inhabitants could not agree on which of the straggling settlements should boast a baker so they made it equally inaccessible to everyone. Moreover, there is no indication that it is a bakery, except for the piles of brushwood fuel around the low, ancient buildings. To be served it may be necessary to summon Kyria Maria from the fields!

Excursion from Ano Meria to Ag Georgios Bay The map of any island tends to indicate beaches in the obscurest of places, none more so than Ag Georgios at the most northerly tip of Folegandros.

The last bus stop but one (or two) is for Ag Antreas, and between the bus shelter so marked and the kafeneion next to the chapel of that saint, a track makes off to the right (*Chora behind one*). It starts as almost a side-street past a few houses, before bending to the left and becoming a well engineered, laid stone mule track. This initially drops quite steeply, levels out round the prominent chapel of Ag Sostis and then descends steeply again towards Ag Georgios Chapel and Bay. The path is surprisingly well used by mule trains 'servicing' local fields.

The walk takes about fifty minutes and allows glorious sea views. At the bottom the path joins a broad, tree-lined river-bed for the last fifty metres to the beach. The small bay is deserted off-season, but is used by fisherman during the summer months. One side is lined by low, stone-built sheds, each housing a small fishing boat behind closed doors. A row of tiny cottages is built above the jetty, and the whitewashed chapel of St Georgios nestles amongst the trees of the backshore. The beach is shingly with some sand, but rocky below the waterline. As the bay faces north, it is difficult to escape the Meltemi, which can cause large waves accompanied by a lot of seaweed.

A Mykonos bell tower. Acknowledgement to Anne Merewood.

The 'dustman' calls, Naxos. *Acknowledgement to David & Liz Drummond-Tyler.*

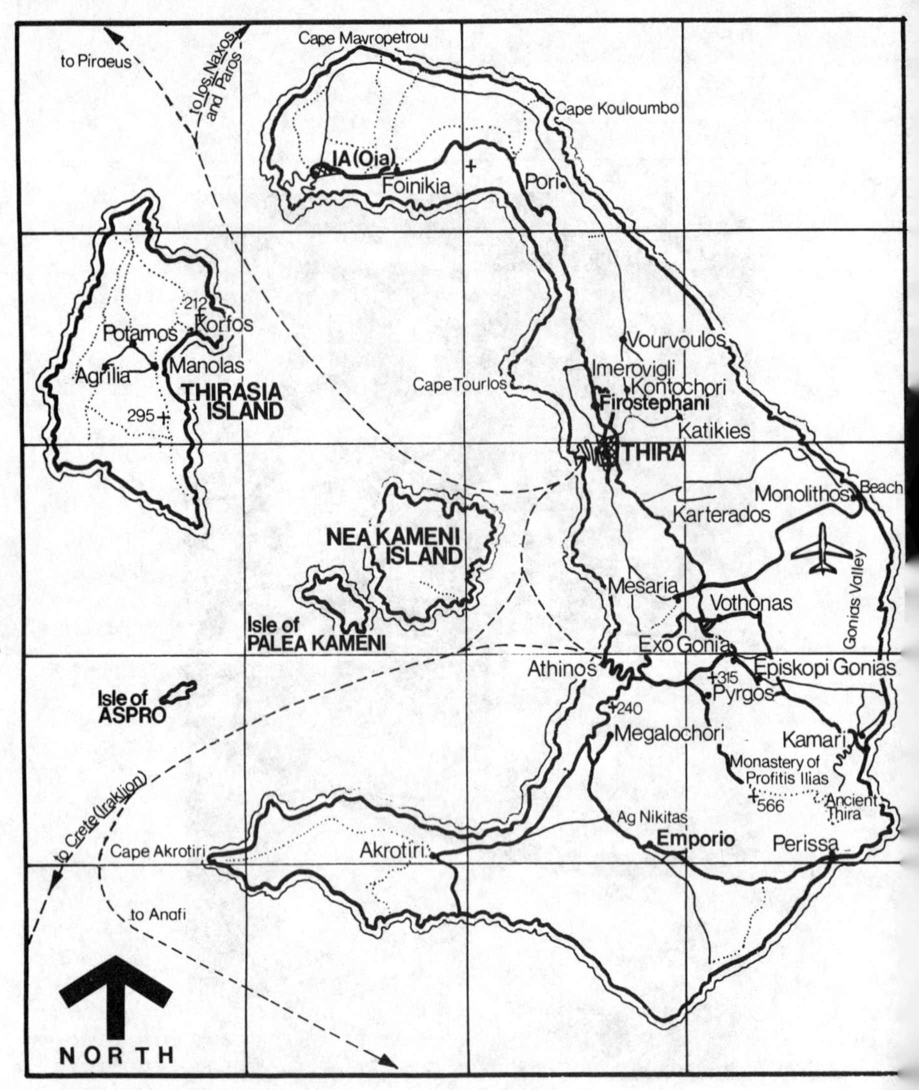

Illustration 26 Santorini island

10 SANTORINI (Santorine, Thira, Thera) & Thirasia Cyclades Islands - Eastern chain

Visually ★★★★★
Otherwise ★★

FIRST IMPRESSIONS Stunningly dramatic coastline; country lanes; churches; barrel roofs; donkeys; crowds, crowds & more crowds; too few buses, ferries & taxis to cope; expensive; cruise liners; duty-free shops; dogs everywhere.

SPECIALITIES Stunningly dramatic coastline; cruise liners; excellent island wines & subsequent lack of retsina; tomatoes; export of pumice stone, china clay & rock soil for cement making; 'breakfasts' (Thira Town).

RELIGIOUS HOLIDAYS & FESTIVALS include: 23rd May – Feast, Karterados; 19th-20th July – Festival, Profitas Ilias; 15th August – Feast, Episkopi (Mesa) Gonia; 1st September – Feast, Thira; 20th October – Festival, Ag Artemiou Church, Thira; 26th October – Festival, Ag Dimitriou, Karterados.

VITAL STATISTICS Tel prefix 0286. The island, shaped like a half saucer (or a foetal 'old man in the moon'), is up to 17km long, between 1¼ and 12km across and has an area of about 95sqkm, with a population of 7,500, of which approximately 1,500 live in Thira, the capital.

HISTORY There are a couple of fundamental differences with the Cycladean island 'norm'. One was the Cretan, or more correctly the Minoan 'connection', which ended rather dramatically, in about 1520 BC. The other was the more than usually Machiavellian and multifarious in-fighting and coups of the medieval Venetian ruling families.

The Minoan link and other interwoven items fostered the possibility that Santorini was part of the lost city of Atlantis, popularised in the writings of Plato and Egyptian papyrists. Perhaps it was 'geological justice' that the island originally formed by volcanic activity, some 20-25,000 year ago, should be blown in half by an enormous eruption, circa 1600 BC. It is postulated that the tidal waves resulting from this cataclysmic eruption almost completely destroyed the ancient Minoan civilisation on the island of Crete. Not that this was to be the last volcanic activity experienced by the island. In fact the present day complex of five islands owes its form to a series of volcanic activity, the last as recently as 1950. After the 'big bang', the islands of Santorini, Thirasia and Aspro and an enormous bay or 'caldera' were in position. Explosions, eruptions and discharges over the years eventually formed the other offshore islands of Nea and Palea Kameni. Two particular periods of activity merit a mention. The first, in 1650, lasted for several months and created an islet 7km off the eastern shore, the shock waves of which were recorded as being heard in Chios, flooding Ios and Sikinos, causing havoc on the shores of Crete and 'filling the farms of Santorini with sea'. Now known as the Kouloumbos reef it lies about 18½m beneath the sea's surface. The other event was as recent as 1925, when an island appeared above the surface which finally enlarged the existing Nea Kameni. Folklore associated the island of Nea Kameni with vampires, so much so that the Greeks had a saying similar to our '...coals to Newcastle', which roughly translated advised '...don't bring a vampire to Nea Kameni, there are enough already'.

Another item of Medieval note perhaps owes its inclusion to my sense of the unusual (or my unusual senses!). It appears that the Turks, at some stage, granted governorship of a group of Cyclades islands including Santorini to a Jew, one Joseph Nazi.

GENERAL Extremely tourist-popular islands usually have their charms diminished to the point of vanishing, as in the case of say Kos (Dodecanese) and Mykonos (Cyclades). There is often an exception to any rule and Santorini could be that anomaly. Despite years of cruise liner visits, serried ranks of backpackers and swarms of package tourists, the sheer beauty, the stunning visual effects of the cliff-hanging towns and the loveliness of the countryside continue to triumph, just. Santorini can still weave its magic charms, even around hardened travellers who should be innured to any island's wiles. If natural beauty were not enough, fate decreed that the dice should be further loaded in Santorini's favour, with the comparatively recent discovery of perhaps the most interesting of all such archaeological digs, the Akrotiri excavations. It must be pointed out that the island should be avoided 'like the plague' in the height of summer months. For that matter, it is difficult to contemplate how long Santorini can rise above the hordes of visitors at any time, now that the airfield can take fully fledged jumbo-jets.

Santorini is a humid island (as is Mykonos) and is supposed to be 'good for the skin, bad for the bones'. The prevailing wind is so strong and water so short that the vines grow low to the ground, gaining their nourishment from the humidity.

Deviating from the format usually adopted makes descriptions easier so the Introduction is modified to allow for the unusual complications caused by there being three main ports of call, all on the west coast. They include Ia (Oia) in the north, Thira(Phira, Fira), the capital, in the centre, and Athinos (Athinos, Athiniou) to the south. The traditional ports of Ia and Thira have now largely been superseded by the new port of Athinos, where the larger ferries almost always call. The smaller ferry-boats often make the older ports their docking point but difficulties are caused by ferries sometimes berthing at one, two or all three. Those steeped in the general vagaries of the ferry-boat system will need no assuring that the operators make the most of this additional obstacle, maximising the uncertainties that are already the lot of the hapless traveller. To the water-borne disorientated, identification of the ports will help. Ia and Thira are ostensibly similar, with the small, and pretty harbour facilities nestling at the bottom of steepling cliffs. The relative position of the Islands of Thirasia and Nea Kameni helps detection, as does the reminder that only Thira has a cliff-top cable car. The Port of Athinos is a large, comparatively modern quay about which there is nothing quaint.

When ferries call in at Ia and or Thira it is quite common for passengers to be transferred to 'bum' or passage boats, even the small **MV Ios** transferring its clients in this fashion.

THIRA (Phira, Fira): capital & port (Illustration 27) Possibly one of the most amazingly and breathtakingly situated capital town's, not only in the Cyclades but in Greece. The rambling, brilliant white buildings, spotted by the occasional blue church dome, skirt the cliff-top ranging along, as well as up and down, the multi-coloured and layered edge circling the east of the enormous caldera. The impact is quite staggering. It is no coincidence that so much publicity material as well as guide books and travel brochures feature a picture of the view from the town, looking out to sea. Unfortunately, this riveting beauty has resulted in an 'overwhelm' of tourism, some of which is represented by a comparatively rarified species, the cruise liner passenger. These latter craft moor at the foot of the Thira cliff-face and disembark their clientele into ship's boats. Once landed, a few 'donkey up' and some climb the steep zig-zag of steps, but most use the cable car.

For many years the only way from the harbour to the town was via the 550/650 steps and a band of donkey men still exercise a firm monopoly on the path. Those who give in to their vaguely menacing presence have to fork out about 300drs for the bumpy ride. Visitors brave enough to shoulder aside the massed barricades of skittish donkey flesh, and drivers, face a 25/35 minute climb. That was the state of affairs until about six or seven years ago when the muleteers agreed to the installation of the cable car, as long

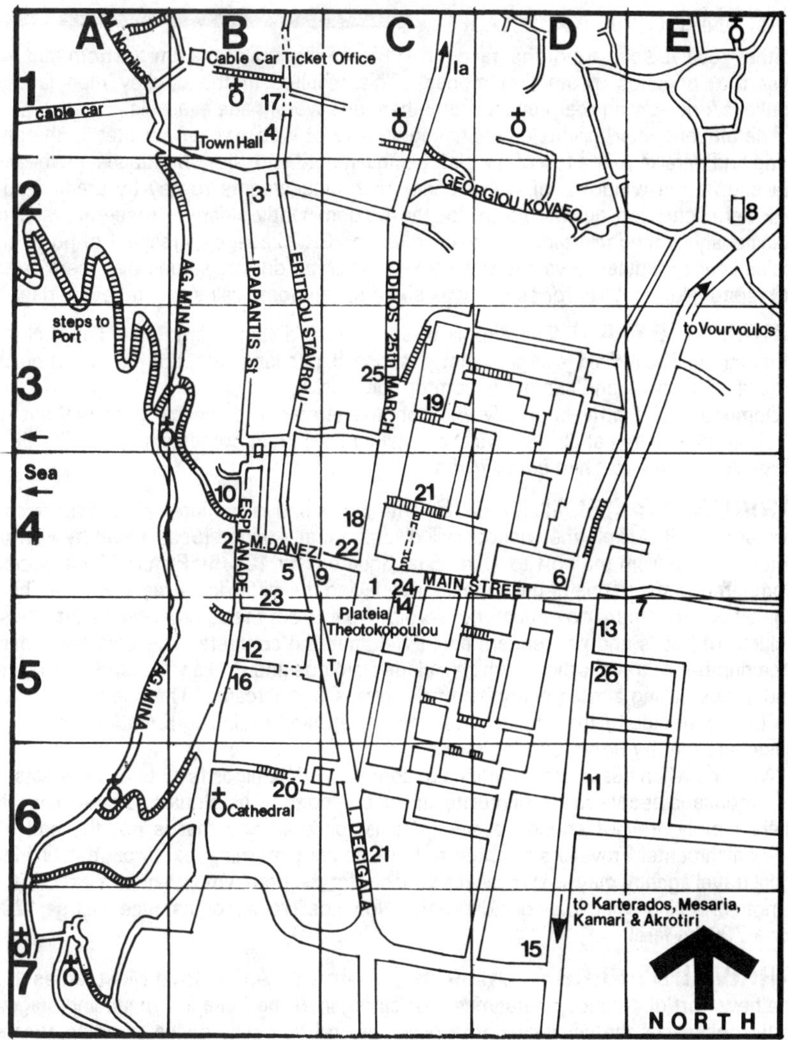

Illustration 27 Thira

Tmr 1C4/5	'Bus' Square, Plateia Theotokopoulou
2B4	Hotel Lucas
3B1/2	Archaeological Museum
4B1	Kamares Hostel
5B/C4/5	Hotel Tataki
6D4/5	Hotel Lignos
7D/E4/5	Hotel Antonia Roussou
8E2	Hotel Thirassia
9B/C4/5	Cafe-bar The Pleasure
10B4	Nicks Taverna
11D6	Olympic office
12B5	National bank
13D/E4/5	Self-service store/Baker
14C4/5	Damigos Tours
15D7	Clinic
16B5	OTE
17B1	Local Museum
18C4	Port police
19C/D3/4	Town police
20B6	Post Office
21	Public toilets
22B/C4/5	Pelikan Travel
23B4/5	Kamari Travel
24C4/5	Laundry
25C3	Dentist
26D/E5	Nomikos Travel
T	Taxi rank

Tmr =Town map reference
Fsw =facing seawards
Sbo =Sea behind one
Fbqbo =Ferry-boat Quay behind one

as they received a share of the 'take'. In 1985 the owners of the funicular omitted to pay over the 'brigands' protection money'. This resulted in the donkey men (and their donkeys?) occupying the premises until the funds were made available.

The affluent 'liner' clientele, emanating an aura of wealth, have resulted in the streets lining and parallel to the top of the cliff, being jammed with sleek boutiques, jewellery and gift shops, the windows of which shriek with inducements to pay by credit card. No junk here, only top quality goods for the predominantly elderly, prosperous and often ridiculously clothed dilettantes. The oft repeated GROC adage (in respect of ports on the cruise liner schedule) to vacate town when the ships dock assumes that there are days of respite. Not so here, for as many as six or seven boats call each and every day.

ARRIVAL BY AIR The airport is some 7km distant from Thira Town close by Monolithos. The airfield is large, as international flights land here, but the airport buildings are still quite small and can get uncomfortably packed.

Domestic flight arrivals simply walk off the tarmac into the car park without going through the building at all. ***Rooms*** and hotel owners meet domestic flights. The Olympic Airways bus fare to Thira costs 70drs.

ARRIVAL BY (ISLAND) BUS With larger and larger inter-island ferries coming into service, it is likely that visitors will disembark at Athinos (*See* **Arrival by Ferry**) and catch the bus from the port to Thira 'Bus' Square (*Tmr* 1C4/5), Plateia Theotokopoulou. Compared to the patina of quiet wealth overlaying the cliff-edge streets, Plateia Theotokpoulou is rather more downbeat, no, sordid. Apart from the summer-time heat, the sheer volume of buses and passengers could well melt the concrete. This square is encircled by a number of travel offices, which include Damigos and Pelikan Tours, as well as stalls and shops selling almost everything from pizzas to postcards. There is a bus timetable on the south side of the square (often incomplete and excluding Kamari & Perissa). The buses are met by Room offering mamas.

At times when buses are scheduled to connect with Athinos ferry-boat arrivals as many as a thousand people can 'accumulate' in and around the 'Bus' Square. On these occasions there simply are not enough buses or taxis to cope, and that is not the end of the admonishments. Travellers tempted to book an early morning taxi through their friendly, local travel agency may well receive a voucher for the prepayment and not a receipt. That is not surprising when it is considered that Nomikos Travel, for instance, charge 1200drs for a 700drs fare!

ARRIVAL BY FERRY – Athinos (Athinios, Athiniou) Most ferries dock at the new Port of Athinos, sometimes also calling in at the Thira Town landing stage. The latter possesses the usual cluster of buildings and four self-service tavernas, where the food is frankly nauseating, as is the treatment of the donkeys used to transport overweight Americans up the hill.

Athinos is a damned big quay edged by unattractive, concrete faced restaurant/cafe-bars with plenty of signs advertising their wares. These include an 'Official Exchange' next door to the *Restaurant Volcano*. A small stall is convenient for a snatched cup of coffee, but plastic cups are the order of the day (perhaps they lost too many china ones). Other 'attractions' include a Tourist Information office and the rather undesirable looking *Athinios Motel* (*sic*) advertising 'Rooms Avalable Here' (*sic*).

A veritable swarm of hotel buses line up to meet disembarking clients and, if everything is in order, there will be several island buses waiting. Destinations include Thira (of course), Kamari and Akrotiri. Even in early and late summer the buses get extremely crowded and it is advantageous for ferry-boat travellers to be as close to first off as is possible. Despite patrons being packed in like sardines, fares are collected by a conductor who has to climb over the passengers. The fare to Thira Town is 100drs per head.

The ferries are also met by Room owners from the various parts of the island who, when they have bagged a client or two, stuff them on the particular bus, often with one of their children to act as guide. It can be somewhat disconcerting. If not 'selected' my advice is to consider heading for Karterados, for which reasons *See* **Route One**.

Should the 'rites of arrival' be considered disconcerting, departure is downright disquieting. Apart from the uncertainty of a ferry-boat's port or ports of call, it will probably be necessary to catch a bus to make the connection (and Santorini island is often an early morning stop). Furthermore the ferries, especially the smaller craft, may well be overbooked, which will not matter as long as port officials do not decide to have a head-count. On one occasion Georgio of Nomikos Travel kindly arranged to deliver us to Athinos, casually advising that it would be possible to board the ferry at Thira but... the boat was rumoured to be at least thirty passengers over the limit. As it was docking at Athinos first, we would be best to board the craft there. 'You bet your sweet... it was'! Tickets should be purchased the day before a planned sailing, which might ensure a place, added to which there are no, repeat no, ticket offices or sales at Athinos

Extra buses are usually laid on to meet the ferries and they start operating from Thira Town as early as 0600hrs. If it is necessary to catch a taxi, the fare from Thira to Athinos costs about 700drs. Some camp out on the stoney foreshore round a rock or two to the south of the quay, which might be compulsory if arriving very late at Athinos. On the other hand the desperate should not forget the *Athinios Motel*.

Ferry-boat timetable (Mid-season)

Day	**Departure time**	**Ferry-boat**	**Ports/Islands of Call**
Mon	0745hrs	Thira II	Ia(Santorini),Ios,Naxos,Paros,Piraeus(M).
	1900hrs	Kimolos	Siphnos,Serifos,Piraeus(M).
Tues	0730hrs	Georgios Express	Sikinos,Folegandros,Ios,Naxos,Paros,Piraeus(M).
	1400hrs	Daphne Express (Excursion boat)	Ios,Paros,Naxos.
	1730hrs	Portokalis Ilios	Iraklion(Crete).
	2400hrs	Golden Vergina	Anafi,Ag Nikolaos(Crete),Sitia(Crete), Kasos,Karpathos,Rhodes.
Wed	0715hrs	Santorini Express	Sikinos,Folegandros,Ios,Naxos, Paros,Syros,Piraeus(M).
Thur	0745hrs	Thira II	Ia(Santorini),Ios,Naxos,Paros,Piraeus(M).
	0815hrs	Georgios Express	Ios,Naxos,Paros,Piraeus(M).
	1730hrs	Portokalis Ilios	Iraklion(Crete).
	2000hrs	Golden Vergina	Piraeus(M).
Fri	0715hrs	Santorini Express	Ios,Naxos,Paros,Piraeus(M).
	2200hrs	Golden Vergina	Anafi,Ag Nikolaos(Crete),Sitia(Crete),Kasos, Karpathos,Diafani(Karpathos),Chalki,Rhodes.
Sat	0745hrs	Thira II	Ia(Santorini),Folegandros,Sikinos,Ios,Naxos, Paros,Syros,Piraeus(M).
	0815hrs	Georgios Express	Ios,Naxos,Paros,Piraeus(M).
	1730hrs	Portokalis Ilios	Iraklion(Crete).
Sun	0700hrs	Kimolos	Folegandros,Ios,Kimolos,Milos,Siphnos, Serifos,Piraeus(M).
	0815hrs	Georgios Express	Ios,Naxos,Paros,Piraeus(M).
	1400hrs	Daphne Express (excursion boat)	Ios,Paros,Naxos.
	1430hrs	Portokalis Ilios	Iraklion(Crete).
	1800hrs	Santorini Express	Ios,Naxos,Paros,Piraeus(M).
	2100hrs	Golden Vergina	Folegandros,Milos,Piraeus(M).

Hydrofoil timetable (Mid-season)

Mon	1230hrs	Nearchos	Ios,Paros,Naxos.
	1800hrs	Nearchos	Iraklion(Crete).
Wed	1015hrs	Nearchos	Ios,Paros,Mykonos.
	1800hrs	Nearchos	Iraklion(Crete).
Fri	1030hrs	Nearchos	Ios,Paros,Naxos.
	1700hrs	Nearchos	Iraklion(Crete).

Please note these tables are detailed as a GUIDE ONLY. Due to the time taken to research the Cyclades, it is IMPOSSIBLE TO 'match' the timetables or even boats . So don't try cross pollinating...

THE ACCOMMODATION & EATING OUT

The Accommodation A wide range of hotels, pensions and ***Rooms*** most of which are extremely expensive. Prices, in recent years, have been increased by very large amounts. The town fills up early on in the day as most tourists head for Thira. I would not stay here, but then it could be argued that I consider Karterados the centre of the island (*See* **Route One**).

The cliff-edge hotels are fearsomely expensive apart from the:-

Hotel Lucas (*Tmr* 2B4) (Class D) Old Port Steps Tel 22480
Directions: On the left of the steps down to the Old Port.

Comparatively inexpensive considering the location. A double room with en suite bathroom costs about 3500drs. The donkey droppings ensure a healthy insect population.

From the top of the Port steps, follow the pebbled Ipapantis St, hedged in with expensive tourist shops, towards the cable-car station. At the Archaeological Museum (*Tmr* 3B1/2) it is possible to turn left or right. Both routes have a few ***Rooms*** signed. The left-hand choice passes the Town Hall and then right along Odhos M Nomikos to the cable car ticket office. Selecting the right-hand choice and then turning left (in effect completing the other side of the square) leads along narrow Odhos Eritrou Stavrou and, after a roofed-in section, a left-hand turn on to Ag Ioannis advances to the head of the cable-car. This latter route leads past a tourist office, the *Asimina Hotel & Pension* and, on the left of Odhos Eritrou Stavrou, the:-

Kamares Hostel (*Tmr* 4B1) Eritrou Stavrou St Tel 23142
Directions: As above.

This youthful, recommended hostel offers rooms in which a dormitory bed costs from 450drs. It overflows early due to the establishment's popularity . There is a cheap breakfast bar next door.

A few paces beyond the *Kamares Hostel* is a local Museum collection,in a rather splendid building.

The other inexpensive hostel type accommodation is the:-

Youth Hostel Tel 22722
Directions: About 350m along the main Ia road, north of Thira Town from the 'Bus' Sq and on the right, close to a church.

The signs loudly proclaim that this is the authorised establishment. An inside dormitory bed costs 500drs, whilst one in the open air is charged at 400drs. The busy bar, open to non residents, is a magnet and a breakfast costs 170drs. The office opens daily, 0800-1300hrs & 1700- 2300hrs.

Continuing along the Ia road to Firostephani village, which is now a suburb of Thira, gives a wide choice of ***Rooms***, pensions and hotels. These include the:- *Margarita* (Class E, tel 22764), only double rooms en suite costing 2750drs, increasing to 3800drs (1st July-30th Sept); *Aphrodite* (Class E, tel 22161), where a single room sharing a bathroom is priced at 1900drs, a double room sharing costs 2300drs & a double en suite 2899drs, increasing to 2700drs & 3160/3800drs (1st April-31st Oct), and the *Sofia* (Class E, tel 22802) with double rooms, en suite only, costing 2500drs, rising to 3000drs (17th June-30th Sept).

A slip road angles off to the left, beyond a taverna, alongside a prominent, twin royal-blue domed church. Close to a railings fenced municipal building turn left, as if to proceed in the direction of Thira, following the path which parallels the cliff-face. Alongside the track is:-

Pension
Directions: As above.

The owners are obliging and a double room, sharing hot showers, costs 2500drs at the height of season. An example of their pleasant attitude is that they don't expect guests to depart early on the day of their departure if the ferry is not until late afternoon.

One removed along this path, still in the direction of Thira, is the:-
Hotel Gallini (Class C) Tel 22095
Directions: As above.

Mr Roussos owns another hotel imaginatively named the *Gallini II* as well as the *Taverna Roussos*. The Firostephani Mr Big! All rooms have en suite bathrooms with a single costing 2800drs & a double 3400drs, increasing to 3400drs & 4000drs (1st July-3400drs).

This caldera edging path, which emerges in town by the cable car, is the source of a number of ***Rooms***. On the right (*Sea to the right*) are houses, here and there, signed unsafe where they have started to slide down the multi-brown coloured volcanic cliff-face.

Back in Thira, another rich, convenient vein of ***Rooms***, generally 'ethnic and provincial' in style, is in the large, central block of buildings immediately to the east and down from the 'Bus' Square (*Tmr* 1C4/5). The area is laced with alleys. Hotels and pensions close to the centre of town include the:-
Hotel Tataki (*Tmr* 5B/C4/5) (Class D) M Danezi St Tel 22389
Directions: Ascend the lane on the right-hand (*'Bus' Square behind one*) corner of which is Pelikan Travel. Signs include 'Best music and drinks in Santorini' & 'We have heating and hot showers in the rooms'. God knows why the heating?

All rooms have en suite bathrooms. A single room costs 2600drs & a double 3000drs, rising to 3000drs & 3600drs (1st June-30th Sept).

Hotel Lignos (*Tmr* 6D4/5) (Class E) Tel 23101
Directions: Descend the Main Street from the right-hand corner of the 'Bus' Square (*Damigos Tours on the right*) and the hotel is on the left, at the junction with the Vourvoulos/Akrotiri road.

All rooms have en suite bathrooms with a single room priced at 2000drs & a double 2500drs, increasing to 3000drs & 3800drs (1st April-30th Sept).

Hotel Antonia Roussou (*Tmr* 7D/E4/5)
Directions: From the *Lignos Tmr* 6D4/5), almost directly across the main road, to the left of the Self-service store/bakery.

Doubles en suite cost 4000drs.

There are also ***Rooms*** in the row of buildings in which the Olympic office (*Tmr* 11D6) is located, on the far or east side of the Akrotiri road.
Hotel Thirassia (*Tmr* 8E2) (Class E) Tel 22546
Directions: Still advancing from the *Lignos* (*Tmr* 6D4/5), turn left along the Vourvoulos road and the hotel is on the left.

Single rooms sharing a bathroom cost 1500drs, a double room sharing 2500drs & a double en suite 3000drs. These prices increase to 2000drs & 3000/4000drs (1st July-31st Aug).

To end the accommodation paragraph it is enough to urge readers to stay elsewhere, anywhere other than Thira Town. I favour Karterados. For those who wish to stay in another beautiful, cliff-hanging town, go to la (*See* **Route Two**).

The Eating Out Yes, well! When a town harbours establishments such as the Paradise Video Music Club, serving 'Sangria Cup'... then the portents for the inner man, or woman, are not good. Added to this, prices generally are expensive. But all is not lost. Note that few Thira eateries have a patio, unless well shielded, as the winds are usually very strong. As Santorini is a noted wine producer, little if any retsina is available, which some might regard as a bonus...

The Pleasure (*Tmr* 9B/C4/5) M Danezi St
Directions: From the 'Bus' Square (*Tmr* 1C4/5) turn west and climb the lane, on the corner of which is Pelikan Travel. The Pleasure is half-way up, on the left.

Not the smartest cafe-bar I have frequented, in fact it is rather 'doo-hickey'. As is often the case there is no patio, due to the wind. On the other hand this simple, home-spun cafe-bar, which masquerades as a restaurant, is excellent value. A smiley, middle-aged Mama makes breakfast a speciality and the 'Nes' served is some of the best and cheapest I have had anywhere in Greece. An excellent breakfast of eggs and bacon costs 170drs, a tea 50drs, a Nes meh ghala 70drs, yoghurt and honey 140drs, fresh orange juice 120drs and a beer 80drs. Omelettes are available.

Cheek by jowl, if not next door, is the *Petros*. This is a pleasant, covered in, elongated alleyway establishment but smarter and more expensive.

Restaurant Helidoni

Directions: Diagonally across the street from the *Pleasure* and down some steps.

Not exactly my prime choice as it is a 'greasy' spit-roast outfit serving the usual unacceptably priced meals. A meal for two of grilled octopus, a pork chop & chips, a plate of giant beans and a bottle of wine (530drs) cost 1750drs. No inexpensive wines are available.

The Ia road out of town is a fruitful source of eating houses. These include a busy cafe-bar about 300m towards Firostephani and on the left, down a set of steps from the road. Almost all of the customers are locals, if not regulars. Further on is:-

The Flying Greek

Directions: About 200m short of the Firostephani turning.

Apart from good, if rather pricey food, the owner is a dead ringer for Louis, he of the American soap Taxi. Perhaps he is a twin as he acts in a similar fashion. All orders are simply barked at the nearest waiter, not written down. This enables the patron to reprimand the hapless chap concerned when he is unsure what food is for whom, when it arrives. Addition is done on the 'back of the tablecloth' with the clients help. One wonders how the VAT man calculates this lot.

Taverna Roussos

Directions: Further along the Ia road and up the Firostephani slip road. This blue painted taverna is about two buildings before the church.

Comes recommended so all should be well but arrive early as the locals know about it and eat here (How unreasonable). Later on in the evening, the choice is severely restricted.

The really expensive offerings can be found ranged along the town's cliff-top road and the upper part of the Port steps. The *Kastro Cocktail Bar & Restaurant*, opposite the cable-car building is a good example of this genre. Another is:-

Nicks (Nicholas) Taverna (*Tmr* 10B4)

Directions: Descending the Port steps and on the right.

The view is magnificent, the prices reasonable but, in the past, the food has been rather unsatisfactory. Sample prices include moussaka 215drs and stuffed aubergines 150drs.

The *Taverna Nikh* across the steps might be an equally good bet.

THE A TO Z OF USEFUL INFORMATION

AIRLINE OFFICE & TERMINUS (*Tmr* 11D6) Down the road from the right-hand corner of the 'Bus' Square (*Tmr* 1C4/5) (*Damigos Tours to the right*), right at the junction of the Vourvoulos/Akrotiri road and on the left. The office opens weekdays between 0900-1645hrs. Santorini makes a surprisingly wide number of inter-island connections, but the services are so popular with the locals that it is difficult to get a seat.

Aircraft timetable (Mid-season)

Santorini to Athens (& vice versa)

Daily	0720hrs
Mon, Tues, Wed, Fri, Sat & Sun	2050hrs
Mon, Thur, Fri & Sun	2350hrs
Return	
Daily	0600hrs
Mon, Tues, Wed, Fri, Sat & Sun	1930hrs

BANKS The **Commercial Bank** have an office on the 'Bus' Sq (*Tmr* 1C4/5) and the **National Bank** (*Tmr* 12B5) is off to the right of a path connecting the angled 'Taxi' St (Odhos I Decigala) and the Esplanade (Odhos Ipapantis). This latter bank operates a separate 'Exhcange'(*sic*) office, behind the main building, alongside a vine covered patio/garden with seats. Normal weekday hours in addition to opening between 1800-2000hrs on Monday, Wednesday and Friday evenings, for exchange only. But note that long queues form every day.

BEACHES Not surprisingly, mindful of the location, none.

BICYCLE, SCOOTER & CAR HIRE The majority of the firms are located either side of the main road to Ia, from the 'Bus' Square. The average island scooter hire fee is about 1500/1800drs a day, including fuel, but Vespas in Thira average 1500drs and can be found as low as 1000drs per day off season. Take note that Nomikos Travel quote 1500drs low season and 1800drs high season. The moral is locate your own rentals.

BOOKSELLERS There are plenty of overseas paper & magazine shops.

BREAD SHOPS There is a Baker in the Self-service store (*Tmr* 13D/E4/5) bordering the Vourvoulos/Akrotiri road.

BUSES Pull up on the Plateia Theotokopoulou or 'Bus' Square (*Tmr* 1C4/5).

Bus timetable (Mid-season)

Thira Town to Ia
Daily 0830, 0930, 1000, 1100, 1130, 1230, 1300, 1330, 1400, 1500, 1600, 1630, 1730, 1800, 1830, 1900, 1930, 2030, 2130, 2230, 2330hrs.
Return journey
Daily 0730, 0900, 0930, 1030, 1100, 1200, 1230, 1300, 1330, 1430, 1500, 1600, 1700, 1730, 1800, 2000, 2100, 2200, 2300hrs.
One-way fare: 80drs.

Thira Town to Kamari
Daily 0730hrs until 2230hrs, every 30mins.
Return journey
As above.
One-way fare: 85drs.

Thira Town to Perissa
Daily 0745, 0900, 1000, 1100, 1145, 1245, 1340, 1400, 1530, 1630, 1730, 1830, 1930, 2030, 2130, 2230hrs.
Return journey
Daily 0700, 0800, 0850, 1005, 1055, 1200, 1215, 1315, 1440, 1535, 1635, 1735, 1825, 1935, 2025, 2135hrs.
One-way fare: 100drs.

Thira Town to Akrotiri
Daily 0830, 1000, 1100, 1200, 1400, 1600, 1700, 1830, 2000, 2130hrs.
Return journey
Daily 0800, 0930, 1030, 1130, 1330, 1530, 1630, 1800, 1930, 2100hrs.

Thira Town to Athinos
Depart 1½hrs prior to scheduled ferry-boat departures.
One-way fare: 100drs.

CABLE CAR (*Tmr* A/B1) Saves donkey haggling or walking. A one-way trip costs 350drs.

COMMERCIAL SHOPPING AREA None. The narrow lane, second right off Odhos M Danezi (*From the 'Bus' Square*) is lined with vegetable stalls. As already mentioned, the Esplanade cliff-top street, Odhos Ipapantis, is jammed with high quality gift, boutique and jewellery shops (very Greek island, don't you know!). The 'Bus' Square is bordered by stalls, shops and travel offices selling everything from pizzas to tour tickets. There is a periptero at each side of the Square. Odhos Erythou Stavrou, one back and parallel to Odhos Ipapantis, is initially lined with gift and tourist shops.

DISCOS Yes, a number including Disco Blue Bell close by the Bus Square.

FERRY-BOATS & FERRY-BOAT TIMETABLES *See* **Arrival By Ferry**.

FERRY-BOAT TICKET OFFICES *See* **Travel Agents & Tour Offices**.

HAIRDRESSERS There are several, including one next door to the Dentist (*Tmr* 25C3), on the left of the Ia road and another further up the same road, on the right, just before the turning down to the Youth Hostel.

LAUNDRY (*Tmr* 24C4/5) Edging the Main St down from the 'Bus' Sq. Not coin-op and charges about 500drs per wash, depending on the weight.

LUGGAGE STORE Koudouri Travel and Pelikan Travel, on the 'Bus' Square, take in bags at 100drs a piece.

MEDICAL CARE

Chemists & Pharmacies A number including one on the Main St from the right-hand corner of the 'Bus' Square (*Damigos Tours to the right*). A rota is operated out of hours.

Clinic (*Tmr* 15D7) On the corner of the Vourvoulos/Akrotiri and one-way roads into the centre.

Dentist One (*Tmr*25C3) on the left of the Ia road from the 'Bus' Sq.

Doctor There is one beside the road to Karterados, between the Baker (*Tmr* 13D/E4/5) and Nomikos Travel (*Tmr* 26D/E5).

NTOG None, which is a surprising omission for a town of this importance. *See* **Ia** and **Athinos**.

OTE (*Tmr* 16B5) On the Esplanade, Odhos Ipapantis. Only open Mon-Fri between 0745-2145hrs.

PETROL There is a filling station on the Akrotiri road.

PLACES OF INTEREST Who needs anything more than the position! To supplement this there is an:

Archaeological Museum (*Tmr* 3B1/2). Open daily between 0845-1500hrs, Sunday & holidays between 0930-1430hrs and closed Tuesdays. Entrance costs 200drs.

'Local' Museum (*Tmr* 17B1) Actually called the 'Megaran Gyzi Cultural Centre' and housed in an old 'Family Mansion' which survived the earthquake. Open daily between 1030-1330hrs & 1700-2000hrs.

Excursions The various travel agents have packaged a number of options including boat trips to the Volcano on Nea Kameni island. It is best to shop around and try and establish which office is offering the best value. Similar tours can differ in cost by several hundred drachmae. The 'round the bay' trips, which more often than not encompass the Volcano, the hot springs on Palea Kameni and either Manolas Harbour on Thirasia island or the northern port of Ia, cost about 1200drs whilst a foreshortened 'volcano and hot springs' job costs some 650drs. One hopes that there are readers who will decide to simply get off at Thirasia Island and stay (*See* **Excursion to Thirasia Island** at the chapter end).

I am assured by participants that the round-the-island coach trip is good value. One particular package includes the Akrotiri excavations, The Monastery of Profitis Ilias, a visit to a wine maker (and tasting) and an afternoon on Perissa beach.

POLICE

Port (*Tmr* 18C4) On the Ia side of the 'Bus' Square, bordering Odhos 25th March.

Town (*Tmr* 19C/D3/4) On the right, 10/20m along the Ia road from the 'Bus' Square.

POST OFFICE (*Tmr* 20B6) Bordering the 'Taxi' St of Odhos I Decigala.

TAXIS (*Tmr* T B/C5) Rank along Odhos I Decigala. The street rises quite steeply so the taxis rank from the top backwards – Irish I know but... The phone is at the corner of the fork where I Decigala angles off from the approach to the 'Bus' Square. The taxis pull up in the queue at the front and then as cabs depart from the back, take the handbrake off and roll backwards to the 'front' of the rank! Sample fares include Thira Town to Ia 550drs, to Athinos Port 700drs and to the Airport 400drs.

TELEPHONE NUMBERS & ADDRESSES

Clinic (*Tmr* 15D7)	Tel 22237/22236
Police, town (*Tmr* 19C/D3/4)	Tel 22649
Taxis (Main Square)	Tel 22555

TOILETS There is a public toilet (*Tmr* 21C4) to the right of the main road to Ia, almost opposite the Port police office, and another (*Tmr* 21C6) edging Odhos I Decigiala, at the other end of town.

TRAVEL AGENTS & TOUR OFFICES Naturally enough, quite a few including:-

Damigos Tours (*Tmr* 14C4/5) Tel 22226

Directions: Bordering the 'Bus' Square.

Helpful and impersonal, but the human traffic is overwhelming.

Pelikan Travel (*Tmr* 22B/C4/5) Tel 22478

Directions: Also bordering the 'Bus' Square. Open daily between 0800-2200hrs.

Atlantis Tours Tel 22965

Directions: On the west side of the 'Bus' Square.

Kamari Travel (*Tmr* 23B4/5) Tel 31390

Directions: In a lane off Odhos I Decigala.

One of the oldest agencies in town.

Nomikos Travel (*Tmr* 26D/E5) Tel 22660
Directions: From the 'Bus' Sq turn down the Main St on to the Vourvoulos/Akrotiri road. Turn right and the office is across the road beyond the Self-service store/Baker and prior to the Olympic office. The 'Head office' is in the village of Karterados.

Most of the Thira Town businesses also have offices at one or two of the major resorts.

ROUTE ONE

To Akrotiri via Karterados & Mesaria (14km) with detours to Monolithos, Kamari, Pyrgos & PerissaA gently downwards sloping road, lined with shady trees, passes a petrol station to the right, a rather untidy car breakers and repair workshop to the left. After about 1½km, alongside a bus stop and the rather surprisingly named *Restaurant Sweet Home Zofos*, there is a turning off to the left to:-

KARTERADOS (2km from Thira Town) The poorly surfaced side road drifts by a 'dead' bus to the left and a roller skating rink (yes, a...) on the right, sloping and gently winding through the surrounding vine fields. On the left is the *Hotel Cyclades*, almost opposite which, across the field, is *Rent Rooms*. Another 100m on and the first village square is reached. On the left is Nomikos Travel (Pension Prekas) followed by the *Glaros Bar*. Edging the other side of the road is the *Hotel O Ghiannis, H Tatakis*. The 'Council' have thoughtfully installed an orange coloured, pedal operated, rubbish bin (against this hotel's wall) which is planted with pot plants! Also on the left, beyond the *Glaros Bar*, another square opens out. This is bordered by, amongst other businesses, the small office of Halaris Travel Tourist Information, which also hire scooters, *Taverna Coral No 2* and *Taverna Neraida*, in front of which is a monument. This last establishment hires out scooters and has Greek dancing on Wednesday nights.

I am informed that Halaris (the scooter man) started up at the same time as Nomikos opened their office. Nomikos stuck to travel and Halaris to scooter hire until the latter moved into travel.... Naturally Nomikos Travel now rents scooters!

Beyond the *Neraida*, the 'Main' Street falls away to the left, on to another large, dusty square. The far side of this is a small General store and, alongside the local telephone office, the *Hotel Gina*, as well as ***Rooms***. From the far, left-hand corner a wide track makes off towards the coast (of which more under Monolithos) edging a small ravine and passing three magnificent churches below road level. One of these 'sports' a Feast Day on the 23rd May. Beyond the *Gina* is a scooter outfit, hidden away around to the right but this may well be the repair depot for the 'front line' boys. Around to the left, down from the edge of this third plateia and up again, the other side of a gulch, is *Hotel Michael* (previously known as the Pension Nickle).

Back at the second square, with *Taverna Neraida* on the left, a lane opposite leads away to the right past the *Kafeneion Astron*, on the right. Beyond the *Astron*, the lane jinks left and then right past several 'dead' buses, on the left, and behind which, across some waste land, are two buildings with ***Rooms***. The lane becomes an alley, on the right of which is a well stocked General store, dropping downhill and curving left to a fork. At this junction, to the right proceeds back up to the main road, whilst to the left descends along a narrow, wall enclosed cleft. Beyond the single campanile of a simple church, reached through a wrought iron gate, and on the right is *Rooms Kavalari*. This lane is decorated (as are some of those in Ia) with flower outlines painted on the paving stones. As it descends it becomes overgrown and runs out, eventually, in a series of cliff cave donkey stables let into the low hillside. Before reaching the end, about 60m beyond *Kavalari Rooms*, a path to the left advances to another ***Rooms***.

The village possesses a number of examples of the Santorini barrel-vaulted roofs, rarely seen elsewhere on the Cyclades, and obviously adopted to help combat earthquake tremors. Here as elsewhere on the island, the churches have separate campaniles (similar to those on the Ionian islands) attached at the roof of the main building.

I realise I have spent a disproportionate amount of time on such a small village but Karterados has a number of plus points for the independent traveller. It is only a twenty minute walk (uphill) to Thira Town, there is a regular bus service and the villagers have, without formal permission, carved a 2½km roadway eastwards to Takki Beach which is, in effect, the far, left-hand end (*Fsw*) of Monolithos Beach. This location must offer a thought provoking alternative base to the 'steaming', crowded, costly capital.

THE ACCOMMODATION & EATING OUT

The Accommodation It must be pointed out that a night-time's sleep is often disturbed in any Santorini accommodation, more especially due to the early morning ferry-boat departures. This results in much pre-dawn banging about as yet another batch of travellers clatters out to catch the relevant bus. In order of approach from the main road are the:-

Hotel Cyclades (Class D) Tel 22948
Directions: As described.

A neat, two storey building. All rooms have en suite bathrooms with a single room priced at 2125drs & a double 2980drs, rising to 2620drs & 3705drs (1st July-30th Sept).

Nomikos Travel, which now occupies the ground floor of the old Pension Prekas building, still lets out the upstairs rooms. A double room, with en suite bathroom, is charged at about 2500drs.

Hotel O Ghiannis, H Tatakis (Class E) Tel 22552
Directions: As detailed.

All rooms have en suite bathrooms, with a single room costing 2170drs & a double 2530drs, increasing to 2575drs & 3160drs (1st July-30th Sept).

Hotel Gina (Class E) Tel 22834
Directions: As described.

All rooms have en suite bathrooms. The single room rate starts at 2500drs & a double room 3000drs, increasing to 3000drs & 3400drs (1st April-30th June) and 4000drs & 4400drs (1st July-31st Aug).

Hotel Michael
Directions: As aforementioned.

Not difficult to miss as the approach path is illuminated by red and white mushroom lights. Another decorative feature is an imitation canon – one cartwheel and axle, the other painted on the wall with a black plastic drainpipe forming the gun barrel. A nice, quiet place. A double room with en suite bathroom, and lots of hot water but no balcony, starts off at 1600drs but the height of summer rate is 4000drs. Breakfast is charged at 200drs.

Hotel Karterados (Class E)
Directions: On the edge of the village, some 50m further on from the *Hotel Gina's* front door.

Once again, pleasant and quiet with en suite bathrooms plus a balcony, with tables and chairs, allowing a view out over the airport and the mountains. Early season charges at 1600drs are less than the official rate of 2500drs but the requested high season price of 3800drs is some 300drs more than the 'official' charge. Incidentally this height of summer price hike is commonplace on Santorini. Single rooms, with en suite bathroom, start off at 1500drs, rising to 2000drs (16th June-15th Sept).

Rooms Kavalari
Directions: As detailed.

Mr & Mrs Kavalari are very nice, as are their charming daughters who assist in running this accommodation. The family are eager to please and guests may well be greeted with a glass of cold water and a plate of sweets. Pleasant, clean rooms with a balcony and a shared bathroom, which exhibits a few of the usual 'defects', but the water is hot, as long as the relevant electric switch is turned on. A single room costs from 2000drs & a double room starts at 2300drs. Incidentally, the family live in a home let into the hillside behind the main accommodation block. This strange feature is repeated down the lane with the pueblo-style, white painted buildings jutting out from the rock face.

Nomikos Travel
Directions: Described in the preamble.

Nomikos has accommodation over and above the office but I have to advise that my 'mail bag' is heavy with criticism in respect of this business. This is a salutory lesson to me for going OTT in the first edition in which I acclaimed young Georgio and his business. It appears that the office policy is to add whatever surcharge is deemed necessary to cover overheads to not only accommodation placed but, for instance, taxi fares. Even the travellers cheque commission fee is more expensive than other offices in Thira Town. An agency should receive their finders fee from the supplier of the service not the client. There you go. One correspondent in respect of his dealing with Nomikos referred to 'being saddened, nay gob-smacked!'

The Eating Out

Glaros Bar

Directions: As described.

The owner is a large chap ('weight lifter' large) Assisted by his similarly sized son. Both are friendly. Breakfast, drinks and cocktails are accompanied by modern music. A large bottle of beer costs 100drs, a tasty pizza, sizeable enough for two, is priced at 600drs.

Souvlaki Cafe

Directions: Next door to *Glaros Bar*.

Take away, as well as sit down and comes well recommended apart from which they serve open local retsina (80drs a ½ litre). Offerings include souvlaki in spiced pita bread (90drs), the best pastry in town, chicken on the spit and chips (250drs).

Taverna Neraida

Directions: As detailed.

The young patron is extremely efficient but the waiters appear to get lost, wandering about with trays of food looking for the relevant clients. A meal for two of 2 vegetable soup, 2 roast pork with potatoes & carrots, a litre bottle of retsina, 2 Greek coffees and 2 ouzos cost a reasonable 1180drs. A local barrel wine is available at 200drs a kilo, which, although slightly cloudy, is jolly good value, compared to bottled wines at 500-600drs a bottle. They serve an excellent breakfast.

A meal for two, at either the *Neraida* or the *Coral*, of kalamares, fassolakia freska, a Greek salad, chips and a large bottle of retsina will cost about 1000drs.

Kafeneion Astron

Directions: As described.

For those tempted to eschew the smarter tourist tavernas, this small establishment might seem a heaven-sent opportunity. The kafeneion only sports a narrow concrete verandah and sustenance is served inside. Our one and only visit brought forth one extremely 'so, so', murky stew.

Returning to the main route, this continues to descend as far as:-

MESARIA (4km from Thira Town) The village is up to the right, the main road passing through a large tree shaded crossroads on the edge of which is a sandy, low wall enclosed square or plateia. The buses stop here.

The road to the village 'Chora' ascends a dry river-bed, dividing around a football ground. There are two or three old, lovely but semi-derelict mansions in the upper reaches of the meandering village,as well as a number of the distinctive, barrel roofed buildings.

Straddling the main road crossroads are a few shops, a mini-supermarket, a tour office, a couple of restaurants and hotels. Bread is distributed from the baker in the Upper Village. Mesaria is rather distant from Thira Town to use as a base, but there are a number of hotels. Standing on the approach to the crossroads, from the Thira Town direction, and on the right are the:-

Hotel Artemidoros (Class C) Tel 31640

Single rooms all have an en suite bathroom starting at 2720drs, whilst a double room sharing a bathroom or with en suite bathroom costs 3265drs, increasing to 3355drs & 4030drs (1st-30th Sept) and 4110drs & 4930drs (1st July-31st Aug).

Hotel Andreas (Class E) Tel 31693

All rooms share the bathrooms with a single room priced at 1200drs & a double 1500drs, increasing to 1500drs & 1900drs (1st May-30th Sept).

These two hotels are followed by the *Kanal Pub* and Santorini Rent-A-Car on the corner.

Adjacent to the village street (or right at the crossroads) is the:-

Restaurant Mario
Directions: As above.

Nice food. A meal for two of kalamari, a bacon omelette, a bottled beer, $\frac{1}{2}$ litre of retsina and 2 bottles of soda cost 920drs.

The other side of the Plateia is a small cafe, convenient for waiting bus passengers. Straight on (in the Akrotiri direction) and to the right are the:-

Hotel Loizos (Class C) Tel 31733
Directions: As above.

All rooms have en suite bathrooms with singles costing 2260drs & a double 2710drs, increasing to 3160drs & 3800drs (1st July-15th Sept).

and:-

Hotel Apollon (Class D) Tel 31792

All rooms have en suite bathrooms, single rooms priced at 2080drs & a double at 2600drs, increasing to 3070drs & 3840drs (1st July-15th Sept).

On the other side of the road is the office of Kritikakis Tours and the:-

Hotel Messaria (Class E) Tel 22594
Directions: As above.

Single rooms have en suite bathrooms and are charged at 1085drs, rising to 1760drs (16th July-30th Sept). Double rooms sharing a bathroom start at 2260drs & increase to 2710drs, while double rooms with an en suite bathroom cost 2350drs rising to 2890drs.

In the ground floor of the *Messaria* is a mini-market with a public telephone.

There is a cafe and the *Hotel Margarita* on the corner of the turning to:-

MONOLITHOS (7km from Thira Town) The road towards the coast passes a turning off to Episkopi (or Mesa) Gonias and Kamari. Beyond this, the highway has to divert around a very large extension to the Airport, which now almost fills the Gonias Valley. Older maps detail the road ploughing straight on, in an easterly direction. If it did, the likelihood is that travellers would be crushed beneath the wheels of one of the 'big boys' that land with regularity.

There are hardly enough dwellings to earn the nomenclature village. The road bends round a chapel, let into a singular, large rock outcrop, and continues down to the right-hand edge of a black sand beach. Yes, the broad beach is fine, black sand enclosed by rocky moles into which the waves roll. The foreshore is kelpy for a metre or so, after which the sea is very clear. As with other black sand beaches, the surface at mid-day is almost impossible to walk on with bare feet. A certain amount of nude bathing is tolerated, but goodness knows what that does to the skin in contact with the beach! The broad backshore is rimmed by groves of arethemusa trees, beneath which the locals park their cars. This is, in turn, backed by a dusty, packed earth wasteground on the far, inland edge of which are two tavernas, set in amongst a jumble of buildings and power cable posts. The far taverna sports a distinctly rickety shower head. Incidentally a gang of 'chaps', complete with wheelbarrow, keep the beach clear of sea-borne debris.

To the left (*Fsw*) is a bleak factory 'D Nomikos 1922' with a single, tall black chimney. This is not derelict, as may appear, but only winds into operation for the summer tomato canning season. On the factory wall a painted sign proclaims 'Rooms To Let'. Striding out beneath the roof overhang, along the wall to the rear of the factory, leads to dry gulch countryside with a number of single-storey houses untidily scattered about. But none of these appear to have accommodation.

To the left (*Fsw*), beyond the rocky mole, a sandy track curves along a narrow shore, past oil tanker mooring buoys and some industry. This is bordered, on the land side, by a porous, sandstone larva cliff, wind and sea tortured, with the occasional dwelling let into the face of the rock. The rather kelpy sea-shore loops on in a series of small coves to a tree planted headland, beyond which the path becomes rather rocky. After about

1½km there is a small, untidy taverna where the track heads inland to Karterados.

Back on the main road to Akrotiri from Mesaria, after about ¾km a left-hand turning spurs off for a:-

DETOUR TO KAMARI This route passes by:-

EXO GONIA (5km from Thira Town) A little village piled up and spread over the hillside. The road is in a thoroughly bad state hereabouts. Down the steep decline leads to:-

EPISKOPI (Mesa) GONIAS The settlement has a rather unique, 11th century Byzantine Church, Panaghia Episkopi, in which the faith has alternated, over the years, between Orthodox and Catholic. The Venetians, whilst masters of the island, changed the religious aspect to Catholic, only for the Turks to allow it to revert to the Orthodox. It is also here that Santorini's largest Panayieri is celebrated, on 15th August.

The route from Kamari to the Mesaria-Monolithos connection is only metres away. Turning right leads along a pleasantly gum tree-lined avenue, similar to a Dordogne county road. This passes a wine factory, on the right, offering samplings and, at the outskirts of the seaside resort, *Camping Kamari*, a rather basic site.

KAMARI (10km from Thira Town) The site of the port of 'Ancient Thira', which city once topped the 370m mountain closing off the right-hand side of the bay. Since then Kamari has gone steadily downhill! The package tourist development has ensured this is now a thoroughly horrid, expensive place.

The road terminates at the right-hand end of the seaside village where a fleet of about twelve small fishing boats and caiques still pull up on the beach. The shore is planted out with masses of sun-beds and lots of umbrellas, as well as beach mounted rubbish bins. The sea-bed is too steeply shelving for the comfort of 'littlies'. The 'sprawl' edges the shore of this one-time, small fishing hamlet that has grown and grown and... The concrete Esplanade is planted with arethemusa trees and lined with taverna/restaurants, gift shops, travel offices, discos as well as hotels, pensions and ***Rooms***. Next door to the very expensive *Hotel Kamari* is the well run Kamari Tours (Tel 31455), who represent *Sun Med*, operate a book exchange library and change travellers cheques and currency.

The National Bank of Greece opens Monday to Friday between 0900-1300hrs. Other seafront hotels include the *Sunshine* and the *Nikolina*. There are scooters and pedaloes for hire and dozens of tavernas and cafes. Eating and drinking out is costly. Two large cans of beer cost 400drs in the bar/restaurant to the right (*Fsw*) of the bus terminus. I would rather stay sober!

On a closing note aircraft swing close by on their approach to the runway, panning from left to right (*Sbo*).

Hotels, all of which have en suite bathrooms, include:- *Sunshine* (Class B, tel 31394), where a single room costs 2825drs & a double 3395drs, rising to 4180drs & 5335drs; the Class C *Akis* (Tel 31670), with a double room at 4025drs, increasing to 4800drs; *Artemis Beach* (Tel 31198), with a single room charged at 3850drs & a double 4700drs, escalating to 4700drs & 654drs; *Astro* (Tel 31366), the single rooms of which cost 2600drs & a double room 3200drs, rising to 3300drs & 4200drs; *Kamari* (Tel 31243), with single rooms priced at 3050drs & a double 4000drs, increasing to 4500drs & 5700drs (1st July-30th Sept); *Kasteli* (Tel 31122), with doubles priced at 3000drs, escalating to 3500drs (1st May-15th June & 16th Sept-20th Nov) and 4800drs (16th June-15th Sept); *Orion* (Tel 31182); *Poseidon* (Tel 31387), with singles at 2440drs & doubles 3070drs, rising to 2710drs & 3430drs (1st May-30th June) and 3930drs & 5060drs (1st July-30th Sept); *Zephyros* (Tel 31108), where a single is charged at 3400drs & a double 3800drs, increasing to 4600drs & 5000drs (1st July-30th Sept); the Class D *Acropole* (Tel 31012); *Aspro Spiti* (Tel 31441), with singles costing 3200drs & doubles 4200drs, rising to 4000drs & 5000drs (1st July-30th Sept); *Blue Sea* (Tel 31481), where a single room costs 2200drs & a double 3000drs, escalating to 2600drs & 4000drs (1st July-30th Sept); *Golden Sun* (Tel 31301), with double rooms sharing a bathroom priced at 1535drs & with en suite bathrooms 2125drs, rising to 2125drs & 2710drs (1st July-30th Sept); *Nikolina I* (Tel 31253), where a double room is priced at 3200drs, increasing to 4200drs (15th June-15th Sept); *Sigalas* (Tel 31260); *Ta Kymata* (Tel 31694), with a single room costing 2900drs & a double room 3500drs, rising to 3900drs & 4500drs (1st July-30th Sept); the Class E *Andreas; Asteria* (Tel 31002), with double rooms costing 2500drs, escalating to 3500drs (16th June-30th Sept); *Dionyssios* (Tel 31310), doubles only priced at 2350drs, rising to 3160drs (1st July-30th Sept); *Ghiannis Kapelos* (Tel 31166), where a double room is priced at 2800drs, increasing to 3200drs (1st July-31st Aug); *Nikolina* (Tel 31253), with single rooms sharing a bathroom priced at 1800drs, a double room sharing 2000drs & a double room with en suite bathroom 2500drs, rising to 2000drs & 2500/3200drs (15th June-15th Sept); *Nina* (Tel 31697), where a single room costs 1625drs & a double 2075drs, increasing to 2170drs & 2710drs (1st July-30th Sept); *Prekamaria* (Tel 31266), with a double room priced at 2000drs, escalating to 2500drs (1st June-30th Sept) *Villa Elli* (Tel 31266), yes the same as the *Prekamaria* where a single room costs 2000drs & a double 2500drs, rising to 2500drs & 3000drs (1st July-30th Sept). Phew!

ANCIENT THIRA (2km) From the right-hand side of Kamari Bay a very steep, winding, flint road hairpin ascent ends at a roundabout on the saddle of a ridge. Prior to the roundabout a mountain path makes off to the right for Pyrgos, another track crosses over the ridge down to the seaside village of Perissa whilst the other path climbs steeply up on the spine of the ridge towards the Ancient City, passing through an entrance gate. Admission is free and the site is open daily between 0930-1330hrs. The return journey by donkey takes ½hr each way and costs 750drs. No, I did not torture one of the poor beasts with my bulk.

From the mountain top there are magnificent views and on a clear day... it is possible to see as far as the mountain tops of Crete, to the south, and the island of Anafi, to the east. The site, which dates back to the 9th century BC, was excavated, in the 1890s, by a German archaeologist. The remains are the usual 'Greek village reduced to ground level rubble'. Apart from the more scholarly matters, one of the houses bore a phallus in relief inscribed 'To my friends'! A terrace exhibits carvings of dancing nude boys and scratched graffiti, expressing admiration in verse (Was this the ancients' version of the modern-day blue movie?). Do not attempt the walk from Kamari at the height of the midday sun if there is not a strong Cycladean wind blowing,nor without wearing a pair of strong shoes.

Returning to the Thira Town to Akrotiri main road, from Vothonas the road snakes along the mountainside to the:-

DETOUR TO PYRGOS (8km from Thira Town) A very pleasant hillside village badly knocked about by the 1956 earthquake. The surfaced road peters out on an irregular square to one side of the pretty houses and alleys that ascend the steep slopes. To the immediate left of the square is a very convenient taverna and patio up a few stone steps from the road, with an equally convenient 'squatty' toilet next door. The taverna 'fails' to display a menu and single courses can cost as much as full-blown meals on other islands, so ask first. There is a baker, mini-market, Post Office, scooter rental, tourist shop and, once upon a time, a Venetian Castle, now disappeared but recorded in a quarter of Pyrgos, called Kastelli.

From Pyrgos village the road strikes out and up to:-

Monastery Profitis Ilias (10km from Thira Town) The 560m mountain top is not only the provenance of the monastery but television and radio masts as well as a radar station, but that's progress. The monastery, built in the early 1700s, makes a worthwhile visit having a fine exhibition of icons, manuscripts, paintings, relics and a museum. Visitors may visit the old cells, workshops and the main building. Weekday admission is between 0800-1300hrs & 1500-1800hrs at a cost of 150drs. Magnificent views but the monastery is on the excursion bus trips so you won't be alone. And do not forget to be fully dressed – shorts are a no, no.

It makes a lovely 2½ hour walk to keep going along the path to the seaside villages of Kamari or Perissa.

Back on the main road, a little further on from the Pyrgos turning, is the tortuous, steeply descending road down to Athinos Port (*See* **Arrival by Ferry**). After 1½km or so, a left-hand thoroughfare heads off through Ag Nikitas for the:-

Detour To Perissa The route advances past a side turning to the left to the lovely village of:-

MEGALOCHORI (circa 8km from Thira Town) A Mrs Koyla, a nice 'Mrs Big', has accommodation where a double room costs about 2200drs. She spent six months in Kings Lynn, in her teens, and would like to make the village a 'tourist centre' – with the help of relatives. Her mother runs the local supermarket and a cousin the taverna. I wish her all the best.

EMPORIO (9km from Thira Town) A large, provincial, rural village with many churches, low and high. The main square is the bus turn-round point and a taxi rank. On the far side of the square is the *Hotel Archea Elefsina Adenauer* (Class D, tel 81250). The rooms have en suite bathrooms. A single room costs 1360drs & a double 2015drs, rising to 1740drs & 3300drs (1st July-15th Sept).

To the right of Emporio is a line of 'dead' windmills, scaling the heights, whilst after 6km the road runs into the outskirts of:-

PERISSA (15km from Thira Town) The long, straight avenue to the village passes through an unsightly scattering of new building sprawl in amongst which are many ***Rooms***, a *Youth Hostel* on the right, several discos as well as a large campsite, also on the right, alongside the beach. Almost a 'mirror image' of Kamari with the headland and main village to the left and the black, coarse, sandy beach curving away 'for ever' to the right. But note there the similarities end for Perissa is 'a Clacton' to Kamari's 'Frinton' and is a much less expensive location at which to eat out. A 'for instance' is the:-

Delfini Fish Taverna
Here a well travelled correspondent advises me he and his wife enjoyed one of the best fish dishes they had eaten in Greece. Some claim. A meal for two of 1 kalamares, 1 plate of Gopas, a salad, 2 beers, 2 ouzos and 2 coffees cost 1180drs. A dinner of 2 fish soups (a meal in itself, with scorpena, potatoes, carrots, onions & celery), a large bottle of retsina, 2 sodas, 2 coffees and 2 ouzos cost 1280drs.

Close to the Bus terminus, a taverna serves large bottles of beer for 60drs.

One writes village but as there must be twelve small hotels it is almost a town, towered over by mountain cliff-faces, topped off by radio beacons and dominated at beach level by a large church. Beyond the church, to the left (*Fsw*), is the Main Square on which the buses park and our 'friends' Nomikos Travel have an office which transacts exchange and stores left luggage. The centre of Perissa sports an open-air cinema, a 'crazy' golf course (Ugh), mini-markets, *Restaurant Popeye Grill* (Double Ugh!), *Mr Quick Fast Food* and scooter hire.

The sea edge is cleanish, despite which smelly rubbish is sometimes piled up in cardboard boxes on the backshore. As for Kamari, the sea-bed shelves steeply and thus is unsuitable for 'littlies'. Pedaloes are to be found and the development peters out in a scrubbly, messy sprawl.

Keeping to the left (*Fsw*) and starting out on the rough, wide track towards Ancient Thira, leads to a number of ***Rooms*** as well as the *Hotels Marianna* and *Artemis*, all in unlovely surroundings.

A friend let me into the secret of one out-of-the-way spot that helps to alleviate Perissa's shortcomings. About ¾km back up the road to Emporio, there is a track across the fields to the left (*Sbo*), just before a church on the right. This leads, after a kilometre or two, to the *Taverna/Hotel Georgios*. Highly recommended and has a seawater pool.

Hotels, which all have en suite bathrooms, include the: *Thira Mare* (Class C), with a single room priced at 2400drs & a double room 3400drs, rising to 3500drs & 4500drs (1st July-30th Sept);

Christina (Class D, tel 81362); *Santa Irini* (Class D, tel 81226), with a single room costing 2300drs & a double room 3950drs, increasing to 3400drs & 4950drs (11th June-20th Oct); *Zorzis* (Class D, tel 81244), where a single room is priced at 1550drs & a double 2250drs, escalating to 1650drs & 2400drs (1st Sept-31st Oct) and 1850drs & 2800drs (1st July-31st Aug); *Boubis* (Class E, tel 81203), with a single room, sharing a bathroom, costing 1300drs, a single room with an en suite bathroom 1800drs & a double room en suite 2500drs; *Maroussiana* (Class E), with double rooms en suite costing 2800/3000drs; *Meltemi* (Class E, tel 81325), where a single room is priced at 1720drs & a double room 2000drs, rising to 2280drs & 2700drs (16th May-30th June & 1st-15th Oct) and 2840drs & 3400drs (1st July-30th Sept); *Nota* (Class E, tel 81209), with a single room costing 2000drs & a double room 3000drs, escalating to 2500drs & 3500drs (1st June-31st Oct); *Perissa* (Class E), with single rooms costing 2000drs, double rooms, sharing a bathroom, priced at 2000drs & double rooms en suite 3000drs, rising to 5000drs & 4000/6000drs (1st June-31st Oct), and the *Rena* (Class E) with double rooms charged at 3160drs.

Returning to the main road at **Ag Nikitas**, a surfaced lane, to the left, cuts off a large corner. The gently undulating, agricultural countryside is planted with the low vines, typical of the island, and dotted with the occasional small chapel. Almost immediately after the main road is rejoined there is an isolated pension to the left, absolutely in the middle of nowhere.

AKROTIRI (14km from Thira Town) A pleasant, old village built round and up a rocky spur around the edge of which more modern development is spreading along the road. There are several houses with ***Rooms***, a mini-market, doctor, and the *Hotel Paradise*. There are a number of attractive tavernas, particularly the:

Restaurant Maria *Directions*: On the right of the main road (*Heading towards the excavations*), just beyond the square.

Maria and her husband are very friendly, pleasant people. A delicious meal for two of moussaka, chicken, meatballs with rice, souvlaki, a village salad, bread, 2 Cokes, a beer and a bottle of water cost to 900drs.

Akrotiri Excavations My general lack of enthusiasm for piles of archaeological this or that may have filtered through to readers. But here and there a particular site captures even my pedestrian imagination, and this is just such a one. Make no mistake about it, Akrotiri is an emperor of archaeological remains, nay a God. Enough to say that if a visitor came blindfolded to Santorini and only saw these remains, then that would be enough.

Another prejudice involves guides (the human type), or more correctly evading paying for a guide. I prefer to enjoy pottering about on my own with one of the coloured brochures, usually imprecisely translated into English and customarily available at the admission point. Well forget it, and stump up and hope you are lucky enough to join a group with young, bespectacled Nena as your mentor.

The discovery of this ancient town provided undeniable proof of the island's close connection with Crete and, as with Pompeii, the larvae and ash preserved many buildings, even multi-storey ones, in their originally constructed shape. Furthermore many of the door and window frames, fireplaces, even lavatory systems were preserved in place. Of course the most dramatic finds were the frescoes and murals. Worryingly, for the inhabitants of Santorini, Athens has got its grasping hands on these, as well as much of the best pottery and jars. The authorities there are keeping them safe, supposedly until Santorini has its own, new museum! Other islands have heard that story. The Greek Father of the Akrotiri excavations, Professor Marinatos who commenced his dig as recently as 1967, must be spinning in his grave. This reminds me to point out he died of a heart attack, 'on the job' as it were, tumbling into one of his own trenches – rather reminiscent of one of those spooky Raoul Dahl short stories.

It would appear that the original inhabitants had sufficient warning of the impending disaster to remove nearly all their personal items and almost every living thing. To date, only a piglet's skeleton has been found – an archaeological 'Marie Celeste'. Chillingly, the guide books written before the discovery of this site, refer to the locals vivid description of spectral figures observed in the area, over many years.

The site is open daily between 0845-1500hrs and on Sundays & holidays between 0930-1430hrs. Admission costs 300drs. A last word of advice is to arrive early as the site is covered by dexion supported, semi-translucent roofing. By midday, it gets very hot beneath this shield.

Down the slope from the excavations, the road runs out on a backshore of large black boulders and pebbles, set in a wide bay. Besides the shore is the *Hotel Akrotiri* (Class C, tel 81375) with en suite rates for a single room are 2900drs and those for a double room 3400drs.

From the 'Dig' it is possible to take the 500m dirt road to the *Red Beach Taverna*. This is run by friendly Louie who spent twenty years as a steelworker in Indiana, USA.

I am reliably advised that a path leads off by a small chapel, up a rocky hill to another cove with, on the far side, a splendid and 'accommodating' cave.

ROUTE TWO

To Ia (10km) and back to Thira Town via Vourvoulos The main road to Ia climbs quite steeply from the Thira Town 'Bus' Square past Firostephani, now a suburb of Thira Town, on to:-

IMEROVIGLI (Merovigli) (1km from Thira Town) To one side of the main road a very steep, short, country lane climbs to this unexceptional, dusty but pleasant village. The church at the entrance to the village is a convent (Irish, yes..!). Businesses include a taverna, mini-market, scooter hire and the large *Hotel Katerina* (Class E, tel 22708). This hotel enjoys possibly the most impressive and spectacular location anywhere on Santorini. I accept that is quite a claim but it overhangs the caldera on a steep cliff, wedged between two jutting rock faces. The owner shamefully capitalizes on this advantage by grossly charging in excess of the official rates, which, for an E class establishment, are sufficient unto the day. All rooms share the bathrooms and the catalogued prices for a single room are 1700drs,a double 2550drs, increasing to 2350drs & 3500drs (1st July-30th Sept).

The Venetian island capital of Tourlos and a castle used to be located to the left of Imerovigli (facing north), on a promontory below the village.

It is a pity that the poorly surfaced main road to Ia is hemmed in by a mountain range which blanks off the incredible view. To some extent this inconvenience is compensated for by the dramatic drop to the flat, fertile plain way below to the right.

There is a way of enjoying the incredible western views and scenery, that is to make the 2½hr walk along the path from Imerovigli. This edges the precipitous drop but is deep gravel and difficult in places. Walkers should wear a solid pair of shoes.

The advent of Ia is signalled by, to the right, the small hamlet of **Foinikia (9km from Thira Town)** Immediately after the Foinikia turning is the:-

Foinkia Taverna which is to the right as the road skirts the village. The taverna is beautifully laid out with abundant red and purple bougainvillea abundant. It offers a useful alternative to Ia eateries. A delicious meal for two of tomato soups, pork steaks, a salad, beer and bread cost about 1700drs.

The taverna is followed by, on the right, a sign to a *Youth Hostel* (where a bed costs 500drs), after which is another board indicating the:-

Atlantis Villas

Directions: A short scramble up a steep country path to the left.

This is a superb hotel complex, a sensational, cliff-hanging cluster of dazzlingly white apartments. Originally they were hillside draped, traditional cave dwellings which have been converted into spacious, separate 'villas', each with its own patio, kitchen facilities and bathroom. The rooms are complete with many original fittings (for example, hole-in-the-wall cupboards and four piece entrance doors) and are an excellent 'model' set of conversions. No doubt the former inhabitants (who squeezed families of up to eighteen in number into one 'double apartment) are despairingly incredulous that tourists pay around 11,000 per double, per night to stay here! Admittedly the price includes breakfast and the use of the marvellously situated swimming pool. In addition to all this is the magnificent location with views over the dark brown streaked, sheer drop to the right, Thirasia island across the incredibly deep blue bay and, to the left, the west coast of Santorini curving away in a series of rocky inlets.

IA (Oia) (10km from Thira Town) (Illustration 28) The village evinces a slow, leisurely pace but is most definitely on the 'day-trip excursion' circuit. Residents are in a rather similar situation to those staying on small, offshore islands where trip-boats flood and ebb every day, leaving the place almost deserted overnight. As elsewhere on Santorini it is a plus point to have inside seating and many restaurants advertise sheltered patios and inside dining areas so clients can get out of the howling wind.

The pedestrian-only Esplanade Odhos N Nomikou, edges the precipice of this cliff-hanging settlement while the main road, more a bypass, curves around to the right past the Bus Square (*Tmr* 1C1) ending up on the Town Hall Plateia (*Tmr* 2B2). The diversion of the two roads happens alongside the large, cobalt blue domed Church of Ag Lazaros. Incidentally, one item Ia is not short of is churches. At the last count there were some forty crammed into the village.

Taverna Laokasti & Rooms to Rent (*Tmr* 14F2) Tel 71343
Directions: On the right of the main road, opposite the Church of Ag Lazaros.

This is about the best offering in Ia, though it does not enjoy a privileged position, compared to other tavernas which overlook the caldera. However, the service is pleasant, the food excellent and good value. Despite advertising 'pizzeria', the taverna serves mainly Greek food. A meal for two of beans, rice with peas, macaroni with beef, a bottle of water, a Coke and bread cost about 850drs. A dinner of stuffed tomatoes, a hamburger steak, a tomato salad, chickpeas, a beer, Coke and bread cost 900drs – very reasonable for Ia. They also have very pleasant rooms to let, complete with bathroom and a kitchen with cooking facilities. Double rooms cost some 3500drs whilst a very large split level room for four, including bathroom/kitchen, costs 7000drs.

An arrowed sign on the wall of the Church of Ag Lazaros points along the Esplanade to an extinct office of the National Bank of Greece. The first 100m or so of Odhos N Nomikou is rather bland, after which the surrounds become extremely picturesque, a definition not allowing for the startling drop to the left. Ia suffered far more than Thira in the 1956 earthquake, resulting in a number of ruined buildings with wired off roof terraces still drunkenly clinging to the cliff-face terraces.

A sign to the left indicates the whereabouts of a baker followed by:-

Rooms For Rent Delfini Tel 71272
Directions: As above.

Splendidly situated and cliff-hanging, with a nice terrace. The young proprietor speaks English. A double room en suite costs some 2750drs.

Hotel Fregata (*Tmr* 3D/E2) (Class D) Tel 71221
Directions: Fifty metres on, almost opposite a souvenir shop alongside the *Hotel/Cafe-Bar Marinos*.

This is a super hotel, well situated with an interesting (ex sea captain?) owner and nice breakfast bar. It has a splendid, wide balcony overlooking the caldera. A double room, sharing or with en suite bathroom, starts at 2915drs, rising to 3780drs (July-Sept).

A few paces further on is the:-
Hotel Anemones (*Tmr* 4D2) (Class E) Tel 71220
Directions: As above.

A single room, sharing a bathroom, starts at 1225drs, a double sharing costs 1755drs & a double en suite 2240drs, rising to 1590drs & 2275/2925drs.

Beyond the hotel, also on the left, is a well stocked general store. A taxi rank is signposted to the right (fare to Thira Town about 550drs, the Airport 700drs) and there is a general store on the left. From hereabouts the tavernas and restaurants straddle the road 'in earnest'.

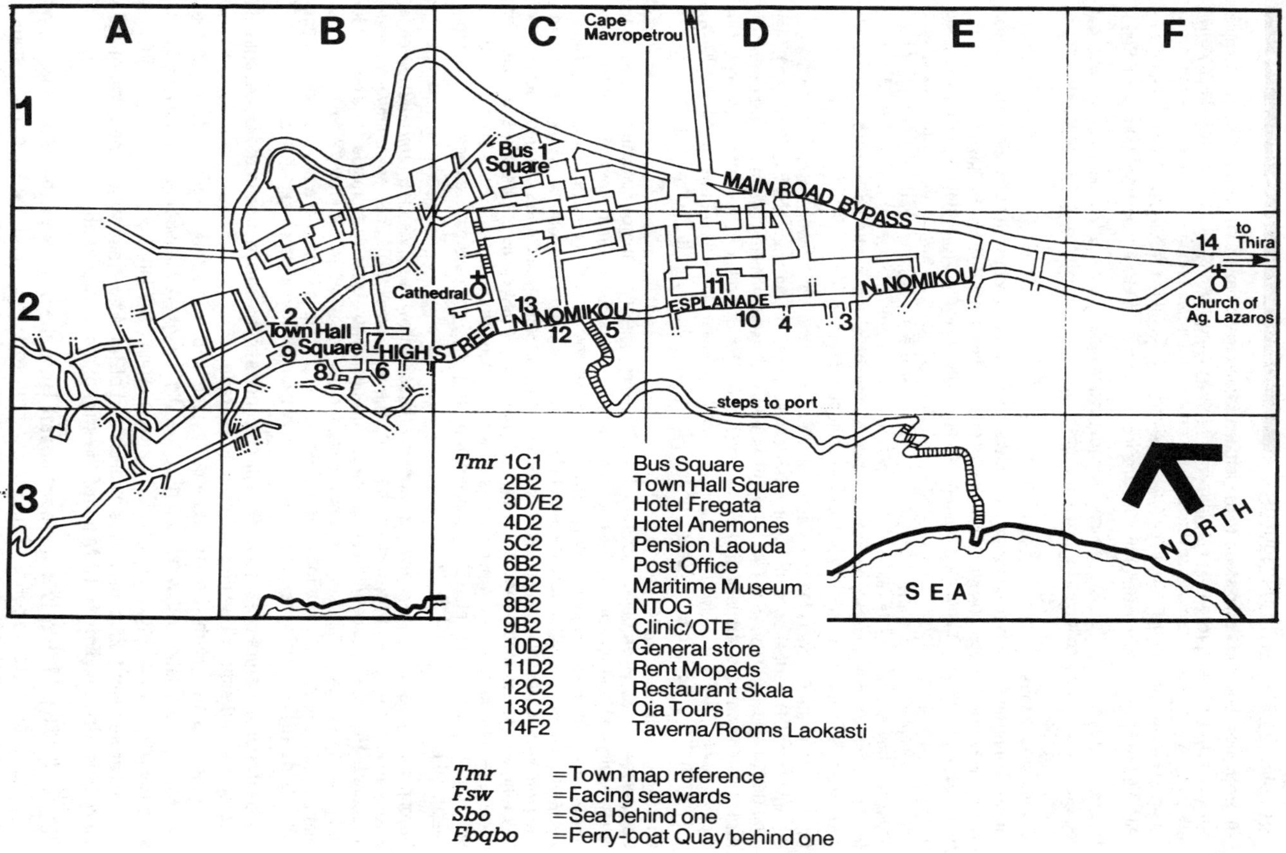

Illustration 28 Ia

A green sign, pointing down steps to the left, indicates the way to:-

Christos Fitros Houses (Pension Laouda) (*Tmr* 5C2) (Class B) Tel 71204

Directions: As above.

Rather spartan with single rooms, sharing the bathroom, costing 1750drs, a double room sharing 2340drs & with an en suite bathroom 3060drs, increasing to 2270drs & 3040/3970drs (April-Sept).

Twenty metres beyond *Pension Laouda* the street is straddled by Nikos/Zorbas disco/cocktail bar and video music joints, followed by a couple of gift shops, opposite which are more steps leading to:-

Restaurant Skala (*Tmr* 12C2)

Directions: As above.

It has seating on a terrace overlooking the caldera. Many tavernas with such a position are pretentious and charge high prices but the Skala is reasonably priced. The service is excruciatingly slow! One (very) harassed waiter dashes about, but he cannot cope. The numbers of clientele are swelled by the position of the taverna, adjacent to the top of the steps which lead down to the harbour. Exhausted climbers collapse here for replenishment. The Skala is also a fun place to watch the high jinx of the mules as they realize they've reached the top – passengers are occasionally pitched off. When the food finally arrives it is generally excellent. A meal for two of (delicious) stuffed peppers, a moussaka, a tomato salad, a bottle of water and a beer cost about 850drs.

On the right is the Panaghia Platsani Cathedral (*Tmr* C2), to the side of which steps lead to the Bus Square (*Tmr* 1C1). Further on, to the right, is the folksy Karvounis Tour office (Tel 71209/71205).They offer book-exchange, trips to the island of Thirasia, as well as ferry tickets and money exchange. On the left and down some steps is the Post Office (*Tmr* 6B2) and another thirty metres walk, opposite the *Pub Sphinx*, is the small Maritime Museum (*Tmr* 7B2) which opens daily between 1100-1200hrs & 1700-1800hrs. Beyond the Museum, on the left and up a short lane, is the:-

NTOG (*Tmr* 8B2) Tel 71234.

Open weekdays between 0800-1500rs & 1700-2200hrs. These are approximations as the staffing is rather unreliable. The office is located in a plain, bare wooden floored room. An efficient lady dispenses information, somewhat grudgingly. The lists available include interesting details of *Traditional Settlements* in Ia. The latter vary from a double bed studio with bathroom, to a 9 bed apartment, complete with a fully equipped kitchen. For those contemplating a week in this charming location the following will give an idea of prices. Per night charges for a 2 bed studio are 3,000drs, a 3 bed/flat and kitchen 4000drs, while a 4 bed 'pad' is 6500drs, 5 beds from 7500drs and 9 beds 14,000drs. For further details of this interesting scheme write to EOT, Paradosiakos Oikismos, Oia, Santorini Island, Greece.

Beyond the NTOG office are a few gift shops on the left followed by the OTE (*Tmr* 9B2) which is across an arch from the Clinic, both on the right. The new, small OTE office open between 0900-1200hrs & 1600-2000hrs daily, except Sundays. An unusually pleasant lady 'presides'. A short stride or two along an alley on this side of the street leads to the Town Hall Square (*Tmr* 2B2) whilst, to the right, is an old-fashioned store followed by Trident Travel. This is located in a tiny, provincial office with signboards advertising tickets to almost everywhere. The owner is a larger-than-life Mr 'Fix-it'.

An intriguing feature of Ia is that the various shops, similar to Nisiros in the Dodecanese, display painted signs depicting the purveyors trade.

Hereabouts the 'High' Street becomes a lane and a left fork tumbles down to the remains of the Castle and what is left of the Old Town. A misleading and long defunct sign still points to a long extinct NTOG office on the castle lane.

There are smelly public lavatories at each end of Ia and a 'squatty' on the edge of the dusty 'Bus' Square (*Tmr* 1C1). Many of the streets are painted with flower outlines.

Detour To Thira Town (via the east coast) From the vicinity of the 'Bus' Square, a surfaced track makes off in a northerly direction to curve round the eastern coastline, which makes a most interesting alternative route back to Thira Town.

Once adjacent to Cape Mavropetrou, the road as far as Cape Kouloumbo becomes a track. This undulates through scrub and gorse moorland backed by terraced landscapes with low volcanic cliffs bordering a coarse, sandy beach and sea-shore. The clean beaches are almost deserted and only accommodate the occasional, isolated sun worshipper.

Here and there the shore narrows down, become rather kelpy with black boulders and shingle, fringed by low sandstone cliffs.

From Cape Kouloumbo the only sign of life is an infrequent chapel or house set in the undulating countryside. The track as far as the hamlet of Pori can be difficult, in places, for two-wheeled powered vehicles, so beware. The surface is often thick, shifting sand which makes for spills and accidents.

PORI (5km from Thira Town) The enterprise exhibited in originally opening *Panaghia Rooms for Rent, Restaurant Low Prices*, seems to have been wasted. The establishment may open up at the height of the summer but cannot otherwise be relied on as even a 'way-station'.

VOURVOULOS (2km from Thira Town) A truly agricultural settlement. A wide path makes down to the sea, an inland track forks to the right, back to Thira Town via Kontochori, whilst the left track staggers off to the hamlet of:-

KATIKIES (1km from Thira Town) Some maps propose all sorts of roads here and there, in this area, with connections to the Karterados coast roadway. Ignore them. There is a track to the sea, signposted 'Beach', but actuality is only a small sea mole and shelters with crude doors cut into the cliff-face by fishermen.

From Katikies the road rejoins the Vourvoulos route to the outskirts of Thira Town.

EXCURSION TO THIRASIA ISLAND

Ia is the best point of departure for an excursion boat to Manolas Harbour. The trip takes about ½hr and the port village is, as are the western towns of its bigger brother, reached by mounting about 300 steps up the cliff-face. This is a ¾hr climb or a 350drs donkey 'jolt'. Fortunately, there is a cafe-bar at the top. Some 100m along the main thoroughfare is a taverna and mini-market, beyond which is a taverna with accommodation. The settlement is a jumble of starkly white, small cubes haphazardly muddled together.

For a better beach than the pebbles of the Harbour it is necessary to cross the island by the reasonable track to the inland villages of either Agrilia or Potamos and then strike out for the coast.

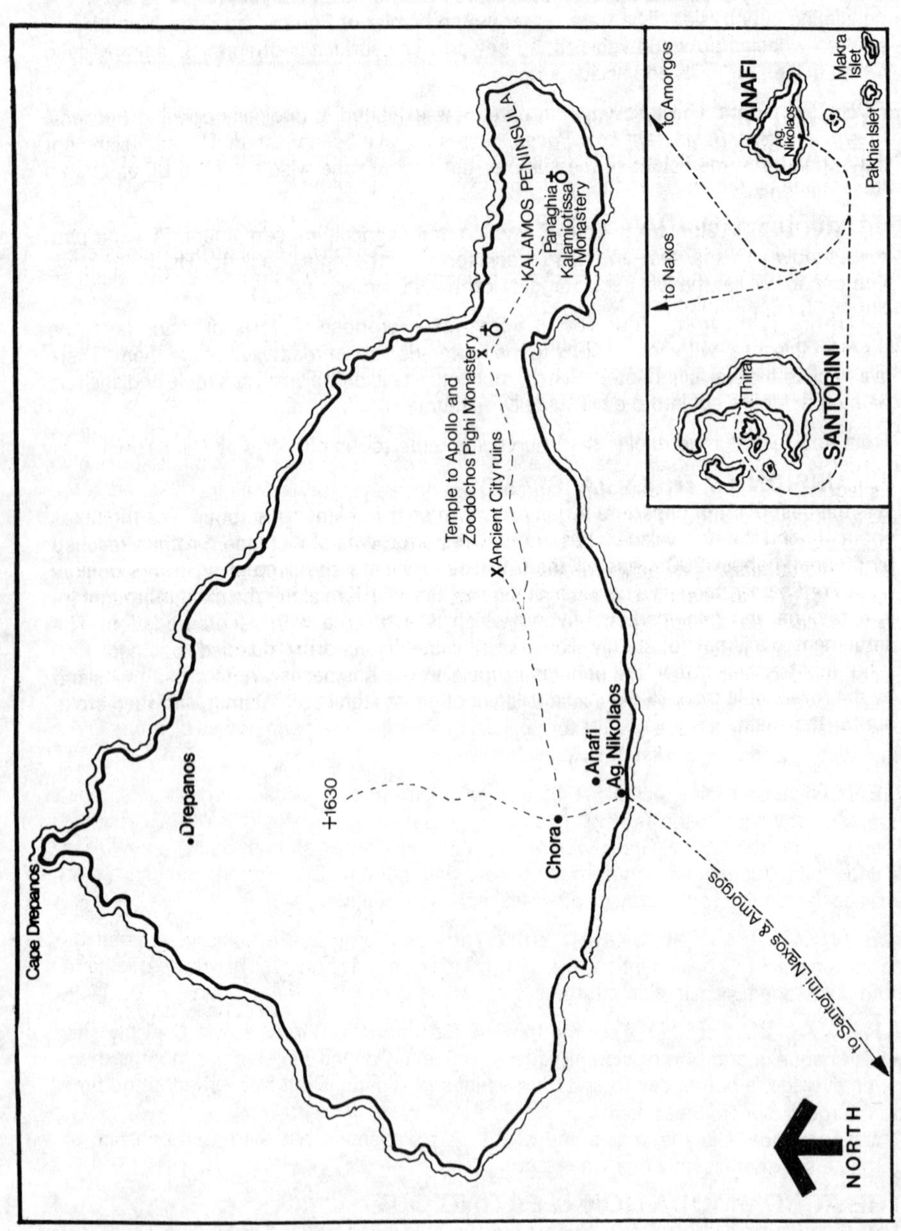

Illustration 29 Anafi island

11 ANAFI (Anaphi, Anaphe) Cyclades Islands - Eastern chain

FIRST IMPRESSIONS Wind; flies; barren landscape & what a climb to the town!

SPECIALITIES Saligari (snails) - eaten only in September; Mizithra cheese; Brusko wine – made by the locals and very strong – one glass is enough.

RELIGIOUS HOLIDAYS & FESTIVALS include: 15th August – Festival, Panaghia Kalamiotissa Monastery; 8th September – Panaghia Kalamiotissa Monastery. An image of the Virgin Mary was found on a bamboo plant or 'kalami', hence the island's saint being Ag Kalamiotissa.

VITAL STATISTICS Tel prefix 0286. The island is squarish in shape, with the Kalamos headland at the eastern end. The population fluctuates, according to the time of year, but averages about 200, most of whom, live in the Chora.

HISTORY Fable has it that the island emerged from the sea at the command of Apollo, in order to shelter Jason and the Argonauts, who were beset by a storm. Quite possibly this legend relates to the Santorini 'big bang'. In any case, Apollo was worshipped here and a temple dedicated to him was located close to the nearest of the two monasteries, Zoodochos Pighi.

The word 'anaphi' actually comes from the ancient Greek, meaning 'no snakes.' According to local legend, no snake can survive here, whilst the neighbouring islands are, or were, covered in them.

The Russians ruled briefly, in the sixteenth century, and more recently, during the Second World War, Anafi was under Italian rule. According to the older locals, the Italian soldiers were well liked and the island 'enjoyed' a peaceful war. During the Greek civil war, Anafi became a place of exile for political prisoners. Here again, it was all rather low-key, with the prisoners billeted in the locals' houses.

GENERAL Until fairly recently Anafi was an 'undiscovered' island, with no roads, cars, hotels or anything associated with tourism. However, with the more intrepid tourists searching for 'the original Greek way of life', this is no longer so true. Sadly, a new road is under construction, leading from the port to the Chora. On completion, I imagine Anafi will acceleratingly, go the way of other lesser known islands.

AG NIKOLAOS (or Skala): port Ferry-boat arrivals are, initially, greeted by depressing mounds of cement and gravel, and little else. The port itself is a tiny settlement, both dusty and unremarkable but it fulfils its *raison d'etre* as a way-station.

ARRIVAL BY FERRY To write this is a focal point for ferries would possibly give an erroneous impression of vibrant activity. However, during the summer months there is, on average, a boat a day to and from various destinations but be warned, at no time do the room owners meet them.

The Ferry-boat Quay is at one end of the port settlement but there is no chance of getting lost – there is only one way to go.

THE ACCOMMODATION & EATING OUT

The Accommodation A few ***Rooms*** are available in the port but not many. These are quickly snapped up by the more faint-hearted and, dare I say, sensible tourists who do not wish to make the strenuous and exhausting climb to the Chora. However, there are more ***Rooms*** available at the nearest beach, which is some ten minutes walk to the right (*Sbo*) of the port.

The Eating Out There is a grand total of two tavernas and one rather small bar, rather inappropriately called *The Crazy Shrimp Disco Bar*.

Taverna Akrogiali
Directions: The first taverna after disembarking from the ferry.

More a place for a quick snack, while waiting for the ferry, than a delicious Greek meal. The tables inside are grabbed quickly because of the swirling dust clouds outside.

Taverna Marie
More in the style of 'the Greek taverna' but again, mainly packed with people waiting for a ferry.

THE A TO Z OF USEFUL INFORMATION

BEACHES

Beach 1: About ten minutes walk to the right (*Sbo*) of the port, along the cliff edge. Quite a pleasant little sandy beach, with clear water but rather windy. There are quite a few ***Rooms*** here, at reasonable prices and a lot of people camp on the beach itself. The beach also boasts a couple of small tavernas which are packed day and night.

Beach 2: Follow the path along the cliffs to the right (*Sbo*) for about thirty minutes. This is a long, sandy beach, an ideal place for those who want to be quite alone. Be warned and carry a torch if planning to stay late.

BICYCLE, SCOOTER & CAR HIRE None, at least until the new road is completed. The island does boast one private car.

BREAD SHOPS Bread can be bought at the general shop next to the *Akrogiali Taverna*.

COMMERCIAL SHOPPING AREA Two small general shops sell the basics. Being a traditional place, everything shuts quite early and is not influenced by middle of the night ferry arrivals.

DISCOS There is one tiny (and I do mean tiny) disco, the *Crazy Shrimp Disco Bar* sited on the corner of the path leading up to the Chora. During peak season it gets very packed.

FERRY-BOATS At the moment, there are few boats which call here. On average, there is one a day, including about two per week from **Piraeus**.

Ferry-boat timetable (Mid-season)

Day	Departure time	Ferry-boat	Ports/Islands of Call
Sun	1700hrs	Golden Vergina	Santorini,Sikinos,Folegandros,Milos,Piraeus(M).
Mon	2000hrs	Olympia	Ios,Naxos,Paros,Piraeus(M).
Wed	0200hrs	Golden Vergina	Ag Nikolaos(Crete),Sitia(Crete),Kasos, Karpathos,Diafani(Karpathos),Rhodes.
	0500hrs	Delos	Santorini,Ios,Naxos,Paros,Syros,Rafina(M).
Thurs	0800hrs	Caique	Santorini.
	1600hrs	Golden Vergina	Santorini,Piraeus(M).
Sat	0200hrs	Golden Vergina	Ag Nikolaos(Crete),Sitia(Crete),Kasos, Karpathos,Diafani(Karpathos),Chalki,Rhodes.

Please note these tables are detailed as a GUIDE ONLY. Due to the time taken to research the Cyclades it is IMPOSSIBLE TO 'match' the timetables or even boats . So don't try cross pollinating...

FERRY-BOAT TICKET OFFICES There is an office (Tel 61218), alongside the *Akrogiali Taverna*. The man who runs it speaks a little English and is very helpful.

MEDICAL CARE Don't be ill in the port, the only doctor is at the top of the hill, in the Chora.

POLICE & POST OFFICE *See* **The Chora**.

TOILETS The only public facilities consist of bushes! The taverna's toilets are not to be recommended.

EXCURSION TO PORT SURROUNDS Boatmen will 'ferry' passengers to all and any coastal location but are rather expensive. Clients should ensure they arrange their return... otherwise there will be a very long walk or swim. The boatmen wander round the small port offering tourists their services and can usually be beaten down on the opening demands.

THE CHORA: capital & only village (Illustration 30) The small village is located on the site of a Venetian fortress, of which little or nothing remains. Bits of pottery can still be found lying around.

The Chora is, for all intents and purposes, one long passageway with small pathways leading off. A charming place full of nooks and crannies, and little else. There is a deserted ambiance to the place. The locals are shy but extremely friendly and helpful. Various paths promisingly make off into the hills, but don't go too far.

THE ACCOMMODATION AND EATING OUT

The Accommodation None of the room owners meet the ferries, so finding accommodation is left totally to the visitor. This does not mean that there aren't any rooms, on the contrary, almost every house provides accommodation. Signs are almost non-existent, so it is necessary to knock on doors and in high season, rooms are like gold dust.

Signs for ***Rooms*** can be found almost at the top of the path from the port, at the Supermarket (*Tmr* 1B2) and also at the Cafe Estiatorio (*Tmr* 6A2).

The Eating Out Limited, which is only to be expected in a place of such a small size.

To Στεκι Taverna (*Tmr* 3A2)
Well frequented by the locals which is not surprising as the food is delicious, although limited in choice. At the weekend, there is often impromptu, traditional dancing, but diners should watch their heads – the locals throw bottles and visitors are encouraged to join in.

Cafe Estiatorio (*Tmr* 6A2)
More of a daytime watering hole, with a choice of about two dishes and little else.

Anafi Ouzerie (*Tmr* 7A3) A new addition to the village, which to date the locals avoid. However, it possesses a terrace overlooking the bay and is a very pleasant evening location. They serve breakfast.

Cafe Cypros (*Tmr* 8A4)
A traditional, rather grubby 'kafeneion' where most of the old men and the 'pappas' sit, all day. It serves a nice breakfast and the friendly owner is the president of the village. He doesn't speak English but is marvellous at sign language.

THE A TO Z OF USEFUL INFORMATION

BANKS None.

BICYCLES, SCOOTER & CAR HIRE None.

BOOKSELLERS A limited selection of second-hand books are available at the Tourist shop (*Tmr* 2B2), at the top of the path from the port.

BREAD SHOPS The one Baker (*Tmr* 5A2) is next to the school, opposite the path to the port.

BUSES None.

COMMERCIAL SHOPPING CENTRE Two small Supermarkets (*Tmr* 1B2 & 11A4) and two small Tourist shops (*Tmr* 2B2 & 9A4).

DISCOS Surprisingly, there is one – The Windmill Disco, to be found out of the village, beyond the ruin of the windmill.

MEDICAL CARE There are no chemists but there is a Doctor (*Tmr* 13A5), whose house is to be found just past the square. Emergencies are airlifted by helicopter to Santorini.

OTE None.

PLACES OF INTEREST None.

POLICE There is a policeman whose house (*Tmr* 10B4) lies down the path, opposite the *Cafe Cypros*.

POST OFFICE (*Tmr*12A4) A very small unit, close to the square.

TOILETS The various cafes and tavernas all have one, even if they are rather primitive.

Excursion To The Monasteries There are two monasteries. About 5km along the path is a branch to the left which leads to the old 'Kastelli' or original settlement (ancient Anaphe), but this has been deserted for the last 800 years. At some 7km, in the Kalamos Isthmus, is the **Monastery Zoodochos Pighi**, built in the 1830s. Most of the structure was destroyed in the 1956 earthquake, killing a lot of the monks. There is also a Temple of Apollo close by, the ruins of which are still visible. Still further, on the Kalamos peninsula, is the older **Monastery Panaghia Kalamiotissa**, built around 1710 and repository for the miracle working icon of the island saint.

The path is a total of about 10km. Being a dry island, walkers must take drinking water despite which the monasteries are worth seeing and the scenery is fabulous.

Episkopi Church, Sikinos. *Acknowledgement to David & Liz Drummond-Tyler.*

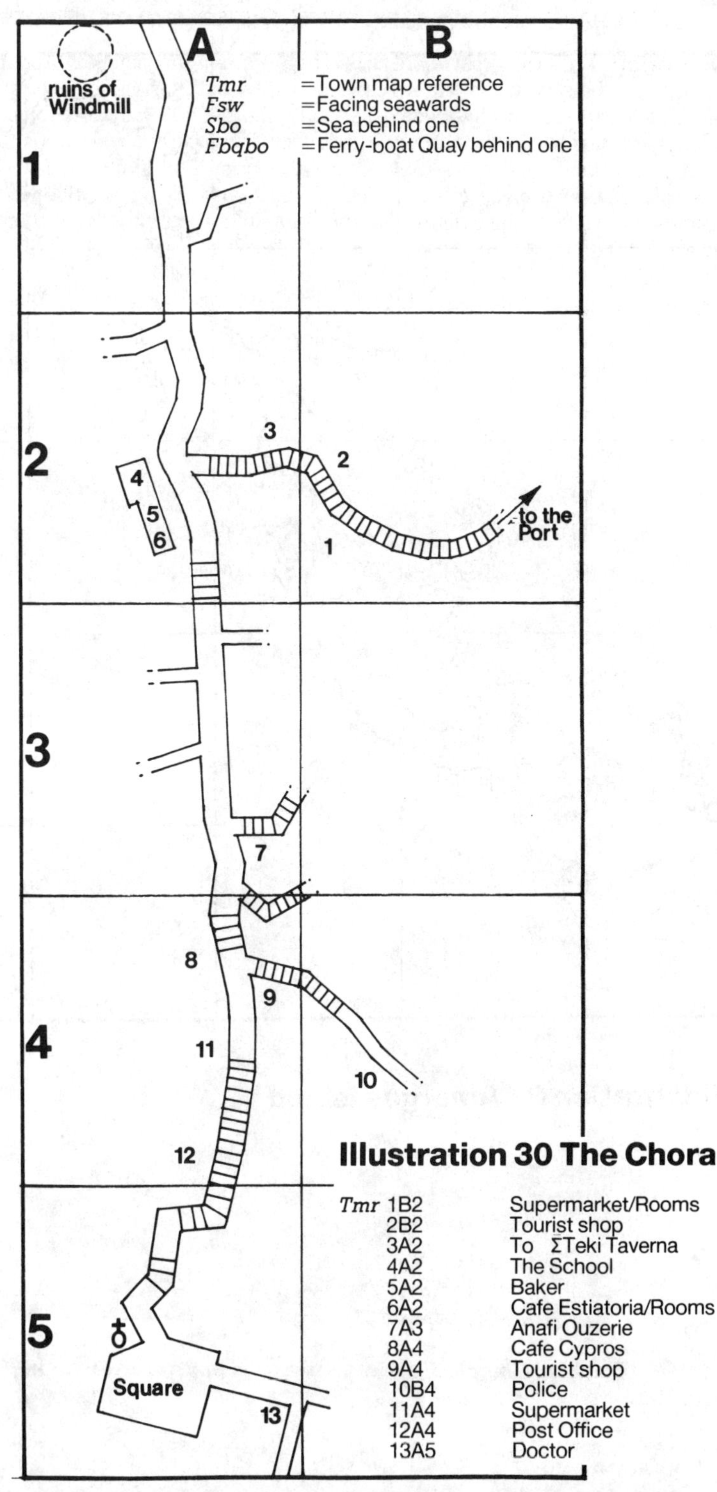

Illustration 30 The Chora

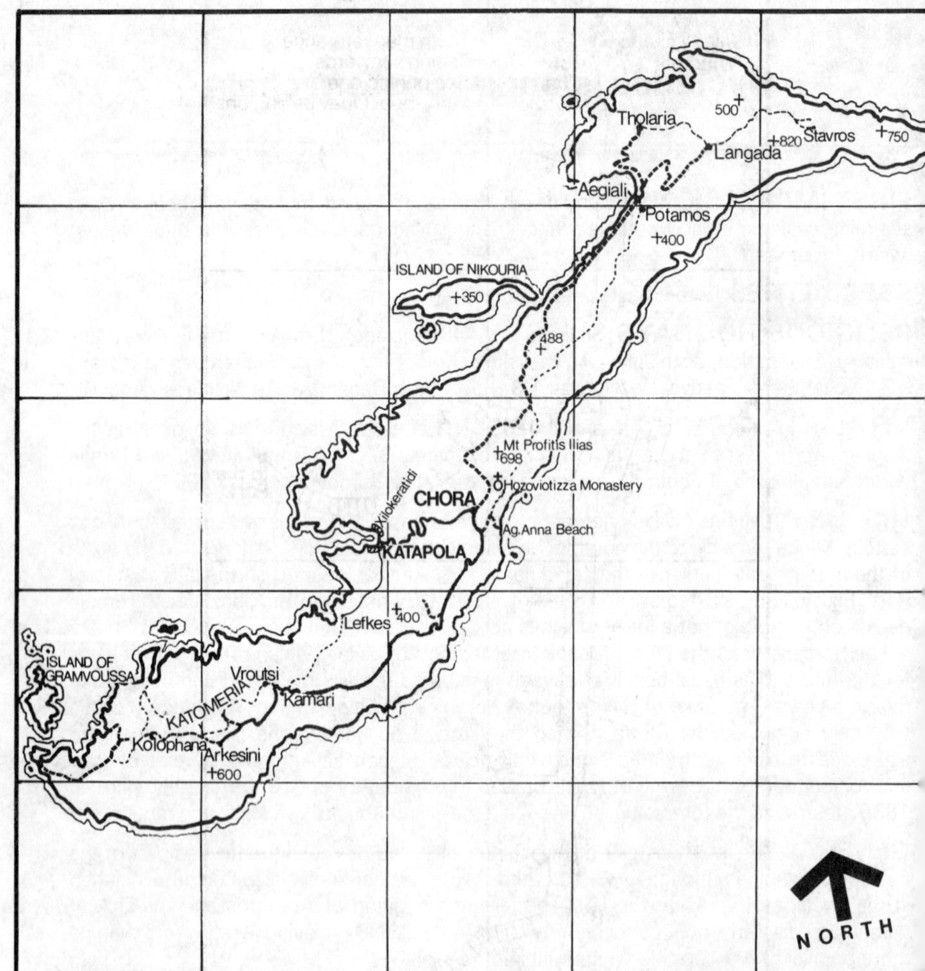

Illustration 31 Amorgos island

12 AMORGOS ****
Cyclades Islands - Eastern chain

FIRST IMPRESSIONS Splendid sea cliff vistas; parched, mountainous countryside; sea-mine casings; older women's white, triangular headscarves; flies that bite; wasps; 'weirdo' tourists.

SPECIALITIES Herbs; pastelli (sweetbread).

RELIGIOUS HOLIDAYS & FESTIVALS include: 15th August – Festival Panaghia Ag Epanochori; 26th July – Ag Paraskevi, Kolophana; 14th September, Stavros; 21st November – Festival Hozviotizza Monastery; 8th December Ag Nikolaos, Aegiali.

VITAL STATISTICS Tel prefix 0285. The elongated island lies obliquely in the Aegean, north-east to south-west. It is approximately 32km in length and up to 11km in width with an area of about 130sq km. The population numbers some 1,800.

HISTORY It seems unlikely now, but in days of antiquity the island sported three city states, 'Minoa' on a hill to the south of and close by Katapola Port; 'Arkesini' to the north of the modern-day hamlet of the same name and 'Aegiali' situated on the site of Aegiali Port. Excavations at Aegiali, in 1888, revealed a Gymnasium, Stadium and a Temple dedicated to Apollo, not a lot of which is now discernible.

The Romans used the island for the incarceration of exiles, which rather set the tone for the future. The usual bunch of savage marauders mauled the island and inhabitants over the years. The Duke of Naxos took Amorgos under his wing, in 1209, and a castle was built alongside the Chora. During the Turkish occupation the island women are supposed to have contributed significantly to the wealth of Amorgos by dint of their embroidery output, the fame of which spread throughout Europe. Unfortunately a fire, in 1835, destroyed the forests which once clad the island, thus the arid hills and mountains.

GENERAL The most easterly of the islands accepted by the authorities as part of the Cyclades grouping although it will be noted that I consider Astipalaia should be included in the Cyclades (*See* **Chapter 14**). The far-flung position of Amorgos and the lack of numerous daily ferry-boat connections results in the island receiving less visitors than its more popular and accessible western neighbours.

For some years, up to 1986, the Government made efforts to encourage tourists to visit the smaller islands of the Eastern Cyclades, including Amorgos, offering a certain amount of free ferry travel out of the high season. This policy seems to have succeeded to a degree, since this facility has now, in the main, been discontinued and the islanders are far more alive to tourism. However, in spite of the increased number of visitors and tourist facilities, relatively speaking, the Amorgots seem reluctant to go the whole hog in joining in the Western European holiday 'dream machine'. This is best exemplified by their reluctance to advertise accommodation at all, let alone the usual rash of billboards and scrawlings. Additionally, prospective landlords can be very selective. The eating and sleeping facilities available tend to cater for the 'wanting to get to know the island and islanders' type of tourist, rather than the 'sun, sea, sand and sex' brigade – modest yet comfortable accommodation, pleasant but simple tavernas, and a prevailing atmosphere of peace and quiet.

The island is rugged and the barrier of its mountainous spine creates the feeling that the two ends of Amorgos have evolved as distinct islands. Access is through the southern, main port of Katapola and the northern port of Aegiali. Caiques and ferries are still the easiest means of travel between the two. Until recently the only overland route was a mule path from the Chora across the mountain range to Potamos, and thence to Aegiali – a journey of some 4 to 5 hours. A rough road, wrested from the unyielding terrain, now runs between the two, following the rocky coastline in its latter stages. This was substantially completed at least five years ago, but has never quite been finished thus neither buses nor taxis venture forth. The sole regular journey is made by a four wheel drive jeep to take the school children from Aegiali to Chora on a Monday morning and bring them back on a Friday afternoon. Additionally, in the high season months, a vehicle ventures forth twice daily. Despite this road connection, most islanders still prefer the ferry. In the north, unsurfaced roads now link the villages of Tholaria and Langada to Aegiali, and they enjoy a regular bus service as does Katapola to the Chora.

As Katapola Port is reserved and quiet (to the point that the arrival of a bus is an event), so Aegiali Port is rather more thrusting. The latter not only boasts beaches (which Katapola does not), but more 'forthcoming' accommodation. Both ports offer, either side of the busiest summer months, that peace, calm and tranquillity that must have been the mark of most Greek islands before the tourist boom really took off.

KATAPOLA: main port (Illustration 32) I have read the occasional guide book that refers to the towering cliffs edging the Bay of Katapola – well there must have been some rapid erosion because this port lies in an indented, 'U' shaped bay edged by comparatively soft, gentle, rolling hillsides. The location is evocative of Vathi Ithaca.

Really the settlement is two, no three village/hamlets with Katapola the ferry-boat port to the right of the bay (*Sbo*); Rachidi, the rather drab, central settlement, set back from the bottom of the bay and dominated by a twin tower church, and Xilokeratidi, a small fishing boat hamlet to the left of the bay, with some lovely, aged, flower bestrewn buildings and remnants of an Old Quarter.

It is difficult to describe, and as difficult to understand, why Katapola 'feels low', as if a visitor is stepping down or docking at a development where height has been diminished. I think the effect comes about at those ports where the houses do not climb the hillside and or are not hemmed in by mountains. Over to you reader.

An unusual architectural feature is the large number of doors sporting Roman style door lintels or, more correctly, pediments.

ARRIVAL BY FERRY Ferry-boats dock at the quay (*Tmr* 1A/B3), a pace or two prior to the Main Square (*Tmr* 2B3/4). With the increase in tourism, ferries are tending to arrive at a more reasonable hour (early evening), rather than the nocturnal visits of previous years. As a result accommodation is more widely advertised by room owners, even if there is still some 'reluctance' on their part. When a particular boat's arrival is very late at night, the convenient park benches, close by the tree dominating the Main Square, will prove a convenient place to rest one's head. Late night arrivals should ensure they don't fall into the large goldfish pond between the tree and the periptero.

The residents tend to rise at the crack of dawn and go to bed early, most tavernas are shut by 2300hrs and siesta is observed, between 1300-1700hrs.

The local fishermen still communicate across the wide bay with blasts on a conch shell, which can sound rather like a ferry-boat's hooter.

THE ACCOMMODATION & EATING OUT

The Accommodation Despite the escalating increase in tourists, the phenomenon of unadvertised, unproclaimed rooms is still, oddly, prevalent. In addition, compared to, say, Astipalaia, accommodation is overpriced. All or any rooms cost 1900/2200drs, sharing a bathroom, regardless of size, shape or position! On the other hand, even in the height of season months, it is not difficult to locate a bed.

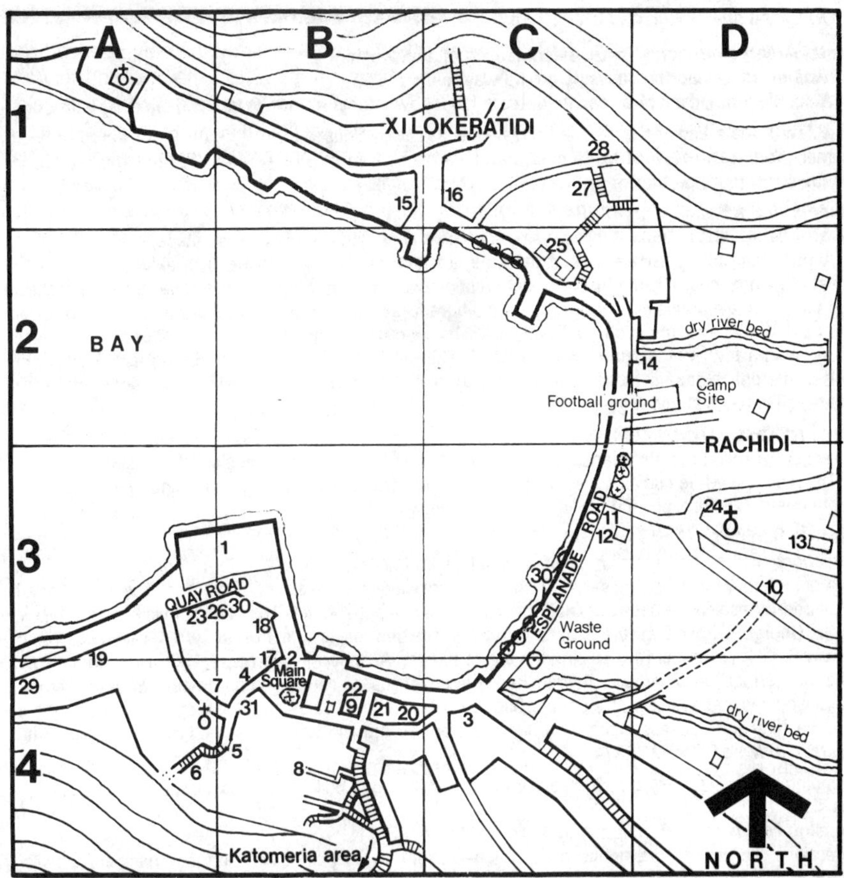

Illustration 32 Katapola

Tmr 1A/B3	Ferry-boat Quay	19A3/4	Cafe-Pub Diogenis
2B3/4	Main Square	20B/C4	Ferry-boat Ticket office
3C4	Hotel Amorgos Beach	21B4	General store
4A/B3/4	Port police	22B4	Baker
5A/B4	Rooms Voula Beach	23A/B3	Dairy & Grocers shop
6A/B4	Pension Tassia	24D3	General store
7A/B3/4	George Simidalas	25C1/2	Grocers's shop
8B4	Pension Minos	26A/B3	General store/OTE
9B4	Pension Amorgos	27C1	Rooms
10D3	Dimitries Rooms	28C1	Rooms
11C/D3	Public Gardens	29A3/4	Restaurant Minos
12C/D3	Town Hall/Rooms/Doctor	30	Moped hire
13D3	Rooms	31A/B4	Pharmacy
14C/D2	Rooms		
15B/C1/2	Pension/Taverna Ο ΓΑΒΑΛΟΣ	*Tmr*	=Town map reference
16B/C1/2	Taverna/Cafe-bar ΒΙΤΖΕΝΣΟΖ	*Fsw*	=Facing seawards
17B3/4	Taverna To Akroyiali	*Sbo*	=Sea behind one
18B3	Taverna To Mouragio	*Fbqbo*	=Ferry-boat Quay behind one

Hotel Amorgos Beach (*Tmr* 3C4) (something of a misnomer).
Directions: Bordering the quayside on the way round the bay.
A double room, if anybody can be bothered to 'show', costs from 3000drs with en suite bathroom.

The few streets and the quay road radiate off the Main Square (*Tmr* 2B3/4). From the right-hand corner (*Sbo*) a narrow lane leads past the office of the Port police (*Tmr* 4A/B3/4). Where the lane bends sharp right, on the left is:-

Rooms Voula Beach (*Tmr* 5A/B4)
Directions: As above, next door to a large butchers shop and up a few broad steps.
A very neat set-up with a row of cabins in addition to the main house. The elderly owner, who meets the ferry-boats, has a 'habit' of underestimating the number of rooms still vacant. If the cabins are full, the main house is proffered, a very different proposition. Instead of a pleasant outlook over the garden, these rooms might well have a small window looking out on to the back of an abandoned fridge with a few weeds and flowers beyond. The only 'plus' is a private bathroom and kitchen, of sorts. The official rate is 1800drs, but haggling might reduce this to 1500drs – still too much for an unattractive room in mid-May.

Pension Tassia (*Tmr* 6A/B4)
Directions: Proceed up the steps, jink right, then left and on the left, up against the hillside.
The blue and white cubicles are set round two and a half sides of an attractive courtyard. A double room costs 2200drs, sharing a bathroom – one between two...

George Simidalas (*Tmr* 7A/B3/4) Tel 71291
Directions: Follow the lane round a short distance and on the right, opposite a church.
A quiet family man, George served in the Merchant Navy and speaks some English. The large ground floor bedrooms share a bathroom and the rates include a hot shower. The bathroom is kept spotlessly clean. George, whose pleasure is to fish from his little benzina, is selective and will not take the 'great unwashed'. It is rumoured that blondes are preferred! A double room costs 1900drs, mid-season. The roof terrace has a bamboo shaded area where mattresses can be laid out to cope with the height-of-season influx at a cost of 300drs per bed, probably the best value on the island. Additionally, there is a washing line , access being by a flight of steps to one side of the house. George also runs the *Restaurant Minos* (*Tmr* 29A3/4).

Standing on the Main Square (*Sbo*), across a 'look-alike' for a builders yard is a large house displaying the sign:-

Pension Minos (aka. Pension Ann N Koveou) (*Tmr* 8B4) No 75
Directions: To get to the establishment it is necessary to walk along the lane, one back and parallel to the quay road, take the first alley to the right, which breaks into steps, and then the first right again. The wrought iron gate to No 75 is let into a stone arch and gives access to a lovely garden.
The pleasant, helpful landlady speaks no English. A double room with a balcony and access to a kitchen, with fridge and gas rings, costs 1500-2000drs (mid-season), depending on the length of stay. The bathrooms are shared, the water is hot all the time and both bedrooms and bathrooms are kept immaculately clean. Table and chairs are set out outside in the lovely garden.

Pension Amorgos (*Tmr* 9B4) Tel 71214
Directions: Left (*Sbo*) along the quay road from the Main Square and on the right, behind the baker.
Comfortable, modern rooms with towels and soap provided in a comparatively noisy location. The rooms at the front have balconies overlooking the 'Marina' part of the harbour but no chairs to sit on! Rates for first floor double rooms, with en suite bathroom, are 2000drs and 1500drs for a second floor double room with a washbasin but sharing a bathroom.

Around the bottom of the bay, across a little bridge and on the right is a large area of waste ground. A rough track winds away to the right to Rachidi, (the 'middle' village), cutting off the corner and ending up opposite:-

Dimitries Rooms (*Tmr* 10D3)
Directions: As above or turn right from the Esplanade, alongside the Public Gardens (*Tmr* 11C/D3), and keep to the right along the track. For 'info' make enquiries at the Town Hall (*Tmr* 12C/D3).
A young Scottish couple originally recommended these 'digs' in which use of a kitchen is included. A double room, sharing the bathroom, costs 2000drs, mid-season. This accommodation is owned by a 'pair' of brothers, one of whom, Yannis, runs a boat to the many coves of Katapola Bay.

The bottom of the bay Esplanade skirts a tree-lined, narrow, grey, scrubbly beach on the left and waste ground to the right. On the right, alongside the Public Gardens is:-

Rooms (*Tmr* 12CD3)
Directions: As above, over the Electric Company office and the Town Hall. The front garden, which is full of bamboos, has two busts and there is a flagpole on the roof.

A large first floor balcony but rather basic accommodation.

From alongside the Town Hall, a road advances to the heart of the 'middle' village, dominated by a large church. The road 'trifurcates' (if there is no such word to describe dividing into three, there should be). The right-hand track leads off to the already described ***Rooms*** (*Tmr* 10D3) whilst straight on, ascending a comparatively broad street, rises past:-

Rooms (*Tmr* 13D3)
Directions: The house is positioned on the left, behind a black wall and well maintained garden. A quiet, pleasant and secluded location.

Rates are 2000drs for a double room with hot water and a nice view.

Prior to the Esplanade turning the far corner of the bay, beyond the campsite track, the beach is (still) narrow, grey, scrubbly and pebbly, but enlivened by a resident family of ducks. To the right is a stone littered football ground and a tree or two to the side of the Kentia Bar. Behind and overshadowing the latter is the skeleton of a large building, possibly an embryonic, L-shaped hotel with a 'grand entrance' at the side. Further on is:-

Rooms (*Tmr* 14C/D2)
Directions: As above.

A very pleasant choice with rooms as well as cabins 'out the back'. A double room with en suite bathroom costs 2000drs a night.

The bay and quay road turns abruptly left. Beyond the narrow, stony, scrubbly foreshore, on which a number of local boats are beached, there is an irregular square, on either side of which are the:-
Pension Taverna Ο ΓΑΒΑΛΟΣ (*Tmr* 15B/C1/2) & the **Taverna/Snackbar** ΒΙΤΖΕΝΣΟΖ (*Tmr* 16B/C1/2).
Directions: As above.

There are also rooms belonging to this set-up,away up the hillside. A double with its own cavernous toilet, but shared shower, costs 2000drs. Not recommended. Poorly furnished with handles falling off doors, nails for hooks, an ill-fitting toilet door grating on the floor with resultant horrific noises and above all, grubby – no dirty.

The rooms in the taverna have use of a fridge and kitchen but are even worse. The shared bathrooms are very dirty. Those at the front are large, with access to an enormous terrace balcony overlooking the harbour.

Higher up the hill are (at least) two houses with ***Rooms*** (*Tmr* 27C1 & 28C1). The first mentioned (*Tmr* 27C1) is owned by an old lady who demands 2000drs for a narrow double bed in a room accessed through her living room, sharing a bathroom reached through the living room and kitchen. The other house (*Tmr* 28C1) is nice, clean with 24hr hot water and one bathroom for two adjacent rooms, costing 2000drs... But it is necessary to pass or be passed through by the other occupants!

Camping

Camp Site
Directions: From the Esplanade, proceed along the bottom of the bay towards the far village of Xilokeratidi. On the right is a private road which crosses tree-edged farmland to the D category, shadeless, stony site.

Very basic facilities, but there is a shower/toilet block as well as a tiny taverna, where a spaghetti costs 200drs and a salad 180drs. Costs per person are 200drs, with children under 10 free and a tent is charged at 100drs.

The Eating Out With flotilla sailing becoming even more popular, the number of yachts ever present is beginning to upset the balance, as elsewhere in the Aegean. There is a definite move towards up-market eating houses and cocktail bars. Despite this, two of the original tavernas are still 'on the go'. Possibly the most convenient is:-

To Akroyiali (*Tmr* 17B3/4)
Directions: On the edge of the Main Square.

In the main the wife runs the taverna. Her small, nervously busy, balding husband operates a small fishing boat. He and his crew are usually to be seen, early in the morning, wearing wet weather gear, on the quay edge opposite the taverna, sorting out the fish from the nets. They are usually surrounded by a semi-circle of stray cats, crouched at a respectful distance, who dash in and out to grab the waste bits and bobs thrown in their direction. The taverna opens early, even for dawn ferry-boat arrivals. Much of the food served during the day is baked in large stainless steel lined units, half-boxed in beneath the verandah. Goodies include loukoumades and tasty cheese pies. A traditional breakfast for two of yoghurt, honey and coffee cost 250drs. The usual caveats apply to the precooked, tray dishes by mid-afternoon, early evening – they can become tired.

To Mouragio (*Tmr* 18B3)
Directions: West along the quay, opposite the Ferry-boat Quay (*Tmr* 1A/B3).

This old-fashioned, averagely priced taverna appears rather shabby and the patron is usually stern faced. I have seen him smile when lobster is on the menu. In the evening the establishment is very popular with the flotilla crews, especially when the aforementioned lobster is available – now you realise why the proprietor smiles. There is a television inside. A number of cats ensure that no food is wasted. Examples of prices include 900drs for one portion of moussaka, one of oven baked fish, a plate of peas and carrots, half litre retsina and bread, and 880drs for one portion of squid, one of chicken & chips, a plate of stewed aubergines and tomatoes, retsina and bread. In general there are not many of the 'cheaper' dishes available but a meal for two of delicious briam, a Greek salad bread and 2 beers only cost 850drs.

With the advent of the OTE, his once exclusive metered phone is not so much in demand.

Cafe Pub Diogenis (*Tmr* 19A3/4)
Directions: Towards the far, sea-end of the quay road, beyond and almost 'chair by table' with the *Minoa Restaurant*.

Despite management changes, the 'offerings' continue to be of a high culinary standard. A meal for two of 2 stuffed tomatoes, a Greek salad, tzatziki, a bottle of retsina, bread, a Coke, 2 ice-creams and 2 coffees cost 1500drs.

Two more establishments 'at this end' include an expensive looking restaurant where the waitresses were non-Greek, the bottles of wine of the more expensive type and the clientele well-heeled. The board outside proclaims the specialities of the day which might include fried shrimps. To sample the 'delights' one feels obliged to 'dress'. The second is the *Cafe-bar Apenanti*, more in the style of a cocktail or wine bar offering crepes, salads, yoghurt, fruit salad, ice cream, milk shakes, refreshments, long drinks and cocktails.

Kafeneion To Kamari
Directions: Next door to the Baker (*Tmr* 22B4)

Possessed of a split personality. During the day more a cafe, starting with breakfast which includes eggs and bacon, and continuing throughout the day with take-aways of cheese pies (80drs), bougatses (80drs), sausage rolls (90drs) and pizzas (100drs). In the evening it 'wears' a taverna face, when the fare is predominantly grills. Sample prices are chicken (250drs), veal (610drs), beefburgers (160drs) and fish kebabs are also served. Cakes and coffee are available throughout the day until it closes, usually at about midnight. The landlord is not averse to a weeny bit of overcharging or 'rounding up' and stays open for late night ferry arrivals.

On the other side of the bay, in Xilokeratidi, there are a couple of cafes as well as the *Taverna/Cafe-bar* ΒΙΤΖΕΝΣΟΖ (open for breakfast onwards) and the:

Taverna O ΓΑΒΑΛΟΣ (*Tmr* 15B/C1/2)
Directions: As above.

This last establishment can be a fun place to eat, being a small, family run concern. Total chaos ensues when more than a dozen diners sit down at the same time. As fish is always on the menu at least twenty cats watch every mouthful. A meal of fish (300drs), meatballs & chips (250drs), salad (200drs), bread (40drs for two) and two half-litres of retsina (from the barrel - 80drs each) cost 950drs. It is as likely that the first retsina will be consumed before any food arrives.

Before closing off this section, to the front and one side of the Ferry-boat Ticket office (*Tmr* 20B/C4), is a bar well worth patronising, being a traditional, turn-of-the-century Greek 'watering-hole'.

THE A TO Z OF USEFUL INFORMATION

BANKS Yes, well there's the rub. The island is rather short of banks, in fact there are none which transact foreign exchange. Change facilities are operated by the rude, surly man in a General store (*Tmr* 21B4), opposite the charter yacht portion of the quay, who I wouldn't use on principle, and the polite gentleman (gentleman in the old sense of the word) who operates the ferry-boat ticket hatch and now changes both foreign notes & travellers cheques. The Chora Post Office 'banks' travellers and Eurocheques.

BEACHES The bottom of the bay between the Katapola side and Xilokeratidi has two narrow strips of dirty grey, coarse sand and pebble beach but...

On the Katapola side, it is possible to walk to the open sea end of the quay road, beyond the *Cafe Pub Diogenes*, and take the track behind the last of the houses. This advances to a very narrow, scrubbly sliver of beach in front of a walled garden. Unfortunately the sea bottom pebbles are slimy and weedy, there are sea-urchins and some tar. Further along this track is a statue facing the bay, followed by a large chapel, with a tripod-hung bell, after which there are two, very tiny, thumb-nail sized beaches.

On the Xilokeratidi side, a track progresses uphill past the cemetery, a small statue set on a flat rock in the sea and on to a low headland which juts into the sea and is surmounted by a chapel with a few small coves on the near side. A steep path descends from the cemetery in the direction of two narrow, rocky and secluded coves. The access to the chapel headland and the beach beyond (which is better than the beaches on the near side) is now by way of a flight of concrete steps (dated 11.10.87). The beach looks inviting from above and several difficult 'goat tracks' can be followed. The beach is shingly sand with a scrubbly, scruffy backshore, and no shade, other than up against the cliffs, at the far end. Getting into the water is not as easy as it might be, with rough weed covering the stony bottom, but swimming in the sheltered bay is excellent. Is this a recommendation or not?

From the harbour it is possible to take a boat to one of the many little coves in the bay. On arrival, depending on which one is selected, it is possible to sunbathe with or without clothes. But girls – a warning! It is rumoured that one of the boatman (Yannis) is prone to wandering hands. This apart, he is a very nice chap, full of local knowledge who, with his brother, owns *Dimitries Rooms*.

BICYCLE, SCOOTER & CAR HIRE A seemingly pointless activity, bearing in mind the general lack of roads and the bus service. Despite this there are two moped firms (*Tmr* 30A/B3 & 30C3).

BREAD SHOPS The Baker (*Tmr* 22B4) is to the left (*Sbo*) along the quay from the Main Square, past (*To Kamari Taverna* and on the far side of the narrow square in which is mounted a very large, incongruous 'tower of a water fountain'.

BUSES The old Dodge bus has gone to the 'great depot in the sky' and has been replaced by three modern vehicles. With this tripling of the fleet, routes now include the Chora, Ag Anna Beach & the Monastery, as well as a daily foray into the south-western hamlets, collectively known as Katomeria. The Ag Anna Beach road is an unpaved track which winds breathtakingly down the mountainside with amazing views of the cliffs and sea. The bus stops at the second large bend to let people off for the Monastery, prior to snaking down to a rough turning point close to the shore. The third, 'Katomeria' bus, on its return, joins in the Chora, Monastery and Ag Anna Beach merry-go-round, adding yet another twist to the timetable mysteries.

Bus timetable

Katapola to The Chora (& on to the Monastery & Ag Anna Beach)
Daily: 0800-2300hrs, every hour on the hour.
Return journey
Daily: 0800-2300hrs, every hour on the hour.

Ag Anna Beach to The Chora (& on to Katapola)
Daily: 0800-2300hrs, twenty minutes to the hour.

Monastery to The Chora
Daily: 0800-2300hrs, ten minutes to the hour.

Katapola to the Katomeria area
Daily: 1030hrs.
Return journey
Daily: 1600hrs.

One-way fares:	Katapola	to the Chora	60 drs.
		to the Beach	100drs.
		to Katomeria	250drs.
	Chora	to the Beach	60drs.

Fares are 'variable'. It is possible to sneak a grand round trip from Katapola to the Chora, Monastery, Ag Anna Beach and back to the Chora for 100drs!

COMMERCIAL SHOPPING AREA In the narrow alley off the Main Square, alongside *To Akroyiali Taverna* (*Tmr* 17B3/4), is a Mini-Market, on the right, and further along, on the opposite side, a large Butchers shop. On my last visit, I observed the latter unload a delivery of frozen boxes of chicken and meat labelled Hungary, (the country, not a state of physical deprivation). There is a Dairy & Grocer's shop (*Tmr* 23A/B3) opposite the Ferry-boat Quay and a periptero on the Main Square. As already indicated the owner of the General store (*Tmr* 21B4) is surly and uncouth.

The 'middle' village also has a General store (*Tmr* 24D3) and there is a little Grocer's shop, (*Tmr* 25C1/2) (entrance to the rear of the building) in Xilokeratidi.

FERRY-BOATS If only for the cheap copy they provided, it is a shame that the decrepit, staggering, characterful rust buckets, the Miaoulis and the local Marianna, have finally been dispatched to the great harbour in the depths. The Marianna, ("last winter, big wind blow – Marianna fall over") has been replaced by the **Skopelitis**. This is captained by the son of the greengrocers next door to *To Mouragio* and is owned by a Mr Skopelitis of Donoussa island. The latter gentleman used to run a small fishing caique, of the same name, in the waters around Donoussa. The Skopelitis is about the same size as the Marianna, capable of transporting a couple of cars, several donkeys, a few mopeds and building materials. In the high season the Skopelitis calls at Aegiali (Amorgos) and Donoussa twice a week; Iraklia, Koufonissi and Shinoussa three to four times a week. It leaves Naxos at 1500hrs on Monday & Wednesday for all four islets as well as Amorgos.

Readers will be delighted to hear that our old friend the **Kyklades** was seen to drift into port again, in 1988, but the timetable, unsurprisingly, remains a total mystery to all and sundry.

Perhaps this would be the point at which to discuss the matter of port identification. A number of visitors, on their very first call to Amorgos, can disembark at the wrong port as night-time recognition is difficult. A general rule, when approaching from the west, is that northern Aegiali is the first port of call while from the east, it is Katapola. Secondary pointers are that Aegiali's quay is an enormous finger pier set in a huge bay, while at Katapola the quay is a small affair at the centre of the settlement, close to the Main Square in a much smaller sea inlet. One last word is to remind travellers proceeding north of Aegiali not to miss the wonderfully dramatic and mountainous coastline, to which the ferry-boats cling.

Ferry-boat timetable (Mid-season)

Day	**Departure time**	**Ferry-boat**	**Ports/Islands of Call**
Mon	0600hrs*	Skopelitis	Aegiali(Amorgos),Donoussa,Koufonissi, Shinoussa,Iraklia,Naxos.
	2000hrs**	Kyklades	Aegiali(Amorgos),Astipalaia,Rhodes.
Tues	0330hrs	Nireas	Aegiali(Amorgos),Astipalaia,Kalimnos,Kos, Nisiros,Tilos,Simi,Rhodes.
	0600hrs*	Skopelitis	Koufonissi,Shinoussa,Iraklia,Paros,Naxos, Mykonos.
	1800hrs	Naxos	Naxos,Paros,Piraeus(M).
Wed	0600hrs*	Skopelitis	Aegiali(Amorgos),Donoussa,Koufonissi, Shinoussa,Iraklia,Naxos.
Thurs	0330hrs	Olympia	Aegiali(Amorgos),Astipalaia,Kalimnos,Kos, Nisiros,Tilos,Simi,Rhodes.
	0530hrs	Schinoussa	Aegiali(Amorgos),Donoussa,Naxos,Paros, Syros,Piraeus(M).
	0530hrs	Skopelitis	Ios,Santorini.
	2000hrs	Nireas	Paros,Piraeus(M).
Fri	0400hrs	Delos	Naxos,Paros,Syros,Rafina(M-1430hrs).
Sat	0530hrs	Schinoussa	Aegiali(Amorgos),Donoussa,Naxos, Paros,Syros,Piraeus(M).
	0700hrs*	Skopelitis	Koufonissi,Iraklia,Paros,Naxos,Mykonos.
	1930hrs	Olympia	Paros,Syros,Piraeus(M).
Sun	0400hrs	Delos	Naxos,Paros,Syros,Rafina(M-1430hrs).
	0700hrs*	Skopelitis	Koufonissi,Iraklia,Paros,Mykonos.
	0800hrs	Nireas	Aegiali(Amorgos),Astipalaia.

1630hrs	Nireas	Donoussa,Koufonissi,Shinoussa, Iraklia,Naxos,Paros,Syros,Piraeus(M).

* Returns same day, in 'the reverse order'.
** Likely to be up to 4½hrs late at Amorgos.

Please note these tables are detailed as a GUIDE ONLY. Due to the time taken to research the Cyclades it is IMPOSSIBLE TO 'match' the timetables or even boats . So don't try cross pollinating...

FERRY-BOAT TICKET OFFICE (*Tmr* 20B/C4) The initially gruff gentleman who runs this pokey little hut is helpful and kindly. The office is positioned to one side of the covered verandah in front of a magnificently rustic cafe-bar. It opens every day, including Saturday & Sunday, but closes for the 1300-1700hr siesta.

HAIRDRESSER There is one in Xilokeratidi, near the quay. It opens Tues, Wed & Thurs (1100-1400hrs & 1700-2000hrs) and Fri (1500-2000hrs).

MEDICAL CARE
Chemists & Pharmacies (*Tmr* 31A/B4) Along the narrow side-street from the Main Sq, beyond the Port police.
Dentist In Rachidi, beyond ***Rooms*** (*Tmr* 13D3) and on the left.
Doctor (*Tmr* 12C/D3) In the Town Hall building.

OTE There are two metered phone booths in the General store (*Tmr* 26A/B3) or head for the Chora. Generally overseas services from Amorgos are appalling.

POLICE
Port (*Tmr* 4A/B3/4) In the narrow lane off the Main Square.
Town In the Chora.

POST OFFICE *See* **The Chora**, but there are two post boxes close to the Ferry-boat Quay.

TAXIS A taxi rolls up to and down from The Chora, but is very difficult to locate.

THE CHORA (Amorgos): capital (Illustration 33) The choice of whether to stay in Katapola or the Chora is very much a personal decision. Certainly the Chora is closer to the Greek ethos. ***Rooms*** in the village are simple and cost between 1000/1200drs & 1800drs for a double bed with the use of a shower.

I wouldn't advocate walking from the port up to the Chora but some might wish to walk back down. By the very rough, rubbly donkey path the descent takes about 45-50 minutes, whilst following the main road windings occupies about one and half hours.

At the outset to the Chora village is a small, irregular 'Bus' Square (*Tmr* 1), where the buses park. Alongside the bus stop is the conveniently located *Welcome Cafe*. A bottle of beer costs 85drs. On the left is the OTE with ***Rooms*** above. There is one overseas booth and the office opens Monday-Friday between 0800-1510hrs.

The 'High' St wanders through the main village. Spread along its length are are several ***Rooms***, a taverna or two, a couple of general shops, a grocers, a baker, an Agricultural Bank (*Tmr* 3) (which does not yet transact exchange) , on a stepped square, and further east the Post Office (*Tmr* 4). This latter office exchanges Eurocheques and travellers cheques, sells postcards, air letters and maps. There is a phone booth which can be used for international calls (with good luck!). Referring back to the Agricultural Bank, they are, in the busier holiday locations, dipping their toes into the foreign exchange merry-go-round. Maybe this branch will follow suit, sometime.

On the way along the High St, towards the Post Office, is the:-

Taverna ΡΩΔΗ (Pomegranate).
Directions: As above.

This establishment is run by a Frenchman and his Greek wife. They serve out-of-the-ordinary dishes, barrel retsina, freshly squeezed orange juice and sangria – which goes down rather well after a hot walk to and from the Monastery/beach. Not the most inexpensive offerings. Two large tumblerfuls of sangria, 2 large slices of 'fruits, nuts, honey and cognac pie with an excellent pastry top, ½litre of retsina and 2 excellent coffees cost 1000drs. The menu may well include gazpacho, chicken pie, vegetable pie and huge vegetable omelettes. There is seating for some eight inside and a similar number outside, at tiny tables in the shade of the wall.

The Chora also has a few discreet , pleasant and quiet bars (in sharp contrast to some of the indiscreet, unpleasant and noisy bars of Aegiali), the nicest of which is the ΛΟΖΑ *Taverna/Cafe*. This is signposted to the left off the Chora's 'High' Street, in a tranquil square. A snack lunch of 2 spaghettis in sauce and 2 Fantas cost 660drs.

Still proceeding eastwards (towards the rising sun in the early morning), the street crosses the rather strange area of 'The Wells', a grouping of water holes where 'Camping is Forbidden'. Between 'The Wells' and the telephone dish mast is a large kafeneion.

The village is dominated by the indistinct remains of the castle. This was built on top of a curious rock outcrop (similar to The Chora of Ios), and is overlooked by a hilltop row of windmills. These are in various states of decay and disfigured by a complex, 'Meccano-like' radio mast and reflector.

EXCURSIONS TO THE CHORA SURROUNDS

Excursion to Hozoviotizza Monastery This is about an hours walk east from the Chora, beyond the area of 'The Wells', and past the large square school building (*Tmr* 6) on the left. Turn right at the large, spacious junction, leaving the stone-wall-enclosed area to the left. Note that to keep straight on and bear round to the left proceeds on to the Aegiali track.

These days most visitors catch the bus but...

Almost immediately the landscape falls sharply away and walkers are clinging to a sheer amphitheatre of rocky mountainside, similar to being located on a saucer almost tilted in the upright position. Way down below is the sea with the mountains encircling the saucers edge. Follow the precipitously descending goat track as it zig-zags down the hillside until it crosses a dirt track road. Here, turn left along the track, and keep on round the cliff edge to the wrought iron gates let into a modern rock slab wall.

Hozoviotizza Monastery The nine hundred and one year old (900 years in 1988), white, cliff-hugging monastery stands out even more starkly (if that is possible), because it is hangs limpet-like to a drab brown, grey and orange mountain rock-face. A steep, stepped path climbs to the monastery.

There are a number of legends regarding the *raison d'etre* of the institution, most revolving around an icon miraculously found washed up on the shores of Amorgos. Quite honestly in the Medieval Ages the Mediterranean must have almost been awash with unmanned rowing boats ferrying icons hither and thither. Be that as it may, various Government inspired 'compulsory grabs' have robbed this once very wealthy religious order of its widespread properties, gifted over the centuries, to naught but a few acres. The monasteries' own pamphlet sets the scene, well illustrating the raw anger of the few remaining monks, focusing on the State acquisitions of their property in 1952. Obviously the brothers were pretty 'cheesed off' with this latter day Dissolution of the Monasteries. I wonder if there was anything left for the further Government takeovers in 1988?

Visitors MUST ensure they are dressed properly, that is to the standard demanded here and elsewhere in religious houses throughout Greece. There is no dodging the issue at this monastery, a fact reinforced by a notice on the gateway prior to the long climb up to the building. Visitors arriving in shorts and or without a respectable shirt/blouse will be turned away. Recently a motley, somewhat unsavoury selection of shirts, skirts and long trousers have been hung up by the door, but don't rely on it.

After a short guided tour, in Greek, one of the three monks will refresh visitors with a cup of Greek coffee, a glass of water and a Turkish delight. This is served in a little upper anteroom. Incidentally, beneath a cloth and rather out of place in this medieval atmosphere,

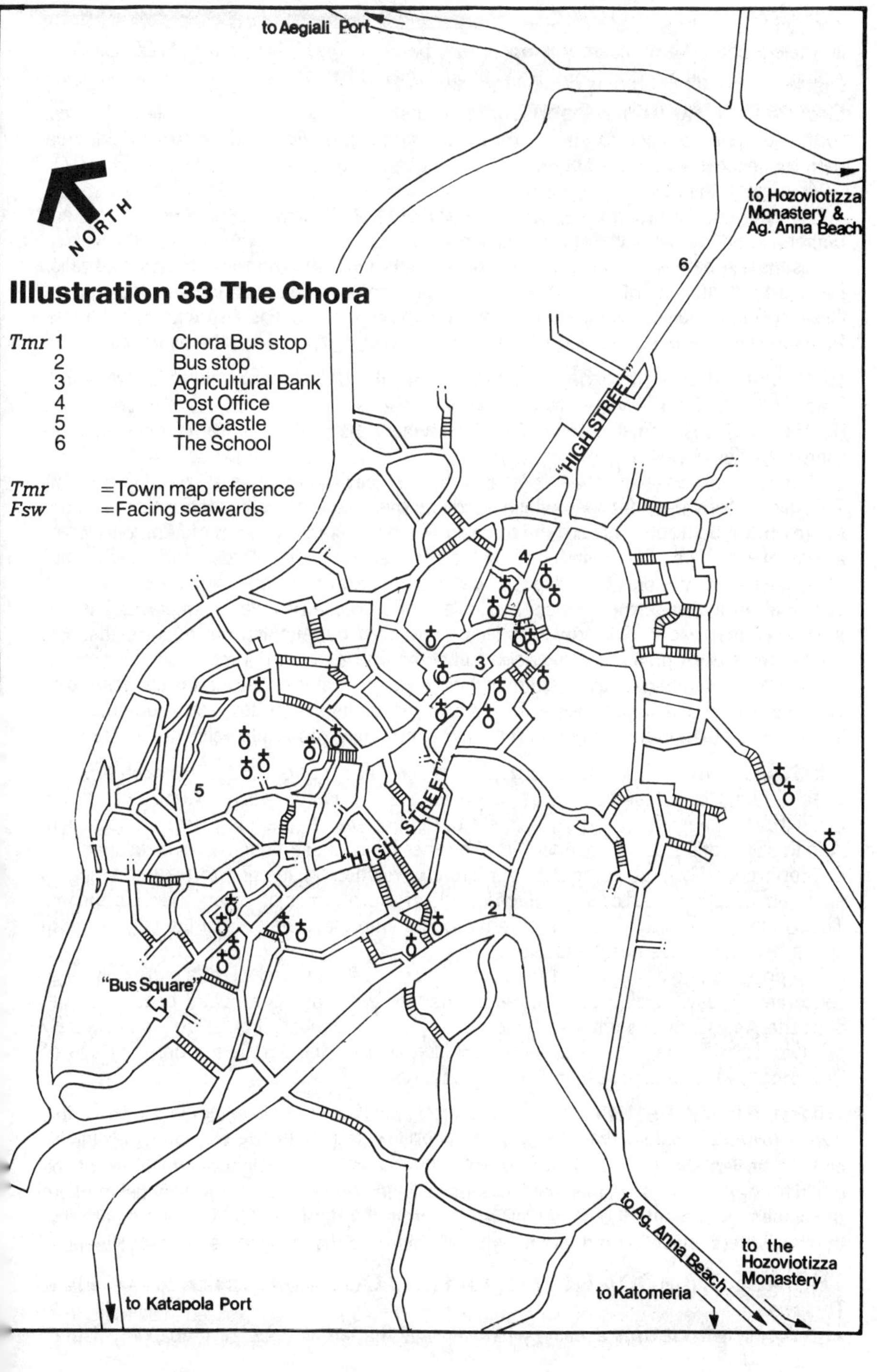
to Aegiali Port
NORTH
to Hozoviotizza Monastery & Ag. Anna Beach
6
Illustration 33 The Chora
Tmr 1 Chora Bus stop
2 Bus stop
3 Agricultural Bank
4 Post Office
5 The Castle
6 The School
Tmr =Town map reference
Fsw =Facing seawards
"HIGH STREET"
4
3
5
"HIGH STREET"
2
"Bus Square"
1
to Ag. Anna Beach
to the Hozoviotizza Monastery
to Katomeria
to Katapola Port

is a telephone. The monastery is open daily between 0800-1400hrs & 1700-2000hrs. Admission is free but donations are welcome, nay obligatory.

Excursion to Ag Anna Beach From the outskirts of the Chora either follow the track to the right (as opposed to the left for the Monastery), or zig-zag down the hillside goat path for another 40 minutes or so.

Most catch the bus.

From the bus turn-round, a broad, new staircase leads down to Ag Anna Chapel and bathers lie on the flat slabs of rock hereabouts.

A separate path from the bus turn-round leads through (worrying) mounds of fallen rock, around difficult little outcrops to the clean, grey pebble beach where access to the clear, brilliantly blue waters is easier than from the rocks. There is a spring of fresh water (now on tap) which is very useful for the campers who stay here in the peak season.

Excursion to the Katomeria Region From the Chora there is a wide, well-made road, allowing fine sea views to both sides of the island which include Katapola in the distance. There is a small restaurant/taverna where the mule track from Lefkes joins the road, near Kamari.

From Katapola a stepped lane ascends from the quay by the General store (*Tmr* 21B4). This joins a fairly new dirt road which winds up over the inland shoulder of the hill above the town. On the top of this are the remains of the ancient settlement of Minoa, to which a footpath detours. The unsurfaced motor road, scarring the hillside from which it has been blasted, serves only the villages of **Lefkes** and **Sarani**. Despite the latters' prominent portrayal on the map, they consist, in reality, of a couple of dwellings apiece. The last section of the road is overgrown as it is rarely used by anything but quadrupeds. The original mule track then takes over again until the Chora route.

The track switchbacks quite spectacularly down to a dry river-bed, up the other side and over the hills towards the villages of **Kamari** and **Vroutsi**. Beyond Vroutsi lies the large village of **Arkesini**, situated on a surprisingly level and fertile agricultural plateau.

AEGIALI (Aigiali, Agiali, Egiali): port (Illustration 34) This northern port is as different from Katapola as say an olive and a glass of retsina. Aegiali has a few distinct advantages over Katapola, the most important of which is the splendid beach. Additionally eating out is cheaper. On the other hand, these benefits have resulted in a disproportionately large number of the 'great unwashed' in addition to the wide ranging spectrum of cultures and classes which include a fair proportion of 'hippy-style' Europeans. The 'Undesirables' have, it is rumoured, brought with them the evils of fighting and drug abuse, which amuses not the locals.

The port is located on the right-hand (*Sbo*) corner of the broad 'U' of a extremely large and dramatic bay. Edging the bottom of the bay is a long, tree edged beach. Almost opposite Aegiali, on the left-hand side of the gulf is a number of small coves backed by precipitous cliffs. High in the mountains which encircle the port is the upper village of **Potamos**, as well as the settlements of **Langada** and **Tholaria**.

ARRIVAL BY FERRY The Ferry-boat Quay (*Tmr* 5) is massive for a port of this size. It marks the right-hand boundary of the village which spreads and climbs up the hill and to the left (*Sbo*), around the waterfront. At the bottom, right-hand corner of the boulder edged quay is a small, phallic shaped 'I-know-not-what'. The local fishing fleet of caiques moor inside the quay wall which forms the Harbour. The ferry-boats are met by the owners of accommodation, who are more forthcoming here than at Katapola.

THE ACCOMMODATION & EATING OUT *See* **Excursion to Langada & Tholaria.**

The Accommodation Usually, whatever time the ferries dock, disembarking visitors

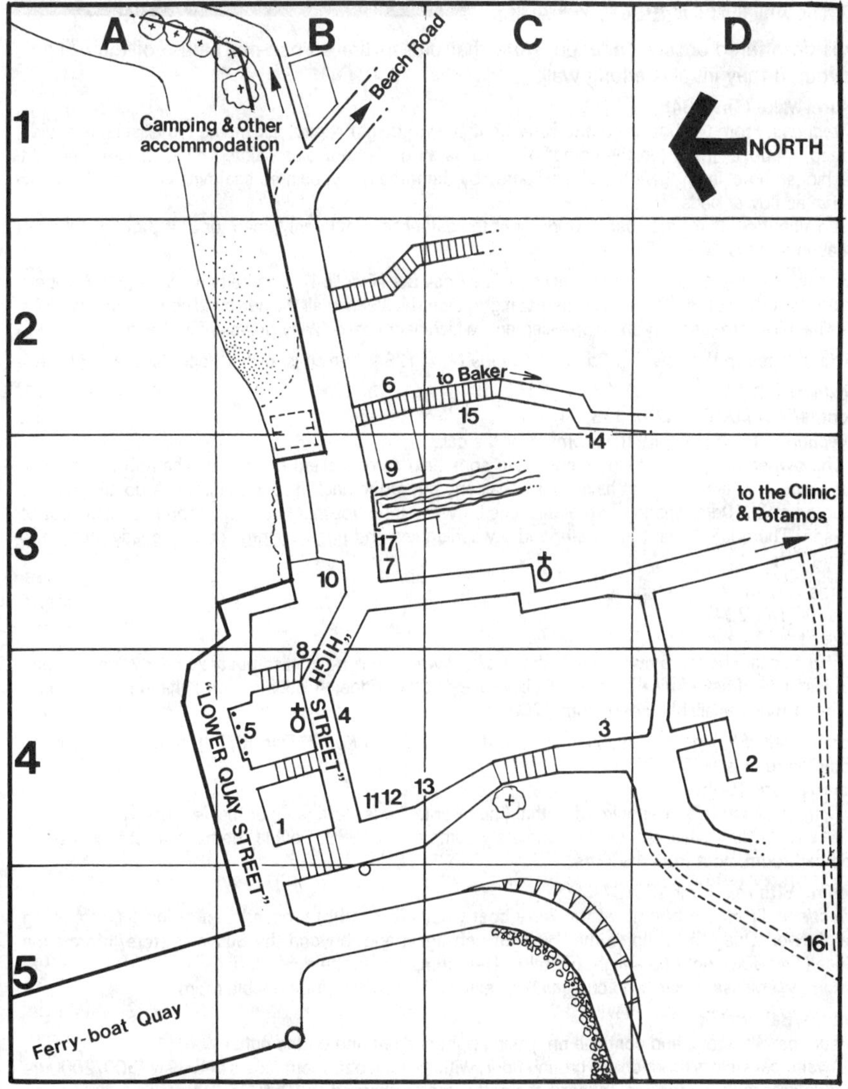

Illustration 34 Aegiali

Tmr 1B4	Hotel Mike	12B4	Rooms Stefanos
2D4	Rooms	13B/C4	Rooms/ΜΑΓΈΙΑ Cafe
3C/D4	Restaurant/Taverna To Korali	14C2/3	Rooms/Bakery
4B4	Taverna To Limani	15B/C2/3	Rooms Efthimia
5A/B4	Taverna Βιλai	16D5	Rooms
6B/C2	Cafe Asteria	17B3	Butcher
7B3	General Hardware store		
8B3/4	Store/OTE	*Tmr*	=Town map reference
9B3	Souvenir store/'Information office'	*Fsw*	=Facing seawards
10B3	Old Kafenion	*Sbo*	=Sea behind one
11B4	Rock Bar	*Fbqbo*	=Ferry-boat Quay behind one

will be offered accommodation. Note that due to the spread-out nature of the village's layout, it may involve a long walk.

Hotel Mike (*Tmr* 1B4)
Directions: From the bottom of the Ferry-boat Quay, straight ahead, ascending the hillside, is a wide, steep, stepped street (on the corner of which is an old, bright blue painted mine casing). This old-fashioned hotel is on the left and highlighted by the three green painted sea mine casings which now serve as flower beds.

En suite double rooms cost 3400drs, but the establishment is only open for 2 or 3 of the height of season months.

Next up the steps, beyond the *Hotel Mike*, is a Rock Bar (*Tmr* llB4). This belts out very loud European 1985 (not Greek pre 1950) music and at night, disturbs sleep in all the surrounding rooms. It is awful, but happily patronised by the hippy element, which seem particularly prevalent in Aegiali.

A few paces up the street is *Rooms Stefanos* (*Tmr* 12B4), which is in the 'Rock Bar area of blight'.

Next on is:-

Rooms/ΜΑΓΕΙΑ Cafe (*Tmr* 13B/C4)
Directions: As above, with the rooms over the cafe.

The owner is a pleasant lady whose two sons help carry a client's luggage. The rooms are small but clean. Those at the front have a large balcony but at the back they are quieter. A double room is charged at 2000drs, sharing two bathrooms between three rooms, but prices drop noticeably out of season. There is constant hot water and a washing line and pegs are provided. The lady meets the ferry-boats.

At the very top of the stepped street is:-

Rooms (*Tmr* 2D4)
Directions: As above.

This pleasant house is owned by Nikita and Ireni who speak no English but are a happy, kind couple. For instance. if asked nicely, they will allow use of their fridge. A double room, sharing a bathroom, with hot water available, costs from 1200drs.

To the right (*Sbo*)and accessed either from the *Taverna To Korali* (*Tmr* 3C/D4) 'terrace' or from the Potamos road is:-

Rooms (*Tmr* 16D5)
Directions: As above or enquire of Pothiti (mum) or Lefkeris Vetri (son) at the *Taverna To Korali*.

A new building which should be absolutely complete in 1989. Double rooms, two of which share one bathroom, cost from 1500drs.

Rooms Efthimia (*Tmr* 15B/C2/3)
Directions: From the bottom of the Ferry-boat Quay (*Tmr* A/B5) proceed east or left (*Fbqbo*) along the 'Lower' Quay St on up to the 'High' St, left again and, beyond the Souvenir store/Information office (*Tmr* 9B3), right up a flight of stairs. The rooms are on the right.

Run by a pleasant man who charges between 1500-2000drs for a double room.

Rooms/Bakers (*Tmr* 14C2/3)
Directions: As above and continue on, jinking right and left and on the right.

A vast, cavernous room on the ground floor, with en suite bathroom, costs between 1500/2000drs or a tiny room up on the roof, sharing the bathroom, is charged at 1000/1500drs.

Before leaving this 'district of the town', enquiries at the aforementioned Souvenir store (*Tmr* 9B3) might well prove fruitful.

For another, rather distant 'accommodation lode', ignore the road but skirt the first messy bit of beach. Then walk along the wide, concrete path skirting the main beach until reaching a large, flat bridge. Beyond this is an old cylindrical buoy set in the shore and a run-down, faded cafe-bar complex on the far right backshore. To the right is an irregular path over some waste ground which connects with the rough track round from the village. Turn left (*Sbo*), and on the left is:-

Lakki Rooms to Rent
Directions: As above, with a large water-tower adjacent. The buildings are spread out on a large patch of land.

Michael Gavalas is the proprietor. The accommodation is fairly basic but well looked after with a double bed costing between 1000-2000drs in mid-season.

Hotel Askas Tel 73333

Directions: Further along the wide track here and on the right.

Not really a hotel but a modern, nicely equipped, elongated, pension, to which a second storey was added in 1988, with the rooms off the long corridors. The owners, Lefteras and Costas Sinodinos, are very pleasant and willing to please, but with limited English. To understand anything more than a simple request they might well send off to the fields from whence a relation emerges to translate. The very pleasant, spacious en suite double rooms cost 2500drs per night in mid-season. One of the brothers runs the catering side of the team and a very reasonably priced breakfast is available on a shingle covered patio surrounded by orchard trees. Coffee, bread, honey and jam for one costs around 150drs. This is a very nice choice and should be considered by those travellers wishing to remove themselves from the 'excesses' of the port.

Camping In a pretty unsuccessful attempt to reduce the number of beach-sleepers, the village authorities established a very basic campsite. This is located in the middle of the backshore, the other side of the beach track. It makes the Katapola site appear luxurious by comparison, being extremely basic. There are two minute toilet/shower blocks, and that's it! The electricity and water supplies are indeterminate, to understate the case. Despite this, charges are the 'standard' 200drs per person and 100drs per tent. As a result, most people continue to camp on the beaches!

The Eating Out Not now the cheapest Aegean location but still inexpensive.

From the bottom of the Ferry-boat Quay (*Tmr* A/B5), the referred to wide, stepped street ascends the hill. On the left is the:-

ΜΑΓΕΙΑ Cafe (*Tmr* 13B/C4)

Directions: As above.

An excellent location for a breakfast but it is not cheap. Two Greek breakfasts and four teas cost 500drs. The young owner is laid back – no, more uninterested, indolent and unfriendly, almost to the point of rudeness.

All is not lost though because almost at the top of the same street, on the left, is the:-

Restaurant/Taverna To Korali (*Tmr* 3C/D4)

Directions: As above with tables both sides of the pedestrian way.

I am delighted to report this remains a really first-rate taverna run by friendly and hard working 'Mrs' Pothiti and her son, Lefkeris. Father and brother have a fishing boat so the Korali has the first and best seafood which may include lobster, swordfish, kalamares, atherina and sardines, in addition to the more run-of-the-mill types of fish. If this were not enough the taverna is a wonderful spot from which to watch the evening sun setting over the slope of Cape Akrotiri, diagonally across the bay. A lunch-time meal for two of spaghetti with sauce, brown bread, a Coke and soda and 2 coffees was a very inexpensive 520drs. A couple of extremely enjoyable evening meals for two were:- kalamares (300drs), swordfish (550drs), a Greek salad (180drs), ½ litre of retsina (100drs and bread at a cost of 1170drs; a dish of octopus & macaroni (250drs), pastitsio (260drs), Greek salad (160drs – yes I know), retsina and bread for 810drs, all in.

One other useful, nay vital aside is that the owner is very knowledgeable in respect of the ferry-boat schedules. He has been known to confirm his opinion by telephoning a 'source of information'.

Another good news if rather more 'working man's', 'all day and night' taverna is:-

To Limani (*Tmr* 4B4)

Directions: In the narrow 'High' St parallel to the waterfront, behind, above and opposite the church.

'We serve on the roof too' where, incidentally, waiting at table is much speedier and quieter. The *To Limani* has a cavernous, neon lit dining room with a few tables across the lane. Two interesting, large, mural wall paintings adorn the interior – not outstanding but a cut above the usual. The taverna substitutes for an evening club and meeting place. The cheerful atmosphere is that of a French bistro where Greeks and tourists intermix, gathered round the tables in animated conversation. A varied menu with meatballs (piled up like profiteroles) a speciality but as they are fast moving (no, not that sort of 'fast moving'!) there is no problem. A 'splurge' meal for two of swordfish, souvlakia, a Greek salad, a beer and a coke cost 1700drs, but the swordfish was 700drs of that bill! A more modest order for two included 1 pork chop, 1 tasty lamb in pasta, a Greek salad, bread, 2 kortaki retsina, 2 coffees and 2 (poor) brandies at a price of 1100drs. Through the bar, up a step or two, are clean lavatories complete with a shower head.

This establishment conveniently stays open for the arrival of late night/early morning ferries. Although the quay is blinded from the taverna by buildings, the boats announce their presence with a strong blast of the horn. Due to the distance to the end of the Ferry-boat Quay, and the chance that it might be quite a rush, it is a good notion for those departing to dump their bags up there, prior to ambling off for the evening's entertainment – but don't leave 'valuables' in the luggage!

There are a number of other establishments scattered about including the 'dead' *Taverna Βιλαι* (*Tmr* 5A/B4) on the waterfront, below the church; the more often than not 'dead' *Cafe Asteria* (*Tmr* 6B2), beyond George Vassalos' Souvenir shop, and a *Kafeneion*, almost side by side with the *Asteria*. The first taverna along the 'Beach Road' is good, traditional and inexpensive, whilst the *Selini Taverna*, the second beach eatery, is less Greek, less inexpensive and belts out rock music.

THE A TO Z OF USEFUL INFORMATION

BANKS None but *See* **Information Office, A To Z** or the **Post Office, Langada, Excursions to Aegiali Surrounds**.

BEACHES The immediate shoreline, beyond a rubbly quay area, is a small, sandy stretch on which the locals pull up the occasional boat. The sea in the lee of the quay can be subject to a sheen of spilled fuel.

Despite the sign 'Forbidden Public Nudity & Camping on the Beach', a number of visitors 'wild' camp in the trees edging the first part of the splendid sweep of sand that edges the long shoreline.

Although the shore is a bit pebbly, to begin with, it soon becomes sandy, getting better the further round one proceeds, with a fine sandy bottom to the shallow shelving sea-bed. The sea is blue, clean and inviting.

The further part of the fairly narrow beach is lined by a high stone wall, through which is a gateway with a painted wooden board proclaiming 'Wild herbs, fruit and vegetables, Rooms to let' in Greek, English, German and French. At the far side of the huge bay are a number of coves. The first has a large, sandy beach, the second is rough sand and shingle and the third is rocky.

BOOKSELLERS None but *See* **Information Office, A To Z**.

BICYCLE, SCOOTER & CAR HIRE None, but there are donkeys to hire from the *Selini Taverna*, on the beach. When they can be bothered, the cost is 400drs per hour.

BREAD SHOPS The Baker (*Tmr* 14C2/3) is up the steps alongside the *Cafe Asteria* He is often to be observed shouldering cooking trays containing various taverna 'meals of the day' which he 'ovens'.

BUSES A single, modern bus provides a regular service from Aegiali to Langada and from Aegiali to Tholaria. There is no road, but two or three mule tracks, between Langada and Tholaria.

Bus timetable

Aegiali Port to Langada

Daily: 0640, 1000, 1300, 1600, 1900, 2030, 2210, 2400hrs.

Return journey

Daily: Approximately ten minutes later.

Aegiali Port to Tholaria

Daily: 0710, 1100, 1400, 1530, 1800, 2000, 2130, 0030hrs.

Return journey

Daily: Approximately ten minutes later.

Plus:-

A vehicle, variously reported as a van, Mini-van or Range Rover, runs twice daily to the Chora, 500drs each way. Leaves Aegiali 0915hrs & 5pm, returns 1015 & 1800hrs' Yes! Incidentally, this 'service' only operates during the height of season months. It is rumoured to be run by Nikos, he of 'The Taverna' at Langada.

COMMERCIAL SHOPPING AREA There is a small, cramped, rather primitive Store (*Tmr* 8B3/4) beyond the church and on the left. This Aegean 'Harrods' doubles up as a very 'doo-hickey' telephone exchange. Okay, it possesses an extremely primitive telephone box and an old-fashioned switchboard but the (lack of) connections here is even more noticeable than at Katapola. The old boy chalks up, not always reliable, ferry-boat information on any bit of cardboard or whatever is to hand. He also sells ferry tickets. In a block opposite the Kafeneion (*Tmr* 10B3) are a cafe, a General Hardware store (*Tmr* 7B3) and a Butcher (*Tmr* 17B3).

FERRY-BOATS *See* **Ferry-boat Timetable, A To Z, Katapola**, George at the 'Information office' (*Tmr* 9B3) or the landlord of the *Taverna Korali*.

FERRY BOAT TICKET OFFICE There is a 'sales point' now, in the General store (*Tmr* 8B3/4).

INFORMATION OFFICE (*Tmr* 9B3) Tel 71252/71346

Directions: Towards the east end of the 'High' St.

Actually, George Vassalos' Souvenir shop but, as the sign boldly proclaims:-

'(EXCHANGE)
(RENT ROOMS)
STAMPS – FILMS
BUY & SELL BOOKS HERE
GENERAL (INFORMATION)
RENT A DONKEY NOT A MOTORBIKE'

The items in brackets are, George explains, "...taped over during August because the travellers in this month are crazy and keep asking stupid questions like 'Where does the bus to Astipalaia (another island) leave from'! After August I remove the tape and continue as an Information Office". Fair enough.

George is a most likeable, helpful young man and a mine of information, some inconsequential, some extremely useful..."don't buy bottled water, the tap in the Main Town Square is excellent" (*See* **Water, A To Z**). Mind you the small area he refers to, across the way, is more a building materials yard. Of more consequence, this is one of the only places in Aegiali at which to exchange money. The shop has some pleasant souvenirs including an interesting island map drafted by a German professor. The preponderance of 'other' Europeans, results in their being few English books for exchange and a 150drs charge is made for a swop. George is often assisted by a friend, and during the quieter hours the pair of them sit on the shops verandah dispensing advice and the odd drink.

MEDICAL CARE There is a Clinic half-way up the steep, wide, unmade road to the Upper Village of Potamos, on the right.

OTE (*Tmr* 8B3/4) More a General store.

POST OFFICE *See* George at the **'Information Office'** or go to the Post Office in Langada.

WATER During the height of season months, in 1988, Aegiali suffered from a drastic water shortage, the likes of which I have not witnessed previously. The port was without running water for several days of one visit. Enquiries uncovered the fact that this was the sixth water stoppage of the summer and that in July there was no water for fifteen consecutive days. Although the village has piped spring water from the mountains this cannot always cope with the numbers of tourists. Then the port becomes entirely dependent on visits from a water supply boat. But due to disputes over payment, when the Government does not pay the subsidies *ad nauseam*, the (privately owned) boat does not deliver! Strangely, or not, depending on your view of the Greek mind, there is no rationing of water at all, during 'times of plenty' – everyone uses as much as they like until it ceases to flow!

EXCURSIONS TO AEGIALI SURROUNDS

Excursion to Potamos The 'Chora' village is up the precipitous hillside, ascending the track that starts out as a lane opposite the old Kafeneion (*Tmr* 10B3), jinks around the church and widens out into a broad, unsurfaced road.

Potamos is an 'up and down' hillside settlement with a Town Hall and a school. In the right-hand part (*Sbo*) there is a post box on the wall, close by the village shop. This latter business is only recognizable by a pile of empty crates outside and the owner lives next door. An OTE phone (0800-1400hrs & 1700-2130hrs) is in the same building and next door is the *Taverna To* ΗΛΙΟΒΑΣΙΛΕΜΑ (The Sunset) – aptly named.

Excursion to Langada (Lagada) & Tholaria There are buses now but to make the 45 minute walk to Langada, rather than taking the zig-zag, unsurfaced road, proceed to the minor crossroads on the way up to Potamos. Select the left-hand turning and clamber through the olive groves

LANGADA This is truly a beautiful village, in addition to which, there is *Taverna/Rooms Nikos*, one of the best establishments of its kind in the Cyclades and deserving of a five star recommendation. The taverna is situated at the bottom of the village, looking down the narrow valley through which the donkey track winds up from below. It is on the right at the point where the track ends and has two wide terraces with tables, the front being covered by a vast bougainvillea tree. Nikos has eight lovely double rooms costing from 2000drs, with en suite bathroom (and hot water), as well as a balcony. This is an extremely peaceful spot to stay.

Nikos' cuisine is far above average island fare, and the menu includes imaginative dishes, such as pork in lemon sauce and aubergines in cheese & onion sauce. A huge feast for two of 3 aubergines, a Greek salad, a plate of tzatziki, bread and a large bottle of white wine cost 1400drs. Beat that. If this were not enough, retsina is available from the barrel. Oh 'taverna heaven' on earth.

Beside the taverna is a baker's which sells brown bread, and along the same lane there are a few small kafeneions. Also in the village are four General stores, the Police station for the Aegiali area (just off the Main Square) and a Post Office in 'someone's living room', complete with a telephone. The latter conducts exchange, as does the large village store near the taverna, and is open weekdays between 0800-1330hrs & 1700-2300hrs. It is run by Mr Vlavianou and his English wife Anna, who has been resident in Langada for some twelve years. They are assisted by their children, who speak English.

The 'Village Store' has a small inconspicuous entrance but once inside... The little old lady has an unbelievable amount of goods stacked in the confined space. There is everything from'Calor'gas to cut out cardboard puppets, yoghurt to shoes and shirts to shampoo.

At the top end of the village it is possible to pick up a mule track, which stays fairly high up on the mountainside. The route passes above an old settlement, of which a few houses are still inhabited, and after about an hour reaches:-

THOLARIA After Langada this village is rather disappointing as it is not nearly so pretty but there are great views out over the island. A great many of the street's steps and flat roofs are painted with simplistic floral designs, some even with 'Peace' and 'Love'!

There are four tavernas, one of which is the *Panorama*. This is nearest the bus stop and has a wide terrace, just below the big church. Apart from good and reasonably priced food they have a few basic rooms at a cost of 1500-1700drs.

Despite the fair amount of new building in progress there isn't a baker or a stores.

Incidentally, the conventional route to Tholaria is to advance to the far end of the bay from Aegiali Port and wind up the rough path, or take the unsurfaced road.

Close by Ag Anna, Naxos. Acknowledgement to David & Liz Drummond-Tyler.

The baker, Ano Meria, Folegandros. Acknowledgement to David & Liz Drummond-Tyler.

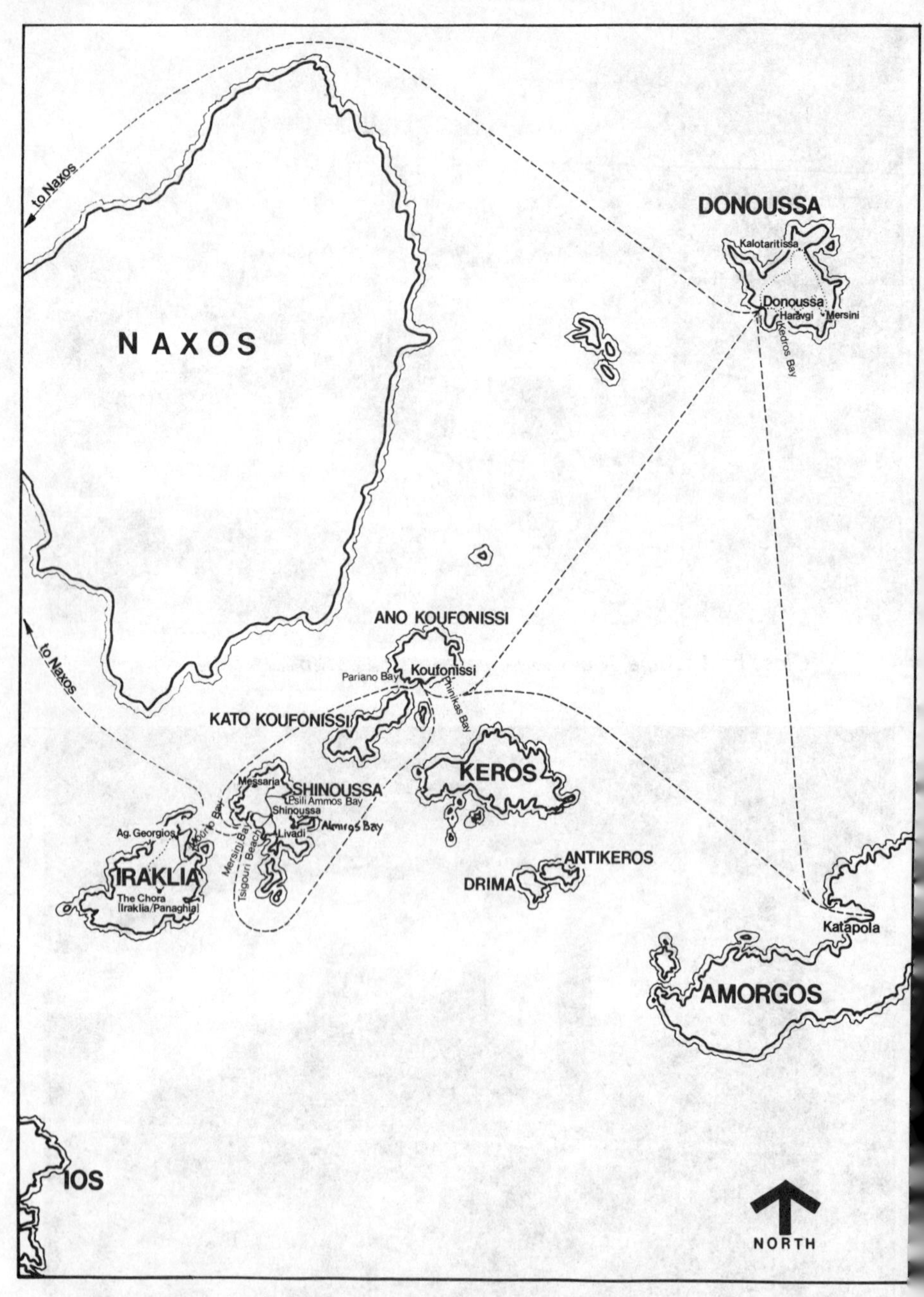

Illustration 35 The Small or Back islands

13 DONOUSSA, KOUFONISSI, SHINOUSSA & IRAKLIA
Cyclades Islands - Eastern chain

These four and others, sometimes known as the *Small Cyclades* or *Back Islands*, are grouped in a scattered archipelago. This circles the east and south coast of Naxos.

DONOUSSA (Dhenoussa, Dhonoussa) *****

FIRST IMPRESSIONS Sandy beaches; rough donkey tracks; choppy seas.

SPECIALITIES None.

RELIGIOUS HOLIDAYS & FESTIVALS None outside the national celebrations.

VITAL STATISTICS Tel. prefix 0285. The population is 115 & the island's area is 13sq km.

HISTORY Tied in with that of Amorgos and Naxos. In recent times the island has only been settled for a couple of hundred years, when farmers and fishermen ventured here from Amorgos. Previous to that it was a pirates lair.

Over the past thirty years or so the population has halved.

GENERAL The island finally caught up with the twentieth century in the last ten years or so. Running water and electricity were installed in 1981 and a full-blown Ferry-boat Quay, in 1988. Donoussa has, to date, remained a relatively little visited, wild island, surrounded by unpredictable seas and currents. It is frequently cut off in the winter months, for up to 15 days at a time, as happened in 1988. Even in the summer months, the island is prone to being cut off in adverse weather conditions.

As the modern-day conveniences began to 'show', so did the tourists and enough stop off now to over-fill the island's forty rooms, in peak season months. Visitors may well continue to increase as facilities improve, because the island has some marvellous, sandy beaches and, to date, a delicious flavour of Greece of yesteryear.

DONOUSSA: capital & port (Illustration 36).

ARRIVAL BY FERRY The larger ferry-boats now dock at the new quay (*Tmr* 1) and caiques no longer need to act as pass boats.

The smaller **Skopelitis** still berths at the old, tiny quay (*Tmr* 2), beneath the tavernas, which makes for much easier unloading of supplies. Unfortunately this selection causes continual confusion amongst departing passengers who, more often than not, wait some distance away, at the end of the new Ferry-boat Quay! If any further turmoil is required... entry on to the Skopelitis is usually from the stern end, but at Donoussa it is from the bow... Disembarking passengers waiting in the aft can often be seen charging through the boat at top speed, just before the boat is about to depart.

THE ACCOMMODATION & EATING OUT

The Accommodation Donoussa has about forty rooms, few of which are advertised, though one large building, behind the church, has painted on the wall 'Rooms at Tel 9584793'. The best place to get information is at the *Blue Lagoon Cafe* (*Tmr* 4), above the baker. The extremely helpful young owner, who speaks both English and German, will point the way to the best places or even negotiate with islanders, on the spot. Double room prices range between 1200-2000drs per night, but the most basic may well be without running water, let alone hot water.

Unfortunately Donoussa simply cannot cope with the influx experienced between 15th July-15th Aug.

The Eating Out Not a vast choice, or varied menus for that matter, but pleasant enough. The choice of meals rather depends on what the boats unload.

Cafe/Taverna To Kyma (*Tmr* 3)
An old-fashioned cafe-turned-taverna, for the summer months. The establishment also doubles as a general store and is open all year round. Fishermen play cards here in the afternoon but the tourists congregate for meals. A meal for two of pistachios, a Greek salad, 2 lemonades and bread cost 800drs.

The shop sells maps of the island (60drs) as well as black & white line drawing postcards – the only ones available of Donoussa, to date.

Blue Lagoon Cafe (*Tmr* 4)
'BREAKFAST' is painted boldly on the outside wall in blue. The premises are above the baker, but entered from the street at the rear of the building. The rooftop terrace is pleasantly bamboo shaded. Two yoghurts, bread, 2 coffees and a bottle of water cost 520drs, which is not cheap. However, the young owner, who speaks English, is extremely friendly and helpful. Apart from assistance with accommodation he also advises enquirers about directions but his ideas in respect of the duration of walks is wildly optimistic. He may change some foreign money but prefers German marks to English pounds. (The young follow-me-lad obviously doesn't remember who won the last war! Perhaps he knows who triumphed in the ensuing economic battle.) Incidentally the toilets are spotless.

Also in the centre of 'all this activity' is the *Taverna Meltemi* (*Tmr* 5). Half-way across the beach, on the backshore near the palm trees, is the large *Taverna Aposperitis* where 2 coffees cost 140drs.

THE A TO Z OF USEFUL INFORMATION

BANKS None and the 'Post Office' doesn't change money either. The owner of the *Blue Lagoon* might, but travellers are best advised to bring sufficient for the day, or days.

BEACHES The superb, sandy town beach stretches away around the bay. There is a sign forbidding nudism and camping, which thankfully is respected. Those who want to 'nude', or camp, cross the town beach and head up the concrete path over the headland to another excellent, sandy beach.

There are beaches at Livadia, near the village of Mersini, and Kalotaritissa. It is a 1½hour walk to Mersini on the circular donkey path and a 5 hour walk to Kalotaritissa.

BREAD SHOPS The Baker (*Tmr* 4) produces bread (but not until after 1000hrs) as well as a wonderful variety of cakes and sweetbreads. However, the island only benefits from his services between 15th June-1st September as he spends the rest of the year baking in Athens. Outside this period bread is brought in from Naxos.

COMMERCIAL SHOPPING AREA There are two General stores (*Tmr* 3 & 6).

FERRY-BOATS *See* **Amorgos, Chapter Twelve**.

MEDICAL CARE A Doctor is housed in the 'Village Hall', next to the Church. His clinic opens weekdays between 0700-1300hrs & 1800-1900hrs. He doubles up as a pharmacy. A dentist visits the island at allotted times.

OTE Surprisingly yes. A new tiny office is open weekdays between 0900-1200hrs & 1800-2100hrs, Saturday between 9000-1200hrs & 1800-2000hrs and is closed Sundays.

POLICE None.

POST OFFICE Not really a Post Office – more the office where the post is counted, housed in the 'Village Hall'. Thus there isn't any exchange facilities.

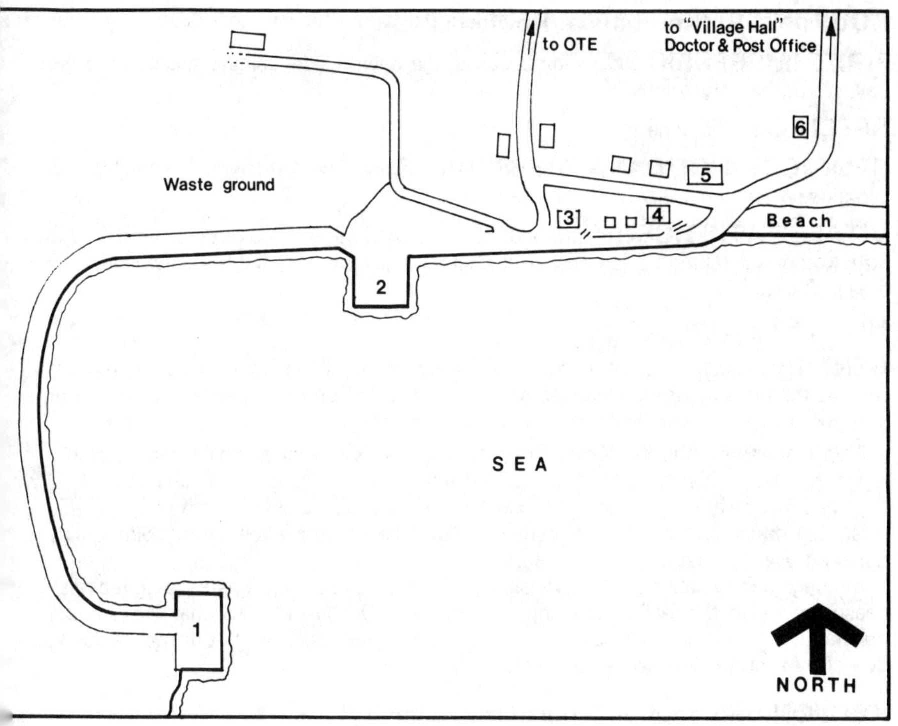

Illustration 36 Donoussa 'Town'

Tmr 1	Large Ferry-boat Quay
2	Small Ferry-boat Quay
3	Taverna 'To Kyma'/General store
4	Baker/Cafe Blue Lagoon
5	Taverna Meltemi
6	General store

Tmr =town map reference
Fsw =Facing seawards
Sbo =Sea behind one
Fbqbo =Ferry-boat Quay behind one

KOUFONISSI (Koufonisia, Koufonisi) ****

FIRST IMPRESSIONS sandy beaches; flat countryside; caiques anchored in the bay, not at the jetty; windy.

SPECIALITIES None.

RELIGIOUS HOLIDAYS & FESTIVALS include: 23rd April - Panaghia, Ag Giorgios.

VITAL STATISTICS Tel. prefix 0285. Ano Koufonissi has a population of 240 & Kato Koufonissi 10 from 2 families. Ano Koufonissi is extremely flat & low lying with an area of 3.8 sq km.

HISTORY See Naxos.

GENERAL The generic name Koufonissi covers two small islands. Ano (upper) Koufonissi has the majority of the inhabitants, all of them being concentrated into the town of Koufonissi. Kato (lower) Koufonissi is all but deserted.

Two features of Ano Koufonissi are remarkable – its lack of anything approaching a mountain, even a hill, and its thriving population. This is coupled to a flourishing fishing fleet of some forty caiques. In sharp contrast to nearby Shinoussa, which was primarily a farming rather than a fishing community, Koufonissi's population has remained fairly constant over the last fifty years or so.

Although still a relatively unknown island, the concentration of tourists during the peak season can give the feeling of being overcrowded. Despite the fact that facilities are constantly being expanded, scarcity of rooms, and even food, are not unknown during July and the first two weeks of August.

KOUFONISSI: capital & port (Illustration 37).

ARRIVAL BY FERRY The new Ferry-boat Quay (*Tmr* 1) was completed a few years ago, turning the town into the port. Until then the island's harbour was over the low hill at Pariano, where boats still dock in bad weather.

From the quay, a cement road leads round to the right towards the main town. The bay is jam-packed with fishing boats lying at anchor.

THE ACCOMMODATION & EATING OUT

The Accommodation The island has around two hundred beds, and the number is growing rapidly. At present the rooms are full to overflowing between 15th July and 15th August. There are some rooms beside the main street into the town and more in the big new pensions behind the Port Beach. Rooms cost from 1600-2000drs for a double.

Accommodation is also available at Phinikas Beach, where there are two large, new, blue and white arched tavernas with rooms.

The Eating Out The establishments are concentrated around the back of the beach and along the main street of the town. Prices are reasonable, as is fish, but the menu depends on the supply boat. In the peak months some tavernas run out of food, later on in the evening. The windmill on the hilltop nearby is in an excellent state of repair and has been converted into a cafe. There is another Cafe (*Tmr* 2) at the junction of the beach road & main street.

THE A TO Z OF USEFUL INFORMATION

BANKS None, but *See* **Post Office**.

BEACHES Plenty and excellent. The Port Beach looks good enough, being long and sandy, but it is nothing in comparison to the string of three, long, sandy beaches which stretch along the coast at

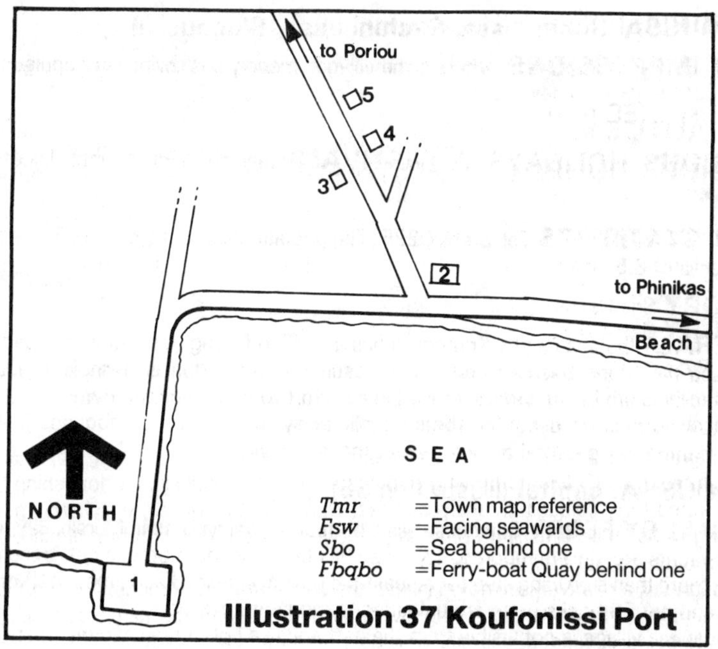

Illustration 37 Koufonissi Port

Tmr	1	Ferry-boat Quay
	2	Cafe/General store
	3	Post Office
	4	OTE
	5	Ferry-boat Ticket office

Phinikas Bay (so called because of the lone palm tree or 'Θοινικατ'). A rough, unpaved road leads over the low rise from Koufonissi Port to the beaches – about a 20 minute walk. Some scant shade is provided by low trees, and 'wild' campers abound. With the latter in mind, the owner of the first beach taverna has thoughtfully erected free showers and toilets at the back of the beach. He is also energetically building more rooms at this very attractive spot.

More sandy beaches can be found at Poriou which are accessible by unpaved road.

BICYCLE, SCOOTER & CAR HIRE None.

BREAD SHOPS There is a baker in Koufonissi Port.

BUSES None.

COMMERCIAL SHOPPING AREA The Cafe (*Tmr* 2), at the junction, doubles as a General store selling everything. There are a couple more stores tucked away in the body of the Port.

FERRY-BOATS *See* **Amorgos, Chapter Twelve.**

FERRY-BOAT TICKET OFFICES There is an office (*Tmr* 5), on the right (*Sbo*) of the main street.

MEDICAL CARE Koufonissi used to have the only doctor amongst the islands of Shinoussa and Iraklia but now each island has its own, which doubles up as a pharmacy. The dentist visits occasionally.

OTE (*Tmr* 4) Opposite the Post Office, on the main street. Open between 0800-1300hrs & 1700-2000hrs, weekdays only.

PLACES OF INTEREST Fishing boat voyages and trips across the narrow channel to Kato Koufonissi can be arranged with local fishermen. Kato Koufonissi has three small beaches and lots of fish.

POLICE The island policeman's beat also covers nearby Shinoussa and Iraklia.

POST OFFICE (*Tmr* 3) Yes, and it transacts exchange.

SHINOUSSA (Schinoussa, Skchinoussa, Skinoussa) ****

FIRST IMPRESSIONS Where's the village; friendly but dwindling population.

SPECIALITIES None.

RELIGIOUS HOLIDAYS & FESTIVALS include: 25th March, Theotokou, Messaria.

VITAL STATISTICS Tel. prefix 0285. The population is a 'dubious' 190. The island has an area of 8.5 sq km.

HISTORY See Naxos.

GENERAL Whereas nearby Koufonissi has a thriving fishing population, the people of Shinoussa have long been farmers. As a result the population is dwindling fast. The tourist facilities are being well advertised in an effort to stem the 'outflow'.

The town's nearest beach is 15mins walk away, but the island abounds in sandy beaches, there being a total of nineteen, at the last count.

SHINOUSSA: capital (Illustration 38).

ARRIVAL BY FERRY Shinoussa has a perfect natural harbour at Mersini Bay, where several yachts are always moored. The quay has been 'under improvement', resembling nothing more than a building site, for at least the past five years. Each time the **Skopelitis** docks, another 50 bricks or so are unloaded... and so it goes on.

The (capital) village is not visible from the port and is a hot, fifteen minute, dusty, uphill walk away.

Mersini Bay has one shingle beach and one narrow sand beach. Besides the latter is a large taverna with rooms. There is a new ***Rooms*** block set down in an orchard.

THE ACCOMMODATION & EATING OUT

The Accommodation All facilities (sixty rooms) are along the long main street of the straggling island capital. Entering the village from the Port, there is a large white building, with blue shutters *Rooms Pothiti* (*Tmr* 11) on the left. This is owned by a large, friendly lady who says, with a wink "We bargain". Double rooms with shared showers and solar heated water (ie none after lunch) cost between 1500-1800drs.

Less expensive, but more basic accommodation, is available at the Cafe (*Tmr* 10) where a double room costs 1200drs.

The Eating Out An assortment of cafes-turned-taverna (for the summer season) serve whatever the two ferry-boats bring in, at a reasonable price. The *Pizzeria* (*Tmr* 6) is run by a very helpful young man, who also produces an island map (which sells out by mid-August) and will offer information in a smattering of English. Despite the title, the restaurant also serves traditional Greek food. A lunch-time meal for one of beans, a Greek salad, a beer, bread and an island map cost 700drs. No bottled water was stocked but island well water is served, which doesn't cause any ill-effects, despite an earthy taste.

THE A TO Z OF USEFUL INFORMATION

BANKS None. The *Pizzeria* (*Tmr* 6) will transact exchange, if a client is desperate. The 'Post Office' (*Tmr* 2) is a 'living-room' affair and not to be relied on. Bring all the funds required.

BEACHES As aforementioned, the island has nineteen beaches, most of them sandy. The best, Tsigouri Beach, also happens to be closest. Take the first track to the right after entering the village from the Port. It is fifteen minutes walk and has a taverna with a couple of basic rooms.

Other beaches near Shinoussa 'town' are Livadia and Almiros. Proceed to the end of the street, beyond the *Pizzeria* (*Tmr* 6). Where the road divides into two dirt tracks, turn right for Livadia. This

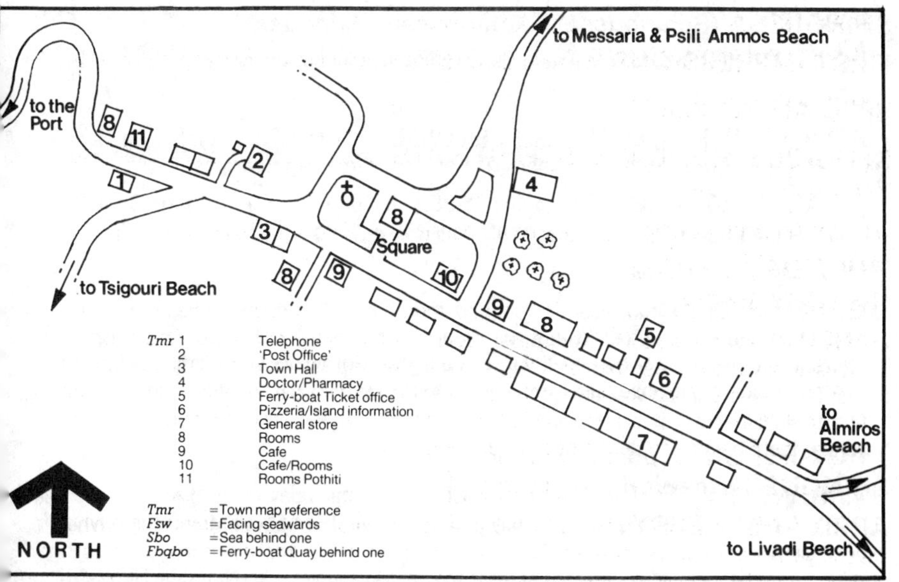

Illustration 38 Shinoussa Town

passes between wheat fields and is about a twenty minute walk from the settlement's centre. Not a very inspiring, narrow, sandy and grassy beach, but the bay enjoys protected, calm waters. The couple who own the land and fields behind the beach claim they intend to set up a campsite here.

The left fork leads down a stony track, again through fields, to a left turn where proceed along a narrower track. Where this ends climb over the wall crossing a large wheat field to the wild, sandy, 'Minoan-flavoured' Bay of Almiros. This choice is also twenty minutes from the town.

To reach the beach at Psili Ammos, close to the tiny hamlet of Messaria, either hitch a tractor ride or walk, for some forty five minutes, to Messaria. From there battle on another for another ten minutes for the beach.

BREAD SHOPS In 1987 the *Pizzeria* (*Tmr* 6) also 'tripled up' as a baker, but in 1988, not surprisingly, he decided it was too much work. Bread is thus brought in from Iraklia and Naxos.

BUSES None but tractors will give a lift.

COMMERCIAL SHOPPING AREA The Cafe (*Tmr* 9) stocks some goods, as does the *Pizzeria* (*Tmr* 6). Opposite the latter is a small shop (*Tmr* 7) run by a frightening man. He advertises 'We sell everything you want. CIGARETTES' on the iron railing outside. Indeed, he seems to stock everything from second-hand clothes to toothpaste.

FERRY-BOATS *See* **Amorgos, Chapter Twelve**.

FERRY-BOAT TICKET OFFICE Surprisingly there is one (*Tmr* 5) along a path and up the outside steps of the white house, next door to the *Pizzeria*. Ferry-boat timetables are displayed outside which is useful. However, the office is only open evenings.

MEDICAL CARE The Doctor/Pharmacy (*Tmr* 4) is in a squat modern building, not far from the church.

OTE Yes..! The island has three telephones. One is the Doctor's, one is 'illegal & private'(!) and the third is a public telephone (*Tmr* 1). The last mentioned is on the right, entering the village from the Port and down a few steps, through a big blue door (Good luck).

POLICE *See* **Koufonissi**.

POST OFFICE A 'living-room' affair (*Tmr* 2), up a scruffy, dirt track on the left on entering the village. They may change currency if an enquirer is lucky.

IRAKLIA ****

FIRST IMPRESSIONS Tranquillity; remoteness; lack of facilities.

SPECIALITIES None.

RELIGIOUS HOLIDAYS & FESTIVALS include: 23rd April – Ag Georgios Church, Ag Georgios; 8th November – Taxiarchis Church, Ag Georgios.

VITAL STATISTICS Tel. prefix 0285. The population is 100 or 95 or 140, depending on the authority! The area of the island is 17sq km.

HISTORY *See* **Naxos**.

GENERAL Of the four islands grouped together in this chapter, Iraklia is the least developed and the quietest. It has two villages, the port Ag Georgios and, inland, the Chora (more generally known as Iraklia or Panaghia. Both have some fifty inhabitants.

A few modern, purpose built rooms and tavernas provide the only facilities for tourists on the island.

AG GEORGIOS: port (Illustration 39).

ARRIVAL BY FERRY The boats dock at the small quay (*Tmr* 1) in the deep inlet of Ag Georgios. One boat fills the quay and it is a five minute walk down the bay to the port village.

THE ACCOMMODATION & EATING OUT

The Accommodation Between the 15th July-15th August the island's thirty rooms are full. Outside this period Room owners meet the ferry-boats with enthusiasm. The owner of *Rooms Alexandra* (*Tmr* 6) is usually decked out in a T-shirt advertising Rooms in three languages!

There are some bedrooms at the *Taverna/Cafe Melissa* (*Tmr* 3) as well as the *Taverna* Βαγγασ (*Tmr* 4). Double rooms vary from 1600drs (basic) to 2200drs (with hot water).

The Eating Out There are five tavernas in the port area: three in Ag Georgios and two by Livadia At the *Taverna* Βαγγασ (*Tmr* 4) pizzas cost 550drs, veal 400drs, a small retsina 110drs and a beer 90drs.

The larger beach taverna at Livadia also has two rooms which cost 1900drs, sharing a shower, which 'enjoys' sporadic hot water.

THE A TO Z OF USEFUL INFORMATION

BANKS None, nor exchange,'not nothing.'

BEACHES Two excellent, sandy beaches are within easy reach of Ag Georgios Port. One is in the bay and the other is at Livadia, some fifteen minutes walk over the hill. The Livadia Beach is particularly impressive – vast, sandy and practically deserted, with two tavernas on the backshore.

BREAD SHOPS The island bakery is in the Chora – a wood-fired affair. Bread is delivered daily to the port at around 1100hrs. Some of the output is shipped to Shinoussa. The *Taverna/Cafe Melissa* (*Tmr* 3) sells bread.

BUSES Mmhh! Once a day it is possible to hitch a lift with the bread van to the Chora. To effect the pick-up, hang around at the junction where the asphalt road leaves Ag Georgios Port for Livadia and the Chora.

COMMERCIAL SHOPPING AREA There are two General stores in the Chora. The *Taverna Melissa* (*Tmr* 3) offers some goods.

FERRY-BOATS *See* **Amorgos, Chapter Twelve**.

MEDICAL CARE The Doctor spends alternate days in the Chora and the Port.

OTE There is a metered telephone in the *Taverna/Cafe Melissa* (*Tmr* 3).

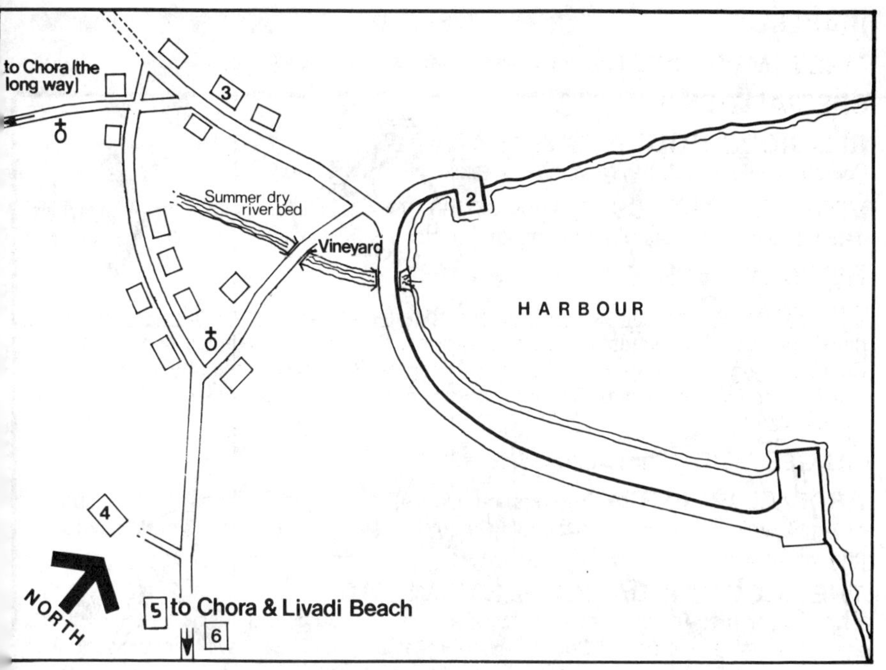

Illustration 39 Ag Georgios Port, Iraklia

Tmr 1	Ferry-boat Quay
2	Fishing boat Quay
3	Taverna/Cafe Melissa/'OTE'/ 'Post Office'/Rooms/General store
4	Taverna Rooms Βαγγασ
5	Taverna
6	Rooms Alexandra

Tmr =Town map reference
Fsw =Facing seawards
Sbo =Sea behind one
Fbqbo =Ferry-boat Quay behind one

POST OFFICE The unofficial location is the *Taverna/Cafe Melissa* (*Tmr* 3). What isn't?

The CHORA (Panaghia/Iraklia) This is a good hour's walk from the Port, up the road which first passes by Livadia Beach. The road is paved in parts, not in others. To avoid walking, hitch a lift with one of the tractors/jeeps which,occasionally pass by, or take the bread van.

The Chora is a very down-to-earth, whitewashed settlement. The big, white domed church, Panaghia, gives the settlement its common name. The town stands half-way up the mountain. There are two general stores, one kafeneion but no rooms nor tavernas.

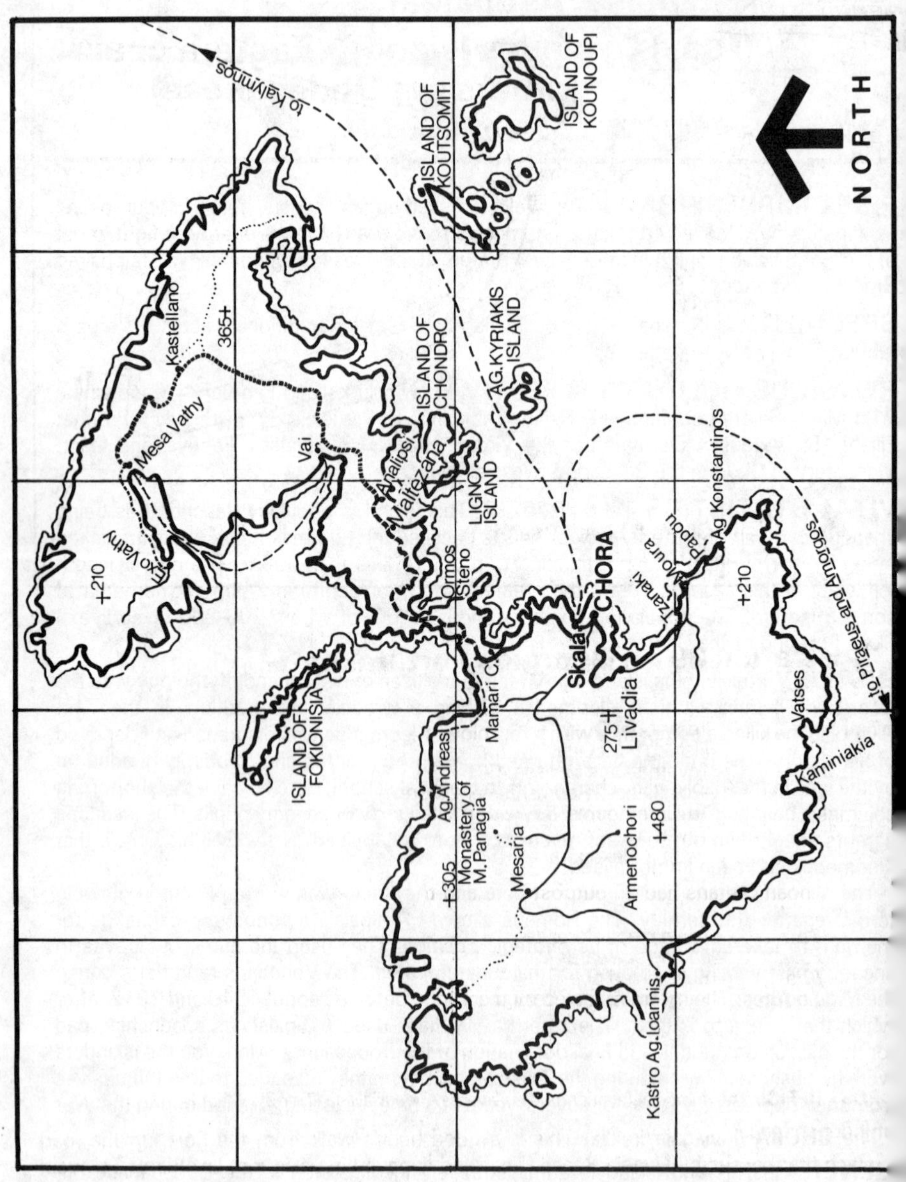

Illustration 40 Astipalaia island

14 ASTIPALAIA (Astypalaia, Astypalea, Astipalea) (I say) Cyclades Islands - Eastern chain (others say Dodecanese) ★★★★★

FIRST IMPRESSIONS Water wells 'dressed up' as chapels; colourful, purposeful fishing fleet; well looked after cats – so much so they even have the energy to fight, most of the night; fishing with dynamite; steps & more steps; 'yassou' becomes 'ya'; fair haired Greeks; flies; aridity.

SPECIALITIES No snakes; curiously elaborate females traditional costume; hares & rabbits; 'Gasosa' lemonade.

RELIGIOUS HOLIDAYS & FESTIVALS include: 2nd February – Candlemas; 21st May – Saints Constantine & Helen; 2nd July – St Panteleimon; 20th July – Prophet Elijah; 15th August – Dormition of the Virgin; 29th -31st August – Festival and feast, Monastery of St John the Beheaded (west of island).

VITAL STATISTICS Tel prefix 0242. This island is popularly described as being shaped like a pair of butterfly wings. This is because the two major land areas are linked by a tiny, narrow neck of land, thinning to probably less than 300m. The overall length (or width in this case) is 18km, the greatest width (or depth) is 24km with an area of some 99sq km. The population numbers about 1,100, of whom 700-800 or so live in Skala Port and or the Chora.

HISTORY Possibly the island's most famous citizen of history and mythology was the disgraced Olympian athlete Kleomedes. During a wrestling competition, in the 71st Olympiad, he killed a competitor with a foul blow. Kleomedes was disgraced and deprived of his victory. The one-time hero returned home pretty miffed and, probably goaded on by the lads in the 'public bar', charged off to the local school. Here he gave the supporting columns a bear hug, pulling the roof down and killed sixty or seventy pupils. The incensed parents sought him out to exact revenge, only to be advised by the Delphic Oracle that Kleomedes had been immortalised.

The Minoan Cretans had an outpost here and the island was written about in glowing terms regarding its fertility. The Romans allowed Astipalaia autonomy in exchange for the right to take advantage of its strategic position. They used the numerous coves to anchor whilst waiting in ambush for marauding pirates. The Venetians ran affairs during the Middle Ages. They were followed by the Turks, between about 1540 and 1912, after which the Italians took over. The latter-day Romans used Astipalaia as a launching pad for the assault on Rhodes and final domination of the Dodecanese. Mark you the islanders were no pushover. Twice during the Turkish occupation they managed to free themselves from their oppressor's yoke, for several years at a time, including a period during the War of Independence.

GENERAL This arid island is administratively incorporated in the Dodecanese but surely this can only be the stroke of a mandarin's pen? Astipalaia is almost more Cycladean than many of the other Cyclades islands. Typically the Port dwellings corkscrew up to a dramatic Chora, topped off by a splendid Venetian castle. Furthermore the ferry-boat connections from the Cycladean outposts are far more frequent than those from the Dodecanese islands. Admittedly there is the mandatory Dodecanese style, Italian inspired, colonnaded Municipal building, even if it is rather insignificant. During their suzerainty the Italian overlords restored the hilltop castle but there all similarity with its administrative brethren ends.

A mark of islands that have been isolated and outside of the main stream is the occurrence of a particular physical peculiarity. Astipalaia's own abnormality is hereditary deafness and it is not uncommon to observe lip-reading natives. Certainly Astipalaia has managed to remain rooted in the Greece of yesteryear. Many of the now, generally lost Hellenique niceties are still to be found here, in spite of increasing penetration by the tourist industry.

The few beaches are not golden sand, more grey pebble and often dirty, a shortcoming more than compensated for by the contented and intrinsically Greek nature of the inhabitants and their environment. Beneath the everyday comings and goings beats a throbbing pulse of island life, both rich in characters and those daily happenings that weave the priceless pattern of everyday Greek existence. A touching example of the islanders disposition is illustrated by the Grandfather of the family that runs the beach taverna, Το Ακροψιαλι (*Tmr* 10B1). A Simiot fisherman, he rowed single-handed all the way to Astipalaia to marry his sweetheart, a distance of some 130kms.

The islanders' reserved nature is balanced by an overwhelming friendliness that blossoms after the first few days of acquaintance. On the other hand a visitors initial impression may be of some disappointment as there are few of the manifestations expected by many hedonistic holiday-makers nourished on a diet of discos and 'fast food'. But persevere. The natural charm of the people and the location may well weave a spell that will hold the true Grecophile tightly in its untidy, somewhat messy, but lively bonds. Certainly it is one of the few islands on which I have had to exercise all my willpower to break the spell and get on the ferry-boat.

If the natives of Amorgos go to bed early, Astipalaians make up for it as they rise late and don't seem to stop until early next morning. Visitors should note that Astipalaia does not really come to life until the end of June, with the official start of the season being around 20th May – in line with other islands.

SKALA: main port (Illustration 41) The harbour is dominated by the Kastro topped Chora. The buildings stretch all the way up from the pleasantly scruffy and intimate port, which exhibits few concessions to tourism. In fact the Skala is bustling and noisy, with goats 'baaing', cats fighting, people ambling home late and the fishermen rising early. The old, 'dead' Electricity Generating station (*Tmr* 1C5) still tends to dominate the left-hand (*Sbo*) side of the port, as do the mass of fishing boats and the Meccano-like OTE reflector tower that almost brushes the corner of the *Hotel Paradissos* (*Tmr* 2B4/5). The *Paradissos* building fronts up this corner of the Esplanade, if that is not too smart a descriptive word for the Skala waterfront.

It is rather as if the squashed up port, set in dry hillsides and surprisingly undeveloped, was an afterthought, a dropping from the Chora's table that splashed on the pebble, shale beach. Perhaps the most eye-catching sight is the Italian constructed Municipal building (*Tmr* 7A/B2/3). On many islands similar edifices would be tarted up, perhaps even gleaming but not here. Everyone is too busy for that sort of bull – the despondent structure moulders and peels.

ARRIVAL BY AIR! One island map details an airport in the area of Maltezana. Enquiries are met by the advice that the man, his donkey and a wheelbarrow, once engaged in the construction work have been spasmodically replaced by a full construction team – when finances permit. Local opinion varies in respect of the year in which the facility will be complete. In the meantime, to maintain enthusiasm, an Olympic Airways agent has been appointed!

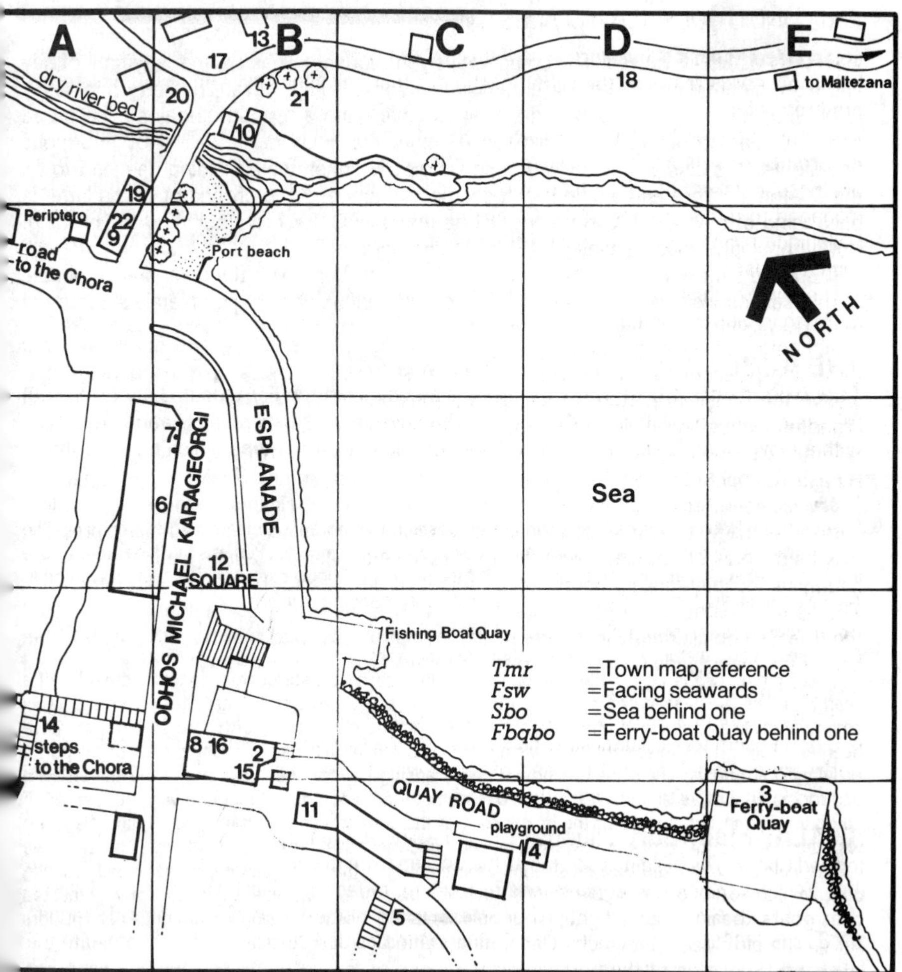

stration 41 Skala

1C5	The 'dead' Electricity Generating station
2B4/5	Hotel Paradissos
3E5	Ferry-boat Quay
4C/D5	Public toilets
5C5	H Monaxia Rooms & Restaurant
6A/B3	Hotel Astynea
7A/B2/3	Municipal Administrative Building/Police
8A/B4/5	Cafe-bar
9A2	Cafe-bar
10B1	Taverna To Akpoγiaγi
11B/C4/5	Baker
12B3/4	'Port Square'
13B1	General store/Grocers
14A4	Butcher
15B4/5	A Economou, Ferry-boat ticket office
16B4/5	OTE
17B1	Hotel/Restaurant Australia
18D1	Hotel Vangelis
19A/B1/2	Cafe/Taverna Albatross
20A/B1	Moped hire
21B1	Rooms
22A/B1/2	Gournas Tours

ARRIVAL BY FERRY The comparatively infrequent ferries are met any time of day and night by hotel and room owners, including some from Livadia. The Ferry-boat Quay (*Tmr* 3E5) has been enlarged and travellers have quite a few strides along the broad concrete road to get to the Esplanade At night the quayside is well lit by enormous floodlights. It is also endowed with a smart, newly constructed building destined to be the Customs offices and a cafe-bar. It seems that any budding proprietor of the latter is only being offered a short lease but will be responsible for fully equipping the building. Not surprisingly, a lessee was, in 1988,proving hard to find.

There are sufficient hotels, pensions and rooms to cope with the comparative dribble of mid-season visitors. Even the height-of-season 'influx' fails to completely swamp the available facilities and there are always rooms of some sort in the Chora.

THE ACCOMMODATION & EATING OUT

The Accommodation The walk along the quay from the Ferry-boat Quay (*Tmr* 3E5) passes the public toilets (*Tmr* 4C/D5) and the now defunct Generating Station (*Tmr* 1C5) with a playground to the fore. Beyond the latter is a flight of steps which climb to the:-

H Monaxia (*Tmr* 5C5) Tel 61290
Directions: As above.

Advertises 'Rooms to Rent & Restaurant'. Its position,next to the old generating station,is not the most attractive and the whole establishment looks somewhat rundown. Perhaps this area will improve when the gutted skeleton is rebuilt as offices for the electricity supply company. In common with other Astipalaia establishments, *Monaxia* does not open very early in the year.

Hotel Paradissos (*Tmr* 2B4/5) (Class D) 24 Michael Karageorgi Tel 61224
Directions: Along the quayside and directly to the forefront.

A family run, 1930s style hotel. Although the public corridors, surrounds and lobby are a bit of a shambles, the position must be one of the finest on any Greek island where I have stayed (This comment excludes the upper end, purpose built holiday hotel centres). Furthermore the rooms have been excellently modernised and possess panoramic balconies allowing a splendid view of the port's activity. The renovation included a shower head hanging point and an extractor fan in the en suite bathrooms as well as lampshades for the bedrooms. Mark you, 'not all that is revamped glitters', if you grab my meaning. Some of the box frames of the comfortable spring mattress's have been left with sharp edges that bite into unwary sleepers... and the loose, brass button mattress holders 'rise up like soldiers with fixed bayonets' during the night. But this is nit-picking, unwarranted, carping criticisms, the cavils of a malcontent rather than the measured, objective, value-judgement expected of a level-headed observer! All rooms have en suite bathrooms with a single room priced at 1500drs & a double 1800drs, rising to 2000drs & 2300drs (1st June-31st Aug).

Hotel Astynea (*Tmr* 6A/B3) (Class D) 21 Michael Karageorgi Tel 61209
Directions: Further to the centre of the port.

Depending on the viewpoint of an onlooker this building has and still is either being renovated or demolished – its difficult to tell. Joking(!) apart the hotel is undergoing fundamental refurbishment with typical Greek thoroughness. Massive new concrete pillars, seemingly unattached to the rest of the building, are being inserted, but early in 1988 the work had once again been halted. It appears to have been in this state for a year or two.

Where the quay road joins Odhos Michael Karageorgi, a surfaced road starts on the steep, winding journey to the Chora. Prior to the first, sharp bend, there are three hotels, the:-

Viva Mare
Directions: As above.

Although there is a bias to apartments, double rooms are available at 2000drs per night.

Hotel Aegean (Class D) Tel 61236
Directions: As above and further up the road, on the left.

Pleasant, rooms with balconies overlooking the bay. All rooms have en suite bathrooms. A single room costs 1000drs & a room 1500drs, increasing to 1500drs & 2000drs (1st July-31st Aug). and the:-

Hotel de France
Directions: In the apex of the first bend of the steeply rising road. Such is the climb that the 1st storey

prior to the bend, becomes the ground floor, round the corner.

The rooms are very small cubes. As the owner is an expatriate baker from Marseilles, clients can have croissants for breakfast. The hotel also incorporates a smart looking bakery and patisserie as a further outlet for his Franco-Hellenic style of baking.

Hotel Australia (*Tmr* 17B1)

Directions: Along the port beach Esplanade, over the river-bed and on the left as the road rises and swings round the edge of the bay.

A second storey has been erected, which is actually ground level at the rear owing to the steepness of the surrounding hill. The hotel 'houses' eleven double rooms which face out on three sides of the building and have en suite bathrooms as well as balconies. The front bedrooms allow a superb view of the port and Chora. A room costs 1000drs, early season, including solar heated water and clean towels. Naturally rates rise during the summer but remain reasonable.

Hotel Vangelis (*Tmr* 18D1)

Directions: Further along the road to Maltezana, on the seaward side.

This new hotel is used by package tour operators, particularly the British company *Twelve Island Holidays*. It is in a superb location overlooking the whole of Skala and has its own steps down to the rocky shoreline.

There are ***Rooms*** to either side of the steps from the port to the Chora.

The Eating Out

Cafe-Bar (*Tmr* 9A2)

Directions: The first of a number of 'dead', 'half-dead' and alive cafe-bars 'hunched' side-by-side along the 'slipshod' Esplanade. A few chairs and tables are scattered about beneath the trees which edge the beach wall.

Cafe/Taverna Albatross (*Tmr* 19A/B1/2)

Directions: At the far end of the row.

Serves an interesting mezes.

Το Ακροψιαλι (*Tmr* 10B1)

Directions: Further along the Esplanade in the direction of Maltezana. Roughly where the tree cover ends, a small, oblique flight of steps angles down to the beach. At the far end, across a summer-dry river-bed, is the delightful, backshore edging taverna.

A very 'smiley' lady and her family run the business. Apart from the narrow verandah, tables and chairs are placed on the pebbly backshore. In addition to the standard menu there is a fresh and often out-of-the-ordinary 'meal of the day'. The food is excellently prepared, portions are generous and the prices are reasonable. Why eat anywhere else? A typical meal for two of dolmades (280drs), a rabbit stew (390drs), a Greek salad (180drs), one tzatziki (100drs), a plate of chips (70drs), a bottle of kortaki retsina (120drs) and bread cost 1150drs. An outstanding meal for two of a tzatziki, 2 enormous fish soups (large boiled fish with separate egg & lemon soup), 2 kalamares, 2 galabourikos, a litre of retsina and bread cost 1400drs. Other sample dishes include chicken and chips 270drs and fillet fish & chips 290drs. In addition to the nice china plates, cotton tablecloths grace the tables. If the cooking were not good enough, their charming, simple wish to please, combined with the *au natural* atmosphere, marks this as a truly memorable taverna. I hope readers will agree.

Amongst other establishments that stretch up the hill of the Maltezana road is the:-

Restaurant Australia (*Tmr* 17B1).

Directions As above.

An engaging, friendly lady and her quieter husband run this splendid taverna. It has to be admitted that the dining area inside is not particularly attractive, being large, modern and reminiscent of a canteen, but the terrace is a pleasant area, sheltered by a vine. An excellent dish of casseroled beef and potatoes (cooked in a pressure cooker! – 650drs for two), a Greek salad (150drs), half litre retsina (120drs) and bread (30drs for two), cost 950drs, again with nice china and tablecloths. The husband speaks good English (presumably picked up in Australia) with a heavy Greek accent.

Continuing up the hillside is a smart restaurant, popular with local Greek families, and the Disco Faros.

Back in the centre of the Skala, almost alongside the Generating Station are two perhaps three, 'eateries'. I understand these properties are only available on short, two to three year leases and thus change hands fairly often. 1988s offerings included the 'Satellite Walk', lit in the evening with blue and white fluorescent tubes. Another is the *Fish Restaurant/Cafe* Ορυαυακησ, followed by the *Restaurant Astipalea*, a rather lively establishment.

It is a shame that the once locally run, characterful Cafe-bar (*Tmr* 8A/B4/5), adjacent to the *Hotel Paradissos*, has been given a more modern, trendy face-lift and is run by an Athenian couple who only attend for the main season.

THE A TO Z OF USEFUL INFORMATION

AIRLINE OFFICE The Olympic Airways agency is run by a travel agent in the basement of the *Hotel Viva Mare*.

BANKS None. The *Hotel Paradissos* (*Tmr* 2B4/5) is the local agent for the Ionian Bank, and a shop in the ground floor of the *Hotel Aegean* acts for the National Bank. However, being agents entails using their own cash for the transactions and, not surprisingly, this frequently runs out. An easier and cheaper alternative for exchange facilities is the Post Office in the Chora.

BEACHES The port beach is adequate if rather small and scrubbly, consisting of shale and grey pebble. The locals careen their smaller fishing boats, which adds to the general mess. The sea is excellent for a swim even if the beach is not ideal for comfortable sunbathing. A refreshing sight is the number of Greek mothers and children who disport themselves, including the older, usually more ample ladies, who often bathe fully clothed, wearing a straw hat and when finished wrap a loose shift over everything.

The best beaches are generally inaccessible by land, although the hardy traveller may be able to reach Ormos Ag Ioannis on foot.

BICYCLE, SCOOTER & CAR HIRE Mopeds can be rented from Skala, the Chora and Livadia. The average cost for a one person machine is 1000drs a day. The Skala outfit (*Tmr* 20A/B1) is at the far, Maltezana end of the Esplanade where is a painted sign. This was erected by an enterprising Athenian who arrived on the island with eighteen clapped-out mopeds. It is rumoured that he is disenchanted with hirers abandoning defunct machines at far-flung corners of the island. It remains to be seen whether he continues with this 'nice little earner'.

BREAD SHOPS Excellent crusty loaves are available from the Baker (*Tmr* 11B/C4/5), close to the *Hotel Paradissos*. Also *See* **Hotel France, The Accommodation**.

BUSES Two, tiny, modern buses terminus on the Port Square (*Tmr* 12B3/4), above the sweep of the street on to the Ferry-boat Quay. The drivers are drafted in from Athens which causes operating problems if one or the other falls ill... thus the timetable can prove to be illusory.

Bus timetable A timetable is pinned up on the Square, but as a sighting shot the following may help.

Bus timetable
Skala Port to Livadi, via The Chora
Daily: 0900, 1015, 1130, 1230, 1320, 1500, 1730, 1815, 1915, 2015, 2115hrs.
One-way fare to Livadia 50drs.
Skala Port to Vai
Daily: 0930hrs.
This bus connects with the boat which travels at 1000hrs from Vai to Vathy.
Skala Port to Maltezana
Daily: 0930, 1100, 1200, 1340, 1530, 1745, 2145hrs.
One-way fare to Maltezana 100drs.

COMMERCIAL SHOPPING AREA None but there are just enough outlets to keep the wolf from the... On the other hand a certain amount of steep walking is necessary because 'complete shopping cover' is only available by including the Chora. There is a small but useful General store/Grocers (*Tmr* 13B1) on the far corner of the cove, a Butcher (*Tmr* 14A4), close to the outset of the Chora steps, and a periptero, close by the crossroads. The *Hotel Paradissos* has a dark, cavernous and cluttered single room store which advertises 'Free tax drinks'.

A closing note must be made in testament to the unknown salesperson who, once upon a time, descended on the unsuspecting shopkeepers and, no doubt with a very smooth line of patter, flogged them not only unquantified numbers of cans of flykiller, but umbrellas and innumerable Japanese porcelain figures. The flykiller, yes, but the umbrellas and ceramics...? It spoils a good story to come clean but there is a cogent reason for the number of incongruous items on display. Astipalaia is administratively one of the Dodecanese islands and is thus a Duty Free Area. This privilege was bestowed by Athens to mark the reunion of the Dodecanese with Greece in 1947. Items exempt include furs, alcohol, perfume, tobacco, leather, gold and pottery.

For other shops, *See* **The Chora**.

DISCO The Disco Faros, on the cliff-top road to Maltezana, has been in business for a few years.

FERRY-BOATS As has been pointed out the Cyclades connection is more frequent than the Dodecanese link.

Ferry-boat timetable (Mid-season)

Day	Departure time	Ferry-boat	Ports/Islands of Call
Tues	0545hrs	Olympia	Kalimnos,Kos,Nisiros,Simi,Rhodes.
	0600hrs	Kyklades	Rhodes.
Thurs	0600hrs	Olympia	Amorgos,Syros,Piraeus(M).
Sat	0545hrs	Olympia	Kalimnos,Kos,Rhodes.
Sun	0400hrs	Olympia	Amorgos,Naxos,Syros,Piraeus(M).

Please note these tables are detailed as a GUIDE ONLY. Due to the time taken to research the Cyclades, it is IMPOSSIBLE TO 'match' the timetables or even boats . So don't try cross pollinating...

It has to be pointed out that an overall air of uncertainty cloaks the ferry-boat movements in respect of Astipalaia – even more so then usual.

FERRY-BOAT TICKET OFFICES The only ticket issuer is **A Economou** (*Tmr* 15B4/5) in the *Paradissos* block. On the other hand **Gournas Tours** (*Tmr* 22A/B1/2), on the right (*Sbo*) of the bottom of the Chora road, is the best source of information in respect of the timetables!

MEDICAL CARE Oh, ho, ho. *See* **The Chora**.

NTOG No. Best to enquire of Louise at Gournas Tours (*Tmr* 22A/B1/2) (*See* **Travel Agents & Tour Offices, A To Z**).

OTE (*Tmr* 16B4/5) Oh, yes. Still an interesting 'little office' located in the ground floor of the *Hotel Paradissos*. It is run by a couple of engaging fellows who have distinct ideas of what should happen when duty and pleasure clash – duty goes out of the window. The office is faded and uncared for, although the 'lads' have encouraged some large pot plants to flourish. The opening hours are weekdays between 0730-1500hrs and Saturday & Sunday between 0900-1400hrs. There is a bench seat outside and prospective clients may well need it whilst waiting for the staff to return from their other activities.

The *Hotel Paradissos* has a metered telephone but it is rather public and a bit of a crush, being located in the store.

PLACES OF INTEREST *See* **The Chora**. Really the sub-heading might well have read 'Characters of Interest', but it is not surprising in this mildly frontier-town atmosphere that the place should support more than its fair share of 'personalities'.

There are a number of small offshore islets and island beaches which can be reached by trip boat or 'Sea-Taxi'. A couple of skippers run the boats from Skala harbour but the excursions are now rather more organised, through the offices of Gournas Tours (*Tmr* 22A/B1/2) (*See* **Travel Agents & Tour Offices, A To Z**). No more totally disparate characters than two of the trip boat captains can be imagined. Captain Roussos is a slight, one-eyed and one-handed Greek fisherman. The story goes that these injuries happened when Roussos, planning another dynamiting trip, decided to double his 'bait' by sawing one of his grenades in half...! Captain Pete, a Welshman, is a piratical but friendly expatriate with a rather wild, 'lived-in' appearance. Some say he has a problem with the 'inebriations'. His craft is recognizable by the stylised eyes painted on the bows. Rumour only rumour, has it that Pete drives the craft rather hard which may, or may not, have something to do with the occasional breakdown... Outside of the cartel, he also offers to ship a boat load of tourists anywhere they like for 3000drs a head, but apparently he has difficulty filling the space.

Whilst writing about characters, it is worth mentioning a Captain Nicolis from the Dodecanese. He drives a grey-hulled, sponge and sword-fish boat and is a frequent visitor to the island, in the season. Captain Nicolis sings and dances superbly and can often be found livening up proceedings in one of the Chora bars. Try Mikalis's or Artemis.

After the island fishermen have landed their mid-afternoon catch, they have a habit of spending the siesta spreadeagled on their nets, in the lee of the *Hotel Paradissos*.

POLICE The town police are located in the Municipal block (*Tmr* 7A/B2/3).

POST OFFICE *See* **The Chora**.

TAXIS A car or three slink on to the Port Square (*Tmr* 12B3/4). The Livadia fare costs 200drs and Maltezana 600drs.

TOILETS There is an absolutely 'mind-boggling', brightly white painted facility (*Tmr* 4C/D5) close by the Ferry-boat Quay. I write 'mind-boggling' for the two cubicles of this squatty are in such an indescribable condition that I hope the flies can't make it down to the waterfront tavernas!

TRAVEL AGENTS & TOUR OFFICES Apart from the ferry-boat ticket biased office of **A Economou** (*Tmr* 15B4/5), there is the excellent:-
Gournas Tours (*Tmr* 22A/B1/2)
Directions: At the outset of the Chora road.

I am reliably advised that Gournas in Greek indicates a donkey trough, which doesn't seem to have too much to do with the delights of a tour office. This agency is run by Louise Edeleanu, an English girl from Kent. She is a proverbial mine of information, having spent a number of summers on the island. Louise also runs the *Castro Bar* in the Chora. Although she does not issue tickets for the boats, she knows as much as anybody as to when they are running, since she is the local agent for *Twelve Islands* and has to meet their clients from the ferries. Otherwise her work consists of letting accommodation as well as organising fishing and beach boat excursions and outings. Daily boat trips to Ag Konstantinos Beach depart at 1030hrs and return at 1730hrs, for a cost of 300drs. On Tuesday, Thursday and Saturday a boat leaves for Vatses and Kaminiakia Beaches at 1030hrs, coming back at 1700hrs for 600drs. On Monday, Wednesday and Friday the boat heads off to Ag Kyriakis and Koutsomiti Beaches at 1100hrs, returning at 1700hrs for a price of 600drs. The office opens daily between 1000-1200hrs & 1900-2100hrs.

Louise advises that there would be considerably more accommodation available in the Chora but private rooms must be licensed by the authorities. As the inspecting officers are unwilling to come out from Athens, not much progress is made. It is not easy for accommodation to be let unofficially, as the jealous hotel owners 'tell tales' to the police, even when they are bursting at the seams. Sounds very familiar.

THE CHORA: capital (Illustration 42) A truly Cycladean Chora which is split into two, the 'Middle', or saddle level and the Upper Castle level.

The 'Middle' level encompasses the Town Hall and the 'Library' Square; a Post Office (*Tmr* 1A1), which transacts currency exchange, opens between 0730-1415hrs and is on the side of the road down to the Skala; a well-stocked, reasonably priced, 'self-service' Grocery store (*Tmr* 5A1), next door to the Post Office and owned by a cuddly Australian speaking Greek lady; further on is a Petrol station (*Tmr* 2B1), selling Sosco and open daily between 1000-1200hrs & 1700-1900hrs, closed Sundays but rather unpredictable; a large warehouse type Supermarket (*Tmr* 3B3/4), with above average prices, beside the Library; a Baker (*Tmr* 4B4), behind the aforementioned supermarket, down some steps from 'Library' Square; a *Taverna* (*Tmr* 8A3) and *Mikalis Bar* (*Tmr* 6C/D2), with a balcony, adjacent to the Skala steps. The Clinic is buried beneath the Town Hall (*Tmr* C/D3), on the lower square. The road towards Livadia is dominated by eight windmills in fairly good condition and one ruin. Beyond the last windmill, up on the right, is a Dentist.

The 'Upper' or Castle level is reached along either of two steep uphill streets. This area possesses a heavily restored Venetian Castle which is circled by a very pretty parade with an oleander planted walk on the far, Livadia side. There are masses of churches; higgledy-piggledly, Medieval private houses and innumerable, if discreet bars. These include *Artemis Cafe-bar* and the *Castle Bar*, the latter located in an alley beside a church, almost to the front of the Castle promontory. The strange thing is that the Chora has no tavernas, only kafeneions and bars, therefore to eat it is necessary to descend to the Skala. Perhaps this is the reason that the bars do not open before late evening and stay open until early morning. For instance the *Artemis*, which serves home-made ice-creams as well as drinks, opens between 1700hrs and 0200/0300hrs next morning.

The 13th century Castle has a church over the vaulted entrance and contains a mass of part covered alleys, old houses and Ag Georgios Church built on the site of an ancient temple. To one side of the port, to the east of the bluff stands the large Panaghia Portaitissa Church, founded in 1764.

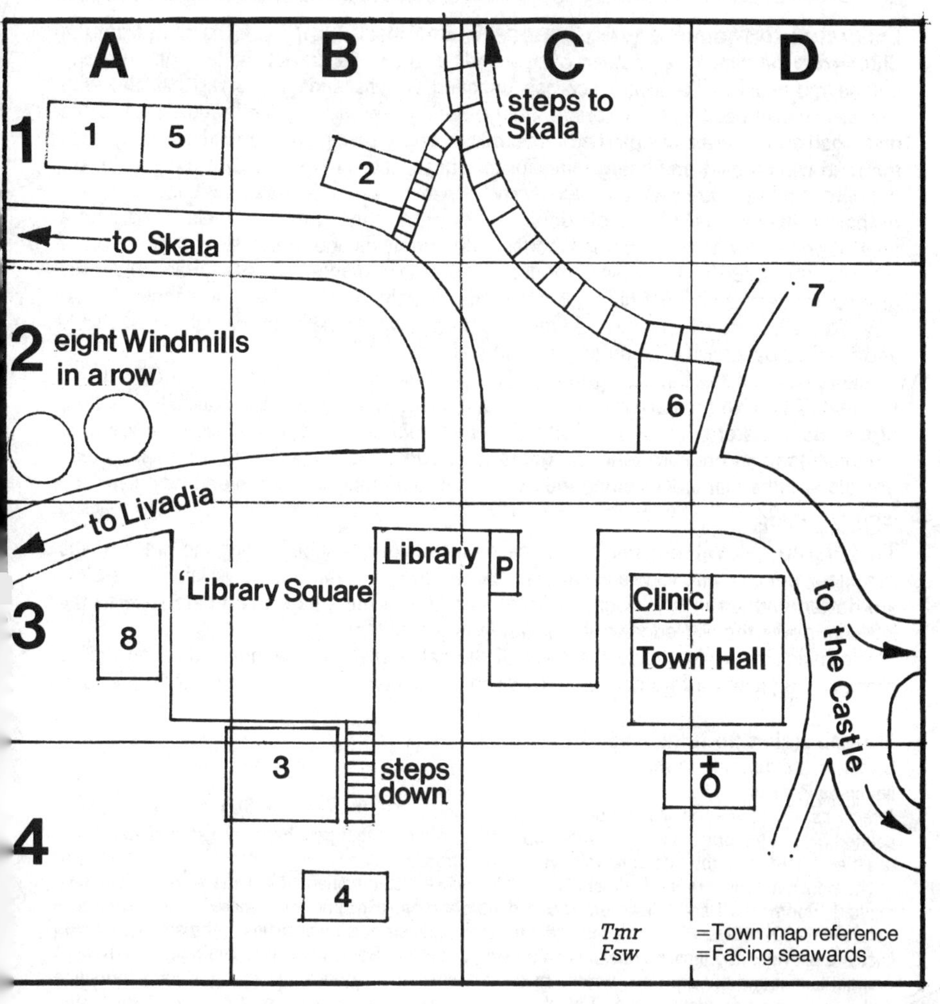

Illustration 42 The Chora

Tmr 1A1	Post Office	5A1	Self-service Grocery store
2B1	Petrol station	6C/D2	Mikalis Bar
3B3/4	Supermarket	7D1/2	Moped hire
4B4	Baker	8A3	Taverna

Excursion to Monastery Ag Ioannis & Beach (10km) Take the road from the Chora past the windmills. Instead of descending to Livadia, select the left road heading up the mountain. This soon becomes unpaved and ascends the steep hillside, with excellent views back to the Chora and over the 'narrow part' of the island. Keep to the main road and ignore any side roads. Eventually, after curving around the back of Livadia, the road climbs past an underground military base, the fences of which are visible. On the right is a helicopter pad, marked 'H' and a road to the left leads to the base. Continue on past a turning that angles off down to the right, staying on the 'main' road past a chapel, on the left. On the right is a house with two fields and trees below. At the top of the rise, the road divides. Select the left fork, usually marked by a large arrow on the ground made of pebbles. This track descends, shortly, to the locked Ag Ioannis Monastery. To the left, a slice of cultivated terraces drop towards the beach, which is just visible and reached by a path after a thirty minute walk.

The remains of the Kastro Ag Ioannis is not visible as it is up on the mountainside, to the right. There isn't a road or visible track and a local guide would be required. The story of the castle's storming, by the Turks, is that an old lady was left outside the walls by the inhabitants in order to tend the goats. The Turks found and 'persuaded her to tell'. She did and the marauders found their way in, slaughtering her and everybody else.

ROUTE ONE

To Livadia (2km) From the Chora the surfaced road wanders over the crest of the mountain, bringing into view a very green, cultivated valley, throughout which homesteads are dotted and set in dry mountainsides. Just before the crest, a concrete road to the left cuts down the cliff-edge to the nearside of the bay.

The main, bus road circles the back of the valley plain and wanders through walled groves of agriculture to junction with the main 'Highway' – an unmade, stony river-bed.

LIVADIA (2km from the Chora)

Close to the junction is the:-

Nicholas Pension

Directions: As above, on the left and can be recognised by the enclosing wall. The latter is high, painted blue at the bottom and white on top, with a blue and gold gate beneath a stone lintel. There is a blackboard mounted bus timetable on the wall opposite.

The pension, which is run by Nicholas and his wife, is unidentifiable by name because it is only marked 'Rooms To Rent'. Clean and basic double rooms, with spotless, shared bathrooms, cost between 1200-1600drs. Visitors can use the kitchen and sit outside at tables in the garden. Clothes lines are provided, so (unfortunately) is an outside television. Some balconies overlook an orchard of orange, lemon and banana trees which smell heavenly! The only drawback is the echoing footsteps and verberating bathroom doors. The showers are solar heated, so should be used early in the afternoon. The owners are super friendly and helpful which ensures this is an extremely pleasant pension at which to stay. If the rooms are full enquirers will be offered a mattress in the orchard for the first night! Depending on the ferries, there will always be vacant rooms within one or two days of a guest's arrival, even in the peak season.

The river-bed 'Highway' is also walled right up to the beach backshore which forms the tree-lined and shaded, grey, rough sand and pebble surfaced 'Esplanade'! There are expectations that this is to be concreted, in 1989.

On both sides of the 'Highway', prior to the 'Esplanade', are ***Rooms***. On the right-hand corner, where the 'Highway' joins the 'Esplanade', is the *Cafe/Restaurant Yesenea*. This pleasant taverna is run by a young family with two small boys, and is frequented by local Greek families. On the other side of the 'Esplanade' is a bus stop – but no timetable.

The messy beach is made up of light brown shale and pebbles. A number of small boats are anchored in the clear sea, close to the shore. The backshore is fringed by a continuous, narrow but comparatively thick stand of trees.

From the 'Highway' junction to the right (*Fsw*) along the 'Esplanade' are ***Rooms***, as well as a number of tavernas set in amongst the trees and squalor. A periptero-cum tiny store, with telephone, is located in the remains of a half-demolished public toilet block. There is a post-box fixed to one of the remaining walls. Just beyond the periptero is the *Taverna Thomas* where tasty food is served so fast that the waiters don't have a moment to stop and talk. A 'blow-out' lunch for one of a fish soup, stuffed tomatoes & peppers, a Greek salad, bread and a kortaki retsina cost 890drs. At the far end is the *Taverna Stefanida*, which has been extended by a second storey in order to house a disco. The owner, a young Australian with a Greek wife, arrived in Astipalaia two or three years ago, bringing with him large, colourful Aquabikes. These are available for hire, although their stability leaves a lot to be desired when the meltemi blows. In fact, their use was forbidden by the police until the proprietor obtained a rescue boat. Surf boards are also available.

To the left (*Fsw*) from the 'Highway' junction is similar to the right-hand side but more so. Beneath the trees are piles of rubble with goats, hens and other assorted domestic animals scratching and fighting it out. The extensive tree cover almost camouflages the concrete block houses and a taverna. The owner of the latter is a rather surly, roly-poly but he serves the very nice 'Gasosa' island lemonade.

It appears that many Chora residents shut shop for the summer months and migrate to Livadia, opening up other little shops. In general a double room is cheaper here than in Skala, averaging 1500drs mid-season.

The track south of Livadia passes along the hillside above a series of beaches, the first of which has a cafe-bar and one small block of ***Rooms***.

A footpath from Livadia also leads to the beaches Tzanaki and Moura. The track ends at Ag Konstantinos, a grey sand beach similar to but smaller than that at Livadia. One advantage is that there are less people. However trip boats compensate, daily! Nude bathing and 'wild' camping is the order of the day. A road to the right, just before Ag Konstantinos, leads into the brown hillsides to... nowhere, so ignore all maps which indicate otherwise!

ROUTE TWO

To Maltezana (9km) & beyond This is a two hour walk, over arid, shelterless countryside for those not prepared to wait for the bus, pay the taxi fare or hire a moped. The road, which is surfaced all the way to Maltezana (or Analipsi), climbs the east side of the Skala cove. Just beyond the 'city limits', as the road curves round the headland, a new petrol station is under construction. The town dump soon appears on the seaward side, and just beside it a new, large house. There appears to be quite a bit of construction work underway and it is pleasant to be able to report that these are not new hotels but private houses. The dowry system is still going strong in Astipalaia, and fathers vie with each other to see who can provide the most splendid house for their respective daughters.

After 1km, the road descends to the first of a series of bays. This is marked 'Marmari B' on the maps – if a reader is lucky enough to acquire one. This reminds me to point out that there are two maps. The one with square photos is quite good. The other with two circular photos on a bright blue background should be avoided as it marks wide thoroughfares where only tracks exist and tracks which are non existent. The local responsible has the trite answer that "It doesn't matter very much – there's really only one road on the island and they won't get lost"! Returning to the narrative, the peace of pleasant 'Marmari B' bay, with colourful fishing boats moored in the near corner, is shattered by the constant throb of the new Generating station which has replaced the one at the port. This unit is now fully operational, despite the generators going missing and the engineers taking as long as possible over the job because they and their families so enjoyed their stay on Astipalaia.

The next bay is marked 'Marmari C' with the almost obligatory indication of a cluster of dwellings. Actuality is one solitary farmhouse, situated on a rise to the left of the road, at the near end of the bay. The steeply shelving, narrow 'beach' is made up of big pebbles and both sides of the road are lined with small trees. On the left, and hidden behind thick screens of bamboo, is the rustic:-

Campsite Anatoli

Directions: Signposted from both the Chora and Skala, from which it is some 2km in distance.

The site is pleasantly shaded by bamboos and has a cafe which serves inexpensive meals. The per person charge is 350drs and a tent costs 100drs per night.

Further round the curve of the bay the beach becomes a broad swathe of pebble with the sea bottom mainly composed of shelving 'biscuit rock'.

Detour to Ag Andreas

A road to the left is marked by a wooden sign on which yellow paint indicates the *Taverna Ag Andreas*. A translation of the message reads 'Alone in the wilderness' which is rather too apt a description... The track leads around the wild bay, past a noisy, unsightly and dusty gravel mine to end at the shack-like taverna, beside a small jetty. The owner tries hard to persuade visitors to eat seafood. He also informs callers that there are plans to extend the jetty, build a harbour, develop the area, and so on... a severe case of wishful thinking. He also claims the taverna will be open summer and winter alike but this is his first year and if it lasts another year, it will be surprising. There are rumours of caique connections to Vathy but little sign of them. Apparently the ferries dock here when the weather is very rough, preventing them from docking at Skala port. 'Rumours' of a road to Ag Andreas, from the Chora, reveal scant evidence of a goat path...

Returning to the main route, the road climbs over the headland and drops slowly down to an almost identical, but more open and treeless, bay. At the near end there are some interesting, low-level cave dwellings and ruins of more recent habitation. The road continues, further back from the sea than at the previous bay as the shingly beach is broader. On the left the land is under cultivation and a few villas are being built. Fields hereabouts are still tilled with a wooden plough drawn by a horse or donkey, or both yoked together.

Beyond the bay the road snakes up over the hillside and skirts the northern shore with splendid views of the offshore islands, before dropping down to the narrowest neck of land. This is described on the map as Stavros (Greek for cross). This could apply either to the cross formed by the strip of land and the sea inlets on either side, or to the tiny chapel by the roadside at this point. It must be a bleak place in winter as a small waiting room has been added to the chapel entrance in memory of one of the congregation. The passage here from one 'butterfly wing' of the island to the other is guarded by a ferocious dog, fortunately securely chained to his packing case kennel. The neck of land is so narrow, it gives the impression that one could touch the sea on both sides.

Beyond Stavros, the road skirts a series of coves which make up Ormos Steno. The middle cove is clean with some kelp, a sandy sea-bed, a fairly broad beach and pleasantly tree planted backshore, set in which are a couple of water wells. The other beaches have narrow shore lines and all are tar polluted.

From the hillside at the far side of this bay are lovely views and, in a 180 degree sweep, a walker can take in the north-western headlands, the Chora spiralling up its castle topped hillside, past the southern inshore islands, resembling basking whales, and on to the airport under construction. This last looks as though it is making progress, jutting out horizontally from the hillside and culminating in a vast embankment just short of the sea.

Just beyond and completely overshadowed by this structure is:-

MALTEZANA (9km from Skala) Both young and old villagers are very smiley and friendly but any traveller who expects a substantial development will be disappointed. Upper Maltezana smacks of a Mexican adobe village and is an untidy sprawl but most of the settlement is set in a verdant oasis which supports a widespread farming community. The approach is along a concrete surfaced, bamboo lined road which curves round to the waterfront of the bay.

Taverna & Rooms Obelisk

Directions: Prior to the sharp bend of the final downhill run to the quay and on the left.

A modern, smart taverna (but don't be put off). To the rear are nicely appointed, clean, if flashy chalet twin rooms which cost 2500drs for a night. The owner Panayiotis now promotes these 'For newlyweds'! Mmhh. I'm not sure Maltezana is a honeymoon resort, but there you go. Incidentally the name 'Obelisk' was selected after the companion of the comic strip Asterix... Panayiotis, once an engineer, is welcoming, friendly and a mine of information, and the food served is good.

Why not ask Panayiotis for directions to the 'Chapel Mosaics', some ten minutes walk into the countryside. No, then I will direct. Back along the road towards Skala, by Remezzo Bar, is a straight track which makes off inland towards an off-white, chapel-like building, set in an enclosure of prickly pears. Keep to the left and head over the rise in the ground towards a startlingly white chapel. Proceed through a rustic gate, across a cacti-littered gorge, past a stone walled enclosure, to the right of a large bread oven, past the face of a dwelling to the low stone wall of the chapel, on the left. Lo and behold, one's own archaeological discovery. There, to the nearside of a small agricultural building and forming a backyard, are mosaics and column bases with the columns lying on the ground, as are the capitals. All this and no guided tour or museum fee. Oh Greece of yester-year.

For the antithesis to *Taverna Obelisk*, it is only necessary to stop off at the small, thoroughly rustic kafeneion around the bend in the road. It is on the right, immediately prior to the municipal looking buildings, alongside which the bus pulls up. The kafeneion has the date 1956 set in the wall but the old, jolly lady and her nearly blind husband look as if they have been here a century or two. Outside, in a narrow alley, is a vine shaded bench seat backed by green painted, beaten out olive oil drums. A few metres further down the street is the *Taverna Seihelles* which serves a slow and comparatively expensive Greek breakfast, of honey, yoghurt and coffee, for about 190drs.

At the bottom of the street is an inordinately large quay set in a smallish, tree edged bay. There is the semblance of a narrow beach to the left (*Fsw*) and a stony, weedy sea-bed. The clearly visible sea bottom is not only weedy but is littered with bits and bobs and home to a lot of sea urchins. A sunken city is supposed to lurk in the Harbour area. Be that as it may, I would not chance the sea urchins.

The track to the left circles round the horn of the bay, past a small toilet block, set in the trees, towards the headland bluff, whereon is the occasional dwelling close by the water's edge. Incidentally the toilets, new some three or four years ago, have gone to rack and... They register very high on the Richter scale and now require dynamiting.

Over the headland the track becomes a pedestrian way to another scrubbly cove with a grey, stony beach.

Excursion to Exo Vathy To get to Vathy it is possible to risk the very rough road/track which is just passable by moped, though the final section is more a footpath than a track. A much better idea is to take the twice daily caique from Vai, just beyond Maltezana. The boat leaves Vai at 1000hrs and returns at 1750hrs (after which it returns to Vathy). It is only a twenty minute trip (400drs return, 200drs for children).

Exo Vathy Here is the *Taverna Galine*, run by a family from Rhodes, whose parents/grandparents live at Vathy all year round. The taverna serves lunchtime meals to visitors. For example 2 octopus, feta cheese, a Greek salad, 3 beers, a bottle of water and bread cost 1170drs. A sign outside reads 'Pleas maked servations at the Tavern

Galine before meal times' (*sic*). The taverna has ***Rooms*** and the star of the place is friendly Dina, a 13 year old who serves as waitress, translator and a source of information.

Unfortunately because of the fjord-like inlet of Limin Vathio, the water is not so crystal clear as might be hoped. There is a scrubbly, sandy beach at the bottom of the bay, with an *ad hoc* shelter providing the only shade. The scene is topped by a sparkling white chapel. Fishermen from the nearby islands, including Kalimnos, while away the day here. Exo Vathy has a generator serving the taverna and rooms, but not the other, numerous scattered homesteads, which are surprisingly well looked after and obviously lived in.

There is no sign of the road marked on the map between Exo and Mesa Vathy. Presumably it served the now abandoned gravel mine in between the two villages. A rough goat track leads back to Mesa Vathy but there aren't any rooms or even a taverna.

Episkopi Church, Sikinos. *Acknowledgement to David & Liz Drummond-Tyler.*

Potamos Church, Amorgos. *Acknowledgement to David & Liz Drummond-Tyler.*

A view from Potamos, Amorgos. *Acknowledgement to David & Liz Drummond-Tyler.*

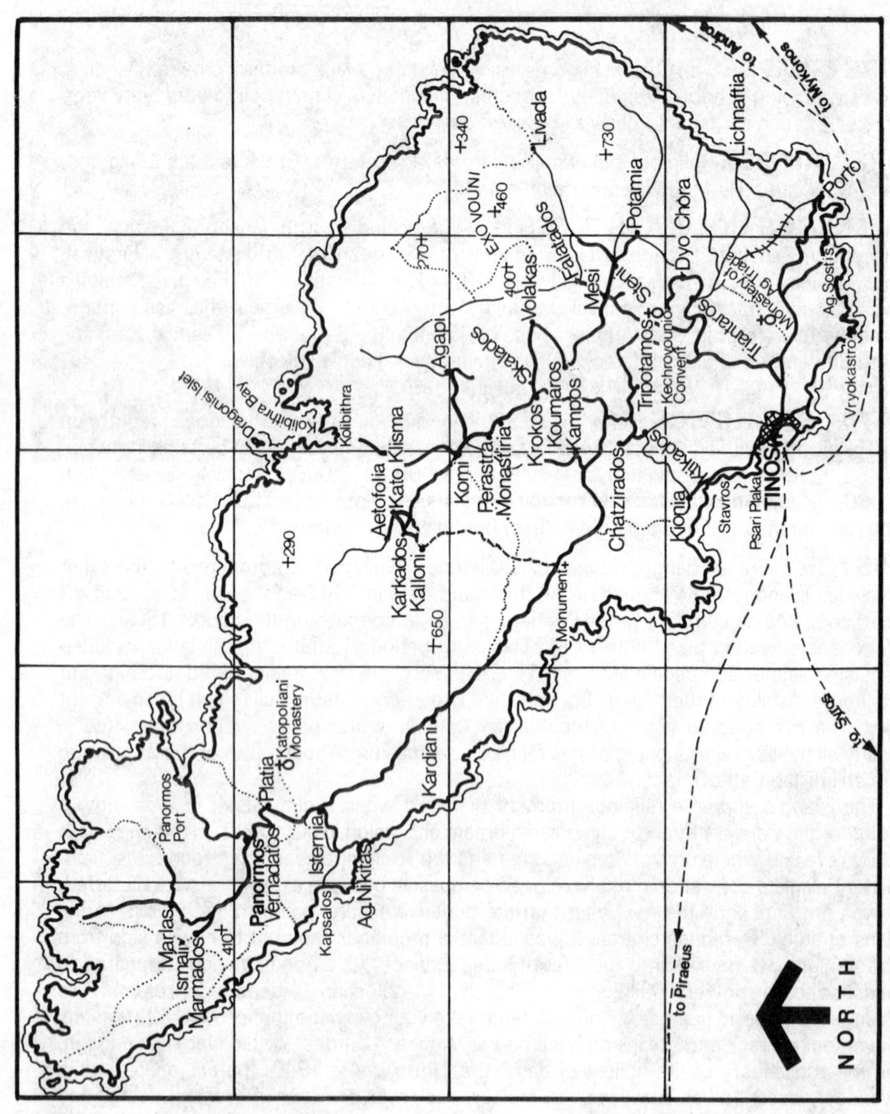

Illustration 43 Tinos island

15 TINOS (Tenos) ★★★★
Cyclades Islands - Eastern wing

FIRST IMPRESSIONS Pilgrims; sick children; black-clothed crones; candles; *exvotos*; driving schools; Venetian dovecotes; (distinctive) church bell towers; very large donkeys; green rocks; wild passion flowers; ouzeries.

SPECIALITIES Religion; loukoumades; frontalia omelettes; Greek tourists & pilgrims; red, American style fire hydrants; green marble.

RELIGIOUS HOLIDAYS & FESTIVALS include:- 30th January – Festival, the Discovery, Panaghia Evangelistria (or Church of Megalochari); 25th March* – Festival, the Annunciation, Panaghia Evangelistria; 23rd July – Festival, Ag Pelegia, Panaghia Evangelistria; 26th July – Festival, Isternia; 15th August* – Festival the Assumption, Panaghia Evangelistria; 31st August – Festival, Isternia; 8th September – Festival, Kardiani; 14th September – Festival, Isternia; 11th November – Festival, Kardiani.

* *The most important 'holy' days around which it is simply not worth travelling to or from the island.*

VITAL STATISTICS Tel prefix 0283. The island is 34½km in (diagonal) length, up to 15km wide, with an area of 194sq km and, some say, 64 villages but certainly between 40-50. Estimates of population vary between 9,000 & 12,000, of which some 3,000-4,000 live in the capital. Another rumour suggests there are up to 750 chapels, churches and monasteries and as many dovecotes, but I have not counted.

HISTORY For a change, an individual historical background compared to the other Cyclades islands. The Venetians took the island over in 1207 and managed to beat off the Turks, not succumbing to their general sweep of conquest in the middle 1500s. The Venetians stayed in place until 1714. This extra period of stubborn resistance included repulsing nine or so specific assaults. The defenders' ability to resist owed not a little to the impregnability of the now all but vanished Exobourgo Castle, built close by an ancient city. The five hundred years occupation by Catholic worshipping overlords resulted in nearly all the inhabitants being of this religious persuasion. About a fifth of the population are still of the Catholic faith.

The island's supreme religious moment occurred when a nun, Sister Pelagia, now a Saint, of the Convent Kechrovounio had a dream and vision in July 1822. In this the Virgin Mary revealed where an icon depicting her and the Archangel was to be found, in a field. Sister Pelagia's conviction must have been persuasive because excavations soon started. It was not until early the next year that the buried 'treasure' came to light, close to the ruins of an old Byzantine church. It was indeed a propitious moment to have a sign from the Almighty, two years into the War of Independence. As a bonus the icon appeared to possess healing powers. Building of the Church of Megalochari (Blessed Virgin) or Panaghia Evangelistria (Good tidings or Annunciation), take your pick, commenced in 1832. Things never looked back and the island became the 'Aegean Lourdes'. If this were not enough, on the anniversary of the holiest of days, the 15th August 1940, the *Elli*, a Greek ship (variously described as a cruise liner, cruiser, destroyer or warship) dressed overall and preparing to join in the religious celebrations, was torpedoed. Although never conclusively established, it was assumed that this dastardly attack was made on the instructions of the 'fascist swine Mussolini and his murderous blackshirted thugs'. And this was prior to War being declared between the two countries. Golly, gosh, the bounder! To the Greek a Hellenic Pearl Harbour with religious overtones, if you see what I mean!

After the theatrical... the island was famous for its stone masons and islanders Giannoulis Halapas, N Gyzis and N Lytras achieved artistic renown.

GENERAL In general, guides tend to refer to the Holy status of the island and the consequential quiet, dignified, religious milieu that presents itself to a visitor. Holy Tinos island may be, but quiet and dignified, no.

Tinos, the main town and port, is an appealing mix of old and new. The forty or so villages of the hard-working agricultural communities are attractively spread out amongst the neat, country hillsides. There are a number of extremely inviting beaches and sufficient spots in which to hide away, as the urban Greek is not a great explorer. This accounts for the almost deserted nature of one or two seaside beauty spots, even in high season.

Most of the islanders are friendly which, combined with their pleasant surroundings, should ensure they remain carefree, 'happy-go-lucky' and generally satisfied with their lot. Outwardly they are but this mien cloaks a psychotic discontent, an almost paranoic distrust of their near neighbours, Mykonos. For instance, the Delos/Mykonos link and the thought of all those tourists going 'astray' really gets beneath the average Tiniots skin. One story relates that the Mykonos pelican was kidnapped by the islanders of Tinos. The resultant furore became so serious that it is supposed to have reached Prime Minister level. After the wretched bird was returned, so as not to be outdone, the Town obtained its own resident pelican. This is to be found in and about on the waterfront restaurants. The hostility stretches back for years though and Tiniots woefully repeat the one hundred year old folklore story regarding their devious neighbours stealing copious quantities of beach sand, yes one hundred years ago.

The obsessive religious beliefs of the older islanders have had interesting social consequences in respect of tourists. Certainly, until comparatively recent years, negroes were considered by elderly ladies to be children of the devil.

This most agreeable island is a cross between Patmos in the Dodecanese and Paros, its close Cycladean cousin. The countryside has just the right mixture of soft mountains, verdant plains with golden green, fields of hay and rivers of olive trees. Churches and chapels vie with Venetian Gothic dovecotes for the available space. These undoubted attributes should make it a prime target for both package and backpacking holiday-makers. Fortunately, to date, the island has remained outside the main stream of the overseas summer onrush. The island is 'invaded' but the majority of the tourists are Greek and, apart from the height-of-the-season months, most resorts remain nigh on empty.

TINOS: capital & main port (Illustration 44) A bustling, busy town which greets the disembarking traveller with a Grecian bazaar, strident and swarming even on Sundays. 'Even' is a misnomer as the town is more active on Saturday and Sundays than the weekdays, due to the high percentage of Greeks who spend weekends on the island. This is so much so that it is best to arrive at any other time than a Friday, depart any other day than Sunday and avoid weekends, if at all possible.

ARRIVAL BY FERRY The mainland port for Tinos is Rafina (*See* **Chapter Two**) from whence daily inter-island connections are made by, for instance, the **FB Eptanissos**, which also calls at Andros, Mykonos and Syros. In the popular summer months, a daily ferry-boat also operates out of Piraeus. The boats conveniently dock (*Tmr* 1B/C3) almost at the bottom of the High St, Leoforos Megalocharis, which ascends arrow-like to Panaghia Evangelistria Church.

THE ACCOMMODATION & EATING OUT

The Accommodation Though plentiful, accommodation tends to be expensive due, in the main, to the all-year round numbers of Greek pilgrims, tourists and sick searching for a cure. This influx is in addition to holiday-making Athenians who traditionally visit those Cyclades islands nearest to the mainland. Others include Andros, Kea and Kithnos.

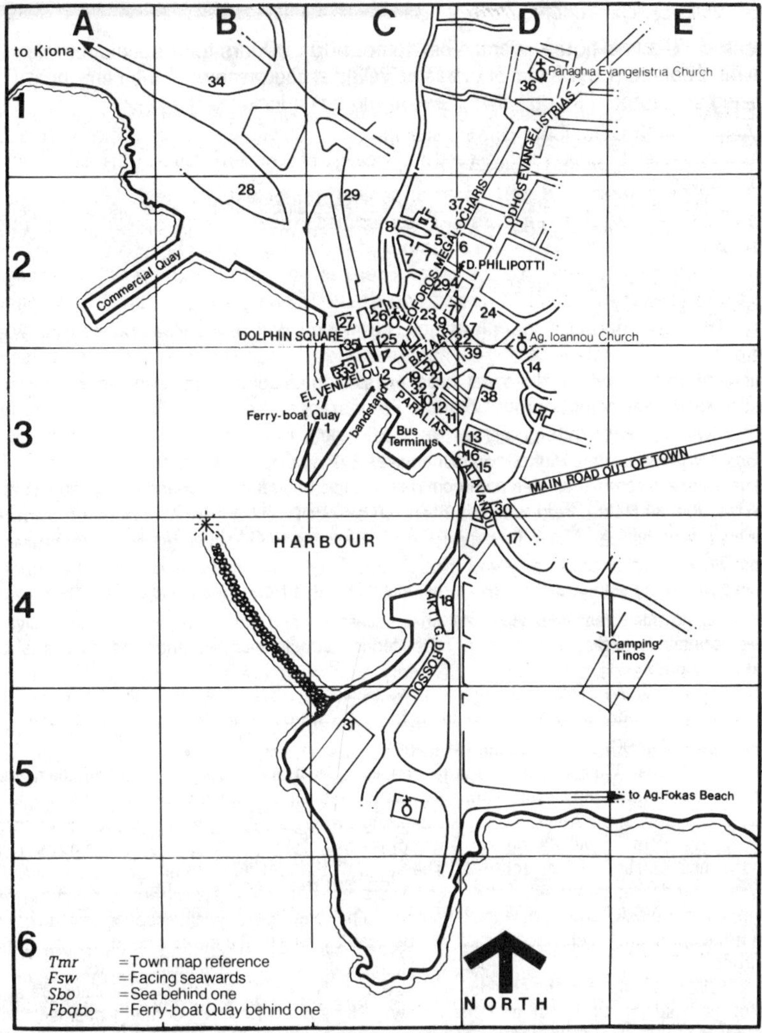

Illustration 44 Tinos Town

Tmr	
1B/C3	Ferry-boat Quay
2C3	Bandstand
3B/C2/3	Hotel Aegli
4C/D2	Hotel Meltemi
5C/D2	Hotel Theoxenia
6C/D2	OTE/Post Office
7	Rooms
8C2	Fountain
9C/D2/3	Rooms Stratis
10C3	Hotel Poseidonion/Pizza Spagetti(sic)
11C/D3	Hotel Delfinia
12C/D3	Bus office
13C/D3	Bakers/Rooms
14D2/3	Hotel Eleana
15C/D3	Hotel Avra
16C/D3	Port police
17D3/4	Hotel Tinion
18C/D4	Rooms O Giannis
19C3	Souvlaki Pita
20C2/3	Taverna To Koytoyki
21C/D2/3	Taverna Michalis
22C/D2/3	Cake shop
23C2	Restaurant To Xinari
24D2	Taverna Good Heart
25C2/3	Greengrocer/Fruit shops
26C2/3	Taverna Dionisos
27C2/3	Baker
28B1/2	Childrens' playground
29C/D2	Town Hall/Municipal Tourist office
30D3/4	Estiatopion O Zefiros
31C5	Taverna Vintsi
32C3	Commercial Bank
33C3	National Bank
34B1	Moto Mike
35C2/3	Market
36D1	Panaghia Evangelistra Church
37C/D1/2	Museum
38D3	Galerie Cybele
39C/D2/3	Town police

Mid-season, 'C' class hotels average between 2500-3000drs for a double room.

Radiating out from the Band Stand (*Tmr* 2C3), at the bottom of the Ferry-boat Quay and facing up Leoforos Megalocharis, accommodation includes the:-

Hotel Aegli (*Tmr* 3B/C2/3) (Class D) 7 El Venizelou Tel 22240
Directions: To the left (*Fbqbo*) in amongst and over a gaggle of taverna/restaurants that line this stretch of the Esplanade.

Well, I intimated accommodation was expensive. Here a single room & a double room, sharing a bathroom, cost, respectively, 2500drs & 3000drs, whilst rooms with en suite bathrooms cost 3400 & 3990drs.

Climbing the High St gives access to the:-

Hotel Meltemi (*Tmr* 4C/D2) (Class C) 7 D Philippoti/Leoforos Megalocharis Tel 22881
Directions: Bordering the side-street to the right, prior to the OTE/Post Office (*Tmr* 6C/D2), and on the right.

A modern hotel, in which all rooms have en suite bathrooms, with single rooms priced at 1750/2050drs & double rooms 2350/2760drs.

Hotel Theoxenia (*Tmr* 5C/D2) (Class B) 2 Leoforos Megalocharis Tel 22274
Directions: On the left of the High St, opposite the OTE/Post Office building.

Modern. A single room, sharing a bathroom, is priced at 1180drs, a double room sharing 1925drs & a double room en suite 2390drs, which rates increase, respectively, to 1280drs & 2000/2700drs (16th March-30th June & 16th-30th Sept) and 1500drs & 2400/3500drs (1st July-15th Sept).

Rooms (*Tmr* 7C2)
Directions: Down the side-street alongside the nearside of the *Hotel Theoxenia* and on the left.

Continuing along this street advances to a small square, in the Old Quarter, with an impressive but waterless fountain (*Tmr* 8C2) dated 1797. To the left is a street which descends and 'crescents' back round to the High St.

From the Band Stand (*Tmr* 2C3), the narrow, ascending 'Bazaar Alley', Odhos Evangelistrias, 'struggles' through a maze of stalls, shops and cafe-bars towards Panaghia Evangelistria Church.

Rooms Stratis (*Tmr* 9C/D2/3) 37 Evangelistrias Tel 23166
Directions: Up 'Bazaar Alley', beyond the large fountain and in a narrow alley to the left, on the nearside of a Herb shop and opposite a bread shop. The steps to this first storey pension are on the right.

Stratis, the helpful, smooth-talking, English speaking owner, is a young man of supreme confidence in his own judgement as well as the excellence of his establishment. His judgement remains, to my knowledge, unsurpassed but the rooms...! The steps to the first floor decant onto a narrow, dirty balcony decorated by unkempt red, pink and white geraniums, the pots of which are filled with cigarette ends and bottle tops. A corridor runs the length of the building from a small reception area, peppered with information, and a tiny kitchen, which can be used by guests. To either side of the corridor are the bedrooms. The conversion of the old building was carried out at minimal cost. Not only are the bedroom walls paper-thin but the corridor acts as a sounding box. The bathroom facilities are at the far end of the building and do not let the side down. There is (still) no lock on the gentlemen's toilet and the bolt on the ladies' toilet/shower continues not to work. A notice declares 'For Any Troubles You Have Call Stratis' with a phone number. Some twenty to thirty minutes later he arrives and, to be fair, he could not be more friendly. The rooms are clean with a single from 1000drs & a double 1500drs.

Stratis also owns some modern chalet bungalows, close by *Camping Tinos*, in which room rates appear to be acceptably priced.

In the next lateral street up Odhos Evangelistrias from *Rooms Stratis* are **Rooms** (*Tmr* 7C2/3 & 7D2/3), to both left and right of the crossroads.

Hotel Poseidonion (*Tmr* 10C3) (Class C) 4 Paralias Tel 23123
Directions: Along the Esplanade to the right (*Sbo*) of the Ferry-boat Quay and above an expensive cafe-restaurant and the *Pizza Spagetti* (*sic*).

A single room with en suite bathroom costs 2200drs & a double room en suite 2700drs.

Hotel Delfinia (*Tmr* 11C/D3) (Class C) Paralia Tel 22289
Directions: Further south along the Esplanade, across the 'Bus ticket office' (*Tmr* 12C/D3) side lane, and there are a row of expensive cafe/restaurants. Above one of these is the hotel.

Considering the position, surprisingly not over-expensive. All rooms have en suite bathrooms with a single room en suite priced at 2000drs & a double room 2570drs, increasing to 2340drs & 3080drs (1st June-30th Sept).

Still proceeding along the Esplanade advances to an initially wide street on the left, by a Taxi rank. This street leads to the Church Ag Ioannou.
Rooms (*Tmr* 13C/D3).*Directions*: As above and over a Bakers on the right-hand side of the street.

Hotel Eleana (*Tmr* 14D2/3) (Class D) Ag Ioannou Tel 22561
Directions: Continue along the street to the pretty, little Ag Ioannou Church around which the road divides. Select the right-hand,church-hugging lane.

Very well commended, although on the expensive side. A single room, sharing a bathroom, costs 1750drs & with en suite bathroom 2000drs, whilst a double sharing costs 2490drs & en suite 2700drs.

Further on round the corner and to the right, along the lane of Odhos Anton Mochatoy, advances to an irregular square, bordered by two ***Rooms*** (*Tmr* 7D3).
Hotel Avra (*Tmr* 15C/D3) (Class C) Paralia Tel 22243
Directions: Back on the Esplanade, beyond the Port police office (*Tmr* 16C/D3) and opposite a smelly section of the waterfront where the benzinas are moored.

Has the appearance of an English country town hotel. A single room sharing a bathroom, costs 1550drs, a double room sharing 2035drs & a double with an en suite bathroom 3240drs.

Beyond the *Hotel Avra*, the next turning left is the main road east out of town, the Esplanade end of which is a Rent-A-Bike and car hire stretch. A street to the left divides round a small triangular island. Close by the corner are two separate ***Rooms***. About ½km further uphill along the main road and on the left, just before the last scooter hire firm, which is on the opposite side of the road, is:-
Rooms
Directions: As above, over a greengrocers shop and a very good supermarket, and distinguishable by the yellow shutters.

A double room en suite costs 1800drs in the high season.

Hotel Tinion (*Tmr* 17D3/4) (Class B) 1 C Alavanou Tel 22261
Directions: From the junction of the main road/Esplanade keep up the lane (that proceeds on to *Camping Tinos*) and on the left.

Single rooms sharing a bathroom cost 1775drs, a double room sharing costs 2215drs & an en suite double room 3545drs.

This lane continues on, widens and runs out in scrubbly, new development and waste ground.
Camping Tinos (*Tmr* D/E4/5) Tel 22344
Directions: On the right, behind a stand of trees.

This is an exceptionally good, well run site operated by an extremely nice, friendly middle-aged couple. They opened some six years ago and are rightfully very proud of this splendid place.

Facilities include a bar, cafe, small supermarket, kitchen & laundry rooms, spotless toilets & showers, postbox, 'clinic' (a room where anyone who is sick is 'rested' and the doctor called), international phones and moped hire. This 'herd' of now 2 year old mopeds cost around 1400drs a day each. The pitches are shaded and there are two shelters for 'sleeping bag' areas if it rains or is windy. Charges are between 300-400drs per person, 150drs for a tent, 250drs for hire of a tent and all within 100m of the beach. They also have bungalows with en suite double rooms costing from 1750drs, which must represent the very best value in town.

Rooms O Giannis (*Tmr* 18C/D4) Akti G Drossou
Directions: Almost round the corner from *Tinos Camping*, along the waterfront and at the far right-hand end of the Esplanade, here named Akti G Drossou.

Hotel Oceanis (Class C) 3 Akti G Drossou Tel 22452
Directions: Next door to *Rooms O Giannis*.

A single room with en suite bathrooms cost 2300drs & a double room 3200drs.

Also mentioned in dispatches are the: clean, friendly, smart Greek *Hotel Aphrodite* (Class C, tel 22456) 23 P Navarhou – once a *Thomson* hotel, but withdrawn due to complaints whilst the owner Maria was pregnant, where all bedrooms are complete with en suite bathrooms and single rooms are priced from 2760drs to 3175drs & double rooms between 3400drs-3910drs; the *Hotel Argo* (Class C, tel 22588) in Odhos Angali, excellent with good facilities where en suite single rooms cost 2600drs & double rooms 3220drs.

For further accommodation *See* **Beaches, A To Z**.

Camping *See* **The Accommodation**.

The Eating Out In the town, the continuous flow of Greeks keeps prices high and the establishments rather 'typecast'. Generally there are few low price snack-bars, some reasonable priced tavernas and a great many expensive cafe-bars and waterfront taverna/restaurants. Meal prices are pushed up by the various taxes being charged as an extra and wines tend to be expensive, more so as retsina is not always available – A fact which might delight some readers. As is often the case, the competition does not result in lower prices but much 'schlepping', shouting and 'encouragement', nowhere more so than in the area of the port where there is the widest choice of eating places. It is worth noting that a number of kafeneions off the waterfront only serve Greek coffee.

On, and to one side of Odhos Evangelistrias, are a number of widely differing establishments including:-

Souvlaki Pita Stall (*Tmr* 19C3).

Directions: Almost immediately on the right of the street, in the covered section of 'Bazaar Alley'.

A good value 'handful' cost 60drs.

The first side lane to the right off Odhos Evangelistrias is a narrow alley in which:-

Taverna To Koytoyki (*Tmr* 20C2/3)

Directions: As above and on the left.

A rather run-down, ramshackle, oddly festooned cafe-bar/taverna advertising 'OK Boy You Satisfied 100 Per-Ent' (*sic*). The contents of the pots and pans were 'thought provoking'. The character who runs the place dresses in white, sports a chef's hat and obviously once enjoyed a popular following but I cannot do more than make a mention.

and:-

Taverna Michalis (*Tmr* 21C/D2/3)

Directions: The establishments is a few metres further along the same lane and on the same side, with some tables lining the pavement.

Not particularly noticeable at first but to be recommended, if rather expensive. The young couple work hard. A dinner for two of moussaka, a Greek salad, 2 beers and bread cost 1240drs.

On the other side of the lane, back towards 'Bazaar Alley' and on the corner of a side lane, is a:-

Kafeneion

Directions: As above.

Super loukoumades and passable, if rather Greek tasting, Nes. Okay, not so passable but what the coffee lacks is more than compensated for by the price differentials with the waterfront chaps. Two black Nes, an ouzo and a plate of loukoumades (90drs) cost 236drs while on the Esplanade one Nes with milk and a yoghurt costs in excess of 280drs. The waterfront has one saving grace, the *Self Service Cafeteria*, for details of which read on.

Back on and two side-streets further up Odhos Evangelistrias, and on the right is the:-

Cake Shop (*Tmr* 22C/D2/3)

Directions: As above.

The lively owner not only stocks a range of drinks but tasty pies, cakes, ice-creams and bread.

Almost opposite the cake shop is a narrow lane (on which are *Stratis's Rooms*) which jinks on to a square edging the High St, Leoforos Megalocharis. On the left is:-

To Xinari (*Tmr* 23C2)

Directions: As above.

A pizza restaurant pleasantly located but the prices 'reflect' the linen tablecloths and Spanish style, high-backed chairs.

Back to Odhos Evangelistrias, climbing beyond the crossroads and the next turning right leads to:-

The Good Heart (*Tmr* 24D2)

Directions: As above and on the right.

'Cleanliness, Good Care'. A clean establishment, the interior of which is dominated by a rather out-of-place, snowcapped mountain scene. The owners are very pleasant. Perhaps prices are kept low by the inexpensive waiter service which includes the wife, aided and abetted by their three children. The youngest and most enthusiastic is a 4½ year old, blond, cherubic girl with curly hair. On the menus is a good value, house speciality – frontalia omelette. The 'filling' is mainly sausage and chips. A meal for two of 2 'frontalias', beans (the tastiest I've ever eaten), 2 beers and bread cost 1120drs.

Back on the Esplanade, at the outset of Leoforos Megalocharis and almost immediately on the right is a small triangular piece of pavement on which is:-

Kostas Cafe-bar Ouzerie

Directions: As above.

Specialises in octopus mezes which,naturally, accompany glasses of ouzo.

On the other side of Leoforos Megalocharis, an alley sallies forth (at the outset of which are two side-by-side Greengrocer/Fruit shops (*Tmr* 25C2/3), to open out on to an irregular shaped Church Square, an Old Quarter and a maze streets.

Dionisos Taverna (*Tmr* 26C2/3)

Directions: As above and edging the square, with tables and chairs attractively spread about.

Average fare at above average prices (there are lots of fishy things on the menu) with a 'pushy', 'allo, allo' waiter.

From the bottom of the Ferry-boat Quay (*Tmr* 1B/C3), the Esplanade to the left (*Sbo*), jinks round the end of a row of restaurant/tavernas. Once past the corner, on the right is 'Dolphin Plateia', a square dominated by the sculpture of a dolphin. The plateia is edged on two sides by tavernas, as is the alley that heads off towards the Bakers (*Tmr* 27C2/3). Further on, the Esplanade widens out and curves to the left, around the back of a large, childrens' playground (*Tmr* 28B1/2), the *Tinos Mariner Cafe-bar* and the Adonis Yacht Club – no, not quite the same as a British yacht club!. In front of this island site, a massive concrete way leads to an equally large expanse of commercial quay. Before the playground, across some public gardens, are a number of bars and tavernas surrounding a square, in the middle of which is a statue of an overweight eagle. The establishments include the Lapito cocktail bar and the expensive looking *Taverna Zyros*.

Along the Esplanade to the right (*Sbo*) from the Ferry-boat Quay is one establishment which may not be a 'jewel in the crown', but it is a good hedge against the almost outrageous cost of most of the other waterfront cafe-bar/restaurants. This is the *Pizza Spagetti* (*sic*) in the ground floor of the *Hotel Poseidonion* (*Tmr* 10C3). Further along the Esplanade, beyond the main road out of town and the *Camping Tinos* street, are two side-by-side restaurants/tavernas, one of which is the:-

Estiatopion O Zefiros (*Tmr* 30D3/4)

Directions: As above and next door to the *Coffee shop Euripidus*.

A little cheaper than the other, more central competitors but a similar style of service.

Before leaving the subject, at the far right-hand end (*Sbo*) of the Esplanade is the:-

Vintsi Taverna (*Tmr* 31C5)

Directions: As above.

More an up-market, northern working mans club style of building than a taverna. Advertises 'live' bouzouki music and only opens the doors late evening. Reputedly excellent value for a night- out.

THE A TO Z OF USEFUL INFORMATION

BANKS There are two banks which cash Eurocheques. The **The Commercial Bank** (*Tmr* 32C3) is alongside a flight of steps from the small, Esplanade 'Cathedral Steps' Square, which ascend to the Catholic Cathedral. The **National Bank** (*Tmr* 33C3) is let into the row of restaurant/tavernas to the left (*Sbo*) of the Ferry-boat Quay and offers pleasant and efficient service.

BEACHES The two rather unsatisfactory town beaches, are:-

Beach 1. West, or left (*Sbo*), and around the corner from the Commercial Quay (*Tmr* A/B2). A large, pebbly cove.

Beach 2. Ag Fokas beach which is south-east, or right (*Sbo*) along Akti G Drossou and up the slope to the left of a ruined church. After 100m or so, the road descends to the left of the headland and edges a narrow, tree-shaded, pebbly beach, with new buildings under construction on the backshore.

For those prepared to strike out, hire a taxi or in possession of transport, there is the option of:-

Beach 3. The last mentioned beach borders the sea all the way to a rocky outcrop, beyond which the surfaced road runs out alongside *Bill and Jim's Cafeteria*. (Oh dear!). The latter establishment doubles up as a disco at night. A little further along, at the outset of this beach, is the Disco Asteria. The backshore is much broader than Ag Fokas but less shaded, although there are small arethemusa trees scattered about. The very long stretch of beach extends all the way to the large headland of Vryokastro and there are many more people here than on the aforementioned beaches. This is hardly surprising as, despite being initially pebbly, the sea bottom is pleasantly sandy after a metre or so and about a third of the way along the shore widens and becomes sandy with a gently shelving sea-bed.

Half-way along is the:-
Golden Beach Hotel (C Class) Tel 22579
Directions: As above.

This has bedrooms and cabins to let. Very nice double rooms now cost 3300drs, rising to 4700drs in high season.

Alongside the *Golden Beach* is:-
Furnished Rooms To Let
Really self-contained cabins, complete with a fully equipped kitchen containing a cooker, sink and fridge. The breakfast bar divides off the 3 beds and there is an en suite bathroom with shower. The cost is 4000drs a day, reduced for a week's rent and with the goat thrown in as well! Quite a proposition for a family, in a splendid location.

From here on there is only about one person per 100m of beach which finally peters out on the nearside of the conical Vryokastro headland. A track progresses over the bluff to a very small, quiet cove with a kelpy beach and stony sea bottom. A number of nude bathers may be found discreetly lounging on the various, 'pocket handkerchief' sized bits of shore.

BICYCLE, SCOOTER & CAR HIRE 'Rental Alley' is on the main road east out of the town, with establishments on either side. The daily rate for a scooter averages 1500drs a day. Petrol is extra.

My favourite outfit, at the other (west) end of town, is:-
Moto Mike (*Tmr* 34B1) Tel 23304
Directions: Situated at the west end of the Esplanade, across a small triangular garden from the childrens' playground.

The owner, Costas, a cousin of Stratis, he of the Pension on Odhos Evangelistrias, is a very friendly, helpful young man who speaks excellent English. Due to Costas involvement with the Municipal Tourist office (*Tmr* 29C/D2), brother Mike is more than likely to be in attendance. He is also pleasant, if less self-assured. The scooters are in good condition and the office/repair shed opens at 0800hrs, closing mid-evening. Incidentally, mounted on the wall is a useful, town plan. The hire rates are 900drs for a single person moped and 1500drs for a 50cc Vespa.

BOOKSHOP Apart from a scattering of shops that keep a selection of tourist guides, foreign newspapers and magazines ranged in a semi-circle around the Esplanade bandstand (*Tmr* 2C3), there is a Bookshop half-way up Leoforos Megalocharis, on the left. *See 'Galerie Cybele'*, **Places of Interest, A To Z**, for details of second-hand books.

BREAD SHOPS A Baker (*Tmr* 27C2/3) is located on the far side of the building that edges the 'Dolphin Plateia'; about a third of the way up Odhos Evangelistrias is a Cake shop (*Tmr* 22C/D2/3) which sells bread; another Baker is located in the second side-street to the left of Leoforos Megalocharis, with a ***Rooms*** sign in the window, and there is a Baker (*Tmr* 13C/D3) on the right of the street to Ag Ioannou Church, with ***Rooms*** over the top.

BUSES The Bus terminus (*Tmr* C3) is on a rectangular extension jutting into the Harbour from the Esplanade. The ticket office (*Tmr* 12C/D3) is across the Esplanade from the terminus, in a short alley, the other side to the *Hotel Poseidonion*. The timetable is chalked on a board inside the office. Drivers are very pleasant and helpful.

Bus timetable (Mid-season)
Tinos Town to Panormos (Pyrgos) **via Kampos** (NW of island)
Daily: 0600, 1100, 1400hrs.
Return journey
Daily: 0700, 1200, 1515hrs.

Tinos Town to Steni (NNE of the town)
Daily: 0700, 1100, 1400, 1700hrs.
Return journey
Daily: 0750, 1145, 1430, 1730hrs.

Tinos Town to Kalloni (NW & middle of island)
Daily: 0630, 1400, 1600hrs.
Return journey
Daily: 0700, 1500, 1645hrs.

Tinos Town to Porto (SE coast)
Daily: 0800, 1600hrs.
Return journey
Daily: 0815, 1615hrs.

Tinos Town to Kiona (S coast, W of town) (from 15th June only)
Daily: 0900, 1000, 1100, 1200, 1300, 1400, 1600, 1700hrs.

COMMERCIAL SHOPPING AREA The religious overtones blanketing the town don't result in a Sunday shut-down. No way. If anything, the activity is more frenzied, with even the siesta swept to one side in order for the shopkeepers to take advantage of the weekenders prior to their exodus on the **CF Eptanissos**, late Sunday afternoon.

Odhos Evangelistrias ('Bazaar Alley') is a narrow pedestrian street jam-packed with stalls and shops selling souvenirs, meat, fruit and vegetables, cakes and drink, pictures and religious items including candles. In the first side lane to the right is a cigarette kiosk and in the second side-street, beyond the Souvlaki pita stall, there is a splendid fruit and vegetable shop.

A morning display of produce appears on the kerb edge of the 'Cathedral Steps' Plateia. There is a small Market building (*Tmr* 35C2/3) bordering 'Dolphin Square'. The whole of this square is taken up by traders in the early morning and to one side is a well organised Supermarket. There are others scattered about the town.

To one side of Leoforos Megalocharis are two Fruit and Vegetable shops (*Tmr* 25C2/3), side-by-side, at the outset to the first alley on the left. Lastly, but not least, there are two peripteros, one on the 'Cathedral Steps' Square, to the right of the Bandstand, and another to the front of *Kostas Cafe-Bar Ouzerie*, at the bottom of Leoforos Megalocharis.

DISCOS None in the inner town, but elsewhere the situation is as normal. To make up for the lack of discos there are a number of 'Cocktail Music Bars' on the periphery of the 'Old Quarter' (How Greek!). These include Georges Place, open until 0300hrs, and the Seagull Bar run by Anna, a large, blonde, Dutch girl who speaks five languages. *See* **Beach 3, A To Z**.

FERRY-BOATS The craft moor to the large quay (*Tmr* 1B/C3) from which the town conveniently radiates. The biggest influx occurs on Friday/Saturday with a mass departure on Sunday afternoon. The Rafina ferry-boats are extensively used by the Greeks.

Nowhere is the hardiness of the old, black-dressed Greek 'ladies' better exemplified than when boarding the **Eptanissos**. They rush the boat, sweeping everything before them. When I last travelled this route they actually swept me off my feet, all 16½ stone of me plus my heavily laden back-pack. An out-of-height-of-season disadvantage for inter-island travel is that Tinos, in common with Andros, is rather off the 'well-worn' Piraeus/Cyclades ferry-boat lanes. It is thus sometimes necessary to bus between the mainland ports of Rafina and Piraeus, via Athens.

Ferry-boat timetable (Mid-season)

Day	Departure time	Ferry-boat	Ports/Islands of Call
Daily	1100hrs	Eptanissos/ Bari Express	Gavrion(Andros), Rafina(M).
	1530hrs	Naias II/ Panagia Tinou	Piraeus(M).
	1550hrs	Panagia Tinou/ Naias II	Piraeus(M).
Daily (Exc Fri & Sun)	2000hrs	Eptanissos/ Bari Express	Mykonos.
Thurs	2000hrs	Kithnos	Syros.
Fri	2100hrs	Bari Express	Mykonos.
Sun	2300hrs	Eptanisso	Syros.

One-way fares: Tinos to Piraeus 1162drs; duration 4½hrs.
to Rafina 1115drs; " 4hrs.
to Mykonos " 1hr.

Please note these tables are detailed as a GUIDE ONLY. Due to the time taken to research the Cyclades, it is IMPOSSIBLE TO 'match' the timetables or even boats. So don't try cross pollinating...

FERRY-BOAT TICKET OFFICES Spread about the waterfront and thickest in the area of the Bandstand (*Tmr* 2C3).

HAIRDRESSERS Both gents and ladies.

LAUNDRY A dry-cleaners and laundry is alongside the *Taverna Dionisos* (*Tmr* 26C2/3). A second launderette is on the right (*Sbo*) at the outset of Leoforos Megalocharis.

MEDICAL CARE

Chemists & Pharmacies One close by the Commercial Bank (*Tmr* 32C3), on the Cathedral Steps Square, and another opposite the baker in the side street to the left of the High St.

Doctors & Dentists There are two doctors and one dentist housed in a large white building on Plateia Litra, opposite the *Restaurant To Xinari* (*Tmr* 23C2). The doctors' names are Kostas & Socrates Kardamitsis and the dentist is Elefetheros Kardamitsis. They must all be brothers!

MUNICIPAL TOURIST OFFICE This was inaugurated in 1986 and is located on the ground floor of the Town Hall (*Tmr* 29C/D2). The latter is a large, square, white building on the right of Leoforos Megalochoris, one block before the OTE. The office is run by Costas (he of the excellent English and Moto Mike!). They have room details, timetables and much other useful information.

NTOG *See* **Municipal Tourist Office, A To Z**.

OTE (*Tmr* 6C/D2) On the right and half-way up Leoforos Megalocharis. The office is open Mon-Sat between 0730-2200hrs and closed Sunday and holidays.

PETROL There are three stations, almost side-by-side about 1km east of town on the main road.

PLACES OF INTEREST

Cathedrals & Churches

The Panaghia Evangelistria (*Tmr* 36D1). This church dominates and overshadows the town, sitting on top of the hill which is approached up the quite steeply climbing Leoforos Megalocharis. The preliminaries have been briefly outlined (*See* **History**). Once through the principal wrought iron gates, the main body of the church is reached across a colourful, pebble mosaic courtyard and up a majestic flight of marble steps. The dark interior is festooned with icons, masses of suspended lamps, candlestick and hanging exvotos, some of which depict the miraculous reason for their being donated. An outstanding example is the trading ship modelled in silver with a fish attached to the hull. This was given in thanksgiving by the captain of a boat which was holed beneath the waterline and foundering in a storm. The ship and crew were saved by a large fish getting stuck in the breach. The miraculous icon is mounted inside and on the left. Continuous streams of pilgrims place candles in a battery of candle-sticks. After only a few minutes these are snatched away to be reduced in an incinerator. I hope the pious communicants are not aware of this apparently callous commercial disregard for their act of worship and or contrition. Beneath the main church is a chapel in which is the excavated hole where the icon was originally found as well as the fountain which started up soon after the discovery. Close by the chapel, in an aisle, is a ritualistic pile of stones on which the icon was supposed to have been found and now covered with candles. Also in this area is the 'Elli Mausoleum' containing a portion of the torpedo that sank the ship, in 1940.

Other buildings include a Museum dedicated to island artists and hung with their pictures and displaying various sculptures, a Byzantine Museum exhibiting mainly 18th and 19th century icons and a picture gallery.

Day-Trips Local trip-boats ply daily to the islands of Delos and Mykonos, leaving the harbour at 0900hrs, spending 2½hrs on Delos and 5hrs on Mykonos, to return at 1800hrs for a cost of 1500drs. The travel offices also advertise 'day trips to Andros' but these are simply arranged on the scheduled ferry-boats and not trip boats.

Fountains There are two particularly large and interesting fountains, one on Odhos Evangelistrias and the other, dated 1797, at the upper end of the Old Quarter (*Tmr* 8C2). From the small, paved square on the side of which is situated the last mentioned fountain, a narrow, walled lane makes up the hillside with lovely gardens on either side. This pretty, stepped way thins out above Panaghia Evangelistria.

Galeria Cybele (*Tmr* 38D3) Worthy of a mention, although I rarely list this type of establishment. The shop is next door to a very old building, on the right-hand side of the street leading to Ag Ioannou Church. A pleasant, French speaking old lady presides over a shop full of antiques and, more importantly, second-hand books. Those who purchase a book (200drs) may be able to swop others at no extra charge. She also sells inexpensive postcards and often gives customers a painted pebble as a memento.

On some summer Sunday evenings the Town's Brass Band slumps around the edge of the Esplanade rotunda (*Tmr* 2C3) and inharmoniously thump their way through a routine.

Museum (*Tmr* 37C/D1/2) A modern building bordering the left-hand side of Leoforos Megalocharis. Exhibits include a collection of the usual mix. Open weekdays between 0900-1500hrs, Sunday & holidays 1000-1430hrs and closed Tuesdays.

POLICE

Port (*Tmr* 16C/D3) Situated in a building to the side of the Esplanade.

Town (*Tmr* 39C/D2/3) Crammed into a large building in a narrow lane off Odhos Evangelistrias. The extremely helpful and pleasant offices will help tourists in distress.

POST OFFICE (*Tmr* 6C/D2) Shares the same building as the OTE, on the right of Leoforos Megalocharis. Open the usual weekday hours.

TAXIS There are two main ranks on the Esplanade, to the right (*Sbo*) of the Ferry-boat Quay. One is on Bus Terminal Sq (*Tmr* C3) and the other is on the corner of the side-street to Ag Ioannou Church.

TELEPHONE NUMBERS & ADDRESSES

Doctors & Dentist	Tel 23133
First Aid Centre	Tel 22210
Municipal Tourist office (*Tmr* 39C/D2)	Tel 22234/23733
Police (Panormos)	Tel 31371
Police, town (*Tmr* 29C/D2/3)	Tel 22100/22555
Taxi rank	Tel 22470

TOILETS On the edge of the 'Dolphin Square', alongside the Market building (*Tmr* 35C2/3).

TRAVEL AGENTS & TOUR OFFICES *See* **Ferry-boat Ticket Offices**.

ROUTE ONE

Tinos Town to Kionia (5km) This coastal road curves past the Commercial Quay (*Tmr* A/B2), leaving the *Hotel Asteria* on the right, a small stony beach on the left and then cuts inland from the Psari Plaka headland, before dropping down to:-

STAVROS (2½km from Tinos Town) A chapel on the hillside of the cove overlooks a small harbour with the possible remains of an ancient Stoa stretching into the sea. Incongruously the latter is now used as a modern-day benzina moorings. The chapel equally incongruously, and irreverently, doubles as a cafe-bar in addition to which there are tables on the quayside.

Further on towards Kionia and on the right, alongside the road, is a field in which there are a scattering of archaeological remains including a temple, an altar and a well. This is an ancient pilgrimage site dating back to the 4th century BC.

KIONIA (5km from Tinos Town)A small settlement that has 'benefited' from plush hotel development. The beach starts out sandy with a pebble seashore. Towards the far end, beyond a low, small, rocky promontory, both beach and sea bottom are sandy. The backshore is edged by a very smart hotel.

The road 'encourages to deceive', turning sharply on to a concreted watercourse, alongside a particularly grand hotel, only to run out in a rocky river-bed.

Hotels include: the *Tinos Beach* (Class A, tel 22626) where a single room starts at 2700drs & a double 4200drs, increasing to 3600drs & 5200drs (1st-30th June & 16th-30th Sept) and 6700drs & 8900drs (1st July-15th Sept).

ROUTE TWO

Tinos Town to the south-east coastal villages The main road from Tinos Town climbs to a fork around which are clustered three petrol stations.

The right-hand turning sallies forth and, after about 2km, passes the **Monastery Agia Triada**, a very old, picturesque monastery with a church, a handicraft museum, library, a fountain and a mausoleum. During the Turkish occupation this was a secret and forbidden school for Greek children ('Krifo Scholio').

Not much further on, an unsigned, right-hand turning at the next fork (4km) leads to:-
AG SOSTIS (7 km from Tinos Town) A lovely, sweeping, sandy beach set in low-rise hills. The backshore of the beach is edged by low dunes supporting small, sparse arethemusa trees. An outcrop of rocks divides the beach in two.

Over the low headland is:-
PORTO (AG IOANNIS) (7½km from Tinos Town) To reach this dignified, new, low-rise 'Costa' development it is necessary to return to the last mentioned fork in the road. The very smart *Rafael Bungalows* epitomises the quality of the building taking place. Despite this 'up-market' attention, the beach close to the 'Bungalows' is rather scrubbly with some kelp heaped about. The sea bottom is sandy, the low backshore dunes are being sorted out and the beach extended around the curve of the low headland. There is a taverna with accommodation on the left, just beyond the right turning to the beach. On the right of the road to the beach is the *Taverna Adonis*.

It is possible to make a cross-country run to the last south-east coast village to be detailed, which is good news as some cartographers slip in a non-existent road from Portos back to the inland village of Triantaros. The initial section of the existing track is poorly surfaced but improves prior to emerging above the village of:-

LICHNAFTIA (11km from Tinos Town) The road to this very North Welsh 'look-alike' ends above the village. It is necessary to scramble down the path and keep to the right along the nearside property wall. This emerges at the far right-hand edge of a tree and property lined, pebble and sand beach. The path to the left, parallels the shore. It passes a rustic fountain and wanders up and down the water running slate steps of the 'High St' before simply petering out.

The sea bottom is large pebbles, the foreshore fine pebbles, with very fine shingle in amongst the right-hand rocky headland. And that is that. Visitors are not encouraged. No smiling Greeks here and possibly the only sight of a (miserable) local will be the disappearing view of a back. There isn't a taverna or even a kafeneion, but this spot does offer secluded, perfect peace.

To return to Tinos it is possible to climb the long, wide, winding and unsurfaced road to the pretty but also unfriendly village of **Triantoros**. From here travellers can wander around the fascinating hill and mountainside villages of, for instance, **Steni**, **Mesi**, **Skalados**, **Tripotamos** *ad infinitum*. If I have not already rambled on about it, there is no doubt that Tinos is a fascinating island on which to spend several weeks walking from village to village.

ROUTE THREE

Tinos Town to Panormos Port via Panormos (35km) Repeat the climb out of Tinos Town to the petrol stations, as described in **Route Two**, and select the left sweep at the fork. This proceeds on up to the mountainous interior of the island.
After about 5km a right fork leads to:-
Kechrovounio Convent Built in the 12th century on the site of a religious establishment reputably founded in the 8th/9th century. Its most famous celibate was, of course, St Pelagia who, in 1822, had the vision revealing the existence and location of the island's miraculous icon.

The main road continues to wind around hillsides dotted with chapels and dovecotes (in about equal numbers), to the village of:-
KAMPOS (14km from Tinos Town) Here is a taverna and Ag Aikaterini Church was

built in 1771, during the brief Russian occupation. The village was the birthplace of Loukia Negreponti, later to become Sister Pelagia (yes she).

Kampos is one of the points from which it is possible to make the fascinating:-

Detour To Kolibithra Four kilometres from Kampos, the track reaches the spread out village of:-
KOMI Set in a lovely, rich agricultural valley. By the bridge is the road to Kolibithra.

The other, more adventurous route is from the main road 3½km beyond Kampos village. The junction, with the unsurfaced turning to the right, is marked by an old quarry, abandoned machinery and, on the left, a flat stone monument. The latter is in the style of a dovecote and commemorates I know not what. The track descends through the villages of **Kalloni**, **Karkados** and **Kato Klisma**, on the north-west edge of a fertile valley prior to:-

KOLIBITHRA (Kolympithra) 22km from Tinos Town) The final approach is a drive along a flat valley bottom to a large, broad, gloriously sandy beach which stretches away to the left. To the right-hand side (*Fsw*) is a swampy river which runs into the rocky edged Bay of Kolibithra. The sea entrance almost seems to be blocked off by an islet. Around a bluff to the right is a deep-set, small, sandy beach cove spoiled by some tar. Above the cove, to the right, are six terraced-house apartments, a restaurant/cafe/souvlaki bar and, on the far side, overlooking the edge of the beach is the admirable, rustic *Drakonisi Taverna*. This is run by a smiling, round-faced man who will rustle up omelettes and a Greek salad, in addition to the more usual coffee and liquid refreshment.

Opposite the taverna, back across the cove, on the beach edge is a toilet and shower block but cross your legs as its usually locked. In fact Kolibithra is a lovely spot unless you are dying to use the toilets!

A map maker (who shall remain nameless) has depicted a secondary track from the village of **Aetofolia** to Isternia, which would be jolly useful if it existed. Path, yes but certainly not negotiable by wheeled vehicles. I shall say no more...

Returning to the main road at the dovecote monument, the stretch of mountainside road to **Kardiani** village allows, here and there, tantalising glimpses of pleasant looking coves and the occasional hamlet, way down below to the left. These are only accessible by donkey or boat, more's the pity. Out to sea, in the distance, Syros island basks in the Aegean Sea.

ISTERNIA (28km from Tinos Town) A picturesque, 'hanging garden' village to the right of the main road and a convenient crossroads to various other villages. Close by is a saddle ridge lined with old but substantial windmills, one of which has been quaintly converted. Adjacent are some rather strange, Romanesque buildings.

The left crossroad turning descends steeply to the port of:-
AG NIKITAS (30km from Tinos Town) The original marble paved muletrack down the steep hillside to this lovely, small seaside hamlet is still in existence, even if the new road has chopped bits out of the path.

I imagine this port was once destined for greater things in the sphere of tourism, but the one hotel, passed on the way into the village, is still deserted and closed. I am fairly certain that Ag Nikitas, also known as Ormos Isternian, was the port to the upper village as far back as the Roman occupation.

Out of the height-of-season hardly a tourist is to be seen, other than a few Greeks. To the right (*Fsw*) is a rather oversize commercial quay, probably a relic of the days when marble exporting was a viable proposition. To the left, an unmade track 'shambles' on parallel to the narrow, pebbly beach,on which are drawn up a number of benzinas.

On the waterfront is the *Cafe, Ouzerie, Restaurant Ormos* This is owned by a large, friendly, ex-merchant seaman who speaks some English and a limited fare is available.

Continuing up and over a small bluff leads to a lovely cove to the left (*Fsw*) of the bay. A sandy sea bottom and beach 'saucers' steeply up to a sandy backshore, where are planted out tree saplings. Well worth the trek.

On the way down (or up,depending..) the mountainside to Ag Nikitas, a track to the right, which degenerates into a stony donkey path, leads to:
Kapsalos (30km from Tinos Town) A lovely cove with sandy beach and sea-bed.

Returning to the main road, close by the Isternia ridge, is a track that makes off to:-
Katapoliani Monastery This was built in 1786 and is guarded by an unfriendly dog, fortunately kept within the bounds of the monastery by wire mesh. A track rises steeply past the building but becomes impassable, except on foot.

The main road winds down the north face of the mountainside to the island's largest village or, more correctly, the town of:-
PANORMOS (Pyrgos, Pirgos) (33km from Tinos Town) The still descending main road circles around the left side of Panormos. Where the bus pulls up on the bypass is a large shelter and wall mounted town plan. A paved pedestrian way ascends past a small museum, on the left, to the pretty, profusely flower and tree planted, higgledy-piggledy settlement which is, in effect, a Chora.

To the left, at the top of the pedestrian way, is a baker (nice bread) and general store across from which are ***Rooms***, where very basic doubles, sharing the bathroom, cost from 1000drs.

To the right of the pedestrian way, the winding 'High St' passes a new OTE on the left then a rustic Post Office (exchange) before opening out on to a very interesting, irregular plateia. The far side of this tree shaded square is edged by a rather 'OTT' fountain, the doubled arched structure of which would not disgrace a Town Hall. One of the two sources of sustenance is a kafeneion advertising 'vegetarian seafood' whilst the other, a cafe-bar, seems more conventional. Famous for sculptures and icons, a number of small businesses continue to keep the traditions alive.

The north-western end of the island is mountainous with a number of hamlets and villages nestling here and there. The most renowned is **Marlas**, famed for its marble quarries and stone masons.

A further 3½km on and the main road (from Panormos) runs out in:-
PANORMOS PORT (36½km from Tinos Town) A pleasant, quiet, rustic port with a very large quay at the end of an equally large concrete quay road, which skirts the right-hand side of the harbour. A number of benzinas moor in shallow water close to the quay. The reason for the inordinately big port facility is that a lot of marble used to be shipped from Panormos, reputably the safest Tinos harbour. To the left is a small, scrubbly beach.

There are a side-by-side restaurant and a coffee-bar, a couple of stores and one gift shop. There are two ***Rooms*** but they fill quickly, when vacancies occur. This is not surprising as an en suite double room, in high-season, is only charged at 1500drs. An inexpensive rate for Tinos.

To Korali Taverna, Aegiali, in preparation for a feast day, Amorgos.

Acknowledgement to David & Liz Drummond-Tyler.

A local ferry-boat undergoing repairs at Ag Giannis Detis, Paros.

Acknowledgement to David & Liz Drummond-Tyler.

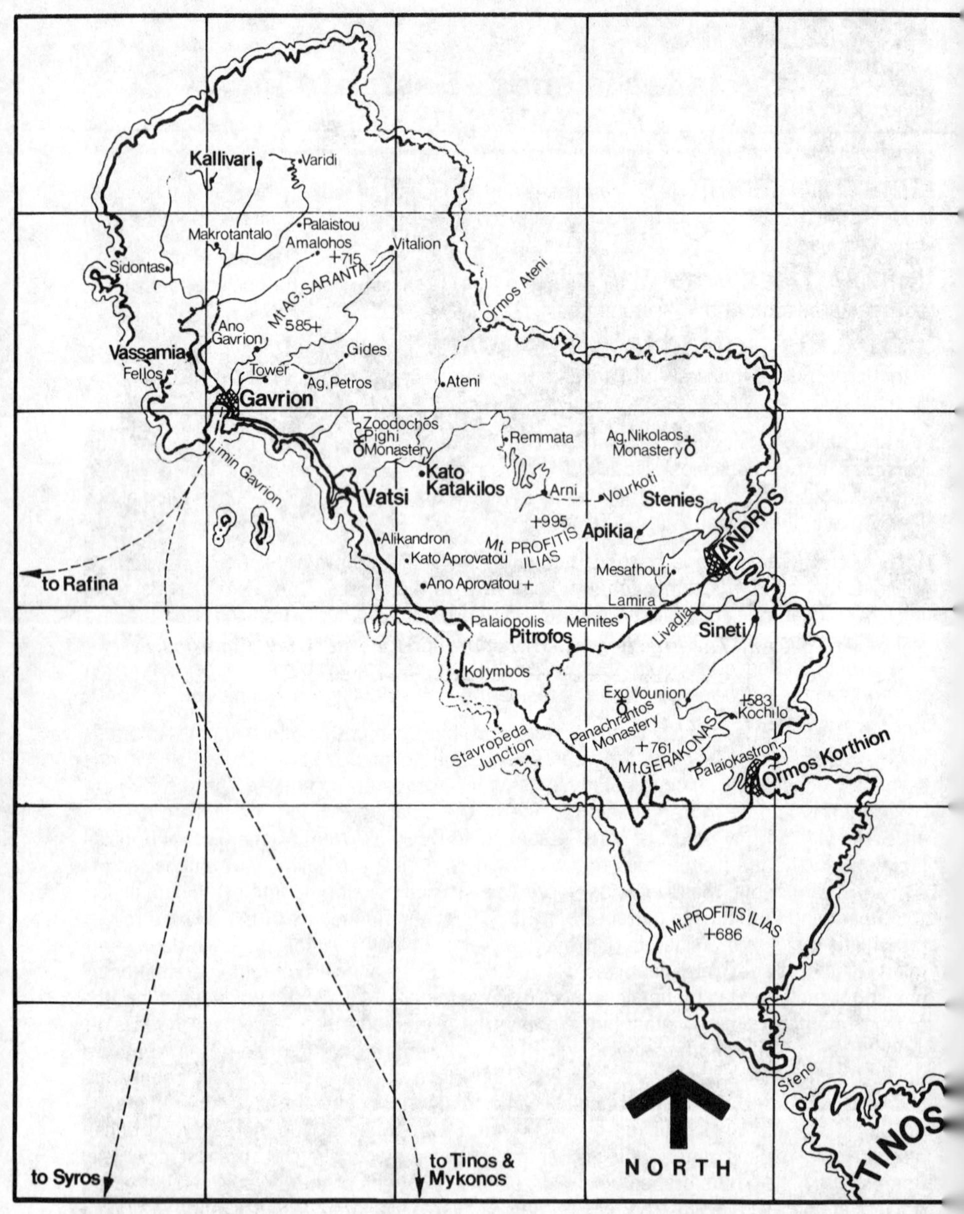

Illustration 45 Andros island

16 ANDROS ★★★★
Cyclades Islands - Eastern wing

FIRST IMPRESSIONS Verdant island; space & breadth; flowers & wonderful scents; prosperity; Greeks on holiday; red roofs; neat villages; unplastered walls; well cared for dogs.

SPECIALITIES Mineral water; unique walls; 'frontalia' omelette (includes potatoes, sausage & bacon or pork – scrumptious).

RELIGIOUS HOLIDAYS & FESTIVALS include: 27th July – Feast of Ag Panteleimon, the Monastery of Panachrantos; 6th December – Feast of Ag Nikolaos, the Monastery of Ag Nikolaos.

VITAL STATISTICS Tel prefix 0282. The most northerly & second largest of the Cyclades islands (to Naxos). Up to 39½km from NW to SE, up to 16km in width with an area of about 373 sq km. The population numbers approximately 10,000,of which about 1,800 live in the capital, Andros Town.

HISTORY The average historical mix although the Andriots appear to have caused their various overlords rather more difficulties than most other Cycladean islands. This may have been due to the large number of Albanians who settled on the island during the Middle-Ages.

Andros experienced an Axis troops 'fall-out' (as did, for example, Cephalonia in the Ionian) with the Germans bombing the resident Italian soldiers into submission, in 1943.

GENERAL Geographically a very large island, but despite this massive physical presence Andros somehow gives the impression of being much smaller. In part this is not surprising considering the comparatively puny size of the main centres. The scruffy port of Gavrion would be more suitable for one of the small island, 'off-the-cuff' ferry-boat calls; the villa holiday resort of Vatsi (Batsi) could be swallowed by many other popular locations, without a hiccup, and Andros Town, is a disappointment, not only lacking a Cycladean Chora but 'masquerading' more as a seaside development than the capital. On the other hand nothing can detract from the soft, awesome beauty of the island's rolling mountains which are divided by large fertile plains. Wealthy Athenians have developed many of the villages into neat, red tile roofed, tidy, bi-annual commuter settlements, nestling in the tree-clad mountainsides. Moreover the plenteous supply of water supports not only rich agricultural vistas, but cypress tree plantations that 'march' up the hillside amphitheatres. The south-eastern fishing port of Ormos Korthion does not let the side down, for here lurks the Greece we know and love so well. That messy 'beauty' of chickens, goats and donkeys rooting and grazing amongst unkempt backyards; unmade, pot-holed streets; lanes that run out in the tumbling stones of summer-dry river-beds; old, graceful houses deteriorating in amongst new, stark, skeletal, precast concrete frames with fishing nets draped wherever. Other evocations of the Greek islands are also present at nearby Palaiokastron, where there is even dilapidated property, and the untidy port of Gavrion.

Although Venetian dovecotes are not so numerous as on Tinos, the Andriots have their own countryside quirk – the unique walling in which a large, triangulated plate of stone is placed sideways in to the wall.

The combination of the comparatively low numbers of package holiday-makers and the continuing, but now meaningless rumour that Andros is the preserve of rich Greeks,has tended to keep independent travellers to a low level and helped maintain some of the island's spirit and traditions. If all this were not enough there are lovely, relatively empty beaches. Is it any wonder that Andros is a favourite holiday and weekend stop-off for mainlanders?

Visitors should note that signposting, especially off the main roads, is very poor but the islanders are very friendly and will be more than helpful.

If the Meltemi is blowing, stay on the south-west, not the east coast.

GAVRION: main port (Illustration 46) Not a very prepossessing place, although it may well grow on a visitor if allowed the time to weave its spell. The appearance is certainly not improved by the expansion of the car and lorry parking which has created an untidy, ugly waste ground, south or to the right (*Sbo*) of the Ferry-boat Quay (*Tmr* 1C3). The port and village is to the right (*Sbo*) of the encircling bay, with a small, haphazard, shanty bungalow development on the backshore of the beach at the bottom of the bay. Almost the whole settlement borders the 'High St-cum-Esplanade' reminiscent and not dissimilar to a Yukon mining town. However, there are signs of impending development and a 'sprucing up', especially in the area of the new Post Office.

ARRIVAL BY FERRY Rather out of the ordinary, the ferry-boat port of Gavrion is not the capital, a main town or even an important holiday resort. Another relatively unusual and 'unwelcome' practice is that the boats are not met, even by a handful of Room owners. However the local buses, up to twelve taxis and the *Camping Andros* van attend a ferry's docking.

All the above leaves a disembarking traveller with a dilemma – to stay in Gavrion or make for Vatsi (Batsi) or Andros Town. Bearing in mind my views on the general unattractiveness of Andros Town, I would plump for Gavrion or possibly Vatsi as the first stop-off.

An important point to bear in mind when planning itineraries is that Andros is a mainlanders weekend resort. You have been warned.

THE ACCOMMODATION & EATING OUT

The Accommodation As intimated, there is not a superabundance of places to stay and it is best to get a move on and grab what is on offer. Fortunately, almost opposite the Ferry-boat Quay (*Tmr* 1C3), is one of the best places to stay.

The Hotel Galaxy (*Tmr* 2C/D2) (Class D) Tel 71228

Directions: Half-left (*Sbo*) from the bottom of the Ferry-boat Quay and across the Esplanade.

Mikali, the amicable proprietor, is almost shy and does not push himself forward to procure clients so it is necessary to take the hotel by 'the horns', as it were. Fortunately, and mistakenly, the smart look of the place tends to put off waverer's so the fleet of foot and mind will ensure themselves accommodation. The rooms are comfortable and, naturally, those positioned to the front overlook much of the port's activities. All rooms have en suite bathrooms. A single room starts off at 1500drs & a double room 1800drs, rising respectively to 1700drs & 2400drs (1st June-30th Sept). The water is hot. The ground floor is most conveniently taken up by a spacious cafe-bar/restaurant. The friendly waiters speak some English and Mikali allows luggage to be stored in his mezzanine office. Two coffees and an ouzo cost 200drs.

Radiating out from this hotel are:-

Rooms G Mamais (*Tmr* 3A/B1) Tel 71219

Directions: Left (*Sbo*) from the Ferry-boat Quay, past the town statue and right down the side-street to the nearside of the building containing the smart *Hotel Gavrion Beach* (*Tmr* 4A1/2). At the bottom of this short road and on the right-hand corner.

A Mama runs this neat accommodation with a double room sharing the bathroom costing (mid-season) from 1000drs.

The Hotel Gavrion Beach (*Tmr* 4A1/2) (Class C) Tel 71312

Directions: As above.

Smart, flag-draped and expensive. Air conditioned, double rooms with en suite bathrooms cost 2800drs, increasing to 3200drs (1st July-15th Sept). Breakfast costs 300drs.

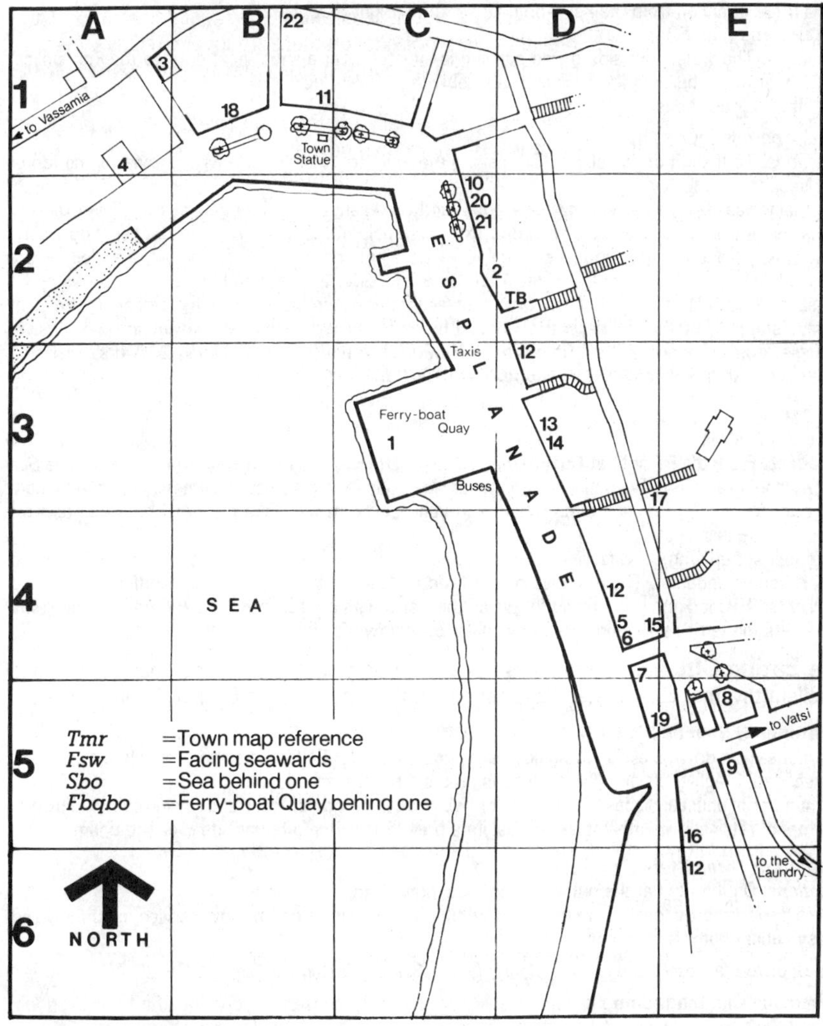

Illustration 46 Gavrion

Tmr			
1C3	Ferry-boat Quay		
2C/D2	Hotel Galaxy	13D3	Ferry-boat Ticket offices
3A/B1	Rooms G Mamais	14D3	Ferry-boat Ticket offices
4A1/2	Hotel Gavrion Beach	15D/E4	OTE
5D4	Rent Rooms	16D/E5/6	Mobil Petrol Station
6D4	Port police	17D/E3/4	Town police
7D/E4/5	Bar Veggara	18B1	Post Office
8E4/5	Estiatorion O Balmas	19D/E5	Agricultural Bank
9E5	Restaurant Three Stars	20C/D1/2	Bar Idrousa
10C/D1/2	Giorgios Rent-A-Rek (sic)	21C/D2	Mouragio Self-service Restaurant
11B/C1	Baker	22B1	Rent A Bike Tasos
12	Supermarkets	TB	Telephone Box

In the other direction from the Ferry-boat Quay, to the right (*Sbo*) is:-

Rent Rooms (*Tmr* 5D4)

Directions: The waterfront side of the building is situated over a shop, next door to the Port police. To the rear of the building the back lane is level with the first-floor.

A bit of a 'doss house'.

Hotel Aphrodite (Class B) Tel 71209

Directions: To the left of and about 150m along the route to Vatsi out of Gavrion, towards the top of the rise in the road.

Actually classified as a pension, not a hotel, and represents extremely good value. This excellent establishment is run by the bald, friendly, extremely helpful Fransisco and his mother who cleans scrupulously – everything is spotless. The showers are hot and towels and soap are provided, as are extra blankets and an electric fire, if required. On the hillside, the pension has very nice views and a pleasant garden full of flowers. There is a 'main accommodation block' of rooms and another row of rooms, 'stepping' up the hillside, with shared bathrooms. The latter are very pleasant and inexpensive. A single room, sharing the bathroom, costs 1600drs & a double room sharing 2000drs, whilst en suite singles are priced at 2000drs & doubles at 2900drs.

Camping

Camping Andros Tel 71444

Directions: From the Ferry-boat Quay (*Tmr* 1C3) turn left (*Sbo*) along the waterfront as far as the *Sea Star Kafeneion* and turn down the lane on the far side. This makes a junction with the back road where turn right for the 2km distant site. Those with vehicles might well take the Vatsi road and turn off where the signs indicate.

A super set-up with good facilities and a cafeteria at which a number of locals eat – there can be no better recommendation. The attentive owner lived in America for a time and is mindful of satisfying his clients. A varied and good menu for which the last orders are accepted at 2200hrs. The campsite van meets the ferries and there are a few chalet bungalows for rent.

The Eating Out Although there is not a great deal of choice, Gavrion has at least one excellent taverna, able to stand against all but the very best the Cyclades has to offer.

Estiatorion O Balmas (*Tmr* 8E4/5)

Directions: Turn down the alley alongside *Bar Veggara* (*Tmr* 7D/E4/5). This opens out on to a pleasant, tree shaded, irregular square. The taverna is on the far right-hand side.

A number of unusual dishes with a meal for two of veal, potatoes, bread and retsina costing 750drs. The 'open' retsina is an interesting, special little brew. Dishes on offer include liver and briam.

Restaurant Three Stars (*Tmr* 9E5)

Directions: On the right at the outset of the Vatsi main road.

Well patronised by locals who get good attention, but visitors don't! Slow service, cold food and greasy cutlery but it is inexpensive.

Next door to the *Hotel Galaxy* is the *Mouragio Self Service Restaurant* (*Tmr* 21 C/D2).

See **Andros Camping, Camping**.

THE A TO Z OF USEFUL INFORMATION

BANKS There is an **Agricultural Bank of Greece** (*Tmr* 19D/E5) but to date it has not indulged in exchange transactions, despite one or two, here and there, going over to tourist dealings. This branch may, one day. *See* **Post Office, A To Z**.

BEACHES The flat, narrow beach at the bottom of the bay is around to the left (*Sbo*) from the Ferry-boat Quay. Local benzinas are anchored in the shallow water for the first half of its length but it will do as a stand-by. There is a small, rustic kafeneion on the backshore.

BICYCLE, SCOOTER & CAR HIRE I suppose my favourite outfit must remain:-

Giorgos Rent-A-Rek (*sic*) (*Tmr* 10C/D1/2) Tel 71466

Directions: A pavement area to the left (*Sbo*) of the *Bar Idrousa*, which serves as an office!

My recommendation is not based on a clutch of high quality machines, far from it. Perhaps his choice of business style says it all. The round faced, moustachiod Giorgos is an ex Merchant Navy radio officer who speaks excellent English. He is a happy, engaging character. Most of his steeds are in a pretty ropey condition although at least three new machines have been added to the stable. The small mopeds cost from 1000drs, medium sized, 1500drs and the larger Vespas 2000drs.

The rivals are **Rent-A-Bike Tasos** (*Tmr* 22B1), along a side-street on the far side of the baker, and someone who operates from alongside the *Bar Veggara* (*Tmr* 7D/E4/5). Giorgos remains convinced that the other guys won't be able to stand the heat of his competitive pressure!

BREAD SHOPS There is a Baker (*Tmr* 11B/C1) to the left (*Sbo*) of the Ferry-boat Quay, immediately behind the Town Statue. He also sells pies and doughnuts.

BUSES They terminus alongside the Ferry-boat Quay, on the waste ground.

Bus timetable The schedules tie in with the ferry-boats *See* **Buses, Andros Town**.

COMMERCIAL SHOPPING AREA As in Kea island, shops open Sunday morning. There are a number of Supermarkets (*Tmr* 12C/D2/3, 12D4 & 12D/E6).

DISCO The Disco Mararound (Wot!) is 500m beyond *Pension Aphrodite* on the left of the Vatsi road, around the second small headland. The set-up also advertises pizzas but they are expensive.

FERRY-BOATS Rafina is the mainland port serving the island, there being no Piraeus connection.

Ferry-boat timetable (Mid-season)

Day	Departure time	Ferry-boat	Ports/Islands of Call
Daily	1330hrs	Eptanissos/ Bari Express	Rafina(M).
Daily (Excl Fri & Sun)	1730hrs	Eptanissos/ Bari Express	Tinos,Mykonos.
Thur	1730hrs	Kithnos	Tinos,Syros..
Fri	1830hrs	Bari Express	Tinos,Mykonos.
Sun	2030hrs	Bari Express	Syros,Mykonos,Tinos.
	2030hrs	Eptanissos	Tinos,Syros.

One-way fare: Andros to Rafina 765drsl duration 1½hrs.

Please note these tables are detailed as a GUIDE ONLY. Due to the time taken to research the Cyclades, it is IMPOSSIBLE TO 'match' the timetables or even boats. So don't try cross pollinating...

FERRY-BOAT TICKET OFFICES Two side-by-side (*Tmr* 13D3 & 14D3), almost opposite the Ferry-boat Quay. Very friendly and helpful with the times chalked up outside.

LAUNDRY There is a laundry (not coin-op) housed in an enterprising villager's front room! Ascend the Vatsi road hill and turn right along a side road immediately before the *Three Stars Restaurant*. The sign 'Laundry, Tel 71327' is on the restaurant wall. This leads up a sharp incline – select the first dirt track to the left, and the establishment is in the first big house (three storeys) on the right. Racks of clothes hang in the window.

OTE (*Tmr* 15D/E4) At the far right-hand *Sbo* end of the Esplanade, down the lane alongside the *Bar Veggara*. It is often difficult to make an international connection from this office, which only opens weekdays between 0730-1510hrs. There is a phone box (*Tmr* TB C/D2/3) on a street corner – often surrounded by stacks of wooden fish boxes and hardly visible!

PETROL Towards the far right of the waterfront (*Fbqbo*) is a Mobil petrol station (*Tmr* 16D/E5/6), open between 0800-1300hrs & 1600-2000hrs, including Sundays.

POLICE

Port (*Tmr* 6D4)**Town** (*Tmr* 17D/E3/4) Very friendly and will help with accommodation.

POST OFFICE (*Tmr* 18B1) This is now housed in a new building, across the first narrow side-street beyond the baker's. Transact exchange.

TAXIS Queue to the left (*Sbo*) of the Ferry-boat Quay and as many as twelve meet the boats.

TELEPHONE NUMBERS & ADDRESSES

First Aid	Tel 71210
Police, town (*Tmr* 17D/E3/4)	Tel 71220

TOILETS A cleanish, concrete block on the waste ground area, in front of the Petrol station.

TRAVEL AGENTS & TOUR OFFICES *See* **Ferry-boat Ticket Offices, A To Z**.

ROUTE ONE

Gavrion Port to Vassamia, Fellos & beyond The route to the north of the island runs off round the bottom of the bay and along the road behind the *Hotel Gavrion Beach*. Once at the far side of the flat agricultural plain backing the bay, the road commences to climb and the rural country lane leads on up into massive, rounded mountains with gentle valleys cuddled in their curves.

From the village of **Vassamia** (4½km) a paved road, which soon becomes a track, meanders off left, by an abandoned bulldozer, tumbling down to a couple of very pleasant seaside coves set in rather 'moth-eaten hills. The first of these coves is the larger of the two, both have sandy beaches and discreetly set in the surrounding hillsides are the bungalows of affluent foreigners.

On this northern coastline there are other 'secret' coves but travellers will require a strong conveyance or very long, strong legs. One of the spots recommended by the locals is **Zorko Beach** accessed via **Kallivari** village but it is necessary to ask the way. The signposting to the little hamlets in this area, as elsewhere on the island, is very poor, if not non-existent,excepting that to **Amolohos** which, for some reason...!

ROUTE TWO

Gavrion Port to Andros Town (35km) The main road to Andros Town climbs from the right-hand (*Sbo*) side of the Esplanade. Thence across the headland that forms one side of Limin Gavrion. From the hill-top are pleasant views to seaward of a group of inshore islets. The road descends to sea-level where there is a very small cove which is hardly worth a mention in the light of the others to come. Hereabouts a dusty track heads into the surrounding hillsides.

Detour to Ag Petros Tower Once off the main road, a left fork leads to *Andros Camping* (*See* **Camping, Gavrion Port**). The right-hand, surfaced road, initially signposted Ag Petros and then confusingly Vitalion, leads to the:-

Tower of Ag Petros (St Peter) Frankly not so dramatic as the pre-publicity would suggest. Quite the most outstanding feature is the neatness of the workmanlike masonry. The structure is the subject of much conjecture as to the date and reason of its construction. Was it a fort, store or signalling tower?

Returning to the main route, a little further along the sea-level road is a lovely, but shadeless sandy beach with two tavernas at the far end. Over a low, small headland is another attractive, shallow shelving,sheltered, small, sandy beach cove backed by dunes. Beyond a rocky outcrop is a longer, very sandy beach on the near edge of which is the Pell Mell Disco and a taverna complex. The *Hotel Perrakis* (Class B, tel 71456) is across the road. Here all rooms have en suite bathrooms with a single room priced at 3380drs & a double 3870drs, increasing to 5500drs & 6100drs (1st July-31st Aug).

Detour to Zoodochos Pighi Monastery A track into the interior from this latter cove snakes up to:-

Zoodochos Pighi Monastery (10km from Gavrion Port) There are a number of island monasteries worthy of a visit including Panachrantos (south-west of Andros Town), and Ag Nikolaos (north of Andros Town), but Zoodochos Pighi is the most accessible. Originally a monastery but, since the 1920s, more correctly, a convent. The date of foundation wavers between the 9th and 14th century AD so it seems a pity that the celibates are now down to about five or six. This loss in numbers has unfortunately put a stop to the weaving once practised and for which the monastery was famed. Visitors should call before 1100hrs and although the views are excellent the buildings are drab.

VATSI (Batsi) (8km from Gavrion Port) (Illustration 47) The main road bypasses this Greek 'St Ives' – part port, part summer resort, with the holiday aspect

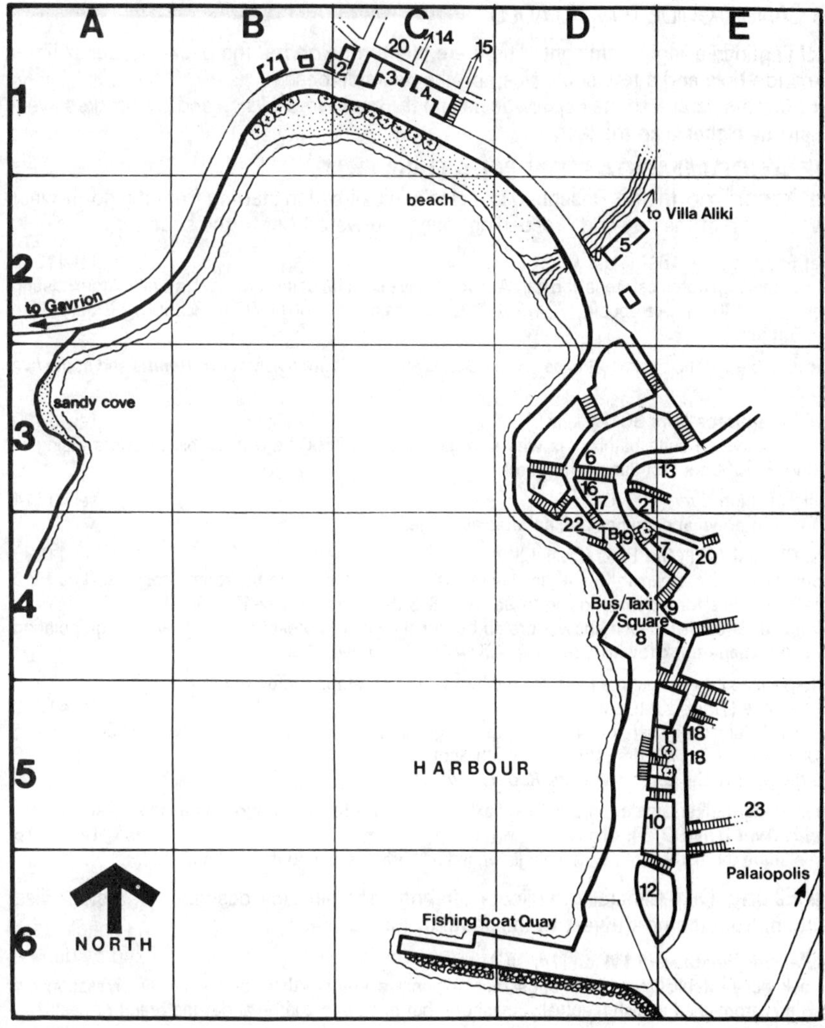

Illustration 47 Vatsi

Tmr 1B1	Hotel Skouna	15C/D1	Rent-A-Car Andros
2B/C1	Hotel Glari	16D3	Pharmacy
3C1	Hotel Karanassos	17D3/4	Newspaper shop
4C1	Pension/Restaurant Lykion	18E5	Bread shops
5D2	Hotel Chryssi Akti	19D4	Koxuli Fruit & Vegetable shop
6D3	Hotel Krinos	20	Doctors
7	Rooms	21D/E3/4	Post Office/OTE
8D4	Bus/Taxi Square	22D3/4	Port police
9D/E4	Hotel H Avra	23E5	Town police
10D/E5	Takis Taverna	TB D3/4	Telephone box
11D/E5	Square		
12D/E6	National Bank exchange office	*Tmr*	=Town map reference
13D/E3	Siroco Cafe/Taverna	*Fsw*	=Facing seawards
14C1	Rent-A-Bike George	*Sbo*	=Sea behind one
		Fbqbo	=Ferry-boat Quay behind one

becoming increasingly dominant. There are plenty of ***Rooms***, the package tourist firms have a toe-hold and a few souls sleep on the nearside beach.

The streets parallel to the Esplanade rise up the contoured hillside and are progressively one storey higher than the last.

THE ACCOMMODATION & EATING OUT

The Accommodation Described in a clockwise direction starting from the north-west (Gavrion) end of the bay and proceeding round the waterfront to the south.

Hotel Skouna (*Tmr* 1B1) (Class C) Tel 41240
A combination of hotel, cafeteria and bar. All rooms have en suite bathrooms with a single room costing either 1000/1300drs & a double 1724/2300drs, increasing to 1300/1600drs & 2500/2800drs (16th July-16th Sept).

In the area behind the package-holiday *Hotel Glari* (*Tmr* 2B/C1) are a number of ***Rooms*** and some five villas to let.

Hotel Karanassos (*Tmr* 3C1) (Class C) Tel 41480
All rooms have en suite bathrooms with a single priced at 2000drs & a double 2600drs, rising to 1500drs & 3200drs (1st June-15th Sept).

Pension Lykion (*Tmr* 4C1) (Class B) Tel 41214
A rather run-down appearance and no rates available.

Hotel Chryssi Akti (*Tmr* 5D2) (Class C) Tel 41236
A 'look-alike' for a 'Spanish Costa' holiday resort block. The en suite bedrooms cost 2100drs for a single & 2500drs for a double, rising to 2600drs & 3250drs (21st July-15th Sept).

Alongside is a small beach-shower prefab, but for the use of hotel clients only, and a sign pointing down an unmade track towards the *Villa Aliki – Rooms to Rent 30m*.

The Esplanade curves round a bluff, from which a flight of steps climbs to the:-
Hotel Krinos (*Tmr* 6D3) (Class D) Tel 41232
'Provincial'. All rooms share bathrooms with a single costing 750/1000drs & a double 1550drs, rising to 900/1150drs & 1700drs (16th June-15th Sept).

To the right of the same steps are ***Rooms*** (*Tmr* 7D3).

Further along the Esplanade, on the 'Bus/Taxi' Square (*Tmr* 8D4) and opposite a small quay, is the:-
Hotel H Avra (*Tmr* 9D/E4) (Class D) Tel 41216
Rooms share the bathrooms with a single priced at 1500drs & a double room 2000drs.

The Eating Out Generally mediocre offerings and similarly described in a clockwise direction, from the north-west to the south of the Harbour.

The Pension/Restaurant Lykion (*Tmr* 4C1)
A 'Greek' busy establishment. In amongst more expensive offerings they serve an extremely reasonably priced macaroni cheese dish – actually spaghetti, but need one quarrel about the brand of pasta?

Siroco Cafe/Taverna (*Tmr* 13D/E3)
Directions: To the rear of the *Hotel Krinos* in a pleasant situation.

A rather restricted menu featuring pasta and pizza dishes. The proprietor is helpful. A meal for two, with wine, averages 1000drs.

In the area of the 'Bus/Taxi' Sq (*Tmr* 8D4) are diverse restaurants, including a row of establishments edging the square. Towards the Fishing boat Quay is *Takis Taverna* (*Tmr* 10D/E5). Prior to *Takis* are two flights of steps. These ascend to a pretty, small square (*Tmr* 11D/E5) around and off which are at least four restaurants.

THE A TO Z OF USEFUL INFORMATION

BANKS The **National Bank of Greece** (*Tmr* 12D/E6) borders the promenade, one postcard shop past *Takis*, opposite the Fishing-boat Quay. Opens for exchange, only Wednesday & Friday, between 0900-1300hrs.

BEACHES Again clockwise from the north.
Beach 1 Across the bay, opposite the Fishing boat Quay, and a small sandy cove.
Beach 2. The main beach stretches from close by the *Hotel Skouna* (*Tmr* 1B1) all the way round to

the *Hotel Chryssi Akti* (*Tmr* 5D2). Mainly coarse sand with a scattering of large pebbles, a shingly foreshore and sea bottom. There are pedaloes and wind surfers at the north end.
Beach 3. A lovely looking, small, sandy outcrop edging the quay adjacent to the 'Bus Taxi' Sq but smelly. I suspect sewage outfalls here!
A small water taxi ferries clients to various beaches in the area of Vatsi. To the south are the sandy beaches of Delevoyas and Ag Marina, a 25/30 minute walk along the coastal track. The path starts out from the Memorial on the side of the acute bend in the Andros road, south from Vatsi.

BICYCLE, SCOOTER & CAR HIRE Rates average about 1500drs a day for scooters and firms include:-
Rent-A-Bike George (*Tmr* 14C1) On the left, behind the *Hotel Karanassos,*in the basement of a villa.

Rent-A-Car Andros (*Tmr* 15C/D1) Down the street to the south side of the *Hotel Lykion*. Advertises 'Moped Express' (the mind boggles!).

BOOKSELLERS (*Tmr* 17D3/4) More a purveyor of foreign newspapers. Ascend the angled flight of steps to the 'Κοχμλι Fruit & Vegetable' shop and left up the inclined and stepped alley. The shop is on the right, to the nearside of the pharmacy.

BREAD SHOPS Actually two (*Tmr* 18E5), one of which is a Baker, and separated from each other by a restaurant. To get there from the south of the 'Bus/Taxi' Sq, climb the stone steps to the tree shaded square (*Tmr* 11D/E5).

BUSES They 'terminus' on the side of the 'Bus/Taxi' Square. I have to own up (here, as elsewhere) that the Andros island bus timetables are complicated and those displayed at Andros Town, absolutely unfathomable. Daily services to Gavrion, Andros Town and Ormos Korthion.

CINEMA A local, open-air job, behind the *Hotel Glari* (*Tmr* 2B/C1). Shows start at 2110hrs and entrance costs 140drs.

COMMERCIAL SHOPPING AREA No market but for a village this size it is amply provided with shops. These include 'Κοχμλι Fruit & Vegetable' (*Tmr* 19D4), reputed to be housed in one of the oldest dwellings in Vatsi. There is a periptero on the edge of the 'Bus/Taxi Square'.

DISCOS At least three including the 'Chaf', at the top of the hill where the Vatsi turn off meets the main road, which advertises 'Wet T-Shirt Parties'. (Golly gosh. I've dreamt of...).

FERRY-BOAT TICKET OFFICES *See* **Travel Agents & Tour Offices, A To Z.**

MEDICAL CARE
Chemists & Pharmacies (*Tmr* 16D3) On the lane, one back and approximately parallel to the Esplanade, quite close to the *Hotel Krinos*. Opens weekdays between 0900-1330hrs & 1800-2100hrs.
Dentist Telephone Mr Vastardis on 41450 for surgery, Monday, Wednesday & Friday.
Doctors There is a surgery (*Tmr* 20E4) in the alley that angles off to the left, standing with the Post Office (*Tmr* 21D/E3/4) on the left. The notice requests clients to telephone and the telephone number is 41555 or 71379. Another doctor is signposted to the left (*Sbo*) along the back lane behind *Hotel Karanassos* (*Tmr* 3C1).

OTE (*Tmr* 21D/E3/4) Shares a building with the 'doo-hickey' Post Office and is most easily reached up the flight of steps alongside the *Hotel Avra*. Opens weekdays only between 0800-1300hrs & 1700-2000hrs. The Post Office opens the standard weekday hours.

PETROL There is a petrol station on the main road that bypasses Vatsi, on the Andros Town side.

POLICE
Port (*Tmr* 22D3/4) In a small modern block.
Town (*Tmr* 23E5) The police station (Tel 41204) is up a steep flight of steps, towards the south end of the Harbour. It has no name but can be identified by the flagpole and two small balconies with blue railings. They will help find accommodation.

POST OFFICE *See* **OTE, A To Z.**

TAXIS Not surprisingly park on the waterside of the 'Bus/Taxi Square' (*Tmr* 8D4).

TOILETS None, so hold on or make use of a convenient taverna.

TRAVEL AGENTS & TOUR OFFICES Not so much Travel Agents, more ticket offices combined with souvenir shops, side-by-side on the south-east side of the 'Bus/Taxi Square. *Andros Travel* is 'housed' in the ground floor of the *Skouna Hotel* (*Tmr* 1B1).

From the Vatsi bypass, a surfaced road of about 4½km in length heads inland for the:- **Detour To Kato Katakilos, Ateni & Ami** The Ateni stream flows through the village of:-

KATO KATAKILOS The three tavernas not only serve reasonable food at acceptable prices but put on a show of music and dancing in the evenings. On summer Saturday nights they roast a pig. If transport is not available the 1½hr walk is most agreeable (if you must).

From Kato Katakilos the upper hamlet village of **Ano Katakilos** is only a hop, skip and a jump (perhaps a little bit further than that).

An extremely rough, 7m track bumps to:
ATENI (16½km from Gavrion Port) This small village unfurls down a lovely river valley, past cultivated fields on which cattle graze, all the way to the sea. Here are two splendid sandy beaches overlooked by a hillock capped by a small chapel. These shores remain almost empty throughout the summer, even at the height-of season, but no refreshments are available.

From Kato Katakilos another track winds up the slopes of Mt Profitis Ilias, through the hamlet of **Remmata**, to the lovely, lush, mountaintop village of:-
ARNI (20km from Gavrion Port) Well worth the journey although, even at the height of the summer, it can be cloud-bound. There is a cafe-bar.

There are signs that the unsurfaced, rough track around the mountainside to **Vourkoti** will, one day, be made into a paved thoroughfare. There is a restaurant/taverna in the village so why not make the trek before there are coach parties and a hamburger bar?

Returning to the main route to Andros Town, the road rises from Vatsi to skirt the steep mountainside. En route, to the left, are the villages of:-
KATO & ANO APROVATOU Both possess tavernas and Kato has ***Rooms*** and a cafe bar. A path from the Kato section of the main road descends to an attractive and peaceful beach.

On a beautiful, giant curve in the lush mountainside, sprinkled with stately cypress trees, is the clean and neat, hillside 'hanging' village of:-
PALAIOPOLIS (17km from Gavrion Port The terraced hillsides are kept verdant by the numerous springs high up the steep sides of Mt Kouvara. No wonder the ancients chose this area for their capital, possibly destroyed in the 4th century AD. Part of the remains are supposed to lie beneath the sea below the village, in the long, straight edged cove bordered by a stony foreshore and beach. As is often the way, the most notable find, a statue, the 'Hermes of Andros', is now on display in Athens.

The stepped path down to the beach starts out from the main road, opposite a little shrine with a kafeneion one side and a taverna on the other. Incidentally the latter offers en suite double rooms for 1750drs – on request, not advertised. On the way down turn right along the first path into which the steps run, over a bridge and keep straight on past a fountain (on the right), beyond the steps that run off to the left. After the next bridge, and further steps down, at the cross paths keep almost straight on, leaving steps to left and right. Where the path breaks into another flight of steps, keep straight on leaving a flight to the left. Okay? Don't blame me if you make a false move...

Returning to and after another 7½km of main road, at a windswept, exposed, scruffy ridge, is a 'T-junction. To the left is the turning for Andros Town, which road descends along a natural cleft in the mountains to left and right. The road straight on skirts Mt Gerakonas to tumble down to Ormos Korthion. Incidentally, the highways are poorly surfaced in patches,from this junction,to both Andros Town and Ormos Korthion.

Selecting the left-hand option, the road and its immediate surrounds down the valley are messy, as are the villages of **Koumani**, **Messaria** and **Messa Chorio**. Furthermore, they are almost sprawling, urban outposts of Andros Town. Admittedly the dramatic hillside surrounds are Samos-like in their verdancy and clad with masses of trees including cypresses. Out of these, to the left, peek the neat, almost densely populated, red tile roofed villages of **Menites** (famous for its mineral waters), **Lamira**, **Strapouries** and **Mesathouri**. Many of the houses in these villages are owned by Athenian commuters who winter on the mainland and summer on the island.

ANDROS TOWN (35km from Gavrion Port): capital (Illustration 48)

This is no Chora, and the Old Town rather resembles a Greek 'Eastbourne or Weymouth'. I remain disappointed, although it has been described as attractive. Oh well, beauty is in the eye... Maybe I suffer from vision defects.

Many of the official buildings are imposing, 19th century 'Municipal' and a notable feature is that the long High Street is a marble paved pedestrian way. The town is built on a high headland promontory that juts out into and divides up Kastrou Bay, leaving a beach way down below on either side.

The worthy citizens make little or no attempt to accommodate tourists and those lodgings available are usually taken up by Greeks. Because of this, and the layout of the town, I propose to stray from the usual arrangement and progress from the outset of the main street, proceeding towards the castle topped islet at the sea-tip end of the promontory.

The **Police station** (Tel 22300) is followed by the **Post Office** which is housed in a modern building, and transacts exchange. The **OTE** (*Tmr* 1A4), on the left side of a large paved square, is open weekdays between 0730-2100hrs. Opposite, on the other side of the square, is the **Hospital** (*Tmr* 8A4 - tel 22758). Where the square narrows back down to the pedestrian way High Street, there is a **Taxi Rank** (*Tmr* A4 - tel 22171), and a **Periptero** with two telephones.

To the right, a side-street leads onto the very scruffy, sloping **'Bus' terminus** Square, (Plateia Olga), *Tmr* 2A/B4). At the far side of this is the messy Bus office building (*Tmr* 3B4), with, on the wall, the:-

Bus timetable (Mid-season)

Andros Town to Stenies

Mon-Fri	0715, 0900, 1145, 1340hrs.
Sat & Sun	0800, 1145hrs.

Andros Town to Gavrion via Vatsi

Mon & Tues	0645, 1015, 1415, 1545hrs.
Wed	0645, 1015, 1415hrs.
Thur	0645, 0830, 1015, 1415hrs.
Fri	0645, 0830, 1015, 1415, 1545hrs.
Sat	0830, 1015, 1340, 1545hrs.
Sun	0845, 1450, 1900hrs.

Andros Town to Ormos Korthion

Mon-Fri only	0715, 1015, 1415hrs.
Return journey	
Mon-Fri	0700, 1700hrs (yes, only 2 buses back, 3 out....).

"enquiries in respect of return bus times are met with polite shrugs or "It comes back from Gavrion immediately"! The timetables are confusing and in Greek.

On the right of Olga Square is a *Station Restaurant* (*Tmr* 4B4), which is signposted from the High St – 'The Stations Restaurant in Olga Square, Bus Station offers fine food at fair prices. Only the freshest local prouce is u-sed in our kitchen, we also do take-away service'(the whole sign is *sic*) In reality the this establishment is a greasy shack, round the back of which are **Public toilets** (*Tmr* 5B4).

From Olga Square a lane winds along and up and down the side of the headland to Plateia Kairis, the Main Square, passing, on the way, more Public Toilets (*Tmr* 5B3).

Returning to the High St, there are a brace of **Chemists** (*Tmr* 13A2/3) and, on the right, the **Ionian and Popular Bank** (*Tmr* 6A/B3). Prior to the Bank is a **Baker**, who sells cheese pies and sausage rolls, for 60drs each, with a **Greengrocer** in the basement. Opposite the Bank, a side-street falls rapidly towards the left-hand beach, on the right of which is a **Galaktopolieo** selling fresh yoghurt. On the far side of the Bank, a flight of steps rises steeply to the:-

Hotel Aegli (*Tmr* 7A/B3) (Class C) Tel 22303
Directions: As above.

If accommodation is available, a single room, sharing the bathroom, starts at 1250drs, double rooms sharing 1650drs & doubles en suite 2250drs, increasing, respectively, to 1550drs & 1900/2750drs (1st July-15th Sept). This hotel also advertises Rent-A-Car.

Opposite the steps to the *Hotel Aegli* is the *Cafe-bar Anemosa*, and, next door, the **Renate** tourist shop (*Tmr* 9A/B3). The latter sells ferry-boat tickets to Rafina and nearby islands. Yiannis, the helpful owner speaks good English, and is an agent for Olympic Airways. Ferry-boat times are displayed on boards outside.

A few metres down the road, on the same side, is the **National Bank of Greece** (*Tmr* 10A/B3). The High St runs out on Plateia Kairis, with, round to the right, a well situated Restaurant with views over the broad, right hand beach. There are a couple of cafes, and a more popular Restaurant, just to the left of the covered archway through which the street passes into the 'Old Town'.

To the left of Plateia Kairis, a steep street drops down to the sea, passing the **Archeological Museum**, open daily between 0845-1500hrs and Sundays & holidays 0930-1430hrs. Entrance costs 200drs. Beyond the aforementioned is the **Museum of Modern Art** from which emanate various loud, vibrating and 'bonging' noises. Its worth popping in, if only to see the amazing display 'Vibrations of the Sea' constructed from wood, metal and electromagnets, which makes this variety of weird sounds. This museum is open daily between 1000-1400hrs & 1800-2000hrs and entrance is free. Both museums are closed on Tuesdays.

On the right of the covered way leading to the 'Old Town' is a **Bookshop** selling foreign newspapers. Alleys branch off either side of the 'headland' lane and on the right is a path down to a few tiny fishing boat quays. The main lane passes by a large blue and white domed church and flowery square, twisting between pretty white houses. Prior to reaching the end of the rock is a **Naval Museum** (*Tmr* 12C2), to which entrance is free. It is open between 1000-1300hrs & 1800-2000hrs daily, except Tuesdays, but the exhibits are not very stunning. Beyond the museum the way peters out on a rather barren, paved square at the end of the bluff. This plateia is dominated by a large statue of an 'Unknown Sailor' peering seawards, with a ditty-bag slung over his shoulder. This commemorates all Andriot seaman ever lost at sea.

The narrow headland, hemmed in by a rocky coast, is tipped by the now ruined Venetian castle built on a tiny rock islet. The castle's state of repair was not helped by German bombing, in 1943, designed to quell mutineering Italian troops, then in occupation . On the way back to Plateia Kairis, a lane branches off to the right (*Castle behind one*) through what is left of an Old Chora and which is not yet overwhelmed by new development.

The beach to the right (*Fsw*) of Andros Town promontory is an expansive stretch of sandy shore. To the left of the headland is a narrow beach bordered by an Esplanade road. This leads past a heavily tree shaded seaside development with a number of restaurants and two houses with ***Rooms***. The road, alongside which is a small petrol station, circles to the right, past a Yacht Club, the very smart 'Naval Club' and lido, followed by a small craft harbour. Opposite the latter is the 'Disco Remedzo', the owners of which must have friends in 'High Places' as it is officially signposted from many kilometres away.

Hotels with en suite bathrooms include:- the Class B *Paradissos* (Tel 22187) with singles costing 2500drs & doubles 3500drs, rising to 3000drs & 4500drs (1st July-31st Aug) and the *Xenia* (Tel 22270), where singles are priced at 1900drs & a double 2650drs, increasing to 2270drs & 3250drs (1st July-15th Sept).

ROUTE THREE

Andros Town to Stenies (5km) From the left-hand (*Fsw*) town beach, a surfaced road proceeds to **Ormos Yialia**, a pebbly, small beach hemmed in by towering cliff headlands and large trees to landward. There is a cafe-bar restaurant as well as wind surfers and pedaloes for hire.

From the seafront the road winds up the hillside to a fork in the road from which the left-hand route advances to the village of:-

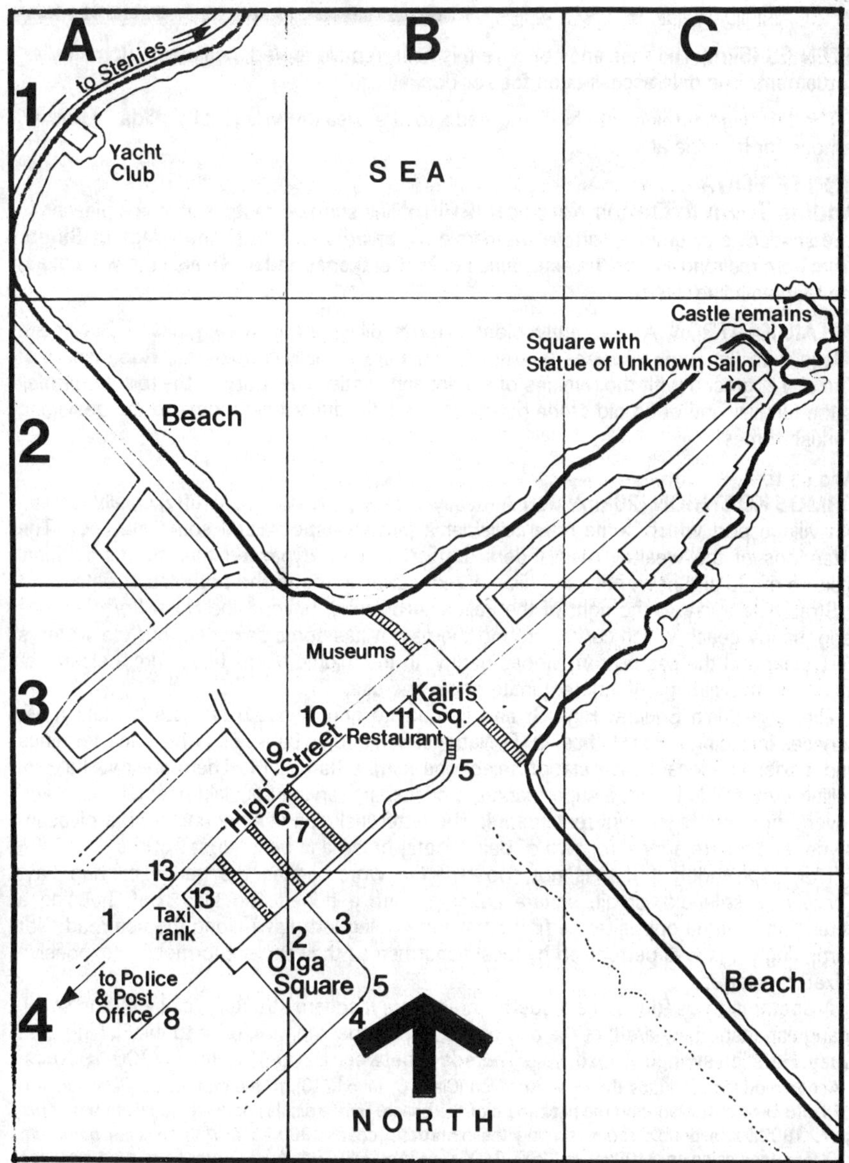

Illustration 48 Andros Town

Tmr 1A4	OTE	10A/B3	National Bank
2A/B4	Olga Square	11B3	Supermarket
3B4	Bus office	12C2	Naval Museum
4B4	'Station Restaurant'	13A2/3	Chemists
5	Public toilets		
6A/B3	Ionian & Popular Bank	*Tmr*	=Town map reference
7A/B3	Hotel Aegli	*Fsw*	=Facing seawards
8A4	Hospital	*Sbo*	=Sea behind one
9A/B3	Ferry-boat Ticket office	*Fbqbo*	=Ferry-boat Quay behind one

STENIES (5km) The road ends prior to this neat, red tile roofed, rich mans 'Roman Villa' settlement. The only access is on foot or donkey.

The left-hand turning, at the fork, leads to the wealthy village of **Apikia** (Apoikia), famous for its mineral springs.

ROUTE FOUR

Andros Town to Ormos Korthion (20km) The shortest route is across a pleasantly tree shaded, agricultural plain via the hamlet of **Livadia** and on to the village of **Sineti**. From here the road climbs the extremities of Mt Gerakonas and down again to wind along the mountainside past:-

PALAIOKASTRON A pleasantly older, almost dilapidated, more typically Cycladean village with flat roofed houses, some of which are actually dilapidated. Goodness me! The site is graced with the remains of a Venetian castle. The story of the fort's downfall is the familiar one of an old crone betraying the beleaguered defenders to the besieging Turkish forces.

And so to:-

ORMOS KORTHION (20km): port A messy, 'rustic', 'provincial', scruffy, smelly, spread out village port which some may consider a pleasant spot – and some may not! The attentions of the wealthy mainlanders appear to have bypassed this more traditional mixture of old and new, neat and dilapidated, surfaced roads and potholed streets.

Stretching away to the right of the Paliokastron road, beyond the *Hotel Korthion*, is a long, sandy beach which curves around the bay. It has some seaweed, but the water is very clear and the sea bottom slopes gently. In the middle of the beach are a cluster of 'dead', grim buildings of indeterminate origin and use.

The large Main Square, High St and immediate grid layout of streets contain most services including a Post Office, OTE, National Bank, Ionic Bank, Bus office and terminus and taxis. The local Police station telephone number is 61211. There are two bakers, selling very edible bread; a supermarket; a snackbar, serving souvlaki pita; chemists and several not-very-high-class restaurants. The latter includes *O Kalogridis* with a pleasant owner and where a meal for two of beans, feta, bread and beers cost 750drs.

The 'Esplanade', if that is not too smart a word, edges the gently curving bay. There is a splendid, small, square building, with a ridged and tiled roof, housing a kafeneion/taverna opposite the first small jetty going left (*Fsw*) along the sea road. Not surprisingly it is well patronised by local fishermen as they serve enormous, inexpensive mixed omelettes.

A doctor is to be found in a modern, three storey, square structure, close by the small, triangular shaped square(!) at the end of the 'Esplanade' (ho, ho), prior to the Fishing boat Quay. He is 'on syringe' Tuesdays & Thursdays between 0900-1300hrs & 1700-1900hrs.

Accommodation includes the *Hotel Korthion* (Class C, tel 61218), to the right of the Palaiokastron road into Ormos Korthion, on the backshore of the beach. Here a single room with en suite bathroom costs 1800drs, a double room, sharing the bathroom, costs 1900drs & with en suite bathroom 2100drs, increasing to 2100drs & 2200/2400drs (21st July-20th Aug). Across the road from the *Korthion*, and slightly to one side, is the *Villa Korthion* (Tel 61122), with apartments to rent costing approximately 2500drs for a double.

Another source is:-

Rainbow Rooms For Rent Tel 61344

Directions: Almost the first side street to the left of the Palaiokastron road heading into the port. This smart, fairly modern building is at the far end, on the right and to one side of a spacious, scruffy garden/backyard.

Stellios, a friendly, chunky young man, who speaks excellent American, runs this pleasantly decorated establishment. His personality infuses the place and the entrance hall reflects the atmosphere. A double room, with en suite bathroom, costs 1700drs for one night, and less for a longer stay.

The 30km main route back to Andros Town, via the Stavropeda junction, leaves Ormos Korthion along the back of the beach, then branches off to the right via the lonely hamlet of **Korthion**, which is blessed with a disco...! The road crosses a patchy, agricultural plain prior to climbing up and through the mountains towards the high escarpment road edging the west coast. The roads are not well signposted, in fact there are no signs at all.

A Katapola back-street, Amorgos. Acknowledgement to Anne Merewood.

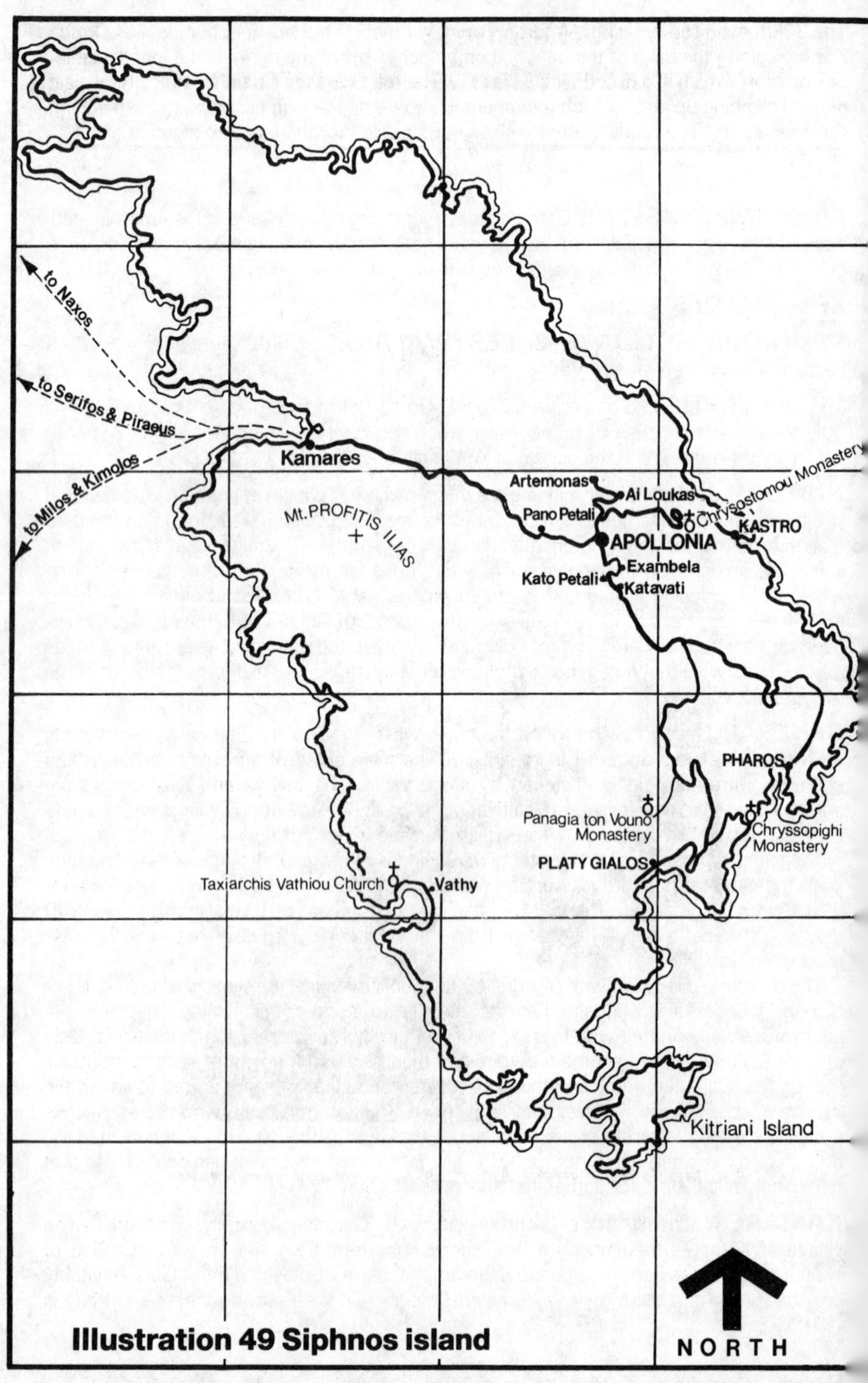

Illustration 49 Siphnos island

17 SIPHNOS (Sifnos) ★★★★
Cyclades Islands - Western chain

FIRST IMPRESSIONS Greek holiday resort; few flies; cats & dogs look well fed; neat countryside; fanciful ceramic chimney pots; clean, neat, almost smug; green & cultivated; relatively unspoilt, dovecotes & windmills.

SPECIALITIES Pottery.

RELIGIOUS HOLIDAYS & FESTIVALS include: 6th September – Feast & Festival, Taxiarchis Vathiou, Vathy.

VITAL STATISTICS Tel prefix 0284. Up to 20km from top to bottom & some 10km wide with an area of some 74sq km. The population numbers about 2,000 of which 1,600 or so live in the capital of Apollonia & its satellite villages.

HISTORY Gold and silver mines gave the island great wealth in antiquity and resulted in Siphnos being the largest contributors to the mainland Delphi Treasury. It is rumoured that this tribute to Apollo irked the islanders, not a little. So much so that instead of sending a golden ball, the equivalent to a tenth of their production, they conceived the wheeze of producing a gold leaf wrapped replacement. When found out they incurred their God's wrath and he caused the mines to sink out of sight. The Siphniots cup of woe overflowed when the Samos tyrant Polycrates attacked the island and levied an enormous tribute. Otherwise Siphnos generally followed the average, 'run-of-the-mill' history of the rest of the Cyclades.

GENERAL The approach around the north-west coast to the port of Kamares leads the visitor to expect an arid island. Not so. The main areas of agriculture are neat and intensive with many fields enclosed by stone walls. The valleys and river gorges are perhaps the most impressive, the cultivation being sprinkled with dwellings and magnificent castellated dovecotes between which cascade 'rivers' of flowering oleanders.

The initial impression of tidiness and well-being is reinforced throughout the island and even the cats, dogs and ducks appear well fed. On an island frequented by Greeks for their own holiday jaunts, it would be unseemly of tourists, or animals, to intrude AND they don't! What a delightful change from the sweltering hordes of blistering holiday-makers on, say, Paros.

The beaches, piled high with plaudits by the publicity blurb, are worthy of praise, if not quite so wonderful as suggested by the more flowing and poetic aclaim. They certainly are profusely signposted with messages urging the 'hordes' to behave themselves. Only at Platy Gialos do they become crowded and then only in the height of season months.

Even the buses run on time in this well ordered and pleasant land, added to which the service is possibly the most extensive in 'all of Greece'. For those who prefer 'shanks pony', the island is fertile ground for 'super walkies'. Although I have drawn readers' attention to the latter, I shall not go 'OTT' as I try to keep my pedestrian activities to that 'absolutely necessary' for authorship and survival. Okay.

KAMARES: main port (Illustration 50) The clean, orderly port and fishing village of Kamares (resembling a hot, sunny Frinton-on-Sea) has an aura, a milieu of wealth. It is impressively positioned in an amphitheatre of massive mountains inevitably crowned, here and there, by the occasional chapel. On the right, the horse-shoe bay is bordered by a tree-lined Esplanade, backed by Mt Profitis Ilias which climbs to a height of 893m; the bottom centre of the bay is filled out by a magnificent sweep of beach and rocky cliff-faces blank off the left-hand side.

ARRIVAL BY FERRY The Ferry-boat Quay (*Tmr* 1A4) is at the very top end of the right-hand (*Sbo*) side of the port. The boats are usually met by Room owners but mainly those with expensive offerings. It may well be best to locate one's own accommodation, which is perfectly possible, even in August. The buses meet the ferry-boats, even late night arrivals, as do the taxis and most of the village. The bus gets very, very crowded despite which the *cognoscenti* might well travel directly to, say, the village of Pharos.

THE ACCOMMODATION & EATING OUT

The Accommodation The possibilities have increased over the years, so much so that there is enough to go round in the height of summer months. On the other hand, Room owners tend to quietly stand and watch – giving nothing away. From the bottom of the Ferry-boat Quay (*Tmr* 1A4) are:-

Rooms (*Tmr* 2B5)
Directions: Turn left (*Fbqbo*) at the bottom of the Ferry-boat Quay along the Esplanade. The building is across the road from the small fishing boat quay, next door to the *Restaurant* ΑΥΡΑ and above Katsoulakis Tourist Agency.

Despite the owners being rather laconic, they are pleasant enough and this must rate as a 'find'. The very clean rooms are all of a sufficient size, are fitted with bedside lamps and have balconies. The bathroom is pleasant with towels provided. The roof area looks out over the whole bay and has a washing line with pegs. Rates for a double, sharing the bathroom, range from 1500drs-2500drs.

Rooms (*Tmr* 3B5)
Directions: Three buildings along from Katsoulakis Tourist Agency, to the nearside of a flight of steps, above the Εστιατοριον Η Μεροπη.

Rooms (*Tmr* 4B5), No 47
Directions: Immediately beyond the flight of steps alongside the Εστιατοριον Η Μεροπη, which establishment manages them.

A double room ranges between 1500-2500drs.

Rooms No 46 (*Tmr* 16B/C5)
Directions: Next door to No 47 and above a Ferry-boat Ticket office.

Average rates.

Hotel Stavros (*Tmr* 5C5) (Class C) Tel 31641
Directions: Further on along the Esplanade, beyond a large church, a flight of steps and on the right, above the family owned supermarket/gift shop/information office/ferry-boat exchange office *et al*.

The accommodating(!) young man, his mother, aunts and other family, all pitch in to run this establishment and the *Pension Kamari*. Now no specific singles on offer. A double room, sharing the rather basic bathrooms, is charged at 1650drs & with an en suite bathroom at 2100drs, increasing to 2235/2800drs (1st July-15th Sept).

From close by the area of *The Old Captain Bar* (*Tmr* 6D5), the beach starts off along the bottom of the bay and the backshore is sprinkled with unofficial camping. Turning along the rough beach backshore road and on the right, at about mid-way, some 60m back from the shore (about square F3 if there were one!) is the:-

Hotel Boulis (Class C) Tel 32122
Directions: As above.

A new, large complex which offers '45 spacious bedrooms, wall to wall carpeting in rooms and marble in all spaces...' Yes, there you go! Owned by the Boulis family, who also run the *Restaurant O Boulis* (ΜΠΟΥΛΗΣ)(*Tmr* 8C5) bordering the Esplanade. Despite the hype, the prices for the en suite rooms are acceptable. A single room starts at 2400drs & a double room 3000drs, rising to 3400drs & 4250drs (1st July-31st Aug).

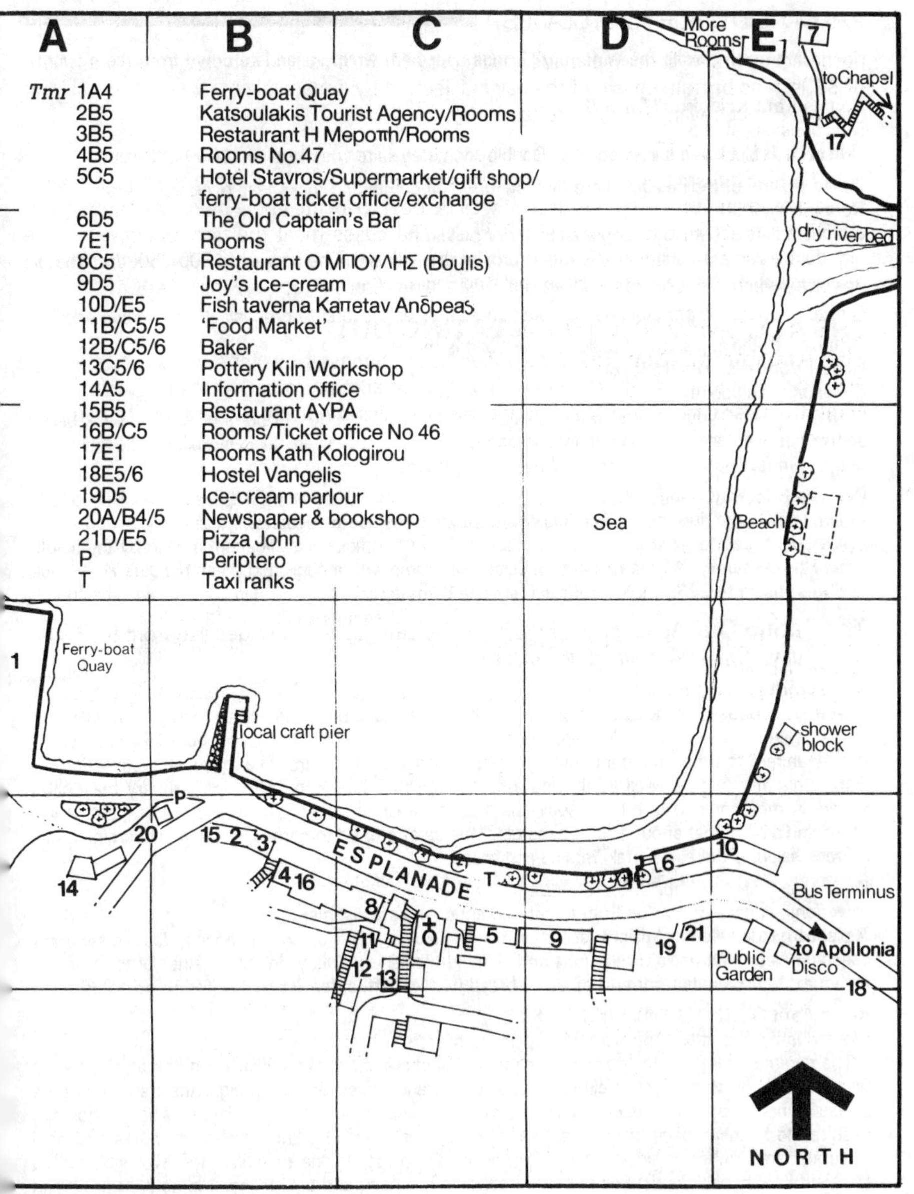

Illustration 50 Kamares

Tmr =Town map reference
Fsw =Facing seawards
Sbo =Sea behind one
Fbqbo =Ferry-boat Quay behind one

Continuing north across the wide, dry Livadas river-bed, which meanders down from the mountain gorge, is:-

Rooms Kath Kologirou (*Tmr* 17E1)

Directions: As above.

A newish block in a super location. Double rooms en suite cost between 2000-3000drs

At the far end of the beach, where the bay turns the corner and rocks take over, is:-

Rooms(*Tmr* 7E1)

Directions: As above, in amongst a cluster of buildings.

A double room en suite, in this rather provincial building, costs between 1500-2500drs. The old peasant couple who manage the place speak no English at all.

Further on, past the aforementioned accommodation, are several ***Rooms***, all at the average price.

Returning to the Esplanade/Apollonia main road is the:-

Hostel Vangelis (*Tmr* 18E5/6)

Directions: As above.

The 'unofficial' youth hostel where charges range between 500-700drs a night for a bunk bed in somewhat cramped accommodation. Reasonably priced meals are also available. The toilet and washroom facilities are supplemented by a roof garden.

Pension Kamari (Class B) Tel 31641

Directions: On the right of the Apollonia road, beyond the Bus turn-round.

A modern, comfortable three story pension (that's the official classification) owned by the helpful *Hotel Stavros* family. All rooms have en suite bathrooms with a single priced at 1650drs & a double 2065drs, rising to 2235drs & 2905drs (1st July-15th Sept)

The Eating Out As for accommodation, the eating places are detailed from the Ferry-boat Quay (*Tmr* 1A4) round the Esplanade.

Restaurant ΑΥΡΑ (*Tmr* 15B5)

Directions: Opposite the local craft pier with tables and chairs pleasantly spread out on the quayside.

The 'waitress may well be the charming, humourous, if absent-minded girl of about 16 years, whose mind wanders to other, more interesting matters than clients' orders. The menu alternatives include 'lump' this and that, as well as the more prosaic dishes! The menu offerings are very reasonably priced. A meal for two of a large souvlakia & chips, a Greek salad, tzatziki, a plate of giant beans, bread and a beer cost about 1095drs, as did 2 plates of stuffed tomatoes, chips, an aubergine salad, a Greek salad, 1 Coke, a kortaki retsina and bread.

Εστιατοριον Η Μεροπη (*Tmr* 3B5)

Directions: A pace or two on from the aforementioned establishment.

A pleasant little cafe-bar, mainly used by the locals. Average fare at average prices. Used to serve the cheapest Nes 'meh ghala' in the port and a 'mind-blocking', cloudy, 'open' retsina. Ouzo is served with mezes. A breakfast for two of jam & bread (for 1), coffee, tea & yoghurt (for 1), cost 300drs.

Restaurant O ΜΠΟΥΛΗΣ (Boulis) (*Tmr* 8C5)

Directions: Further along towards the Esplanade church.

The taverna tables line the quay across the road and are shaded by a scattering of mature trees. In fact most of the waterfront is cluttered with chairs and tables set in amongst the trees. Run by a pleasant, hard-working, welcoming family who positively want to show diners 'what's cooking', despite the kitchen space being fairly cramped. It is only fair to point out that my notes also said 'leisurely' and 'rather brusque'. Several good meals, a recent one of which, for two, included an excellent kolo kithaki yemiste as a starter between 2, 1 spaghetti bolognese, 1 lamb & pasta, bread and 1 litre of retsina for a cost of 940drs. Breakfast for two cost 350drs (bread, jam and coffee). Inside the building is an interesting picture of Old Kamares – have a look.

Joy's Ice Cream (*Tmr* 9D5)

Directions: Beyond the *Hotel Stavros*.

Surprise, surprise, they serve a range of ice-creams and fruit juices, but not much joy here, more a rather aggressive response.

Why not try the left-hand (*Sbo*) ice-cream parlour (*Tmr* 19D5), almost directly across the street from the 'Captain's Bar'. This is run by the smiling, happy Manoli and his wife.

Ψαροταβεγνα Καπετεν Ανδρεασ (Fish Taverna Captain Andreas)(*Tmr* 10D/E5)
Directions: Bordered by the road to Apollonia on one side and the beach on the other. The tables and chairs are set out on the curve of the backshore, amongst the shelter of some trees.

Somehow the menu and cooking put me in mind of the French Mediterranean, as do the charges, which are expensive. The meals, with an emphasis on fish, are excellent which at these prices they should be. If the patron's wine is unsatisfactory he changes it without question. A meal for two of 1 beetroot/spinach salad, 2 'dreamy' swordfish steaks (550drs per kilo), 2 chips, bread and a bottle of 'cellar Vin Blanc' cost 2000drs.

It has been pointed out that there is (at least) one good taverna at the far north side of the bay(*Tmr* E1).

THE A TO Z OF USEFUL INFORMATION

BANKS None but the *Hotel Stavros* office (*Tmr* 5C5) changes currency and travellers cheques. *See* **Banks, A To Z, Apollonia**.

BEACHES The fine sandy beach, which fills the bottom of the very long bay, has only one shortcoming – the extremely slow gradient of the sea-bed. It is a long wade to achieve more than knee-height – ideal for 'littlies'. It has to be admitted that the foreshore gets a little messy towards the far end of the great sweep. Nonetheless a beautiful beach and clean sea, second only to Milopotamos Beach, Ios island. At the near end is a small block of beach showers which are charged at 40drs a head. This facility is necessary to cope with backshore 'wild' campers. Pedaloes are rented at 350drs an hour and windsurfers cost 600drs.

BICYCLE, SCOOTER & CAR HIRE

Sifnos Car Hire Tel 31793/31661

Directions: Beyond the 'wasteground' Bus terminal, on the left-hand side of the Apollonia road.

A two seater moped costs 1500drs and a car from 4500drs a day. But do not forget that the bus service is so excellent that vehicle hire seems to me to be rather unnecessary. (Sorry Sifnos Hire).

BOOKSELLERS There is a English/foreign language book and newspaper stall (*Tmr* 20A/B4/5) near the Information office, close to the Ferry-boat Quay.

BREAD SHOPS The Baker (*Tmr* 12B/C5/6) also sells cold bottled water. The shop is reached through the archway alongside *Restaurant Boulis* and round to the right, behind the 'Food Market'.

BUSES The main turn-round area is at the outset of the Apollonia road and only buses connecting with a ferry-boat arrival carry on down to the quay. Lots of 'horn' on arrival and prior to departure.

Incidentally, the service in the bar alongside the bus turnround is polite and attentive and this establishment has a toilet in the building opposite a tourist information office.

Bus timetable (High season)
There are timetables everywhere.

Kamares Port to Apollonia, Artemonas, Platy Gialos
Daily: 0730, 0830, 0930, 1000, 1030, 1130, 1230, 1300, 1330, 1430, 1500, 1515, 1530, 1630, 1730, 1830, 1930, 2000, 2030, 2130, 2200, 2230, 2330, 2430hrs.

Platy Gialos to Apollonia, Kato Petali, Kastro
Daily: 0700, 0745, 0900, 1030, 1200, 1315, 1400, 1515, 1600, 1730, 1900, 2015, 2045, 2230, 2330hrs.

Artemonas to Apollonia, Kamares
Daily: 0700, 0815, 0900, 1000, 1100, 1200, 1230, 1300, 1400, 1430, 1445, 1500, 1600, 1700, 1800, 1900, 1930, 2000, 2100, 2130, 2200, 2300, 2400hrs.

Artemonas to Apollonia, Platy Gialos
Daily: 0700, 0900, 0930, 1000, 1100, 1130, 1200, 1300, 1400, 1500, 1600, 1630, 1700, 1730, 1800, 1930, 2000, 2100, 2130, 2200, 2300, 2400hrs.

Artemonas to Apollonia, Pharos
Daily: 0700, 0830, 1030, 1100, 1230, 1330, 1530, 1630, 1800, 1830, 2030, 2215hrs.

Pharos to Apollonia, Artemonas
Daily: 0730, 0900, 1100, 1130, 1300, (via Kato Petali), 1415, 1600, 1700, 1830, 1900, 2100, 2300hrs.

Kastro to Kato Petali, Apollonia, Artemonas
Daily: 0730, 0800, 0915, 1045, 1215, 1330, 1415, 1545, 1615, 1745, 1915, 2030, 2115, 2245, 2300, 2400hrs.

Pharos to Apollonia, Platy Gialos
Daily: 1100, 1700, 1900hrs.

Platy Gialos to Apollonia, Pharos
Daily: 1200, 1800, 2000hrs.

OPharos to Kamares
Daily: 0900, 1415, 2100hrs.

Kamares to Pharos
Daily: 1000, 1515, 2200hrs.

Artemonas to Apollonia, Kato Petali, Kastro
Daily: 0700, 1030, 1315, 1515, 1730, 1900, 2045, 2230, 2330hrs.

Kastro to Kato Petali, Apollonia, Artemonas
Daily: 0730, 1045, 1330, 1545, 1745, 1915, 2115, 2245, 2400hrs.

Kastro to Kato Petali, Apollonia, Kamares
Daily: 0815, 1215, 1415, 1915hrs.

Kamarea to Apollonia, Kato Petali, Kastro
Daily: 0830, 1300, 1500, 2000hrs.

Kastro to Kato Petali, Apollonia, Platy Gialos
Daily: 0915, 1615, 2115hrs.

Platy Gialos to Apollonia, Kato Petali, Kastro
Daily: 1000, 1700, 2200hrs.

Kastro to Kato Petali, Artemonas, Pharos
Daily: 1045, 1745hrs.

Pharos to Artemonas, Kato Petali, Kastro
Daily: 1130, 1830hrs.

COMMERCIAL SHOPPING AREA None, but the ground floor of the *Hotel Stavros* (*Tmr* 5C5) is almost a 'shopping mall' of opportunities, including a supermarket.

Through the archway alongside the *Restaurant Boulis* is a 'Food Market' (*Tmr* 11B/C5/6) – actually an old fashioned store.

A ceramics and pottery kiln workshop (*Tmr* 13C5/6) is to be found by climbing the steps alongside the large Esplanade church.

DISCO One beyond the public garden, at the outset of the Apollonia road.

FERRY-BOATS Well served and connected to the Eastern chain by the **Kimolos** whilst the **Ionian** sails the more traditional north-south route.

At least one small excursion boat makes the all important transverse connection with the pivotal Cycladean ferry-boat island of Paros.

Ferry-boat timetable (Mid-season)

Day	**Departure time**	**Ferry-boat**	**Ports/Islands of Call**
Mon	1300hrs	Kimolos	Ios,Thira(Santorini).
	2200hrs	Delos	Milos.
	2300hrs	Kimolos	Serifos,Piraeus(M).
Tues	0945hrs	Delos	Serifos,Kithnos,Rafina(M).
	1400hrs	Schinoussa	Serifos,Piraeus(M).
	2000hrs	Kimolos	Milos,Kimolos,Syros.
Wed	1100hrs	Kimolos	Serifos,Kithnos,Piraeus(M).
	1500hrs	Ionian	Kimolos,Milos.
	2000hrs	Ionian	Serifos,Kithnos,Piraeus(M)*.
		(*This boat arrives at 0200hrs but passengers can stay onboard until 0700hrs).	
Thur	1900hrs	Kimolos	Milos.
	2300hrs	Kimolos	Serifos,Kithnos,Piraeus(M).
Fri	2200hrs	Kimolos	Milos,Piraeus(M).
Sat	1400hrs	Ionian	Milos,Piraeus(M).
	1430hrs	Schinoussa	Serifos,Piraeus(M).

	1500hrs	Kimolos	Milos,Kimolos,Ios,Santorini.
Sun	1130hrs	Ionian	Serifos,Kithnos,Piraeus(M).
	1430hrs	Kimolos	Serifos,Kithnos,Piraeus(M).

For Paros island connections See Ferry-boats, A To Z, Paroikias, Paros (Chapter Five).

Please note these tables are detailed as a GUIDE ONLY. Due to the time taken to research the Cyclades, it is IMPOSSIBLE TO 'match' the timetables or even boats. So don't try cross pollinating...

FERRY-BOATS TICKET OFFICES

Katsoulakis Tourist & Travel Agency (*Tmr* 2B5) Tel 31700

Directions: At the Ferry-boat Quay end of the Esplanade.

The most professional outfit but the young women assistant is still rather sour-faced. They are also 'Authorised AGENGY (*sic*) Olympic'.

Ticket Kiosk Shop (*Tmr* 16B/C5) No. 46

Directions: Also at the west end of the Esplanade.

Sells tickets for the **Ionian**, **Schinoussa** and the 'local' Paros connection.

'Hotel Stavros' Ticket Office (*Tmr* 5C5)

Directions Mid-Esplanade.

This office also sells tickets for the **Delos** and **Schinoussa**.

MEDICAL CARE All in Apollonia.

MUNICIPAL TOURIST OFFICE (*Tmr* 14A5, tel 31977). Conveniently situated behind a small public garden on a layby not far from the end of the Ferry-boat Quay. Inaugurated in 1985, the office opens daily in the summer; Mon 0915-1500hrs & 1800-2400hrs; Tues 0915-1400hrs & 1700-2200hrs; Wed 0915-2100hrs; Thur & Fri 0915-1500hrs & 1800-2400hrs; Sat 0915-2100hrs and Sunday 1015-2000hrs. These 'openings' are timed to tie in with the arrival of the ferries. The staff have remained very enthusiastic, pleasant, keen, helpful and speak some English. Luggage can be stored here. Another 'twin' office has opened in Apollonia.

PLACES OF INTEREST There are trip boat excursions to the south-western harbour of Vathy. They depart every day, at 1000hrs, from the inland side of the Ferry-boat Quay (*Tmr* 1A4). They leave Vathy between 1430-1600hrs and, at the height-of-the-season, there are up to three boats a day.For other routes to Vathy *See* **Places of Interest, A To Z, Apollonia**.

TAXIS Two ranks (*Tmr* T), one at the bottom of the Ferry-boat Quay and the other on the water's edge opposite the *Hotel Stavros*.

TRAVEL AGENTS & TOUR OFFICES *See* **Ferry-boat Ticket Offices** & **Municipal Offices, A To Z**.

ROUTE ONE

To Apollonia (5km) The road picturesquely climbs the mountainside beside an intensely cultivated valley gorge. The stone wall bordered, dry river-bed is awash with oleanders in and amongst which are the occasional small dwelling and dovecote. At Pano Petali, on the outskirts of Apollonia, there is a petrol station.

APOLLONIA: capital (Illustration 51) Busy and active Apollonia is a town rather than a Greek island Chora. But the nomenclature town is incorrect as the settlement is more the epicentre of a cruciform development of hamlets and villages spread across the ridge and saddle of busy, neat, agricultural hills enclosed by tidy terraces. Apollonia encompasses, from north to south, the villages of **Artemonas**, **Ai Loukas**, **Pano Petali**, **Kato Petali**, **Arades**, **Katavati** and **Exambela**. Despite the height of summer tourist influx it remains unspoiled.

THE ACCOMMODATION & EATING OUT

The Accommodation There is not as much as might be hoped. The buses park on 'Bus & Museum' Square (Inset *Tmr* 1B2/3), on the far side of which is a convenient Kafeneion (Inset *Tmr* 2A/B2), even if the old boy is a bit surly. On the west side of the square is counter selling souvlakis.

Along the narrow street connecting 'Museum' Sq with 'OTE' Sq is the:-

Hotel Sophia (Inset *Tmr* 5B1/2) (Class C) Tel 31238

Directions: On the left with a restaurant occupying the ground floor.

Despite conflicting comments, one fact is certain – the proprietor is psychotic about the 'fluence' required to heat the water. As a result 'shower power' is only switched on for very short intervals per day. Rooms all have en suite bathrooms with a single costed at 1330drs & a double 1950drs, rising to 1355drs & 2360drs (1st-15th April & 1st July-10th Sept).

Hotel Anthoussa (Class C) Tel 31431

Directions: A modern building next door to the OTE (Inset *Tmr* 6C2) and above a famous patisserie.

Single rooms with en suite bathroom cost 1810/2260drs & a double room en suite 2080/2710drs.

South, along the main road to Pharos and Platy Gialos, is the:-

Pension Apollonia (Inset *Tmr* 7D2/3) (Class B) Tel 31490

Directions: On the left.

A long, single storey *Auberge* style building, close by the side of the road. All rooms share the bathrooms. A single room costs 1085drs & a double room 1400drs, increasing to 1445drs & 2080drs (1st-20th April & 1st July-31st Aug).

Almost opposite the *Apollonia* is ***Rooms*** which have received favourable comment.

From the top of the 'Museum' Sq (*Tmr* 1B2/3), opposite the Post Office, a narrow alley bears off alongside the elongated, tree-planted and seat scattered public garden. After about 30m, across the way from the Town police station (Inset *Tmr* 8B/C2), another narrow lane, Odhos Stylianou Prokou, sets off at right-angles climbing and snaking upwards. On the right, alongside a small plateia, is the:-

Hotel Sifnos (Inset *Tmr* 9B5/6) (Class C) Tel 31624

Directions: As above.

Double rooms only with en suite bathrooms, costing 2000drs which prices increase to 3000drs (1st July-31st Aug).

A chance meeting with an amply proportioned lady, Madame Aliopi Nicolou, failed to give me any more than the phone number for her ***Rooms*** (Tel 31459/31255). Nonetheless double rooms in her house cost 2000drs. It may help out!

The Pharos road is edged by a petrol filling station, alongside which is:-

Angelos Rooms

Directions: As above.

A highly recommended choice, even if a 'bit out of town'. The couple are most considerate and the rooms have mosquito coils fitted 'as standard'. Each of the two floors possess a communal refrigerator and there is a washing line and pegs. The ground floor rooms start off at about 1000drs. The first floor rooms cost from about 1500drs but they have the advantage of a veranda with marvellous views down the valley.

For other ***Rooms*** *See* **Places of Interest, A To Z**.

The Eating Out Apart from the Kafeneion (Inset *Tmr* 2A/B2) and the souvlaki snackbar on 'Museum' Sq (referred to under **The Accommodation**), the best all round value taverna/restaurant 'in Town' must be the:-

Restaurant Cyprus

Directions: On the 'Museum' Sq (Inset *Tmr* 1B2/3), between the Post Office and the souvlaki stall.

Well recommended, especially if the various tributes stuck in the window are any indicator. They include the poets acolade:-

'This man is a brilliant cook
Concerning hygiene just take a look
I have travelled this island wide
Who needs an Egan Ronay guide?
This man's cuisine is one of the best
The food is hot, put it to your test'.

The owner has added the following notice:-

'Dear Customer,
Behind this ugly entrance of the Restaurant Cyprus is hidden a wonderful garden. You can enjoy a dream of blue flowers in the shade. It is worth it'!

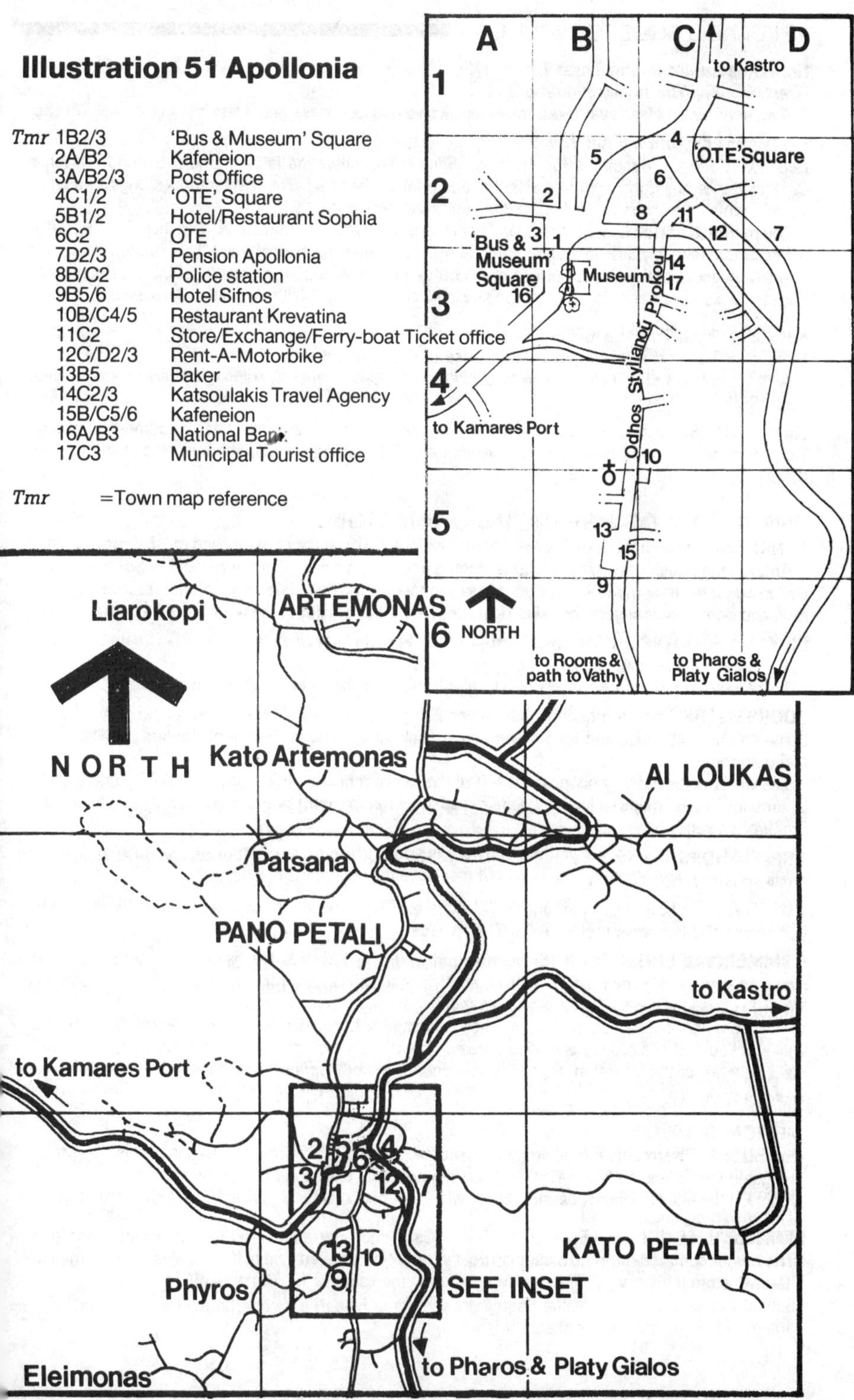

Illustration 51 Apollonia
Tmr 1B2/3 'Bus & Museum' Square
2A/B2 Kafeneion
3A/B2/3 Post Office
4C1/2 'OTE' Square
5B1/2 Hotel/Restaurant Sophia
6C2 OTE
7D2/3 Pension Apollonia
8B/C2 Police station
9B5/6 Hotel Sifnos
10B/C4/5 Restaurant Krevatina
11C2 Store/Exchange/Ferry-boat Ticket office
12C/D2/3 Rent-A-Motorbike
13B5 Baker
14C2/3 Katsoulakis Travel Agency
15B/C5/6 Kafeneion
16A/B3 National Bank
17C3 Municipal Tourist office
Tmr =Town map reference
A
B
C
D
1
2
3
4
5
6
to Kastro
'O.T.E.'Square
'Bus & Museum' Square
Museum
Odhos Stylianou Prokou
to Kamares Port
NORTH
to Rooms & path to Vathy
to Pharos & Platy Gialos
Liarokopi
ARTEMONAS
NORTH
Kato Artemonas
AI LOUKAS
Patsana
PANO PETALI
to Kastro
to Kamares Port
KATO PETALI
Phyros
SEE INSET
Eleimonas
to Pharos & Platy Gialos

Hotel/Restaurant Sophia (Inset *Tmr* 5B1/2)
Directions: *See* **The Accommodation**.

A meal for two of freshly cooked meatballs & chips, local cheese and a litre of retsina cost 750drs.

Restaurant Krevatina (Inset *Tmr* 10B/C4/5), Stylianou Prokou St.
Directions: *See* the directions for the *Hotel Sifnos*. The Krevatina is on the left, beyond the Argo Cocktail Bar on the right, opposite a church and prior to the hotel. The restaurant is alongside a small square, which the chairs and tables of the establishment fill.

The patron, Nikolaos Lantsis, presides over an inexpensive but varied menu. This includes swordfish but unfortunately only a large, costly bottle of retsina. A meal for two of swordfish, ratatouille, a plate of green beans, Greek salad, potatoes and a bottle of retsina cost in excess of 2000drs. Despite the prices the establishment is well patronised and closes from 1400hrs until early evening.

Kafeneion (Inset *Tmr* 15B/C5/6)
Directions: To the side of Odhos Prokou, close to the *Hotel Sifnos*.

A delightful, old style kafeneion with backgammon 'prominent'. A frappe coffee and a lemonade cost 150drs.

Edging 'OTE' Sq, in fact next door to the OTE (Inset *Tmr* 6C2), are the tables of a smart patisserie located in the ground floor of the *Hotel Anthoussa*. They spread across the terrace and the front of the OTE office.

THE A TO Z OF USEFUL INFORMATION

BANKS The **National Bank of Greece** (Inset *Tmr* 16A/B3) is at the Kamares end of 'Museum' Square.

An Exchange desk (Inset *Tmr* 11C2) is located in a large shop straight on (*'Museum Sq' behind one and to the left*) from the Police station. This emporium not only sells dairy products, sliced meats, food and some ironmongery, but also operates a ferry-boat ticket office – for the **FB Ionian**.

BICYCLE, SCOOTER & CAR HIRE Rent-A-Moto-Bicycle (Inset *Tmr* 12C/D2/3) is situated between 'OTE' Sq and *Pension Apollonia*, on the right.

There is also an outfit on the left of the road leaving Apollonia in the direction of Kastro.

BOOKSELLERS The 'Boomerang' International Agency borders 'Museum' Sq (Inset *Tmr* 1B2/3), between the Post Office and the souvlaki stall. They stock a wide range of foreign newspapers and magazines.

The Gift & Haberdashery shop,on the left of the road connecting 'Museum' and 'OTE' Squares,sells a number of useful maps including a gem in respect of Kastro, written and illustrated by a John Barkett Smith of England.

BREAD SHOPS There is a Baker (Inset *Tmr* 13B5) on Odhos Stylianou Prokou, the other side of the small square to *Hotel Sifnos*.

BUSES Park on both 'Museum' and 'OTE' Squares. The service, as has been written, is first class. For details *See* **Bus timetables, A To Z, Kamares**.

COMMERCIAL SHOPPING AREA North from 'OTE' Sq, towards the hamlet of Artemonas, is an excellent 'provincial' supermarket, on the right. Where the bus stops for ten minutes, on the Artemonas leg of the bus journey, is a baker who sells mouthwatering tiropites for 30drs.

The aforementioned Grocery shop (money exchange & ferry-boat ticket office) (Inset *Tmr* 11C2) is well stocked and has a dairy and sliced meats counter. On the right of the road connecting the two main Squares, at the 'Museum' Sq end,is a butcher and shop. Opposite the 'Museum' Square souvlaki stall is a periptero.

MEDICAL CARE
Chemists & Pharmacies A pharmacy is situated on the left of the narrow lane which heads off alongside the Kafeneion (Inset *Tmr* 2A/B2), in a northerly direction from 'Museum' Sq.
Clinic On the left of Odhos Vássalopoulou, which connects 'OTE' Sq (*Tmr* 4C1/2) with Artemonas.

MUNICIPAL TOURIST OFFICE (Inset *Tmr* 17C3) Odhos Stylianou Prokou. A spacious office with ferry, bus, accommodation and excursion boat information situated next to Katsoulakis Tourist Agency. They will store left luggage. The opening hours are the same as for Kamares office.

OTE (*Tmr* 6C2) Open weekdays 0800-1300hrs & 1700-2200hrs; weekends & holidays 0900-1300hrs & 1800-2140hrs.

PLACES OF INTEREST Naturally a plethora of churches, as well as the Museum, but one of the big attractions of Siphnos island is the opportunity to walk the many paths and tracks. I am aware that I rarely laud the delights of marching about the countryside but... This is an island where 'walkies' pays off, especially as no particular trek is of inordinate length and nearly every route passes at least one, if not two interesting churches and or monasteries.

Walking all the way along Odhos Prokou, beyond the *Hotel Siphnos*, leads to a ridge at the top of Apollonia Town, whereon a children's playground and several windmills. Incidentally there are ***Rooms*** advertised here.

From this ridge there is a donkey track to:-

VATHY (1hr 40mins from Apollonia) This route covers an old path as much of the surface is paved marble. Keep to the track, past a sign to the right to Mt Profitis Ilias which is followed by another for Vathy. There are a few 'red-herring' paths but, even allowing for getting lost a couple of times, the walk shouldn't take more than two hours. The route passes a ruin and some splendid churches.

Vathy is simply delightful. The harbour and sandy beach of this fishing boat and pottery port are set in a decanter shaped inlet. There are some sixteen ***Rooms***, three tavernas and unofficial backshore camping, as well as the 16th century Byzantine Taxiarchis Vathiou Church. The church celebrates festivals on the 6th September and the 8th November.

POLICE The Police station (Inset *Tmr* 8B/C2) is on the left of the alley branching off at right angles from the north end of 'Museum' Sq. The small hut-like office is open Saturday as well as weekdays and the officers will help in a search for accommodation, but they do not speak very much English.

POST OFFICE (Inset *Tmr* 3A/B2/3) On the left of 'Museum' Sq (*Facing north*). Transacts exchange.

TAXIS Rank on both Main Squares.

TELEPHONE NUMBERS & ADDRESSES

Clinic	Tel 31315
Police (Inset *Tmr* 8B/C2)	Tel 31210

TRAVEL AGENTS & TOUR OFFICES Apart from the Exchange office (Inset *Tmr* 11C2) (*See* **Banks, A To Z**), there is the:-

Katsoulakis Travel Agency (*Tmr* 14C2/3) Tel 31000

On the left of Odhos Stylianou Prokou. The friendly young lady speaks clear English.

ROUTE TWO

To Pharos from Apollonia (7km) The surfaced road strikes south from Apollonia through the outlying village of **Katavati** and, after some 2km, forks left off the main road to Platy Gialos.

The last section of the route is paralleled by a lovely river gorge, full of oleanders, set in farming country.

PHAROS (Faros) (7km from Apollonia) A small, sleepy, one-time port, now an *ad hoc* holiday resort and certainly where I would head if not staying in Kamares Port.

On the left of the road into the settlement, just before the village, is an unnamed taverna reached by a set of steps from the roadside. Great fish, great service and the friendliest cats on the island.

The buses pull up to the left of the hamlet, on the edge of the fishing boat quay which not only frames this side of the bay but is at right angles to the waterfront.

On the left of the quay (*Fsw*) are the rather rustic *Rooms* (Tel 31822) and a small, basement gift shop that sells tourist bits and bobs.

Proceeding along the waterfront to the right are *Rooms Stela Kakaki* where mid-season doubles, sharing a bathroom, cost from 1500drs; a Chalet owner (Tel 31989) with double rooms from 2000drs and the *Restaurant To Kima (Mesimeriatis)*. The latter's midday lunch menu is native in content with dishes such as Siphniot chick-peas in lamb stock.

The evening servings are more touristy and expensive. A meal for two of moussaka, giant beans, Greek salad, 2 beers and bread cost 900drs.

The young lad who served the super breakfasts at the *Restaurant To Kima* has now set up on his own at the left-hand end of the first beach – the *Mermaid Bar*. If a client can wrest him away from his friends and or games of backgammon he may even serve one! He offers a 'Euro Breakfast' – coffee or tea, fruit juice, bread, butter and honey or a 'Super Breakfast' as above plus eggs, bacon and chocolate cake – yes chocolate cake.

This first beach is small and sandy with a coarse sand sea-bed and a pebbly backshore on to which 'expires' a dried up river-bed. A notice requests, 'Please love this beach as we do'. Behind and to the left of the beach (*Sbo*) is the *Pension Fabrica*, a recently restored Venetian style stone building. This is most attractive accommodation with wonderful views. Some rooms have balconies and all rooms have en suite facilities as well as hot water. A nice touch is the mosquito 'machine' fitted in each room. Furthermore, the tablet is changed every day! Rates are from 2000drs per night for a double room. From the far end of the first beach, steps ascend to a pocket-sized and pretty 'Old Quarter' draped over a prominent headland. Hereon are several rudimentary ***Rooms*** overlooking the sea, on the tip of the promontory. Double rooms, en suite, cost from 1500drs,but the shower water is cold.

Beyond the bluff is another small, very sandy beach, with some kelp at the centre, backed by a stone wall and bulrushes at the far end. A lot of 'wild' camping takes place in the olive grove behind this beach. 'Nudes bathe', despite the sign prohibiting the same.

ROUTE THREE

To Platy Gialos from Apollonia(10km) From the Pharos fork, the main road loops past the **Monastery Panaghia ton Vouno** built in 1813. Further on is the paved side road past the expensive looking *Hotel Fiora* (Class B, tel 31778) where all rooms have en suite bathrooms, with a single room costing 1330drs & a double 1935drs, increasing to 1810drs & 2395drs (11th June-15th Sept). There certainly are superb views. Progressing leads to the beautifully sited:-

Monastery Panaghia Chryssopighi Built in 1650,on a rocky cape,and founded because of the discovery of a glowing icon in the sea, which makes a change from the usual rowing boat legends. The fissure twixt monastery and the shore is attributed to Holy intervention. The story goes that three local women were set on by pirates, who no doubt had other thoughts in their minds than ballroom dancing. The ladies prayed to the Virgin Mary who caused an earthquake and the cleft, which, understandably, shook the pirates no end.

To the left of the monastery car park, a sandy track descends to a very pleasant, popular sandy beach set in a bay and whereon are two good tavernas, but no accommodation.

Returning to the main road, the route descends through the surrounding hills to:-

PLATY GIALOS (Plati Yialos) The road parallels the long, flat sea-shore. The landward side is edged by stone-walled fields of olive trees and the plain is ringed by hills. The occasional apartment and private house edges this side of the thoroughfare.

The sea side of the road is fringed by a row of single storey dwellings, at least five tavernas, a restaurant, snackbar, tourist shop and the two storey *Panorama* (Class D).

The left-hand (*Fsw*) side of the bay is bordered by a gathering of fishermans cottages with benzinas and a fishing caique or two anchored in the shallow water. The beach at this end is stony with some kelp whilst the sea bottom has biscuit rock and pebbles.

There are two small, low quays between which a flock of ducks and drakes swim back and forth. About centre of the sandy beach is a fascinating jumble of low buildings. To the left (*Fsw*) is a ceramic kiln with all the paraphernalia necessary to produce the pottery.

To the right is a simple terrace, conspicuous by a solitary shower head. This is backed by once rudimentary ***Rooms*** to which a two storey addition has been 'bolted on'. The rather mercenary landlady demands 2000drs for a double room en suite.

The bus pulls up to the right of centre of the bay and prior to the last stop, on the beach side, is the delightful *Pension Angeliki* (Tel 31688). This is run by Angeliki Gerontopoulou and her taxi driving husband. The rooms have en suite bathrooms.

To the right the beach becomes progressively more stony, as does the sea bottom, and terminates by the:-

Hotel Platis Gialos (Class B) Tel 31324

Directions: As above.

A simple but expensive looking three storey building let into the rock that edges this end of the bay. Appearances do not deceive! All rooms have en suite bathrooms with a single room costing 2980drs & a double room 3750drs, increasing to 4200drs & 5000drs (1st July-15th Sept).

The backshore has occasional clumps of trees and signs 'Do not swim naked in the crowded beaches. Withdraw to isolated places' and 'Please keep Sifnos clean. Cleanliness means health and civilisation'. Despite this last admonishment the beach is a little messy.

Camping Plati Yialos

Directions: A stony track leads off the main road at the far right-hand end of the beach (*Fsw*), just before the main road 'comes to an end'. It is about a 500m climb. The track is signed 'Camping' and 'Vathy', as it is possible to walk via the campsite to Vathy, but the track is badly marked and it is very easy to get lost.

This is the island's one official campsite, which opened in 1987. As yet there are few facilities and very little shade, as most of the trees are only about 1 metre high! Facilities include showers & washing rooms, and a reception selling cold drinks as well as a few other necessary bits and pieces. Charges are 300drs per person but nothing for the tent.

ROUTE FOUR

To Kastro from Apollonia (3½km) Why not save the best to last? As nobody can take the Kastro away, reserve it for a treat.

KASTRO (3½km from Apollonia) The bus makes the short journey along the road which drops steeply down to a saddle bordered by some windmills and pulls up on the right flank of the massive headland, which is swathed by a Medieval fortress.

There are ***Rooms*** to rent on the hillside at the outset to the Kastro, just before the windmills, right opposite the sign which marks the entry to the village.

The Kastro is a really very beautiful, clean, whitewashed Chora, dramatically positioned on the promontory that falls away sharply on either side into the sea, way below. The streets are in terraced tiers, climbing the hilltop in the fashion of a layered cake.

The antiquity and continuous development of the site is no better evidenced than by the bits and pieces of ancient columns and headless busts haphazardly incorporated into the facades of various houses. There is a plentiful 'supply' of churches as well as an Archaeological Museum. The original castle walls have all but disappeared.

There are very few concessions to tourists apart from *Zorbas Taverna*, *Rooms Helen Lempesi*, 'Green Grocery & Snack, The Star' and a postbox, all scattered throughout the alleys and lanes. Some of the pedestrian-only ways form bridges to the top floors of the lower houses, while some are arched and covered by buildings whose first floors connect overhead.

The approach road to the Kastro dips on to a 'bridge-like' hillside saddle, on the left of which are three remaining windmills. These are interesting in that they are constructed in the style of the Cretan models. That is they are built with a rounded front, elongated main body and flat back instead of the archetypal, circular Cycladean pattern. A snackbar has been set into the side wall of one of two of the mills that stand almost side-by-side.

To the right of the main road, as it approaches the flank of the Kastro, is a steep mountainside drop to the small, stony, beautiful cove of Ormos Seralias. A rocky track winds and wanders down to the narrowing and diminutive backshore. This and a dry valley river-bed are almost crowded out by a clutter of buildings. One of these was once a tannery, another is a domed church, alongside which is a restaurant.

On the other side of the mountain to the Kastro and high above Seralias Bay is the:-
Monastery Chrysostomou Founded in 1550 and once a convent. Its claim to fame is that it served as headquarters of the island opposition to the Turkish overlords, including an illegal school to educate children in traditional Greek customs.

To the left of the main road, just before the windmills, an unsurfaced, short track ends abruptly overlooking the craggy, sea edged, cliff-face. On a small blob of headland, almost at sea-level, is the blue domed Church of the Seven Martyrs. On the side of this track are the foundations of what may (still) be a projected hotel. If this is so, why not visit the Kastro before the 'delights' and demands of 20th century holiday-makers ruin this lovely city of antiquity and manage what 3,500 years of turbulent island history have failed to inflict – its despoliation.

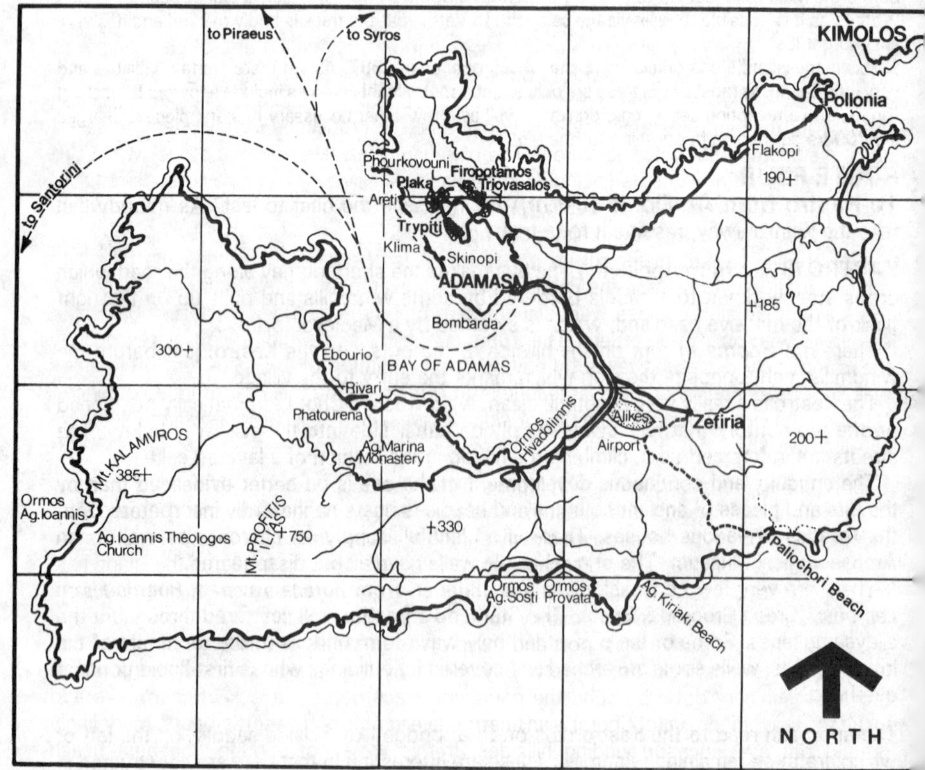

Illustration 52 Milos island

18 MILOS (Melos, Milo) & Kimolos Cyclades Islands - Western chain

Milos ★★★
Kimolos ★★★★★

FIRST IMPRESSIONS Attractive sea approach; dramatic coastline; the island appears to be under reconstruction by mining & quarrying; saline water; old men's attire includes a cummerbund.

SPECIALITIES Venus de....; mineral mining; hot thermal springs.

RELIGIOUS HOLIDAYS & FESTIVALS include: 7th May – Feast & festival, Church Ag Ioannis Theologos (south-west of island); 8th September – Feast of Birth of Virgin Mary, Church Panaghia Korfiatissa (Plaka).

VITAL STATISTICS Tel prefix 0287. The island has an area of about 160 sq km, is roughly 20km wide, 13km deep and would resemble a flattened circle if it were not for the huge horseshoe bay that almost divides the island in two. The population numbers between 4500 & 5000.

HISTORY The volcanic nature of the rocks and the 'apple-like bite-of-bay' points to an ancient volcanic eruption that tore out the centre of the island.

Milos served as an important Minoan outpost and has been mined and quarried throughout the centuries. Has anybody considered the predilection for Minoans to select sites associated with volcanic action? The obsidian, a glassy, volcanic stone, was used for all manner of implements (including knives as well as spear and arrow heads) prior to perfection of the treatment of metal ore. Apart from the mining activities, the history has tended to follow the Cycladean historical 'norm'.

Admittedly the Athenians cut-up pretty rough, in about 450BC, when the islanders refused to side with them in the Persian wars. An example was made to discourage this 'backsliding' so all the males were slaughtered, the women carried away and the island colonised with mainland settlers. The Turks, during their rule, did not physically occupy the island, only extracting taxes by envoy. The population of the main port of Adamas was supposedly stiffened by a large influx of Cretans, during the War of Independence.

During the First World War the Bay of Adamas was used as a harbour by large numbers of Allied warships.

GENERAL The association with Venus often convinces visitors to believe that this most southerly island of the Western Cyclades will be 'a jewel in the Aegean Sea'. Readers who prefer to be let down slowly should not read on, for Milos is not everyone's dream, more a disturbed sleep. Probably not wildly attractive to start with, the island has, for thousands of years, been and still is under constant attack by the mining industry. This has resulted in a 'chewed', manky appearance to the scenery.

The dusty, unattractive main port and town of Adamas lies on the edge of a huge bay but just the islands luck, not a pretty bay. Certainly the various concentrations of ore moving machinery dotted around the periphery exacerbates the lack of charm. To add insult to injury, the Plaka (or Chora) is an unattractive jumble of four settlements, muddlingly draped out over the surrounding hillsides. If this were not enough, the best beach (Paliochori) is a comparatively long bus ride across the island. Perhaps the best feature of Milos is the not unattractive northern fishing boat port of Pollonia, from whence can be caught a caique for the adjacent island of Kimolos. Now there's a different 'cup of retsina'. How the beautifully simple, lovely island of Kimolos can have remained unsung for so long is a mystery to me. Even the local guide, which comments on all the neighbouring islets, declines to give Kimolos more than a passing mention. Perhaps its larger neighbour has kept the wraps firmly on the undeniable attractions of Kimolos in case it should detract from the 'delights' of Milos. If so it is quite understandable for Kimolos is a 'rose amongst the thorns' of Milos.

In defence of Milos it has to be pointed out that the islanders are very friendly; much of the countryside, not 'under the machine', is fertile; there are some superb beaches, more especially on the south coast; it is very easy to escape the height of season hordes and accommodation is plentiful, even in August.

Those visitors tempted to leave Milos almost as fast as they can catch the next boat might like to hang on and allow the island's charms to weave their spell.

ADAMAS: main port (Illustration 53) A rather dusty, unattractive mishmash of a port with a large Ferry-boat Quay and the main development of the town sprawling away to the right (*Sbo*). Set in a ring of hills and with a southerly aspect, if there is no wind the port becomes hot and sticky. This, combined with the dust resulting from the continuing mining activity, often makes it necessary for the streets to be wetted down – by tanker. With so much waterfront it would be nice if there were glorious beaches but...

ARRIVAL BY AIR The small, dusty airstrip lies to the south of a large, still worked salt bed, about 4½km from Adamas. The term airport is rather grand for this collection of 'large garden sheds'. I hope the eager expectations of arrivals are slowly deflated but if the airport lives up to passengers hopes, the drive along the seashore of the huge bay will probably allow doubts to intrude. But some may like what they see...

ARRIVAL BY FERRY The approach to the port flatters to deceive as the ferry-boats run down the lip or east shoreline of the very large Bay of Adamas. To the right, about 8km offshore, is the comparatively large, uninhabited island of **Antimilos**, a sanctuary for chamois. The boats cut in between the untenanted, inshore islets of **Akradies** and Milos island. They steam past some fascinating geological formations as well as the colourful, picturesque, 'Venetian', fishing hamlets of **Phourkovouni**, **Areti**, **Klima** and **Skinopi**. The buildings of these settlements cling so low to the waters edge that an onlooker can only marvel that the wash of the larger ferry-boats doesn't swamp them. These 'ports' are only inhabited during the summer months, the citizens returning to the Plaka for the winter.

Even the last sandy headland, around which the boats sweep, tends to mislead, keeping a travellers hopes high but... The ferry-boats dock at the large, prominent quay (*Tmr* 1C4) and are met by any number of hotel and Room owners.

On a warning note it is worth bearing in mind that the ferry-boats often sound their hooters rather too early, before rounding the headland, which masks this notice of their impending arrival.

THE ACCOMMODATION & EATING OUT Accommodation, does not pose a problem, even in the month of August. On the other hand eating out does.

The Accommodation At the cliff wall end of the quay is a Tourist Information kiosk (*Tmr* 33C3/4). This is rarely manned, or 'womaned' for that matter, but much useful information is displayed, including accommodation details.

Around to the left (*Sbo*) of the Ferry-boat Quay (*Tmr* 1C4) is the pleasant, cosy, package holiday hotel development at Lagada Beach (*Tmr* A3). Of the three or four hotels, at least one has Rooms, the:-

Hotel Delfini Rooms (*Tmr* 2A2/3) (Class D) Lagada Beach Tel 22001
Directions: From the end of the quay, follow the cliff-face waterfront track to the small beach cove. The modern hotel is third block back and one building in from the road as it heads up the valley.

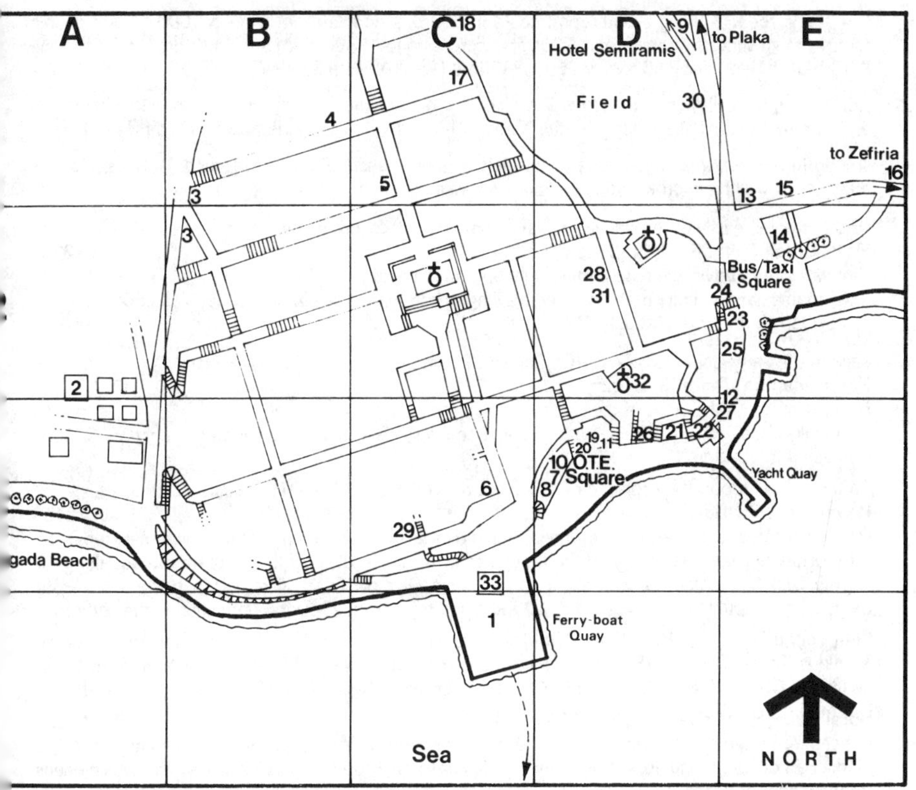

ustration 53 Adamas

Tmr	=Town map reference
Fsw	=Facing seawards
Sbo	=Sea behind one
Fbqbo	=Ferry-boat Quay behind one

r 1C4	Ferry-boat Quay
2A2/3	Hotel Delfini Rooms
3A/B1/2	Rooms (a pair)
4B/C1	Kanaris Rooms
5B/C1/2	Hotel Corali
6C3	Hotel Adamas
7C/D3	Rooms
8C/D3	OTE
9D1	Olympic office
10C/D3	Milos Tours
11D3	'Tourist' office
12D/E2/3	Averkios Tours
13D/E1/2	Hotel Georgantas/Maggies Fast Food
14E1/2	Cafe-bar Restaurant
15E1/2	Hotel Meltemi
16E1/2	Hotel Milos
17C1	Rooms
18C1	Antonios Rooms
19D3	Cavo D'Amore
20D3	Post Office
21D3	Restaurant O Φλοισβος
22D/E2/3	Taverna O Κυξηγος
23D/E2	Cafeteria Milos
24D/E2	'Charcoal' Taverna
25D/E2	Commercial Bank
26D3	National Bank
27D/E2/3	Newspapers
28D2	Baker
29C3	Unisex Hairdresser
30D1	Pharmacy
31D2	Clinic
32D2/3	Catholic Church
33C3/4	Tourist Information Kiosk

A single room, sharing a bathroom, costs 1390drs, a double room sharing 1600drs & a double room with en suite bathroom costs 2250drs, increasing to 1530drs & 1840/2800drs (1st-30th June & 16th-30th Sept) and 1860drs & 2500/3480drs (1st July-15th Sept).

North along the valley from the *Hotel Delfini*, on the right of the road, at the junction with a backward angled street that climbs steeply up the 'Chora hill', are two neighbouring ***Rooms*** (*Tmr* 3A/B1/2).

A little further on, a flight of steps to the right rises to *Kanaris Rooms* (*Tmr* 4B/C1). Note this area may just as well be approached in an anti-clockwise direction.

Another hotel, easily accessible if you have come this far round, is the:-
Hotel Corali (*Tmr* 5B/C1/2) (Class C) Tel 22204
Directions: As above, the next turning right and on the right.
All rooms have en suite bathrooms with a single room priced at 2000drs & doubles 2500drs, rising to 2800drs & 3500drs (1st July-15th Sept).

Back at the Ferry-boat Quay (*Tmr* 1C4), close by is the:-
Hotel Adamas (*Tmr* 6C3) 2 Griara Tel 22322
Directions: Up on the crest of the cliff overlooking the waterfront.
Actually classified as a pension with double rooms only. They share bathrooms at a cost of 1500drs, increasing to 2500drs (1st July-31st Aug).

To the right (*Fbqbo*), the Esplanade widens out on to the lop-sided 'OTE' Square. On the left is:-
Rooms (*Tmr* 7C/D3) Tel 22183
Directions: As above, next door to the OTE and over a small office, up a flight of external steps.
Unfortunately the owner lives at the far end of the town. That is off the Plaka main road, along the narrow lane that branches to the left, prior to the Olympic Office (*Tmr* 9D1), beyond the *Hotel Semiramis*. A double room costs from 2000drs and triple from 2500drs, both sharing the bathroom.

Both Tour offices (*Tmr* 10C/D3 & 11D3) lining the 'OTE' Square offer accommodation advice, as will Averkios Tours (*Tmr* 12D/E2/3) on round the corner. The Esplanade follows the waterfront to the 'Main' or 'Bus/Taxi' Square (*Tmr* E2), so nicknamed because both buses and taxis park here!

Hotel Georgantas (*Tmr* 13D/E1/2) (Class D) Tel 41636
Directions: Bordering the north side of the 'Bus/Taxi' Sq, on the corner of the Plaka and the Zefiria roads. Part of the ground floor is occupied by *Maggies Fast Food Self-Service Restaurant*, which opens for the height of season.
All rooms share the bathrooms with a single starting off at 1800drs & a double 2990drs, rising to 2000drs & 3500drs (1st July-31st Aug).

A few metres along the Zefiria road, that circles round the bay, separated from the waterfront by a *Cafe-Bar Restaurant* (*Tmr* 14E1/2) and a grubby lorry-park, are the:-
Hotel Meltemi (*Tmr* 15E1/2) (Class C) Tel 22284
Directions: As above but only a step or two to the side of the 'Bus/Taxi' Sq.
Neat, if rather pricey. All rooms have en suite bathrooms with a single room priced at 2300drs & a double 2990drs, rising to 2915drs & 3500drs (1st July-31st Aug).
and the:-
Hotel Milos (*Tmr* 16E1/2) (Class C) Tel 22087
Directions: As above. but further along the road to the east.
Pleasant looking but the situation, behind an old warehouse in the lorry park area, leaves something to be desired. The en suite room rates also leave something to be desired, with a single room costing 2200drs & a double 2800drs, rising to 2800drs & 4000drs (1st July-31st Aug).

Hotel Popi (Class B) Tel 21988
Directions: A 'room or so' further along the Zefiria road.
Actually rated as a pension, despite which it is jolly expensive. En suite single rooms cost 2000drs & en suite doubles 2500drs, rising to 3800drs & 4500drs (1st July-15th Sept).

Proceeding along the Plaka main road, the previously referred to lane that angles off to the left (*Sbo*), beyond the *Cafeteria Pub Dream* (*sic*), advances to the:-
Hotel Semiramis (Class D) Tel 22117
Directions: As above and on the left.
All rooms have en suite bathrooms. A single room costs 2125drs & a double 2170drs, increasing

to 2400drs & 2440drs (16th May-15th June), and 2935drs & 2980drs (16th June-20th Sept).

Returning to the 'Bus/Taxi' Sq, a narrowing lane climbs and curves from the top, left-hand side (*Sbo*) of the plateia skirting a field on the right. Beyond the second flight of steps and a lane to the left, is:-

Rooms (*Tmr* 17C1)
Directions: As above.

The lady is very nice, plying guests with bottles of cold water and fruit. She only has two simple double rooms sharing the one bathroom. One of the twin beds is a camp bed but there is a bedside lamp, wall hooks, a washing line and the water is hot all day and night, even if the pressure is rather low. She charges some 2000drs a night.

This lane is fairly busy and noisy at night. Alongside the house is a side-street to the left which leads to *Kanaris Rooms* (*Tmr* 4B/C1). Carrying on down the dip in the street, almost to the outskirts of the development, leads to:-

Antonios Rooms (*Tmr* 18C1) Tel 22002
Directions: As above and on the right.

A large, purpose-built pension displaying a number of unique features in addition to the more usual failings. The plumbing must have been subject to last minute adjustments as several pipe runs are laid over the floors of the corridors with resultant bumps and humps. The walls are so thin that guests in rooms next door to the bathrooms are party to the most intimate and shared moments. The cavernous bathrooms contain conveniently large waste-bins, which I'm afraid to report are rarely emptied. For some reason the corridors echo loudly and the pleasant rooms are devoid of cupboards, hanging capacity being furnished by one those 'sassy', sagging, material covered frames. Prospective 'roomers' must not get the impression that the building is not solid and well constructed. For instance the window and balcony door units are very expensive, aluminium framed modules – which, incidentally, don't lock. A double room costs from 1800drs & a triple from 2500drs

The Eating Out The use of the port by a fairly small-time, Swiss yacht organisation has not resulted in such a diversity of choice as one would expect, if the experience of other 'flotilla islands' is anything to go by.

On the way round from the Ferry-boat Quay (*Tmr* 1C4), where the Esplanade widens out on to the 'OTE' Square, is the:-

Cavo D'Amore (*Tmr* 19D3)
Directions: Next door to the Post Office with a double awning stretching into the road.

Chatty and expensive with beer served in large glass mugs! Pizzas, tost, ice-creams, a fast food menu but prices are almost double those of the 'Bus/Taxi' Sq *Cafeteria Milos*. Say no more. Breakfast for two costs 550drs (350drs at the *Milos*).

Further along the Esplanade, side by side, are two similar restaurants with much the same offerings. They are the *Restaurant Mariana* and the:-

Restaurant Ο Φλοισβοσ (*Tmr* 21D3).
Directions: As above.

The owner is smooth and attentive enough until a client's order is taken, after which interest and memory fails. The service is quicker for attractive young women! Every so often a dish ordered is forgotten but the food is fresh and consistently good, even if the portions are small. A meal for two of 1 squid with macaroni, 1 beef & chips, 1 green beans, 1 taramosalata, bread, 1 beer and 1 coke cost 1250drs.

On the corner, where the Esplanade bends sharply around to the left (*Fbqbo*), is the:-

Taverna ΚΥΝΗΠΟΣ (*Tmr* 22D/E2/3).
Directions: As above.

A meal for two of 1 stuffed tomatoes, 1 stuffed aubergine & chips, a salad, 1 beer, 1 Coke and bread cost a very inexpensive 800drs.

Alongside the 'Bus/Taxi' Sq is possibly the best value in the port, the:-

Cafeteria Milos (*Tmr* 23E/E2)
Directions: As above, on the left. Attractively the cafe has tables and chairs the other side of this wide section of the Esplanade, by the waterside.

The striking, driving lady keeps the cafe-bar open all day, and quite a lot of the night. During the day a sign advises 'No help here, self-service please' she only employs waiters in the evenings. Her English is peppered with the catch-phrase 'Bravo darling, sit down'. Prices seem to vary from day to day. Two baklava and 2 coffees cost 280drs and 2 breakfasts (and coffee) 350drs. Certainly this must represent a reasonably priced, friendly alternative to the other quay front, snobby outfits. Additionally there is a cave-like toilet.

Next door is the:-
Cafe-Bar Aktaion
Directions: As above.
A smarter, more expensive alternative to the *Milos* and serves beer in cans. Need one say more?

Still on the same side of the road, towards the crossroads of the 'Bus/Taxi' Sq, is a small, sandy, rectangular yard to the left (*Sbo*). This is empty in the day, edged on the far side by a dusty chandlers. Lo and behold, at night opens up the:-

'Charcoal' Taverna (*Tmr* 24D/E2)
Directions: As above.
The limited menu is now also written in English and this is one of the all round, best value establishments in Adamas serving charcoal cooked food. The dishes on offer include individual sticks of souvlaki (at 65drs a stick – clients ordering so many sticks), beef steak (in actuality minced beef) and large pork cutlets. The meat dishes are accompanied by excellent Greek salads, large helpings of chips and big plates of correctly prepared tzatziki (I'm salivating whilst writing!). One drawback is the lack of retsina (although some would regard this as a plus point or three), only *Demestica* being available. A meal for two of 4 souvlaki, 1 beefsteak, 1 tzatziki, a plate of feta, ½ bottle of red wine, a bottle of water, a Coke and bread cost 1355drs.

Cafe-Bar Restaurant (*Tmr* 14E1/2)
Directions: Alongside the taxi rank and well shaded by mature trees, with tables and chairs pleasantly spread about.
Sophisticated, but should be avoided if cost is a primary concern. The patron is a vast, profusely bearded man in his late 30s. Waiter service only with 500gm tin of beer costing 150drs.

THE A TO Z OF USEFUL INFORMATION

AIRLINE OFFICE & TERMINUS The office (*Tmr* 9D1) is to the left of the Plaka main road and is open daily between 0800-1430hrs, except Sundays.

Aircraft timetable (Mid-season)
Milos to Athens
Daily: 0750, 1825hrs.
Mon & Fri 1040hrs.
Return journey
Daily: 0645, 1720hrs.
Mon & Fri 0935hrs.
One-way fare: 4200drs; duration 45mins.

BANKS There are two, the **Commercial Bank** (*Tmr* 25D/E2) and the **National Bank** (*Tmr* 26D3).

BEACHES
Beach 1: From the Ferry-boat Quay (*Tmr* 1C4), to the left (*Sbo*) is a small cove, bordered by a plethora of new hotels and the 'Venus Village' complex. The backshore of the coarse sand beach is pleasantly tree shaded but the sea bottom becomes rather weedy. There are a number of fishing boats anchored inshore. Windsurfing costs 1000drs an hour. A certain amount of 'wild' camping.
It is possible to walk on past a tiny cove to the lighthouse headland, some hot water springs and a sandy foreshore.
Beach 2: Almost a 'bayful' really, with the tree-lined main road, east from Adamas, edging the bay most of the way round to the junction with the Zefiria turning. A 'representative' stretch is close by the petrol station. Lots of unofficial camping.

BICYCLE, SCOOTER & CAR HIRE Various outfits including **John's Corner**, wedged between *Cavo d'Amore* (*Tmr* 19D3) and a Tourist office (*Tmr* 11D3). He hires mopeds at a cost of 1000-2000drs per day and cars from at 6000drs per day.
Averkios Tourist Office (*Tmr* 12D/E2/3) Tel 22191
Directions: On the left of the Esplanade, between the private yacht quay and the Bus/Taxi Square.

Averkios, a pleasant, 'streetwise young man, with very good English, is not too bothered about hiring out his machines. A Vespa costs 1500drs a day, but the extensive number of rough tracks created by the mining companies makes for extremely difficult navigation, once off the few surfaced roads. It is possible to spend hours and hours lost, wandering about the scarred, chewed, dusty, loose-surfaced hill and mountain paths. In fact it must be a moot point if it is worth hiring a powered conveyance because not only are the number of attainable destinations limited but, due to the appalling road surfaces, there are even more accidents on Milos island than is usual. You have been warned.

BOOKSELLERS (*Tmr* 27D/E2/3) More a vendor of foreign language newspapers. I have no doubt that this unprepossessing man will, on 'high days', change his vest. Maybe not!

BREAD SHOPS (*Tmr* 28D2) A baker who sells cheese pies. To reach his premises either climb the steps alongside the *Cafeteria Milos* (*Tmr* 23D/E2) and take the first street on the right, or climb the half-left lane from the Bus/Taxi Square and cut down the first left, almost acutely back on oneself.

BUSES A reasonably widespread. efficient service with an 'interesting' cross-country journey to Paliochori. The buses gather on the side of the 'Main' Square (*Tmr* E2) where there is displayed an up-to-date timetable. Not only do the buses run on time but the drivers are very helpful.

In high season months almost any bus will connect with Kimolos caiques, as the boats run about every two hours and tie in with the various buses. Early or late in the summer, to make the return journey to Kimolos island in one day, it is essential to catch the first bus to Pollonia (0645hrs). Conveniently, the smart *Hotel Meltemi* cafe-bar opens early enough to enjoy a life-reviving coffee before mounting the bus. The coffee is reasonably priced and hot but this cafeteria is rather expensive.

Bus timetable (Mid-season)

Adamas Port to Plaka & Trypiti

Daily: 0730, 0830, 0930, 1030, 1130, 1230, 1330, 1500, 1630, 1730, 1830, 1930, 2030, 2130hrs.

Adamas Port to Pollonia

Daily: 0645, 0915, 1115, 1315, 1615hrs.

Adamas Port to Paliochori Beach

Daily: 0940, 1030, 1120, 1510, 1610, 1700hrs.

COMMERCIAL SHOPPING AREA No particular market, but a number of shops are concentrated at the outset of the narrowing lane that climbs from the left (*Sbo*) of the Bus/Taxi Square (*Tmr* E2). Here are three general stores as well as a fruit and vegetable 'importers' and a butcher. There is a shack-like greengrocers on the Esplanade, close by the Commercial Bank (*Tmr* 25D/E2), but the quality is not very good. There are a considerable number of 'back of donkey' sales pitches as well as a supermarket on the left of the Zefiria road around the bay.

DISCOS Disco Milos is adequately signposted from the quay area and Cocktails Pub 82 does its best to be heard on the neighbouring islands from its eyrie above the *Charcoal Taverna* (*Tmr* 24D/E2).

FERRY-BOATS The main craft is the **CF Kimolos**, supplemented by other inter-island craft.

Ferry-boat timetable (Mid-high season)

Day	**Departure time**	**Ferry-boat**	**Ports/Islands of Call**
Mon	0200hrs	Golden Vergina	Piraeus(M).
Tues	0800hrs	Delos	Kimolos,Siphnos,Serifos,Kithnos,Rafina(M).
	2200hrs	Kimolos	Kimolos,Syros.
Wed	0950hrs	Kimolos	Siphnos,Serifos,Kithnos,Piraeus(M).
	1830hrs	Ionian	Siphnos,Serifos,Kithnos,Piraeus(M).
Thur	2200hrs	Kimolos	Siphnos,Serifos,Kithnos,Piraeus(M).
Fri	1730hrs	Golden Vergina	Folegandros,Thira(Santorini),Anafi, Ag Nikolaos(Crete),Sitia(Crete),Kasos, Karpathos,Rhodes.
	2400hrs	Kimolos	Kimolos,Piraeus(M).

Sat	1630hrs	Kimolos	Kimolos,Folegandros,Sikinos,Ios,Thira(Santorini).
	1700hrs	Ionian	Piraeus(M).
Sun	1300hrs	Kimolos	Siphnos,Serifos,Kithnos,Piraeus(M).

One-way fare: Milos to Piraeus 1512drs; duration 7½hrs.

Please note these tables are detailed as a GUIDE ONLY. Due to the time taken to research the Cyclades, it is IMPOSSIBLE TO 'match' the timetables or even boats . So don't try cross pollinating...

FERRY-BOAT TICKET OFFICES Milos Tours (*Tmr* 10C/D3), on the 'OTE' Sq, acts for the **CF Kimolos**, which is unfortunate as the proprietor is a rather unpleasant, surly man. Open between 0830-1330hrs & 1730-2200hrs. **The Tourist Office** (*Tmr* 11D3), also on 'OTE' Sq, sells tickets for the **CF Ionian & CF Delos**.

HAIRDRESSERS Hope (*Tmr* 29C3) A Unisex hairstylist located on the hill in front of the Ferry-boat Quay. It is accessible up some steep, rickety concrete steps that scale the cliff-face.

MEDICAL CARE
Chemist & Pharmacy (*Tmr* 30D1) One on the left of the Plaka road.
Clinic (*Tmr* 31D2) In the same street as the Baker.

MUNICIPAL TOURIST KIOSK (*Tmr* 33C3/4) An information kiosk is located at the land-end of the Ferry-boat Quay but is rarely, if ever staffed. However much useful information is stuck on the windows, which includes bus & ferry-boat times, taxi fares, opening hours (museums) and accommodation details.

OTE (*Tmr* 8C/D3) One of the first buildings at the outset of the Esplanade, from the Ferry-boat Quay. A small office, open weekdays between 0800-1300hrs & 1800-2200hrs, weekends/holidays between 0900-1300hrs & 1500-2140hrs.

PETROL There is a Petrol station some 450m along the bay encircling road. Closes on Sunday. There is another Filling station just before Plaka, on the road from Adamas. Open Sundays.

PLACES OF INTEREST
The Catholic Church (*Tmr* 32D2/3) A date 1827 is inscribed in the plaster. The building lies obliquely to the street and is neatly 'snuggled' in and around by surrounding buildings.

On 'Navigation light' point, Bombarda, west of Adamas, is a monument to French sailors killed in the Crimean War.

Round island trip Averkios Tours (*Tmr* 12D/E2/3) runs a trip boat that circumnavigates the island. Considering the various interesting rock formations this must be an interesting day out. The boat departs at 0900hrs, returning at 1830hrs for a cost of 1500drs. Sailings depend on the weather.

POLICE
Port Over an office on 'OTE' Sq (*Tmr* D3).

POST OFFICE (*Tmr* 20D3) Bordering 'OTE' Sq and alongside which a wide flight of steps climbs up to the 'Old Quarter' hillside. Above the Post Office is the Customs.

TAXIS They rank on the 'Main' Square and a board lists the 'going rate' charges including: Plaka 250drs, Pollonia 500drs, Paliochori Beach 600drs, Voudia 600drs, Ag Kiriaki Beach 600drs and Provatas 500drs. Probably a taxi is the best way of getting to some of the more isolated beaches. The drivers are very friendly and informative as to which beaches are best under certain conditions, taking into account prevailing wind direction. The shops sell excellent postcards of the various Milos island beaches. It is a good idea to pick a beach and ask the driver if he can get there! Fares are per 'load' – it costs 600drs for one or four people to Ag Kiriaki Beach. Furthermore it is possible to pre-arrange a pick-up time with a driver. Certainly some routes are better managed by taxi than by moped as many tracks are very sandy, making for an 'exciting' ride.

TELEPHONE NUMBERS & ADDRESSES

Doctor	Tel 22027
Taxi rank	Tel 22219

TRAVEL AGENTS & TOUR OFFICES *See* **Ferry-boat Ticket Offices.**

ROUTE ONE

To the Plaka (& Catacombs) (6km) I have lumped together the various hill-top villages under the one, all encompassing name Plaka. The Plaka is the Chora village close by the now disappeared Kastro. The other settlements, which include **Pera Triovasalos** (where a Petrol station), **Triovasalos**, **Firopotamos**, **Plakes**, **Trypiti**, and **Mili**, distantly circle a rather weed infested, modern-day stadium.

TRYPITI (6km from Adamas Port) Here are windmills, an Ancient Theatre and very early Christian catacombs. It would appear these date back to the 1st century AD, the islanders possibly being converted to Christianity by St Paul on a voyage from Crete. The burial site was probably the final resting place for between 2,000 and 5,000 islanders.

The catacombs are worth a visit for which catch the bus to Trypiti. The road, the last right turning before entering Trypiti village 'proper', is signposted 'katacoums' (*sic*) and is the same thoroughfare which drops down to the beach and delightful village of **Klima**.

A very steep, slithery path makes off about a third of the way down (beyond the second hairpin bend). After 50m are some 'rennovated', lovely stone terraces complete with shaded seats and platforms, with wonderful sea views – Lord knows why they didn't finish the cliff-path too!

The well-preserved catacombs are open between 0900-1500hrs (give or take 30mins) and entrance is free. Unfortunately it is only possible to walk around a very small section of the underground passages. The 'plus' is that they are excellently and tastefully displayed with a little, clay-mounted light in front of each tomb. The lights stretch away into the distance giving a superb overall effect.

Nearby are remains of the Ancient Theatre and it was at Trypiti, in a field, that a farmer found the 'Venus de Milo'. It is possible that the French broke the hands off in their haste to remove the statue, as a contemporary report refers to their position.

PLAKA (6km from Adamas Port) The bus pulls up at a 'T' junction, with the main body of the village to the left and a Clinic (Tel 21222) to the right, on the edge of a small, 'unsatisfactory' Main Square. From the latter a signposted track leads down to the coastal hamlets of **Phourkouvouni** and **Areti**.

The confusing bus timetable includes the following detail:-

Bus timetable (Mid-season)

Plaka to Adamas

Daily: 0630, 0750, 0850, 0950, 1050, 1150, 1250, 1450, 1550, 1650, 1750, 1850, 1950, 2050, 2150hrs.

Plaka to Pollonia

Daily: 0630, 0900, 1340, 1550hrs.

Plaka to Paliochori Beach

Daily: 0940, 1030, 1115, 1220, 1515, 1610, 1700, 1740hrs.

The Town police station (Tel 21378/21204) is close to the bus turn-round and taxi rank, on the Main Square.

Around the edge of the Plaka are ***Rooms***. There is an OTE and Post Office (which transacts currency exchange). The Plaka is an absolute pedestrian maze with a couple of friendly cafe-bar tavernas and a 'disturbing' number of pharmacies (do they know something we don't?). The Folk Museum is very difficult to locate as the signs run out, as do the indicators to a baker. This latter is down steps to the left, after climbing to a location from whence there is a lovely panorama of the north coast and the Bay of Firopotamos.

The signs for the Archaeological Museum also disappear but best to ignore them – it is located just below the Post Office. The spacious, well laid out, but sparse exhibits are displayed in a building which has the best lavatories on the island. A minimum of three staff oversee this delightfully air conditioned museum.

From the part marbled terrace of the Church of Panaghia i Korfiatissa (a repository for various icons and treasures) are stunning views out over the Bay of Adamas and the western island. The site of the Old Kastro is marked by a rock hilltop church.

ROUTE TWO

To Paliochori Beach (9½km) The main road east of Adamas skirts the huge bay at sea level. Stretches of the fairly narrow foreshore are suitable for bathing, if rather scrubbly, with the backshore and edge of the road irregularly planted with trees. The inland side, in the main, resembles a lunar landscape with mines and machinery littered all over the place. The occasional mine working pierhead projects into the bay. Furthermore there is not a taverna in sight.

Opposite the very large, Electricity Generating plant (3km), is a pleasant little beach and remarkably hot water, a thermal spring. (I thought it was the Generating station outflow).

The inland road curves off alongside the Generating plant to:-

ZEFIRIA (5km from Adamas Port) Now a small, almost insignificant, village set in an agricultural plain, but once the island's capital with a one-time population of about 5,000, seventeen churches and two bishops, one Orthodox and one Catholic. Much of the prosperity (from the 8th century AD to 1793) was derived from pirates who used the island as a base, but earthquakes, pestilence and sulphurous fumes caused the inhabitants to abandon the site. Well that is all except the modern-day *Taverna/Restaurant Madam Loula* – 'All information here' and Greek evenings as well!

The first time traveller can be forgiven for not noticing the Paliochori Beach turn-off, which is in the village prior to the prominent church. The signpost is almost invisible but is there. The route to the beach becomes nothing more than a narrow, unmade, rough track snaking through farmland and up over the hills to:-

Paliochori Beach How the bus company envisaged this as a scheduled route I'm not sure. The beach is on the day trip boat excursion schedule. The settlement is encircled by extensively quarry-scarred countryside which, with the shack-like nature of some of the buildings, imparts a 'frontier feel' to the place.

There is a large, central, clean beach of grey sand with a pebble sea's edge and two wing coves. The steeply shelving shore results in small breakers when the wind is in a particular direction.

To the left (*Fsw*), up a rough and sandy track, is the *Artemis Taverna*.The inordinately large building has a neat, gravel laid patio. To the right of the bus pull-up is the *Taverna Paliochori*. Generally prices here are no more than slightly above average.

There are three sets of ***Rooms*** available, one of which is 'Rooms To Rent' with telephone numbers summer 22101, winter 21788.

To reach the cove to the right-hand (*Fsw*) it is necessary to clamber through a low rock tunnel. The smell of sulphur is very strong and the cliffs are stained a dirty yellow. There is some 'wild' camping, a little more litter and some nude bathing.

The small, rather lovely cove to the left is only accessible by climbing over a pile of rocks edging and tumbling into the sea. The low cliffs hem in the narrow, pebble beach and there are rocks in the deep, dark coloured sea-water.

ROUTE THREE

To Ag Kiriaki Beach (10km) As for **Route Two** as far as the Paliochori Beach track beyond the turning off from the Zefiria road. A signposted, difficult, sandy surfaced trail progresses to:-

Ag Kiriaki Beach (10km from Adamas Port) The beach is wide and sandy and sits between two low-lying hills, with one or two houses in the background. The sea is extremely blue and clear.

To the right (*Fsw*) a sand track leads to the single storey *Ag Kiriaki Taverna*, which serves good food midday and evenings.

There are a row of red-doored, rather basic ***Rooms*** at this lovely, isolated spot. Bedrooms share the bathrooms with singles costing from 1750drs, doubles from 2000drs and triples 2300drs.

This location is a great place to get away from it all, though some round the island trips stop here for lunch.

ROUTE FOUR

The Western island As for **Route Two** as far as the Electricity Generating station, where the main road continues to curve round the bay. Soon after the turning off to Zefiria is a very large Alikes or salt works. At the far end of this (4km from Adamas Port) is a paved road to the 'doo-hickey' Airport – a shack or two and a small runway.

Ormos Hivadolimnis (6km from Adamas Port) Tucked into the nearside of a promontory and perhaps one of the finest beaches on the island, with a clean, small cove and a big sweep of sand.

The road turns slightly inland and makes a junction with a cross-country track to the south coast, across an agricultural plain (yes agriculture, not mining) to either:-

Ormos Provata (8.5km from Adamas Port) A lovely sandy cove, with a steeply shelving shore, some kelp and six little boat-houses.
Or the indistinctly signed:-
Ormos Ag Sosti (8.5km from Adamas Port) Two small coves with tiny, sandy beaches bounded by rocks, both set in low crumbling hills and connected by a track.

The main road climbs steeply up into the unattractive mountainous area surrounding Mt Profitis Ilias, towards the Middle Ages **Ag Marina Monastery** (11km from Adamas Port). This is set in a pleasant, lush garden. The road becomes an unsurfaced track and there is some cultivation. A very steep path drops down from the side of the monastery to the edge of the great bay and perhaps the prettiest area of the island, more especially:-

Phatourena (12½km from Adamas Port) Along with the other locations bordering Adamas Bay to the north from here, this attractive sweep of sandy beach is rather inaccessible, except by trip boat from Adamas Port. This is a pity because adjacent **Rivari**, the lagoon, Ag Nikolaos and, further up the coast, the sandy beach and scattered houses of **Ebourio** are well worth a visit, or two. Even further to the north of the bay are two small, sheltered beaches and the Church of Ag Dimitris set on a small headland.

A seven kilometre trek, circling Mt Profitis Ilias to the north and then cutting through a cleft between Mt Kalamvros, leads to the:-
Church of Ag Ioannis Theologos (Siderianos) This overlooks a bay of the same name and is the site of great celebrations. The story goes that when miscreants attacked the church, the worthy worshippers begged St Theologos to intercede. He caused the door to harden 'as iron' and when an assailant on the roof attempted to shoot at those sheltering inside, the pistol seemed to explode in the man's hand, both pistol and severed limb falling into the building. These grisly reminders of the fortuitous salvation were preserved as was a tatter of cloth affixed to the front of the door, supposedly that of a woman's dress torn as she scrambled inside, in the face of the pirates' onslaught.

ROUTE FIVE

To Pollonia (9½km) On the way to the north-eastern fishing port, the route passes:-

FLAKOPI (Phylakopi) (7½km from Adamas Port) This important archaeological location, once the site of three cities, overlooks the pleasant beach of Papafranga and the Bay of

Flakopis. It comes as no surprise, considering the location, that one of the city civilisations was Minoan. With the decline of Flakopi, about 1100 BC, Klima, to the west of Trypoti, assumed the mantle of island capital. Off the coast are the islets of **Glaronissia**.

POLLONIA (9½km from Adamas Port) A pretty, typical, quiet fishing port set in a small, semi-circular bay with the hamlet and quay to the right (*Fsw*). Centre is a narrow, tree-lined, sandy beach running around to the left of the bay on the far horn of which are a surprising number of Greek villas and holiday homes.

The bus parks at the outset to the port hamlet, close by a fork in the road. A street makes off to the right (whereon scooter hire). The waterfront road to the left, which is edged by buildings, runs out on the quay.

There are ***Rooms*** everywhere, both to the right and left of the bay. I would guess they are never full. A very nice looking block is to be found by continuing up the hill,from the bus stop,to a large, white house with plastic pot plants on the wall and green shutters. A double room en suite costs from 2000drs. They also hire mopeds for 1500drs per day. The *Cafe* ΛΗΛΛΗΣ,on the quayside,has Rooms at the going rates.

The *Cafe/Restaurant Petrakis*, the first on the quayside, cooks delicious apple pies (bougatsa) for 90drs. A nice breakfast for 2 including tea, coffee, yoghurt with honey, bread & marmalade costs 350drs.

There is 'wild' camping beneath the trees on Pollonia beach, around a toilet block which bears a 'No Camping' sign!

Bus timetable

Pollonia to Adamas Port

Daily: 0710, 0930, 1045, 1130, 1230, 1430, 1700, 1800, 2000hrs.

EXCURSION TO KIMOLOS ISLAND *****

Area 36sqkm and a population of about 1,000 The name is the Greek for chalk.

The caique boat to Kimolos As long as the weather is clement the caique makes the ½hr duration sea crossing from Pollonia to Kimolos island. The boat departs from Pollonia quay daily at 0730, 0900, 1000, 1130, 1400 and 1600hrs (in mid-summer), returning the same day at various times(!), but connecting with the return bus to Adamas. The return boat fare costs 300drs. The boatman is something of a character. He 'messes around' in the boat some 40 minutes before it's due to leave, thus causing all round panic among potential passengers. He also appears to enjoy steering very close to the rocks.

In summer the boat stops on the way to Psathi at an excellent, long sandy beach and calls back later to collect people. As times vary it is best to ascertain exactly when he plans to leave... Communication can prove difficult, unless a traveller speaks Greek, as the only number he knows in English is 'fifty'! The passage passes by a couple of islets with cargo ships lurking at anchor here and there. In the middle distance, to the right, is the large uninhabited island of **Paliegos**.

In indifferent weather conditions it is more reliable to catch the inter-island **CF Kimolos** (*See* **Ferry-boats, A To Z, Adamas Port, Milos**).

GENERAL The island has been the scene of much mining activity in the past, but somehow less intrusively than Milos. The low, chalky white cliff faces of Kimolos evince the occasional evidence of quarrying and shore to ship loading gear. Originally chalk was the deposit extracted but a crushed stone used for chemical purposes is still excavated.

At **Palaiokastro**, on the west coast side of the island, on a 430m hilltop, are the remains of a Venetian castle and a very old church; to the north-east is the hamlet of **Klima**, a beach and,further on,sulphur springs at **Prassa** (about 6½km).

I have written before that a guide book author experiences a certain amount of conflict when a 'find' is made – to tell or not to tell. Now of course it all depends on what idiosyncrasies (or bigotry?) take your fancy. Whatever, I must nominate Kimolos as one of the slowly decreasing circle of islands on which I would wish to be landed in order to enjoy peace, a lack of modern day 'necessities' and unaffected, old fashioned, Greek island charm. Can one say more?

PSATHI: port The port is set in comparatively gentle hills, the middle of the range being crowned by the Chora. To the right of centre, the peaks are spotted with windmills.

Ferry-boats dock at the end of the small quay, to the extreme right (*Sbo*) of the lovely harbour cove , and are met by a swarming mass of humanity who dash helter-skelter to and from the ship. The inter-island caique berths at about the middle of the quayside.

Stretching along the rest of the bay,to the left,is a pebble beach backed by a scattering of trees and buildings. The first quarter of the backshore has a narrow concrete track up against which is a combined kafeneion-cum-simple-store. The proprietor is a smiley, gold-toothed man. No food is served here, just drinks.

Fifty metres to the right (*Sea still behind one*), at the end of the boat quay, is the *Snackbar Spiros* The amusing, if taciturn owner serves an excellent meal though the menu is limited, depending on supplies. Spiros says "very good..." for whatever is on the menu! A very good value, tasty repast for two of 2 meatballs & rice, tomato salad, tzatziki, 1 beer, 1 coke and bread cost 750drs.

About three hours to the west is a long sweeping beach but the port seems sufficient to me and is in reach of a taverna or two... At about 10 o'clock, weather permitting, there is a boat trip on one of the local fishing boats to the neighbouring, uninhabited island of **Paliegos**, for those who wish to indulge in skinny-dipping.

To the Chora The steep uphill path passes a really very large, private house,which it is rumoured belongs to the owner of the **CF Kimolos**.

One hundred and fifty metres up the hill is *Rooms for Rent* Ε ΜΕΛΑΝΘΗ (Tel 51392). This is a nice looking, single storey block gathered round a patio where a double room costs from 2000drs.

The ascent takes about 20 minutes and on the way there is, to the right, the sight of a large cemetery and a glimpse of a fishing village (*See* **Oupa**).

CHORA (Kimolos) A crumbling, twisting confusing maze of lanes and alleys which often end above a ruin or in a backyard animal enclosure. A number of lovely old churches, two tavernas and one kafeneion. Alongside the large Cathedral is the Police station. Above the Chora are six windmills, one of which is still in working order. From these heights are superb views.

The steep, concreted 'main road' into the Chora, from the uphill route, passes by, on the left, a bakery, and the *Taverna Nikos* (open evenings only). Continuing on the same street and bearing right passes the smart, modern Clinic and, further up, a 'no name' taverna-cum-general store. Next door are ***Rooms***. The Chora also has a Post Office, *en route* to the church, which changes Travellers cheques. Along the main street, up from the public fountain, is *Taverna/Rooms Bohouris*. This offers beautifully clean rooms with en suite facilities, hot water, balconies and power points (that work). A double room costs from 1900drs per night and there is a metered telephone. The establishment is owned by Nicos Ventouris, a 50 year old man who gives the appearance of being very gruff, but is, in reality, a softy. The food is excellent and cheap. At the weekends the locals 'volta' and gather here for music and impromptu dancing – the real thing.

From the Chora, left around a hillside gorge, descends to:-

OUPA A stunningly beautiful, simple fishing village built into and around the rocky hillsides. The boatsheds and stores are cut into the rock with the living accommodation above. The community spreads out over the rocks and cliff, spanning the voids and fissures with makeshift bridges. To the right (*Fsw*) is a small, semi-circular bay edged by a pebbly beach, on the far side of which are a row of surprisingly large, modern 'lock-up' style boat sheds. The rather stony sea bottom of the cove is riven by a narrow band of sand enabling bathers to walk painlessly into the sea. Unfortunately there isn't a taverna, not even a kafeneion, but what a delightful spot to while away part of the day.

The Kouros of Flerio, Naxos. Acknowledgement to David & Liz Drummond-Tyler.

Beyond Drios 'en route' to Kanala, Kithnos. *Acknowledgement to Anne Merewood.*

Piso Livadi beach, Paros. *Acknowledgement to David & Liz Drummond-Tyler.*

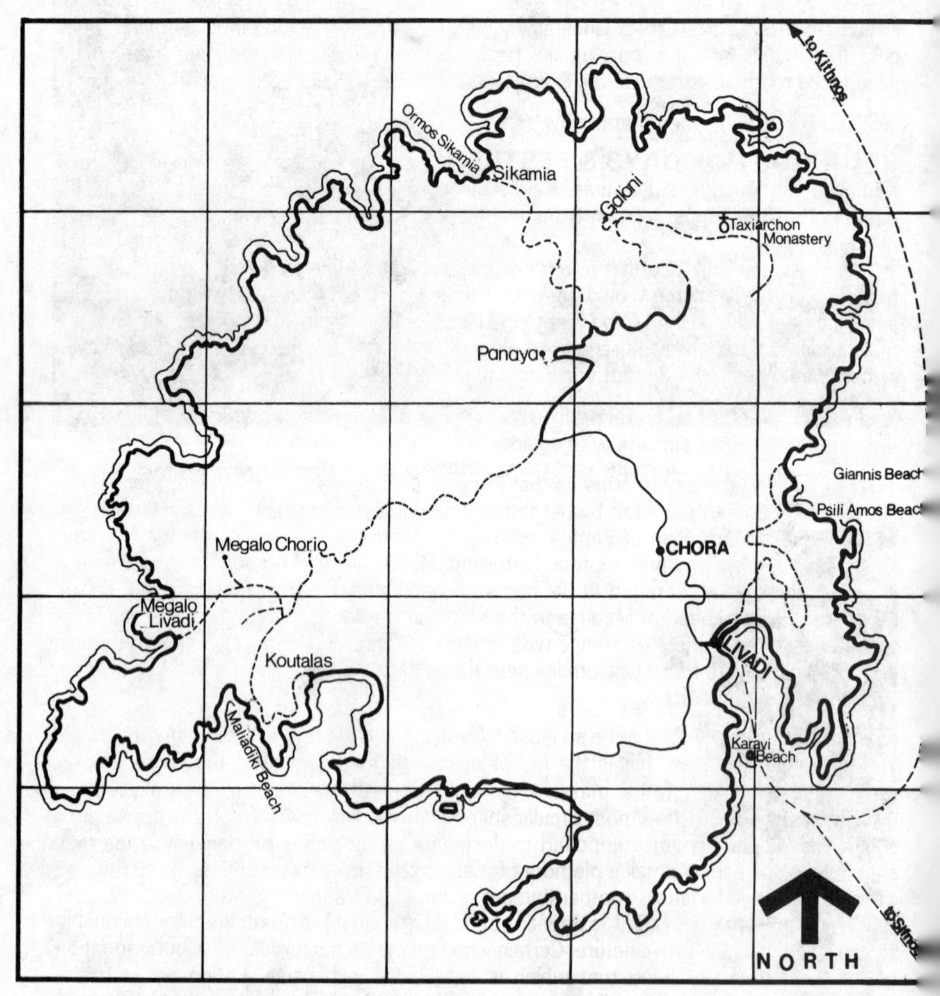

Illustration 54 Serifos island

19 SERIFOS (Seriphos) ★★
Cyclades Islands - Western chain

FIRST IMPRESSIONS Generally secretive, unfriendly inhabitants; womens' bonnets (koukoula); intrusive pop music; beautiful butterflies; wild buddleia; fine mules; unsurfaced roads; charter caiques & flotilla yachts; Greek holiday island; winnowing.

SPECIALITIES None that I know of.

RELIGIOUS HOLIDAYS & FESTIVALS include: 5th May – Festival, Ag Irenes, Koutalas; 6th August, Ag Sotiras, Kalo Amebli (south coast); 15th August, Panaghia, Ramos; 15-16th August – Feast & festival, Pirgos; 7th November – Festival, Monastery of Taxiarchon.

There is a local folk-tale that at a Panaghia, the first couple to dance around the olive tree closest to the church would get married very, very soon. Naturally fights broke out amongst pairs who wished to be first to the tree (Foolish, idealistic things...). The weapon of attack was traditionally a branch. An old saw went 'It is best to be stabbed by a Turk, rather than beaten by a Serifiot wielding a staff'... or words to that effect.

VITAL STATISTICS Tel prefix 0281. The almost circular island is up to 8km from side-to-side & top to bottom, with an area of 70sq km. The population is about 1200.

HISTORY Mythology informs us that Princess Danae and her son Perseus landed on Serifos, having been set adrift by her father. Perseus killed Medusa, the ghastly gorgon, at the request of the King of Serifos, who really wanted the lad out of the way in order to have his wicked way with mother. Unfortunately for these lecherous designs, Perseus returned home early. Enraged at his hosts unchappish behaviour, Perseus held up and 'showed' the dead head of Medusa to the King and his court, who turned to stone.

Historically the island's existence was rather humdrum, following the usual Cycladean succession of overlords. The Romans sent exiles here, as they did to a number of other unprepossessing islands.

GENERAL For an island to be so close to Siphnos and yet be so totally different should be impossible, but then that is the joy of discovering and travelling the Greek islands.

The mountains seem rather massive, old and rounded. The peaks are centrally located which, combined with the almost circular shape of the outline, gives a blob-like appearance to the island. The name is supposed to designate dry, which is probably why the map makers are so keen to detail a plethora of massive but non-existent rivers, in addition to innumerable paved roads – another figment of the cartographer's mind.

The worthy citizens of Serifos appear not to want tourists, or perhaps they are unable to overcome their secretive nature. Certainly no one meets the ferries, so accommodation has to be ferreted out and that which is available is expensive. Eating out is rather prohibitive and often unrewarding. Apart from these drawbacks the best beach close to the port remains unsignposted; the scenically picturesque Chora makes little attempt to welcome visitors and the buses only travel between Livadi and the Chora. This lack of bus routes makes it difficult to connect with the two or three other extremely rewarding, but widespread seaside hamlets. Admittedly the roads are nothing more than rather fearsome tracks through the interior. Even the bus drivers, so often a source of useful information on other islands, are uncommunicative. If the so-helpful citizens of Milos could have some of the attractions of Serifos island, they would probably be very grateful.

Perhaps I have painted too dismal a picture. Livadi is situated in an extensive bay, with every possible attraction dotted about its periphery; there are one or two exceptional beaches within fairly easy reach of the port; the Chora is an acceptable example of its genre and the seaside hamlets of Mega Livadi, Koutalas and Sikamia are each unique in their style and type.

LIVADI: port (Illustration 55) Originally a small-time fishing village, fortuitously sited adjacent to a lovely sweeping beach at the end of a horseshoe bay. The attempt to become a 'big-time' holiday resort has resulted in a disjointed 'mishmash' circling the water's edge.

On the left (*Sbo*) is the massive Ferry-boat Quay (*Tmr* 1D/E4/5) followed by a concrete walk towards the caique and yacht quay (*Tmr* 2B3/4). The village spreads up the 'High' St. From hereon, all the way round to the far edge of the bay, is a spread-out, rather scrubbly and 'tacky' ribbon of development skirting the water's edge. This includes tavernas, restaurants, hotels, private homes, discos, pensions, rooms, cafe-bars and a few shops that slowly thin out as one progresses. This disparate growth may be the result, in part, of the high incidence of cruise caiques and charter yachts. It certainly is strange that such a pretty location has grown or developed (if that is not a contradiction in terms) as it has. The surfaced quay road runs out on the Main Sq, the rest of the shore encircling 'Esplanade' being nothing more than a dirt track enhanced by the number of mature trees spread along the backshore.

Livadi has its resident 'character', the grizzled, small, lean man who masterminds the port's rubbish. He is easily recognisable by the oversize Wellington boots into which are tucked tight jeans, into which is tucked a check shirt. A large pair of dark glasses perch on the end of his dew-drop nose and his chin sports several days 'pepper and salt stubble', all topped off by a grimy yachting hat. He totters back and forth with ever larger boxes of rubbish, that is when he is not lavishing attention on his possibly eternally land-bound, small benzina fishing boat fitted with an impossibly oil begrimed engine. Livadi is almost one of the only Greek island locations where pop music (not Greek) is intrusive.

ARRIVAL BY FERRY It is quite a hike to the village centre and ferries are not met by owners of accommodation. As there is little in the Chora and not much spare in Livadi, it is important to locate a bed, quickly. The bus and taxis meet some ferries.

THE ACCOMMODATION & EATING OUT Rooms, at the height of season, are almost non existent and owners will only accept pre-bookings for a minimum of a week. Meals tend to be expensive, probably as a result of the large numbers of charter yachts and cruise caiques that call.

The Accommodation From the Ferry-boat Quay in a clockwise direction:-

Areti Guest House

Directions: From the side of the Skorpios Disco Bar (*Tmr* 3C5), a flight of steps climbs the hillside. The pension is on the left (*Sbo*).

A double room costs from 2000drs.

Pension Cristi

Directions: On the other, right side of the steps to the *Areti*, with similar rates.

Alongside the caique and yacht quay (*Tmr* 2B3/4), the 'Esplanade' is wide enough to form a 'Main' Square where the buses park. At right angles to the waterfront is the short 'High' St at the top of which is a T-junction. The right-hand (*Quay behind one*) turning makes off for the Chora.

'Bakery' Rooms (*Tmr* 4A4)

Directions: On the right (*Quay behind one*) of the 'High' St , over the village baker.

Now let as suites, from 3000drs a night, by the adjacent Serifos Tours.

Further along the Chora road are steps alongside the modern building containing the Port police (*Tmr* 5A3). These drop down to ***Rooms*** (*Tmr* 6A3)

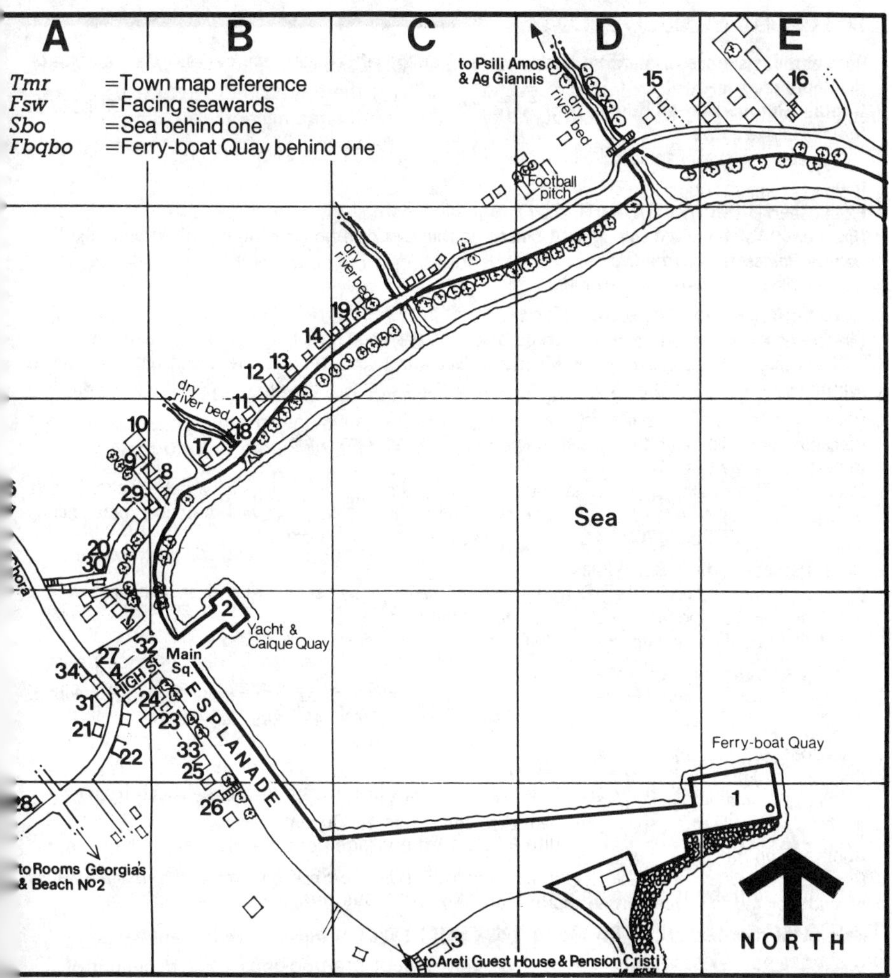

ustration 55 Livadi

r 1D/E4/5	Ferry-boat Quay	18B3	Perseus Restaurant
2B3/4	Yacht & Caique quay	19B/C2	Restaurant O Σtamathς
3C5	Skorpios Disco & Bar	20A3/4	Restaurant
4A4	'Bakery' Rooms/Baker	21A4	Restaurant Pizza
5A3	Port police	22A4/5	Tootsie Hamburgers
6A3	Rooms	23A/B4	Zachararoplasteion Μεδογσα
7A/B3/4	Captain George Rented Rooms	24A/B4	Central Kafeneion
8A/B3	Hotel & restaurant Cavo d'Oro	25B4/5	Taverna O Mokkas
9A/B3	Hotel Serifos Beach	26B4/5	Restaurant To Διεθνε
10A/B3	Pension K Potas	27A4	Serifos Travel
11B2/3	Hotel Perseus	28A4/5	Rent-Bykes
12B2/3	Hotel Maistrali	29A/B3	Butcher/Gift shop
13B2/3	Albatross Rooms	30A3/4	Karavagia Rock Cocktail Bar
14B/C2	Rooms	31A4	'Telephone' shop
15D1	Pension Erotas	32A/B4	Peters shop/Rooms
16E1	Rooms No 119	33B4/5	Mini-market
17B3	Kafeneion No 46	34A4	Grocery shop/store

Back at the unsurfaced waterfront 'Esplanade' and on the left, beside a narrow alley that emerges on the Chora road, is:-

Captain George Rented Rooms (*Tmr* 7A/B3/4) Tel 51274

Directions: As above.

A double room with an en suite bathroom in this lively area costs from 1500drs.

Beyond Froggies Pub (*sic*), a cul-de-sac advances past:-

Hotel Cavo D'Oro (*Tmr* 8A/B3) (Class E)

Directions: As above, on the right. A smart, newish block in the ground floor of which is the Self-Service *Restaurant Cavo d'Oro*.

A double room costs from 2500drs.

Hotel Serifos Beach (*Tmr* 9A/B3) (Class C) Tel 51209

Directions: As above. Another modern building, this one shutting off the end of the cul-de-sac.

They accept *American Express* and *Diners* credit cards, which 'benefits' are reflected in the charges. All rooms have en suite bathrooms with a single room costing 1960drs & a double 2350drs, rising to 2635drs & 3160drs (July-Sept).

Perhaps more in line with the budget of some readers' pockets is the:-

Pension K Potas (*Tmr* 10A/B3)

Directions: This delightful pension is hidden away in charming surroundings behind the *Serifos Beach*. Slide down the alley to the right of the hotel and turn left along the back wall. A double room sharing a bathroom costs from 1700drs & with an en suite bathroom 2300drs.

Hotel Perseus (*Tmr* 11B2/3) (Class B) Tel 51273

Directions: Continue round the bay along the 'Esplanade', over a summer-dry river-bed spanned by a footbridge, and on the far side of the *Restaurant Perseus*.

Actually classified as a pension. A double room en suite costs from 2000drs.

Hotel Maistrali (*Tmr* 12B2/3) (Class C) Tel 51381

Directions: From the *Hotel Perseus* this hotel is the next building east beyond the *Pizzeria Restaurant*.

Double rooms en suite start at 2940/3360drs & rise to 3720/4320drs (July-Aug).

Albatross Rooms (*Tmr* 13B2/3)

Directions: Almost next door to the *Hotel Maistrali*.

Cell-like rooms but a very pleasant looking building in a nice position with an oleander bush-tree to the fore. A double room sharing the bathroom costs from 1800drs mid-season.

Rooms (*Tmr* 14B/C2)

Directions: This accommodation is on the nearside of an *Ouzerie/Snackbar* from which emanate waves of loud rock music. A forked tree is prominent.

Beyond the river-bed path to Psili Amos and Giannis Beach, at the far end of the bay are:-

Pension Erotas (*Tmr* 15D1)

Directions: As above, at the back of a long plot.

Rooms

Directions: Next site along but may only open for the height-of-season months.

and:-

Rooms (*Tmr* 16E1) No. 119

Directions: In the corner of a track that bends back from the waterfront,in the shadow of the hillside that blocks off this end of the bay.

Rather spaced out with a 'cabin-like' hut end on. There is a large tree towards the back corner of the yard.

The beach here is rather scrubbly consisting of sand and pebbles with a few small boats anchored in the shallow water.

A 'new' area of accommodation, which may prove a saving grace, is along the road to Beach No. 2. From the junction of the 'High' St with the Chora road, a street to the left (*Quay behind one*) advances past *Tootsie Hamburgers* (Ugh). Prior to Rent-Bykes (*Tmr* 28A4/5) is the No. 2 Beach road. First on the left is:-

Rooms Georgia's *Directions*: As above.

Georgia is much more friendly than other Serifot accommodation owners (which is not difficult). A double room costs from 1800drs. She will offer a bed on the patio if full. All the best Georgia.

Also *See* **Psili Amos Beach, Excursion to Livadi Port Surrounds.**

The Eating Out I am advised that the reason for the expensive restaurant meals is that the owners do not work the establishments themselves, preferring to let them out to managers on short term leases. This makes for costly overheads...

Kafeneion (*Tmr* 17B3) No 46
Directions: A simple, square building with a raised patio about a quarter of the way round the bay.
Very popular and the best value coffee in town. Unfortunately the owner and his wife close for siesta (1300-1500hrs) and fairly early in the evening.

Perseus Restaurant (*Tmr* 18B3)
Directions: A little further on round the bay from the Kafeneion above. 'Smarty' and very expensive. The pricing is probably not the fault of the manager, more a result of the referred to system of leases, but that does not make the meals any cheaper.

Εστιατοριον Ο Σταματησ (Restaurant O Stamatis) (*Tmr* 19B/C2)
Directions: On towards the dried up river-bed/road, at the centre of the bay.
Looks as if it should be satisfactory, with reasonable prices, but very slow, lackadaisical and often 'confused' service. A meal for two of 2 spaghetti bolognese, a tomato & cucumber salad, bread, a beer and a coke cost about 800drs.

The Restaurant (*Tmr* 20A3/4)
Directions: Close to the village centre and next door to the Kovaki Gift Shop, which is itself alongside the Karvagia Cocktail Bar.
Possibly, on average, the best food served in Livadi, although the *Restaurant Pizza* (*Tmr* 21A4) might have cause to object. A meal for two of giant beans, Greek salad, chips, beer, coke and bread cost 765drs. A small plate of briami is very expensive, the bread pricey and the costly list of wines is only saved by the availability of a bottled retsina (an oversight?). On the other hand the service is polite and very speedy.

Tootsie Fast Food Hamburgers (*Tmr* 22A4/5)
Directions: Along the 'High'St , left (*Quay behind one*) up the slope at the T-junction and on the left.
Normally I do not list establishments inspired by North America and serving such unrepresentative offerings as hamburgers (150drs) and chips (60drs). But they do offer a souvlaki pita for 80drs.

Almost directly across the road is:-
Restaurant Pizza (*Tmr* 21A4)
Directions: As above.
The only reason I have not sampled the menu is that the establishment is on the caique and cruise yacht itinerary, with the mandatory top table courier exuberantly leading communal jollities. I have been unable to bring myself to rejoice with them.

Zacharoplasteion Μεδουσα (Medusa) (*Tmr* 23A/B4)
Directions: Bordering the Esplanade front, to the right (*Fsw*) of the 'Main' Square, in a row of breakfast cafe-bars/cake shops and bars.
A reasonable breakfast and changes money.

Central Kafeneion (*Tmr* 24A/B4)
Directions: In a block alongside an 'up-market' gift shop (which accepts *American Express* and *Diners* credit cards).
A very pleasant spot at which to enjoy an evening drink.

Two smart restaurants, that cater for the affluent 'yachties', edge the Esplanade – the *Cafe-Bar Fish Taverna O Mokkas* (*Tmr* 25B4/5) and the *Restaurant* ΤΟ ΑΙΕΘΝΕ (*Tmr* 26B4/5). An alternative is the 3-wheeled popcorn cart that parks on the 'Main' Sq.

THE A TO Z OF USEFUL INFORMATION

BANKS None but there are one or two offices that change foreign notes and travellers cheques, including Serifos Travel (*Tmr* 27A4, tel 84005), and the *Zacharoplasteion* Μεδουσα (*Tmr* 23A/B4).

BEACHES

Beach 1. Well really one big beach almost all the way round the bay. The beach proper commences approximately opposite the *Perseus Restaurant* (*Tmr* 18B3) and keeps on to the far right-hand (*Sbo*) side. The nearside is sand and fine shingle, whilst the middle section is very pebbly sand grading to coarse sand in the area of the track to Psili Amos. The scrubbly far end is sand and pebbles. As the season progresses and accommodation gets scarcer so 'wild' backshore camping increases.

Beach 2. Ormos Livadakia This can be reached from the track close by the Ferry-boat Quay (*Tmr* 1D/E4/5), up the steps adjacent to *Skorpios Disco & Bar* (*Tmr* 3C5), or along the street to the left of the 'High' St T-junction. A once 'sweet' bay edged by a tree-lined, narrow, sandy beach. There is now a Windsurfing school to the nearside, the 'Great Unwashed' extensively and unofficially camp out in the summer and backing the shore is a smart, new, nameless hotel.

Beach 3. Karavi beach Take the path beyond Ormos Livadakia. This is a comparatively deserted location about forty minutes from the port with a few holiday homes on the backshore slopes.

BICYCLE, SCOOTER & CAR HIRE Rent-Bykes (*Tmr* 28A4/5) is a friendly firm. The English speaking owner has well maintained scooters costing 1500drs a day, complete with a full tank of fuel. Office hours are between 0830-1930hrs.

BREAD SHOPS The Baker's (*Tmr* 4A4) edges the 'High' St.

BUSES Two conveyances, one manufactured in the 1930s which only runs when it 'feels well'. As explained in the Introduction, the service simply connects Livadi to the Chora, although with the amount of road reconstruction taking place surely it can only be a matter of time before the coverage is expanded. The schedules are totally flexible but the buses run frequently and 'in tandem', as it were. The bus to the Chora is often jam-packed despite which the plump, young and very pleasant bus conductress still manages to force her way between the passengers collecting fares. One 'highlight' of the trip is the inevitable moment at which the buses meet, one going up and one down. The 1930s bus is loaded with tools for emergencies and may well stop for repairs and or to take on fuel, en route! The Livadi turn-round is on the 'Main' Sq, alongside the caique and yacht quay (*Tmr* 2B3/4).

Bus timetable

Livadi Port to Chora There is no 'real' schedule, the buses running between 0700-2300hrs (or 2400hrs, if there are enough passengers) – every 20mins or 30mins, when full!

One-way fare 60drs.

COMMERCIAL SHOPPING AREA None, but some stores are in unexpected locations. For example there is a self-service store O ΜΑΡΙΝΟΣ in a large building curiously situated behind the *Kafeneion No 46* (*Tmr* 17B3), to one side of which is a small general shop. The owner of O ΜΑΡΙΝΟΣ is extremely rude, grumpy and unpleasant. A little closer to the centre of the village is a side-by-side Butcher's and Gift shop (*Tmr* 29A/B3). Alongside the Karavagia Cocktail Bar (*Tmr* 30A3/4) is a narrow lane (which joins up with the Chora road) in which is a Butcher's shop. On the corner of the 'High' St and the Esplanade is Peters shop (*Tmr* 32A/B4), selling gifts, foreign papers and magazines, alongside which is a Periptero with a not very effective metered phone. Across the road is a Supermarket, more a disorganised store, which also sells tickets for the **FB Ionian**. Separated from this store, by a cafe-bar, is an up-market Gift shop where are accepted *American Express* and *Diners* credit cards. Further south along the Esplanade is a well-stocked Mini-Market (*Tmr* 33B4/5). On the left of the Chora road is a Grocery shop/store (*Tmr* 34A4) where tickets for the **CF Kimolos** are sold.

DISCOS A remarkable collection probably as a result of the port calls of the aforementioned caique and charter yachts. They include Froggies Pub and, close to the Ferry-boat Quay, is Skorpios Disco & Bar – 'Add a sting to your holiday disco'!

FERRY-BOATS Quite well connected with the other Cyclades islands if travellers are prepared to chop and change boats and bear in mind the excursion boat connections between Siphnos and Paros.

Ferry-boat timetable (Mid-high season)

Day	Departure time	Ferry-boat	Ports/Islands of Call
Mon	1200hrs	Kimolos	Siphnos,Ios,Thira(Santorini).
	2100hrs	Delos	Siphnos,Milos.
	2300hrs	Kimolos	Piraeus(M).
Tues	1045hrs	Delos	Kithnos,Rafina(M).
	1530hrs	Schinoussa	Piraeus(M).
	1900hrs	Kimolos	Siphnos,Milos,Kimolos,Syros.
Wed	1215hrs	Kimolos	Kithnos,Piraeus(M).
	1345hrs	Ionian	Siphnos,Kimolos,Milos.
	2115hrs	Ionian	Kithnos,Piraeus(M).
Thur	1800hrs	Kimolos	Siphnos,Milos.
	2400hrs	Kimolos	Kithnos,Piraeus(M).

Fri	2100hrs	Kimolos	Siphnos,Kimolos,Milos,Piraeus(M).
Sat	1300hrs	Ionian	Siphnos,Milos,Piraeus(M).
	1330hrs	Kimolos	Siphnos,Milos,Kimolos,Ios,Sikinos, Folegandros,Thira(Santorini).
	1530hrs	Schinoussa	Piraeus(M).
Sun	1300hrs	Ionian	Kithnos,Piraeus(M).
	1530hrs	Kimolos	Kithnos,Piraeus(M).

One-way fare: Serifos to Piraeus 1140drs; duration 5hrs.

Please note these tables are detailed as a GUIDE ONLY. Due to the time taken to research the Cyclades, it is IMPOSSIBLE TO 'match' the timetables or even boats. So don't try cross pollinating...

FERRY-BOAT TICKET OFFICES Not so much offices, more stores with a niche from which tickets are sold. These include the Grocery store (*Tmr* 34A4) alongside a tiny church bordering the Chora road and agent for the **FB Kimolos** and the Supermarket, on the corner of the 'High' St and the 'Main' Sq, selling tickets for the **FB Ionian**.

MEDICAL CARE Not a lot. For pharmacy items try the various stores. There is a Clinic with a resident doctor in the Chora.

OTE There is a metered telephone in the 'Main' Sq Periptero and a 'Telephone' shop (*Tmr* 31A4) alongside the 'High' St/Chora road T-junction.

PETROL A petrol station edges the Chora road but supplies can be indeterminate.

POLICE

Port (*Tmr* 5A3). On the right of the Chora road.

POST OFFICE *See* **The Chora**. There is a post-box mounted on the wall, almost opposite the Bus turn round, between the smart Gift shop and the money-changing Zacharoplasteion.

TAXIS When available, park on the 'Main' Sq.

TRAVEL AGENTS & TOUR OFFICES

Serifos Travel (*Tmr* 27A4) Tel 51484

Directions: In a small office on the right of the Chora road, opposite the tiny church.

The sign says 'You ask, we've got it'. Certainly they are very helpful and offer details of accommodation (but not rooms in August!). They also market 'Round the island trips' but these tend to only run when full enough – they are apt to be cancelled at the last minute . Note there aren't any other excursions or trips – anywhere. The office opens daily between 1000-1300hrs & 1800-2100hrs.

WATER In the height of summer months the drinking water often has to be turned off, usually siesta hours. The Chora similarly suffers.

EXCURSIONS TO LIVADI PORT SURROUNDS

Excursion to Psili Amos & Ag Giannis Beaches The unsignposted, just about 'moped friendly' track sets out beyond the football pitch (*Tmr* C/D1) along a stony river-bed which is attractively hedged in and overgrown by oleanders and bamboos. I have not written dry because even as late as June the river trickles and water lies in pools. Ignore all 'alluring' and misleading branch paths off to the right – stick to the main route. It is about a 3/4hr walk up and over the hillsides to:-

Psili Amos Beach The rough track passes by above the lovely, clean, golden sand cove with small arethemusa trees planted on the edge of the low, sand dune backshore. The sea is delightfully clean and there is one taverna and one cafe.

The owner of the taverna is quite a character and now lets out ***Rooms*** in a new block on the slope. They may well even have accommodation available in mid-August, but insist on upwards of three nights stay. A double room costs from 1500drs. The taverna has an outdoor beach shower.

On the steep hillside, between the taverna and the track, a house appears to have been built in direct line with the winter storm culvert – some erosion has already taken place!

Ag Giannis Beach Another fifteen minutes walk on from and larger than Psili Amos. At the nearside, the coarse sand beach blends into large pebbles, backed by a grove of trees. There are a number of private dwellings.

ROUTE ONE

Livadi Port to the Chora (2km) The main road progresses up the very fertile and profusely tree-planted plain that backs the port. This runs out in an ever narrowing valley against the side of the mountains.

THE CHORA If the ascent is made by bus it circles round at the top, far or north end of the Chora. The village, which I think looks most picturesque from the port, is draped around a precipitous hilltop, spilling over and down its flanks.

Immediately prior to where the bus stops, there is a Public Toilet block edging the road with separate men and women's cubicles, clean squatties and urinals. Opposite is an OTE office open between 0800-1430hrs.

Of the three or four ridge mounted windmills, one has been renovated and is now a home. To the side of the small 'Bus Square' are three cafe-bar kafeneions (one serving snacks) and two tavernas.

There are a few advertised ***Rooms*** and just above the 'Bus' Sq, on the left opposite a main flight of steps, is:-

Stavros Taverna & Rooms
Directions: As above.

Stavros is a very large, benign, slow moving man with a popular taverna and fabulously situated accommodation. His food is both good and inexpensive. A meal for two of 2 dolmades, 4 stick souvlakis, 1 meatballs, a Greek salad, bread, 2 beers and a Coke costs 1350drs, whilst a Greek breakfast for two and 4 coffees cost 450drs.

His accommodation is at the far end of the village just beneath the Kastro. Though the rooms are small the views are stunning from this mountainside location. A double room starts off at 1500drs. All in all an excellent establishment at which to make a base.

Climbing the steps to the right of the 'Bus' Sq (*Square behind one*) gives access to the large, marble paved 'Town Hall' Square. The latter building is an impressive ochre tinted edifice, constructed in 1908. It has a distinctive roof balcony with cast iron railings of sculpted swans. Alongside is a church and a dark interiored general store 'lurks' on the edge of this square. From the terrace of another church, below the castle walls, facing south out over Ormos Livadi are some impressive views including those over the port.

Descending from the Chora 'Bus' Sq, the main road passes a Clinic, Post Office, which changes money, the Police station, a number of kafeneions and a few tavernas.

It makes a pleasant alternative to walk back to the port via the wide steps that cross and recross the serpentine windings of the main road. It takes between ½ and ¾ hour down. Incidentally, if readers feel the need for excessive exercise, it is a ¾ to 1hr hard climb up.

A path also makes off from the Chora to join up with the track between Livadi and Psili Amos Beach.

ROUTE TWO

The Chora to Ormos Sikamia (6km) & Taxiarchon Monastery (7⅓km) From the Chora to beyond the junction (2km) of the Mega Livadi and Sikamia roads is a steep ascent up the mountainside. At the junction the road for Sikamia climbs on up to the right, for a short distance, to a crest marked by an ugly chapel. From here are glorious views down the mountainside to the Bay of Sikamia.

The maps mark the villages of **Panaya** and **Galani** as being on the roadside, but they are off to one side, down steep access tracks, the one to Panaya being surfaced. Whilst berating the cartographers, it is best to totally ignore the roads marked in yellow and note that signposting is very poor. The Panaya church dates back to the 10th century.

After another 2km, between the villages of Panaya and **Pirgos**, a left-hand, unsurfaced turning tumbles very roughly and steeply down a lovely, intensively farmed valley to:-

Ormos Sikamia (6km from the Chora) The lovely and unspoilt bay is backed by extensive dunes hosting groves of bamboos with some plastic litter scattered about. The beach is sandy, the sea clear and clean and the backshore is a sand and pebbles mix planted with occasional clumps of trees.

There is no taverna, 'no nothing' apart from some new buildings spread out amongst abandoned, older dwellings. The 'High Street' is a sandy track, winding between the dunes and outcrops of bamboo. A delightful spot with donkeys and mules in the ascendancy but the bay is sometimes visited by the round the island excursion trip boat.

A final word of warning in respect of the track surface to Sikamia must be 'TAKE CARE' and if at all unsure of riding a scooter, do not attempt the journey as it is tricky.

By keeping to the right at the turning down to Sikamia, a part surfaced, part rough track loops round a further 3 km to:-

Taxiarchon Monastery (7⅓km from the Chora) A fortified religious house built in the 16th century and possessing Byzantine manuscripts and 18th century icons.

It is possible, on foot, to double back to the Chora, a distance of a further 3km, by continuing on beyond the monastery through the very pretty village of **Kallistos** (¾km) which is set in a lush valley.

ROUTE THREE

The Chora to Mega Livadi (7km) & Koutalas (7¼km) A turning off to the left from the road to Ormos Sikamia, at about 2km, is well signposted. The route is actually a rough surfaced track which descends to a fork in the road (5⅓km).

The right-hand turning bypasses the tiny village of **Megalo Chorio** (to the right) and bears off down to:-

MEGA LIVADI (7km from the Chora) The track runs up the side of a widening agricultural plain, hesitating by some building ruins and remnants of ore wagon tracks, for this was a mining town and port. Vestiges of the erstwhile activity still litter the area including the lattice framework of a freighter loading span projecting out over the water.

The last 20m of paved path tumbles down on to the near or left side (*Fsw*) of the rather closed-in, small bay. The stony backshore of the mature tree lined beach runs parallel to the sea's edge taking in a stony football pitch. The beach is made up of a scrubbly foreshore and a broad sandy strip. The landward side of the track is edged by a hotchpotch of buildings including a kafeneion, a store and a taverna, where they can rustle up a nice lunch time snack, but no accommodation.

The locals may or may not be delighted to welcome visitors to this once thriving town that 'died' some forty years ago. Vivid reminders of the glorious past remain at the far end of the waterfront where there is an amazing old colonial house in ruins, fronted by palm trees and a scattering of oleanders – very South American. On the far, cliff side of the bay is a big cave and a monument which appears to commemorate the dead of a 1916 strike. Were they shot?

Returning to the left-hand turning back at the fork, the unsurfaced road loops around a large headland, past a footpath down to **Maliadiko Beach**, and runs along the near right-hand side (*Sbo*) of a very large bay on which nestles:-

KOUTALAS (7¼km from the Chora) The track passes rusting reminders of erstwhile quarrying activity, for Koutalas was also once a mining town.

The very spacious bay is divided up by a large church topped bluff in the middle distance. Only a scattering of buildings now perch on the gentle mountain slope, that hems in the narrow tree-lined, shingle beach and small pebble foreshore. The scant community of fishermen support a 'Hillbilly taverna', the owner of which is delighted to minister to travellers' requirements, but there isn't any accommodation.

Both the seaside hamlets of Mega Livadi and Koutalas are delightful places in which to while away a day but be mindful that ***Rooms*** are not available.

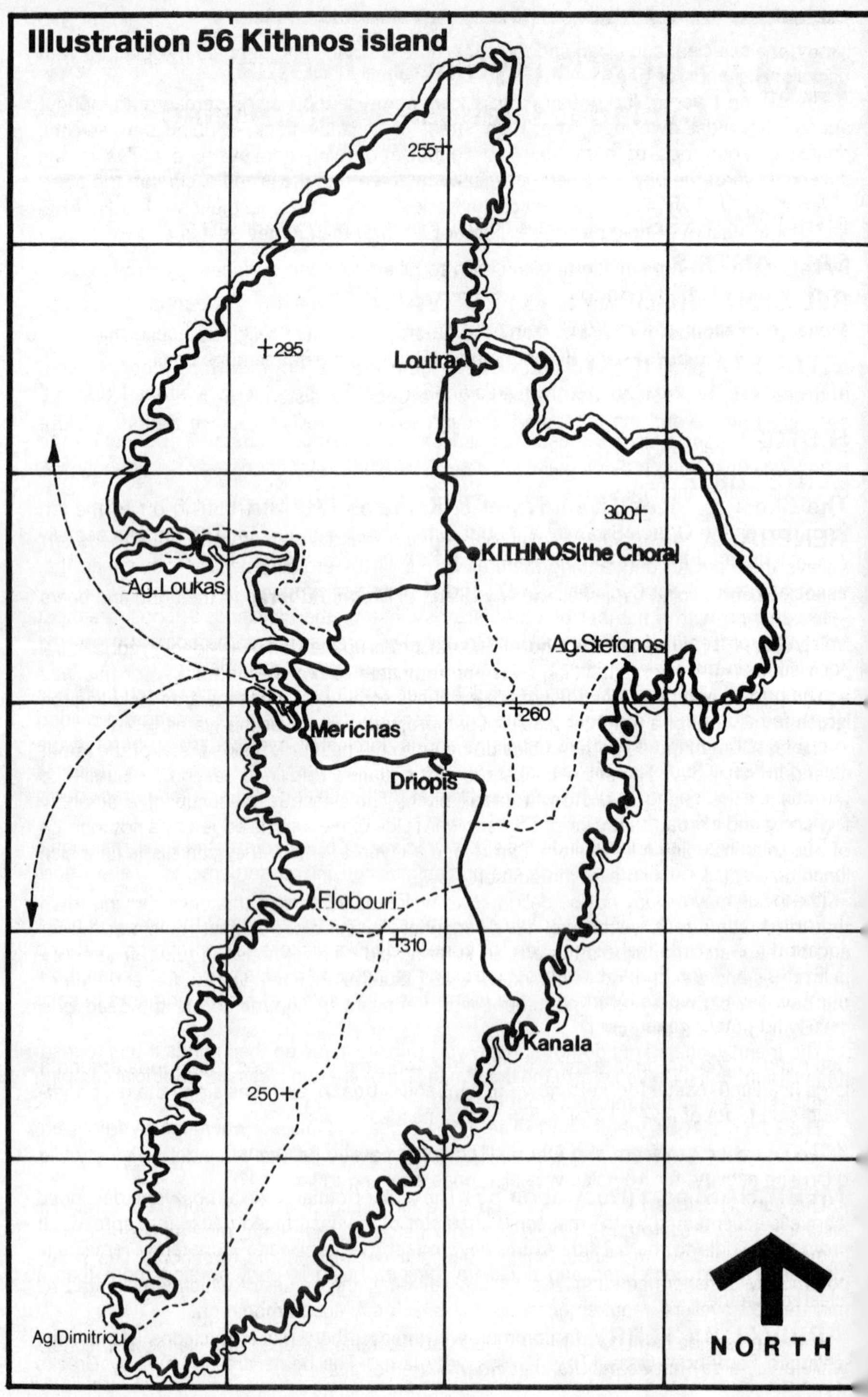
Illustration 56 Kithnos island
255
295
Loutra
300
KITHNOS(the Chora)
Ag.Loukas
Ag.Stefanos
260
Merichas
Driopis
Flabouri
310
Kanala
250
Ag.Dimitriou
NORTH

20 KITHNOS (Kythnos, Thermia) ★★★
Cyclades Islands - Western wing

FIRST IMPRESSIONS Greek holiday island; friendly inhabitants.

SPECIALITIES Basket weaving; cheese.

RELIGIOUS HOLIDAYS & FESTIVALS include: 8th September – Festival, Monastery Panaghia, Kanala (SE coast).

VITAL STATISTICS Tel prefix 0281. Kithnos is 22½km from top to bottom and, at the widest, 11¼km across with an area of 86sq km. The population numbers 1,500.

HISTORY Apart from the usual Cycladean story, nothing outstanding although the island was once infamous for snake infestation. Additionally Kithnos was supposedly one of the original island city states.

GENERAL A comparatively small, dry and arid island. Apart from the river-beds and valleys there are no outstanding features or out-of-the-ordinary beauty, other than that associated with most Cycladic islands – if that were not enough.

In common with a number of other islands close to the mainland, Kithnos is almost solely the preserve of holiday-making Greeks. This presents accommodation problems for visitors in the peak summer period and more especially weekends.

The port of Merichas was once a small hamlet with a few old red-tile roofed buildings scattered along the backshore. I write once, for now the settlement is almost crowded out by small, round edge cubic dwellings and is dominated by a six storey hotel at the far right-hand (*Sbo*) side of the bay. Despite this, the port still manages to radiate a 'frontier settlement' milieu with only a section of the beach edging 'Esplanade' track being concrete surfaced.

The other island villages include the attractive fishing port of Loutra, the small residential beach resort of Kanala as well as the undistinguished inland settlements of the Chora (Kithnos) and Driopis.

For reasons that are difficult to pin down with more than hunches, the island is not a location that excites the imagination, or conversely lulls visitors to contentedly drift into a lazy *laissez-faire*. Perhaps the most intriguing pastime is to guess, or try to divine, how the bus service works. Mark you, the island has been selected for experiments in solar and wind power generation.

The friendly inhabitants do not appear, yet, to have made up their minds if this tourism fad will last, or if it is even worth the drachmae. There are two pleasant, unofficial camping beaches, one only five minutes from the port.

The island can be water-short. The listed times and places when the hydrants are turned on does not seem to tie up with any of the island locations!

MERICHAS: port (Illustration 57) The rather frontier town atmosphere described above is accentuated by the makeshift character of the unsurfaced tracks that spread out from the middle to the far side of the bay. In fact the 'Esplanade' constantly remains in danger of being completed and tidied up, despite being in part, nothing more than a cleared swathe.

ARRIVAL BY FERRY In common with many other smaller Cyclades islands, the enlarged Ferry-boat Quay (*Tmr* 1D1) is very large. The boats are not met by Greeks bearing 'accommodation', despite most of the population appearing to turn out. Admittedly luggage-laden travellers wandering down the quay road may well be 'accosted'. The bus drives up to the quayside to await the arrival of the larger ferry-boats. This alludes to the fact that a small ferry-boat connects with the mainland port of Lavrio in addition to one or two of the larger ferries which include Kithnos on their itinerary.

Visitors might contemplate making directly for the delightful fishing port of Loutra.

THE ACCOMMODATION & EATING OUT

The Accommodation Even the Greeks are asked to vacate their rooms over weekends, so visitors should be 'quick about it' and consider stopping off during the week. The problem is that accommodation is often booked by long standing holiday-makers from one year to the next.

One convenient aspect is that most of that on offer is on the left-hand (*Sbo*) side of the bay. Two-thirds of the way along the quay road, prior to a periptero (*Tmr* 2E3/4) about which more later, a flight of steps lead up to the higher level, Chora road. Opposite the top of the steps, across the road is the:-

Kithnos Hotel (*Tmr* 3E3) Tel 31247
Directions: As above.

A very pleasant hotel, the excellent rooms of which are complete with sensibly sized, nicely fitted en suite bathrooms. If possible get a front room facing over the bay but more importantly just get a room, back or front. A double room en suite in mid-season costs from 1750drs. There was once a restaurant on the ground floor, but now only the *Cafe-bar/Zacharoplasteion O Merichas*. This is a pity as good eating places are at a premium. Mind you they serve a good 'standard' breakfast for 180drs. They also offer a splendid '½ a melon filled with ice-cream' for 200drs – delicious.

The Periptero (*Tmr* 2E3/4) on the left of the quay road is run by a very friendly man with some English. A sign proclaims ***Rooms*** which in fact refers to the *Hotel Kithnos*. The periptero owner ascertains the up-to-date position regarding accommodation by simply bellowing up the stone retaining wall!

Rooms (*Tmr* 4E2/3)
Directions: A private house just before the quayside Ouzerie.

Average room rates.

Rooms (*Tmr* 4E5) Tel 31243/31425
Directions: At the outset of the Esplanade, close to the junction of the quay and Chora streets, is the Driopis road which encircles this end of the village. The building is almost immediately on the left.

A private house charging the going rates.

Rooms (*Tmr* 4D5)
Directions: Off the first small square along the 'Esplanade' (*Fbqbo*), opposite a *Souvlaki Snackbar*.

Rooms (*Tmr* 5C/D4/5)
Directions: Above the *O Yialos Restaurant* and bordering the 'Esplanade'.

Rooms (*Tmr* 6C/D5)
Directions: In the street parallel to the waterfront and over the first supermarket on the left.

Rooms (*Tmr* 7B/C5/6) Tel 31248
Directions: Further west along the 'Esplanade' is a wide, dry river-bed at right angles to the waterfront. The accommodation is on the right (*Sbo*) above the Baker.

An extremely pleasant choice with en suite double rooms costing from 2500drs.

Rooms (*Tmr* 4B5)
Directions: Still in a westerly direction, towards the *Hotel Possidonion* and on the left, two buildings before *The Sunshine Cafe-Pub* (Ugh).

Rooms (*Tmr* 4A5)
Directions: To the left and in the shadow of the massive six storey *Hotel Possidonion*.

Hotel Possidonion (*Tmr* 22A5/6) (Class C) Tel 31244
Directions: At the far end of the Esplanade (*Fbqbo*). Quite visible!

All rooms have en suite bathrooms with a single room priced at 2000drs & a double 2500drs, increasing to 2300drs & 3000drs (July-Sept).

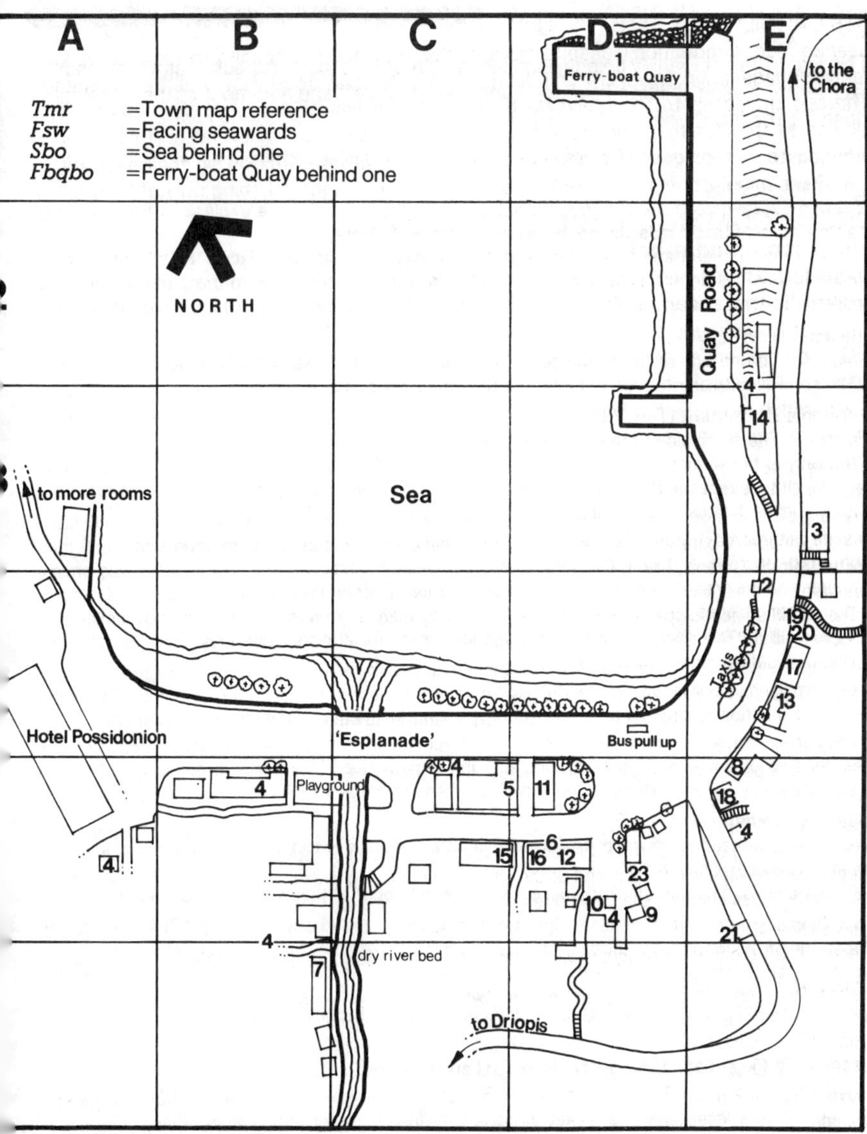

...ustration 57 Merichas

...1D1	Ferry-boat Quay	12D5	Souvlaki Taverna
2E3/4	Quayside Periptero	13E4	Kafeneion
3E3	Hotel Kithnos	14E2/3	Quayside Ouzerie
4	Rooms	15C/D5	'Front Room' office
5C/D4/5	O Yialos Restaurant/Rooms	16C/D5	Supermarket
6C/D5	Supermarket/Rooms	17E4	Disco Kavos
7B/C5/6	Baker/Rooms	18D/E4/5	Gift shop ticket office
8E4/5	Cafe-bar	19E4	'Ionian' ticket office
9D5/6	Souvlaki snackbar	20E4	Pharmacy
10D5	O Antonis Restaurant	21E5/6	Shell Petrol Station
11C/D4/5	Porto-Bello Snackbar	22A5/6	Hotel Possidonion
		23D5	Scooter hire
		T	Taxi rank

The Eating Out Frankly no one establishment redeems the ports lack of any gastronomic excellence. Young children have to supplement the staff and a number of the restaurants close for the afternoon.

In the absence of any good tavernas in town, I would recommend readers to eat at the:-

Cafe-Bar (*Tmr* 8E4/5)

Directions: A low, shed-like building, within which a 'laid-back' atmosphere, close by the junction of the Driopis and Chora roads across the way from the waterfront.

The young proprietor and his aides-de-camp are 'hunky', pleasant and friendly. He speaks tolerable English and serves an excellent pizza – the salads are very nice too. A pizza costs 550drs, a bacon omelette 220drs, a salad 120drs, a beer 85drs, a Nes meh ghala 60drs (110drs at *O Yialos*!).

Snackbar (*Tmr* 9D5/6)

Directions: To one side of the small square at the outset of the 'Esplanade' (*Fbqbo*).

The souvlaki pita on offer are not 'giro' cooked and cost 80drs.

O Antonis Restaurant (*Tmr* 10D5)

Directions: The south side of the square with an attractive trellis, plant covered patio.

Not only is the service lackadaisical to non-existent but the food is tired and lukewarm much of it being lunch time reheats. Prices do not assuage these shortcomings. Dishes include stuffed tomatoes 225drs, beans 170drs, moussaka 290drs, beer (500gr) 85drs and feta 75drs.

The 'Esplanade' is paralleled by a street one block back which peters out in the river-bed.

Porto Bello Snackbar (*Tmr* 11C/D4/5)

Directions: In a singularly ugly building, spanning the two streets described above.

The establishment's speciality is lobster but I usually manage to turn a deaf ear to the siren calls of this costly dish. The sloppy service,which epitomises the general shortcomings of eating out in the port is overlaid by yucky pop music.

Ο ΓΙΑΛΟΣ (O Yialos) Restaurant (*Tmr* 5C/D4/5)

Directions: Pleasantly situated bordering the 'Esplanade' with tables on the beach backshore

The service is quick and they do offer a wide choice of less common but very expensive dishes. A meal for two of 2 veal & vegetables, one egg and tomato salad (tiny portion), one bottle of water, bread, 2 coffees (100drs each!) and a baclava cost an outrageous 1790drs!

'Souvlaki' Taverna (*Tmr* 12D5)

Directions: Squeezed in between the forgettable *Cafe-Snackbar Byzantio* and a busy supermarket, in the street parallel to the waterfront.

As the title suggests, a 'souvlaki house', which is just about all they serve at 70drs a stick.

Two Kafeneions deserve a mention. One is at the outset of the Chora road (*Tmr* 13E4), with tables across the street in the trees dividing the road from the Ferry-boat Quay. Two coffees cost 130drs. The other, an *Ouzerie* (*Tmr* 14E2/3), borders the quay road and is built over and round a fisherman's shelter. They serve retsina, inexpensive ouzo, with good mezes, as well as nice cakes and stay open until late into the evening. This is an excellent position from which to survey the Ferry-boat Quay.

THE A TO Z OF USEFUL INFORMATION

BANKS None. A 'Front-Room office' (*Tmr* 15C/D5), in the street behind the *O Yialos Restaurant*, 'trebles up' as a local ferry-boat ticket office, cigarette wholesaler and change office. Total chaos reigns and they charge 100drs commission for Eurocheques.

BEACHES The narrow, tree edged, dirty, grey coarse sand beach is scrubbly, even unacceptable. Restaurant tables encroach on the stony backshore. That is the bits of the backshore that are not piled high with building materials, shale and lumps of concrete. Additionally the sea bottom is made up of slimy pebbles covered with weeds.

A number of fjord-like bays with beaches lie to the north of the port to which a small blue hulled cabin boat runs a water-taxi service. This water-taxi service is one of those that inexplicably hides its light... for some obscure reason. The first of these beaches is a five minute walk along the Chora road. Round the first headland, a path and steps angle down to a very pleasant, narrow, coarse sand cove set at the end of a fertile valley. To the right-hand side of the path down are ***Rooms*** in a house set into the hillside. There is a church at the far side of this cove and the beach is planted with small arethemusa trees, in amongst which some 'wild' camping. The grey, coarse sand beach is in surprisingly good condition, considering the presence of the campers. The sea edge is biscuit rock, except at the far side, but the quickly shelving sea-bed is sandy. Disadvantages are that the flies bite and the location fills up. A taverna fulfils most of the bodily functions and requirements, having an accessible toilet and the usual fare. No menu is available and they do not open until 1400hrs. To the right (*Fsw*) is the small islet of Ag Loukas which is attractively connected to the mainland by a narrow neck of sand and is a worthwhile destination, using the water-taxi.

BICYCLE, SCOOTER & CAR HIRE Another island on which the admittedly erratic, at times baffling, bus service and convenient taxis invalidate the need to hire transport. Despite this there are two moped/scooter hire firms. One is in the large building on the right of the Chora road, midway between the waterfront and the *Kithnos Hotel* (*Tmr* 3E3), and the other (*Tmr* 23D5) edges the small square west of the Driopis road. At the latter a 2 seater moped costs 1700drs per day.

BREAD SHOPS A Baker (*Tmr* 7B/C5/6) is on the right of the 'River-bed Road' off the Esplanade and about half-way round the bay.

BUSES The buses park (*Tmr* D4/5) on the broad stretch of concrete at about the point where the Esplanade and quay road run into each other. Despite the timetable being stuck up all over the place it is a confusing service, so much so that even the Greeks get excitable about it!

For what it is worth, here are my notes. Incidentally one of the buses 'owns' an infernal horn which plays a loud 'tune, frequently to announce an impending departure:-

Bus timetable (Mid-season)

Merichas Port to Kanala via Driopis
Daily: 0710, 1000, 1200, 1345, 1700, 1930hrs.
Return journey
Daily: 0730, 1030, 1230, 1415, 1730, 2000hrs.
One-way fare to Driopis 60drs & Kanala 110drs.

Merichas Port to Chora & Loutra
Daily: 0700, 1100, 1230, 1715, 1900, 2115hrs.
Return journey
Daily: 0730, 1000, 1200, 1315, 1615, 1815, 2015hrs.
One-way fare to Chora 60drs & Loutra 90drs.

Chora to Loutra
Daily: 0715, 0915, 1115, 1245, 1600, 1730, 1915, 2130hrs.
One-way fare Chora to Loutra 60drs.

Chora to Merichas
Daily: 0745, 1015, 1215, 1330, 1630, 1830, 2030hrs.

These last 2 seem rather to contradict and confuse the first 2....

When questioned the bus driver advises "There is always a bus to Chora meeting the ferry"? A point to note is that the Merichas to Loutra bus does not (always) enter the Chora, but stops at the junction on the outskirts.

The wise use the taxis which operate on a share basis and cost from 250drs for two from the Chora to Merichas Port (or vice-versa). One or two of the drivers are under the misapprehension that they are at Le Mans, especially the dark, handsome driver in his late 30s. A journey with him is inevitably accompanied by many a blast on the car's horn, which is programmed to produce a 'Colonel Bogie' effect. Oh goody!

As an aside, I must admire the gall of a Greek garage owner from Piraeus. He addressed himself to one driver of a bus on which we were passengers saying he had left his purse at the hotel and would he, the driver, mind lending him 2000drs... and the driver did just that.

COMMERCIAL SHOPPING AREA None but well served by two Supermarkets (*Tmr* 6D5 & 16C/D5) side-by-side in the street, parallel to the waterfront. Both display a public telephone sign.

DISCO I have not sampled the delights but the Kavos (*Tmr* 17E4) is centrally situated.

FERRY-BOATS An interesting situation where, apart from the 'mega' inter-island ferry-boats connecting with Piraeus, there is a smaller boat connection to the mainland port of Lavrio.

If a reader or traveller thinks 'I protest too much...' in respect of the Greek ferry-boats and their operation, Kithnos may be regarded as an island benchmark. It is one of those locations where all the truths will out. Whereas I have even been praised by other guide book authors for daring to list ferry-boat details, it has to be admitted that Kithnos (and Kea) steer one towards the brink. I nearly wrote drink, which would have been equally apposite.

The daily (except Wednesday) height of summer connection between Lavrio-Kithnos is made by the bright blue **Kithnos** car ferry. The **FB Ioulis Keas II** only runs between Lavrio-Kea-Lavrio, or at least that is the theory but it does turn up one or two days a week!

The **Kithnos** calls at Kea, *en route* for Kithnos, once a week (on Sundays) but never on its way back. Thus it is still necessary to go back to Lavrio to return to Kea but... A joker in the schedules, the once a week **Theoskepasti**, makes an appearance connecting Rafina(M), Kea and Kithnos. Now a reader might well be reaching for the tranquillizers! I simply cannot understand why it is necessary to return to Lavrio to connect between the two islands. There have been rumours that this cock-eyed arrangement is to be amended, but if you believe that, then flying pigs will come as no surprise. Incidentally, the **FB Ioulis Keas II**, is an ex Merseyside craft.

Ferry-boat timetable (Mid-high season)

Day	**Departure time**	**Ferry-boat**	**Ports/Islands of Call**
Mon	1700hrs	Kithnos	Lavrio(M).
	1930hrs	Delos	Serifos,Siphnos,Kimolos,Milos.
Tues	1230hrs	Delos	Rafina(M).
	1700hrs	Kithnos	Lavrio(M).
	1730hrs	Kimolos	Serifos,Siphnos,Milos,Kimolos,Syros.
Wed	0100hrs	Theoskepasti	Kea,Syros,Tinos,Andros,Rafina(M).
	1200hrs	Ionian	Serifos,Siphnos,Kimolos,Milos.
	1400hrs	Kimolos	Piraeus(M).
	2300hrs	Ionian	Piraeus(M).
Thur	0245hrs	Kimolos	Piraeus(M).
	1600hrs	Kithnos	Lavrio(M).
	1630hrs	Kimolos	Serifos,Siphnos,Milos.
Fri	1600hrs	Kithnos	Lavrio(M).
	1915hrs	Kimolos	Serifos,Siphnos,Kimolos,Milos,Piraeus(M).
Sat	1130hrs	Ionian	Serifos,Siphnos,Milos,Piraeus(M).
	1800hrs	Kithnos	Lavrio(M).
Sun	1430hrs	Ionian	Piraeus(M).
	1600hrs	Kithnos	Lavrio(M).
	1730hrs	Kimolos	Piraeus(M).

One-way fares: Kithnos to Lavrio 845drs; duration 4hrs.
to Piraeus 1025drs; " 4hrs.

Please note these tables are detailed as a GUIDE ONLY. Due to the time taken to research the Cyclades, it is IMPOSSIBLE TO 'match' the timetables or even boats . So don't try cross pollinating...

FERRY-BOAT TICKET OFFICES The **Kimolos** is represented by the Gift shop (*Tmr* 18D/E4/5) tucked in the corner of the Driopis Road. This shop also has a metered telephone and bus timetables stuck in the window.

Tickets for the **Ionian** are sold from the small office (*Tmr* 19E4) on the right of the Chora road, prior to the *Kithnos Hotel*. They also advertise ***Rooms***.

The 'Front-Room' office (*Tmr* 15C/D5) in the street behind the *O Yialos Restaurant* represents the **Ioulis Keas II**.

MEDICAL CARE
Chemists & Pharmacies There is a Pharmacy (*Tmr* 20E4) on the right of the Chora Road.
Clinic *See* **The Chora**.

OTE & POST OFFICE *See* **The Chora**. Note there is a metered telephone in the Gift shop (*Tmr* 18D/E4/5) but lines are very difficult to obtain.

PETROL A Shell petrol station (*Tmr* 21E5/6) edges the Driopis Road.

TAXIS Bunch up at the outset of the quay road (*Tmr* T E4). *See* **Buses, A To Z** for further details.

ROUTE ONE

Merichas Port to Loutra (8km) via The Chora Apart from the bottom of the valley bottoms, the countryside is arid with multi-terraced hillsides. The road from the port winds up a fertile valley, the summer-dry river-bed of which is prettily and profusely flowered with oleanders and buddleia.

KITHNOS (The Chora) (5km from Merichas Port) Set on a high, rolling, agricultural plain, but lacking the traditional whitewashed hill-capping beauty associated with the 'standard model' Chora.

There is no accommodation (that I could find) but the village is well resourced with a bread shop, general stores, Clinic, butcher, several kafeneions, a smart taverna, greengrocers, a Post Office and OTE, all widely spaced out throughout the settlement.

The buses park on a square at the outset to the Chora. The OTE is off round to the right and right again, alongside a clock tower. The Post Office changes travellers cheques, Eurocheques and foreign currency notes.

The road from the Chora snakes down to the large plain backing:-

LOUTRA (8km from Merichas Port) Situated on an attractive bay at the end of a wide river valley. Loutra is a truly 'lovely' fishing village inhabited by friendly people and now graced with a yacht marina. Note the beauty is not that of poets and artists, more that associated with *au naturel*,Greek working settlements.

The site has been a spa since ancient times, hence the name Loutra derived from the word for bath ('Lutra'). The thermal waters are delivered to the baths at two temperatures, 40°F and 70°F, one suitable for rheumatism and the other for ladies wishing to have babies – but for the life of me I cannot remember which is for whom!

The left-hand (*Fsw*) horn of the bay has a bluff dominated by a white wall enclosed church, an old mining jetty and the ruins of a castle, beyond which is a small cove.

To the right-hand side of the bay is a continually running, warm, brown coloured stream that bubbles over a wide, stony river-bed, edged and contained by a low concrete border. Across the stream, in an English moorland setting, is, incongruously, a baker in an unfinished, red brick building with blue doors. To get to the 'ovens' it is necessary to follow the stream and bear left.

The final approach to the spread out village is dominated by the very large:-

Xenia Anagenissis (Class C) Tel 31217

Directions: As above.

In the front and to the side are various outbuildings, including a church and the thermal baths for which the hotel must have been created. All rooms have an en suite bathroom with a single priced at 2000drs & a double 2500drs, increasing to 2300drs & 3000drs (July-Sept). If accommodation is available breakfast will cost an extra 350drs.

The main road approaches the village down the right-hand (*Fsw*) side and turns sharp left along the front of the *Xenia*, leaving, to the right, a spindly tree fringed, large square of wasteland. The far, sea edge of this latter area is bordered by the backshore of the coarse sand and pebble beach and the left-hand side by the back of the buildings lining the 'High' Street. The main road traverses to the foot of a cliff-face, which hems in the left side of the village, where it makes a junction with the 'High' St. The bus parks on an earth-surfaced square to the side of the 'High' Street which drops away to the right to run out on the left of the beach

The 'High' St has ***Rooms*** on both left and right. The left-hand buildings are set into and on top of the steep hillside that edges this side of the development.

Rooms to Rent Delfini Tel 31464/31468

Directions: On the right of the 'High' Street. There is a sign in the hall 'Please don't let the doors to hit and generally don't make a noise at the times...'.

A double room with en suite bathroom costs from 2500drs.

Next door to the hotel is a gift shop. The grand-papa of the proprietors chatters to passers-by. If they are English he calls them into the shop in order to proudly display his personal letter from Field Marshall Lord Alexander. This commends him for assistance rendered to the Allies during the Second World War. All the time the conversation is punctuated by his repetitious phrase "Bad business", his English being rather rudimentary, despite six years spent in London.

The 'High' St also contains a supermarket, two ferry-boat ticket offices, a kafeneion, a small store and a ramshackle Post Office, transacting currency exchange and often closed when the manager pops off for a coffee.

From the bottom, sea end of the 'High' St, the beach stretches away to the right (*Fsw*). The backshore is bordered by the large area of waste ground. In amongst the trees nestles a small block of changing room cubicles and there are usually pulled up a number of small fishing boats. The centre section of the foreshore is made up of fine pebbles and the sea bottom is sandy, whilst at the far end, by the stream outfall, the beach is coarse sand and pebbles.

To the left of the bottom of the 'High' St, a clean, fine sand 'Beach Road' curves round past a restaurant and then another restaurant. A surfaced street angles up the hillside to a supermarket and ***Rooms***, whilst the beach runs out on the edge of a small, concrete fishing boat quay. When the boats land, a swarm of villagers surround the fishermen who sell their catch from the quay. The 'Beach Road' and main beach are kept very clean by a 'council workman'.

Despite the mention of accommodation this is an unusual location in that enquiries regarding Rooms are met with the advice that they are only available to Greeks. It certainly is a very popular holiday resort with them, so why does it not get more than a mention in most guide books? In conclusion, Loutra is 'a find'.

ROUTE TWO

Merichas Port to Kanala (8km) via DriopisA similar road to **Route One** climbs to the village of:-

DRIOPIS (4km from Merichas Port) More spaciously laid out than Kithnos village and rather more representative of a Chora, with pleasantly tiled roofs and to one side overlooked by old, hillside windmills. There is a baker who prepares awful looking bread.

As with Kithnos village, the main road bypasses Driopis despite conflicting detail on the official maps. Beyond the still uncompleted, huge, twin towered Byzantine Church of Ag Kostodinos, the road winds steeply downhill to the seaside development of:-

KANALA (8km from Merichas Port) Not at all typical, this neat, verdant, modern holiday resort, with a few ***Rooms***, sits on top of a tongue of headland, flanked by a bay to either side. Flowers, trees and roses bedeck the gardens.

The bus pulls up on the widened section at the road end, to the right (*Fsw*) of the village. There is a water tap and bread is sold here daily, from the back of a van.

To reach the left-hand, small cove climb the steps by the bus pull-up, pass between the houses, over a wall, and down the track. The beach is coarse sand and pebbles, with biscuit rock at the sea's edge and a sandy sea bottom. No taverna but a pleasant spot.

To the right-hand is a very small, generally crowded cove with a tiny, rock edged, sandy beach. Beyond this and a rocky outcrop is the large main bay. Access to both is through the large gates at the front or sea end of the 'Bus' Sq,which advances down a sloping Public Garden on a zig-zag stone path. This is sheltered from the sun by closely packed fir and pine trees as far as a concrete fishing boat quay. The lower path leads to the first small cove. The upper path continues on and over a low hillside to a spread out bay with a narrow, sandy, fine shingle beach and some buildings behind the wall edged backshore. The latter include a Pension, cafe-bar and breakfast restaurant. Some 'wild' camping takes place in the shade of the few spindly arethemusa trees. The large, centre-of-beach taverna slowly serves a limited but nice menu. A lunch time meal for two of 2 stuffed tomatoes, a curdy cheese and bottled water costs 850drs.

Naoussa, Paros, close by the Cathedral. *Acknowledgement to David & Liz Drummond-Tyler.*

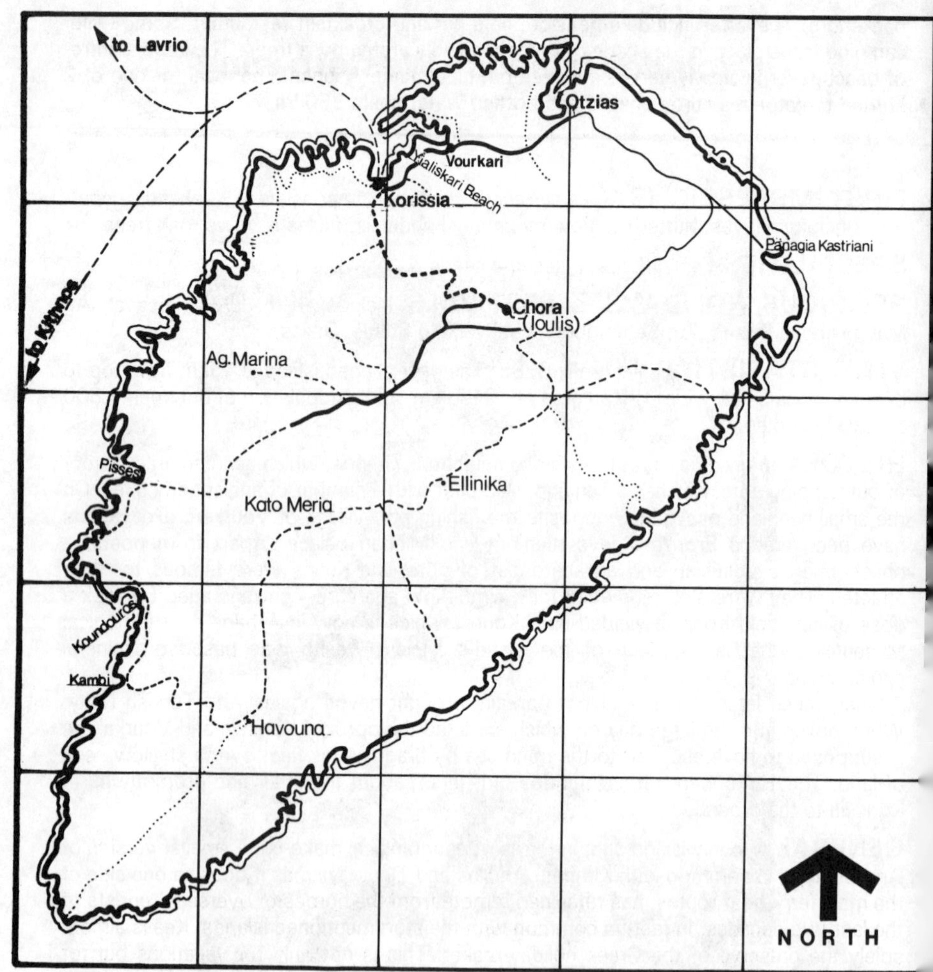

Illustration 58 Kea island

21 KEA (Tzia) ★★★
Cyclades Islands - Western wing

FIRST IMPRESSIONS Expensive accommodation, impossible at weekends; generally unhelpful natives; butterflies; low mountains; buddleia; mules & cows; oak trees.

SPECIALITIES Pasteli (bars of sesame seeds & honey).

RELIGIOUS HOLIDAYS & FESTIVALS include: 17th July – Festival, Ag Marina above Pisses; 7th September – Festival, Ag Sostis, Otzias.

VITAL STATISTICS Tel prefix 0288. The pear shaped island is 19km from top to bottom, up to 9½km wide with an area of 121sq km, and a population of between 1,600 & 1,700 people.

HISTORY In vivid contrast to its close neighbour Kithnos, which accrued little history of outstanding note, Kea has a rich and vivid past with a number of ancient city sites. On the small headland of Ag Irini, opposite the fishing port village of Vourkari, excavations have uncovered a Bronze Age settlement and Minoan palace. Apart from poets, a philosopher, a politician and an anatomist of note, the Keans were famous for their athletes. They were also renowned for a simple old age cure – citizens aged 60 took a dose of hemlock! Korissia yielded up a Kouros which is now in Athens Archaeological Museum – what isn't? Much of the island's ancient wealth was based on mineral exploitation.

Later, much later, a Greek ship's Captain wrought havoc against the Turkish Navy. When boxed into the large bay on which are sited the ports of Korissia and Vourkari he is supposed to have escaped to the open sea by dragging his fleet over a shallow neck of land. The Turks were rather 'miffed' and 'terse' about the affair and promptly burnt Korissia to the ground.

GENERAL A lovely island and, in terms of geographical make-up, a smaller version of Andros. Kea, in common with Kithnos, Andros and Tinos, lying as it does to one side of the main ferry-boat routes, has remained remote from the hordes of overseas tourists of the last two decades. In fact, in common with the aforementioned islands, Kea is almost solely the preserve of the Greek holiday-maker. This is not only for vacations but for weekends as well, which is the rub. During the summer weekends the island is crowded, bursting at its limited seams, with all the paltry 150* or so beds taken. So bad is the situation that even the Greeks have to take to the beach. This pressure is reflected in the islanders' attitudes to foreign visitors, for they are, in the main, disinterested with a tendency to rudeness. During the week Kea reverts to a sleepy, none too busy island.

The cost of rooms is high, shopping is expensive, scooter hire pricey and eating out is in the price bracket experienced on some of the more tourist packed islands. A further word or two of caution must advise that Lavrio, the mainland port servicing Kea, is unlovely and the ferry rates are rather expensive.

Despite the foregoing, readers should not be put off as the island is extremely attractive. The port of Korissia is endearing, even if the adjacent beach is not of a high quality. One cove further on, there is a splendid beach, followed by the pleasant, seaside, private yacht and fishing boat hamlet of Vourkari. The main town, Ioulis is no whitewashed show piece, but a fine example of a working Chora. Additionally, there are a number of other,

**There are another 150 beds at the Class B Kea Beach, Koundouros. Apart from the location and expense, the hotel is not really the sort of place at which a traveller can just drop in.*

if rather far-flung beaches and the most lovely agricultural hillside routes running the length of the island.

KORISSIA: port (Illustration 59) A pleasant enough harbour village which is rather reminiscent of and similar in layout to Katapola Port, Amorgos The setting sun lighting up the hillsides across the bay is a lovely sight, which can be watched in perfect comfort from one of the quayside kafeneions.

ARRIVAL BY FERRY The point on the quay where the ferries dock (*Tmr* 1B/C4/5) is rather narrow and claustrophobic, being hemmed in by a steeply rising hillside on which is an eye-catching, green pavilion type building.

Bearing in mind the general shortage of accommodation, especially over the weekends, it is best to get a sharp move on. The boats are rarely, if ever met by Room owners added to which there is an additional twist to the plot, namely that the proprietors operate through a co-operative.

THE ACCOMMODATION & EATING OUT

The Accommodation As prefaced in **Arrival by Ferry**, most of the available Rooms are part of a collaborative association which is handled by the:-

Tourist Office (*Tmr* 2C5) Tel 31256

Directions: Edging the waterfront quay where it widens out, opposite the taxi rank.

The private house owners of accommodation leave the letting to this basement office, which is down a few steps in the square, low building. The office is rumoured to be moving further along the quay, closer to the Ferry-boat Quay. Not only is the renting of accommodation centralised but the prices are structured, so much so that the door of the office exhibits a price guide. The standards are not outstanding and 'C' class is in effect 'village rustic'. When the Rooms run out, there is little anyone can do. The shoulders are shrugged and that is that. Best to telephone and book in advance. The office opens daily between 0930-1300hrs & 1900-2200hrs.

Hotel Karthea (*Tmr* 3E4) (Class C) Tel 31222

Directions: A large, modern building at the far end of the quay, where the Esplanade bends round.

All rooms have en suite bathrooms with a single priced at 2000drs & a double 2400drs. Double room prices increase to 3000drs (1st July-15th Sept).

Another hotel is the:-

Motel Tzai Mas (*Tmr* 4E1/2) (Class B) Tel 31305/31223

Directions: Along the beach road and on the left, beyond the school, set in a tree shaded position backing on to the beach. A low rise modern hotel.

When available, the double rooms en suite cost 2630drs with breakfast charged at 250drs.

Incidentally, across the road are two private houses with accommodation (*Tmr* 5E2 & 6E2) The one closest to the port, left up the river-bed road and on the right is:-

Rooms (*Tmr* 6E2)

Directions: As above.

This is the house of the lady who advertises her accommodation on a fence close by the ticket office, at the mainland port of Lavrio – 'Rooms for Rent with Bathrooms *Kopissia* Tel 0288 31355'. Not cheap though with double rooms from 2500drs.

From the *Hotel Karthea* (*Tmr* 3E4) along the Esplanade in the direction of the Ferry-boat Quay, there is a sign which proclaims ***Rooms*** but do not expect too much from the direct approach.

On my last visit we stayed in a ladies house (*Tmr* 7C5) behind a Taverna (*Tmr* 8C5). This was 'C' class accommodation with an en suite bathroom. Mmhh! The ceiling of the bedroom was untreated hardboard, there was no lampshade, the bathroom door would not shut, the shower control was 'iffy' and it would have been difficult to swing a wet flannel. But it was a bed and I had spent the previous night on the beach, when it had rained. Say no more.

At weekends even the Greeks have to sleep out beneath their motorbikes, or in their cars so a few pointers are discussed, for which *See* **Beaches, A To Z**.

The Eating Out Generally prices are medium to expensive.

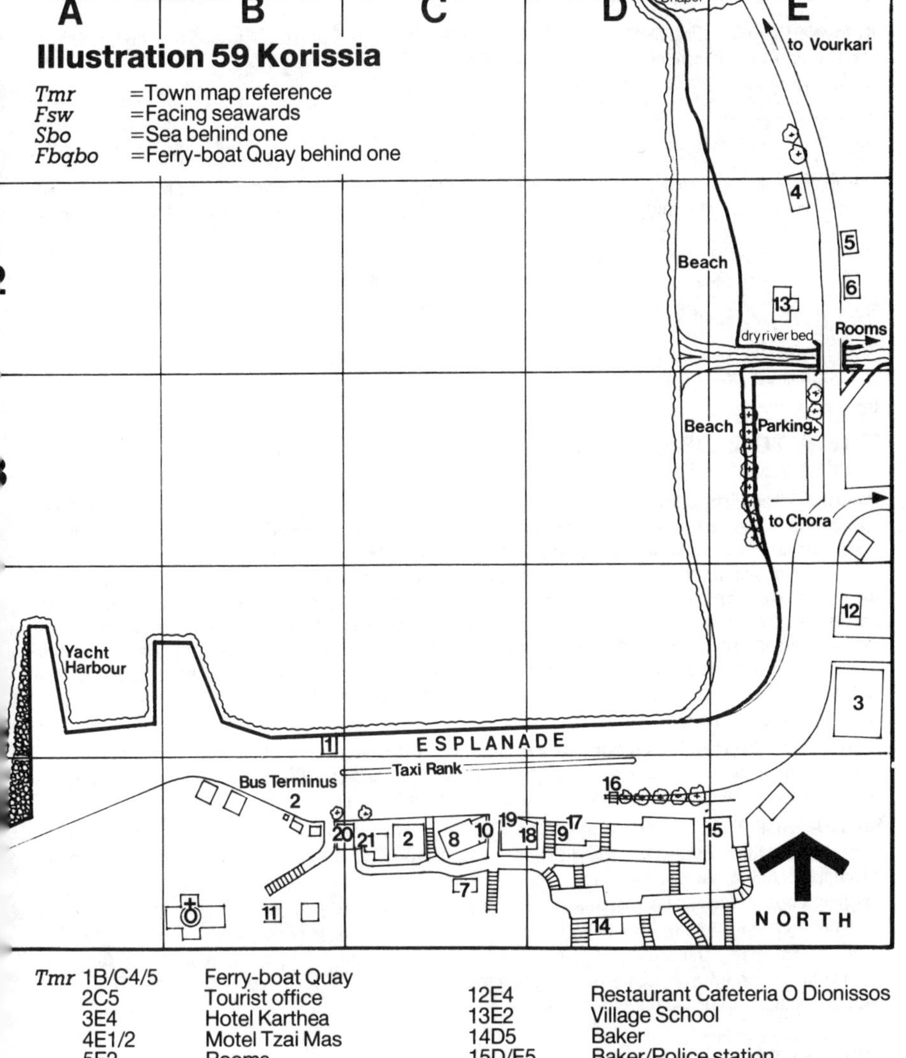

Tmr			
1B/C4/5	Ferry-boat Quay	12E4	Restaurant Cafeteria O Dionissos
2C5	Tourist office	13E2	Village School
3E4	Hotel Karthea	14D5	Baker
4E1/2	Motel Tzai Mas	15D/E5	Baker/Police station
5E2	Rooms	16D5	Telephone box
6E2	Rooms	17D5	Butcher
7C5	Rooms	18C/D5	General store
8C5	Taverna/Restaurant/Rooms	19C/D5	General store
9D5	Kafeneion ToΥntaς	20B/C5	'Hole-in-the-wall' Periptero
10C5	Grocery shop	21B/C5	Ferry-boat Ticket office
11B5	Port police		

Kafeneion Τογυτασ (*Tmr* 9D5)
Directions: About centre of the Esplanade, flanked by a butcher and steps.
The owner is no 'smiler' but opens early and serves good coffee.

Taverna/Restaurant (*Tmr* 8C5)
Directions: Borders the Esplanade with steps to the right (*Sbo*) of the building and a squashed up grocery shop to the left.
Fast, friendly, disorganised service with good meals served in a pleasant atmosphere of controlled chaos overseen by the middle-aged, rather disinterested owner who masterminds the bills. Bags of shouting. Closes for siesta but serves food up to, if not after, midnight. Those that might think it took time to be served should wait until they ask for the bill...
Oh, by the way, the owner has ***Rooms*** to let but he is in the co-operative.

Restaurant Cafeteria Pizzeria O Dionissos (*Tmr* 12E4)
Directions: Across the side-street from the *Hotel Karthea*.
A surprisingly large establishment with a spacious terrace patio. They serve a jolly good breakfast and there are acceptable toilets, both of which may be necessities to those who have over-nighted on the beach.

THE A TO Z OF USEFUL INFORMATION

BANKS No. *See* **The Chora**.

BEACHES The unattractive port beach occupies the bottom of the bay and is dominated by the red tile roofed, white walled school. Small boats are beached at the nearside, in amongst the scrubbly backshore of grassy, low dunes. Some attempt is made to bulldoze the sand about.
From the middle to the far side of the beach, where a small chapel tops a sea-hugging rocky outcrop, the indifferent, fairly clean beach of sand mixed with pebbles is not very wide. The foreshore and immediate sea bottom is weedy and pebbly whilst the road edge is lined with arethemusa trees. As the far side is approached the surface becomes almost entirely pebbles. There are some almost derelict changing cubicles and a concrete pad. A number of tubular frame, bamboo roofed shelters are dotted about. These allow some overnight shelter, but my 'favourite' location, if there can be such a thing, is the porch of the village school (*Tmr* 13E2).

BICYCLE, SCOOTER & CAR HIRE One establishment is **Moto Kea** on the right of the Chora road. There is little or no chance of hiring at the weekend. Motorbikes cost 2000drs a day, including petrol. A rather bandit-like atmosphere and no telephone, so do not breakdown too far away.

BREAD SHOP There is one Baker (*Tmr* 14D5) on a small irregular square reached up the steps alongside the Kafeneion (*Tmr* 9D5) and another (*Tmr* 15D/E5) at the bottom of the quay road over which is the Police station.

BUSES A good service but a limited number of destinations. A timetable is stuck to the glass pane of the waterfront public telephone box (*Tmr* 16D5) as is a ferry-boat schedule.
On Wednesday, Thursday and Sunday the service expands its horizons making for far-flung destinations (marked with asterisks*). The timetable details an 'AX' followed by a number. This is the registration number of the particular bus.

Bus timetable

Monday

Ioulis(Chora) to Korissia	0515hrs
Korissia to Ioulis	0930hrs
Otzias, Vourkari, Korissia, Ioulis	0930hrs
Ioulis, Korissia, Vourkari, Otzias	1045hrs
Ioulis, Korissia, Vourkari	1045hrs
Otzias, Vourkari, Korissia, Ioulis	1300hrs
Vourkari, Korissia, Ioulis	1300hrs
Ioulis, Korissia, Vourkari, Otzias	1545hrs
Korissia, Ioulis	1630hrs
Otzias, Vourkari, Korissia, Ioulis	1830hrs
Korissia, Ioulis	2030hrs
Ioulis, Korissia	2130hrs

Tuesday

Ioulis, Korissia	0715hrs
Korissia, Ioulis	0800hrs

Otzias, Vourkari, Korissia, Ioulis	0930hrs
Ioulis, Korissia, Vourkari, Otzias	1015hrs
Otzias, Vourkari, Ioulis	1300hrs
Ioulis, Korissia, Vourkari, Otzias	1545hrs
Otzias, Vourkari, Korissia	1900hrs
Korissia, Ioulis	1930hrs
Ioulis, Korissia	2100hrs
Korissia, Ioulis	2130hrs
Wednesday	
Ioulis, Korissia	0515hrs
Korissia, Ioulis	0800hrs
Otzias, Vourkari, Korissia, Ioulis	0930hrs
Ioulis, Korissia	0945hrs
Korissia, Ioulis	1030hrs
Ioulis, Pisses*	1100hrs
Otzias, Vourkari, Korissia, Ioulis	1300hrs
Pisses*, Ioulis	1430hrs
Ioulis, Korissia	1515hrs
Ioulis, Korissia, Vourkari, Otzias	1600hrs
Otzias, Vourkari, Korissia, Ioulis	1800hrs
Korissia, Ioulis	1930hrs
Ioulis, Korissia	2100hrs
Thursday	
Ioulis, Korissia	0715hrs
Korissia, Ioulis	0800hrs
Otzias, Vourkari, Korissia, Ioulis	0930hrs
Ioulis, Korissia, Vourkari, Otzias	1015hrs
Ioulis, Korissia, Vourkari	1010hrs
Otzias, Vourkari, Korissia, Ioulis	1300hrs
Ioulis, Korissia, Vourkari, Kastriani*	1600hrs
Kastriani*, Vourkari, Korissia, Ioulis	1830hrs
Korissia, Ioulis	1930hrs
Ioulis, Korissia	2100hrs

Friday
As Monday but the 1045hrs bus departs at 1015hrs, the 1630hrs at 1600hrs and the 2130hrs at 2100hrs.

Saturday	
Ioulis, Korissia, Vourkari, Otzias, Kastriani*	0915hrs
Vourkari, Korissia, Ioulis	0930hrs
Korissia, Ioulis	1030hrs
Ioulis, Korissia, Vourkari, Otzias	1030hrs
Otzias, Vourkari, Korissia, Ioulis	1230hrs
Otzias, Vourkari, Korissia, ioulis	1300hrs
Ioulis, Korissia, Vourkari	1600hrs
Vourkari, Korissia, Ioulis	1830hrs
Korissia, Ioulis	2100hrs
Ioulis, Korissia	2130hrs
Sunday	
Ioulis, Ellinika*, Katomeria*, Havouna*	0630hrs
Havouna*, Katomeria*, Ellinika*, Ioulis	0800hrs
Otzias, Vourkari, Korissia	0930hrs
Ioulis, Korissia, Vourkari, Otzias, Kastriani*	1000hrs
Korissia, Ioulis	1030hrs
Kastriani*, Otzias, Vourkari, Korissia, Ioulis	1200hrs
Ioulis, Korissia	1445hrs
Ioulis, Ellinika*, Katomeria*, Havouna*	1530hrs
Korissia, Ioulis	1900hrs
Ioulis, Korissia	1915hrs
Korissia, Ioulis	2100hrs

Incidentally, the buses 'terminus' towards the west end of the Esplanade.

COMMERCIAL SHOPPING AREA None, but a Grocery shop (*Tmr* 10C5), Butcher (*Tmr* 17D5), two General stores (*Tmr* 18C/D5 & 19C/D5) and a small, 'hole-in-the-wall Periptero' (*Tmr* 20B/C5). Fruit & vegetable vans ply their trade daily, including Sundays. This reminds me to mention that Sunday does not deter the island worthies from trading and even the baker opens in the morning.

DISCOS Disco Kea is close to the Chora road, beyond the olive oil factory, possibly 1½km distant.

FERRY-BOATS The island is not on the large inter-island ferry-boat itineraries. The year round connection is with the mainland port of Lavrio on an ex-Merseyside ferry, 'The Royal Daffodil'. This was purchased by a Greek company in 1977 and renamed the **Ioulis Keas II**.

In the height-of-season months another boat, the **Theoskepasti** connects the mainland port of Rafina with the island once a week, proceeding on to Kithnos.

Ferry-boat timetable (Mid-high season)

Day	**Departure time**	**Ferry-boat**	**Ports/Islands of Call**
Daily		Ioulis Keas II	Lavrio(M).

One-way fare: Kea to Lavrio 560drs; duration 2½hrs.

Please note these tables are detailed as a GUIDE ONLY. Due to the time taken to research the Cyclades it is IMPOSSIBLE TO 'match' the timetables or even boats . So don't try cross pollinating...

It will be noted, that as things stand, it is necessary to return to Lavrio to connect with Kithnos but there are rumours, innuendoes and hints at changes for the better, sometime?

Please note these tables are detailed as a GUIDE ONLY. Due to the time taken to research the Cyclades, it is IMPOSSIBLE TO 'match' the timetables or even boats. So don't try cross pollinating...

FERRY-BOAT TICKET OFFICES Only one (*Tmr* 21B/C5) close to the Ferry-boat Quay and slightly set back. The unsmiling, uncommunicative man also runs a grocery shop. The office opens prior to a ferry-boat's departure but allow ½hr to purchase tickets. No one is allowed on board without a ticket so queues form, with the occasional native holding up matters for agonisingly long periods.

Do not miss the marvellous panoramic photo of the port and surrounding area hanging in the office.

MEDICAL CARE *See* **The Chora** for both Clinic and Pharmacy.

OTE *See* **The Chora**.

PETROL There is a Shell petrol pump beyond the Ferry-boat Quay.

POLICE (*Tmr* 11B5) The office is on the hillside, looking down over the ferry-boat docking point.
Town (*Tmr* 15D/E5) At the bottom end of the waterfront quay above a bakers. They are no help in finding accommodation.

POST OFFICE More a post box, close by the 'Tourist office' (*Tmr* 2C5). *See* **The Chora**.

TAXIS The rank is opposite the 'Tourist' office (*Tmr* 2C5).

TELEPHONE NUMBERS & ADDRESSES

Police	Tel 22300

TRAVEL AGENTS & TOUR OFFICES Tourist Office (*Tmr* 2C5). Apart from the discourse under **The Accommodation**, the office sells maps and a guide book.

ROUTE ONE

From Korissia Port to Panaghia Kastriani (10½km) The surfaced road borders the port beach and curves round the edge of the bay and the small headland to dive down to:-

Yialiskari Beach (1km from Korissia Port) A very pleasant, popular, small, sandy beach cove backed by verdant groves of gum and tamarisk trees. The foreshore sports some green weed. On the nearside is a beach taverna, a public toilet and tap water. Despite signs forbidding the same, a few wild camp at the far end of the beach.

Beyond Yialiskari the road parallels the sea but a little up the slope of the hill. On the far horn of land that encircles the bay, set close to the shore, are the abandoned but sturdy buildings of a once thriving industrial activity. This was probably a tanning factory (for which last process the prolific island oak trees were a necessary ingredient). Keep an eye open for some Andros style walling.

The stone wall edged road curves sharply right, down past a public toilet to the busy waterfront of:-

VOURKARI (2½km from Korissia Port) Once a fishing port but now host to a multitude of motor boats, yachts and a few, very large private caiques mooring bow or stern-on to the quay. Some craft anchor at the left-hand side of the quay. The waterfront, which forms the through road, is busy and the port smart, as one would expect with this amount of money swilling about. Bench seats, street lights and 'no swimming' signs – not very Greek really.

The right-hand side of the quay is lined by the buildings, businesses and homes of Vourkari. The taverna/restaurants include the self-proclaimed 'world famous' *Taverna Aristos,* where the menu prices are rather more expensive than those of Korissia. There is a supermarket.

Across the bay is the chapel topped promontory of Ag Irini whence a number of archaeological finds referred to in the Introduction. At the far end of the quay, where the water is very shallow, are moored a number of speed boats, inflatables and small power boats. The Disco Medusa is 300m beyond Vourkari.

The road now climbs and leads inland across to:-

Otzias (5½km from Korissia Port) A very pleasant, deeply inset, circular bay with, along the right-hand edge, a narrow, sandy beach, edged by young tamarisk trees. To the left is a wide, coarse sand, rather scrubbly beach with a few rocks dotted about and some beach shelters (similar to those at Korissia Port). On the right of the road is a taverna and, just beyond, a fresh water tap across the way from a toilet block. Unofficial camping occurs in the groves of trees.

From the edge of the bay the now unsurfaced track zig-zags steeply up (and down) very dry, arid, stony hillsides to a final saddle connecting to:-

Panaghia Kastriani (10½km from Korissia Port) Naturally enough, from this church and monastery topped hill, the views are splendid. The original church was erected in 1708 at the site where an icon of the Madonna was found by shepherds attracted to the strange glow. A larger church was added in 1910.

The last 5km,from Otzias to Kastriani,can prove an unpleasantly hot walk at the height of the day.

ROUTE TWO

Korissia Port to The Chora (Ioulis) (5km) The road to The Chora is very pleasant, passing through lovely countryside, even if the road surface is appalling. To make the steep climb the road serpentines through old terraced hillsides (similar to Siphnos) and the buses really labour up the last section. By keeping to the left the road spills out on to a small plateia at the outset of the:-

CHORA (Ioulis) (5km from Korissia Port) The smart square is edged by a Post Office, a pharmacy, a hardware-cum-general-cum-drink store and the chic *Restaurant Piazza Delia Pizza.* The buses and taxis pull up here, but be careful not to park illegally as the police are prone to turn up and levy on-the-spot fines! A sign directs those in need of medical care the 50m to the Clinic.

The covered way from the square (the right-hand wall of which is muralled and behind which is an art shop), leads to a 'kafeneion cluttered' junction with the 'High' Street.

To the left up the 'High' St, steps, more steps and left again through the remnants of the old Kastro walls, an archway and then right progresses to the:-

Hotel Ioulis (Class B) Tel 22177
Directions: As above.

Actually classified as a pension, the provincial building is faded 1930s in style with an impressive tree-shaded patio. From the terrace is a splendid panorama looking out over the mountain slopes, Korissia Port, the sea and, in the distance, the island of Makronisos* that lies between Kea and the mainland. To the side of the patio is the 'imaginatively' named *Bar Panorama*. A single room sharing a bathroom costs 1500drs, rising to 1700drs (1st July-15th Sept). A double room sharing a bathroom costs respectively 1900drs & 2400drs and with an en suite bathroom is priced at 2360drs & 2800drs.

Back at the 'Kafeneion Junction', to the right ascends the steeply rising 'High' St. This passes a large, three storey Museum, the OTE (open weekdays between 0730-1510hrs) as well as a baker and butcher, all on the right, and, on the left, the impressive 'comic opera' Town Hall. This municipal edifice really is an extraordinary building with the rooftop balcony pedestals topped off by rows of statues and a kafeneion in the basement.

The 'High' St continues to rise, curving to the left beyond a formal tree-planted square and a 'doo-hickey' dress shop, only to narrow down into a musty, narrow street. On either side are various legal offices. On the right is a paper shop which is also an agent for the National Bank, and the:-

Hotel Filoxenia (Class E) Tel 22057
Directions: As above.

All rooms share the bathrooms with a single costing 1350drs & a double room 1450drs, increasing to 1450drs & 1800drs (16th May-30th Sept).

Opposite the hotel, in a covered way, is another baker and further along the lane, on the left side of a slow right-hand curve, is a building with a British Railway style fretwork canopy, resembling nothing less than a station waiting room.

This street, now a path, departs the outskirts of the Chora and 'stutters' along in fits and starts. Opposite a church cemetery and a dovecote, across a small valley ravine, and set in heavily terraced hillsides is the famed Lion of Kea. This is supposed to date back to the 6th century BC. Frankly it looks like a Cheshire cat to me. Rosemary reminds me that, assuming the season is correct, a 'stolen' fig from the trees shading this stone walled path is a treat.

Glancing backwards, the Chora tumbles down the hillside and across a wide saddle to a pinnacle of rock. The red tile roofed houses are those of a working town, not a whitewashed monument to a life and a world long disappeared – to be gawked at by neck-craning tourists. Incidentally, a number of the building facades incorporate bits and pieces of ancient masonry in the door uprights and jambs.

ROUTE THREE

Chora (Ioulis) to Ellinika via Pisses, Koundouros, Kambi, Havouna & Kato Meria A circular route out and back to the Chora, in this case in an anti-clockwise direction, but the reader can always travel the other way round.

Initially taking the route back towards the port, the surfaced road required branches off quickly to the left in the shadow of the Chora topped, steep cliff-face. In common with much of this route it climbs to 'contour' at a comfortable height. A left-hand turning cuts round above the Chora to join up with the return track of this circular route, which is signposted OTE leading, as it does, to the southerly mountain top mounted dish reflector.

After about 4km a path stretches away to the right towards the ruined tower in which nestles the Chapel of Ag Marina. Another ½km or so and the road surface deteriorates to that of a rough track and dips down a verdant valley, planted with cypresses and olive trees, to:-

Pisses (8km from the Chora) A sandy, fairly clean beach with, at the left-hand, a taverna/cafeteria possibly with ***Rooms***. The owner is Basilis Denegas Tel 22122.

Makronisos island, referred to under* **Lavrio, Chapter Two, was, between 1946-1974, an infamous place of detention for political prisoners.

Koundouros (11km from the Chora) It is with mixed feelings that this resort (yes a resort) is described. The developers of the Kea Beach holiday complex (Class B, tel 222810) have, in addition to the hotel, built a series of classical style windmills to house guests as well as at least four swimming pools and a tennis court. If this were not enough, on the second of a series of small coves, on a beautifully sandy beach, are organised 'fun and games'! Oh and don't let me forget the plastic matting laid down to save the hedonists feet from getting sandy! Room rates start at 3450drs for a single & 4600drs for a double room, increasing to 5175drs & 6900drs.

The third cove appears to be private and the fourth, with a kelpy beach, has a taverna, the *Manos Taverna*. It is sometimes difficult to get served as assorted distractions side-track the staff from other than desultory interest in clients.

The fifth cove is stony while the sixth and last is:-

Kambi A lovely, lonely situation with a coarse sand and pebble strip of beach and a sandy stretch of foreshore. A summer dry river-bed, lined with buddleia, is set in neat agricultural holdings and runs out on the backshore. Two tidy, wide stone paths make off inland, one to a chapel. On the north side are a few stone walled fishermens' cottages that have been tastefully converted to private homes.

One other attractive looking cove is left to the right as the track winds up from the coastal strip, but access is only by boat, foot or donkey.

HAVOUNA (17km from the Chora) More a widespread collection of agricultural, stone-walled houses and farm buildings.

A rocky path heads off across craggy hillsides to the most southerly point of the island. The immediate landscape (or more correctly the mountain top) is dominated by the aforementioned OTE reflector and mast. The tracks are rather confusing hereabouts with no signposts but they join up on the other side of the hamlet. Away down to the right, on the edge of Poles Bay, are the remains of the Ancient City of Karthea, but I am not sure where the path takes off to make the 3km or so excursion.

The rest of the 12km journey, high up on the mountainside, passes through beautifully neat,agricultural countryside interspersed by profuse groves of olive and oak trees.

In common with many of the island's countryside dwellings, the external plastered stone walls are not whitewashed, often making them difficult to see, melding as they do with the surrounding rock-bestrewn land.

The track finishes up overlooking the lovely Chora with distant views of Korissia, a fitting point at which to conclude.

INDEX

A

Artwork:Jonathan Duval & Geoffrey O'Connell
Plans & maps:Graham Bishop & Geoffrey O'Connell
Typeset:Disc preparation by Willowbridge Publishers

Output:Unwin Bros.
Tables & Headings
Typeset:County Productions

Enjoy a **real** holiday to the full!

The Alternative Holiday Guides provide all the relevant information and expert guidance required for your chosen holiday pursuit. The Guides look at specific activities rather than holiday centres and contain useful ideas for travel, tours, equipment, dos and don'ts and local information.

The Alternative Holiday Guides

Exploring Nature in North Africa

Julian Cremona and Robert Chote
An essential companion for anyone venturing into the fascinating and varied landscapes of Morocco, Tunisia and Algeria, countries so far unspoiled by package tourism. Julian Cremona and Robert Chote have amassed a wealth of information on what to see and how to get there, in the process identifying an exotic new destination for the more adventurous holiday-maker. Their recommended routes encompass many of the region's greatest natural and cultural phenomena, from the high peaks of the Atlas mountains and the desolate beauty of the Sahara, to the teeming kasbahs of Fez and Marrakech.
Paperback 1 85253 161 4

£9.95

Golfing in Europe

Eric Humphreys
Distinguished golfer and travel writer Eric Humphreys has selected and appraised both the Championship and 'middle-handicap' courses of Europe, producing a guide that can be used either by the serious golfer planning a holiday or tour devoted entirely to golf, or by the enthusiast simply wanting a few hours play on an otherwise 'conventional' holiday.
Paperback 1 85253 106 1

£9.95

Horse-Riding in Europe

John Ruler
The traditional popularity of horse-riding means that it is possible to find a place to ride almost anywhere in the United Kingdom and Europe. John Ruler has selected the very best stables and touring centres, around which a wide variety of horse-riding holidays can be planned, including pony trekking, trail riding, hacking, instructional and special interest holidays. No-one need be excluded by age, inexperience or disability - in horse-riding there's a holiday for everyone. The author's intimate knowledge of this specialised holiday field will help you to choose the safest and most enjoyable vacation for you or your children.
Paperback 1 85253 092 8

£9.95

Deep Sea Fishing Around Europe

Graeme Pullen
Specific information on venues carefully selected by the author to be easy to reach, pleasant to stay at, and which have versatile and productive fishing, making a sporting trip both exciting and enjoyable. "*Overflowing with practical information and advice on everything from taxis to tackle, this book will prove invaluable to anyone planning to fish in foreign waters.*" **Sea Fishing Magazine**
"*The angler's travelling companion - pack it with your passport.*" **Sea Angler**
Paperback 200 pages 40 B/W illustrations 6 maps 1 85253 072 3

£8.95

Exploring Nature in the Wilds of Europe

Julian Cremona and Robert Chote
Full of valuable advice on planning and enjoying nature exploration - from a family holiday to a field trip or major expedition. The authors are highly-experienced and well-travelled, offering detailed information on camping, accommodation, vehicles and transport, clothing, food and cooking, health, money, insurance and photography.
Locations include the Hebrides, Norway, Iceland and Spain. "*The authors have succeeded in making you want to go to see for yourself .. the routes and areas within the grasp of us all.*" **Off Road and 4 Wheel Drive**
Paperback 200 pages 60 B/W illustrations 15 maps 1 85253 059 6

£8.95

Please add 10% p & p for orders by post